ARCHITECT OF JUSTICE

Architect of Justice

Felix S. Cohen and the Founding of American Legal Pluralism

Dalia Tsuk Mitchell

CORNELL UNIVERSITY PRESS
ITHACA AND LONDON

Frontispiece: Portrait of Felix S. Cohen by Joseph T. Margulies. Used by permission of The City College of New York, CUNY.

First published 2007 by Cornell University Press

Printed in the United States of America

Library of Congress Cataloging-in-Publication Data

Tsuk Mitchell, Dalia.
  Architect of justice : Felix S. Cohen and the founding of American legal pluralism / Dalia Tsuk Mitchell.
      p. cm.
  Includes bibliographical references and index.
  ISBN 978-0-8014-3956-8 (cloth : alk. paper)
   1. Cohen, Felix S., 1907–1953.   2. Law teachers—United States—Biography.   3. Legal polycentricity—United States. 4. Indians of North America—Legal status, laws, etc.   I. Title.

KF373.C6185T78 2007
340.092—dc22
[B]

2006035655

Cornell University Press strives to use environmentally responsible suppliers and materials to the fullest extent possible in the publishing of its books. Such materials include vegetable-based, low-VOC inks and acid-free papers that are recycled, totally chlorine-free, or partly composed of nonwood fibers. For further information, visit our website at www.cornellpress.cornell.edu.

Cloth printing   10 9 8 7 6 5 4 3 2 1

For Larry

CONTENTS

ACKNOWLEDGMENTS

This book began with a simple question. At the beginning of my second semester as a Ph.D. student at Yale University, I had to select a topic for a research paper in Johnny Faragher's seminar on Western Americana. When I told Johnny that I was also an S.J.D. student at Harvard Law School, he suggested that, "as a lawyer," I should look at the Felix Cohen Papers and try to figure out how a Jewish guy from New York became the guru of federal Indian law. By the time I completed writing the paper, I knew that Felix Cohen would be the topic of my S.J.D. dissertation; Cohen's road into federal Indian law seemed to resonate with my own path into American legal history.

I was exceptionally fortunate to have Morty Horwitz as a dissertation adviser. Morty sparked my interest in American legal history during my first year at Harvard and helped turn an Israeli graduate student into an American legal historian. Our conversations over the years about the subject (and many others) have been not only extremely helpful but also inspiring and simply delightful. I am grateful to Morty for his ongoing support and help and unrelenting enthusiasm for my work.

Martha Minow was the dissertation's "second reader," a title that does not do justice to the role she played in pushing me to explore the question of American pluralism and to examine the connections between pluralism and Felix Cohen's scholarship. I thank Martha for her help throughout and for her faith in the significance of my work and in its importance to contemporary debates.

Jean-Christophe Agnew, Nancy Cott, and Bob Gordon did not supervise this dissertation, but they were my dissertation committee at Yale. They cheerfully indulged my musing about Felix Cohen and pluralism, even as they knew that writing this book would delay my completing the other dissertation. I am grateful to them for their willingness to share their vast knowledge of American cultural and intellectual history, for their insightful questions, and for their encouragement and support.

I thank Dirk Hartog, Tom Green, Laura Kalman, Sandy Levinson, Dick Polenberg, and Avi Soifer for reading and commenting on the initial manuscript and Willy Forbath and Sally Gordon for reading and commenting on the final manuscript. Their questions and incisive suggestions helped me rethink and rewrite the book. Thanks also to Courtney Rodgers for excellent cite-checking, and to Susan Gooding for her encouragement and for the innumerable conversations about Felix Cohen, federal Indian law, and pluralism.

I owe special thanks to Dan Ernst, not only for reading and commenting on the final manuscript but also for his untiring willingness to engage in conversations about the subject, his comments on drafts, and, especially, for thinking to look for Felix Cohen materials while doing his own research. Thank you, Dan, for all the e-mails, Xeroxed material, and encouragement you sent my way.

Earlier sections of the manuscript were presented at the NYU Legal History Colloquium, the Willard Hurst Legal History Institute, the Colloquium on Constitutional Law and Theory at Georgetown University Law Center, meetings of the American Society for Legal History, meetings of the Working Group on Law, Culture, and the Humanities, meetings of Martha Fineman's Feminism and Legal Theory Workshop, the Annual Yale Native American Studies Conference, the University of Arizona College of Law Faculty Workshops, the George Washington University Law School Faculty Workshops, the UCLA Law School Faculty Workshop, and the University of Oregon Law School Faculty Workshop. I thank the participants in these events for their comments and suggestions.

I am also thankful to Maureen Garmon at the University of Arizona College of Law, Larry Ross at the George Washington University Law School, and archivists at the Beinecke Rare Book and Manuscript Library, the Sterling Memorial Library, the Franklin D. Roosevelt Presidential Library, the Joseph Regenstein Library, the Morris Raphael Cohen Library at City College, and the National Archives for their assistance in finding material and their ability to answer even my most arcane questions.

Financial assistance was provided by the University of Arizona College of Law Summer Research Fund, the George Washington University Law School Summer Research Fund, the Samuel Golieb Fellowship at NYU School of Law, and the Beinecke Rare Book and Manuscript Library.

Early versions of parts of the manuscript appear in " 'A Double Runner': Felix S. Cohen and the Indian New Deal," *Political and Legal Anthropology Review* 25 (2002): 48–68, "Pluralisms: The Indian New Deal as a Model," *Margins: Maryland's Interdisciplinary Publication on Race, Religion, Gender, and Class* 1 (2001): 393–449, and "The New Deal Origins of American Legal Pluralism," *Florida State University Law Review* 29 (2001): 189–268.

Last, but certainly not least, my greatest debt is to Larry. For four years, he heroically tolerated my constant chatter about Felix Cohen and pluralism. He read every draft of the entire manuscript—several times!—carefully edited out the Hebrew (my native tongue), made perceptive comments, and asked extremely probing questions. Most important, he offered love, encouragement, confidence, and a sense of belonging that made every day brighter. It is to him, with love, that this book is dedicated.

ARCHITECT OF JUSTICE

Prologue

The philosopher, legal scholar, and lawyer Felix Solomon Cohen lived a life dedicated to the promotion of a particular vision of the modern American state—a vision of legal pluralism. This image of the state had a profound influence on the transformation of law in the first half of the twentieth century. Its insight was that groups and other associations were political, social, and cultural centers in American life. Therefore, the success of American democracy demanded that they be accommodated within its political and legal structures. Cohen devoted his life to defining the boundaries of group autonomy and group power.

Legal pluralism was informed by British and American theories of political pluralism that held that groups and organizations, created by individuals to pursue common interests, were centers of political life. By exploring the role of groups in society, pluralists attempted to offer a more realistic description of the limited function of the liberal state. Moreover, many political pluralists treated the group model not only as descriptive but also as normative. They saw the state as too broad and abstract a body to command loyalty from individuals, who identified more easily with groups and organizations. In their view, society contained and should contain multiple centers of self-government. They encouraged the growth of diverse groups within the state to facilitate the flourishing of valuable forms of identities, experiences, and viewpoints, all of which could help individuals live rich and meaningful lives.

Legal pluralism was also influenced by legal realism, a jurisprudential movement that emerged in the early twentieth century and peaked during the interwar period. Legal realists rejected classical legal thought, which dominated American legal institutions from the 1880s to the 1930s. Classicists described law as a body of axioms from which judges deduced rules in particular cases.

Legal realists argued that this vision obscured the connections between law and social, economic, and political concerns; realists described law as the outcome of concealed battles over the social utility of diverse activities in a rapidly changing society, especially the activities of organized labor and organized capital. Seeking to formulate law and policy that would better accommodate different visions, interests, and experiences, legal realists stressed the need for empirical studies of the relationship between law and diverse social, economic, and political questions.

Legal realism was grounded in skepticism toward existing values and structures of thought. Yet once realists turned from their critiques to build a better legal system, they were confronted with a difficult normative dilemma—the dilemma of pluralism: did their skepticism imply a nonjudgmental attitude toward all customs and values?

No scholar suspended judgment toward all values and cultures. The uncertainty of such a radically relativist approach was too great for many intellectuals. Instead, legal realists tried different ways out of the dilemma. Some endorsed cultural and ethical relativism but trusted empirical studies (or science) to point to the appropriate system of values. Others challenged absolute structures of knowledge (such as science) but accepted absolute moral values.

The legal pluralist image of the state provided a different resolution to the dilemma. It recognized the diversity of values, experiences, and points of view while limiting the resulting uncertainties. By embracing groups like labor unions as centers where individuals found meaning, legal pluralists maintained a certain skepticism toward universal norms; groups could pursue their own values. Yet pluralists also demanded absolute norms outside group boundaries, for example the norms regulating the power of collectivities (especially corporations). Rather than choosing between relativism and absolutism, legal pluralists saw their task as defining the appropriate balance between group autonomy and the limits of group power—in other words, the normative limits of their celebration of diversity.

The Depression and the New Deal gave legal pluralists a chance to try out their ideas in practice. Recast as New Dealers in Franklin Roosevelt's administration, they sought to combine decentralized economic and political power with national planning. By recognizing groups like labor unions and corporations as power centers, legal pluralists hoped to endorse the diversity that characterized modern society while promoting economic progress and relying upon national planning to limit the destructive potential of capitalism. In this vein, the securities acts of 1933 and 1934 were based on cooperation between government and big business, the Tennessee Valley Authority combined centralized government planning with regional bureaucracy, and the National Industrial Recovery Act of 1933 created the National Recovery Administration to oversee cooperative programs among business, labor, and government (the scheme was held unconstitutional in 1935).

A series of developments beginning in the late 1930s helped redirect the attention of American scholars from collective institutions to the individual as the unit of legal and political analysis. First came wide acceptance of Keynesian economics, which provided economic justification for regulating the economy based on existing consumer preferences instead of planning, a justification upon which the later New Deal fiscal policies were predicated. The individual consumer became the foundation of economic thought. At the same time, amid growing fears of creeping Communism and totalitarianism, constitutional law scholars obsessed about the need to protect the rights of ethnic and racial minorities. While early New Deal policies emphasized the individual's rights to work, to livelihood, to social insurance, and to economic independence, ideals that were compatible with collective rights, legal scholarship from the late 1930s was concerned with the rights of individuals to be different. The earlier pluralist image of the state, with its collectivist focus, was abandoned and the intellectual milieu converged on the ideal of individual rights and liberties.

The individual was also at the core of a new pluralist image of the state that political theorists created in the postwar years. It reduced groups to the instrumentalities of individuals. Groups existed to enhance the ability of individuals to pursue their ends. This new pluralist image of the state assumed that individuals formed multiple interest groups to interact, compete, and trade ends in neutral economic and political markets. Neo-pluralists saw the state as a political compromise between diverse groups. They trusted presumably free political markets to produce shared public goods.

The prominence of interest group pluralism during the 1950s helped obscure the legacy of earlier interpretations of pluralism. The decisions of the Warren Court in the 1950s and 1960s made individual rights and liberties, and thus individuals, the center of American liberalism. In 1971, John Rawls, in *A Theory of Justice,* while insisting on the diversity of selves as a necessary starting point, argued that individuals were capable of ignoring all differentiating individual characteristics and reasoning from the same universal point of view. According to Rawls, this universal original position represented the impartiality of justice.

Rawls's conception of justice has been widely criticized. Many critiques resemble the perspectives of pluralism seen several decades earlier. Indeed, issues of diversity, pluralism, or what we today label multiculturalism account for inexhaustible debates as contemporary political theorists, legal scholars, and philosophers struggle to understand the American state at the turn of the twenty-first century. The story of early pluralism—its rise in the 1920s and 1930s and its demise in the 1940s and 1950s—is the story of the origins of multiculturalism in the 1980s and 1990s.

Felix Cohen was the son of Jewish immigrants—second-generation on his father's side and third-generation on his mother's. Like many American Jews of his generation, he was caught between the world of the immigrant and the world of the American, longing to find a place in American society. Educated both as a philosopher and as a lawyer, Cohen found his sense of belonging in legal pluralism.

In the early 1930s, as Cohen took his first steps as a practicing lawyer, he followed many Progressive-era scholars (including his father, a renowned Jewish philosopher at the College of the City of New York) by rejecting ethnic particularism and emphasizing economic improvement through solidarity and collaboration among groups like labor unions and corporations.

In 1933 Cohen accepted the invitation of a family friend, Nathan Margold, the new solicitor of the Department of the Interior, to help draft the Indian Reorganization Act. The act was meant to end the late–nineteenth-century federal policy of allotting tribal lands to individual Indians and forcing the assimilation of Indians. The New Dealers recast Indian tribes as groups with political and economic autonomy over their reservations and worked to grant them more authority over their economic, social, cultural, and political affairs. This endeavor became known as the "Indian New Deal."

Cohen knew nothing of Indian affairs when he joined the Department of the Interior as assistant solicitor. As he later put it, he was "a New Yorker, from a city where there were no reclamation, public land, Indian or territorial problems,—problems of which [he] had never heard until [he] came to Washington." Influenced by Norman Thomas socialism on the one hand and pluralism on the other, Cohen saw Indian tribes as one of many political and economic groups that would form the foundation of the modern pluralist state. He used his work on Indian reservations to create a model for other groups. This model was based on group self-government and the collective ownership of property. Cohen wanted to empower tribes by advocating tribal self-government and incorporation for the purpose of running their economic affairs.

But Indian tribes were different from the corporations and labor unions that served as a model for legal pluralists. Tribes were more than political and economic groups. They were ethnic and cultural groups as well, with their own values, ethics, and modes of life. Cohen rapidly found himself struggling to apply the economically oriented legal pluralist image of the state to groups defined by race, ethnicity, and culture. Intrigued by this project, Cohen, who had intended to work at Interior for a year, stayed for fourteen.

While at Interior, Cohen supervised a survey of federal Indian law, which he also summarized in the *Handbook of Federal Indian Law,* the first comprehensive, and still definitive, treatise on Indian law. In 1946, a year before he left the department, Cohen helped draft the Indian Claims Commission Act, which established an administrative tribunal to settle tribal land claims against the federal government and which became a model for litigating land claims around the world. In all these endeavors and in his scholarship, he attempted to formulate laws and policies to accommodate the interests and needs of Indian nations as well as other groups.

Cohen never abandoned the assumption that groups were the foundation of the state, but with each attempt to accommodate diverse interests, his legal solution changed. In the late 1930s, witnessing the looming tragedy of Jews in Europe and the palpably missing American response, Cohen realized that it was not enough to describe the state as being made up of many political groups.

Such a description did not justify opening American borders to strangers or protecting strangers' interests. Only a normative argument about the importance of diversity in individual and social life could give the outsider a place in American society. The diversity of groups that characterized American society became for Cohen not only a means of reconciling the tensions created by relativism or a source of a comforting sense of belonging but also an explanation for the strength of American democratic traditions and institutions.

In the 1940s, as others turned to the individual as the basis for social, legal, and political analysis, Cohen stressed the need to protect group rights. Increasingly discontent with the idea that the state's function was limited to setting the boundaries of group autonomy and power, Cohen emphasized the state's obligation to protect the rights of minority groups. This was also the premise of Cohen's *Handbook*. It promoted the protection of tribes' rights and advocated constitutional protection for group rights.

Cohen filled the ideal of constitutionally protected group rights with content in his work to protect the rights of Alaska Natives to use their lands and waters and in his work on Indian land claims. His goal was to create a legal system that could accommodate not only multiple political sovereigns but also cultural sovereignty. He wanted law to honor the values of diverse groups. He wanted American law to recognize aboriginal conceptions of property. He wanted to create an American legal forum respectful of the property traditions of Alaska Natives and Native Americans. Cohen's 1940s pluralist ideal was anchored in the possibility of legally facilitated dialogue among diverse peoples and legal systems.

Amid a world war, Cohen thought that the only alternative to total annihilation was the preservation of diverse cultures. But by the late 1940s, Interior had become less responsive to Cohen's pluralist agenda. In 1948, disappointed with the rapid demise of the New Deal and legal pluralism, Cohen left the department. He devoted the rest of his life to teaching, writing, and advocating on behalf of Native Americans and other minority groups.

Cohen's worldview merged theory and practice. His brilliant article "Transcendental Nonsense and the Functional Approach" (1935) criticized the abstraction of classical legal thought as a form of group violence and argued for the redefinition of abstract concepts as functions of diverse particular experiences. His article "The Relativity of Philosophical Systems and the Method of Systematic Relativism" (1939) stressed that the meaning of concepts depended on many possible external systems of reference. Accordingly, legal change required understanding that legal reality was composed of a variety of interrelated particular and collective experiences and reconstituting different legal systems as broader and more inclusive. Cohen's ideal of constitutionally protected group rights and his defense of aboriginal conceptions of property were attempts to make the American legal system more inclusive.

After he left Interior, Cohen's jurisprudential focus changed, reflecting both the awful realities the world had witnessed and his personal sense of failure at his inability (and that of the other architects of the New Deal) to build a pluralist state. Cohen seemed to have given up the idea of a coherent jurisprudential theory. Instead, he focused on the relationship between language and law. "Transcendental Nonsense" advocated redefining abstract concepts as functions of particular experiences, and "The Relativity of Philosophical Systems" called on legal scholars to study the correlation between propositions in different systems in order to create an inclusive jurisprudential system. In comparison, Cohen's writings in the early 1950s sought to explain the relationship between particular experiences and cultural assumptions as they were reflected in legal language. The analytical focus of his pluralism shifted from finding ways to accommodate diverse interests and values to exploring the cultural reasons for the inability of law (and society) to do so.

Felix Cohen died in 1953; he was forty-six. A year later, in *Brown v. Board of Education,* the U.S. Supreme Court gave its stamp of approval to the modern ideology of individual rights. Three years later, Robert Dahl published *A Preface to Democratic Theory,* which turned pluralism into a procedural theory of democracy. In the past half century, as the struggle of African Americans to be accepted into American society set the parameters around which rights and liberties are discussed, the rights of American Indians (as well as immigrants) have been on the outer margins of the cultural debates.

Shortly before his untimely death, Cohen organized all of his writings under three categories: "Logic, Law, and Ethics," "The Indian's Quest for Justice," and "The Philosophy of American Democracy." He wanted his daughters, Karen and Gene, who were respectively eleven and thirteen years old, to understand their father; he wanted them to know what he was doing when he was not with them. Scholarship was his means of reflecting upon and sharing his experiences and endeavors; it was both personal and public. His wife, Lucy Kramer Cohen, later published Cohen's gift to his daughters as a collection entitled *The Legal Conscience* (1960).

During the past fifty years Cohen's two interests—his jurisprudential interest ("Logic, Law, and Ethics") and his interest in federal Indian law ("The Indian's Quest for Justice")—have been separated in legal thought. For some scholars, Cohen is a legal realist. Indeed, my first exposure to Cohen was in a course on legal realism at Harvard Law School in which "Transcendental Nonsense" was examined as a brilliant realist critique of classical legal thought. For other scholars, Cohen is the guru of federal Indian law. A couple of years after my introduction to Cohen at Harvard, I was introduced to his work on federal Indian law, specifically to the *Handbook,* in a Western Americana seminar in the history department of Yale University. Interestingly, neither group of scholars sought to explore the connections between Cohen's two seemingly distinct interests. As I began examining Cohen's papers, archived at the Beinecke Rare Book and Manuscript Library at Yale, I gradually realized that the link between Cohen's jurisprudential writings and his work on federal Indian law was, in fact, his democratic philosophy ("The Philosophy of American Democracy")—his legal pluralist vision of the modern American state.

While Cohen never labeled himself a pluralist, his voice was the voice of legal pluralism. His legal career and scholarship illustrate the influence of legal pluralism on conversations about rights and liberties during the first half of the twentieth century. These discussions focused not only on protecting the individual from the state but also on the rights of groups and associations. The mid-century ideal of individual rights and liberties grew out of this larger legal scheme, which recognized the multiplicity of groups and associations that characterized modern American society and sought to determine the boundaries of these entities' autonomy.

Cohen's encounters with pluralism were embedded in his personal experiences—his experience as the son of a Jewish immigrant, his political involvement with the socialist movement, his intellectual fascination with legal realism, his professional role in the Indian New Deal, and his reaction to World War II and its aftermath. Like Woody Allen's Zelig, who found himself in the middle of some of the defining moments of the early twentieth century, Cohen was always in the right place at the right time. For the most part his work was behind the scenes and he often did not have the political power necessary to transform his ideas into reality. Still, first, as a member of the Solicitor's Office (with Margold's unwavering support) and later as a Washington lawyer, he left the marks of legal pluralism on a variety of laws and policies affecting Indian nations and other minority groups. Cohen's story is thus the story of the impact of the legal pluralist image of the modern state on the transformation of American thought and American society in the first half of the twentieth century.

The story of legal pluralism is a story about doubts and hopes, failures and successes. As a whole, Cohen's work on behalf of Indian tribes and Jewish refugees failed to accomplish most of his goals. Unconvinced politicians and changing tides in the administration contributed to these failures and to the demise of legal pluralism and the New Deal. But the fall of the legal pluralist image of the state also demonstrates the strong hold on American thought of Enlightenment ideas centered upon the individual even in the face of social and political realities that challenge such ideas.

Cohen's failure to achieve material results must have been disappointing. But Cohen was not one to despair. His faith in the significance of the legal pluralist vision and in the power of law to bring about change ran deep. For Cohen, law was a tool for remedying historical wrongs against Indian tribes, specifically colonization and forced inclusion. Underlying this understanding of the law was Cohen's personal hope that American law could remedy wrongs against Jews, specifically forced exclusion. For a while, he was able to repress the wrongs inherent in using a legal system predicated upon individualism to remedy past injuries to diverse communities. Similar constraints continue to impede contemporary attempts to devise a plural polity, as different others (ethnic, religious, cultural, and political groups) struggle both to escape law's violence and to come under its protection.

Cohen's gradual realization of the law's limits illustrates how in the shadows of the law lurks hope, as constraints may be transformed into possibilities. For those who seek to create a pluralist polity and for those who are affected by such attempts, the law can help facilitate social contacts. Even failed attempts to devise formalistic legal structures to accomplish pluralistic goals create peripheries where pluralism might flourish. Our treatment of different groups and individuals, as Cohen so aptly described it, is the litmus test of our democracy; it reflects "a set of beliefs that forms the intellectual equipment of a generation." In the shadows of the law, doubt may turn to hope.

PART I

Longing to Belong, 1907–1933

CHAPTER 1

A Second Generation

Felix Cohen's most vivid childhood impression was a sense of dislocation and loneliness. As an adult he confessed to his friend Joseph Lash that he "felt horribly lost and lonely when, as a child, [his] family's wanderings would take [him] from the people and places [he] knew."[1] Indeed, the Cohens moved three times before Felix turned eighteen, but they always remained close to the College of the City of New York (CCNY), where Felix's father taught. Felix might have overstated his feelings to encourage Lash, who was contemplating moving to a new place. But his confession captured deeper emotions. Felix Cohen belonged to a generation of ethnically diverse, secular, left-of-center American intellectuals who were both mesmerized and terrified by their multifaceted relationship to diverse cultures and experiences. They embraced modernity, with its freedom and fluidity, but they felt lost, at times alienated, longing to belong in a rapidly changing, pluralist society.

The Cohens

Felix was a third-generation American on his mother's side and a second-generation on his father's side. His parents, Mary (Miriam) Ryshpan and Morris (Moshe) Raphael Cohen, were brought up in the Jewish ghetto of the Lower East Side and impressed by a secular American culture in New York's public schools and the Educational Alliance—an educational and cultural center created by the German Jews of upper Manhattan to acculturate the Eastern European Jews of the Lower East Side to American life.[2] Felix's upbringing was rooted in these impressions.

Mary, born on July 31, 1880, was the second-youngest of Sheba Pearl and

Solomon (Yehusa Shelma) Ryshpan's eight or nine children and the first born in the United States. The family migrated from Russian Poland shortly before Mary's birth and lived on East Broadway, within a block of the Henry Street Settlement. Solomon Ryshpan, who initially worked in the jewelry business and later acquired some real estate in Brooklyn, was "a devoutly orthodox Jew." He believed that his daughters' education should emphasize "their duties to God and family," but, at Sheba Ryshpan's insistence, the three youngest daughters attended the Normal College (renamed Hunter College in 1914) of the City of New York.[3]

After graduating from Normal College, Mary taught at Public School 12 on the Lower East Side and was active in different social organizations, particularly those providing services to families and the poor and those advocating better working conditions for women and women's rights (including the Organization for Rehabilitation through Training, the Henry Street Settlement, and the Women's International League for Peace and Freedom). In 1911, after the tragic fire at the Triangle Shirtwaist Company, which claimed the lives of 146 immigrant workers, many of whom were young Jewish and Italian girls, Mary joined the Women's Trade Union League. Leonora O'Reilly, a founding member of the league, became Mary's lifelong friend.[4] Probably through O'Reilly, Mary also became involved in the Ethical Culture Society, which Felix Adler, a German Jew, founded in 1876 to bring together those who, regardless of religious affiliation, cared about moral betterment. Of particular interest to Mary was the society's Manhattan Trade School for Girls, where O'Reilly taught.[5]

Morris, born on July 25, 1880, was twelve when his parents, Abraham Mordecai and Bessie Farfel Cohen, brought him and his three siblings from Minsk, Russia, to America.[6] For a short period the Cohens lived in Brownsville; then they moved to the Lower East Side. Like millions of Jews who wanted to get away from the anti-Semitism and physical hardship of Eastern Europe, the Cohens came to "the golden land" (di goldeneh medina), where the family continued to struggle to overcome economic hardship. Yet, even if the first generation struggled, in the golden land and the promised city, their children could dream of being assimilated.[7]

Reluctant as they might have been to give up their particular cultures, most immigrants were eager to become Americans. Given the resemblance of Jewish and American cultural narratives (the story of exodus, the covenant, the promised land), Jewish immigrants often experienced the tension between particularism and assimilation more strongly; they had come to America in search of a promised land, seeking to leave behind a history of segregation and discrimination. Many Eastern European Jews associated emigration to the United States with "biblical narratives of flight from oppression and the coming of the Messiah."[8] The possibilities that Americans saw in the western frontier were embedded for Jewish immigrants and their children in the eastern shores of America. "I am . . . grateful," Felix Cohen stated more than five decades after his father had come to the United States, "grateful for the opportunity to serve the country that welcomed my father and my grandparents out of slavery into freedom."[9]

The immigrants' aspirations to assimilate echoed the plans that many American reformers had for them. As millions of immigrants, most of them from poor eastern and southern European towns, poured into the United States, social workers and educators sought to Americanize them—to help immigrants remold their behavior in accordance with the values of mainstream America. German Jews, who were already assimilated and embarrassed by their ethnic brethren, whom they viewed as "uncouth, barbaric, ill-mannered, fanatical," put money and effort into transforming Eastern European Jews into respectable American citizens.[10]

Eastern European Jews had a remarkable culture that developed in conditions of extreme poverty and physical persecution. For centuries their culture was grounded in religious Orthodoxy. But in the nineteenth century, with the influence of *Haskala*, the Jewish Enlightenment, it became more secular, a transformation that was completed in the United States. Jewish writers and scholars, who saw no future in oppressive Europe, helped bring this Jewish culture over to New York City. On the Lower East Side, they drew upon Jewish traditions to turn political socialism into a communal ideology. In newspapers, social gatherings, marketplace interactions, and theatrical productions, the Lower East Side Jewish community constructed "an ethnic identity with a socialist character."[11]

Lower East Side socialism envisioned human fraternity as a means of ending "the exploitativeness, the inhumane competitiveness, the moral frigidity associated with capitalism." Young men and women were drawn to socialism, reading not only Marx but also Tolstoy, Mark Twain, and Theodore Dreiser. They aspired to organize unions and to immerse themselves in the cultural heritage from which they were traditionally excluded. It was their way into American society.[12]

While Eastern European Jews found socialism conducive to the cultivation of their political and ethnic identity and their flourishing as an intellectual community, German Jews feared that socialism would prevent the absorption of Jews as a group into American society. Like Anglo-Saxon reformers, they wanted to Americanize the new immigrants, a project that implicated both an ethnic and a class struggle. Proponents of Americanization asserted both "the superiority of Western 'civilization'" to "'Oriental' outlandishness" and "the contempt of investment bankers, national civic figures and international merchants for petty traders, neighborhood customer peddlers, and tailors." In so doing, they helped to associate "foreignness and socialism, Americanism and respectable (nonradical) trade unionism."[13]

German Jews engaged in well-publicized charitable and educational efforts to acculturate Eastern European Jews. The Educational Alliance was their most successful endeavor. Formed out of a merger between the Hebrew Free School Association, the Young Men's Hebrew Association, and the Aguilar Free Library Society, its goal was "to teach the blessing of American citizenship"—to transform Eastern European Jews into an "acceptable and respectable minority" by impressing upon them the American values of individualism, self-reliance, industry, competitiveness, and upward mobility.[14] The alliance rejected the Yiddish language and emphasized secular culture. The older generation despised it, while their sons and daughters turned to it in search for ideals that could replace their parents' cultural and religious values. Eager to become Americans, they wanted to study hard so that they could rise higher in the American social ladder than their fathers, who were tailors, storekeepers, salesmen, and petty brokers.[15]

Mary and Morris were among these students. They met in 1899 when both attended a lecture series by Thomas Davidson at the Educational Alliance. Davidson, a Scottish scholar, believed that inculcating working-class Jewish immigrants with "Culture" would save them from pessimism, parochialism, and political radicalism. According to Davidson, who was born in poverty, culture was the best defense against "violence and barbarism."[16]

Morris attended the first lecture as a member of the Marx Circle, a group of friends that met occasionally to read and discuss Marx's *Capital* and other socialist scholarship. He wanted to challenge Davidson's argument in favor of the principle of individualism.[17] But, gradually, the lectures became for Morris a stepping-stone into academic life and middle-class America. Davidson's kindness and "paternalistic flattery" helped to transform Morris's convictions. Encouraged by Davidson, who invited him and Mary to his summer school in the Adirondacks, Morris embarked upon the study of philosophy: from Hume and Kant to Plato, Aristotle, and the pre-Socratics. Growing estranged from religious Orthodoxy and his father, who practiced it, Morris found the philosopher's search for an impartial truth the equivalent of the religious quest for the Kingdom of God and of the political search for utopia.[18]

Shortly after Davidson's death in 1900, Morris, Mary, and others formed the Thomas Davidson Society—"an institution that would make no distinction of race or creed, would be open to rich and poor alike, and would be founded upon the principles that Thomas Davidson had sought to perpetuate." Predicated upon the possibility of social harmony, the Davidson Society offered a liberal consensus as an alternative for the unavoidable conflict of Marxism and socialism. Morris, who had previously taught workingmen's classes for the Socialist Labor Party, was conducting classes for the Educational Alliance.[19]

In 1904, Morris left New York City to begin graduate studies in philosophy at Harvard University (he proposed to Mary shortly beforehand). Felix Adler arranged for the Ethical Culture Society to finance Morris's studies. In return, Morris led the activities of the Cambridge Ethical Culture Society.[20] Morris earned a Ph.D. in philosophy in 1906; he and Mary were married shortly after he completed his dissertation. Six decades later, a friend commented that Morris chose metaphysics over the working class.[21]

Assimilationists, Cultural Pluralists, and Cosmopolitans

To be known as a thinker, not a Jewish thinker, not even an American thinker, was Morris's dream, and it was one not easily fulfilled. A father a year after his graduation, Morris struggled to find a teaching position in a philosophy department. He received superb recommendations from William James and Josiah Royce, only to find the doors of philosophy departments locked by pervasive anti-Semitism. Philosophy was taught as an inquiry into the religious and ethical underpinning of American culture, and only those with the correct cultural credentials could teach it. Only in 1912 was Morris appointed to the Department of Philosophy at his alma mater, CCNY. Harry Overstreet, the new chairman, persuaded the college "to overcome its reluctance to allow a Jew to teach philosophy."[22]

Despite, maybe because of, his personal experience, Morris remained an avid advocate of the Enlightenment's universal ideals and criticized attempts to emphasize ethnic or religious differences. He carved a place for himself in modern American society by focusing on the similarities between individuals and groups rather than on their particularities. There were, accordingly, "many human problems, of which Jews, as human beings, [had] perhaps more than their share. But these problems, traced to their ultimate roots in reality, [were] also the problems of other minority groups, and [every] group of human beings [was] . . . a minority in one situation or another."[23] Formerly a socialist, Morris, the philosopher, proposed a democracy committed to social and economic equality as a solution to these human problems, subconsciously bringing the radical socialist traditions of Eastern European Jews to bear upon Western liberalism.

Morris was a centrist. Emotionally and intellectually, he viewed the world in terms of extreme polarities, and he defined philosophical questions in terms that reconciled these extremes.[24] His democratic ideal was a compromise between two conflicting cultural and political positions that were competing to gain a hold among American intellectuals, especially among Jewish scholars, namely the positions of assimilation and cultural pluralism.

Advocates of assimilation, memorialized in Israel Zangwill's play, *The Melting Pot* (1909), urged immigrants to divest themselves of every vestige of their native culture and merge into the presumably homogenous American culture. In response, cultural pluralists, most notably Horace Kallen in his "Democracy versus the Melting Pot" (1915), used a metaphor of "multiplicity in unity" to argue that America ought to remain a nation composed of many cultural or ethnic nations and to urge harmonious cooperation between different cultures.[25] As Kallen put it, American society was like an orchestra, with "each ethnic group . . . the natural instrument, its temper and culture . . . its theme and melody and the harmony and dissonances and discords of them all . . . the symphony of civilization."[26]

While Morris shared the cultural pluralists' sympathies with the immigrants' experiences, he accused them of cultural determinism, of embracing the "very popular racial philosophy of history," that is, "the constant tendency to emphasize the consciousness of race." In contrast, Morris described "liberal America" as "stand[ing] for separation of church and state, the free mixing of races, and the fact that men [could] change their habitation and language and still advance the process of civilization." Morris offered a fluid understanding of ethnic relations and argued that particular cultures, the Jewish culture being an example, were repositories for insights that, when brought together, would allow the development of a more comprehensive conception of national identity. According to Morris, great civilizations could only be achieved when "a mixed people freely [borrowed] from others in religion, language, laws, and manners."[27]

Anglo-Saxon thinkers like John Dewey and Randolph Bourne saw in Morris the fulfillment of their belief that a cosmopolitan approach (unlike cultural pluralism or assimilation) would help individuals attain a more complete human experience and a better understanding of it. While native-born Americans were exceedingly anxious about the influx of immigrants from Eastern and Central Europe, liberal Anglo-Saxon intellectuals hoped that immigrants would help alter the course of American history—from isolationism to internationalism. Writing on the eve of Wilson's decision to join the war in Europe, Bourne described immigration as offering Americans an opportunity "to liberate themselves from 'parochialism,' and to develop in themselves a truly 'cosmopolitan spirit.'" Bourne and his colleagues sought to develop a broad-based national identity and ideology and were eager for immigrants to advance the cause. For Dewey, Bourne, and other cosmopolitans, Morris became a symbol. Jewish immigrants, Bourne believed, were the most useful to the cause. Like their liberal, Anglo-Saxon contemporaries, Jewish intellectuals were impatient with the constraints of particularism.[28]

Eager to be known as a thinker, Morris found a place for himself by mediating the polarities of assimilation and cultural pluralism. An immigrant who never felt he belonged, he embraced in his philosophy a sense of detachment, distrusting "the concrete, the sensual and the active." In his view, assimilation and cultural pluralism emphasized the subjectivity and particularity of race and ethnicity. In turn, cosmopolitanism used universal logic and reason to coalesce particularity and universality.[29] Baffled by the incongruity between traditional Jewish culture, grounded as it was in Orthodoxy, and American culture, Morris developed a new ideal, a cosmopolitan Jewish identity. Ironically, while Morris became a prominent figure in American philosophy (indeed, the first Russian-born Jew to become a member of the American Philosophical Association, and a regular contributor to the *New Republic*), he remained the renowned Jewish philosopher of CCNY or as some put it, "the Paul Bunyan of the Jewish Intellectuals."[30]

Loneliness

Morris and Mary's lifestyle and manners reflected both the values of the Jewish immigrant culture and those of the budding American middle-class culture. For one thing, like other members of the burgeoning Jewish middle class, they moved out of the Lower East Side into the newly developed Jewish neighborhood on Manhattan's Upper West Side.[31] Felix was born there.

Morris and Mary named their three children after philosophers. Victor William, the youngest, born in 1911, was named after William James, whom Morris described as his best friend on the Harvard faculty; it was a striking choice, given Morris's preference for Royce's philosophy. Leonora, born in 1909, was named after Leonora O'Reilly and bore the middle name Davidson, after Thomas Davidson. Yet the complexity of life's passions and concerns—Judaism, philosophy, and politics—was unveiled in the name Morris chose for his eldest son. Felix, born on July 3, 1907, was named after Felix Frankfurter, Morris's roommate at Harvard and a close friend, who would become the third Jewish Justice on the U.S. Supreme Court, and after Solomon Maimon, whom Morris called "the greatest Jewish philosopher since Spinoza."[32] To an outside observer, Felix's life might easily seem to have been an ongoing struggle to understand, adjust to, and overcome the polarities that Morris, a poor Jewish emigrant eager to become an American, sought to mediate.

Morris used to say that Leonora was the dreamer and William the doer. Felix was the thinker. With their parents' encouragement, all three pursued doctorate degrees—Leonora in French literature, William in physics, and Felix in law and philosophy. In so doing, Felix turned out to be "an inestimable boon to his father." As Leonora commented in retrospect, "independent as were their minds, their relationship was one of rare understanding."[33]

Morris's involvement in Felix's upbringing was, however, limited. In part, Morris's detached attitude reflected a stern Jewish upbringing, which Morris himself endured as a child. Morris's father was absent for most of Morris's childhood, traveling between Russia and the United States searching for an opportunity to move his family to New York. When he visited home, Morris felt that his father ignored and humiliated him. When he was seven, Morris moved to live with his grandparents. In his memoirs, Morris described his grandfather, Hirsch Farfel, as belonging to "the stern old school that did not encourage the outward expression of affection" and instead emphasized teaching.[34] Morris, too, never understood why the children were not always reading, "in the books," as a relative put it.[35]

In part, Morris's lack of interest in raising his children reflected an endorsement of American middle-class patterns of gender behavior: men worked while the woman's role was more home-centered than it had been in Eastern Europe. Mary, who deeply believed in Morris's "intellectual promise," was resolved "to keep him sufficiently free of 'petty cares.'" While both had been

"Davidson's philosophic protégés," only Morris would "realize his philosophic potential." Mary ran a household in which the children could develop their potential to the fullest and Morris could work with very little distraction.[36]

As married women were not eligible to teach in public schools, Mary left her teaching position and became the primary caregiver for the children.[37] Mary home-schooled Felix until he was eight years old, teaching him music, languages, and philosophy and introducing him to Anglo-American culture. "She would take us down to the old Park Theater on Columbus Circle for Gilbert and Sullivan," Leonora recalled; "we would go through a whole score of Mikado or Pinafore in the big kitchen in our house."[38] Many friends remembered the adult Felix either reading poetry aloud or leading everyone in a round of German songs.[39]

Mary was also responsible for educating the children in the Jewish tradition. At Morris's insistence, neither Felix nor William had a bar mitzvah; to celebrate Passover, Mary would take the children to her mother's house.[40] Morris, who as a child was fascinated by the study of the Torah and wanted to become a Talmudic scholar, was no longer interested in embracing tradition, not even in celebrating Jewish holidays.[41] In his vision of America, religion was an impediment to inclusion and success.

The Cohens remained in upper Manhattan until 1915. Then, when the precocious Felix was about to enter the public school system, they moved to Yonkers. While the relevant documents do not indicate any reasons for the move, one can speculate that Morris and Mary wanted Felix to be in a public school that was not focused, as many public schools in New York Jewish neighborhoods were, on the induction of new immigrants into American life.[42] Their Felix was to be educated like an American.

Felix entered Public School No. 5 in Yonkers in 1915, graduating with a gold medal; he was the class valedictorian. In 1920, after Felix's first year at Yonkers High School, the Cohens returned to upper Manhattan—to Washington Heights. By then, the neighborhood, originally populated by wealthy Jews, had become a predominantly middle-class Jewish neighborhood. Felix transferred to Townsend Harris High School, then part of a seven-year educational system coordinated with CCNY.[43]

Townsend Harris was established in the early twentieth century on the premises of the new campus of CCNY on St. Nicholas Ave. With views of the Hudson to the west, it was a long way from Twenty-Third Street, where CCNY had earlier been located, and even farther from the "noise and bustle of the lower East Side." Initially, Townsend Harris attracted boys "of every sort from every part of the city," but the student body rapidly became predominantly Jewish, reflecting the influx of immigrants into New York.[44]

Seemingly separate from CCNY students, Townsend Harris boys participated in campus events and extracurricular activities. Sports and clubs brought together boys from distant neighborhoods, broadened their horizons, and made learning more entertaining.[45] Felix was an active and resourceful young adult. Friends and relatives later commented that Felix's presidency of the high school's stamp club offered a glimpse into his negotiating and administrative skills. At fifteen, he received his diploma from Townsend Harris. Then, from 1923 to 1928, he financed part of his college education by dealing in stamps; he purchased stamps from various foreign countries and sold them in the United States.[46]

But, as his letter to Lash suggests, Felix was lonely. The Cohen household was unconventional. Relatives remembered "a great big rambling house" dedicated to intellectual ventures: Morris's library, the many books in Greek, Morris's important friends, such as Oliver Wendell Holmes Jr., Learned Hand, and Benjamin Cardozo.[47] Morris's teaching and Mary's various reform activities kept both parents away for long hours; meals were left for the children on a fireless cooker. Decades later, Felix recalled his distress over his mother's frequent absences from home.[48] There was a certain detachment in the Cohen household, "an arms-length relationship" not only between the parents and their children but also among the children.[49] Felix rarely, if ever, said anything negative about Morris and Mary, but a friend recalled him noting that until his senior year at CCNY, his father had hardly noticed him. Apparently, this was consistent with Morris's attitude toward his students: Morris never approved of students until others commended them.[50]

"And yet many times since then," Felix concluded his letter to Lash, "I found people and places I knew recede into a background that remained part of life—City College, for instance, and Cambridge. I suppose the difference is that I felt I had finished one chapter and was looking forward to the next."[51] A son of a detached philosopher, the American son of immigrants, Felix derived his sense of belonging from his experiences. In every chapter of his life, Felix sought to merge intellect with the experience of participation and community. He established different social clubs where he found intellectual stimulation at the same time that he forged long-lasting friendships. Only a few decades earlier, in an attempt to articulate a modernist alternative to traditional conceptions of scientific logic, Charles Sanders Peirce noted that "unless we make ourselves hermits, we shall necessarily influence each other's opinions; so that the problem becomes how to fix belief, not in the individual merely, but in the community."[52]

The College of the City of New York

> Old memories are come to me tonight
>   And I am all alone with ghosts of years,
>   To know dead hopes returned and joys and tears
> That pass in poignant silhouette in white
> And black, and leave still shadows of their flight
>   Across these walls. Dear Melodies and cheers
>   And low familiar accents haunt my ears
> And scenes of sport and love and toil, my sight.

O City College, castle of the mind,
    I could not see your towers in the sun;
I climbed your stairways, confident and blind;
    The way was pleasant and the way is done.
Within your walls my days of springtime lie . . .
Gray towers melt away in the sky.
                    —Felix S. Cohen (1926)[53]

America's first municipally owned public college, CCNY was established in 1847 at the initiative of Townsend Harris. Harris, a wealthy businessman and the president of the New York City Board of Education, convened a committee to explore the possibilities of establishing a municipal high school or college to educate the citizens of the rapidly growing global metropolis. At the time, New York City had no public secondary schools and only two private institutions of higher education, Columbia College and the University of the City of New York (now New York University). Acting on the committee's recommendation, the state legislature passed a proposal for a public academy or college, which the governor signed. In the referendum that followed, the voters of New York City approved the proposal with overwhelming support. The Free Academy (renamed CCNY in 1866) formally opened on January 21, 1849, on East Twenty-Third Street. It offered a program of study that lasted five years—one preparatory year, followed by four years of college.[54]

Whether or not Harris intended CCNY to change the social order by providing free education to all is debatable. While at times Harris indicated that CCNY would bring together children of the rich and the poor, at other times he suggested that he wanted to establish a vocational school for the sons and daughters of artisans and tradesmen. In reality, while the Free Academy allowed male graduates of all New York public elementary schools who passed the entrance examination to obtain public schooling through college, most of its students were of middle-class background as working families could not afford to dispense with the income from their children's wages. As late as the first decade of the twentieth century, only a small proportion of the population, and an even smaller proportion of working men and women, pursued college education. In short, CCNY's significance was "not . . . its mass effect, but . . . its institutional innovation."[55]

For the better part of the nineteenth century, CCNY was also not distinguished. It remained a combination of high school, college, and trade school, with no eminent faculty or novel teaching methods. But at the turn of the twentieth century, just as CCNY moved from lower Manhattan to its new campus on St. Nicholas Heights in Harlem, a dramatic change began to occur. The establishment of public high schools in New York City and the growing requirement of college education as a prerequisite for admission to the professions made important changes to the curriculum inevitable. When CCNY's board of trustees was ultimately taken over by Progressive reformers, the time was ripe for a curricular reform. New departments were established (including the departments of political science and education), modern courses were added to the curriculum, and the instruction became less "prescribed and uniform" and more "career-oriented individualized."[56]

The student body, which serious working-class Jews of Eastern European origin came to dominate in the first decades of the twentieth century, provided the background for these transformations. Many of them had little choice but to attend CCNY because Ivy League colleges, faced with a rising number of Jewish students, were instituting quotas to limit the number of Jews they admitted (usually about 10 percent). In turn, CCNY admitted anyone who qualified, with no restrictions based on ethnicity or race. Many students were also poor, and CCNY was free.[57]

Jewish students pursued higher education at two to three times the rate of non-Jewish Americans. Jewish men (women were not admitted until after World War II) viewed CCNY as an extension of New York's public schools—a means of assimilation and upward mobility. Many Townsend Harris boys went to CCNY, admitted almost automatically. (Indeed, the "introductory year" of the Free Academy grew into Townsend Harris.) Education was their chance at success.[58]

CCNY transformed the Jewish community, and the Jewish community in return made CCNY into one of the most vibrant institutions of higher education in America. CCNY remained "a form of secularized Anglo-Protestantism" for some time after its student body became predominantly Jewish. Yet its Jewish students created their own culture. "While [students at] Harvard, Princeton, and Columbia were cultivating the 'gentleman's C,' students at City College were making CCNY into a unique institution, with a scholarly, ethnic, and political character all its own." Often labeled the "Jewish University of America," CCNY became a prominent institution, one of the democratizing institutions of a buoyant urban culture.[59] "Between the 1920s and the 1970s, more of its graduates went on to receive Ph.D. degrees than those of any other college except Berkeley. . . . Eight graduates received the Nobel Prize, a record for a public institution." As one observer concluded, "by their desperate ambitions and their feverish hopes" Jewish men transformed CCNY "from a symbol of Jacksonian democracy to a symbol—perhaps *the symbol*—of the new America of assimilation, competition, and mobility."[60] CCNY was the "proletarian Harvard."[61]

Father and Son

Morris had been teaching at CCNY for almost a decade when Felix entered its Gothic halls in 1922. His father's legacy was Felix's anchor. It provided him with a sense of safety and comfort in knowing that he belonged not only with the Jewish intellectual elite but also with the American intellectual elite (however anti-Semitic it often was). But Morris's legacy also burdened Felix with expectations. Four decades later, friends and relatives remembered a pact between Morris and Felix to ignore each other if their paths crossed in CCNY's corridors. Given Morris's stature on the faculty, it is implausible that father and son were able to conceal their relationship. Friends' recollections of the pact, as well as retrospective comments about professors who were astonished to discover the relationship, suggest that only a few were fooled. More important, these comments offer a glimpse into the relationship between Morris, a detached philosopher and father, and Felix, an adolescent seeking his father's approval but trying to avoid being hidden beneath his intellectually imperial shadow. According to friends, only in his fraternity, *Lambda Mu,* did Felix feel that he was accepted on his own merits.[62]

In a subtle way, Felix rebelled. While Morris was known as a fearsome professor, "a brilliant and remorseless practitioner of the Socratic method,"[63] Felix had a friendly disposition.[64] Morris placed science and logic above all disciplines, so Felix turned to the humanities. He majored in languages, taking forty-four credits in Latin, German, French and Greek, with a minor in English.[65] Other than a required course in philosophy with Harry Overstreet, Felix avoided contact with the subject at CCNY. "I would not feel comfortable sitting in a class taught by my own father" a friend recalled Felix saying.[66]

Morris emphasized the life of the mind. He exemplified the traditional Jewish dedication to learning, finding a sense of belonging in the modern world in the study of philosophy. Felix, like other middle-class Americans of his generation, derived his sense of belonging from experience. He loved the outdoors and participatory sports such as tennis. Rejecting Morris's suggestions that he read more during breaks from school, Felix spent summer vacations in the Adirondacks, playing tennis, swimming, hiking, and canoeing with friends.[67]

Felix's rebellion was a generational one. As the Yiddish daily *Der Tog (The Day)* captured it at the end of the High Holidays: "Three generations rejoiced: The old—over the Torah, the middle-aged—over the business page in the newspaper, the young—over the sports page." While Morris was in fact a first-generation American, he was not only sufficiently young when his family immigrated to the United States, but he also developed aspirations that put him, at least culturally, among the second generation. Felix, in reality a second-generation American, could thus assume the identity of the "youthful third generation."[68]

Felix was aware of his youthful rebellion. His letters to Morris from summer vacations in the Adirondacks were playful, especially when compared to the sincere tone of his letters to Mary. "It's all decided," Felix wrote to his father in the summer of 1925; he and his friend were going to canoe and, as he reported to Morris, "have the most wonderful time of [their] lives paddling through the wilderness, sleeping underneath the stars, etc." Quite aware of Morris's concerns, Felix added that they were "both excellent swimmers." But he could not resist teasing Morris. Concluding his letter, Felix wrote that all that was left for Morris to do was "to say 'I don't think you ought to do it, but you're old enough to decide for yourself. Be a thousand times careful,' and sign on the dotted line."[69]

The rebellion ran deeper. Felix rejected not only Morris's emotional and so-cial identity but Morris's approach to philosophy as well. Morris was the epit-ome of a Jewish immigrant seeking to be accepted by the Anglo-Saxon elite. He used his philosophical approach to make the Western and Anglo-American traditions his own by criticizing his contemporaries' "revolt against their eld-ers" and their inability to formulate a coherent vision. He oscillated between the old world of metaphysics and logic and the new functional and experi-mental wave of which William James and John Dewey were the leaders. As an emotional matter, Morris felt safe with the idealists of an earlier generation who, when faced with the destabilizing aftermath of the Civil War, suggested that universal reason and morality existed behind observed temporal changes and constrained the effects of contingency and change. Their solution appealed to him, as he was struggling with the influences, destabilizing in their own right, of immigration and acculturation. As with his cosmopolitanism, Morris's attraction to logic and science reflected a rejection of individuality and subjec-tivity, which he saw as destabilizing, and an endorsement of universalism. In contrast, the pragmatists and empiricists felt sufficiently at home in an uncer-tain world and "feared no loss of moral values, or of intelligibility, in a contin-gent and plural universe." Morris accepted their insights but wished to find a medium that would allow him to hold onto certain aspects of the Western philosophical traditions. As Morris's biographer concluded, "Threatened by the new and skeptical of the old, [Morris] was caught between generations and be-tween countless polarities."[70]

Felix was fearless. Born and raised American, the son of a renowned philosopher, he could afford to indulge himself with new ideas. While avoiding the formal study of philosophy, he organized an informal group of friends, the "Sunday Night Meetings," to read and discuss works of philosophy. They fo-cused on the works of the logical positivists Ludwig Wittgenstein and Bertrand Russell, philosophers whom Morris regarded as nihilistic and whose works Felix and his friends found uplifting. Russell's and Wittgenstein's positivism complemented an intense fascination with scientific study that characterized the early twentieth century. For many who came of age between the wars, ob-jective, scientific studies of society—the social sciences—held the promise of providing alternatives to metaphysical absolutes, which were often religious, and to the parochial ideologies of isolationism and exceptionalism.[71] While Morris was clinging to the old, Felix found the modern approach to philoso-phy, science, and society appealing.

During the academic year, the Sunday Night Meetings were held in the Co-hens' apartment. They discussed different papers and books and at times trans-formed philosophy into theatrical action. For example, in order to illustrate their generation's challenge to conventional metaphysics, the group wrote a musical called *The Dying Metaphysician*. Nicknamed "Meta," the dying metaphysician had "never been really well since [he] gave up solipsism," though he had tried every possible alternative, including realism, idealism, naturalism, and phenomenalism. Meta complained about the loss of "the atom, . . . the soul, . . .

the good, and [ultimately] . . . substance," and he struggled as the doctor refused to allow him to write his "world view." Indeed, the doctor, representing the new realism, only allowed him to paint, or play, or write in rhyme, promising Meta that his problems would disappear once he replaced metaphysics (the "metaphysical notion of learning [which was] pressing on the base of the brain") with "a bromide of, say two parts prediction and one part verification." In a reassuring voice, the doctor announced that not metaphysical thinking but prediction was the focus of modern philosophy. But the difference was a matter of degree, not of kind, and the group proclaimed it so in another play, *Metaphysics on Trial, or Get a Metaphysician.* "Tear the mask off a positivist and what do you find? A metaphysician," they sang. "Things are seldom as they seem, skim milk masquerades as cream" was the theme song of one of their conferences on positivism.[72]

Morris rarely joined Felix's group. When Wittgenstein was the subject of discussion, he joined them but said nothing. Yet Felix's youthful rebellion was not all-encompassing. In summers the group organized conferences in the Adirondacks modeled after Thomas Davidson's summer schools, which Morris had attended almost three decades earlier. In 1930, the group read the galleys of Morris's first book, *Reason and Nature.* Participants remembered a hike to Grassy Springs during which they read the book. They marked one of the trees on the trail "Reason and Nature ⟶ ."[73] In retrospect, one of the participants pointedly explained the group's relationship to Morris and Felix: "To some of us Morris stood in the relation of father, and Felix in the relation of older brother. We were dazzled by their brilliance and agape at their learning. We loved Morris with a certain earthy reverence; we loved Felix quite simply."[74]

Socialism

CCNY was a stronghold of leftists throughout the 1920s. Jewish students, many of whom inherited a streak of socialism from their parents or were exposed to socialism in the city's ghettos in which they had grown up, poured into CCNY in overwhelming numbers. For many of them, socialism, which was blind to ethnic differences and instead celebrated solidarity and the improvement of economic conditions, continued to provide a sense of inclusion, of belonging with others in a struggle against injustice. It allowed them to maintain a unique political identity while rejecting the particularity of ethnic differences. Even as the socialist movement that focused on organizing workers was, in the 1920s, losing its grip on Jewish communities around the city, one could still find its traces among CCNY students. Being second- and third-generation Americans, they drew upon the traditions of "radical politics and working-class organization" to articulate a different kind of socialism—a left-liberal alternative to what they saw as the structural impediments of liberal capitalism. Their early exposure to socialism and other forms of European radical thought allowed them to dissociate themselves from the exclusionary mainstream of American political culture and to articulate other, more inclusive alternatives.[75]

More generally, American socialists reshaped their ideology after World War I shattered notions of solidarity among workers. In the 1920s, Norman Thomas emerged as "the premier American social democrat, the spokesman of a non-Marxist brand of socialism which offered itself as an alternative to both communism and twentieth century capitalism." Along with the Progressive ideology out of which it emerged, Thomas's socialism did not focus on the power of the working class to bring about change but rather on the civic responsibility of a well-bred elite class toward society. It did not advocate the redistribution of wealth but emphasized the importance of individual opportunity. In short, Thomas's was a socialist approach that mediated "between organized society and mass resentment, preventing revolution and chaos through orderly, responsible social change."[76] It was a socialism that allowed many of Felix's cohort, no longer members of the working class but of the educated middle class, to feel at home in America, capable of reforming the world but secure from the dangers of social turmoil. As Lash commented in retrospect, their socialism was a form of intellectual inquiry that embraced skepticism while remaining grounded in the possibility of order.[77] It was a comforting form of socialism.

And it was a socialism that appealed to Felix. While at CCNY, he became involved in a variety of intercollegiate and political organizations like the National Student Forum (a socialist student organization), the League for Industrial Democracy (an organization founded by Upton Sinclair in 1905 and led by Harry Laidler and Norman Thomas in the 1920s), and Norman Thomas's Socialist Party.[78] These were not organizations of working-class Jews but of middle-class Americans. "I seem to have dim memories of a group of about twenty enthusiastic college editors with southern drawls and western tongs, and Bahstan pronunciation . . . discussing the reformation of the world," Felix wrote to his father after a National Student Forum conference held in Woodstock, adding that only one among them, Sam Friedman, was his "religious compatriot."[79] At another conference, held in Bridgewater, Connecticut, Felix was elected "Boss," in charge of "organizing the performances." In a letter to his parents Felix wrote: "I pointed out that this is against all good anarchist principles, but to no avail."[80] In the presidential election of 1928 Felix voted for Norman Thomas.

Yet, while Felix was active in different socialist organizations, he had been memorialized in CCNY history as the editor of the college newspaper, *The Campus*, who fought against compulsory military training on campus with a strong conviction in democratic solutions and tolerance.[81] As we will see, the struggle marked the beginning of a life-long commitment to such pluralist values.

"The choice of acceptance must lie with individual conscience"

The socialism of the 1920s was imbued with pacifism. War was the supreme example of a world gone awry, of "human suffering in its most advanced, brutal, and organized form." Socialists argued that capitalism provided the cultural and emotional environment in which war could thrive—a combination of greed and the egotistical pursuit of self-interest, whether individual or national.[82] For modernists, more generally, war "became a metaphor for far-reaching condemnation of modern culture."[83] Having lost their campaign against America's entry into World War I, pacifists aimed their postwar efforts at limiting the growing influence of the military establishment, believing that an arms race had been a major underlying cause of World War I.[84] In colleges and universities, their struggle focused on the Reserve Officers' Training Corps (ROTC), organized by the War Department in the wake of World War I.

Colleges and universities offered courses in military training as early as 1819. The first institution to offer it was the American Literary, Scientific, and Military Academy, now Norwich University, in Vermont. But on June 3, 1916, President Woodrow Wilson signed the National Defense Act, which brought military training in higher education under a single, federally controlled entity—the ROTC. Between 1917 and 1918, 50,000 officers who received military training at civilian colleges or universities served in World War I. And between 1919 and 1920, the first ROTC commissions were conferred on 133 men.[85]

Originally billed as a "training program," the course became a "recruitment and public relations device." By 1927, eighty-six colleges had mandatory ROTC programs; in forty-four others it was an elective. In fifty-three cities it was also extended to high schools. Pacifists found this development alarming, and by the mid-1920s they were running a nationwide campaign to encourage students and teachers to wage war against the compulsory drill.[86] At CCNY, the fight over mandatory ROTC became a battleground between a student body committed, for the most part, to pacifism and socialism and an administration keen on enforcing patriotism and national loyalty.[87] Due to CCNY's reputation and location, the battle received national and international attention.

CCNY officially started elective military training in the winter of 1917. Explaining the decision, President Sidney Edward Mezes noted that "the great national need, in case of a crisis, is for officers, and the trustees in authorizing the course are offering the students an opportunity for the most effective service to the country." In October 1918 the course became mandatory, but in December, one month after the signing of the armistice, the Student Army Training Corps were demobilized. Then, in February 1919, the board of trustees and the faculty established an ROTC and made two years of military training compulsory for all CCNY students. An additional two years were voluntary. On March 14, 1924, the Student Curriculum Committee recommended that the course be placed on the list of elective subjects. "Leadership, self-control, good carriage and the rest may often be the products of military training," their statement read, "but only when that training is voluntarily undertaken and appreciated. . . . A liberal college should not in any way seek to perpetuate the conditions which make war possible." Seven months later, the Faculty Curriculum Committee rejected their proposal, declaring that the course "formed a concrete method of expressing the students' appreciation of the education offered by the College under the American Institutions." While the students offered no immediate response, on May 15, 1925, a new Student Curriculum Committee recommended abolishing the compulsory drill. They claimed to represent the desire of the student body that "Military Science" not be required for any degree. "Any duty that we owe the City, State, or Country," the Committee's request read, "is surely not fulfilled by making students mechanical dolls. Our purpose as an institution of learning is to turn out a good citizen and a cultured man. By turning out truly good citizens we are more than fulfilling our obligations to the civil authorities." The Faculty Committee did not respond to the report.[88]

Six months after the Student Committee issued its proposal, Felix, as editor-in-chief of *The Campus*, became a spokesman for the students. On November 2, 1925, *The Campus* published an editorial calling for a student referendum on the subject of the compulsory course in Military Science. Nine days later, on Armistice Day of 1925, obviously chauvinistic extracts from the "Manual of Military Training" appeared in the editorial columns of *The Campus* next to an editorial denouncing militarism.[89] The following day, the Social Problem Club adopted a resolution calling for a plebiscite on the question of military training at CCNY, which the student council authorized a day later. In support, Felix published an editorial entitled "Who Wants Millie?" in which he reiterated his call for a referendum to be conducted by the student council. "An editorial invective against military training," he explained, "would have the same harmless effect as the hundreds that have been written on the topic. What will convince the Board of Trustees is not an individual opinion but the combined desires of all. . . . At any rate let us have a vote."[90]

Despite President Mezes's support for compulsory training, the student council continued with its plan. On the eve of the balloting, anti-military articles and statements on both sides from alumni and various faculty members (who had thus far remained astonishingly quiet) filled the front page of *The Campus*. On November 18, 1925, voting began on a student referendum. Over two-thirds of the student body voted in three days of balloting, a number larger than had ever participated in any activity at CCNY. The student body voted "2092 to 345 . . . against the military training course."[91] Five days later, Felix published his last editorial on the subject, "The Last Word," an assessment of arguments in support of and in opposition to compulsory military training and of the importance of freedom of opinion and tolerance in a democratic society.[92]

Pacifists objected to the ROTC because it introduced chauvinism, militarism, authoritarianism, and indoctrination into the educational process under the guise of citizenship training, physical education, and preparedness for peace. "The Last Word" demonstrated that ROTC courses actually allotted no hours to civic education. At CCNY no hours were devoted to citizenship training and only six hours to physical education. Instead, ROTC courses focused on military training (at CCNY, two hundred hours).[93] In retrospect,

Felix noted that the students' battle had not been against bayonets or brutality. Rather, the quotations he published "were simply used to show that talk about citizenship, honor, discipline, education, etc. was a lot of hooey." He also recalled that what bothered him in particular was the glorification of war, "the investing of war with the aura of adventure in the world of youth."[94] Playing war, pacifists argued, did not create good soldiers or citizens, nor did it promote peace.[95] In this vein, "The Last Word" quoted an anonymous "Army Officer": "An army exists to kill men, when ordered, in the nation's quarrel, irrespective of justice." As Felix echoed, "Preparation for war in time of peace is destined to bring war, not peace." It was thus "incompatible with true love of country, real patriotism."[96]

Moving beyond debates between pacifists and advocates of military training, which he portrayed as factual, the essential Felix shone in the concluding remarks of "The Last Word." He "despise[d]" those who ignored, or sought to crush, any opposition to their beliefs, and "respect[ed]" those who expressed beliefs that were opposed to his. "We realize," Felix wrote, "that the sincere belief of our opponent in this matter is as worthy of consideration as is our own. Each is a religious principle. The choice of acceptance must lie with individual conscience."[97]

Here was Felix's rebellion against his father, who, in accordance with his moral universalism, viewed compulsory training as "indefensible from the point of view of ethics."[98] Here was Felix carving his place in the modernist project. Felix embraced the plurality of moral points of view. It was precisely this diversity that made mandatory military training objectionable in his mind. Not a choice among values but tolerance was Felix's intuitive reaction to the plurality of opinions. "The Last Word" advocated toleration of a multiplicity of beliefs and experiences. And it ended as a work of advocacy should. "Our cause is pleaded," Cohen wrote. "Further editorial comments, except in the nature of reply to new criticisms or interpretation of new circumstances, would be superfluous."[99]

The administration's response was negative. Shortly after the publication of "The Last Word" and notwithstanding *The Campus*'s announcement that it would withhold further comment on the issue pending consideration of it by the faculty, President Mezes ordered Felix, as editor of *The Campus*, to refrain from making any further mention of military science in the columns of the paper. On November 25, 1925, *The Campus* responded with three blank columns bordered in black on its front page, carrying a wry statement: "*The Campus* may make no further reference in any of its columns to a certain course at the College." This blank space would appear in several subsequent issues, always with this statement.[100]

Newspapers around the country carried the story and responses to it. Some of the published letters were ruthlessly unsympathetic, noting not only military training was important, but also that those who did not agree were un-American, Communists, and, according to one anonymous author, "ungrateful kikes" who should "get the hell out of here and go back to Trotsky's paradise." "You are a menace to America," another reader wrote.[101]

Such comments must have been painful to the students. No matter how as-similated many of them felt, conservatives in America saw them as Communist Jews. But other letters, many of which were written by academics at other uni-versities, offered consolation. Military training is "undemocratic, barbaric and educationally wholly unwise," John Dewey explained. An editorial in *The Na-tion* followed, noting that "the City College boys . . . deserve the active support of all citizens who love peace, liberty, and the best American traditions of edu-cation." "If the majority of the students were indeed pacifists, they would have the same right to their opinions that those who are not pacifists have to theirs," the American Civil Liberties Union (ACLU) wrote to President Mezes. "I have noted with much satisfaction the student revolt against compulsory military training and with equal regret your view that the course should be retained for its educational and physical value," Richard Rogers Bowker echoed in a letter to President Mezes.[102] Bowker, an 1868 alumnus who founded the first under-graduate newspaper at CCNY, was also among those who sent a letter to the college trustees expressing the wish to join with the students' petition to make the compulsory military training course elective. Bowker strongly denounced the censorship ordered by President Mezes, asserting that it was "contrary to the spirit of our free institution and that the conscription of our youth in time of peace through compulsory military training is likewise incompatible with the spirit of our college."[103]

"Behind the stone surface"

In December 1925, the faculty and board of trustees lifted the ban forbidding *The Campus* to discuss military training but voted to retain the course as part of the prescribed curriculum.[104] In February 1926, the managing board of *The Campus* dismissed Felix as editor. The reason given was Felix's tenure as editor of *Microcosm,* the class yearbook. At the end of the year, the published yearbook included a page headed "Microcosm Honor Roll," which listed "in recognition of Exemplary Valor on the Field of Battle Dec. 19, 1925" the seventeen profes-sors who dissented from the faculty vote in favor of compulsory military drill.[105] Writing to Morris from the Adirondacks in the summer after his grad-uation, Felix noted: "I discover that I have during the past year developed a pleasant faculty—that of enjoying human craziness and stupidity. Protagonists of military science, professors, commencement orators, collegiates, and not least of all the inmates of this madhouse have helped make the past year very pleas-ant."[106] "The little burlesque figures that decorate these walls," Felix's forward to *Microcosm* read, "have, all, the youthful seriousness of purpose that is the no-blest characteristic of the City College man. Yet there lurks behind the stone surface a smile, a sense of proportion. That, too, is part of our College's soul."[107]

The debates carried on beyond Felix's graduation. On December 30, 1926, Felix, at the time a student in the Philosophy Department at Harvard University, presented the reasons for opposing military training in colleges to the annual intercollegiate conference of the League for Industrial Democracy.[108] Then, in 1928, the Military Science course was made "optional with a third year of Hygiene." It was not what the opponents of military training had agitated for, but it was a major step in that direction.[109]

There were also personal repercussions. The admissions committee of the Phi Beta Kappa chapter of CCNY omitted the name of Felix Cohen, a summa cum laude graduate, from their 1926 list for election. Felix's supporters in the chapter, including his father, announced their intention to block any other candidate if Felix was not admitted.[110] In a letter to his mother, who relayed the news to him, Felix proclaimed that although he was "of course . . . sorry to have been even an unintentional cause of the rest of the fellows' being blackballed," the affair made him "much happier than getting in ever would have done. Good old Bowker."[111]

For two years admissions to Phi Beta Kappa were at a standstill.[112] Morris recommended that Felix withdraw his name.[113] But Felix felt that as he had not presented his name in the first place, it was not for him to withdraw. Eventually, a special committee vindicated the integrity of the former editor of *The Campus,* and another committee devised a more democratic rule for voting on admissions. In November 1928 the struggle was terminated. Felix, by then a graduate student both in the Department of Philosophy at Harvard University and at Columbia Law School, became Morris's brother in Phi Beta Kappa.[114]

CHAPTER 2

Multiple Destinies

Felix announced his intention of attending law school immediately upon his graduation from CCNY in 1926. Given his natural abilities as an advocate and his strong sense of commitment to social and political causes, the decision seemed obvious. While many second- and third-generation immigrants saw their choice of a career as unrelated to their ethnic background, a career in law carried with it the promise of continued upward mobility, of acceptance and assimilation. Throughout the 1920s, an average of about 30 percent of CCNY graduates pursued a career in law.[1] Friends and relatives commented that Morris triggered a subliminal desire in Felix's mind by introducing him to prominent lawyers and legal scholars. "Felix saw all those famous judges and legal scholars as he was growing up; he saw how much Morris admired them," a friend suggested, "and how he attacked all the philosophers that came."[2]

The correspondence between Morris and Felix during the summer of 1926 focused on Felix's choice. Morris, who had always been interested in the study of jurisprudence, urged Felix to pursue graduate studies in philosophy before embarking upon the study of law.[3] Writing from the Adirondacks, where he spent his summer vacation, Felix offered a compromise. He told his father that he wanted to study law at Harvard and then perhaps continue graduate studies in law or pursue an M.A. in philosophy. Morris, writing from New York City, persisted. He was anxious for Felix to come to a different decision. Aware of Morris's desires, Felix chose to appear nonchalant. "I don't know how many times I'll change my mind—or care particularly," he explained to his father, then apologized for not reading or thinking much during the summer. "If I haven't written of my 'reading and thoughts' for the past two weeks," he tweaked Morris on a different occasion, it was "as much because I haven't read or thought for two weeks." He had "read the first five books of the Bible," Felix added, assuredly to Morris's dismay, "and discovered among other interesting facts that locusts, grasshoppers, and crickets are kosher." The letter concluded by noting that "besides not reading and not thinking," Felix and his friends "indulged prodigiously in canoeing, swimming, tennising, eating and sleeping." Determined to make his son a philosopher, Morris invited Felix to read some of his articles. "I've always secretly wondered," Felix wrote in response, "why you never encouraged me along that line but I think now that you're right. Far from entering your philosophy with a predisposition in its favor, I'll be a subject for you to convert from Bertrand Russell."[4]

In his typical filial loyalty, Felix proclaimed that he did not think there was "much conflict" between Morris and Russell, as if such announcement would reassure Morris that Felix shared his philosophical approach. But the tone and context of the correspondence between Morris and Felix reflected a growing professional and personal disagreement. Morris and Felix differed dramatically in their assessment of the importance of philosophy and the social sciences to Progressive reform; their divergent evaluations were grounded not only in intellectual convictions but also in Morris's and Felix's distinct feelings about their place, as Jews, in American society.

For Morris, the immigrant who wanted to assimilate, the study of philosophy was a way of connecting with the Anglo-Saxon academic elite. His dissertation, for example, sought to reformulate ethics (specifically Kant's) without reference to religion. Ironically, Morris's was a false promise of acceptance. As his biographer explained, the idealists, with whom he felt aligned, were "materially parochial," seeking to affirm "the goodness and wholeness, not only of being in general, but of American society and the Christian religion in particular."[5]

Felix, raised a middle-class American, was not interested in the study of philosophy. He viewed philosophical contemplations as a prerogative of those who could remain detached from daily events. He did not share Morris's faith in the force of ideas to effectuate radical social and economic changes. As he told the participants of the Eastern Law Students Conference in 1936, "Lawyers have never been creators of social ideals." "That is a task rather for philosophers, inventors, poets, artists, educators, agitators, dreamers." In turn, "the lawyer's highest calling . . . is . . . to capture the dream and to transfer it into the stuff of reality, to bring the ideals of his age into the concrete material of human adjustments and social structures."[6] In short, while Morris cared about abstract arguments, Felix wanted to engage the harder task of developing principles and applying them to factual situations.[7]

Felix was fascinated by the social sciences with their promise of objectivity and their rejection of religious parochialism. He belonged to an intellectual generation that sought to draw on developments in the social sciences to suggest solutions to diverse social, economic, and political problems.[8] Many of this generation viewed the study of law as providing tools with which they could challenge the authority of the Anglo-Saxon elite in American life, ultimately creating a more egalitarian society. Unlike philosophy, the social sciences, particularly law, could effect actual change.

Morris's pressure, however, was not easy to bear. Before too long, Felix changed his mind. He would study philosophy first and then law. A relative suggested that the offer of a Henry Bromfield Rogers Fellowship in Ethics and Jurisprudence at Harvard was the decisive factor; it brought with it a promise of economic independence.[9] Yet in a letter written more than two decades after the events, Felix reflected on the role that one of his generation's representative figures, Roger Baldwin, who would become the first director of the ACLU, had played in making him realize the importance of bringing together modern legal science and traditional, philosophical meditations, what Felix would later describe as the fusion of the social sciences and ethics:

> There was a September evening around a Connecticut fireplace, back in 1926, when I was fresh out of college and trying to decide what to do next, weighing the relative significance of a lawyer's life and a philosopher's. I got to arguing with Roger Baldwin about prohibition and politics; before the evening was over I began to see that neither law nor philosophy had much meaning if they were kept in separate compartments and that even a lawyer's life can be philosophic if one keeps sight of the cosmic interconnections between legal cases and man's social aspirations.[10]

Felix decided to study law and philosophy with an emphasis on the interconnections between them. In the fall of 1926, with a fellowship from the graduate school, Morris's blessing, and an apparent conviction that the study of philosophy and law would better equip him to understand the radical interdependence that characterized modern life and to bring about change, Felix began his doctoral studies in the Department of Philosophy at Harvard.[11] He lived with three roommates in an apartment at 30 Wendell Street in Cambridge.

Cambridge

Boston had played host to the "American mind" for centuries, but in the twentieth century New York City was "the site of the American mood." Beginning in the decade after World War I, as America began its ascendance as the world's most powerful nation, New York was rapidly gaining recognition as "the world's most powerful city." New York had no governing middle class, no consistent moral consensus, and no single university that dominated it as Harvard presided over Boston's intellectual life. Rather, New York's strength was its vibrant diversity. A home to the giants of industry and finance, to a highly visible working class composed of immigrants and their children, and to a rapidly growing African American community, New York had an exuberant secular, popular, and inquisitive culture.[12] It was a culture that Felix associated with CCNY. As he wrote a decade after graduation, CCNY students bore three distinguishing marks: "the mark of labor, the mark of intellectual curiosity, and the mark of cosmopolitan civilization." "I well remember," he added, "that as a graduate student at Harvard, carrying on the City College tradition of questioning and correcting the professor, I found that the practice, which had seemed perfectly natural to my undergraduate classmates, was in the new environment horrifying to some, entertaining to others, and intriguing to still others, but surprising to all."[13]

CCNY was an educational and cultural haven for Jewish students. CCNY's inclusiveness helped make New York City, and America more broadly, a home. And the students, as Felix put it, did not come "to enjoy 'college life,' or to get degrees, or to achieve social distinction," but to learn. They came because they looked forward "to ways of earning a living and ways of recreation" which required "learning of some sort." More important, they came because they wanted to understand their world.[14]

In comparison to New York, which Felix celebrated as the epitome of tolerance and freedom, Cambridge was the place of the Anglo-Saxon elite, with whom he felt no affinity. "Cambridge is duller than ever, except for philosophy," Felix wrote to his father. It simply could not compete with New York's appeal. As he explained to his mother, he felt "growing irritation at the 'superficies' of Cambridge Society, which is not much different . . . from Society in general." "The form of social intercourse," Felix complained, "makes the substance less palatable than it deserves to be—at least to a Bolshevik like myself." "Got an invitation to an affair Monday evening at [William Ernest] Hocking's home, which I promptly accepted," he wrote to Morris on a different occasion. "Since then I've heard a rumor that it's formal. Of course I'll go, and if I see an array of soup-and-fishes I can always ask to see the gas meter and take my exit."[15]

Cambridge was simply not to Felix's liking, and that his girlfriend Lucy, a student of statistics at Barnard, was in New York City probably contributed to his sense of disappointment. But a close circle of friends, many of them from New York, his ongoing interest in sports, and books kept him in good spirits. "I'm really keeping in condition—gym sessions three times a week—nine hours sleep regularly, excluding lectures. Weigh 153 in spite of this exercise, which is more than I've ever weighed," he reported home in the winter of his first year at Harvard. "I've been raiding a secondhand book store lately," he wrote on another occasion. "I've picked up at a dime a piece a couple of eighteenth century editions of Cicero, collected essays of Macaulay, Mill, and Carlyle, a few pounds of Bible, one of the famous Bridgewater treatises, a complete collection of Hood's poems, and many other interesting items."[16]

Felix wanted to be, and not least to succeed, on his own. He continued to feel discomfort at being known as Morris's son. "I'm awfully sorry about dad's suggesting that Sheffer let me off. If I need favors here, really I'm old enough to ask them myself," he wrote to his mother. But he also sought Morris's guidance. His letters home included daily reports about courses, essays he was writing, books he was reading, and Morris's friends on the faculty, especially Alfred North Whitehead.[17]

The Citadel of American Philosophy

For the most part, Felix found his courses interesting.[18] He had great respect
for Whitehead, Henry M. Sheffer, and Ralph Barton Perry, all of whom were
leaders in the fight against idealism. Whitehead, hired by Harvard in 1924,
transformed the study of metaphysics by emphasizing the importance of process, that is, the ongoing movement to transcend and unify the multiplicity of
experiences (which, according to Whitehead, constantly gave rise to new mul-
tiplicities). Sheffer sought to use the notion of inconsistency to develop a system of logic. Finally, Perry revolutionized the study of ethics by critiquing the
idealists' description of personality as "a multiple and mutual affair, social in its
context and determining relations, but not social in its seat or locus." Instead,
Perry suggested that the self was a composition of "multiple interests," that is,
multiple kinds of tendencies and adaptations which were related to each other
through value.[19]

Perry's approach to ethics appealed to Felix's understanding of human needs
in the complex and interdependent modern world. According to Perry, individuals "determined moral goodness by considering the totality of affected interests in order to satisfy and promote them jointly." While Perry conceded that
individuals did not always act prudently to check their interests in relation to
others, he proclaimed that everyone agreed that it was irrational not to do so.
As Perry explained, individuals recognized the existence of conflicting interests
and understood the need to adjust them; moral dilemmas were resolved "when,
and only when, everyone's will was so attuned that each was content with a situation in which all benefited." Each person achieved personal harmony only
by the guidance of universal benevolence. "The concern for all satisfied each,"
and "the result was a cooperative federation in which the community of interests and personal integration were one."[20] For Felix this seemed both rational
and intuitive.

Felix chose Perry as his dissertation advisor. Yet he was not satisfied with the
study of moral philosophy for its own sake. Harvard was "*the* place" to obtain
advanced training in both empirical and metaphysical thought. But the study
of philosophy in Cambridge was too sterile. By the 1920s, intellectuals like
John Dewey and Walter Lippmann had created a buoyant intellectual world
outside philosophy, turning away from traditional forms of inquiry toward the
methods of the social sciences. They saw in the norms of efficiency, rationality,
and expertise, which the newly developing social sciences endorsed, a substitute for the moralism of philosophy. For young New York intellectuals, Jews in
particular, the turn to the social sciences offered a means of infusing traditional
philosophy departments, from which Jews were often excluded, with new ideologies. They did not reject philosophy, but they wanted to make it reform-
oriented.[21] Without an understanding of the connection between the problems
of philosophy and legal, ethical, and social problems, Felix wrote in his disserta-

tion, "philosophy tends to become simply the noblest of games and social reform the most pathetic of humanity's aspirations."[22]

The social sciences satisfied Felix's intellectual curiosity. Taking minors in government, economics, and anthropology, he spent many hours reading law, psychology, political science, and anthropology and auditing the classes of professors such as Roscoe Pound, Felix Frankfurter, William Y. Elliott, and Alfred Tozzer. He disliked economics, concluding "after reading one or two accounts of the law of diminishing returns" that "it was all the bunk" and reduced to the claim that "where production (used in its most general sense) is fixed by a limited number of factors there exists a certain ratio in which these factors must be combined to afford the optimum return." But the course in anthropology was "a great source of consolation."[23]

What triggered Felix's interest in anthropology is unclear. Certainly this was not to satisfy Morris, who made a special point of indicating that he did not think highly of Tozzer. (In response, Felix insisted that even though Tozzer was not brilliant, "he has done some interesting original work in archeology and New Mexico.")[24] It could be that Lucy, who worked with Franz Boas, turned Felix on to the subject. Or else it was his fascination, typical of the generation that came of age in the 1920s, with the primitive mind and magic.[25]

Whatever the original attraction was, Felix was determined to act on it. Having read Ernest Hobson's *The Domain of Natural Science,* he reported to his parents that he found its "discussion of magic" offensive to his "anthropological sensibilities." Foreshadowing a lifelong commitment to learning about and celebrating different cultures, Felix's letter announced his intention to "write an admirable exposition of magic" some day. He wanted to refute the belief, which many philosophers shared and to which he was exposed in Whitehead's class, that cultural customs such as beating gongs when the moon was in eclipse reflected a "primitive" recognition that the universe was inexplicable. Felix believed that such cultural customs reflected a belief in the universe's explicability. Those who beat gongs, he explained, intended to scare the monster that was eating the moon. "They haven't discovered metaphysics yet," he wrote to his parents. "If they had, they would have said 'This is a metaphysical problem we need not discuss here,' and gone ahead to assume a metaphysical answer as do most of the authors I've been reading lately."[26]

In comparison, traditional courses in philosophy, such as Burtt's course on the method and task of metaphysics, seemed tedious, even "putrid." A letter home on a different occasion expressed Felix's sheer excitement about a paper on primitive science and magic only to conclude that "instead of wandering in this fashion I ought to be doing an essay for Sheffer." He wanted to write a good paper, but he did not "just know where to start."[27]

Anthropology was also the most Progressive of the social sciences, due to the development of cultural anthropology, which the doctrine of cultural relativism dominated between the wars. Prior to World War I, the idea that cultures must be understood "in their terms" was merely a methodological injunction, subject to conceptions of cultural hierarchy and progress. After the war, influenced by Franz Boas, "cultural relativism flowered not just as a methodological imperative, but as a moral and intellectual posture." Anthropologists called not only for tolerance toward diverse cultures and folkways but also for "a certain detached skepticism toward the norms of one's own society."[28] And while a certain estrangement from the norms of modern society cultivated cultural relativism, relativism also made young intellectuals feel at home. In a world that celebrated a diversity of cultures and identities, all were welcome. Gone was the idea that America could remain secluded from the world, gone was the ideology of the melting pot. A feeling of alienation from tradition to which many early twentieth-century American writers alluded was superseded by the optimistic appeal of a world where the one was many and the many, potentially, one.

For Felix's generation, New York City embodied this sense of optimism. Felix spent less than two years in Cambridge, revisiting the city on vacations and other opportunities. In the fall of 1928, with a law school scholarship for the highest grade given on the entrance examination (instituted that year "to avoid the human waste of allowing men without requisite capacity to embark upon studies at which they were doomed to fail")[29], he returned to the city as a student at Columbia Law School. "He had a girl [Lucy] in New York City," Morris explained his son's choice to his college roommate, Felix Frankfurter, who had assumed Felix would go to Harvard Law School and had even helped arrange a full scholarship for him. For a while after his return to New York, Felix stressed that Columbia was better than Harvard.[30]

Legal Realism

Legal education at the turn of the twentieth century was informed by classical legal thought.[31] While early nineteenth-century legal scholars endorsed a utilitarian approach, according to which judges determined important policy questions when making decisions, classical legal thinkers embraced formalism. Accordingly, law was like geometry, organized around a few fundamental axioms, drawn from precedents and from which judges could deduce rules to apply to particular cases. Judges declared but did not make law. Law was an autonomous and coherent system, and judicial decisions were the products of internal reasoning, immune to the influences of social, economic, and political interests. The study of law was thus the scientific study of written appellate cases. The professor's task was to teach his students how to draw general principles from a series of cases and how to apply them to the issue before them. Decisions inconsistent with these uncovered principles were deemed wrong.[32]

While classical legal thought dominated American legal institutions between the 1880s and the 1930s, from the turn of the twentieth century Progressive legal scholars and their successors, the legal realists (including Morris Cohen), participated in the general revolt against formalism and absolutism and engaged in a harsh critique of classical legal thought.

Bringing the lessons of philosophical pragmatism to legal thought, Progressive legal thinkers and legal realists argued that law was not an autonomous body of abstract axioms from which judges could deduce rules but rather the outcome of debatable policy judgments about the social utility of diverse activities in a rapidly changing society. Legal realists rejected the idea that law was discovered through internal reasoning. They argued that by depicting law as apolitical, the classicist model obscured the indeterminacy of legal doctrine and the social, economic, and political interests that legal decisions promoted.[33]

Realists believed that by calling attention to the uncertainty and indeterminacy of law, they could make predictions about what courts would do more, rather than less, certain. Oliver Wendell Holmes Jr., whom many legal realists regarded as antecedent and who was a close friend of William James and Charles Peirce, articulated the prediction theory of law, according to which law was "what the courts would do in fact and nothing more pretentious."[34] And Jerome Frank, whose writings have often been associated with the position that judges made decisions based on what they ate for breakfast, stressed that "if we relinquish the assumption that law can be made mathematically certain, if we honestly recognize the judicial process as involving unceasing adjustment and individualization, we may be able to reduce the uncertainty which characterizes much of our present judicial output to the extent that such uncertainty is undesirable. We may augment markedly the amount of actual legal certainty."[35]

The legal realist critique of law's determinacy and certainty was animated by their concerns about the inadequacy of traditional legal rules and categories to address the problems of modern American society. While many historians see legal realism as developing between the wars, the legal realists' scholarship was deeply informed by the distinction between the "law in books" and the "law in action" that Roscoe Pound, later the dean of Harvard Law School, drew around 1910 to explain why the law lagged behind social and economic change. According to Pound, the disparity existed because legal learning continued to reflect the values and categories of an individualistic agricultural society that had evolved into an interdependent and urbanized industrial society.[36] Pound faulted a system of "mechanical jurisprudence" for moving law ever further away from society. He argued that the nineteenth-century deductive method created a closed system of legal rules that supported anachronism as a fundamental principle. To enable law to stay in touch with life, Pound articulated a sociological jurisprudence—"a movement for pragmatism as a philosophy of law; for the adjustment of principles and doctrines to the human conditions they are to govern rather than to assumed first principles; for putting the human factor in the central place and relegating logic to its true position as an instrument."[37]

The legal realists' critique unveiled the political biases of classical legal thought, which realists saw manifested in the classicist argument that private property and contracts reflected natural rights and voluntary choices that should be protected from the coercive power of the state. Classicists asserted that a self-executing market would promote just results. The state was supposed to protect the functioning of the market by leaving individuals free to enter whatever transactions they chose. Unequal results were accordingly conceptualized as reflecting the unequal abilities of individuals. The state could ensure that contractual arrangements reflected the meeting of the minds of the parties involved, but it could not impose on private parties particular conceptions of right or wrong. For one thing, business corporations, which were legally viewed as private entities, could not be forced to take into account the social welfare of workers or the common weal. Between the 1880s and the 1930s, courts used such arguments to strike down protective labor legislation as an unconstitutional interference with the property rights of employers or with freedom of contract.

Legal realists like Robert Hale and Morris Cohen argued that by employing the private-public distinction and by treating the market as natural and neutral, courts had obscured the role of the state in distributing wealth and power and particularly in strengthening the position of business corporations at the expense of workers and consumers. They rejected the distinction between a supposedly noncoercive private sphere of individual rights and a coercive public sphere of state regulation as fundamentally misguided, as all relations among private parties were premised on the existence and enforcement of the law of contracts and property by the state. Private law was thus a form of regulatory public law. Property rights were a means by which the government indirectly coerced some individuals to produce income to the property owners.[38] The law of contract, in turn, put the state's forces at the disposal of one party over another, thus conferring a form of sovereignty on the former. A contract did not reflect an agreement between the parties, but the court's vision of policy and justice.[39] Finally, the supposedly self-executing market was a social construct that reflected prevailing "notions as to policy, welfare, justice, right and wrong, such notions often being inarticulate and subconscious."[40] The freedom of the market was accordingly the freedom of strong individuals and groups to dominate weak ones, with their coercive power being reinforced by state agencies.[41]

Having deconstructed law's politics, many realists turned to the social sciences in an attempt to create a legal system that would be better grounded in social and economic contexts or consequences and would thus be less politically tilted in favor of one group than the classicist model was. In 1897, Holmes told the students of Boston University School of Law that "for the rational study of the law, the black-letter man may be the man of the present, but the man of the future is the man of statistics and the master of economics."[42] And in 1910 Pound emphasized the importance of history, philosophy, and science to the study of law. According to Pound, history could shed light on the periodic movements between rule and discretion; philosophy could illuminate the shadowy relation of ethics and religion to legal conceptualism on the one hand and to the doing of practical justice on the other; science, specifically the social sciences, could show how law dealt with the stuff of life and direct legal research away from books and decisional precedents and into laboratories and field investigations.[43]

In the early decades of the century, such empirical studies were infused with reformist energies, the most prominent example being the "Brandeis Brief," which was submitted to the Supreme Court in 1908 by Louis Brandeis and his sister-in-law Josephine Goldmark in support of a law mandating maximum working hours for laundresses. The brief devoted only two pages to legal precedents and over a hundred pages to sociological data demonstrating that overly long days had negative effects on women and their families. By grounding law in experience and empirical studies rather than logic, Brandeis hoped to obtain a sympathetic hearing for the facts supporting the legislation. He succeeded. The brief persuaded the Court to uphold the law.[44] A milestone in labor law, it was also one of the best practical examples of Progressive (and later realist) jurisprudence. As Holmes put it in his famous *Lochner* dissent, which had become a cornerstone for Progressive and realist thought, "general propositions do not decide concrete cases."[45]

In the late 1920s, the possibility of social reform was treated more skeptically, but the social sciences retained their methodological appeal. Realists engaged in a wide range of functionalist studies, aligning legal research with the studies of economics, sociology, and anthropology, which during these decades produced many detailed studies of the functions of social and economic institutions. Some realists believed that the functions and consequences of legal rules would be better understood through detailed studies of social facts. Others wanted law to reflect social customs. Still others urged that value questions be deferred and that empirical studies of the determinants, administration, and effects of legal decisions and rules be prioritized. At any rate, realism became associated with social scientific studies.

Columbia Law School: Fighting over Legal Education

Young law professors at Yale and Columbia who engaged the social sciences also sought to revise the curriculum to set legal education in the frame of anthropology, economics, political science, psychology, and sociology. In his annual report for the year 1925–26, President Butler of Columbia University noted that there were "signs on every hand that a larger conception of what is meant by the study of the law is making its way in the legal profession as well as among the judges and among the teachers and scholars of the law." Topics like public law, constitutional history, the principles of the social sciences, which at the end of the nineteenth century were viewed as outside the realm of professional legal education, were introduced into the curriculum. And law teachers emphasized the need to teach not only legal doctrine but also law's function as a means of social control.[46]

In 1926, such sentiments led the faculty of the Columbia Law School, one of the bastions of legal realism, to engage in a critical reexamination of legal education, a serious attempt to incorporate more than two decades of Progressive and legal realist scholarship into curricular reform. All involved in the study agreed that law was a means of social control and should be studied as such. To accomplish the task, the faculty recommended changing the formal and artificial categories of law, which obscured the social problems with which law dealt, into categories of human activity. Members of the faculty further urged the inclusion of other disciplines in the required curriculum.[47]

Yet, despite the seeming consensus about the need to expose law students to nonlegal material, the proper way to achieve this change was a subject of intense debate. Led by Herman Oliphant, some professors, including Underhill Moore, Hessel Yntema, and Leon Marshall, believed that the curriculum should incorporate social scientific research into law as an aspect of social organization and focus on the nonprofessional (that is, unrelated to the immediate needs of practice) study of law. They believed "that the time had now arrived for at least one law school to abandon its traditional purpose of preparing students for practice and to become instead a 'community of scholars' devoted 'primarily to the non–professional study of law, in order that the function of law may be comprehended, its results evaluated, and its development kept more nearly in step with the complex developments of modern life.'" Interestingly, Oliphant, Yntema, and Moore were all trained in law, but none practiced law, while Marshall was an economist. Most members of the Columbia Law School faculty, however, contended that while graduates should be adequately trained in the social sciences, the principal function of the school should remain professional training.[48]

For two years prior to these events, the Columbia Law School's dean, Huger W. Jervey, played an important role in mediating the conflicting ideas of members of his faculty. But in the spring of 1926, Jervey fell ill. He was granted an indefinite leave of absence in the summer of 1927 and in February 1928 tendered his letter of resignation. Debates over education turned into arguments about the selection of a successor. When President Butler, without consulting with the faculty's special committee on the deanship, which seemed to be embroiled in disagreement, chose Young B. Smith, the decision was met with "an immediate uproar."[49]

Oliphant, Smith's challenger, left the law school, along with some of his supporters. Assistant Professor William Douglas resigned, effective June 30, 1928, and moved to Yale Law School. Associate Professor Yntema resigned too and, together with Marshall, a visiting professor whose appointment terminated that same day, went to Johns Hopkins University, "where an Institute of Law was being set up under the direction of Walter Wheeler Cook to translate into institutional form his plans for a research school of jurisprudence that would be devoted to the objective study of law as a social institution." Oliphant, too, was heading to Johns Hopkins, but his resignation went into effect a year later, so that he could take advantage of a sabbatical leave due to him. Finally, Moore, who was invited to join the group at Johns Hopkins, "regarded that venture as unsound, and remained at Columbia, speaking to no one, not even to say 'Good Morning.'" He ultimately resigned, effective January 1, 1930, and moved to Yale's Institute of Human Relations.[50]

New Beginnings

Felix began his first year of studies at Columbia Law School in the fall of 1928, shortly after the split. In many respects, his law school experience was typical. He enjoyed the courses in evidence (with Jerome Michael, a close friend and one of the reasons Felix chose Columbia Law School), conflict of laws (with Elliot Cheatham), industrial relations (with J. C. Bonbright), sales (with Karl Llewellyn, with whom he shared a taste for exotic foods and singing),[51] and, more important, utilities and rate making (with Robert Hale) and corporate finance (with Adolf Berle). Felix was a Kent scholar and a book and legislation review editor for the *Columbia Law Review,* a position that allowed him to continue using the author's pen; Felix published three notes and two legislative comments while in law school.

In other respects, Felix's experience already reflected the transformation that Columbia Law School had undergone. Dean Smith and the faculty were resolved to pursue the broadening of legal education. Felix's courses in corporate finance and utility rate making were examples of the new curriculum, grounded as it was in concrete social problems and the methodologies of the social sciences. (The teachers of these courses, Berle and Hale respectively, were given seats on the faculty in July 1928, shortly after the split.) Dean Smith emphasized the changes in the curriculum in his 1930 annual report, noting that the social sciences like psychology, philosophy, economics, and sociology had "much to offer to the student of law, not because they offer a ready solution to legal problems, but because all the different social sciences, including law, deal with different aspects of the same problems, and a satisfactory solution to the problems is more likely if the knowledge to be derived from all sources is better coordinated."[52] In the early 1930s, the teaching staff of the Columbia Law School included professors of finance, economics, accounting, insurance, political science, and philosophy.

A growing focus on the place of law and legal education in society and on the morality of law and legal practice was also apparent in many of the courses given at Columbia in the late 1920s and early 1930s. Michael, for example, revolutionized the study of evidence by examining the psychological and logical bases of the rules. Drawing on collaborative work he had done with Mortimer Adler of the Department of Psychology, Michael used symbolic logic and neo-Aristotelian philosophy to make coherent the system of diverse rules of evidence and to teach students the ethical obligations of lawyers as members of the profession.[53]

Similarly, Hale and Berle brought institutional economics to bear upon the study of the law and emphasized the need to use law, uncertain and indeterminate though it may be, to achieve social reform. Hale's pointed critique of the classical distinction between the public and private spheres and his discerning analysis of property rights as the delegation of sovereign powers to individuals provided the foundation for many of the regulatory policies of the New Deal.

If law was a reflection of collective determination, all law was inherently regulatory and coercive, and any objection to the power of the government to regulate was nonsensical.[54] Berle, who introduced corporate finance into the study of business associations, was one of the coauthors of *The Modern Corporation and Private Property* (1932), which brought Hale's work on property to the study of the emerging large business corporations. Berle and Gardiner Means, his coauthor, argued that because property, especially corporate property, was a means by which the state legitimized the use of nongovernmental coercive power, the state could require those in control of such power to promote public interests. Specifically, corporations could be required to act to benefit the community at large.[55] A strong commitment to the common good, to "introducing a modicum of ethics and fair dealing into the law's treatment of corporate affairs," also characterized Berle's teaching.[56]

The Columbia faculty also participated to a great degree in public service.[57] Karl Llewellyn, who joined the faculty in 1924 and became a major figure in the realist movement, is remembered for his participation in the public crusade against the execution of Nicola Sacco and Bartolomeo Vanzetti, the Italian anarchists who, as a remnant of the Red Scare of post World War I, were convicted of robbery and murder in Braintree, Massachusetts, based on very sketchy evidence. Three days before the execution took place, Llewellyn offered a radio address condemning the Massachusetts legal process.[58] A master of jurisprudence and commercial law (he drafted the Uniform Commercial Code), Llewellyn emphasized in his teaching "the need for viewing law as a 'going institution,' with jobs to do, and with results in life, by which its effectiveness must be tested." He sought to impress upon his students "the fact that they are in law school not to memorize a body of legal propositions but to learn counseling and advocacy, to learn not law but how to be lawyers."[59]

That Felix found the legal realists' analysis (especially that of Berle, Hale, and Llewellyn) intriguing is not surprising. (He maintained contact with them throughout his life.) The legal realists' critique of classical legal thought sat well with Felix's understanding that modern society was composed of a multiplicity of competing interests, his growing fascination with the social sciences, and his belief in the power of law to bring about social change. In 1927, Felix spoke (alongside Norman Thomas) at a demonstration on CCNY campus against the execution of Sacco and Vanzetti.[60] He and Lucy went "to keep the vigil."[61] "The defense of Sacco and Vanzetti," Felix would write in 1936, "mobilized the great intellectual protest of the late 1920's and early 1930's"; it was the closest thing "to a revolutionary movement in this country."[62]

Felix's attraction to legal realism was also personal. Classical legal thought served to maintain not only the economic and political status quo but also the structure of the legal profession. The efforts to synthesize and formalize legal doctrine in the late nineteenth century had strong ties to East Coast Anglophilia.[63] Lawyers who possessed "appropriate social, religious, and ethnic credentials" employed the methodology of classical legal thought to claim a place for themselves as legal scientists and to secure the prominence of the legal profession in society. As the developing corporate law firm set the priorities that shaped professional education, ethics, and the social distribution of wealth, only lawyers who were allowed within its ranks were influential. "Born in the East to old American families of British lineage, they were college graduates (a distinct rarity) who followed their fathers into business and professional careers. They molded the law firm to resemble the corporation; both restricted access to those who presented proper ethnic and social credentials."[64] To those without social capital, like Felix, the critique of classical legal thought offered a cherished place within the legal profession.

Legal Realism: Enthusiasts and Critics

Despite its appeal, the jurisprudence of legal realism had its limitations, which many thinkers, including Morris Cohen, Roscoe Pound, John L. Dickinson, Lon L. Fuller, and Hermann Kantorowicz, were quick to point out.[65] These critics, many of whom agreed with the realist critique of classical legal thought, were often of an older generation, a generation that came of age in the first decade of the twentieth century. They argued that the legal realists who engaged in social scientific studies of society, many of whom came of age in the 1910s and 1920s, failed to articulate a coherent theory about the relationship between the social sciences and law, the empirical and the normative. "The movement reveals quite conspicuously the defects of youth," Lon Fuller wrote.[66] As was the case at Columbia Law School, while the critique of classical legal thought gained widespread acceptance among legal scholars in the early decades of the twentieth century (all of whom might be labeled legal realists), they diverged in their understanding as to how a better legal system would be created.

Many of the realists who engaged in social scientific studies, the "Young Turks," as they might be labeled, turned to the study of society in an attempt to generate acceptable values. They sought to substitute expertise and professionalism as the central forms of legitimation for traditional, religious-based values.[67] Their critics, the "Old Guard," embraced such empirical studies and the critique of religious-based values but called for generalization of ideas and values. "After the actualities of the legal order have been observed and recorded, it remains to do something with them," Pound charged.[68]

The critics feared that detailed empirical studies of fact without generalization would lead either to nihilism or to unchecked absolutism. As Morris Cohen, Pound, and Fuller were quick to indicate, in a diverse society, detailed empirical studies of diverse legal interests offered little guidance as to how law should accommodate this multiplicity of interests, or which customs and principles, if any, should be made universal. Realists would thus have to adopt either a nonjudgmental ethical relativist stand or an unchecked absolutist position, prioritizing one value over another. "The new realists," Pound complained, had "their own preconceptions of what is significant, and hence of what juristically must be." Yet they insisted that their picture was scientific.[69] By seeking to find legal norms in society, others echoed, many social-scientist realists ended up privileging the existing distribution of social, economic, and political power among individuals and groups. As Morris Cohen charged, these legal realists neglected to realize the distinction between "uniformities" of human custom (the subject of "descriptive sociology") and "legal rules" that regulate human activity (the subject of "juristic science"). According to Morris, by viewing law "exclusively as uniformities of existing behavior," the social scientists among the realists were led to the "conservative" dependence of "norms" on "habit and inertia."[70] In short, they adopted an approach that led them to conclude that "what is, is right."[71]

The legal realists who engaged in social scientific studies were not opposed to a general normative program—to the study of what the law ought to be. But they argued that a comprehensive understanding of society—of what the relationship between law and society truly is—was required before such a program could be executed. As Llewellyn explained in his response to Pound, a response that acknowledged Felix's research assistance, legal realism implied a commitment to the temporary divorce between Is and Ought for the purposes of study.

In other words, the "rebels," as Pound labeled them, like their critics, struggled with a question that would trouble scholars ever since—how should law respond to the modern phenomenon of diversity? How should law accommodate the diverse interests that characterized the modern American state? But while scholars like Morris Cohen and Pound assumed that answers would be deduced from a general, normative, and universal theory, those who were impressed with the burgeoning social sciences first went looking for facts.

For example, Llewellyn turned to the social sciences "because attempted change seems useless until one finds the laws of change—what can be changed, and how, and with what result." By using the methods of the social sciences, specifically sociology and anthropology, Llewellyn wanted to expose the faults of classical legal thought. He used sociological analysis of legal culture to demonstrate that "law needed to be studied at the level of detailed particulars, where social relations were guided by the practices and processes, or what he called the 'law-ways,' of groups and subgroups." In the early 1940s, in collaboration with the anthropologist E. Adamson Hoebel, Llewellyn offered a critical analysis of the social customs of the Cheyenne. Hoebel and Llewellyn's famous *The Cheyenne Way* demonstrated not only law's role in shaping behavior and sustaining social cohesion but also how the study of social custom revealed the multiplicity of legal systems and their corresponding cultural and social values.[72]

Published almost a decade after the debates between the young rebels and their critics, *The Cheyenne Way* demonstrated the depth of their disagreements. The law's treatment of diverse interests was not a novel issue, but at the turn of the twentieth century it had received a renewed and changed attention. In the nineteenth century, the recognition of diversity in society was tied to the belief in progress and the assignment of subordinated positions to certain social and cultural groups.[73] At the turn of the twentieth century, the critique of absolutism led to growing skepticism toward existing social norms and values (what historians have described as cultural and ethical relativism, respectively) and toward "traditional foundations of thought and structures of understanding" (what Peter Novick labeled cognitive relativism).[74] This was the core of the realists' critique of classical legal thought—legal realism's negative aspect—which both the social scientists among the legal realists and their critics embraced. Yet, when members of both groups attempted to articulate ways to improve the legal system, they had to come to terms with the normative implications of their skepticism: does skepticism toward one's own legal system and ideals implicate a nonjudgmental attitude toward all customs and values?

Young and old legal realists argued that the law should aim to accommodate the different visions, interests, and experiences that characterized modern American society. This was the essence of the legal realists' argument that law had to be brought in touch with society. Yet neither the rebels nor their critics embraced a nonjudgmental attitude toward all cultures, values, and structures of understanding. Without dwelling on it, they simply refused to accept that skepticism necessarily implied a relativist stand toward all aspects of life. What was intellectually possible and maybe inevitable was not only practically impossible but also personally destabilizing to most of them. A nonjudgmental view of all customs, values, and forms of knowledge involved a level of uncertainty about law and the world that very few could endure. It produced an existential crisis. Still, to recognize a degree of absolutism in the cultural, ethical, or cognitive realm undermined the critique of classical legal thought. Having recognized the tension, legal scholars struggled to find a middle ground—to avoid an emotional and intellectual crisis (maybe even nihilism) on the one hand and absolutism on the other. The debates between the younger and older generation were so heated because they reflected idiosyncratic attempts to resolve the uncertainties that their realist critiques had produced. Individually and as a group, realists struggled to come to terms with modernity, both emotionally and intellectually.

The social scientists among the realists (especially the hard-core social scientists who moved from Columbia to Johns Hopkins and Yale) set out to collect data about the diverse interests, customs, and viewpoints that characterized society. They overcame the uncertainties produced by relativism in part by postponing the normative and in part by departing from cognitive relativism. They put their trust in science as the ultimate form of knowledge and in empiricism as an objective way to verify facts and learn about the world.

Throughout the twentieth century, major critics of legal realism focused on this group of social scientists, noting, as Morris Cohen and Pound did in the 1930s, that in a heterogeneous and changing society, the social sciences offered little guidance as to which customs or principles to adopt. While social scientists who were not legal scholars could remain impartial to any normative program, the legal realists who engaged in social scientific studies could not. Gradually, they sought to discern not only the Is but also the Ought from society. Forced to engage normative questions, they evaded the difficult task of choosing between competing interests and values by portraying society as homogenous and law as a mirror of congruent social interests. Their legal realism, grounded as it was in objective empiricism and nonjudgmental attitudes toward customs and values (what some have labeled ethical relativism), helped suppress the critical stand of legal realism (their cognitive relativism) and obscured the realists' reformist zeal. In their hands, realism became increasingly apologetic.[75]

Other legal realists, like Hale, Berle, and even Morris Cohen, held on to a stronger cognitive relativist approach but continued to believe in the power of certain norms and customs and the disadvantages of others. They sought "to combine a pre-modern, prophetic and essentialist moralistic passion for social justice with a critical modernist sense of the socially constructed character of social categories and institutions."[76] Their legal realism was a combination of skepticism toward traditional structures of knowledge (or cognitive relativism) and a degree of ethical absolutism. It breathed life into the Progressive origins of the social sciences.

A significant public debate over the meaning of legal realism took place in 1931, on the occasion of Holmes's ninetieth birthday. Each group of legal realists wanted to claim Holmes as its antecedent, and Holmes's wide-ranging scholarship provided sufficient ammunition for all. This debate, during which Llewellyn coined the term "Legal Realism," became the springboard for much of the historical analysis of legal realism. But, as Morton Horwitz demonstrated, the ideas originated earlier than the 1930s—in Progressive legal thought, in the debates at Columbia Law School, in the realist scholarship of the 1920s.[77] In 1929, in a dissertation written during his first year of law school, Felix, too, entered the turbulent waters. Originally titled *The Valuation of Law,* his dissertation aimed to articulate an objective ethical basis for the legal realists' critical and skeptical attitude toward traditional customs and structures of understanding. A skeptic about the foundations of knowledge, Felix trusted the scientific method to help him refute the seemingly necessary connection between skepticism and relativism. With a strength of conviction that reflected both intellectual confidence and emotional maturity, Felix believed that if he could *scientifically* eliminate all but one ethical standard, he would prove that one could endorse the critique of traditional structures of knowledge without embracing a cultural or ethical relativist stand. While the young legal realists engaged in empirical studies of society, simultaneously endorsing an ethical relativist stand, and the critics joined cognitive relativism with a certain moral absolutism, Felix set out to reveal, by a process of scientific verification and elimination, first what the end of law should be (the legal ideal) and then the content of that legal ideal (the ethical system that defines it). His dissertation was published in 1933 under the more appropriate title *Ethical Systems and Legal Ideals.* Felix was reportedly amused when one of the galleys came out *Ethical Ideals and Legal Systems.*[78]

Ethical Systems and Legal Ideals

Ethical Systems and Legal Ideals set out to combine the methodology of the social sciences with the discourses of moral and political philosophy—to make
law promote better politics. Criticizing moral philosophers for ignoring facts
and social scientists for neglecting morality, Felix, who believed that ethics was
"capable of scientific treatment," sought to "elaborate a *science* of ethics."[79]
Many legal realists, especially those who rejected ethical relativism, were ultimately content to assume that "there were correct—liberal—answers to the
hot legal questions of the day but that conservative judges couldn't be expected
to reach them."[80] Felix's dissertation in turn drew on the principle of verification established by the Vienna Circle (the idea that assertions are meaningful
only when their content meets a minimal condition about the ways in which
their truth could be empirically verified) in an attempt to establish an objective
connection between the realists' critique (their cognitive relativism) and their
ideological or ethical commitment to Progressive politics.[81] It turned out to be
an example of the difficulties that diversity posed to political and legal reform.

Ethical Systems and Legal Ideals began in legal realism. Felix defined law as "a
body of rules according to which the courts . . . decide cases." Law was not the
outcome of logical deduction from abstract rules but what courts did in fact.
Ethics, for its part, was defined as "the science of the significance and application of judgments of *good, bad, right, wrong, better, worse, best, worst, ought,* and
their derivatives, in so far as these terms are applied categorically." Felix's task, as
he saw it, was to articulate both an objective legal ideal that would serve as the
basis for legal criticism and an ethical theory that would give meaning to that
ideal. Once an ethical system defined the normative factor of law, social scientific studies (economics, sociology, anthropology) could delimit the realm of
"ethically justiciable facts which law can comprehend or affect."[82]

After a relatively short section that explained the need to ground legal criticism in an ethical basis, the second part of *Ethical Systems and Legal Ideals* eliminated different legal ideals as inadequate for the valuation of law. As a legal realist, Felix first rejected the non–utilitarian or intrinsic standards, including the
aesthetic standard, which evaluated law by the logical consistencies of its rules;
the content-based standard, which focused on the expressed content of the
law's commands; and the purpose-based standard, which evaluated legal rules
based on their purpose. According to Felix, in "making scientific inquiry into
the potentialities and consequences of law irrelevant to legal criticism," these
non–utilitarian standards judged only "some abstract phase of the actual legal
command, either its formal relation to other commands, or its bare content, or
its intended purpose." Hence, they could not offer "a universally correct index
to the goodness or badness of law." But Felix also rejected utilitarian standards
such as the promotion of peace, liberty, social interests, and justice. As he
pointed out, while these standards evaluated legal rules based on their consequences, none of them was sufficient to mediate the diversity of experiences

and interests that characterized modern society. "Conflicts between these various ends," he explained, were "at the heart of most social problems and we must find some common denominator for their treatment."[83]

Natural law was another standard of legal valuation, one that Morris adopted. Yet, for Felix, it was inappropriate both because it was a remnant of a religiously based legal system, and, more important, because it was grounded in a separation between practice and ideal. Natural law, as Felix described it, was a universal ideal.[84] "The real problem here," Felix wrote, partially to his audience and partially to his father, "is one of degree. How much uniformity is there between the ideal law for various communities?" Felix's goal was to consider and compare "the needs, powers, and social conditions of different societies" so that he could formulate an empirically verifiable standard by which to evaluate the law.[85] If he could do that, he would refute his father's charge that the young legal realists substituted empiricism for moral inquiry.

Felix concluded that the only common standard for evaluating the law (traceable to Aristotle and Bentham) was the good life. As he put it, it was "a necessary as well as a sufficient ethical basis for the valuation of law." Then, in order to give "a living concretion of this abstract principle" of the good life, the third part of the book turned to ethics.[86]

Felix wanted to ground the concept of good life in "empirically verifiable criteria," but he could not.[87] After a process of elimination and verification, the third part concluded that two theories of ethics appeared "equally valid as explanations of the world of value":

> On the one hand, there is the theory that intrinsic goodness is relative, definable, and identical with a relation to an approving individual. On the other hand, there is the theory that intrinsic goodness is absolute, indefinable, and equivalent in application to positive pleasantness. Between these incompatible alternatives, we have discovered no rational basis or choice, nor have we been able to show with any conclusiveness that other ethical alternatives are untenable. It is in the shadow of these doubts that our legal philosophy must make its very beginning. The conclusion is not a pleasant one. But the stories philosophy tells do not all have happy endings.[88]

Given the inability to find a "rational basis of choice" between the two theories, legal philosophy had to "be reared 'in the shadow of these doubts.'"[89] As between the two theories—one that based judgment on personal approval (Felix labeled it ethical relativism) and one that rested judgment on the scientific study of pain and pleasure (Felix called it ethical absolutism)—Felix chose the latter. Relativism was not only too subjective, it also involved a level of uncertainty and alienation that, emotionally, he could not accept. Felix knew that he could not argue that what pleased many people had more intrinsic value than what pleased only a few. But he could endorse the intuitive assumption that what people found pleasing was good and what they found painful was not. Pleasure, a verifiable sensation according to Felix, gave content to the concept of the good life: "Ethical assertions [were] in this sense verifiable, though the integrity of the measurement [had to] appeal to something as unverifiable as intuition."[90] As Perry, Felix's dissertation adviser, similarly explained, "values were 'objective' because they were inter-subjectively verifiable."[91]

Hedonism also fit Felix's political agenda. "As a lawyer interested in improving the law," one reviewer wrote, Cohen was "naturally attracted by the great reforming impulse that originated with Bentham."[92] He wanted to use Bentham's hedonistic utilitarianism to give content to Morris's ideal of natural law. As Felix explained, while in theory hedonism meant "the translation of the books of the law into the universal language of human joys and sufferings," in practice it meant "the struggle for the attainment of ideals thus discovered."[93] According to Felix, coming up with the means of struggle for these ideals should be the focus of positive legal studies. "If indignant moralists balk at the word 'hedonism,'" Max Radin wrote in his review of *Ethical Systems and Legal Ideals,* "let them read the whole chapter through and discover that Dr. Cohen's hedonism could describe a life of virtuous self-denial."[94]

Yet, as many critics were quick to point out, Felix's choice of hedonism was peculiar in light of his initial goals. For one thing, hedonism was not "a possible and a workable standard for comparing values."[95] Indeed, the appeal of hedonism lay deeper. Felix described hedonism as an objective and absolute formula because it sought to take into account the multiplicity of interests in society without making ethics dependant on a particular point of view or reference.

Having chosen hedonism as defining the legal ideal at the foundation of legal criticism, Felix turned to positive science. "It is the task of positive science," he wrote in the fourth part of *Ethical Systems and Legal Ideals,* "to link the ceremonial show of the legal process with the joy and sufferings of sentient beings." Felix argued that positive social science should focus on three specific inquiries: "What is the systematic interaction between the act of one agency of the law and the acts of all other legal agencies?"—a question that would allow jurists to understand the legal system as a whole; How does "an awareness of law" affect "one's conduct in those fields where law commands and prohibits?"—a question that would help jurists realize what the law could and could not affect; and "What is the significance in human life of such conduct as is directly controlled by the law?" By inquiring into these questions, Felix hoped to uncover how law affected happiness and thus to understand how to make law better promote the hedonistic ideal. "A sound legal criticism will correct Bentham's impressionistic surveys of law's effect on human happiness with a more mature psychology and a richer fund of factual social studies than was at Bentham's disposal," Felix concluded.[96]

Like the social scientists among the legal realists, who argued that legal change depended upon a better understanding of society, an understanding that they sought to derive from empirical studies, Felix turned to positive science to learn about the effects of law on different interests and groups in society. As he explained at the outset, he was "concerned only with the . . . search for the lines of causation which connect law with [happiness], . . . lines which by shifting from one culture to another give to identical legal elements contexts of varied significance in different times and places."Yet, unlike the social scientists, he did not believe in the separation of the Is from the Ought even for purposes of study. Like the critics, and especially like his father, Felix's turn to positive science was predicated upon the assumption that law had to promote happiness. He wanted to find "some factors of constant or universal significance" that could be evaluated based on a hedonistic standard.[97]

Felix's approach was unique. Having failed scientifically to refute the connection between skepticism and relativism, he chose a middle path, focusing on the possibility of convergence between interests and values. Unlike the young social scientists, he did not merely study diversity. He embraced the diversity of experiences as a constitutive element of the legal system. Unlike the critics, he also did not assume the existence of universals. Rather, by subjecting diverse experiences to the hedonistic calculus he hoped to uncover universals, which, in turn, could inform the promulgation of legal rules. As Felix wrote in the conclusion of *Ethical Systems and Legal Ideals,*

> In the clash of incommensurables we are forced to acknowledge confusion and despair or to look beyond our *media axiomata* to some ultimate principle, beneath which the artificial clarity and the essential incompatibility of our subordinate standards together vanish and leave every problem with the mark of quantity and continuity.[98]

While reason led Felix to relativism, faith brought him the belief in universals. The book ended with the following paragraph:

> In the human world of which philosophy is a part the choice of ideals, which is love, and their understanding must co-exist. That understanding without love is empty, that love without understanding is blind, that the good life is found only in the intimate union of these ideals,—the wedding of reason and faith, as the phrase of another age ran,—these are the most important truths to which men have attained.[99]

"The intimate union . . . of reason and faith"

Felix's search for intimacy, both intellectual and emotional, reflected concerns that many early twentieth-century intellectuals shared. Amid tremendous social and economic changes, scholars struggled to understand the place of the individual in the world. "The American spirit," Jean Wahl explained at the time, "was on the look for a new faith: a philosophy wherein there would meet and blend together . . . an idealist conception and the will for practical action, the eagerness after individual effort and the sense of mightier realities in which individual souls are, as it were, immersed."While earlier generations had found a

response to those aspirations in Emerson's transcendentalism or Whitman's democracy, intellectuals in the early twentieth century developed a discourse of
pluralism.[100]

Traced back to William James's 1909 published lectures on *A Pluralistic Universe,* the philosophy of pluralism insisted on the plurality of things as given in
experience and on the impossibility of a single law to traverse all the various
domains of being. A pluralist theory of knowledge insisted on the multiplicity,
whether limited or infinite, of knowers in the world and various forms of
knowledge or truth, none of which could claim epistemological primacy.[101]
Pluralism in ethics implied the existence of a variety of competing ends, among
which policymakers had to choose.

Pluralism was not a novel idea in its empirical form. Anthropologists had
called attention to the diversity of experiences in society throughout the nineteenth century. At the turn of the twentieth century, however, philosophers, especially James and his students, transformed empirical pluralism into a normative theory. Given the multiplicity of experiences and the diverse ways in
which they were interrelated, these philosophers rejected the monistic belief
that human substance became fully divine only in the all-form. Instead, they
urged the will to believe that there might ultimately never be an all-form—
that there was no absolute truth. As James explained:

> Pluralism or the doctrine that it is many means only that the sundry parts
> of reality *may be externally related.* Everything you can think of, however
> vast or inclusive, has on the pluralistic view a genuinely "external" envi-
> ronment of some sort or amount. Things are "with" one another in many
> ways, but nothing includes everything, or dominates over everything.
> The word "and" trails along after every sentence. Something always es-
> capes. "Ever not quite" has to be said of the best attempts made anywhere
> in the universe at attaining all-inclusiveness. The Pluralistic world is thus
> more like a federal republic than like an empire or a kingdom. However
> much may be collected, however much may report itself as present at any
> effective centre of consciousness or action, something else is self-
> governed and absent and unreduced to unity.[102]

The philosophy of pluralism grew out of pragmatism. Like pragmatists, pluralist philosophers sought to substitute empiricism, particularism, indeterminacy, and uncertainty for rationalism, universalism, determinacy, and certainty.[103] Yet while pragmatists emphasized that the understanding of reality was
mediated through experience, pluralist philosophers focused on the complex
nature of reality. Not only was our conception of reality mediated through our
individual experiences, as pragmatists suggested, but reality was also, for each
one of us, one and many at the same time. As James's student Horace Kallen explained, individuals had "separate ideas of the chair, of the table, of the pew."
They had "an idea of them all together. Yet this last idea [was] not made up of
the former separate ones—it [was] a genuine unit, in which the separate ones

[were] parts. The separate ones [were] independent of it and [were] not independent of it—and so on."[104]

In the multiplicity of experiences and in the realization that a complete picture would never present itself, pluralists found a sense of connectedness and intimacy in the world, and they sought to make the concrete intimacy individuals experienced in relationships a fundamental part of reality.[105] In turn, the search for connections and relations, for points of convergence, and the faith in their existence allowed pluralists, Felix among them, to reject absolutism on the one hand and to resist relativism on the other. What the philosophy of pluralism contributed to the debate between relativists and absolutists was thus the ability to embrace diversity without endorsing a nonjudgmental relativist view. The diversity of values that the social scientists among the legal realists seemed to ignore, and that some of the critics ultimately sought to eliminate, was crucial to Felix's pluralist approach.

Law and Politics

Ethical Systems and Legal Ideals was very well received. Some criticized Felix for being "a philosopher who employs the terminology of modern logical analysis with a slightly overwhelming sense of ease."[106] Others argued that the book was written in "a tone of such gentle and charming good sense" that even a certain lay reviewer had found its "legal exegesis . . . so reassuringly simple."[107] But all celebrated Felix's achievement. Hessel Yntema wrote that "the work is concerned with what is perhaps the crucial problem in legal theory today. . . . Its quality is a tribute to the author."[108] Walter Nelles began his confessedly "not . . . adulatory" review by noting that the book "signalizes the coming of age, which must precede maturity, of a mind that is perhaps as precociously full, as clean and clear, as penetrating, and as powerful as was young Jeremy Bentham's when he wrote that brilliant first work, which he did not publish."[109] And Max Radin commented that "Dr. Cohen has written in his youth the sort of book that most men do not manage to write until they have lost the belief that their writing will do any good."[110]

Yet even setting aside Felix's failure to complete his stated task—to refute all potential ethical systems but one—the book had faults. Some questions were not adequately treated. "Is the hedonistic hypothesis . . . helpful . . . in dealing, for example, with private property?" asked Malcolm Sharp of the University of Chicago Law School. "Does contemporary utilitarianism, or does logical idealism, affect the classical justifications of 'individualism,' when studied in relation to the depression?" Sharp wanted to know.[111] "It may fairly be asked whether the radically altered outlook of contemporary psychology and philosophy lends itself so readily to a formulation of ethical ideals in terms of Hedonism," wrote George Adams of the University of California at Berkeley.[112] Cohen's failure to supply a rational system of ethics, noted Kingsley Davis of Pennsylvania State College, was the failure "of rational-individualism" more generally.[113]

And while Max Radin found the central thesis ("that a system of ethical norms must be found for law") correct, he concluded that "it is not quite so good a book as Dr. Cohen will write, if he continues his thinking in these fields."[114]

Felix agreed. In the conclusion of *Ethical Systems and Legal Ideals,* he noted that the significance of his argument was not in supplying a solution but rather in pointing the way to one. As he explained, the solution of legal-ethical problems involved, first, a definition of the good life (and Felix believed that the theory of hedonism offered "the most adequate" definition) and, second, it involved questions of positive science. Fusing these two aspects "to produce material norms of legal activity and standards of legal criticism" was beyond the task of the book.[115] But it continued to engage Felix's attention. In the years immediately after he completed his dissertation, Felix's focus shifted to more concrete legal questions: the status of labor unions, copyright laws, and utilities ratemaking. Yet, what might seem to be different subjects were actually examples of how normative pluralism could be translated into law and policy. Like other legal realists who oscillated between absolutism and relativism, Felix moved from the individual and individual preferences to groups as the focus of political and social analysis. In groups he (and others) found similarities and connectedness in a diverse and multifarious world.

On their face, Felix's writings in the early 1930s, specifically the notes he wrote as an editor of the *Columbia Law Review,* seemed to reflect the different contributions of legal realism to his thought. Two of the notes focused on legislation, a common theme in legal realists' writings (and an alien theme to classical legal thinkers who focused on judicial decisions). Each note was also informed by the realists' argument that the distinction between a public sphere of government power and a private sphere of individual freedom was fictional, especially with respect to property rights.

The first note, "The Bauer-Bonbright Proposal for the Revision of the New York Public Service Commission Law and its Constitutionality," reassessed debates about rate regulation, a very controversial issue in the early decades of the twentieth century. Utility companies maintained that rate regulation was a confiscation of their private property under the doctrine of eminent domain. Drawing on the description of property as a delegation of sovereign powers by the state to individuals put forward by Hale and Morris Cohen, Felix advocated the view (expressed in the Bauer-Bonbright proposal) that rate regulation should be analyzed under a contractual approach. Accordingly, implicit in the utility companies' charters was an assumption of required reasonable rates.[116]

The second note, "The Vestal Bill for the Copyright Registration of Designs," used a realist analysis of the "economic and social consequences of the bill and an ethical evaluation of these consequences" to suggest that the "actual effect of the bill [would] be to aid manufacturers rather than authors or inventors."[117]

Underlying Felix's analysis in both notes, however, was a broader theme, which he more fully articulated in three notes on labor unions ("The Privilege to Disparage a Non-Competing Business," "The Elements of a Fair Trial in

Disciplinary Proceedings in Labor Unions," and "The Judicial Resolution of Factional Disputes in Labor Unions"). These three notes called on the courts to recognize the important role of groups such as labor unions and corporations in the modern social and political life, and thus to recognize group rights. At the same time, they also urged the courts to realize that while groups should have rights as collective entities, the interests of individual members were not necessarily identical with the interests of the collective.[118] "Outsiders, who are accustomed to see the labor union functioning as a single unit in its industrial struggles," Felix wrote, "often forget that the unity attained on the field of battle is temporary, that a labor union, like any other association with important purposes, is a collection of disagreeing individuals irregularly coagulating into opposing factions." Once the potential differences between the one and the many were realized, rules had to be promulgated to provide "the unfairly disciplined individual, group, or local" with recourse to internal remedies or legal aid and to determine the appropriate remedy the union could request in civil courts for enforcing its decrees.[119]

The resolution of certain conflicts between individual members and their union such as the disposition of unions' funds required a determination as to the nature of unions' rights in property. But the subject of union autonomy was broader. It called into question not only the status of groups but also the nature of state sovereignty. "Those who believe that one of the great dangers of modern civilization is the over-centralization in a national state of power over men's lives and those who more particularly hope for the growth of industrial democracy," Felix concluded his analysis, "will welcome a theory which puts the larger share of property rights over union funds in the union itself, and, within certain limits, allows to the union the opportunities for error from which self-discipline and political genius may emerge."[120]

In Felix's opinion, any such theory should combine support for union self-government with the requirement that unions act as trustees both for their individual members and for the community at large. His understanding was informed not only by the realists' conceptualization of property rights, such as rights in union funds, as originating in the sovereign state but also by the works of political scientists drawing on the philosophy of pluralism. Interestingly, while Felix's philosophical pluralism, as articulated in *Ethical Systems and Legal Ideals,* was unique, even idiosyncratic, his political pluralism was shared by other legal scholars. Together they formed a strand within legal realism—legal pluralism.

Pluralism

New political theories—from populism to socialism—proliferated in the early twentieth century. Yet one approach was particularly characteristic of Progressive thinkers. Resisting both the radical collectivist vision of Marxists and socialists and the traditional liberal view of the state as a night watchman, Progressives turned their attention to groups, specifically functional groups, as the fora where individuals found meaning for their ideas and actions. As farmers, workers, professionals, consumers, women, and ethno-cultural groups formed a variety of associations to protect and advance their interests, political scientists used William James's proclamation that "the pluralistic world is . . . more like a federal republic than like an empire or a kingdom"[121] to argue in favor of adding groups, organizations, and associations to the existing array of local and state governments as the bases of the modern American state.[122]

Certain political theorists, such as Arthur Bentley, argued that because individuals organized themselves into groups to pursue their interests, groups and organizations were loci of participation and representation. They believed that by exploring the role of groups in society, they could offer a more realistic description of liberal democratic politics and of the limited role of the liberal state.[123] Other political theorists, such as John Dewey, Mary Parker Follett, and Harold Laski, not only recognized the existence of a multiplicity of centers of self-government in society, but also endorsed this multiplicity as a constitutive element of democracy. These theorists argued that the state was too broad and abstract a body to command loyalty and allegiance from individuals, who associated more easily with diverse groups and organizations than with a unified state entity. As Harold Laski explained, by focusing on the unity of the state, traditional, absolutist or monist visions of sovereignty obliterated differences of class, politics, and religion. There were "no rich or poor, Protestants or Catholics, Republicans or Democrats," only "members of the State"; all groups—"Trade-unionists and capitalists alike"—surrendered their interests to the state.[124] By envisioning sovereignty as distributive or multiple and by encouraging the growth of organizations such as labor unions, these political theorists sought to guarantee the flourishing of diverse and valuable forms of identities, ways of life, experiences, and viewpoints.

Political pluralism, as W. Y. Elliott explained, was a "revolt against the 'Metaphysical Theory of the State.'"[125] The labor union cases, Felix echoed Elliott, presented "directly and dramatically the wavering boundaries of state sovereignty." As he explained, "The line which courts are drawing between those functions in which associations may act with autonomous discretion and those in which their activity comes under state control in the form of judicial direction is an important sector of the battle line about which the perpetual war between political absolutists and political pluralists rages."[126] The future, in other words, "belong[ed] to labor" and to the lawyers who represented labor unions as well as other organizations: "trade unions, industrial unions, consumer organizations, farm organizations, semi-governmental corporations, and forms of associations that have not yet been invented."[127]

Political pluralism was an innovative vision within the boundaries of American liberalism. By focusing on groups as forums in which individuals received meaning for their ideas and actions, political pluralism offered a middle ground between conservative individualism and radical collectivism. It was an alternative to nineteenth-century American individualism on the one hand and twentieth-century European radicalism on the other. "By the 1920s," political pluralism "was displacing the conventional conception of the state."[128]

Legal scholars expanded upon theories of political pluralism to formulate new legal doctrines. Advocates of the workers' right to organize and corporate law scholars drew upon theories of pluralism to portray labor unions and corporations, respectively, as real entities whose existence was both real and distinct from their individual members.[129] Yet while for the most part political pluralists were not concerned about the power that collective entities might exercise (trusting labor unions and corporations to self-regulate their activities), some legal scholars (including Morris Cohen, Hale, and Berle) closely examined the boundaries of group autonomy. They exposed organizations, associations, and corporations as loci not only of individual self-government but also of coercive power (over their members, nonmembers, and other associations), power that liberal legal thought cloaked as free contractual arrangements between individuals.[130] Fearing the power that labor unions or corporations could amass, legal scholars argued that, in principle, collective entities should be allowed to exercise their powers freely but that courts should tame potential abuses of power by imposing on organizations limitations resembling the constraints on sovereign power. They wanted collective entities to exercise their power to benefit the community at large. This was also at the core of Felix's argument that self-governing labor unions were to be trustees for their members as well as the community.

Having argued that groups should exercise their power to benefit society at large, legal pluralists had to give meaning to this assertion in particular contexts. The different developments that led to the rise of big business, Felix wrote as early as 1932, "indicate[d] that capitalism [was] passing beyond a laissez faire, individualistic stage and assuming a collectivist or fascist stage." It was thus left to his generation to determine "what sort of collectivism" it wanted and what legal, political, and economic means would reach that end.[131]

For many legal pluralists, the new collectivism was grounded in a conception of group autonomy or self-government. But group self-government was a means to a broader end. Legal pluralists believed that if individuals could unite to promote their interests (subject to the requirement that group power should be exercised to benefit the society at large), disparities of power, particularly economic power, could be minimized if not eliminated. As became clear when many of them joined the New Deal administration, intellectuals endorsed a legal pluralist image of the state because it promoted a particular social and economic agenda. They were certain that a state built on the grounds of pluralism would promote social and economic equality.

In other words, legal pluralists were not relativists. While many political pluralists, especially labor organizers, viewed the pluralist or corporatist state as a "society of societies," devoid of any moral character or obliging force, legal pluralists feared that without centralized planning, free competition between corporations and other groups, specifically labor unions, would benefit the former at the expense of the latter.[132] As Felix saw it, the idea of a free market of groups would substitute the sovereignty of one group—the corporation—for the sovereignty of the state.[133] Instead of reducing sovereignty to its parts, the legal pluralists' approach was predicated on a strong commitment to government planning. Felix believed that national planning was required to coordinate the plans of different self-governing entities, to balance production and consumption, and to distribute wealth and income.[134]

Legal pluralists never fully resolved the tension between their commitment to group autonomy or self-government and their endorsement of the Progressive agenda in politics and economics. Throughout the 1930s and 1940s, they struggled, many of them in government positions, to mediate this tension. Over time, the attention of legal pluralists shifted from political and economic groups to cultural and ethnic ones. But the premise of their argument remained the same: groups and collective entities were the basic units for legal and political analysis.

Fearing the alienation associated with conservative individualism as well as the inherent class conflict of radical collectivism, legal pluralists advocated a vision of the modern state that was grounded in the possibility of social harmony and community. By accentuating groups, they drew attention away from both class and the individual as important bases of the modern American state. Still, by adopting a pluralist image of the state, legal pluralists of Felix's generation were able to carve a place for themselves in the modernist project.

The legal pluralist image of the state recognized diversity but limited the uncertainties associated with cultural, cognitive, or ethical relativism. Groups and associations were fora where individuals could pursue particular values, subject only to a general economic and political scheme. The role of the state and the legal system was to guarantee that individuals could associate with others to pursue their needs and that no one association or collective entity could use its power to oppress individuals who belonged to other groups (oppression being defined, at least initially, as economic oppression). Beyond administering the allocation of power among groups, law had little role. In short, legal pluralism was a particular way out of the modernist dilemma: by focusing on the diversity of groups, it allowed scholars to endorse a certain amount of skepticism toward the prevailing legal system and ideals. Yet, by viewing self-government as a means to political and economic equality, legal pluralists were able to embrace skepticism without also sanctioning a nonjudgmental attitude toward all customs and values.

Belonging

The pluralist image of the state drew a particular American vision not only of politics but also of ethnicity. The political pluralists' image of the state was the mirror image of Horace Kallen's cultural pluralism, that is, the idea that ethnic and cultural groups were constitutive elements of the modern state. As advocates of assimilation developed educational and social programs to help smooth the immigrants' absorption into the American melting pot, cultural critics such as Kallen drew upon James's philosophy of pluralism to stress the significant contribution of diverse cultural groups to the Western democratic tradition. In their writings, ethnic and racial differences became important sources of, not obstacles to, individual freedom.[135]

Despite the resemblance between political and cultural pluralism, Felix's writings in the early 1930s, as did the writings of other legal pluralists, remained focused on the struggle of labor against capital. In the midst of the Great Depression and its aftermath, Felix clearly saw that law was a tool of capitalism, but he failed to recognize its contribution to racial and cultural hegemony. The attitude of the Socialist Party, whose ranks he joined, toward race relations was indeed "hazy."[136] A second-generation Jewish American, Felix defined his place in American society by rejecting ethnic particularism and by emphasizing the possibility of solidarity and collaboration for the improvement of economic conditions. The sense of belonging that Morris found first in socialism and then in cosmopolitanism, Felix found in the legal pluralist image of the state.

Felix's growing sense of belonging, socially and politically, was one of the causes for the optimism apparent in his writings in the late 1920s and early 1930s. But there were other, more personal, reasons. Perhaps most important, Felix's relationship with Morris had matured. Morris remained critical of Felix's attraction to the social sciences and his perhaps less than rigorous philosophical approach. But he also valued Felix's opinion. In the summer of 1929, shortly after Harvard University awarded Felix his Ph.D., Morris and Felix traveled to the tranquility of the Adirondacks to finish Morris's first book, *Reason and Nature.*

According to Morris, the book would probably not have seen the light of the day if it hadn't been for Felix, who "developed a special skill in belittling the imperfections of [Morris's] writings and persuading [Morris] to publish them." Throughout his life, Felix obsessively edited and published his father's works. In the preface to *Reason and Nature* Morris wrote: "My son, Dr. Felix S. Cohen, has been so helpful in suggestions, criticisms, and preparing the manuscript for the press that I find it difficult to indicate the great extent of my—and the reader's—obligation to him."[137]

The book, which was dedicated to Holmes, was published in 1931. "May I visit you on Sunday March 8 and bring you the first copy of my book on *Nature and Reason* [*sic*]?" Morris Cohen wrote to Holmes to arrange for the presentation of the book as a gift. "I should also like to bring my son who as editor of the Columbia Law Review wants to present you a copy of the March number of that publication which is dedicated to you."[138] "The two visits I paid to [Holmes]," Felix commented years later, "are among life's most treasured occasions."[139]

Shortly after his visit to Holmes, in the summer of 1931, Columbia University awarded Felix Cohen an LL.B. degree and "an award for the best essay written by a member of one of the most brilliant graduating classes." The paper used the conversational method of *Through the Looking Glass* to develop its thesis and enliven the discussion of legal philosophy.[140] During the same year, Felix's team won the law school's moot court competition, at which Judge Benjamin N. Cardozo presided. "And well may you be proud of Felix's performance," Felix Frankfurter reported to Mary Cohen of her son's victory.[141]

Upon graduation, Felix secured a clerkship with Justice Bernard Shientag of the New York Supreme Court. Shientag's politics were to his liking. Shientag had been an industrial commissioner and an ardent advocate of the minimum wage before becoming a judge.[142] Furthermore, working with Shientag, an Orthodox Jew who did not work on Saturdays, allowed Felix to pursue other activities. Determined to be not only a lawyer but also a teacher and a scholar, Felix secured a lectureship position at the Rand School of Social Science. He taught ethical philosophy at Rand in 1931 and 1932. For a year or so after that he taught a course called "Contemporary Legal Thought in America" at the New School for Social Research.[143] In preparation for both courses, Felix collaborated with Morris to compile reading materials in jurisprudence, later published as *Cohen & Cohen, Readings in Jurisprudence* (1951). Morris also sat at the back of the lecture hall when Felix was teaching. "They say he's a chip off the old block," the person sitting next to Morris once commented about Felix. "If you saw the old man you would say he was a block off the old chip" was Morris's reply.[144]

Not only in the world's estimation but also in his father's eyes, Felix was now Dr. Cohen. With a sense of fulfillment and, more practically, with a secure job and the ability to support a family, he asked Lucy to marry him. (They had met in 1926 at a Halloween party; Felix was a senior in college, Lucy a sophomore at Barnard.) Cohen spent three days on a canoe trip through Cranberry Lake weighing "credits" against "debits" to determine whether he had the right to ask anyone to marry him. When he returned to New York, he took Lucy hiking on Fire Island. After several miles Felix turned to her and informed her that at the end of the road he would ask her to marry him. She would have all the time in which to make up her mind, he stressed. Then he listed his faults. It was unnecessary. Lucy apparently had decided to marry him at their first meeting.[145] Six years after proposing, Felix wrote to his father that "the accident of falling in love with a girl named Lucy . . . [had] opened to [him] a world of values, perspectives, and efforts that had never before seemed real."[146]

The wedding took place on Tuesday, September 22, 1931, at the New School for Social Research.[147] "You are hereby ordered to show cause why you should not be present at the marriage of Lucy M. Kramer and Felix S. Cohen," the invitation cards read. Rabbi Stephen Wise, the founder of the modern American Reform movement and Morris's friend, conducted the ceremony. Wise had promised to officiate at his marriage when Felix was a child. Lucy wore a blue satin evening gown; Felix—a brown suit. The next day Lucy went to take a math exam, and Felix was back at work. It was "a nice party last night," he told a friend.[148]

Part II

Building a Pluralist State, 1933–1939

Chapter 3

A Time Ripe for Change

A New Deal

Felix Cohen clerked for Justice Bernard Shientag from September 1931 through June 1932. He found clerking "the easiest job in the world—all the fun of being a judge, with very little of the responsibility." He was impressed with Shientag and the judicial process, especially with the secondary place of "law school law" and the interplay between law and real facts.[1] With Shientag's help, Cohen secured a position with the law firm of Hays, Podell, and Shulman, which, like other Jewish firms in New York, was relegated by the corporate bar's anti-Semitism to the presumably less worthy task of enforcing plaintiff stockholders' rights. Cohen found the firm's reputation for having a social conscience appealing.[2]

Cohen had been with Hays, Podell, and Shulman for less than a year when Nathan Margold, the new solicitor of the interior, asked him to join him for a year to help change federal Indian policy. Margold, who had been Morris Cohen's student and had remained a friend of the family, was impressed with Felix's intellectual ability.[3] More than three decades later, Leonora suggested that Mary Cohen took Margold on daily walks and persistently reminded him of Felix's activities so as to "plant the idea of appointing Felix in Margold's mind." Another relative commented that all were worried that Felix "should get a start."[4]

Indeed, in the years following the 1929 stock market crash, as law firms cut back on new recruits and dismissed recent ones, many lawyers from minority groups (who were usually the first to go) chose government positions. The less fortunate, thousands of Jewish lawyers and other Jewish professionals, remained either unemployed or underemployed throughout the Depression, exacerbating the Jewish community's traditional concerns about the success of the younger generation.[5] But in a Jewish firm like Hays, Podell, and Shulman, Cohen's risk of being let go was minimal. Other reasons seemed to have influenced Cohen who, with no prior experience with Indian affairs, chose to accept Margold's offer (and ultimately to remain at Interior for fourteen years).[6]

It is possible that the Indians' plight against the attempts of missionaries to convert them to Christianity subconsciously triggered Cohen's interest in Margold's offer. Commissioner of Indian Affairs John Collier believed that "the group of people in this country who had the deepest feeling about Indians came from the Jewish faith."[7] Similarly, Theodore Haas, who worked with Cohen at Interior, saw "Cohen's zealous fight for Indian rights [as] rooted in the causes of the flight of his father and grandparents from the oppressive government of Russia to the freedom of America" and, more broadly, in the Hebraic tradition.[8] But the evidence that might support such arguments is typically from statements Cohen made in the 1940s, most often after he had left the department.

Indeed, something else seems to have influenced Cohen's decision. As we will see, the New Deal's zest, the Indians' plight, and, ultimately, Cohen's vision for the modern state brought him to Interior. Here was an opportunity to experiment with pluralism. Cohen's power to effect change was limited by his role at Interior and by the relationship between Congress, Interior, and other departments. But for a while, with Margold's support, Cohen was able to bring legal pluralism to bear upon laws and policy affecting Indian tribes.

The Department of the Interior

The Roosevelt administration's promise of a better future must have influenced Cohen's decision. He wanted to participate in what seemed to be a transformative moment. As Cohen told Lash shortly after he joined the New Deal, he was genuinely "amazed at the amount of idealism floating around" Interior. "One expects enthusiasm in the [National Recovery Administration] crowd, who expect they're ushering in the millennium with golden trumpets," Cohen noted, "but to find it in a staid and stable department like the Interior is a shock." "Even the lawyers around the place," he wryly commented, "who might be expected to inject a shot of cynicism and reaction, are amusedly or sympathetically tolerant."[9]

While the New Deal administration endorsed many Progressive ideas with respect to economic reform, members of Interior under Secretary Harold Ickes were exceptionally progressive in their approach to minority groups. Margold had been general counsel to the ACLU on minority issues (including Indians) and legal adviser on Indian issues at the Institute of Government Affairs before joining Interior at the age of 33. In the early 1930s Margold helped frame the NAACP's legal drive for equality and served (as a volunteer) as a special counsel for the Pueblo Indians in pressing their land-title claims, an appointment that brought him to the attention of Ickes and John Collier.[10]

Collier, the "emotionally withdrawn, forty-eight-year-old native of Atlanta, Georgia," sworn in as commissioner of Indian affairs on April 21, 1933, was a self-proclaimed cultural pluralist. Collier was generally concerned about industrialism's negative consequences, and he believed that civilization would emerge out of the cooperation of local groups. In the early twentieth century Collier worked with immigrant groups in New York, seeking to preserve their particular cultures.[11] In 1920, after a visit to the Taos Pueblo in New Mexico, he determined that because Indian culture focused on "beauty, adventure, joy, comradeship and the relationship of man to God" rather than "the material aspects of life," it was a model for the redemption of American society. In the mid-1920s Collier became the executive secretary of the American Indian Defense Association (AIDA), which he created (and apparently ran singlehandedly) to advocate the preservation of Indian civilization and prevention of government-sponsored assimilation.[12]

Secretary Ickes was eager to help all underprivileged groups. "A blunt-speaking fifty-nine-year-old Chicago attorney" at the time of his appointment, he became deeply interested in Indian welfare while living in his summer home near Coolidge, Arizona, and was among the first members of Collier's AIDA.[13] Ickes became so interested in the plight of Indians that before Roosevelt's election he hoped to be appointed commissioner of Indian affairs. When he was appointed secretary of the interior, he helped secure Collier for the position of the commissioner.[14] In a diary entry on June 8, 1933, Ickes denounced the white man's exploitation of Indians, including the taking of land and the inflicting of disease.[15]

"Even old employees rally enthusiastically to the defense of the oppressed Indian," Cohen wrote to Lash.[16] The time was ripe for change.

Historical Landmarks

The new administration found Indian reservations in disturbing conditions. Throughout the nineteenth and early twentieth centuries, Indian tribes were at the outer boundaries of American society. They were regarded as "distinct political communities" with limited sovereignty, as Chief Justice John Marshall described them in his 1832 *Worcester v. Georgia* opinion.[17] But as domestic dependent nations, not foreign nations, their efforts to maintain their tribal organization proved futile in the face of military conquest, fraudulent or unfulfilled treaties, and the pressure of white settlement that forced them away from most of their lands and ultimately onto reservations.[18]

Worcester v. Georgia was the last in a trilogy of cases in which Marshall defined the relationship between Indian tribes and their lands. In *Johnson v. M'Intosh* (1823), Marshall declared that tribes only occupied their lands while the federal government held title to them.[19] In *Cherokee Nation v. Georgia* (1831), Marshall described the federal government as having a fiduciary position, guardianship, toward Indian tribes, its wards.[20] *Worcester v. Georgia* explained the nature of this trust relationship: only the federal government, not the states, could deal with Indian tribes.[21]

With judicial approval, the federal government transferred many Indian lands to its possession and advanced non-Indian settlement. For one thing, the Indian Removal Act, which was passed shortly after *Worcester v. Georgia* was decided, forced eastern tribes to move west (particularly into the Louisiana Purchase territories). Seemingly in compliance with agreements and treaties, Indians were pushed west of the Mississippi and Indian lands opened to white settlement. Native American narratives with titles like "The Trail of Tears" memorialized the brutality of the removal.[22]

The demand for Indian land influenced federal Indian policy throughout the nineteenth century. During the 1850s, treaties were signed with Indians of the recently acquired Pacific northwest for the cession of large amounts of land while gold seekers "practically annihilated" the Indians of California. In 1854, the Kansas–Nebraska Act authorized negotiations of new treaties with the Indians in the Louisiana Purchase area "through which [Indians] agreed either to accept relatively small tracts of communally owned land designated 'reservations,' or to take up individually owned 'allotments.'" After the Civil War, the reservation policy became applicable to all Indians. Tribes were pushed onto reservations, vacating lands for white settlers moving into western states. The federal government held the title to reservation lands in trust for the tribes, while lands left over after the creation of a reservation were made available to white settlement.[23]

Then, in the last decades of the nineteenth century, reformers and government officials rejected the reservation system. To eliminate it, the General Allotment Act of 1887 (the Dawes Act) sanctioned the distribution of reservation lands to individual Indians. The Dawes Act authorized the president to allot reservation lands that could be used for agriculture and grazing to individual Indians: to each head of a family 160 acres, to each single Indian over the age of eighteen 80 acres, and to each Indian child in a family 40 acres. The federal government would hold allotted lands in trust for the allottee's use and benefit for twenty-five years, during which the allottee was expected to learn farming, irrigation, and husbandry; the allottee could neither sell nor lease the lands. After twenty-five years, the laws of descent and partition of the state or territory where the lands were located would apply.[24]

The Dawes Act was grounded in a classical liberal equation of freedom and prosperity with individual possession of property as well as a messianic belief in the civilizing force of private property. Proponents of the act hoped that, when Indians were introduced to the institution of private property, they would abandon their customs and traditions, become yeoman farmers, and be prepared to assimilate into American society.[25]

Indian tribes had often restricted decisions to transfer lands outside the tribe to tribal leaders. Yet even before the Dawes Act, many tribes held a more individualistic system, similar to the common-law system of private property, to regulate their members' property rights. Some tribes had traditionally endorsed a system of private property, while others embraced such a system after the encounter with the European nations.[26] Still, the Dawes Act aimed to force all tribes to adopt common-law rules of property rights, specifically a conception of absolute ownership, and cared little about particular tribal traditions (which were often based on usage) or, ironically, about the interests of individual owners.

For example, the Dawes Act included no mechanism for land transfers between individual Indians. It made cooperation and coordination among tribal members impossible and deprived Indians of the potential benefits of economies of scale. It was easier for Indians to lease allotted lands to non-Indians (which they were allowed to do) than to transfer them to other Indians. Furthermore, because the act required that a deceased's allotment descend to all of his or her heirs as tenants in common, allotments were rapidly fragmented and fractioned so as to be unusable. As one scholar concluded, "The property system imposed on the Indians by the Dawes Act denied them the ability to reap the economic benefits that private property might have offered. The Indians . . . receive[d] only the cost of the imposition."[27]

Unsympathetic to Indian needs, supporters of the Dawes Act were interested in opening reservation lands to white settlement and railroad tracks. Once all individual Indians residing on a reservation received allotments, the remainder of tribal land was declared surplus and opened to non-Indian purchase. Almost half of the lands owned by Indians prior to allotment were transferred to white homesteaders. Tribes were paid around $1.25 per acre, compared with anywhere from $1.00 to $15.00 per acre paid by white homesteaders for similar lands; the payment was either distributed in per capita payments to individual members or spent by the Bureau of Indian Affairs (BIA), purportedly on the tribes' behalf.[28] As Cohen sarcastically wrote shortly after his appointment, often "it has appeared to some Secretary of the Interior that it would be of great benefit to an Indian tribe to build a transcontinental highway through its reservation or to spend large sums on salaries of departmental employees. If the Indians did not see the wisdom of these expenditures their objections were dismissed as the impertinent remarks of uncivilized people."[29] On many reservations, BIA agents also blocked the allotment of better lands so that it could be declared surplus, leaving Indians with arid or semi-arid lands.[30]

By 1934, tribes had lost control of almost 90 million acres, two-thirds of their 1887 land holdings. In addition to surplus land that went onto the general land market and was sold to non-Indians, individual allotments, which were often too small to farm properly, were leased to non-Indians (by allottees or their heirs) and ultimately sold.[31] Poverty was rampant among Indians, and the achievements of a few individuals who became successful farmers or ranchers helped deepen social and political divisions on reservations. The diverse regulations put in place to carry out the Dawes Act effectively transferred control of Indian lands to the BIA, hastening the disintegration of many tribal governments or at least forcing them to alter their traditional structures. The psychological and cultural blow was devastating. The tribes' ways of life and their values were destroyed, resulting in extreme poverty coupled with a sense of shiftlessness on many reservations.[32]

Land and Assimilation

Federal Indian land policy reflected assumptions about the need to civilize the Indians. From their first encounters with Indians through the nineteenth century, Europeans (and then Americans) justified taking Indian lands by describing Indians as "uncivilized"—as scattered, nomadic peoples, incapable of inhabiting a land. In comparison, the white settlers' westward expansion was God-sanctioned, "civilized" progress.[33]

With the post–Civil War adoption of the reservation system and the subsequent abolition of the treaty system, the internal affairs of the tribes came under direct scrutiny. As Americans came to view the Indian as a vanishing race, government officials and missionary societies joined in an effort to civilize the Indian. Government farmers were employed to teach Indians how to farm their lands, and missionaries were funded to bring tribes the benefits of Christianity and education.[34]

The tribes' strong resistance to these civilizing efforts led government agents to believe that Indians would accept individual responsibility and join in the march of civilization only when forced to fend for themselves on individually owned land. The Dawes Act aimed to accomplish this goal. It implied that Indians could either yield to American individualism and be absorbed into American society or vanish.[35]

In 1889, two years after the enactment of the Dawes Act, Thomas J. Morgan, the commissioner of Indian affairs, dictated a cultural assimilation policy that the Indian Service followed during the first decades of the twentieth century. It saw education as a means of breaking down tribal organization and tribal culture. "Compulsory schooling emphasizing the English language and Anglo-American culture was recommended, and all tribal history and traditions were to be suppressed." According to Morgan, the American "civilization [might] not be the best possible . . . but it [was] the best the Indians [could] get."[36]

A series of laws passed during the first decades of the twentieth century presumably aimed at further assimilation. The 1907 Lacey Act authorized the secretary of the interior to grant to individual Indians control of their "pro rata share" of tribal funds.[37] The 1917 Sells Declaration, which reflected Commissioner Cato Sells's impatience at "the time it was taking to assimilate the Indians," sanctioned a variety of measures, including the rapid issuance of patents-in-fee to individual Indians, to accomplish the swift absorption of Indians into the nation.[38] The 1919 Citizenship for World War I Veterans Act conferred citizenship on every veteran who so desired.[39] The Snyder Act of 1921 expanded the BIA's powers "to expend congressional appropriations for most reservation activities, including health, education, employment, real estate administration, and irrigation."[40] Finally, the 1924 Indian Citizenship Act declared "all non-citizen Indians born within the territorial limits of the United States . . . to be citizens of the United States."[41] Indians were presumably welcomed into the polity but only as long as they relinquished their "old ways."[42]

Even anthropologists, while often rejecting the evolutionary theories underlying forced assimilation, assumed that Indian cultures would gradually disappear, and turned to the task of preserving different tribes' ethnographic records.[43]

Forced-assimilation policies and beliefs supported the disintegration of tribal structure and control over reservation lands. They also helped sustain a new scientific racism, which the rapidly growing capitalist class employed to justify their ruling position. Merging economic and ethnic assumptions, this racial ideology brought together the southern planter aristocracy, keen on promoting Jim Crow laws to control southern populism, and the northern industrialists, interested not only in controlling the immigrant working class but also in "carrying the white man's burden and U.S. industry across Indian lands and beyond the territorial United States."[44] This new capitalist class defined the new American culture—imperial and unilateral, it was committed to the removal of all obstructions to the progress of capitalism.[45]

Changing Tides

By the 1920s, the ideology of the new capitalist class was losing ground among American intellectuals, as was the Progressives' faith in economic and political adjustments to the corruptive influences of industrial capitalism. If Progressives criticized American society for its disparities of wealth and income, their 1920s disciples were concerned about the middle-class biases and habits of modern society. A collection of essays entitled *Civilization in the United States* (1922) castigated urbanization, industrialization, and growing consumerism for their spiritual failures. Instead of economic and political revival, American society required a change of consciousness. Instead of the belief in scientific and technological solutions to social problems, so prevalent in the Progressive era, 1920s intellectuals exhibited growing ambivalence about the advance of science, uncertain whether its promise was a new and more ordered world or a threat to humanity. A sense of individual alienation from one's environment seemed to permeate the 1920s scholarship.[46]

As they became more at odds with the culture of capitalism, American intellectuals grew more attracted to other cultures. Cultural anthropologists led the march. In 1910, Franz Boas's study of immigrants and their children, undertaken for the U.S. Immigration Commission, demonstrated that racial characters, including physical measurements, changed as immigrants stayed longer in the United States. Accordingly, racial differences were cultural, not biological. Some scholars, including many Jewish Americans lobbying against the 1924 restrictive immigration laws, used Boas's study to demonstrate that assimilation was inevitable. They pointed to "the Educational Alliance's American-ization program" as illustrating how education could eliminate "immigrant de-ficiencies."[47] Others drew on Boas's studies to urge the preservation of diverse traditions. In any event, Boas and his disciples ensured that, by the end of the 1920s, "scientific racism" and "hierarchical distinctions between 'primitive' and 'civilized' societies" were "no longer respectable in academic or intellectual circles."[48]

As we already saw, one of the most famous reflections of the cultural atti-tudes of the era was Horace Kallen's cultural pluralism, which was influenced by his interaction with the African-American philosopher and writer Alain Locke and the Harlem Renaissance in New York City, with which Locke was associated and which helped elevate African-American culture.[49] But the at-traction to different cultures was more general. In 1932, sociologist Donald Young, who would later become the president of the American Sociological Association, summarized his generation's intellectual attitude by explaining that "no culture is so perfect that it will not bear improvement by borrowing from almost any other culture."[50]

The American Indian held special appeal. Critics of the capitalist and indus-trial culture turned to vanishing Indian traditions in search of alternative modes of social and cultural organization. Amid waves of nativism, including the rapid growth of the Ku Klux Klan, American intellectuals sought to trans-form Indians from an antithesis to "productivity, profit and private property"[51] into a model for modern society.

Throughout the 1920s many American intellectuals found refuge from the hustle and bustle of city and industry in the Taos home of Mabel Dodge Luhan, a wealthy heiress from Buffalo turned Greenwich Village bohemian, who moved to New Mexico in 1917 looking for alternatives to Western cul-ture. Celebrated artists, writers, and thinkers, including D. H. Lawrence, Geor-gia O'Keeffe, Ansel Adams, and Mary Austin, flocked to Luhan's home. Some later settled in the area.[52] Together, they came to view the culture of the Pueblo Indians as a healthy alternative to the diseases of their own capitalist culture.

Among the friends whom Luhan wanted to interest in the Indian cause was Collier. On December 11, 1920, after repeated invitations, Collier came to New Mexico. In five months in Taos, Collier, who had never before met an In-dian but shared the 1920s critique of capitalist culture, came to believe that the Indians "possessed the fundamental secret of human life—the secret of building great personality through the instrumentality of social institutions."[53] In Taos, Collier had discovered "a 'Red Atlantis' which held secrets desperately needed by the white world. . . . [Indians] had discovered a way to become both 'com-munists and individualists at one and the same time.'"[54] Collier found in Indian culture a middle ground between radical Marxism and conservative individual-ism—he found pluralism in action.

Collier and his contemporaries were not only dreamers, they were also doers. In the early 1920s, many of them collaborated to protect the Pueblo land grants in New Mexico against legislation (including the notorious Bursum

Bill) that sought to deprive the Indians of their rights by forcing them to produce proof of title from a hopelessly confused record of several centuries of Spanish, Mexican, and American land transactions.[55] These joint efforts led in 1923 to the formation of the AIDA, a counterorganization of sorts to the more conservative Indian Rights Association and a vehicle for Collier, its executive secretary, to promote his agenda. The AIDA's work helped secure the passage of the Pueblo Lands Act of 1924, which "established a Lands Board at Santa Fe . . . to 'investigate, determine, and report' the status and boundaries of all Pueblo lands." While it gave non-Indians the right to demonstrate "either adverse continuous possession under color of title since January 6, 1902, supported by payment of taxes on the land, or continuous possession since March 16, 1889, supported by payment of taxes, but without color of title," it reserved the Indians' right "to hire attorneys and to 'assert and maintain . . . their title and right to any land.'" The act also "upheld the right of the Indians to compensation for relinquished land and water rights."[56]

A push for change in federal Indian policy was developing.

Momentum

Throughout the 1920s, policymakers from different ends of the political spectrum criticized the policy of allotment. Several government investigations into the practices of the BIA were pursued, but they ended without specific proposals for reform.[57] In 1926, however, at the request of Secretary of the Interior Hubert Work, the Institute for Government Research undertook an independent review of the policies and practices of the BIA. The Rockefeller Foundation financed the work, Lewis Meriam of the Brookings Institution edited it, and the Johns Hopkins Press published it in 1928 under the title *The Problem of Indian Administration*. Memorialized in the history of federal Indian policy as "the Meriam Report," it outlined how the allotment policy obliterated the economic base of traditional Indian culture and resulted in widespread "poverty, disease, suffering, and discontent" among Indians.[58]

The Meriam Report did not recommend repealing the allotment policy. Rather, it called on the BIA to ensure that Indian lands were not leased or sold to whites. The harshest parts of the report attributed the failures of Indian policy to lack of funds and faulty training and urged the government to educate Indians so that they could assimilate into the social and economic life of American society.[59]

In 1929, President Herbert Hoover, Secretary of the Interior Ray Lyman Wilbur, and the newly appointed commissioner of Indian affairs, Charles J. Rhoads, made education, specifically training to operate irrigation systems, a keystone of federal Indian policy. It seemed a positive turning point in the relationship between the federal government and Indian nations, ostensibly severing cultural policy from Indian land policy. Still, for the most part, Hoover, Wilbur, and Rhoads remained committed to finding better ways to assimilate Indians, either as farmers or as industrial workers.[60]

The Meriam Report and Hoover's response condoned assimilation. But advocates on the Indians' behalf like Collier were calling for a different approach; they viewed the Meriam Report as setting the stage for an overhaul of federal Indian policy. Collier's crusade to safeguard the Pueblo land rights and the economic survival of the tribes was a step in Collier's broader program. While this initial struggle focused on land issues, as Indian policy always had, Collier envisioned an all-encompassing program focusing on the tribes' cultural self-determination.[61] Collier wanted to shift the focus of federal Indian policy from land issues to cultural ones.

Toward a Comprehensive Reform

In late 1929, Collier drafted four letters to Congress, which Wilbur and Rhoads sent to the chairmen of the Senate and House Committees on Indian Affairs, recommending that they be given serious attention. Collier's letters proclaimed that in order to build stable economic bases on reservations, previously allotted lands had to be returned to tribal ownership. Collier further contemplated that if tribes were allowed to incorporate and assisted in the process, allotments could be returned to tribal ownership in exchange for shares in the tribal corporation. Finally, Collier's letters recommended the establishment of a "special Indian claims commission" to settle Indians' claims against the United States.[62]

Collier, who soon after sending the letters began to lose patience with the Rhoads-Wilbur administration, hoped to establish self-governing tribal communities on Indian reservations. He maintained that Indian corporations, or more precisely cooperatives, would help preserve tribal traditions and that, in turn, the views about nature and the individual's place in it that grounded these traditions could benefit industrialized societies.[63] Land policy and incorporation were Collier's means to cultural pluralism.

With help from ACLU lawyers, including Margold, who was chairman of the ACLU Indian Rights Committee from its inception in 1931 until he resigned to become Interior's solicitor, Collier began transforming his vision into legislative goals. They included an incorporation bill and a bill giving authority to tribal councils on numerous matters. Both aimed to strengthen Indian governments.[64]

Then, in 1933, with the support of Ickes and Margold, the new secretary and solicitor, respectively, of the interior, Collier was appointed commissioner of Indian affairs and immediately began developing a network of top officials to support his Indian programs. Ickes did not necessarily understand all of Collier's musings, but he let his commissioner have complete responsibility for the BIA.[65]

During their first year in office, Ickes and Collier pursued different reform policies that did not require congressional approval.[66] Collier raised the number of Indians employed by the BIA's Indian Service to 30 percent of all employees, and he convinced Roosevelt to establish the Department of Indian Emergency Conservation Work, a special division of the Civilian Conservations Corps operated by Indians.[67] Collier also arranged for the inclusion of Indians in relief programs under the Agricultural Adjustment Administration,[68] the Federal Emergency Relief Administration,[69] the Civil Works Administration,[70] the Public Works Administration,[71] the Works Progress Administration,[72] and the National Youth Administration.[73] Schools, hospitals, wells, and sewerage and irrigation systems were built on reservations during Collier's first year in office, while Ickes wiped out more than $12 million in past Indian debts for developments on reservation lands.[74] In 1934, the Johnson-O'Malley Act authorized the secretary of the interior "to provide money for local assistance in the areas of Indian health, education, agriculture and social welfare." Finally, Collier launched a new magazine, *Indians at Work,* to make known these and other Indian efforts to improve their conditions.[75]

These endeavors on behalf of Indian tribes were impressive, but Ickes, Collier, and Margold agreed that if their efforts were to have any lasting consequences, a complete legislative and policy reform was necessary. They wanted to revive tribal governments (and with them, Indian ways of life), a reform that would require not only the provision of economic assistance to reservations but also a new cultural policy and, first and foremost, an end to the allotment policy.

As a first step toward these goals, Collier and Ickes convinced Roosevelt to abolish the Board of Indian Commissioners, a body that was controlled by Republicans who favored assimilation. On May 25, 1933, Ickes, at Collier's request, replaced the board with a "consultant group of social scientists who were experts concerning Indian arts and crafts, cultural anthropology, education, the use of natural resources, regional planning, health, and Indian law."[76]

Other steps toward achieving a comprehensive change of federal Indian policy were also accomplished during the first year of the Roosevelt administration: policy statements guaranteed Indian religious freedom, and the Pueblo Relief Act (1933), which concluded a decade of struggles to protect the Pueblo land rights, transferred tribal funds to tribal control, thus establishing "a precedent of payment to Indians for lands taken without their consent."[77] Furthermore, Ickes instructed all superintendents to stop any future sale of "trust or restricted Indians lands, allotted or inherited."[78]

Then, in the fall of 1933, a decision was made to bring in individuals with expertise in other fields, "with little previous involvement with Indian affairs" and no predisposition to any particular solution to the Indian problem, to prepare a general legislative reform. Felix Cohen and Melvin Siegel were the two assistant solicitors appointed by Margold to draft the bill. Cohen was appointed temporarily on October 19, 1933, and permanently on November 16, 1933.[79] Shortly after his appointment, Cohen described the situation on Indian reservations as "a condition approximating legalized anarchy."[80]

An Expert "with little previous involvement with Indian affairs"

Cohen, a proclaimed Norman Thomas socialist, was self-conscious about join-ing Roosevelt's administration. In a letter written immediately after he joined Interior to "Comrade" Norman Thomas, "whose judgment in these matters [he] most respect[ed]," Cohen apologetically explained why he thought he could "serve the Socialist movement, for a while at least," as a Socialist "within the framework of a capitalist government." Everyone at Interior, he elaborated, shared a "steadfast desire to protect challenged Indian rights against various forms of capitalist exploitation."[81]

There was more to Cohen's feelings about his role in the New Deal admin-istration than his letter to Thomas seems to suggest, although this closing ges-ture to a "steadfast desire" to participate in protecting "challenged Indian rights" against the excesses and abuses of capitalism offers an important clue.

In retrospect, Lucy commented that Cohen was "attracted to Indian law be-cause he had a great feel for the land and the return to the simple life." The In-dian way, about which he had read as a child, held tremendous appeal for him.[82] Taken at face value, Cohen's attraction reflected the attitude of many middle-class men of his generation who shared a nostalgic love of nature and the natural.[83] Read together with his letter to Thomas, however, Cohen's at-traction to the Indians' "simple life" pointed to a stronger conviction. Cohen believed that Indian reservations held a promise for a better national future—a future that would implement his legal pluralist vision.

Unlike Collier, who viewed tribes' cultural self-determination as a constitu-tive element of modern society, Cohen was fascinated by the tribes' communal political and economic structures. Despite, perhaps because of, his attraction to Indian culture, Cohen's understanding of the Indian problem was rooted not in land policy or in cultural concerns but in his legal pluralist vision. He wanted to establish self-governing communities on Indian reservations, communities that would also provide models that other groups could follow. Here was his opportunity to begin forming a state based on a multiplicity of centers of eco-nomic and political power. Given the communal economic structure of many tribes, Cohen believed that it was also an opportunity to ground group self-government in collectivist ownership of property.

In short, for Cohen, a legal pluralist and a socialist, Indian reservations were fertile fields for the cultivation of his vision for the modern state. He was thus especially troubled by the disintegration of the political and economic struc-tures of Indian tribes and the pressing of "capitalist individualism" on Indian reservations "through the allotment of tribal property to individual Indians and through the inculcation of the capitalist psychology." Cohen believed that the administration should correct past damage by encouraging "a communal cere-mony," which for him meant self-governing communities with collective own-ership of property.[84] For a while after he had joined Interior to help draft the

Indian Reorganization Act (IRA), Cohen used to comment that they were "making 'Reds' of the Indians."[85]

Interlude: Legal Pluralism

The intellectuals of the early twentieth century feared that corporations were wearing away the function of the individual producer and with it the nineteenth-century democratic and economic ideals, that is, the power of markets equally to distribute the rewards of individual industry and to help conform individual liberty to socially beneficial ends. For some, individual ownership of property and participation in the market economy were a means of cultivating social and political citizenship. They saw in the corporation's collective ownership a threat to the idea of "ordinary producers" who "shape their world on equal footing." For others, private property was a means of constraining the exercise of public power. They saw in the concentration of power in a few corporations a threat to individual autonomy. As giant corporations obfuscated "the traditional relationships between individual liberty, competition and social utility," Progressives grew concerned about "the problem of the trusts."[86] Was there an alternative? Could the nineteenth-century ideals of civic engagement be sustained in an organizational society?

Three themes characterized the Progressives' debates about these problems. Some advocated decentralizing the economy to subject smaller productive units to local democratic control and to encourage civic participation on the local level. This was the core of Louis Brandeis's attack on the "curse of bigness" and Woodrow Wilson's New Freedom. Others urged the enlargement of national institutions to control the growing business organizations. Here was Theodore Roosevelt's New Nationalism as well as Herbert Croly's call for nationalizing the economy and strengthening citizens' sense of national identity. Still others turned to a new way of thinking about political economy—consumerism. It urged Americans "to confront the impersonal world of big business and centralized markets, not as members of traditional communities or as bearers of a new nationalism, but rather as enlightened, empowered consumers." This was the gist of Walter Weyl's *New Democracy* (1912).[87]

All three positions were attempts to add organization, stability, and reason to what seemed to be the chaotic nature of industrial capitalism.[88] The legal pluralist image of the state offered a different alternative. It sought to balance decentralization with national planning, to recreate the decentralized communities in which Americans had traditionally exercised self-government while encouraging Americans to endorse a new, pluralistic understanding of their national identity. As Horace Kallen put it, "America was a nation composed of many nations."[89]

To create a decentralized economy and sustain the nineteenth-century conception of a polity of producers, many legal pluralists saw not only groups but also collective ownership as the foundation of modern society. They substituted collective production for the concept of the individual producer as the basis for economic and political citizenship, gradually transforming the corporation from a menace to society into a model for collectivist reform. Indeed, some reformers went so far as to suggest that other interest groups (for example, labor unions) should not only organize but also incorporate.[90]

Not everyone who viewed groups as the bases of society accepted collective ownership as typified in the corporate model as the ultimate model for reform. Many political pluralists adopted a contractual vision of groups and associations. So did many supporters of labor organization. While they criticized the law for treating as a single person both the large business corporation and the individual worker, they preferred to view labor unions as voluntary trade agreements meant to achieve better wages, hours, and working conditions and protected under the First and Thirteenth Amendments.[91] While pluralism reflected the impact of collectivism on American legal thought, the contractual approach typified the growing influence of voluntarism.

By the time the New Deal administration came into power, the legal pluralists' collectivist approach and the political pluralists' contractual approach converged in viewing the collaboration among associations and collective entities under a national umbrella as a way out of the Depression. As many intellectuals retreated from the 1920s obsession with culture and returned to the Progressives' political and economic obligations, creating a new economic infrastructure was seen as a first step toward a radically new society.[92] In a sea of despair, combining decentralized economic and political power with national planning, a combination that characterized the legal pluralist vision, offered a shadow of hope.

New Dealers viewed the collaborative work of collective entities as providing the basis for a new market infrastructure, an infrastructure that would reinvigorate national economic growth, which the monopolization of capital and manufacturing had stifled.[93] They focused on collective entities like corporations, or ones that resembled corporations like labor unions, as the foundation for economic and political reform. By emphasizing the efforts of groups and associations across the country, New Dealers hoped to protect individuals from the uncertainties of the market. By delegating power to a wide range of groups and collective entities, New Dealers also hoped to guard against the recurrence of disasters, like the crash they had just witnessed, that could sweep through a national economy. In short, by legitimating the activities of collective entities—whether labor unions, corporations, or, as Cohen came to realize, Indian tribes—New Dealers hoped both to endorse the multiplicity of interests and viewpoints that characterized modern society and to promote economic progress while entrusting national planning to limit the destructive potential of capitalism.

Such aspirations informed many New Deal programs. The securities acts of 1933 and 1934 rested on the assumption that government planning required cooperation with big business and that mandatory transparency and disclosure had to underlie such cooperation. The Tennessee Valley Authority, created in 1933, sought to combine government planning with decentralized, regional bureaucracy. It offered a means of "encouraging small, integrated communities in which workers might remain attached to the land while also gaining access to electricity, transportation, and modern technology." And while according to some commentators the National Industrial Recovery Act of 1933 erred on the side of extreme national planning, it too was rooted in the understanding that collective entities such as corporations and labor unions played an important role in the modern economy and had to be dealt with if the American democratic experiment was to continue to succeed. The act established the National Recovery Administration to oversee cooperative programs among business, labor, and government, particularly to negotiate agreements with employers regarding working conditions and collective bargaining (the scheme was held to be unconstitutional in 1935).[94]

Cohen's plans for reforming federal Indian policy were similar. Informed by the pluralist belief that individuals could best promote their interests by pursuing their ends in semi-sovereign associations with economic and political powers that resembled the powers of the modern state, Cohen turned to a concept of a private corporation with public obligations as a model. He advocated incorporating Indian tribes as a means of ensuring that the tribes' political and economic matters would be dealt with successfully. According to Cohen, incorporation offered a solution to the Indians' economic and political plight.

Ultimately, then, Cohen's willingness to leave private practice and join Roosevelt's administration was motivated by his wish to promote his legal pluralist vision of the state by formulating policies to encourage the growth of (and collaboration among) multiple centers of political and economic power as fora in which individuals received meaning for their ideas and actions. Cohen's ability to promote legal pluralism helped resolve the tension between his involvement with Norman Thomas's Socialist Party and his role in Roosevelt's "capitalist" administration.

"Making 'Reds' of the Indians"

Cohen turned to incorporation and collective ownership as a means of bringing Indian reservations out of many generations of poverty and destitution and of empowering tribes to manage their own affairs. By bringing to Indian tribes the benefits of organization (Cohen even suggested adding the term "incorporated" after tribes' names), Cohen sought to empower Indians in their relationship with the government as well as business corporations that for decades had been encroaching on reservations' lands and natural resources. As he asserted shortly after joining Interior, to leave individual Indians to compete with business corporations in a supposedly noncoercive world was as encumbering as the BIA's control of their affairs.[95] According to Cohen, the role of national planning was to ensure the economic and political survival of Indian tribes.

Once elevated from their desperate economic situation, Cohen trusted Indian tribes to promote their members' interests. His support for Indian self-government and his trust in the Indians' ability to self-govern ran deep. He often repeated the common, albeit historically unsubstantiated, myth that "essential elements of the Federal Constitution were embodied in the Constitution of the Iroquois Confederacy long before they occurred to any white men, and . . . that the Federal Constitution was in part derived from the Constitution of the Iroquois Confederacy." Moreover, Cohen argued that "many other tribes have evidenced a capacity for self-government and an interest in safeguarding natural resources for the use of future generations which is definitely superior to the capacities and attitudes of white groups in these matters." In a telling manner, Cohen insisted that even if, as some argued, the Indians were inferior to their white supervisors, "under elementary principles of American democracy and under the promises of [the New Deal] Administration," any group should be entitled to manage its own affairs."[96]

Yet despite his apparent radicalism, Cohen could not evade the tension inherent in legal pluralism between an endorsement of group autonomy and a commitment to particular economic and political reforms. While encouraging self-government, pluralists also described bureaucratic expertise as a foundation of the modern state. Cohen hoped that tribes would organize around an important economic enterprise and believed that, without community enterprises, the tribes would derive little if anything from the new policy.[97]

Cohen's plan for Indian reform thus reflected the legal pluralists' dilemma. On the one hand, legal pluralists recognized that a plurality of values was constitutive of the modern state and sought to promote and cherish these values. On the other hand, they feared that endorsing all values as equally valid would lead to nihilism. Cohen chose the corporate structure not only because it offered a means of empowering tribes, but also because he believed that a concept of a private corporation with public responsibility offered a satisfactory way out of the pluralist dilemma. What he failed to realize was how foreign the corporate model was to Indian tribes.

As much as Cohen wanted to view Indian tribes as yet another group with economic and political powers, just like corporations and labor unions, Indian nations were unique. They were cultural groups. Cohen was thus in the right place at the right time to bring theories of legal pluralism to bear not only on the treatment of economic and political groups but also on the federal government's dealings with cultural and ethnic groups. Other legal pluralists (and legal realists) may have been able to evade the issue of ethnic and cultural differences but Cohen was forced to address it.[98] As we will see, the tension between Indian cultures and Cohen's initial solution to the Indian problem, as seen in Cohen's struggles to adapt the legal pluralist model to Indian tribes, helped transform not only his understanding of the relationship between the state, groups, and individuals (his legal pluralist image of the state) but also his understanding of his place as a Jew in American society.

CHAPTER 4

Ideals and Compromises

Diversity

Incorporating Indian tribes was a general idea, and more information about each tribe and reservation was required before an appropriate corporate form for tribal governments could be devised. Cohen's initial task was to become acquainted with earlier efforts to reform federal Indian policy, specifically attempts to rebuild tribal governments—the 1920s tribal incorporation movement, previous tribal council bills, and different existing tribal organizations and agricultural cooperatives.[1]

Then, on November 7, 1933, Cohen and Siegel embarked upon a tour of Indian country. "I was to have gone the day before yesterday," Cohen wrote to Joseph Lash ten days before they departed, "but I convinced my boss Margold that not knowing anything about the Department or the Indians I'd make a pretty lousy ambassador. But I'm learning."[2] It is unclear what aspect of Indian law Cohen was studying when he wrote the letter to Lash, but one can assume that his attention was focused on tribal organization. Indeed, the tour's purpose was to gain firsthand knowledge of "existing tribal organizations and agricultural cooperatives" as well as community organizations and to discuss "with Indian tribes . . . problems of self-government and land ownership."[3] Writing to his father from Santa Fe, Cohen noted that his job was one of "research rather than persuasion." He was trying to discover whether the pueblo system of landholding could be used for other tribes, especially ones without the Pueblos' strong religious sanctions.[4] Cohen and Siegel also planned to provide chosen tribal communities with a "tentative outline" of the requirements for their self-government programs.[5]

Meanwhile, the BIA approached anthropologists for detailed information on issues pertaining to the organization plan. On November 20, the BIA sent out a questionnaire to a few dozen anthropologists, asking specific questions about tribes' economic activities and political structures. Of particular interest to the BIA, more likely to Collier, was the pattern of tribes' governments and political processes and the powers that tribal authorities exercised in allocating land rights, in determining property questions, and in enforcing law and social custom.[6]

The BIA described the questionnaire as an attempt to develop a better understanding of tribes' customs and traditions. It was marketed as a means of collecting data about different tribes to formulate better policies to preserve tribal traditions and promote tribes' interests. Informed by cultural anthropology, which called for appreciation of, and tolerance toward, different cultures, the questionnaire sought to unearth the range of historical and social influences that had shaped Indian cultures. Still, the policies of yesteryear determined the scope of inquiry. Despite the desire expressed by Collier (and Interior) for comprehensive change, the questionnaire focused on altering Indian land policy—on ending the policy of allotment. Anthropologists were asked to assess whether the governing bodies of each Indian tribe or group were "competent" to deal with the tribe's economic affairs, especially in the areas of allocation, management, and usage of tribal lands.[7]

Responses from anthropologists began to arrive in early December, just as Interior, including Cohen and Siegel, called back from their tour on December 4, began the process of drafting a bill to change federal Indian policy.

The anthropologists' reports, which were detailed and scientific in style, substantiated Cohen's personal experience of the diverse conditions on Indian reservations. Anthropologists described a wide range of economic undertakings on reservations (farming, agriculture, weaving, pottery, basketry) as well as diverse political organizations and structures.[8] Some Indian groups, like the Pueblos, had an explicit communal structure;[9] some held on to a hereditary or semi-hereditary chieftainship with no formal political organization;[10] some, like the Hopi, maintained religious, aristocratic governments;[11] while some had lost their communal structure and assimilated into the white population.[12] Patterns of land ownership also varied. Some tribes maintained a communal holding of land, while others became satisfied with their individual allotments.[13] Factions and disagreements among tribes about the appropriate government structures or patterns of landholding made discerning Indians' interests rather difficult.

The anthropologists' assessment of the different tribes' propensity toward self-government set additional hurdles on the road to a coherent policy. While some anthropologists described the Indians whom they studied as "just about as competent" to deal with economic matters "as is the average body governing white men, but possibly inclined to be more honest and appreciative of serious responsibility,"[14] other anthropologists feared that the collapse of tribal authorities made the young Indian generation "not conditioned to report to any independent native gov'tal body" and recommended "an extended, slow, cautious, process" to create new tribal governments.[15] Some anthropologists, still, concluded that the Indians were "quite content with the present individualistic arrangement" and within a decade or two would be capable of taking care of themselves.[16]

Cohen found these comments "extremely helpful"; he was very interested in responses that criticized attempts to enforce private ownership on reservations and recommended the establishment of communal political and economic organizations.[17] "I think some suggestions are contained in these letters that will prove important in defining the policy of the Indian Office at next Sunday's conference," Cohen wrote to another member of the bill drafting team.[18]

Interior's Responsibility

More than one policy was required to address the diversity of tribes' economic and political organizations.[19] But the New Dealers did not consider different policies for different tribes an option. Assuredly overwhelmed by the diverse conditions on reservations, they turned to the task of drafting a uniform policy with scientific determination. As anthropologists' letters arrived at the BIA, Lucy, as a volunteer, helped Cohen compile them. Chosen quotes from each letter were classified under specific categories—Land, Self-Government, Communal Life, Approval of Policy, Law and Order, Public Welfare, Religion, Property, Education.[20] Then, through a process of elimination and reiteration, the drafters arrived at four sections for the proposed bill: self-government, lands, law and order, and education.

Collier was the bill's visionary. On January 7, 1934, he called a conference at the Cosmos Club in Washington to discuss the future of federal Indian policy. Collier hoped to unite behind the planned legislation an array of groups, including the AIDA, the Indian Rights Association, and the National Association on Indian Affairs as well as the ACLU, the National Council of American Indians, and the General Federation of Women's Clubs, which had been Collier's closest ally in past struggles. Margold, Roger Baldwin, Cohen, and several Indians were also present. As Collier anticipated, the participants concurred on the need to end the allotment policy, to consolidate Indian trust lands and heirship lands under community ownership, to obtain land for landless Indians, to establish tribal councils and Indian court systems, to create a credit system for tribal economic development, to return the Oklahoma Indians to federal guardianship, and to settle claims arising from broken treaties.[21] These became the guidelines for drafting a uniform federal Indian policy.

Several participants were involved in the drafting process: Robert Marshall, director of forestry, whose role seems to have been supervisory;[22] Ward Shepard, a forestry expert, whose tasks focused on land policy;[23] and Cohen and Siegel, whose draft proposal was the most comprehensive. In retrospect, Collier recalled that the act was drafted by the Solicitor's Office, "particularly" by Felix Cohen.[24]

Collier and Cohen shared mutual respect, but their visions for federal Indian policy were distinct. Collier was a self-proclaimed cultural pluralist. He wanted to preserve and conserve the cultural and social traditions of Indian tribes and to create on reservations "civil liberty, including group and cultural religious liberty within a framework of continuing federal protection and assistance."[25] For Collier, Indian cultural revival was a means of saving American society from what he saw as the ruins of capitalism. Given his focus, Collier's plans for the tribes' economic development were modest—he wanted to raise Indian income to a subsistence level.[26]

Cohen's plans centered around the tribes' economic and political powers. He believed that once Indian communities had become politically autonomous, which required a stable economic base (specifically, but not exclusively, land), cultural self-determination would follow. In short, according to Cohen, economic success promised political autonomy, which in turn guaranteed cultural survival. As he explained shortly after he joined Interior, "The first responsibility of the Interior Department towards our Indian population is to assist them to achieve and maintain that economic independence without which political freedom may prove to be a will-o'-the-wisp."[27]

Eager to help Indian tribes, Cohen did not merely wish to make "'Reds' of the Indians"; he was convinced that Indian society was already socialist as it was. "The Indian," he wrote, was "too deficient in the white man's business equipment, the white man's love of work, and the white man's selfishness to maintain his economic independence when he is turned loose, as an individual, to face the mighty forces of the modern economic world."[28] Accordingly, the new administration's task was to acknowledge the Indians' socialist temperament and to correct the damage caused by earlier attempts to eradicate it. Cohen wanted to allow Indian tribes not only to self-govern but also collectively to own and develop their resources, including land, and to define the boundaries of law and order on their reservations. He believed that such steps would lead to the development and preservation of the Indians' unique cultural capacities.[29]

Both Collier, as the bill's visionary, and Cohen, as the bill's drafter, influenced the initial departmental bill. In some sections of the bill, the clash between their differing visions was apparent; in others, their perspectives coalesced. Together, they made federal Indian law a site for the development of cultural and legal pluralism.

Interior's Bill

The initial departmental bill was completed on February 6, 1934. It was inscribed as "A bill to grant Indians living under Federal tutelage the freedom to organize for purposes of local self-government and economic enterprise, to provide for the necessary training of Indians in administrative and economic affairs, to conserve and develop Indian lands, and to promote the more effective administration of justice in matters affecting Indian tribes and communities by establishing a Federal Court of Indian Affairs."[30] The bill was long and complex, reflecting an extensive collaborative drafting process. It expressed the view that the government should abandon the objectives of destroying tribal organization and assimilating individual Indians and should instead encourage tribal self-government. It was forty-eight pages long and was divided into four titles: Indian self-government, education for Indians, lands, and the court of Indian affairs.[31] The sequence of the titles was carefully thought out, seemingly foreshadowing the order in which Interior would work out the program.[32]

Self-Government

The first title of Interior's bill, "Indian Self-Government," declared the freedom of tribal societies "to organize for the purposes of local self-government and economic enterprise, to the end that civil liberty, political responsibility, and economic independence shall be achieved among the Indian peoples of the United States." Specifically, "one-fourth of the adult Indians residing on any existing reservation" could petition the secretary of the interior for a charter that would grant them "powers of government and such privileges of corporate organization." The secretary would investigate the reservation's conditions and issue a charter defining the territorial limits and the community's membership criteria and prescribing a form of government suitable for its needs and traditions. The charter would be submitted back to the tribe for ratification by "a three-fifths vote at a popular election open to all adult Indians resident within the territory covered by the charter."[33]

The first title followed Cohen's recommendations in a draft he coauthored with Siegel. It viewed tribal incorporation as a means of empowering tribes and preserving their traditions. Each charter was to contain "a concise and definitive list of powers and restrictions of power applicable to the particular community."[34] As Cohen elaborated in a different memorandum, these charters, which would be modeled after municipal or quasi-municipal charters, would allow Indian groups to adopt their own laws and ordinances—in short, to form a sovereign community.[35]

Interior's bill outlined the powers that the secretary of the interior could grant tribes, including the power to organize as a federal municipal corporation; to adopt "a form of government"; to elect "officers, agents, and employees"; to "regulate the use and disposition of property"; to establish courts for the enforcement of rules and ordinances; to condemn and take title to lands or properties; to "acquire, manage and dispose of property"; to sue and be sued; to employ counsel; and to "exercise any other privileges which may be granted to membership of business corporations."[36]

In addition, charters could grant tribal governments the power to dismiss Federal Indian Service employees, to regulate intercourse between members and nonmembers, to enter contracts for public services with the states and the federal government, and generally to administer Indian affairs as a federal agency. But the bill made it clear that the federal government would not be liable for any act or omission by a chartered Indian community.[37]

Interior's concept of a federal municipal corporation treated tribal powers as delegated from the federal government rather than inherent in the tribes' sovereign (or semi-sovereign) status. Accordingly, while the bill described tribes as modern municipal corporations, it also called on tribal governments to "cultivate and encourage arts, crafts, and culture." As other scholars have observed, these two roles placed tribal governments "in the uncomfortable position of having to represent traditional culture while performing contemporary, and basically non-Indian, functions of government."[38]

Moreover, while the bill embraced tribal sovereignty, the charters were also intended to bring all tribes and reservations under a national planning umbrella. For one thing, while the bill anticipated that Indian communities would gradually take over control of their affairs, Interior remained concerned about tribes' abilities to undertake the task. Section 7 of the title on "Indian Self-Government" thus authorized the secretary to enter "temporary and experimental" agreements with any community "for the performance of such functions whenever the community is by charter empowered to perform them." Communities could undertake different functions based on Interior's assessment of their ability to do so.[39]

Because the New Dealers were also concerned about potential abuses of power, the title on "Indian Self-Government" declared that each tribe was expected to guarantee "the civil liberties of minorities and individuals within the community, including the liberty of conscience, worship, speech, press, assembly, and association," as well as the right of any member to abandon the community and be compensated for interests in community assets thereby relinquished.[40]

Cohen's original draft went even further. It sought to restrain community power "to affect two main purposes: (a) the preservation of the resources of the community and (b) protection of individuals against factional discrimination, the arrogance of petty officials and the domination of property interests."[41] As we will see with respect to the third title, as Cohen well realized, the most important power of tribal governments was their power over the communal property, specifically over lands.

Education

The second title of Interior's bill, "Special Education for Indians," focused on the need to train Indians for positions in certain trades and in the BIA. The title directed the commissioner to provide training programs for young Indians (defined as having at least one-fourth Indian blood) to help them qualify for positions in the Indian Office, including "posts in education, public health work, law enforcement, forest management, bookkeeping, and social services." Funds were created to finance this training.[42]

Informed by Collier's cultural pluralism, the title announced that Interior's educational policy would emphasize the significance of Indian culture. Government schools were to bring to Indian communities a sense of their past, culture, and values. A fund would be created for the formal education of Indians and for measures to "preserve and develop the special cultural contributions and achievements of [Indian] civilization, including Indian arts, crafts, skills, and traditions."[43]

The bill's endorsement of cultural pluralism antagonized missionaries and assimilated Indians. But the second title's radicalism was limited. Collier (and BIA officials) seemed to have a clear vision of what Indian cultural contributions were and little patience with tribes or individual Indians who deviated from them. To draw on the observation of D. H. Lawrence, who was Collier's next-door neighbor in Taos in 1921, Collier seemed to set "the claws of his own egotistic benevolent volition" into the Indians.[44]

In contrast, Cohen and Siegel's draft, which did not focus on culture, recommended consulting with anthropologists and educating Indians and BIA personnel "in the realities of [tribal] political and economic affairs" as the Indians saw them. According to Cohen and Siegel, "a carefully documented study of the movement and development of the Indian population since the inauguration of the allotment program" had to support each aspect of the program.[45]

Furthermore, as Cohen elaborated in another memorandum, Indian education was meant to promise that, ultimately, the various political and economic powers vested in Interior in 1934 could be transferred to their true "owners"—the Indians. When all that was secured, the BIA's authority to govern tribal affairs could be abolished entirely. Using wit to enliven his argument, as he often did, Cohen concluded:

> The [BIA] should have no greater powers of government than the Weather Bureau. . . . [T]he Weather Bureau has never attempted to prevent the savage custom of clouds or to impose a model code of conduct upon the winds. . . . [The BIA] could have contributed more to the happiness of its wards and to the richness of its American service if it had emulated the Weather Bureau's illustrious example and restricted its functions to the fields of research and public service.[46]

While Interior officials proclaimed that Indians would be specially educated to enable them to take over BIA positions, they remained unconvinced by Cohen's assertion that the BIA was dispensable. Yet, while he might have not been persuasive on issues of Indian education, Cohen seemed to have had an important effect on Interior's initial land policy.

Indian Lands

Like Collier, Cohen wanted to prevent the future loss of Indian lands and allow the repurchase of reservation lands already lost to non-Indians. Cohen further believed that the federal government should provide Indians with credit so that they could develop their own properties and should encourage communal holding of lands and other resources that could not efficiently be used by individuals.[47]

More important, Cohen saw the tribes' economic structures as a means of promoting the collectivist aspect of his legal pluralist image of the state. His plans for tribes' economic resources were rigid. The proposal he and Siegel developed emphasized that tribes should be encouraged to adopt a system of self-government based on shared ownership and usage of land. Individual Indians were to be required to return their lands to the community; those who wished to remain owners of individual property were to be persuaded, even forced as a means of last resort, to turn over lands they owned to their communities.[48]

According to Cohen and Siegel, a "satisfactory solution of the land problem" required that all Indian-owned lands be controlled by the community. They believed that in order to provide each individual member "some opportunity to wrest a livelihood from the limited resources of the community," unequal distribution of rights to land had to be eliminated. In exchange for lands, Cohen and Siegel suggested that individual Indians would receive an equal interest, not a proportionate one, in the community's assets.[49]

According to Cohen, only collective ownership could correct the damage caused by allotment. "We shall not add to the Indian's freedom by accepting the shallow arguments of those who insist that the Indian will be free when he is given his own individual property, [and] permitted to live under state laws and enjoy freedom of contract," Cohen proclaimed. "The termination of governmental control would not inaugurate Indian freedom. It would only exchange the slavery of bureaucracy for the slavery of poverty."[50] Instead, Cohen wanted to see genuine socialist communities flourishing on Indian reservations.[51]

Cohen and Siegel's insistence on communal ownership and equal distribution of interests was sweeping. In comparison, Marshall did not trust Indians to manage their affairs and cautioned against transferring to Indian communities legal title to lands that the government held in trust for them.[52] And Shepard's analysis focused on halting allotment, bringing back lands that had not been allotted under tribal control, and purchasing new lands for Indians. Shepard recommended teaching Indians "economic self-support" through "the planned development of farming, grazing, and forest communities, where allotment and individual ownership have not gone so far as to make it difficult to bring the people together into communities."[53]

In short, while Cohen and Siegel emphasized collective ownership, Shepard sought to balance collective land ownership with individual rights, and Marshall wanted to subject all Indian activities to government oversight. The third title of the departmental bill, "Indian Lands," struck a compromise between these different recommendations.

First, reversing a policy of fifty years, the title prohibited all future land allotments and restored to tribal ownership lands that had been declared surplus under the respective allotment acts but never settled. Furthermore, in response to tribal needs, the third title provided Interior with a $2 million annual fund to purchase lands for landless Indians and for existing reservations. (One reason for this fund was to consolidate lands otherwise trapped in checkerboarded areas.) To allow for the further consolidation of lands, the title placed serious restrictions on tribes' rights in their current and future lands. Following Marshall's suggestions, the trust period assigned to Indian allotments and unallotted lands was "extended and continued until otherwise directed by Congress," and "sale, devise, gift, or other transfer of Indian lands held under any trust patent or otherwise restricted" were prohibited unless authorized by the secretary of the interior.[54]

As to Cohen's recommendations, his idea of a mandatory return of individual lands to tribal ownership (in exchange for an equal share in the tribal property) was abandoned. But the title declared that all lands allotted under the Dawes Act would be classified into productive units, which could be exchanged for a proportionate interest in the tribal corporation. Furthermore, the secretary of the interior was authorized "to transfer to the tribe any individual Indian's interest in grazing, farming, or timber lands." In exchange, the individual member would be issued a nontransferable certificate, giving the member a proportionate share in the tribal property and the right to continuous use of the property. These certificates (and the right to use) were inheritable but not by nonmembers.[55]

Finally, in accordance with Cohen and Siegel's draft, heirship lands were to be ceded to the community in exchange for a certificate of interest "equal to the proportionate share" that the individual member "would have otherwise received under the will of the deceased" and compensation for improvements. Heirs could also continue to use the land. In short, instead of "inheritable allotments," Indians were to receive "lifetime assignments" of land.[56]

Law and Order

If Cohen's proposal was radical with respect to education and rigid with respect to land ownership, the extent of his legal pluralism was revealed in his and Siegel's advocacy of a system of separate Indian courts, a subject that Cohen explored in detail in a subsequent memorandum called "The Problem of Law and Order on Indian Reservations in Relation to the Wheeler-Howard Bill."[57]

According to Cohen, a system of specialized courts was needed to fill a serious legal gap caused by imperial neglect, that is, that neither the federal government nor the individual states had ever developed any adequate legal machinery to promote law and order on reservations. Specifically, because Indians were expected to administer their own affairs, states had "no constitutional power to regulate either the conduct of tribal Indians or the conduct of [their] own citizens towards such Indians, where the acts in question occurred in Indian country." In turn, unless such matters constituted "intercourse with Indian tribes," they were also outside the reach of federal courts. In addition, the federal government had never assigned to the district courts "general jurisdiction over Indian offenses," nor had the federal government "ever established a comprehensive criminal code covering such offenses." Finally, Courts of Indian Offenses, established on several reservations, could not adequately deal with many of the problems arising on the reservations. In the absence of effective tribal, state, or federal judicial systems, Cohen concluded, "law and order on Indian reservations [had] been entrusted to the unreviewable discretion of the Commissioner of Indian Affairs and the Secretary of the Interior." As Cohen proclaimed, a "condition of anarchy" was "cured only by the introduction of unlimited despotic powers."[58]

Cohen recommended two changes. First, he called for the establishment of community courts with limited jurisdiction over issues arising on the reservation; the courts of the state were to retain jurisdiction over affairs involving non-Indians.[59] Second, Cohen recommended the creation of a special Federal Court of Indian Affairs to "hear appeals from the local courts of Indian communities as well as exercise a limited original jurisdiction in Indian matters."[60] This federal court was to have administrative functions such as the power to rule in advance of controversies, particularly in issues involving the nature of tribal governments' authority.

Cohen's plan reflected a pragmatic realization that the federal courts could easily jeopardize the New Deal reforms. Establishing specialized courts sympathetic to Indian self-government (and his pluralist goals) and appointing special, similarly sympathetic, attorneys to represent the tribes were vital features of his proposal. He hoped that while "the Federal Court of Indian Affairs would be manned by persons endowed with sympathetic understanding of Indian problems," it would command, "by virtue of its Federal status, the respect and cooperation of the white community in its operation upon the delicate relationships between Indians and whites."[61]

Through the establishment of "definite community ordinances," community courts, and a special Federal Court of Indian Affairs, Cohen expected to generate legal stability and political advancement on reservations.[62] The fourth title of Interior's bill endorsed many of Cohen's recommendations. It called for the establishment of "local courts or tribunals to handle the legal problems that arose at the community level" and the establishment of a U.S. Court of Indian Affairs. The national court, which was to consist of seven justices "appointed by the President . . . with the consent of the Senate," was to have original jurisdiction over all legal controversies to which an individual Indian or Indian community was a party and over all matters relating to the affairs, ordinances, or jurisdiction of any Indian tribe (including crimes committed by non-Indians on reservations). The court would also hear appeals from the judgment of any court of any chartered Indian community.[63] Finally, the secretary of the interior was authorized to appoint ten special attorneys who would advise and represent either individual Indians and Indian tribes or the United States acting on the Indians' behalf.

Cohen and Siegel's initial draft also recommended establishing a supervisory board, perhaps "three white men and two Indians," on each reservation to enforce the tribes' rules and ordinances as well as the obligations of the community government.[64] Such a scheme was, however, beyond what others at Interior could embrace. As Marshall explained, creating supervisory boards in 110 different jurisdictions "merely to check up on how the Indians manage their own affairs" would be too expensive and administratively cumbersome, "just what is not wanted with self-government." Ironically, instead of a board composed of Indians and whites, Marshall recommended that BIA inspectors should routinely check on different tribal governments.[65] In other words, Marshall wanted to promote Indians' welfare but did not think Indians were capable of governing themselves. At the very least, he and those who shared his views were indecisive about the limits of tribal self-government.[66]

Cohen, too, was ambivalent. While his discussion of tribal courts and justice seemed to emphasize that the new administration would allow "Indians to choose for themselves to what extent democratic rights will be preserved,"[67] on other occasions Cohen saw fit to require separate Indian courts to protect the liberties guaranteed under the Bill of Rights.[68] In a telling manner, the last paragraphs of Cohen's memorandum on law and order elaborated how courts operating on reservations would familiarize Indians with the administration of justice. Cohen believed that such familiarity would "instill a public sentiment against law-breaking" in Indian groups. He further argued that the local and special courts would offer Indians "sitting as jurors or . . . observing the operations of the court" an opportunity "to learn the fundamental principles of American law and court procedure." While recognizing that conquest often led colonized people to condone violating the conqueror's laws, Cohen anticipated that when tribes were properly introduced to American law, they would model their governance systems, ordinances, and courts after its structures.[69]

In the end, while the fourth title recognized the need for a separate system of Indian courts, it imposed Anglo-American ideas about justice that were often different from the traditional conceptions of Indian justice. It required the Court of Indian Affairs to promulgate rules of evidence and procedure following those in practice in U.S. district courts rather than traditional tribal rules. It also subjected the final judgment of the Court of Indian Affairs "to review on questions of law" in the appropriate district courts as well as the Supreme Court. In other words, even Cohen accepted, uncritically, that in a conflict between tribal traditions and American law, the latter should prevail.[70]

Ambivalence

Interior's bill endorsed a philosophy of pluralism—cultural and legal—that Indians did not necessarily embrace (or, sometimes, understand) and that members of Congress were unwilling to accept.

Furthermore, Collier's and Cohen's ambivalence about the normative limits of their pluralism led them to draft a bill that was inherently self-contradictory. While the bill pronounced as its goal tribal self-government, it delegated almost absolute power to the secretary of the interior to determine the scope of tribes' autonomy.[71] Similarly, the bill reflected a tension between an endorsement of cultural pluralism and a strong commitment to certain cultural ideals. Ultimately, Interior's indecisiveness about pluralism, reflected in every section of the long and detailed bill, offered ammunition to those who criticized the bill for giving too much power to tribal governments and alienated those who wanted tribes to have more powers of self-government.

As if recognizing the faults of his own program, Cohen's initial draft indicated that to state some of its objectives "in statutory terms" was "politically inadvisable." Instead, Cohen and Siegel trusted the process of "reasoning and bargaining" for which "ample leeway . . . [was] provided within the framework of [the] statute," to convince the Indians to endorse some of the policies they advocated.[72] As Cohen proclaimed shortly after the drafting process was complete,

> The problem of securing a measure of freedom for the Indians of this country calls for more than the abolition of obsolete laws, it calls for more than the abolition of undemocratic methods of government. It calls for active, constructive, cooperation of the Government with the Indians in building a form of organization through which the individual Indian can protect and conserve his rights.[73]

At the very least, the finetuning of the new federal Indian policy required the approval of both Congress and the Indians. The New Dealers could not ignore Congress, and they wanted to help the Indians. The dialogue involving members of Congress, who resisted the proposed change, members of Interior, who were eager to bring about change, and members of Indian tribes, who had good reason to fear change, did not always benefit Indian tribes. But in the process of deliberation, the complexities of accommodating diverse interests, as well as the intricacy of the balance between centralized planning and decentralized governments, were revealed. For Cohen, whose role in these deliberations was often limited—he was the legal expert, called upon to explain particular points—the process was educational.

Congressional Hearings

The bill was introduced by departmental request. Senator Burton K. Wheeler of Montana read it in the Senate on February 12, 1934 (S. 2755), and Representative Edgar Howard of Nebraska read it in the House on February 13 (H.R. 7902). It was then referred to the Senate and House Committees on Indian Affairs, chaired by Wheeler and Howard, respectively. The House Committee commenced its hearings on February 22, 1934, and the Senate Committee did so five days later. In both committees, Collier introduced the bill, carefully explicating the problems of the allotment policy, the loss of lands, the erosion of self-government, and the BIA's consequential assumption of power.

Collier announced that the new bill would "curb Federal absolutism and [provide] Indian Home Rule under Federal guidance."[74]

Having explained the need to correct the devastating effects of the allotment policy, Collier introduced the bill's different titles. Title I, Collier emphasized, would add to Indians' existing rights (especially treaty rights). Title II would provide for Indian education and their assumption of important positions in the BIA. Title III would create a land base, while Title IV would establish a long-needed Indian legal system.

Collier emphasized that the bill would not compel Indians to adopt a particular political or economic structure, promising that "the futures of the Indian tribes will be diverse, as their backgrounds and present situations are diverse." He stressed that the bill did not intend to predetermine tribes' futures. Rather, it sought to free tribes from "economic and social imprisonment" and allow them to establish the legal conditions that would permit them to follow their chosen destinies.[75] As Cohen echoed in a subsequent memorandum, the bill was meant to eradicate dictatorship in Indian country.[76]

While there is no reason to assume that Collier and Cohen doubted the accuracy of such statements, in describing the bill as promoting American ideals such as freedom and autonomy they also hoped to make the hearing process smoother. They did not succeed.

Members of the House and Senate Committees resisted endorsing the long and technical bill. Only Title II, which dealt with education for Indians and which was ambiguous as to whether its goal was gradual assimilation or cultural pluralism, did not attract much contention (although Senator Wheeler proclaimed that it segregated Indian children).

Title IV, which incorporated Cohen's recommendation for establishing a Federal Court of Indian Affairs, was strongly opposed in both committees (especially by Wheeler in the Senate Committee). The committees' members were not ready to tinker with a legal system that had lasted for more than a century. When the House Committee called for a joint session with the House Judiciary Committee, Collier decided to sacrifice the Court of Indian Affairs in order to preserve the remaining provisions of the bill.[77] At the beginning of a session in which Charles Fahy, another solicitor at Interior, explained Cohen's memorandum on law and order, Collier signaled that the title was expendable.[78]

Representatives and senators were overtly critical of Indian self-government, endorsed in Title I, and the overwhelming diversity of conditions on Indian reservations magnified their qualms about the suggested policy's prospects. Specifically, the committees' members were concerned that the bill would segregate Indian communities. Representative Isabella Greenway of Arizona thought the bill made Indians less likely to undertake civic responsibilities, while Senator Wheeler claimed that the bill would isolate Indians. Senator Elmer Thomas of Oklahoma accused Collier of creating Indian zoos, and Representative Theodore Werner from South Dakota charged that the bill made it impossible for the Indians to assimilate.[79]

The notion that tribes would have an economy based on collective land ownership, as elaborated in Title III, exacerbated the concerns about segregation. The committees' members described collective ownership as socialistic or communistic. The power of the secretary of the interior to divest individual Indians from their farming, grazing, and forest lands for purposes of land consolidation and the provision calling for the mandatory transfer of inheritance lands to the community augmented these fears. While recognizing the difficulties associated with continuous fragmentation of lands, members of both committees believed that mandatory transfer of land from individuals to the community ran against the grain of American constitutionalism, especially as millions of acres of allotted lands, which had already passed to their rightful heirs, were awaiting lease or sale. While committee members found the issue of tribal self-government problematic, the main controversy during the hearings centered around the section on Indian lands.[80]

The bill's complexity—undoubtedly a reflection of Cohen's brilliant legal mind and possibly his shortcomings as a politician—intensified the fears that the bill endorsed socialism. Representative O'Malley complained that Indians and members of the committee had "no analogy in applying a comparison between a community established under the principles set out" in the bill and tribal communities under the allotment system. Specifically, there was no place in the country where "a proposition of collectivism" similar to the one proposed in the bill was successful. Indeed, as far as many members of Congress saw it, only in "Russia under the Soviets or collectivist village" was there a system that placed "all the land in the community."[81]

"What would an individual Indian who wants to leave the reservation receive in return for his share in communal property?" one representative asked Cohen.[82] He was not satisfied by Cohen's explanation that "the reason we do not provide for that in the bill is that there are so many different situations on the different reservations that we cannot have a uniform procedure."[83]

Cohen, reflecting his political naïveté, was not sympathetic to accusations that the bill advocated socialism. "What was the difference between tribal corporations and business or federal corporations?" he pointedly asked.[84] But Collier took pains to emphasize that the bill did not "introduce any socialistic or communistic idea or device"; it only extended to Indians "facilities of organization" and "modern instrumentalities of business" that were not only "commonplace of American life," but also "indispensable to the prosperity of Americans."[85]

Once emphasizing that the bill sought to extend to Indians cherished American ideals, for example home rule, Collier faced a troubling question: was the bill's ultimate goal cultural, economic, and political self-determination or benign assimilation? Cautious not to provoke resistance from members of Congress who thought that Indians should give up their tribal ways and special status, Collier stressed that the bill would prepare Indians who wanted to assimilate for American life while assisting those who wanted to remain on reservations and practice their traditions. Accordingly, the bill was the epitome of American tolerance. It did not seek "to cause Indians to go in any predetermined direction so far as their habits and religious and cultural preferences [were] concerned." As Collier put it, the bill only aimed to "extend to all Indians that minimum of home-rule in domestic and cultural matters which is basic to American life."[86]

In another attempt to move the debate away from the controversial issues of assimilation versus pluralism and Americanism versus collectivism, Collier stressed the need to remove the BIA's bureaucratic stranglehold on Indian reservations. Echoing Cohen's suggestion that the BIA was dispensable, Collier argued that the bill contemplated that the BIA would become "a purely advisory and special service body." But members of both committees pointed out that the bill placed enormous discretionary power in Interior and its secretary.[87]

Indeed, as much as Collier and other New Dealers tried, they never offered a satisfying reply to Representative Werner's discerning observation that the bill was attempting to do two things—segregate Indians with its land policy and assimilate them through its educational policy.[88] Shepard openly admitted their dilemma: they wanted to give Indians "the benefits of community action without depriving them of the advantage of associating with whites, and without depriving them of the public services that can be rendered by the State and local political agencies."[89]

A Public Debate

Collier was determined to pass the bill, believing that the composition of Congress and the likely support of the president offered an opportunity that would not soon come again. He stopped short of nothing in his attempts to gain support for his reform program, sending copies of the bill to anthropologists and Indian and non-Indian organizations to attract their attention and engage them in a dialogue about it.[90]

The comments Collier received about the bill were carefully read, catalogued, and answered. Many correspondents, including organizations and representatives of Indian tribes, were invited to testify before the committees, and many letters were introduced at the hearings and included in the reports. Indeed, the legislative records of the Wheeler-Howard Bill leave the impression that the entire country was engaged in a long, collective debate about its dealings with Indian tribes.

Many of the responses reported in the hearings strongly supported the bill. They included letters from the General Federation of Women's Clubs, the AIDA, the ACLU, and anthropologists.[91] But the bill was not widely endorsed; some groups and individuals from around the country echoed the concerns of members of Congress about socialism and self-government.

Missionaries and church groups were opposed to the instruction of Indians in their traditions. Catholic priests seemed to accept self-government with few reservations, but other denominations, specifically the Christian Reformed Church, expressed strong misgivings. Groups associated with the Christian Reformed Church in Michigan wrote that if the bill became law, the word *tradi-tion* should be deleted from it. "First, because the minds of our Indian children should not be more polluted with these traditions than they already are"; second, because it was "unconstitutional that the government shall provide money for religious instruction."[92]

Real estate advocates, merchants living on reservations, "cattlemen holding large leases in Indian country," and mining companies were among the major opponents to the new land policy.[93]

Most devastating was the objection of Indian groups. The Indian Rights Association was one of the bill's most vocal opponents. The association endorsed Title II on education but emphasized the need to educate Indians "in a manner that would speed the assimilation process."[94] Flora Warren Seymour, a member of the Board of U.S. Indian Commissioners, which Collier disbanded, charged that the bill would perpetuate segregation of Indian communities, promote communism on Indian reservations, and result in the loss of land, liberty, and rights that the Indians had secured over the years.[95] Joseph Bruner of the National Indian Confederacy echoed Seymour's comments, attacking the bill as a socialist and communist doctrine that would set Indian affairs back two hundred years.[96]

Awakening "sympathetic understanding"

The harsh public criticisms of the bill contributed to fear and confusion on many reservations. Interior attributed some reservations' rejection of the bill to Indians' susceptibility to critiques describing it as promoting socialism or communism and as taking away Indians' citizenship and property rights. Collier and his assistant, William Zimmerman, sent angry letters to superintendents, ordering them to clarify the meaning of the proposed policy. They wanted Indian tribes to know that if Congress did not approve the bill, the allotment policy would gradually erode their land base. More important, they wanted superintendents to clarify that the bill's self-government provisions were "entirely voluntary, that a chartered community [could] adopt as much or as little of the power made available to the community by the bill as it [chose] to adopt, and that no abandonment of Federal responsibilities [was] contemplated or permitted by the bill."[97]

Collier, Zimmerman, Cohen, and their colleagues were convinced that when the Indians "faced this problem squarely, and thought about it in a constructive way," they would endorse the bill.[98] To encourage them to do so, in March and April of 1934, during the hearings, Interior held Indian congresses to explain the bill.

Early Attempts

Reservations were first called to hold official deliberations about the proposed reform on January 20, 1934, before the bill was complete and submitted to

Congress. On that day, Collier sent a circular to "Superintendents, Tribal Councils and Individual Indians" asking that the Indians on each reservation consider "plans for enlarged self-government" and suggest methods of organization for administrative consideration.[99]

The circular was Cohen's idea. Three days earlier he urged Collier to send out to reservations "a concise statement of administrative policy and a request for discussion and counsel" with respect to problems raised by the program. "As I find myself almost alone in believing that it is very important to send out such statement to the field in the shortest order," Cohen wrote to Collier, "I am impelled to state briefly the grounds of this belief." While he did not anticipate the Indians or field administrators would suggest major policy changes, Cohen expected to find their comments "invaluable in shaping or modifying" the bill's details.[100]

Cohen thought that engaging Indian tribes at an early stage would prove valuable once the legislation was passed and, at any rate, would prevent "inaccurate second-hand reports of policy." He wanted tribes to recognize that the bill was "designed not to prevent the absorption of Indians in white communities, but rather to provide for those Indians unwilling or unable to compete in the white world some measure of self-government in their own affairs."[101]

Pragmatically, Cohen recognized that Congress would not favor the program without "considerable Indian support." Accordingly, he stressed that it was vital to send to the reservations "an authoritative statement of policy in terms likely to awaken sympathetic understanding" before the official commencement of the legislative program.[102]

Collier was not entirely convinced that Indians' opinions mattered. Conspicuously, his circular to the reservations did not indicate that a draft bill was almost complete. In fact, it ended with a note:

This study is undertaken for the purpose of determining what legislation is necessary to effect the largest benefits in policy and administrative methods. It is desired, therefore, that the meetings, conventions, or councils of the Indians to discuss this program be held in the *very near future,* and that reports be prepared and forwarded to the [BIA] *not later than February 15, 1934.*[103]

Cohen's pragmatic approach and Collier's unrealistic request for a response within three weeks reflected, yet again, their ambivalence. While they sought to promote self-government, they did not always realize the many intricate aspects of self-determination or each tribe's particular needs.

In response to Collier's circular, some tribes endorsed the proposed policy. But many others were not enthusiastic, and some vehemently objected to it. As thirty-seven Crow Indians wrote to President Roosevelt, they could no more live the way Collier designed for them than "any White person would be dictated to by one American."[104]

For the most part, tribes expressed concerns about any change to the status quo. A long history of broken treaties and unfulfilled promises had left its scars. Many tribes feared that the bill would hinder their rights under existing treaties and take away their American citizenship. Some tribes, including the Arapaho Indians of the Wind River reservation in Wyoming, the Sioux at the Cheyenne Agency in South Dakota, and the Assiniboine and Atsina Indians at the Fort Belknap reservation in Montana, had grown accustomed to the system of allotment; they were concerned that the new system would harm their individual property rights and reinstate outdated government practices.[105]

Other tribes, like the Eastern Band of Cherokees in North Carolina, reminded Collier that they were already self-governing.[106] Still others, perhaps internalizing centuries of colonization, did not think they were fit for self-government.[107] Instead of running their own affairs, they sought government assistance. Specifically, tribes wanted the federal government to purchase more lands for them, to offer social welfare for their needy, and, most important, to allow Indians to attend public schools and colleges all over the country. While anthropologists were concerned about the contempt for Indian customs and traditions that the public schools instilled in young Indians, many tribes wanted their younger generation to be educated in the public school system so that they could better interact with non-Indians.[108] Finally, some tribes who had never before been consulted about policy used the opportunity to voice grievances and requests on issues beyond the proposed bill.

Taken together, the tribes' responses confirmed the wide range of opinions about the appropriate structures of government and property ownership not only among different tribes but also on any given reservation. Indeed, as the anthropologists' reports indicated, reservations were plagued with tensions between older and younger (often more assimilated) generations,[109] between full-blood and mixed-blood Indians,[110] and between landed Indians, who often wanted to keep their lands, and landless Indians.

Whether or not the bill could have accommodated both its supporters and its opponents, the tribes' responses to Collier's circular arrived too late to be incorporated into the initial departmental bill. Fearing, however, that Congress would not pass the bill without a show of Indian support, as Cohen had warned, Collier's opening remarks in the House Committee announced that congresses would be held around the country to discuss the bill with Indians. Collier was not taking any chances. With mounting critiques from different groups and the Indians before the bill was even discussed in Congress, he put much effort into building goodwill with different tribes.

Indian Congresses

Ten congresses were scheduled in March and April to bring different groups of tribes together with Interior representatives to discuss the proposed bill. Officially, Collier noted that the congresses were meant to explain the very complex bill to Indians and receive their responses, but for the most part he wanted

to guarantee the tribes' support. Each congress ended by encouraging participating tribes to adopt a resolution and send it to Congress.

The congresses were clearly "a public relations effort," but in seeking out
Indians' opinions about federal Indian policy, they were a radical feature of the
legislation process. For one thing, Interior worked to guarantee that tribal representatives to the congresses be elected rather than selected by reservation superintendents.[111] The Indian congresses "symbolized a new relation between
the Indians and the Indian Office"—a partnership in creating policy, which Interior hoped would replace the "administrative absolutism" of past years.[112]

Congresses were held in South Dakota, Arizona, New Mexico, Oklahoma,
Oregon, Wisconsin, and California and followed a similar pattern.[113] Collier or
his representative commenced the deliberations by examining the problems
facing Indian tribes. A discussion of the solutions offered in the bill followed,
with particular titles explained by other members of the department. When he
was present, Cohen often described the title on self-government and the title
on Indian courts, stressing that "this law, when it is passed in Congress is only
the beginning of things. In order to mean something, [Indians] will have to
take advantage of it."[114]

Once the bill was introduced and discussed, Collier and other Interior representatives answered the participants' questions, which were to be submitted
in writing. Each congress ended with tribal representatives' statements, commonly indicating that they would take the information to their tribes and tribal
councils for consideration.

The concerns expressed in the Indian congresses echoed letters and resolutions that had been arriving at the BIA's offices for the past few months. Indians remained anxious about any proposed change and perplexed by the complexity of this particular one. Proponents of assimilation were not lured by the
promise of self-government. As Albert Folsom, a member of the Choctaw Nation, explained, the Indians of Oklahoma feared that the bill accorded no benefits to the Indian community and, instead, set out to isolate them and deprive
them of the opportunities of citizenship.[115] In turn, supporters of tribal autonomy worried about the power reserved in Interior. Francis Red Tomahawk, a
Standing Rock Sioux, summarized the general feeling by proclaiming that
while the allotment policy had had devastating effects upon his reservation, the
comprehensive change proposed by Interior was likely to cause as much
harm.[116]

Many delegates remained concerned about the bill's endorsement of communal ownership. Tribes could not see how a proportionate share of tribal
property was equivalent to an individual title, and the secretary's power to
transfer title of individual lands to tribal ownership exacerbated their fears.
Some tribes (especially in the southwest) wanted to know whether communal
ownership would also apply to their cattle. Still others reiterated critiques of
the bill as forcing a communistic or socialistic program on reservations. Joe Irving from the Crow Creek delegation announced that if the bill "were passed

[Indians] could not exercise [their] own rights and . . . might just as well live in Russia."[117]

Factional conflicts, specifically between full-blood Indians who held their allotments and mixed-blood Indians who had already parted with their property, underlay many of the concerns about transferring land to tribal ownership.

Confusion about tribal self-government and anxiety about the proposed land policy were infused with fears that the bill would impede tribal rights to sue for lands previously taken as well as with distrust, even hostility, toward the federal government.[118] "Will another commissioner come out from the seat of government and tell them this community system is a failure?" asked one delegate. "These men sit up here, what do they know about our reservation?" Oliver Bellville of the San Carlos Reservation proclaimed more pointedly. "I want to say to these gentlemen up here that I want them to make it known that the San Carlos reservation is mine and I want to keep it."[119]

Deliberations

Collier, Cohen, and their colleagues were able to dispel some of the distrust, misunderstandings, and fears associated with the bill. Simple gestures during the congresses, such as attentiveness to tribal delegates who did not understand English and required interpretation, and participation in rituals and entertainment activities arranged by the various delegates, increased their credibility. But Interior representatives were also forced to listen. "So far our Congresses have been very adventurous and gratifying," Cohen reported to his parents from San Francisco.[120]

The Indian Office was eager to have the bill passed, emphasizing during the congresses that tribes who would not come under the act were likely to lose their lands and gradually everything.[121] But it also recognized that some features of the draft bill had to be changed—specifically the proposed land policy.

On April 26, Collier presented to the Senate Committee on Indian Affairs a new version of the bill. To accommodate the Indians' requests, the amended bill made the transfer of title from living individuals to tribal control entirely voluntary and prohibited "the disposition of any community or tribal assets without the consent of the tribe or community." The section mandating the transfer of land to the community upon the death of an allottee was changed to include only grazing lands, forests, and farming lands that physically could not be further subdivided. The revised bill also clarified that transfer of land from an individual to the community would not transfer individual rights in minerals, including oil and gas. Finally, provisions were added to prevent "the possibility of having 50 active voters out of a thousand eligible adults bind the entire tribe" and to require a minimum percentage of the adult population for charter approval.[122]

The second bill did not fare better than the initial draft. In the hearing before the Senate Committee, Wheeler, joined by Elmer Thomas, opposed tribal self-government altogether. They wanted Congress to educate Indians to adopt "the white man's way." According to Wheeler and Thomas, once tribes proved capable of handling their affairs, the government should end its special relationship with them. In the House Committee, Will Rogers of Oklahoma continued to question whether Indians understood the bill, and Thomas O'Malley of Wisconsin continued to accuse Interior of attempting to impose communism on Indian reservations.[123]

Fighting for the bill, Collier secured President Roosevelt's support. In identical letters written to Representative Howard and Senator Wheeler, Roosevelt noted,

> We can and should, without further delay, extend to the Indian the fundamental rights of political liberty and local self-government and the opportunities of education and economic assistance that they require in order to attain a wholesome American life. This is the obligation of honor of a powerful Nation towards a people living among us and dependent upon our protection.[124]

The pressure was mounting, but the opponents were not ready to give in. On May 21, members of the House Indian Affairs Committee met for an evening session and redrafted an abbreviated bill, which, after further amendments by the Senate Committee, passed both houses (H.R. 7902, S. 3645) and was signed by President Roosevelt on June 18, 1934. It became known as the Indian Reorganization Act.[125] Tellingly, Howard, who introduced the initial bill, commented shortly before the final bill was enacted that "this program will pave the way for a real assimilation of the Indians into the American community on the level of economic independence and political self-respect."[126]

The Indian Reorganization Act

The IRA was a far cry from Cohen's radical draft or the initial departmental bill, reflecting a range of taming, more conservative influences—the fears of individual Indians owning allotments, the interests of non-Indian groups leasing Indian land or using Indian timber, the concerns of missionary groups operating on Indian reservations, and congressional beliefs about the appropriate relationship between Indians and the federal government.[127]

Drastically shortened from forty-eight pages and four major titles (each divided into several sections) to five pages and nineteen succinct sections, the final version included most of the original ideas with respect to the termination of allotment, tribal incorporation and organization, education, and the BIA's employment of Indians.[128]

The IRA prohibited future allotments, extended the trust period on restricted lands, empowered tribes who would choose to come under the act voluntarily to consolidate lands, restored to tribal ownership remaining surplus lands, and authorized an annual fund of $2 million for the purchase of new tribal lands. Tribes were encouraged to form governments similar to municipal corporations and draft tribal charters of incorporation for managing their economic resources. To help tribes with the drafting of constitutions, bylaws, and charters of incorporation for business purposes, an annual appropriation of $250,000 was authorized. A $10 million revolving credit fund was further created to support economic development on reservations. Funds for advanced education for Indian students were authorized, and states where Indians had enrolled in public schools were given federal funds. Finally, the act authorized incorporated tribes to take on BIA functions and to use state and local services.[129]

On the other hand, the act reduced the title on self-government to a few provisions that provided Indian tribes with very limited powers. Legislators opposed the idea of delegating power and authority to tribal communities. Indian communities' powers to make contracts with federal and state governments, to hire their own employees, or to compel the removal of government employees were left out.[130] Furthermore, the power of tribes and Interior to acquire allotted lands for consolidation was notably diluted. Transfer of individual lands (including heirship lands) to community ownership could only be voluntary.

In addition, two elements included in Cohen and Siegel's draft were completely absent. First, as Collier indicated, the fourth title, the establishment of a system of Indian courts, was eliminated. Second, the act did not allow groups smaller than tribes to incorporate. Its focus was tribal initiative rather than more local, community-centered activities; it thus reinforced and perpetuated the existence of basically artificial units of Indian political, economic, and social life.[131]

Cohen saw Congress's refusal to ground political autonomy and cultural survival in collective ownership as the most devastating alteration to the original draft. A couple of years after the passage of the act, he noted that "in the original Wheeler-Howard Act [he] defended to the best of [his] ability, but unsuccessfully, a provision expressly authorizing the Secretary to dispose of individual Indian lands for the benefit of the Indian owners without their consent." As Cohen explained, he was "convinced that this [was] a sound economic policy, at least with respect to grazing, large-scale farming, and timber operations," but, as he recollected, he was not able to convince others.[132]

In a similar manner, Collier noted that "the parts which did not become law," specifically the section that allowed the secretary to compound allotted lands and Title IV, "were more radical and possibly more fundamental than the parts which went through to enactment."[133] According to Collier, losing those features was "a major disaster to the Indians, the Indian Service, and the program."[134]

Finally, the IRA introduced new features. Section 18 called for a referendum to be held on reservations included under the act within one year (subsequently extended to two years) to determine whether or not the tribe would choose to come under the provisions of the act. Representative Howard initiated the demand for a referendum. It provided that the act would not apply to a reservation where a majority of the eligible voters voted against its application. Tribes that rejected the act would remain under the BIA's direct control. Tribes that accepted it could prepare a constitution, to be ratified by "a majority of the Indians on a given reservation and officially recognized members of the tribe."[135] The establishment of a tribal council and a charter of incorporation would follow. As we will see in the next chapter, the time limit of the referendum requirement put an undue burden both on the Indians and on Interior and produced mistakes that might have otherwise been avoided. As Collier concluded in retrospect, "We had pressed the democratic philosophy not too far; we had not pressed it far enough nor skillfully enough."[136]

CHAPTER 5

In Flux

Referenda

The New Dealers rushed to administer referenda. To create an atmosphere in favor of the IRA, the first referenda were called on supportive reservations, beginning with the plains reservations in Montana and the Dakotas and in the Great Lakes region. The New Dealers hoped that more doubtful tribes would follow if a large number of reservations had already adopted the act.[1]

The initial referenda seemed successful. While reports offer different numbers, it seems that between 172 and 192 Indian groups with a total population of roughly 130,000 chose to come under the act, and between 71 and 78 groups with a total population of roughly 90,000 chose not to do so. In general, large reservations favored the IRA while small bands, like the Mission Indians of California, voted against it. But there were a few notable exceptions of large tribes rejecting the act. The Klamath Indians of Oregon, which already had a well-established tribal government and which proponents of the act pointed to as a model for reorganization, rejected the act. So did the Crow in Montana, described by anthropologist Robert Lowie as "one of the strongest and most cohesive tribes in the plains region." Negative votes were recorded on several other plains reservations—Fort Peck in Montana, Sisseton in South Dakota, and Turtle Mountain in North Dakota—and among the Iroquois tribes of New York (even before the bill was passed, the Iroquois tribes had sought exclusion from it). But perhaps the most devastating rejection of the IRA occurred on June 14 and 15, 1935, on the large Navajo reservation in Arizona and New Mexico.[2]

The number of tribes that chose to come under the act, which Interior officials used to counter continuing opposition to their new policy, did not necessarily indicate widespread Indian support for the act. In addition to selecting reservations for the initial referenda carefully, the New Dealers engaged in subtle coercive tactics. For example, while stressing that tribes who rejected the IRA would suffer no discrimination, Collier also pointed out that such tribes could not benefit from the act's programs. Collier emphasized that the revolving credit fund of $10 million would only be available to Indian chartered corporations, which would be responsible for making loans to individuals and groups. As coming under the act was a prerequisite for incorporation, tribes could take advantage of the revolving loan fund only if they came under the act and incorporated. In addition, tribes that rejected the IRA could not receive the new educational loans or benefit from the fund to purchase new lands, and in general they would be subject to governmental administering of their tribal assets. As Collier put it, tribes that rejected the act would "merely drift to the rear of the great advance open to the Indian race."[3]

Moreover, while the New Dealers described the referenda as giving tribes a voice in determining their future,[4] the referenda were administered in ways that were foreign to tribal cultures. American Indian cultures distrusted haste and urgency. Indians preferred to take their time in making decisions because they viewed such decisions as binding and irrevocable pledges. Decision-making required careful attention and consensus with respect to the present conditions of the tribe and its future welfare.[5] The hasty referenda did not leave room for such considerations.

Adding insult to injury, Interior, in a solicitor's opinion drafted by Cohen, interpreted section 18 ("Wherein a majority of the adult Indians, voting at a special election duly called by the Secretary of the Interior, shall vote against its application") to mean that "a rejection of the Act on any reservation [became] effective only if a majority of all eligible Indians on that reservation cast their ballots against the application of the act." Because several reservations rejected the IRA with a very low voter turnout (less than a majority of the eligible voters), Cohen clarified that "eligible voters who failed to vote would be counted as being in favor of adoption." Even if less than a majority of the eligible voters actually voted, "even if the opponents of the act should have a clear majority of the votes actually cast, . . . the act [would] continue to apply" (unless the secretary required another election).[6] According to one report, "for seventeen tribes, comprising a total population of 5,334, this ruling reversed an otherwise negative vote."[7]

Interior's method of registering negative votes was obviously intended to make a very strong opposition to the act the only way a tribe could opt out. Department officials, particularly Collier, probably knew that a majority of traditional Indians would refuse to participate in any election called by Interior, and that Indians would show their disagreement by not voting on the referenda rather than by casting a negative vote.[8] Still, Margold proclaimed that "it is quite possible that many Indians refrained from voting because they had been informed that rejection of the act could be accomplished only by a majority of the eligible voters. This meant, in effect that voting in favor of the act had no different effect than refusing to go to the polls."[9]

It was left to Congress, which remained ambivalent about its support for the new policy, to place a limit on Interior's good measure of legal competency and to force the New Dealers to recognize the reality of tribal opposition to the act. In 1935, while extending for another year the deadline for holding referenda, Congress amended the IRA to authorize the BIA to count only participating votes. For many tribes, the change was insignificant. Interior was already underway to organize them.[10]

Organization: Preliminary Decisions

As the department administered the referenda, the IRA's opponents, including Indian organizations such as the pro-assimilation American Indian Federation, continued to criticize its ends. Several times during the act's first years, Collier had to defend its goals and the BIA's activities before congressional committees. His success was especially important as many of the act's provisions required congressional appropriation of funds, and Congress had adjourned shortly after the passage of the act, before funds could be appropriated. Indeed, when Congress returned into session, the House Subcommittee on Interior Appropriations dramatically cut many of the funds authorized under the act.[11]

Anticipating an uphill battle to implement the act, Interior hurried not only to administer referenda but also to secure the organization of a sufficient number of tribes before the beginning of a new session in Congress (including the adoption of constitutions, bylaws, and charters). In so doing, they hoped to avoid congressional criticism as well as to clarify the act's permanent implications and deficiencies that needed to be amended.[12]

A newly formed Organization Division (with Cohen as chairman) was responsible for implementing the IRA. Field agents were sent to reservations to provide a link between the BIA's offices in Washington and the tribes (as well as BIA's personnel on the reservations). These agents were responsible for explaining the act to the tribes and the BIA's personnel and for advising them on the organization process, including drafting constitutions, establishing tribal governments, and creating cooperative organizations for economic enterprises.[13]

Tribes were carefully selected for inclusion in the immediate program, taking into account factors such as the tribe's understanding of the act (as reflected in their correspondence with the BIA and their initial reaction to the act), the willingness of the tribe's superintendent to cooperate with the department, and the tribe's adaptability to the organization program. Specifically, Interior looked for tribes whose "economic conditions" could sustain "a community organization program independent of land purchase" and whose organization would be relatively simple, for example, when their existing constitutions were "functioning in a satisfactory manner."[14]

On October 4, 1935, the Confederated Salish and Kootenai Tribes of the Flathead Reservation in Montana adopted the first constitution prepared in accordance with the IRA by a vote of 549 to 123. Secretary Ickes approved it on

October 28, 1935. Shortly thereafter the Rocky Boy's, Lower Brule, and Fort Belknap reservations, with which Cohen had worked since he joined Interior, adopted constitutions.[15]

Organization: Constitutions and Charters

Once a tribe adopted a constitution and bylaws, one-third of its adult members could petition the secretary of the interior for a charter, to be ratified in a special tribal election. To provide tribes foundations for developing constitutions and charters, Cohen undertook a comprehensive study both of existing tribal constitutions and their functioning theretofore and of tribal social, political, and legal traditions, including divisions within tribes. Based on this research, Cohen prepared a compendium of Indian constitutions and a model constitution and charter to help the different tribes in drafting their own.[16]

Cohen wanted tribes to discuss the proposed charters and constitutions rather than adopt them as presented. In a "Basic Memorandum on Drafting of Tribal Constitutions," written shortly after the passage of the act to assist tribes and the BIA, Cohen explained that the different tribes' "experience in self-government, . . . nature of land-ownership, . . . solidarity of the community, and . . . extent of contacts with non-Indians" was so variable that it precluded preparing a single constitution that would fit their divergent needs.[17]

Even if it were possible to create a model constitution, Cohen insisted that it was wrong to do so. He stressed that a constitution had to be the "offspring of Indian hearts and minds." As if responding to critics of the IRA who argued that the Indians were not ready for self-government, Cohen pointed out that while there was no assurance that an Indian community could manage "a form of government manufactured in Washington," there was no doubt that the Indians would understand their own creations.[18] Cohen wanted "the constitution, bylaws and ordinances of each tribe [to] reflect a larger or smaller amount of native material depending upon the extent of acculturation on each reservation."[19]

While insisting that tribes should write their own constitutions, Cohen's memorandum nonetheless discussed the different details to which every constitution should attend. These included the tribal organization's name, which the group could choose—Cohen expected that groups would use their traditional names, "and if incorporated under the Wheeler-Howard Act may add inc. (but . . . they [were] not required to do so)"; the organization's purpose—which would be "to establish Indian self-government and to promote a healthy and satisfactory community life" or "to preserve and develop Indian lands in Indian ownership and to provide the opportunity of economic livelihood for all who choose to remain within the Indian community" or something similar; the territory and membership rules; and the organization of community government—that is, officers and their titles, elections, and government powers.[20]

In retrospect, Cohen stressed how tribal constitutions "were drafted by the

Indians themselves" with technical help from Interior, "local white friends, newspaper editors, missionaries, and other individuals in whom they had confidence." Writing fifteen years after the events, he explained his role as follows:

> What I generally did was to take up a specific problem with the group concerned and then, unless they had already made up their minds as to just how they wanted to treat it, I would take up constitutional provisions already adopted by various Indian groups, explain the various alternative provisions, and then the Indians would make the selection of the provision that most accurately corresponded to their own wishes.[21]

Cohen knew that many tribes chose to imitate the model constitution and bylaws or constitutions and bylaws that had already been adopted by other tribes. He apologetically explained that once the secretary approved a few constitutions, tribes and field agents preferred to adopt similar provisions rather than prolong the organization process by submitting new provisions that might be rejected. The outcome was a multiplicity of similar constitutions.[22]

The constitutions and charters created the political and economic structures, respectively, of the different tribes. Typically, a constitution defined the membership rules of the community, set the foundation for organizing a community council, and enumerated the council's powers. These powers included the power to negotiate with local governments, the states, and the federal government on behalf of the community; to approve or veto transactions in tribal lands and assets; to manage the economic affairs of the community and its funds; to establish ordinances to enforce law and order on the reservation; to regulate members' domestic affairs; and, perhaps most important, to employ legal counsel for the protection and advancement of the rights of the community and its members. The corporate charter transformed the political community into a federally chartered corporation with corporate rights, powers, privileges, and immunities intended to further the community's economic development. Most important, it allowed tribes to use their assets collectively and to benefit from the revolving credit fund.[23]

Tribes were confused about the need to have both a constitution and a charter. They did not understand why they could not continue to follow their traditional, collective ways of managing their resources. Most tribes made the elected tribal government the corporation's governing body.[24] Indeed, why would a self-governing nation need a charter of incorporation in order to use its shared assets? For Cohen and his colleagues, the corporate form was the only structure through which a large number of individuals could collectively own assets. Unable to conceptualize tribes as completely analogous to states or corporations, Interior chose a hybrid—a public/private entity—a political community that derived its power to act from its federal charter of incorporation. Indian tribes were presumed to carry on profit-making businesses commonly associated with private industry. At the same time, tribal corporations had the characteristics of government entities, not only because they were supervised by the federal government but also because they were to pursue public goals and facilitate Interior's Indian policy.[25] Rather than trying to resolve the Indians' confusion over the need for constitutions and charters on a conceptual level (which might have led to more effective reorganization), Interior came up with a cosmetic solution. To prevent confusion between the two sets of documents, it recommended that a charter petition be circulated for signature thirty days after the approval of a constitution and bylaws on any given reservation.[26]

By 1937, according to one report, "sixty-five tribes had established constitutions and thirty-two had also ratified corporate charters. Altogether, between 1936 and 1945, ninety-three Indian groups set up tribal governments, and seventy-four of them had business charters. All but seven of the tribes were organized before 1938, indicating the intensity of the effort."[27] Furthermore, at Interior's urging, thirteen tribes who rejected the IRA, like the Navajos, chose to organize and form tribal councils. As they did not accept the act, they could not participate in any of the programs it authorized; but they could operate like other organized communities.[28]

Failures and Successes

"Seeing the change for the better that has taken place at [the Fort Belknap Reservation] since my first visit eight years ago was gratifying—particularly when one of the leaders of the tribe, who was my bitterest opponent in the fight over the Wheeler-Howard Act and the corporate charter, said to me: "That old no good law of yours is pretty good now."
—Felix S. Cohen to Morris Cohen, ca. 1941 (MRCP)

By the end of 1936, the basic administrative framework of Indian reorganization was complete. Through different acts of Congress, all Indian groups in the United States were brought under the program, including the Oklahoma and Alaska Indians that were excluded from the 1934 IRA.[29] The BIA developed formal procedures for tribal organization and formed new units "to oversee the process and coordinate political and economic programs for the Indians." The Indian Organization Division, which had a small Washington staff and a large group of traveling field representatives, most of whom were Indians, was responsible for helping tribes prepare constitutions and charters and for reviewing the operations of different councils. Interior also created, within the BIA, an applied anthropology staff under the leadership of H. Scudder Mekeel, formerly of Harvard University. It was an advisory board charged with the task of studying the social conditions on reservations and advising BIA staff on tribal constitutions. The applied anthropology staff was disbanded in 1938 due to budget cuts, but anthropologists continued to work with the BIA's Educational Division, "training new employees on Indian cultural differences."[30]

Yet the success of reorganization remained questionable. Ninety-three Indian groups adopted constitutions, but 252 groups were eligible to come under the IRA. Furthermore, only seventy-four groups adopted a charter and thus could benefit from the credit fund.[31] Indeed, while some historians celebrate the New Deal's emphasis on tribal self-government, the ideal of autonomous communities on Indian reservations was never fully achieved. Even among the tribes who were organized, the degree of assimilation of any given Indian group, as well as the number of religious, cultural, and economic divisions and factions that each group exhibited, often determined whether or not self-government under the act would be successful. In this respect, the New Dealers' eagerness to organize as many tribes as possible and their failure to recognize the complexity of tribal life and culture were often hindrances on the road to genuine Indian self-government.

The propensities of tribes in favor of reorganization tracked their degree of assimilation. Generally speaking, tribes like the southwestern tribes that lived on reservations far removed from white settlements, had low intermarriage rates, or were able to evade allotment, often remained unassimilated. Tribes like those in the northern United States and eastern Oklahoma that lived in close proximity to white settlements, had high intermarriage rates, and were subject to allotments, were often highly assimilated. The more assimilated tribes were most opposed to the IRA.[32]

At the same time, unassimilated tribes often found it difficult to understand the act and the structures it created. The IRA was sufficiently complex to confuse an English-speaking lawyer, let alone someone who needed to understand it through translation. Moreover, it was often hard to translate its terms into Indian languages. For example, anthropologist Ruth Underhill reported that the Papagos had "no equivalent words for terms like *budget* and *representative*," used the same word for "*president, Indian commissioner, reservation agent* and *king*," and had "no linguistic distinction between the terms *law, rule, charter*, and *constitution*."[33] Cohen, too, realized as early as the Indian congresses that in many Indian languages there was no word for *self-government*.[34]

Instead of recognizing that "the paraphernalia of American legal and political tradition" could not be easily "transferred to a people whose experience of these institutions was remote or nonexistent" and that even under the best of circumstances, the Papagos and other unassimilated tribes would understand the act only vaguely,[35] the New Dealers continued to assume that, once explained, the American model of self-government would empower all tribes.[36] Mekeel of the BIA's applied anthropology unit traced the Indians' weak response to the act to these conceptual flaws.[37]

Interior also insisted that tribal councils and tribal corporations organize along lines that would enable them "to enter into contracts with other companies and have legal standing in courts." Indian constitutions were modeled on the U.S. Constitution, and tribal councils and corporations were modeled after Anglo-American government structures, "with electoral districts, voting by secret ballot, tribal presidents, vice-presidents, treasurers, and committees." (Defiantly, some tribes who came under the act refused to delegate powers to their governments and continued to make decisions by the entire tribe.)[38] The imposition of Anglo-American traditions was particularly problematic among the unassimilated tribes.

Divisions on reservations, specifically between full-blood and mixed-blood Indians, also influenced whether a given reorganization would be successful. Full-blood Indians were commonly older and less assimilated than mixed-blood Indians. Historically, the BIA tacitly built upon the tensions between the groups to promote policies such as the 1920s establishment of pro-assimilation business committees on reservations. The New Dealers were determined to discourage, if not reverse, patterns of factional government. Yet on many reservations, especially in the northern plains and northwestern states, they reinforced conflicts between mixed-blood and full-blood Indians. As full-blood Indians, distrustful of any forced change, remained passive, "younger men, often of mixed-blood background," dominated many of the tribal councils established under the act. This led many full-blood Indians to resent, if not totally reject, the new councils, which often exhibited disrespect to tribal traditions and the tribal elders.[39]

Furthermore, on many reservations, the mixed-blood Indians were landless, having sold their fee patents. But while full-blood Indians treated them with contempt for having sold their land, they also feared that through their control of the new tribal councils, mixed-blood Indians would "take over the full bloods' allotments and redistribute them to the landless."[40] Such fears were exacerbated when Interior clarified who could vote to adopt a constitution under the act. A solicitor's opinion declared that:

> In the absence of any statutory provision to the contrary, the descendants of enrolled members of a tribe who are not themselves enrolled but who are recognized as members of the tribe, in accordance with tribal custom and usage, have the right to vote on the adoption of a tribal constitution. Similarly, recognized members of the tribe who were, through accident or mistake, omitted from the tribal rolls have the same right to vote (a right which does not carry with it any claims to tribal property) as other members.[41]

Margold's interpretation of tribal membership seemed rather devastating to full-blood Indians, especially in light of Interior's holding that members of a tribe or a group of tribes, irrespective of their residence, were eligible to vote on the question of coming under the act's programs. First, unless a majority of the reservation's residents, usually full-blood Indians, voted to reject the act, it would apply to their reservation. Then, "a majority of the people in the vicinity who could trace their ancestry back to a member of the tribe could adopt a constitution," which, at Interior's insistence, often included similar membership provisions; thus, these people "in the vicinity" could also elect officers. Full-blood Indians were afraid that Interior's different interpretations of tribal membership would turn over their reservations' governance to those Indians who had already sold their lands and were no longer considered tribal members—in other words, to "Indian politicians, whose only loyalty was to their own political career."[42]

The confusion over tribal membership reflected a deeper misunderstanding. Since the inception of the IRA, BIA officials struggled to determine who was eligible for its benefits. They chose to rely on the concept of the tribe—a social construction that was imposed on Indians to help white officials distinguish among different groups and that concealed deep-seated divisions among Indians. By making the tribe the basic unit for political and economic reform, the New Dealers helped sustain "an essentially artificial institution in Indian life" and failed to recognize the many internal and lasting factions coexisting on reservations.[43] When one adds that in the fifty years prior to the passage of the IRA, government officials had sought to break down tribal organization, it is not surprising that many Indian groups viewed the tribal governments established under the act as a completely foreign means of organization.[44]

Divisions within the administration further widened the deep cultural gap between the New Dealers and Indian tribes. Continued congressional opposition, which had eliminated important provisions of Interior's initial draft, was also reflected in ongoing appropriation and budget cuts.[45] Moreover, while the Washington officials who drafted the act hoped to bring about change in federal Indian policy, many local BIA representatives, who had to carry out the change, regarded the new tribal governments as "at best a meaningless addition to the agency and at worst an obstacle to the efficient administration of the reservation." Many of these BIA representatives were appointed before 1934 and supported the policy of allotment. They continued to try to dominate tribal councils, leading tribal members to view the new councils as BIA-controlled. The many conflicts between the BIA Washington office and its local offices over the scope of tribal powers led Mekeel to argue that the reformers' goals were "systematically undermined by the old guard" within the BIA.[46]

Moreover, many reformers in Washington were so concerned about salvaging Indian economies that they, too, were reluctant to divest the BIA of its supervising powers. Many BIA officials did not deem Indian tribes and individual Indians to be capable of managing their own affairs. Tribal constitutions were thus loaded with qualifying phrases, subjecting many tribal powers to administrative review.[47] Indeed, as other scholars have concluded, Indian opposition to the Indian New Deal was "not because they rejected self-government per se but because they wanted free and undisturbed government of their own choosing." They wanted to make their own decisions without having to receive Interior's approval. "They wanted independence."[48] Cohen viewed the BIA's position as the most challenging obstacle in fulfilling the reorganization goals (and one that led him to resign from the position of chairman of the Organization Division).[49]

Given the different assumptions underlying the act and its administration, it is perhaps not surprising that tribal governments never became what the New

Dealers envisioned them to be. Some commentators have gone as far as to suggest that tribal governments became "nothing more than adjuncts to the local
administration, placidly rubber-stamping the decisions made by the [BIA]."[50]

Yet, despite its failure to create autonomous communities on Indian reservations, the IRA aroused "a remarkable degree of Indian political activism."
Councils often engaged in heated debates with the BIA over the scope of their
powers, specifically over the "hiring and firing of agency employees, determination of tribal membership, salaries and perquisites of council members, and
the handling of restricted tribal funds." And while tribal councils were, like
other governments, often self-centered and self-serving, and while many of
their efforts were futile, they began to create a model for modern tribal leadership.[51]

There were other successes. While the New Dealers were unable to revive
long-dormant Indian cultures, they made major contributions to the economic
development on reservations, including the creation of many cooperative livestock associations, and to land restoration. The BIA spent over $1.5 million to
purchase four hundred thousand acres of cropland for Indians. In addition,
seven million acres of grazing land and almost one million acres of surplus land
were returned to Indian control. Finally, the New Dealers initiated a wide
range of conservation and wilderness preservation projects on many reservations, including water development and flood control programs and land nutri-
tional programs.[52]

The most enduring legacy of the IRA were its by-products—studies, opinions, memoranda—which often remained unexplored until a new generation
of reformers and Indians discovered them. One of the most important of these
was Cohen's study of Indian law and tribal powers. It became the foundation
not only for the most comprehensive treatise on the subject, *The Handbook of
Federal Indian Law,* which Cohen authored in 1941, but also for an important
solicitor's opinion, "Powers of Indian Tribes," that Cohen drafted and that drastically transformed the meaning of the IRA and tribal sovereignty.

"Powers of Indian Tribes"

Cohen and his colleagues used solicitor's opinions programmatically to interpret the IRA. These opinions provided statutory and administrative interpretations that balanced the short-term interest in quick administrative solutions
and the long-term need to prevent future changes of policy. Cohen, who
drafted many opinions, often emphasized that his interpretation of the act was
detached, disinterested, and against his own sympathies in situations where the
act did not incorporate his ideas.[53] But gradually he helped reintroduce many
sections of the initial draft that Congress chose to eliminate. "Because the administration which advocated [the act] has been continued in power, and the
bill as passed did give the administration a wide latitude in its grant of powers
under constitutions and charters," Collier pointedly concluded, "the loss of the

feature which gave tribes authority to determine progressively the extent of their own autonomy" became "less important."[54]

"Powers of Indian Tribes," issued four months after the passage of the act, was the most significant of these solicitor's opinions. It focused on section 16 of the final act. Due to the objection of the Senate and House Committees, this section did not include the sovereign powers enumerated in the initial bill. Instead, section 16 declared that the governing bodies of tribes that would be issued constitutions under the act possessed the limited powers specified in the act and "all powers vested in any Indian tribe or tribal council by existing law."[55] Which powers were "vested by existing law" and whether tribes had other powers remained open questions (and made drafting charters and constitutions almost impossible) until October 25, 1934, when Margold issued his opinion on "Powers of Indian Tribes."[56]

Drafted by Cohen, the opinion detailed the powers that were "vested in the various Indian tribes under existing law." It was well crafted, reflecting Cohen's growing attentiveness to the history of Indian tribes and their relationship with the federal government. It also reflected Cohen's realization, albeit limited in scope, that Indian tribes had unique legal and political systems that the American legal system had to accommodate. The opinion thus began by asserting that Indian tribes had traditionally enjoyed full external and internal powers of sovereignty.[57]

Having gone through a long process of committee hearings, Cohen was well aware of Congress's ambivalence about Indian self-government and his own legal pluralist vision. The opinion thus admitted that "conquest has terminated the external powers of sovereignty of the Indian tribes" and brought the tribes' internal affairs under congressional control. Then, having declared Congress's power over tribes, Cohen went on to limit it. "Except as Congress has expressly restricted or limited the internal powers of sovereignty vested in the Indian tribes," Cohen declared, "such powers are still vested in the respective tribes and may be exercised by their duly constituted organs of government." As Congress had never presumed that tribes had these sovereign powers, it was unlikely that they were limited either in legislation or in treaties, especially as Cohen further insisted that dubious congressional actions or statutes were not sufficient to limit tribal sovereignty. In short, the opinion was meant to reinforce tribal political powers and tribal autonomy, which the federal government had not previously recognized.[58]

Among the powers that remained vested in Indian tribes were "the prerogative of any Indian tribe to determine its own form of government"; the power to determine its own membership "subject to supervision of the Secretary of the Interior where rights to Federal property are involved"; the power to regulate domestic relations of its members; the power to prescribe rules of inheritance "except with respect to allotted lands"; the power to "tax members of the tribe and nonmembers accepting privileges of trade or residence, to which taxes may be attached as conditions"; the power to remove nonmembers from the reservation; the power to regulate tribal property, except as restricted by acts of Congress; the power to regulate property and contracts of tribal members; the power to administer justice "except as criminal or civil jurisdiction has been transferred by statute to Federal or State courts"; and the power to prescribe duties of federal employees where powers of supervision were delegated to them.[59]

To these inherent powers Cohen added powers enumerated explicitly in the IRA, including the right to employ legal counsel; the power to negotiate with federal, state, and local governments; the power to prevent future alienation of tribal property; the right to review appropriation estimates relating to the tribe; and the power to establish tribal corporations.[60]

In short, according to Cohen, tribes held sovereign powers "similar to those of any other municipality in the United States, or, to be more precise, similar to those of a foreign state which, as in the case of Hawaii or Texas, had become a part of the United States but except in a few particulars, had been left to operate under local laws which antedated the acquisition." Tribes needed only to delegate these powers to the tribal corporations created under the act. Some of these powers were historical in origin; some could be found in treaty provisions or negotiations. Other powers were simply what Cohen believed were rights that Indian tribes had amassed since their sovereignty had been established. Granted, the powers enumerated reflected Cohen's knowledge about tribal laws and customs at the time. It was thus an incomplete list. But it was an impressive list.[61]

Cohen took pains to emphasize that "there was nothing in Solicitor Margold's opinion that had not been said in substance many times before." During the hearings on the original draft of the IRA, Interior had indeed sought to delegate similar powers to Indian tribes. But there was a significant difference between the department's approach during the hearings and "Powers of Indian Tribes." With Margold's endorsement, Cohen announced that the powers that Congress refused to grant to Indian tribes were "*not delegated powers granted by express acts of Congress, but rather inherent powers of a limited sovereignty which has never been extinguished.*" While delegated powers meant that tribal governments were a part of the federal government, inherent powers preserved an area of tribal political independence that the United States could not abrogate.[62] "Powers of Indian Tribes" thus set the foundation for the modern discourse of tribal sovereignty.

It was an all-encompassing conception of sovereignty. According to Cohen, every group that was "recognized now or hereafter" by the federal government as a distinct entity having the necessary political characteristics was deemed to have always possessed "all the attributes of a sovereign political power whether the group had previously exercised those powers or not." While the BIA failed to allow Indians to review Cohen's opinion and while it would take another generation before Indian tribes fully understood the meaning of the opinion, it was clearly a good beginning.[63]

"Powers of Indian Tribes" reflected lessons learned in intensive interactions with Indian tribes. Cohen wanted to help tribes reinstate their traditional political and legal powers. The opinion attempted to incorporate Indian tribes' political traditions into the IRA. But the rhetoric of power and formal processes remained foreign to many Indians. The concept of tribal government, as the New Dealers understood it, was rooted in Western political philosophy—in the Weberian legitimization of bureaucracy as a form of organizing public power. In Indian culture, leadership (often associated with spirituality) and deliberations were important, not power and organization.[64] Many of the powers enumerated in "Powers of Indian Tribes" were recognized by traditional tribal systems, but Indians had a different conception of them. Elected officials, removal from office, meeting rules, and membership agreements were foreign concepts on Indian reservations.[65]

What was missing from "Powers of Indian Tribes," as it was from the Indian New Deal, more generally, was a deeper understanding of the multiplicity of legal cultures and legal values that characterized modern American society. Cohen intuitively sensed this flaw, even though he could not fully explain it. His distress over this gap was manifested not only in his work on federal Indian law but also in his philosophy, specifically his realist desire to offer an alternative to classical legal thought. As we have seen, powerful as the realist critique of liberal legal thinking was, it left intellectuals like Cohen desperately striving to reconcile relativism in thought and culture with universalism in ethics. In the early 1930s, many of the realists, Cohen among them, saw a middle ground in pluralist political theory and its emphasis on collective institutions as the basis for legal and social analysis. In the mid-1930s, following two years of relatively unsuccessful attempts to reorganize Indian tribes, Cohen again attempted to explore and explain the relationship between law and the multiplicity of cultures in American society.

As the following sections demonstrate, the result was at least twofold. First, at Interior, Cohen drafted two important opinions on law and order on Indian reservations. They sought to reintroduce the tribal court system that Congress had rejected during the deliberations over the IRA and to create a separate legal system on tribal reservations. Second, in 1935 Cohen published the article "Transcendental Nonsense and the Functional Approach," which elaborated his critique of liberal (classical) legal thought and his pluralist alternative to it.[66]

Law and Order

One of the most important powers described in "Powers of Indian Tribes" was an Indian tribe's power to administer justice. Because an Indian tribe had the power to regulate certain activities and relationships of its members (such as marriage), "Powers of Indian Tribes" held that it also had the power to adjudicate "through tribunals established by itself" controversies involving such relationships or activities. In all fields of local government, "the judicial powers of the tribe [were] coextensive with its legislative or executive powers."[67] In other words, the power to establish a tribal court system (separate from the federal courts and the BIA) was derived from the inherent powers of the tribe.

Another solicitor's opinion, "Secretary's Power to Regulate Conduct of Indians" (February 28, 1935), dealt with the status of the old Courts of Indian Offenses, which were established by the federal government in 1883 to bring law and order to reservations. It concluded that the legal authority of the forty-one existing courts was derived not only from Interior's power to create them (specifically, "the secretary general's power to regulate the conduct of Indians . . . derived from his authority to create administrative courts") but also, more crucially, from "the inherent power of the tribes to govern their own members."[68]

This conclusion was in accord with Cohen's idea of a tribal court system. Already in January 1935, he sent to superintendents a draft of a new legal code for Indian reservations that allowed tribes to establish their own judicial systems. Cohen's *Law and Order Regulations* declared that "Indians of the various tribes could establish their own courts," which would exercise civil and criminal jurisdiction over thirty-eight common offenses, "including assault, kidnapping, forgery, reckless driving, and bribery."[69]

Out of sixty superintendents, twenty-two thought Cohen's code suited their jurisdictions. Sixteen opposed it. In California, Oklahoma, the Dakotas, and other areas where tribal governments were destabilized, state jurisdiction seemed necessary, while among the Florida Seminoles, the New Mexico Pueblos, and the Indians of New York, traditional law enforcement worked sufficiently well. Finally, some tribes, according to their superintendents, were so "unaccustomed to modern legal forms" that they "could not effectively administer their own courts."[70]

Most superintendents agreed not to interfere with the functioning of the courts but "insisted on the right to command tribal police." In response, Cohen issued a revised code. It declared that tribes organized under the IRA could establish their own courts. These tribes could pass ordinances rather than rely on "administrative regulations to settle civil disputes." Furthermore, where "tribal funds were available," tribal governments created under the act "could appoint and remove judges without the Indian commissioner's approval and could employ their own police force."[71] Four years later, another solicitor's opinion on the subject of tribal courts, "Law and Order—Dual Sovereignty—Powers of Indian Tribes and U.S." (April 27, 1939), insisted on the power of Indian courts to punish errant members for offenses, even "on the basis of acts committed on unrestricted lands within an Indian reservation." Again, such power was described both as inherent in tribal sovereignty and as historically recognized by the federal government.[72]

While time would pass before the Indians made use of their law and order powers, these opinions ultimately legitimated the creation of tribal courts, not only for tribes that came under the IRA, but also for those who chose to pursue self-government outside the authority of the act and adopted constitutions establishing tribal courts.[73]

Still, as important as these opinions were, their impact was naturally limited to the relatively marginalized field of federal Indian law. This was not true about Cohen's 1935 article, "Transcendental Nonsense and the Functional Approach," which has remained one of the canonical works in twentieth-century American legal thought.[74]

Pluralist Lessons: "Transcendental Nonsense and the Functional Approach"

"What I'm anxious to bite into now is some accurate account of what revolutionary change looks like in a village or small town. All the accounts of revolution I know of are written from the viewpoint of the capital. I'm looking forward seriously to learning something about human nature and its capacities for quick change of patterns when I get down to work with Indian groups under our new bill; and I'd like to profit from past experience. What can you suggest?"
—Felix S. Cohen to Morris Cohen, July 3, 1934 (MRCP)

No necessary correlation existed between legal realism and the programs of the New Deal. But the New Deal administration espoused a conception of law as a form of socially informed expertise, linking the realist emphasis on law's political nature with their professional advocacy of empirical studies. Moreover, the realists' critique of the liberal night-watchman state helped legitimate the new administrative state. It is thus not surprising that, like Cohen, many realists accepted positions in the New Deal administration. William O. Douglas became chair of the Securities and Exchange Commission (SEC); Jerome Frank was general counsel to the Agricultural Adjustment Administration and to the Federal Surplus Relief Corporation, special counsel to the Reconstruction Finance Corporation, and commissioner and chair of the SEC; and Herman Oliphant acted as an advisor to the Treasury Department and other agencies. In addition, Karl Llewellyn "stridently supported President Roosevelt's plan to make certain reforms to the Supreme Court and wanted a constitutional amendment 'expressly and unequivocally enlarging the powers of Congress—preferably under the general-welfare clause.'"[75] Together these realists brought their critique of classical legal thought to bear on the development of law and policy.

The realists' legal work in the 1930s focused on groups and institutions—on creating a pluralist polity. It was informed by Oliver Wendell Holmes's critique of individual (natural) rights as well as Roscoe Pound's characterization of the common law as obsessed with individual rights, and by the social scientists' embrace of group theories. Legal realists focused on the "working rules" by which collective institutions such as labor unions, corporations, or banks functioned. Adolf A. Berle and Gardiner C. Means formulated rules to constrain corporations, Harold J. Laski stressed the importance of administrative agencies, and

Llewellyn's Uniform Commercial Code embodied the working rules of merchants (as a group) as its central normative and interpretive concept.[76]

Legal realists (or legal pluralists) who became New Dealers sought to formulate working rules to allow diverse collective entities to function and coordinate their activities. They wanted to make their theories operational. As Llewellyn explained, their task was "to reconcile the ideology and practices of the older American individualism" with the needs of a corporate-based industrialized economy.[77]

Cohen's focus was similar yet unique. Indian tribes were not only political and economic groups but also ethnic and cultural groups. Cohen's task was to draw on legal pluralism to formulate law and policy affecting a broader range of groups.

Furthermore, after the turbulent early 1930s, when younger legal realists engaged the older generation in jurisprudential debates, most of them became captivated by policy questions and abandoned any attempt to articulate a coherent theory of law. This was especially true of the legal pluralists among them. While recognizing the importance of groups to modern society and working to formulate legal doctrines that set the boundaries of group power, they did not attempt to articulate a legal theory that would complement their efforts. Cohen was different. A legal philosopher at heart, he wanted to develop a jurisprudential theory to legitimate his work (and the work of others) with, or on behalf of, different collective entities.

"Transcendental Nonsense" bore the marks of Cohen's uniqueness. Reflecting the interdependence of theory and practice, it brought Cohen's experience at Interior to bear on his ongoing struggle to articulate a legal pluralist theory of law, a theory attentive to the diverse interests that characterized modern society.

Legal Concepts and Group Conflict

"Transcendental Nonsense" began with a dream, attributed to classical legal thinkers, about the heaven of legal concepts, where one could meet, "face to face, the many concepts of jurisprudence in their absolute purity, freed from all entangling alliances with human life . . . [and] all the logical instruments needed to manipulate and transform these legal concepts and thus to create and solve the most beautiful of legal problems."[78] Then, in a series of rhetorical questions—*Where is a corporation? When is a corporation? What's in a trade name? How high is fair value? When is a legal process "due"?*—Cohen elaborated how by seeking answers to all legal questions in a set of abstract axioms, the classicist method failed to understand the social and political nature of legal problems and thus could not effectively resolve them.

Cohen asserted that legal concepts (that is, due process, trade name) did not have inherent meanings that judges could unearth. Rather, as Indian languages taught him, the meaning of legal terms had to be derived from factual observations. For example, the question of where a corporation was located for purposes of bringing a legal suit against it could not be answered without observing the plaintiffs' difficulties if they had to bring suit against a corporation in its state of incorporation rather than in the state where the plaintiffs resided, as well as the social, moral, and political considerations as to the propriety of putting financial burdens on corporations or their plaintiffs.[79]

This, on its face, was a typical early-1930s realist argument. Realist articles often began by examining a particular field of law and the principle that governed it according to classical legal thought (that is, consideration in contract law or proximate cause in torts). Then, the realist author would offer a different rationale, typically a "purposive" or "consequentialist" rationale, for the particular legal rule. In private law fields like contracts and torts, realists often concluded that "the actual decisions made functional sense, even if the formal rationales were 'transcendental nonsense.'" In the fields of regulatory law, realists often proclaimed that "the latent policy subtext was irrational or the product of an inarticulate, conservative political or economic judgment."[80]

Cohen was more politically radical than other realists, or at least more vocal about it. He saw both private and public law as reflecting conservative politics. His critique of abstract concepts reflected the idea that "the law is itself a system of violence . . . concealed or justified by a social ritual and ideology, a set of forms or phrases, a system of constantly reiterated ideals, which portrays the law as a moral force."[81]

Cohen's association of legal abstraction with systematic violence was threefold. First, he argued that by treating "vivid fictions and metaphors" as "reasons for decisions, rather than poetical or mnemonic devices for formulating decisions reached on other grounds," classical legal thinkers ignored, and were likely to forget, "the social forces which mold the law and the social ideals by which the law is to be judged." Second, Cohen proclaimed that by relying on legal terms rather than addressing the social, political, and economic reasons for their decisions, classical legal jurists engaged in circular reasoning. They purported "to base legal protection upon economic value," not realizing that "the economic value of a sales device depends upon the extent to which it will be legally protected." Finally, Cohen described such circular reasoning as both logically flawed and politically conservative, allowing courts "to create and distribute a new source of economic wealth or power." For example, by using trademark law to prevent B "from exploiting certain forms of language" that A had already begun to exploit, courts forced B to pay A for the privilege of using these forms. "Masquerading in the cloak of legal logic" and the "hypostatization of 'property rights,'" the courts sanctioned the transfer of wealth from B to A.[82]

Cohen's critique went beyond describing law as a system of violence, a description that other realists and pluralists shared. Cohen stressed the role that groups and collective entities played in sustaining law's violence. Accordingly, law was a system of class violence. The first part of "Transcendental Nonsense" drew on Cohen's notes as an editor of the *Columbia Law Review* to describe how the law sanctioned inequalities of wealth and income—in rate regulation, as Cohen explored in "The Bauer-Bonbright Proposal for the Revision of the New York Public Service Commission Law and its Constitutionality"; in the creation of property rights in trademarks, as he discussed in "The Vestal Bill for the Copyright Registration of Designs"; and in the disparate treatment of labor unions and corporations, as he began to explore in three notes: "The Privilege to Disparage a Non-Competing Business," "The Elements of a Fair Trial in Disciplinary Proceedings in Labor Unions," and "The Judicial Resolution of Factional Disputes in Labor Unions."[83]

Furthermore, while Cohen's early notes and the first part of "Transcendental Nonsense" reflected Cohen's endorsement of political pluralism and his interest in class conflict, the second and third parts of the article embraced a more inclusive description of the law as a system of group (class, ethnic, religious) violence. As we will see in the following sections, this was the background for Cohen's turn to functionalism.

Clearly informed by his experience at Interior, Cohen's functional vision of the law was not fully worked out in "Transcendental Nonsense." The article examined only how collective interests and group behavior influenced the law; it did not fully assess the subtlety of law's violence. Enchanting as the article was, it was a work in progress, explained in following articles. But even in its preliminary stage, the article stood out. Drawing on his experience in drafting and administering the IRA, Cohen's functional approach was a precursor not only for an intellectual shift from class to ethnicity (a shift that would be complete only after World War II) but also for a transition from early theories of group pluralism, which emphasized group autonomy, to a theory of law that saw the role of the legal system as facilitating interactions between autonomous groups. As we will see, Cohen would develop this theory as the 1940s began.

The Functional Method: Pluralism in Policymaking

Legal realists (and pluralists) wanted to "get out of the tangle" that classical legal thought's reliance on abstract concepts created. Realists struggled, however, to translate such aspirations into a working theory. Many turned to empirical studies of the administration and effects of legal decisions and rules so as to offer practical solutions to legal problems. Others wanted law to reflect social custom. Cohen belonged to a third group—those who sought to align legal research with the study of the social sciences. These realists engaged in detailed studies of social facts in order to understand the functions and consequence of legal rules. They believed that such studies would allow them to formulate better laws and policies. Specifically, they hoped to disaggregate and contextualize abstract concepts and to restate "principles as 'functional' policies and purposes, rights as practically available remedies, and rules as patterns of results likely to be obtained in particular settings."[84] Cohen labeled this alternative "the functional approach."[85]

The first part of "Transcendental Nonsense" illustrated the negative aspects of the functional method, namely the endeavor to eradicate meaningless concepts and abate meaningless questions. The second part of "Transcendental Nonsense," which focused on policymaking, explicated the positive side of functionalism, namely the redefinition of concepts and the redirection of research. Cohen began by noting that instead of "assuming hidden causes or transcendental principles behind everything we see or do," functionalists sought to redefine concepts as "constructs, or functions, or complexes, or patterns, or arrangements, of the things that we do actually see or do." Similarly, functionalists sought to redirect research away from "classificatory or . . . analytical inquiries" and toward studying "the *significance* of the fact through a determination of its implications or consequences in a given . . . context."[86]

According to Cohen, the functionalist redirection of research had important consequences. In religious studies, it shifted attention away from comparing religious beliefs and exploring the genesis and evolution of religions toward studying "the consequences of various religious beliefs in terms of human motivation and social structure." In anthropology, functionalists substituted studies of "the social consequences of diverse customs, beliefs, rituals, social arrangements, and patterns of human conduct" for studies of "human peculiarities . . . [and] the historical origin, evolution, and diffusion of 'complexes.'" In political science, functionalists rejected the ideal of an absolute sovereignty residing in the state and called attention to the role that collective semi-sovereign entities played in modern society. In economics, the functional method shifted research from the "systematic analysis of economic 'norms' to the study of the actual economic behavior of men and nations."[87]

Cohen had firsthand experience with the functional approach. In 1931, under Judge Shientag's supervision, Cohen undertook a functional study of summary judgment in New York State to determine "what difference, as a matter of fact, the existence of summary judgment procedure makes in the conduct of civil litigation."[88] While drafting the IRA, Cohen found functional anthropology extremely helpful. But while functionalism's positive aspects tied the functional method to Progressive and New Deal politics, the method also had a more conservative bent.

For one thing, by the second decade of the twentieth century, amid concerns about labor violence, urban poverty, waves of immigration, and racial tensions, social scientists increasingly stressed "scientific expertise and administrative efficiency" as a means of producing "ordered, benevolent change." They embraced a "particularist, functionalist objectivism" and stressed the importance of facts over values. By analyzing social problems in an objective and quantifiable manner, social scientists believed that they could minimize disputes and establish a more satisfying social order. Gradually, however, they eliminated facts that did not adapt to the needs of progressive evolution and transformed the scientific (and objective) study of society into an apology for the status quo.[89]

Similarly, many legal functionalists in the 1920s and 1930s judged legal systems based on their adaptation to recognizable social needs. They accepted, without challenge, the function of existing legal forms and institutions, often using speculative functional rationales to legitimate existing legal practices. Furthermore, they assumed that there was an evolutionary progressive path for all societies, with the concept of progress being associated with industrialization, modernization, or economic and political development. Accordingly, functionalists assessed legal forms and institutions based on how well they satisfied the functional requirement of their evolutionary stage, recognizing neither indeterminacy nor multiplicity. Many legal functionalists also embraced an elitist vision of law and policy, ignoring the important role of mass movements and local struggles in bringing about legal change. Finally, they tended to assume a congruity of social interests and to view social conflict as a disruption of the natural equilibrium.[90] As we have already seen, the older generation of Progressive legal thinkers and legal realists criticized these assumptions as failing to realize the norms underlying presumably value-free social scientific studies.

Cohen had much in common with this older generation. His functional method was radical. While he saw a relationship between law and society, his attraction to pluralist theories and his experiences led him both to recognize that social context and historical development were not determined and to move away from elitist versions of policymaking. Cohen realized that different societies, and different groups within a single society, reacted to similar social conditions in diverse ways. More important, he recognized that similar social conditions could generate different legal rules. For him, functionalism was the recognition that modern phenomena were composed of a multiplicity of facts and effects and should be studied as such. Informed by the philosophy of pluralism, Cohen described functionalism as:

> the view that a thing does not have a "nature" or "essence" or "reality" underlying its manifestation and effects and apart from its relations with other things; that the nature, essence, or reality of a thing *is* its manifestations, its effects, and its relations with other things; and that, apart from these "it" is nothing, or at most a point in logical space, a possibility of something happening.[91]

Celebrating diversity was Cohen's alternative to the classicists' attempt to force uniformity on law through abstract concepts.[92] But even the typically more progressive among the social scientists—the anthropologists—did not share Cohen's radicalism. In 1937 when Cohen sought to publish an article in which he asked anthropologists to teach administrators about Indian cultures so that they could promulgate laws and policies that would better fit Indian traditions, he encountered strong resistance.

Cohen wanted anthropologists to help policymakers develop educational and economic programs attuned to Indian cultures, histories, and present needs. He asked anthropologists to teach policymakers about the historical and ethnological grouping of Indians so that they would avoid forcing Indian groups into unfamiliar administrative units. He called on anthropologists to explore what the Indians might consider efficient and respectful work, to explain the nature of Indian land tenure (including individual rights and social responsibilities), and to detail the rules of Indian inheritance. Finally, Cohen asked anthropologists to resurrect "forms of Indian art and recreation," which were destroyed by the forces of colonization, or to help Indians develop their modern equivalents.[93] As Cohen explained to Franz Boas, the article was "a list of jobs that an administrator would like to see done on the scientific [anthropological] front"; it was a "'help wanted' advertisement."[94]

Mainstream journals of anthropology refused to publish the article. Leslie Spier, the editor of *The American Anthropologist,* proclaimed that their journal did not publish applied anthropology.[95] Spier did not elaborate, but his response reflected concerns about Cohen's endorsement of diversity, not merely as an empirical fact to be constrained through universal structures, but as a constitutive element of society that should be normatively embraced. Anthropologist Robert Lowie, who found Cohen's piece "admirable, both in form and substance," explained that anthropologists varied greatly "in their individual attitude towards 'applied anthropology.'" Many believed that, given the small numbers of tribes, in the absence of permanent government policy, tribes would be eliminated as cultural entities within a few years. In their view, Lowie's letter implied, Cohen's call for applied anthropology could impede gradual cultural assimilation.[96]

While most anthropologists embraced the New Deal's economic and political programs as a universal solution to the problem of Indian tribes, not all of them shared Cohen's pluralism. To celebrate the functional significance of diverse cultures was to engage in a normative argument about pluralism that even Lowie found troubling. There was a chasm, he explained to Cohen, "between a normative and a purely descriptive approach." Like Cohen, Lowie believed that "the ethnographer should fully expound whatever he knows that might be pertinent to the purposes of officialdom." Still, Lowie questioned whether the ethnographer should go any further. As he asked, "How can the anthropologist, qua anthropologist, learn and advise which craft activities should be stimulated in response to expectable demands of the market?"[97] Should Interior, Lowie's questions implied, aim beyond protecting the economic and political interests of Indian tribes? Should they embrace cultural pluralism as a normative ideal?

For Cohen the answer was obviously yes. He viewed law as the outcome of struggles between social groups with diverse needs and thus as sanctioning disparities of wealth, power, and status. Law was a system of group violence, and Cohen hoped to use the functional method to bring about change. Recognizing that once a legal system was in place it gained popular support and became hard to transform, Cohen called on reformers not to attack the popular ideals on which the law rested but to show the discrepancy between these ideals and law in action. Then he suggested using functional studies to formulate laws that would be better suited for different groups and would thus improve the conditions of men and women throughout the world.[98] In short, Cohen believed that a functional approach could evade the trap of universalism—the trap of a uniform view of law and policy.

But Cohen was not satisfied with using functional studies only for purposes of better policymaking. While he recognized the power of the executive branch, he also knew the power of the courts to strike down both legislation and administrative programs.[99] The last part of "Transcendental Nonsense" was thus devoted to articulating a theory of adjudication informed by functionalism.

Unlike many realists, who declared the uselessness of legal rules and abstract concepts, Cohen wanted not only to redefine "legal concepts, rules, and principles . . . in terms of verifiable facts and verifiable legal consequences" but also as functions of judicial decisions.[100] He wanted to draw on functionalism to articulate a theory of adjudication and a theory of ethical criticism to evaluate judicial lawmaking. As the third part of "Transcendental Nonsense" illustrated, Cohen's functional jurisprudence recognized both the multiplicity of groups with diverse needs to which the law had to attend and the subtle ways in which such multiplicity influenced judicial lawmaking and its effectiveness. Informed by this vision, Cohen articulated a theory of ethical criticism, the goal of which was the celebration and preservation of diverse interests.

Legal Functionalism: A Pluralist Theory of Adjudication

According to Cohen, the functional approach in adjudication was traceable to Holmes's definition of law as the prediction of what the courts would do in any given case. Accordingly, legal concepts were to be defined as functions of concrete judicial decisions. For example, in determining whether a particular document constituted a contract, jurists should not inquire into the essential nature of the document or the concepts of offer and acceptance. Rather, they should evaluate how courts were likely to view the particular transaction—what elements of the transaction would be viewed as relevant, how were similar transactions dealt with in the past, what factors compelled judges to follow precedents, and what factors might evoke new judicial treatment.[101]

Cohen admitted that this was not a perfect definition. Confusion could potentially arise over what constituted a court or over the distinction between what courts said and what they did. He nonetheless embraced this functional definition because it evaded the equation of law (the Is) with morality (the Ought). For Cohen, classical legal thought's greatest disservice was in hiding the ethical basis of adjudication and thus perpetuating "class prejudices and uncritical moral assumptions which could not survive the sunlight of free ethical controversy." In turn, describing law as a function of judicial decisions implied that not all laws were just, so that all laws were subject to ethical criticism. Indeed, Cohen's functional redefinition of legal concepts involved not only objective description but also critical judgment. Cohen wanted legal scholars to ask not only whether courts would enforce a transaction as a valid contract but also whether they should.[102]

Based on this functional redefinition of concepts, Cohen went on to articulate a theory of adjudication. The younger generation of realists, after having discredited legal doctrine as internally inconsistent and thus indeterminate and uncertain, spent much time (and paper) examining the process of judicial decision-making. For example, Joseph C. Hutcheson, Jr. concluded that judges resolved controversies on the basis of intuition or hunches,[103] while Frank argued that judges' personal biases, traceable to their personal experiences, influenced judicial decisions.[104] Like the older generation of Progressive scholars, Cohen rejected these explanations. "'Realistic Jurisprudence,'" he wrote, represented "a great intellectual advance beyond orthodox legal doctrine, in revealing the difference between what judges *do* and what judges *say*. Unfortunately, neither Mr. Frank, Professor Llewellyn, nor Judge Hutcheson offer[ed] any plausible explanation of *why* judges do what they do or *why* judges say what they say." Cohen was especially critical of the realists' individualistic undertones. "In common with most liberals," he complained, realists sought "to explain large-scale social facts in terms of the atomic idiosyncrasies and personal prejudices of individuals, rather then in terms of a truly realistic analysis of social forces."[105]

Cohen's functional approach described law as a social process. He viewed judicial decisions as being shaped by diverse social forces (the political, economic, and professional background and activities of a judge as well as the judge's biases), and as having diverse human consequences (partly a product of the extent and effects of law enforcement, its acceptance by other courts, and its acceptance by the parties). Accordingly, he wanted to study judicial decisions the way anthropologists would study different tribal societies. For Cohen, jurisprudence was "a study of human behavior . . . as it molds and is molded by judicial decisions."[106] More important, jurisprudence was a study of human social or group behavior. While the first part of "Transcendental Nonsense" suggested that the usage of abstract concepts was a form of class or group violence and the second part called for detailed studies of the needs of diverse groups, the third part elaborated how groups both shaped and were shaped by the law.

Cohen did not fully work out the details of his functional jurisprudence. He explained how the functional approach could help redefine legal concepts, but, as if reflecting the transitory nature of the article, his examination of a functional theory of adjudication was limited. But in the articles written shortly after the publication of "Transcendental Nonsense" we can see more clearly the relationship between this canonical realist article and Cohen's struggles to accommodate the plurality of interests that characterized American society.

Take, for example, "The Problems of a Functional Jurisprudence," written at least in part in response to criticisms of "Transcendental Nonsense."[107] There, Cohen explained that by calling attention to the uncertainty of legal doctrine and by redefining law and legal concepts as functions of judicial decisions, the functional approach made apparent the "element of choice in the judicial process." It thus made "the study of social factors that determine the course of judicial decision an essential part of the lawyer's outfitting."[108] A judge's social and cultural background became a major part of law.

"The Problems of a Functional Jurisprudence" also explained how the pluralist analysis of group-based biases reached beyond the judicial role to the behavior of those groups affected by the law. Informed by his experience administering the IRA, Cohen stressed that "the human significance of the rule of law" was determined by whether or not it was obeyed. Obedience, in turn, hinged on "the strength of the organized desire," which the rule encouraged as balanced against "the strength of the organized desire," which the rule frustrated. Accordingly, to be useful, reform legislation had to create "some independent agency capable of representing the interests of [the oppressed] class in securing enforcement of the legislation." As Cohen concluded,

> Every legal problem, viewed functionally, involves a conflict of interests. The stability of any solution will depend, at least in part, upon a correct appraisal of the desires that will be effectuated or frustrated by the solution. . . . In constitutional as well as in private law, the stuff of which living law is made is not concepts in logical arrangements but conflicting interests diversely organized and pitted against each other in an ever shifting battle line. A realistic appraisal of the human meaning of any legal rule involves us in a measurement of human desires and human powers in every domain of life.[109]

Viewing jurisprudence as the study of group behavior and group interests reached beyond descriptive studies of the reasons for, and consequences of, judicial decisions. Once these reasons and consequences were recognized, the door was open for ethical criticism. As the following section elaborates, Cohen's theory of adjudication involved both objective description and critical judgment.

Functionalism, Ethical Criticism, and Identity

The divergence between Cohen's view of law as a social process and the views of other realists of his generation, who focused on the individual tendencies of judges and statesmen, ran deep. In 1938, in a review of Thurman Arnold's *The Folklore of Capitalism,* Cohen suggested that legal realists could be divided into a right and left wing. The right-wing realists viewed rules and principles as "only noises, without practical significance." Accordingly, "any criticism, in terms of 'rules' and 'principles,' of the decision of judges and statesmen must be 'disingenuous.'" There were no values by which decisions could be judged. Rather, "whatever happens to exist" was justified. In turn, the left-wing realists employed "the technique of realism to strip from legal decisions, economic institutions, and political practices the false coverings of cosmic respectability that shield them from moral scrutiny." They wanted to eliminate those principles that were predicated on class prejudice or hypocrisy and thus could not serve modern society.[110]

According to Cohen, the potential combination of objective description and ethical criticism was the true contribution of the functional method.[111]

Once legal rules were seen as "simply formulae describing uniformities of judicial decision, . . . legal concepts . . . [as] patterns or functions of judicial decisions," and decisions as "social events with social causes and consequences," then, Cohen announced, we were ready for the task of evaluating the law and legal system "in terms of some standard of human values." To his mind, this was "perhaps the chief service of the functional approach." "In cleansing legal rules, concepts, and institutions of the compulsive flavors of legal logic or metaphysics," it made room for "conscious ethical criticism of law." "Transcendental Nonsense" thus concluded with the following:

> The relation between positive legal science and legal criticism is not a relation of temporal priority, but of mutual dependence. Legal criticism is empty without objective description of the causes and consequences of legal decisions. Legal description is blind without the guiding light of a theory of values. It is through the union of objective legal science and a critical theory of social values that our understanding of the human significance of law will be enriched. It is loyalty to this union of distinct disciplines that will mark whatever is of lasting importance in contemporary legal science and legal philosophy.[112]

Such was also Cohen's vision in *Ethical Systems and Legal Ideals,* to which he referred in a footnote in this concluding paragraph. But the Cohen of "Transcendental Nonsense" was different from the Cohen of *Ethical Systems.* When he joined Interior, Cohen minimized the uncertainties associated with cultural, cognitive, and ethical relativism by embracing a vision of the state that focused on collective institutions. His ethical criterion was tied to his vision of the group as the foundation for legal and political analysis. By viewing group autonomy as a means to political and economic equality, Cohen was able to embrace skepticism toward American law (and liberal legal thinking) without also sanctioning a nonjudgmental attitude toward all customs and values; moreover, pluralism gave him, the son of a Jewish immigrant, a sense of identity, of belonging to American society.

Two years at Interior began to transform Cohen's vision. He realized that the role of the legal system could not be limited to guaranteeing individuals' associational rights. Rather, "Transcendental Nonsense" sought to call jurists' attention to the different needs of diverse groups in society and, more important, to the ways in which a judge's group status affected his or her vision of the law. At the same time, Cohen wanted jurists to see that the plaintiff's or defendant's group status determined the extent to which any given decision would be followed and, therefore, its effects. This vision of groups as affecting one's understanding of the law was, again, tied to an ethical criterion, a criterion that Cohen articulated in a separate article called "The Socialization of Morality." It focused on the possibility of social integration of diverse group interests. In the mid-1930s, this possibility minimized the uncertainties associated with relativism.[113]

"The Socialization of Morality" offered a harsh critique of traditional moral theory and the tradition of individualism that grounded it. According to Cohen, the morality of the individualist tradition was devoid of social content. In response to the plurality of interests that characterized modern society, traditional moralists turned to the individual. Instead of addressing the complexity of modern civilization, which transferred important choices from the personal realm to the collective realm (including "matters as peace and war, the distribution and the use of economic power and political force, the functions of scientific thought, of education, and of artistic endeavor, the changing substance of cultures, and the physical conditions of existence"), traditional morality remained fixated on the individual as a universal category of analysis.[114]

According to Cohen, by focusing on the individual, traditional morality made the complexity of modern society oppressive. Cohen's alternative was thus collective morality or an integrated moral order in which complexity became useful.[115]

Cohen's critique of traditional morality and his alternative focused on the need for a moral order that would accommodate complexity and social change. It was tied to the political project of socialism (and Progressivism). Cohen viewed individualist morality as subscribing to one commandment—*laissez faire*—whether in the economic field or in all other realms of life. In turn, an integrated moral order informed "each vocation of civilized life with a social ideal and a clarified moral task." Like Horace Kallen's orchestral vision of America, Cohen's collective morality offered an integrated vision of the social order. As he put it, socialist morality allowed "for specialization, for variation from common norms, for the development of rare human potentialities," just as "the collectivity of a baseball team" left room for a "greater scope for diverse talents . . . than . . . a field of nine runners." In so doing, socialist morality made "universal the material security" required for the existence and flourishing of the human spirit.[116]

Cohen's conception of collective morality reached beyond his political aspirations. For Cohen, individualist morality was associated with the tenets of Christianity and exclusionary attitudes, while collective morality drew on the ancient Jewish and Greek traditions. It was informed by the "moral codes as . . . embodied in the writings of the Pentateuch, in the dialogues of Plato, or in the scholastic summas." Rather than being grounded in the "defense of man against society," socialist morality was grounded in the idea that "man finds the completion of his personality in society." Its focus was not individual liberties and self-aggrandizement but social functions, power, and responsibilities.[117]

This was a moral order in which Cohen felt at home. In its emphasis on power and social responsibilities, the integrated moral order resembled the Jewish tradition of *mitzvot* (obligations); in its emphasis on diversity, it had much in common with the philosophy of pluralism.

Cohen's socialist morality was a stage in Cohen's ongoing search for intimacy in a diverse world. The last part of "The Socialization of Morality" thus explained the metaphysical difference between socialist and individualist morality as lying in "the unit of integration applied to conflicts of human interests." According to Cohen, individualist morality integrated "the conflicting desires of a person into a harmonious pattern of satisfactory living." It endorsed the "metaphysical dogma . . . that the individual is an ultimate unity and society an ultimate plurality." This dogma required that "all the adjustments, balances, and compromises which are the substance of morality . . . take place within an individual life." Hence, individualist morality encouraged the individual to subordinate momentary impulses to more permanent purposes, but it did not attempt similarly to integrate conflicting individual interests by encouraging the subordination of individual desires to more permanent social purposes.[118]

In turn, socialist morality embraced the opposite dogma—a dogma of intimacy and interconnectedness. It revealed "something of the unity of the individual in society itself and something of the plurality of society in the individual life." It encouraged diversity but did not resort to the relativism that Cohen associated with *laissez faire* liberalism. Rather, it encouraged social integration of diverse human interests and desires. According to Cohen, just as the individual could harmonize conflicting interests, so could society. "For in the last analysis," he concluded the article, "the human soul is neither the master nor the slave of its environment. The human soul *is* its environment, seen from within."[119]

Three decades earlier William James pointed out that the question of "the one and the many" was "the most central of all philosophic problems, central because so pregnant."[120] The beauty of "Transcendental Nonsense" lay indeed not only in its sophistication, but also in its reflection of Cohen's inner struggles, particularly his interest in accommodating diverse social groups and his concerns about the uncertainties produced by relativism in culture, thought, and ethics. It was not only a "farewell to dear old jurisprudence and some of its most distinguished followers," as one of Cohen's critics described it,[121] but also an important milestone in the ongoing cultural revolution of the twentieth century. Together with a few other articles that Cohen published in the mid-1930s, "Transcendental Nonsense" sought to shift the attention of legal scholars toward the need to facilitate a society where diverse interests could be integrated into one whole. It was an end, and it was a beginning.

Legal Pluralism: A New Beginning

Shortly after "Transcendental Nonsense" was published, Walter B. Kennedy responded with a harsh critique—"Functional Nonsense and the Transcendental Approach." While admitting that Cohen had destroyed "the temple of legal conceptualism . . . in telling fashion and unique allegory," Kennedy went on to attack each of Cohen's arguments.[122] He cautioned against making law derivative of the social sciences and empiricism, challenged functionalists to come up with a real alternative (rather than merely criticizing the common law), and concluded (most pointedly in a later article) that functional jurisprudence, despite its alleged devotion to facts, figures, charts, statistical curves and tape measures is more empty, airy, elusive and impractical than the legal concepts, principles, precedents and rules which have been the targets for the functional sharpshooters; that there is a lot of "nonsense" bearing the stamp of science which is being peddled about by the traders in the fact-approach; that this "reliable technique" never gets close enough to legal problems to be of any value; that when it does "approach" it walks around the given problem, offers a few generalizations and then departs.[123]

Underlying Kennedy's critique was a generational fear. "It seems timely to warn 'the more intelligent of our younger law teachers and students,'" he wrote, "that youth has an impulsive and insatiable urge to pull things apart just to see how the wheels go round." Turning on its head Frank's equation of the search for legal certainty with "the childish reliance upon the omnipotence of its father," Kennedy suggested "that the itch for *change* in the law may be traceable to the restless impatience of youth seeking utterance in their legal philosophies."[124]

Cohen was a poor target for this line of attack. Genuinely in awe of older philosophies, his approach was motivated by his emotional need to save the old and to constrain the rebels. His deep philosophical understanding of the nature of intellectual revolutions converged with his generally peaceful personality to put him above the factions of his times, always striving toward a more complete understanding of philosophical as well as social problems. As Cohen put it, he objected to "the practice of fighting one's predecessors, alive and dead, to prove the virtue of the lady for whom one fights."[125]

Furthermore, like many second- and third-generation Americans, Cohen could not but celebrate the American legal order; with direction, he believed, law could promote human welfare. As we have seen, his critique of classical legal thought was anchored in his ongoing search for intimacy in an alienating world. Having deconstructed legal discourse into its elementary concepts, Cohen constructed a functional theory of law. It provided an empirical conceptualization of the dynamic relations among law's different components. Intimacy was achieved not by rationality and reason but through a variety of concrete and interdependent experiences.

But Kennedy was also on target. "Transcendental Nonsense," with its buoyant style, could not but have upset the older generation of Progressive legal scholars, particularly Morris Cohen. In a letter to Roscoe Pound in 1938, Morris expressed his request that a footnote reference to Cohen's "Transcendental Nonsense" would bear the initials F. S. "I should not myself, for instance," Morris wrote, "want to be given credit (positive or negative) for my son's brilliant writings. While I naturally admire them immensely I am certainly not always in agreement."[126] Indeed, shortly after the publication of "Transcendental Nonsense," Morris issued a rebuttal. Concealed under the title "On Absolutism in Legal Thought," it began with the following reprimand: "In the reaction against mechanical jurisprudence, against the complacent manipulation of legal concepts in utter disregard of the facts of social life, it is well to be on guard against throwing out the baby with the bath."[127] Morris agreed with his son that liberal legal thinkers had abused traditional concepts, like rights and titles. Both father and son also accepted the importance of concepts and general principles. Still, Morris was taken aback by the pluralist overtones of Felix's approach. For Felix, pluralism was the foundation of the modern state; for Morris, it was an empirical fact that logicians needed to examine and, where possible, reduce.

Specifically, while Morris recognized the plurality of interests and groups in society, he remained convinced of the superiority of scientific knowledge. For example, Felix saw in Einstein's theory of relativity, as it informed relativism in the social sciences, a foundation for a legal theory that would celebrate diversity (including plural forms of experience and knowledge). In turn, for Morris, Einstein's theory of relativity, with its underlying assumption that "common-sense knowledge and ordinary experience were no longer adequate to understand the physical world," undermined democracy by creating "an artificial barrier between the uninitiated layman and the initiated expert."[128] Given his strong adherence to the scientific method, Morris was also a staunch (Kantian) universalist. While recognizing the importance of collective institutions, he continued to believe that the individual should be the premise for legal and political analysis. It is indeed not surprising that Morris often admonished Felix to remember that "it is not enough to be good to mankind as a class. [One had] to be helpful to individuals."[129] Finally, while Felix sought to derive principles and values from multiple experiences, Morris embraced certain principles and values as self-evident.

The differences between Morris and Felix were subtle, but father and son alike alluded to them in their writings and in commentary on each other's writings. Having reviewed "On Absolutism in Legal Thought," Felix wrote to his father that he had no serious quarrel with any of its substance, but he did not like the style. As Felix explained, "The paper fail[ed], by reason of its loose organization to fulfill the interesting promise to drive between conflicting absolutes. It [gave] an impression of gentle meandering."[130]

In this vein, both Morris and Felix viewed "Transcendental Nonsense" as an act of rebellion, a rebellion that would be made complete two years later, on the event of Felix's thirtieth birthday. Responding to a birthday note from Morris, Felix noted his "thrill" at realizing that his father thought he had done "very well for the first thirty years."[131] A couple of weeks later, this time at the event of Morris's birthday, Felix reiterated his feelings. "It is curious," he wrote to Morris, that "you should have had faith that a lump of humanity that appeared about thirty years ago would develop into a projection of some of your own rational values, and the curiousness grows when one considers the college boy that was me some twelve years ago, practically devoid of serious intellectual interest and, as I recall, rather a disappointment to fond parental hopes."[132]

In two years, Felix would become a father to Gene Maura (named after Gene Weltfisch, an anthropologist at Columbia University), whom he described in a letter to Franz Boas as "the newest anthropologist in the family."[133] In his personal life and in his professional life, he seemed to be making strides. As daunting as the task of accommodating the diverse interests of Indian tribes was, he enjoyed it. More important, he believed that his work could become a model for addressing the needs of diverse groups in society. It was not long before he faced the task of doing so. As the following part examines, with the war in Europe and new assignments at home, the mission of building a pluralist state became a task not only of securing autonomy for groups but also of making law more attentive to their particular needs.

PART III

New Frontiers, 1939–1941

CHAPTER 6

First Americans, Misfits, and Refugees

"The corporation lawyer creates his client. In organizing a corporation he brings together individuals—rich, poor, stupid and wise, to make an effective fighting organization that can achieve objectives that the in-dividual members could not achieve. So too, any lawyer who wants to fight oppression must create his client, for oppression exists where men are not organized to secure their human rights, and the legal attack on oppression must always be linked with the campaign of education and organization that puts force behind an abstract legal claim."

Felix S. Cohen, Draft of an Address before the Eastern Law Students Conference, New York University School of Law, March 7, 1936 (FSCP 74/1186)

"As long as there remains in human hearts . . ."

In the mid-1930s Cohen described collective institutions, governments, and international organizations (all of which he labeled governments) as arising "out of agreements between individuals who surrender their liberty of action, or some part of that liberty, in order to escape the dangers of liberty, that is to say, the dangers of one's neighbor's liberty." While one might not have expected such endorsement of the social contract theory from a legal philosopher with strong affinity to utilitarianism, it is important to recall the context in which Cohen developed his ideas. As he saw it, the social contract theory offered an explanation for the piecemeal development of governments. It allowed him to describe governments as constantly "in the process of creation," which, in turn, allowed him to explore his ideas about social integration. In this vein, Cohen suggested that the future would see governments collaborating. He predicted that the creation of an international community would involve sovereigns sacrificing a degree of independence to bring about international peace. In a similar manner, he saw "the first beginnings of industrial peace and industrial government in the collective contract between a manufacturers' association and a labor union."[1]

While Cohen envisioned individuals coming together to create collective institutions, he emphasized that the group remained the unit of legal and political analysis. He encouraged lawyers interested in Progressive reform to focus "on the social interests, the social groups, the social values" that would benefit from social change and to endeavor to "bring the entire organized force of these groups and the entire weight of these values" into the processes of government formation.[2]

This was indeed the premise of *A Socialist Constitution for the Commonwealth of the United States* that Cohen drafted together with a few friends in the mid-1930s. It imagined individuals forming associations that would enter agreements to create a pyramid of collective institutions. Cohen believed that if law and government were viewed "as an ever-shifting balance of conflicting demands and interests," the possibility of ethical criticism would remain alive.[3]

While the group remained Cohen's basic unit for political and legal analysis, he also began more fully to explore the social place of the individual. As Cohen put it, his was a functionalist conception of government—"dealing not simply with words and symbols, but with the actual aspirations and energies of human beings."[4] While his early writings emphasized how collective institutions could promote their members' interests, his focus in the mid-1930s turned to the emotional and psychological role that institutions played in the lives of individuals.

Take, for example, Cohen's assessment of "How Long Will Indian Constitutions Last?" In this 1939 article, written in response to growing critiques of the IRA and calls to repeal it, Cohen attempted to explain why reorganization was not always successful.[5] Cohen proclaimed that tribal governments would only survive (and constitutions last) as long as they performed the important functions that individuals expected governments to satisfy—promote economic security, support the continuity of community life, maintain law and order, manage education and the distribution of resources (gas, water, electricity), maintain health and sanitation, and protect citizens against fire and other natural disasters. At least in part, Interior's failure to organize tribal governments was due to the fact that on many reservations these services, if at all provided, were performed by the Indian Service. Cohen wanted to transfer more power over these functions to tribal governments so that they could perform governmental roles.[6]

Many at Interior agreed (although BIA officials seemed rather content in maintaining their control over Indian reservations).[7] A few years into the process of reorganization, it became clear that Indians had to be educated in the elements of public administration, which many of them found foreign to their traditions. In a similar manner, education in political procedure, laws applicable to Indian nations, treaties, regulations, and the like was required. The economic development was far from successful. Many tribes were reluctant to form community enterprises and lacked knowledge as to how to manage their financial resources. They also required technical guidance in managing land resources and in promulgating and administering tribal criminal and civil codes.[8]

But Cohen's examination of tribal governments and constitutions reached further. For him, tribal governments and other collective institutions could not survive without "the community of consciousness" that they reflected. Above factionalism and assimilation, both of which threatened the continuity of any organization, lay Cohen's pluralist vision. It was based on the understanding that organizations could help individuals promote their interests and on the realization that individuals associated more easily with those similar to them, that "where many people think and feel as one, there is some ground to expect a stable political organization." More important, as "Transcendental Nonsense" already indicated, Cohen recognized the role that individuals' emotions and needs played in their view of the law. "How Long," then, "Will Indian Constitutions Last?" According to Cohen, a constitution was "the formal structure of a reality that exists in human hearts." Hence, "an Indian constitution will exist as long as there remains in human hearts a community of interdependence, of common interests, aspirations, hopes, and fears, in realms of art and politics, work and play."[9]

Not the economic and political interests of Indian tribes but their human needs became the focus of Cohen's scholarship in the late 1930s. It was a subtle but profound shift. For Cohen, a second-generation Jewish American and an active member of Roosevelt's New Deal, America was a community of interdependence, aspirations, and hopes. Here he felt at home, although even in the progressive Department of the Interior he faced remnants of anti-Semitism.[10] In the late 1930s, the increasingly horrifying treatment of Jews in Europe and the absence of a serious American response threatened his feelings. Rather abruptly, the pluralist description of the modern state as composed of many collective political institutions seemed insufficient. It could not protect the interests of groups and individuals outside of American society. Only a normative argument about human needs and America's role in protecting them could support the idea that the *outsider* had a place in modern American society. As we will see, the question became ever more important as Cohen struggled to find a haven for Jewish refugees in the United States—to bring another group under his umbrella of legal pluralism. As we will also see, as other scholars and reformers turned to the protection of human needs, they associated such protection with an ideal of individual rights that helped undermine Cohen's pluralist vision.

A Different Frontier

Jewish immigrants to the United States often referred to America as "*di gold-eneh medina*"—the golden land—the land of opportunities with open doors and sympathy for persecuted minorities. But American society had also exhibited nativist and anti-alien sentiments. Fears that foreigners would subvert American democratic ideals were as prevalent as belief in those ideals. The Anglo-Saxon Protestant majority had also long been suspicious of racial and religious minorities—African Americans, Chinese, Jews, and Roman Catholics. Government immigration policies reflected these sentiments.[11]

Immigration restrictions were imposed against the Chinese and Japanese in the late nineteenth century and, after World War I, also against Europeans. A visa system was instituted at the end of the war, and immigration laws in 1921 and 1924 established limits on immigration from European countries.[12] Then, on September 8, 1930, President Hoover issued an executive order instructing consular officers to refuse to issue visas if they believed "that the applicant may probably be a public charge at any time, even during a considerable period subsequent to his arrival."[13] Combined with the Alien Contract Labor Act of 1885, which prevented immigrants from securing jobs in advance, Hoover's directive meant that "only the independently wealthy" could emigrate to America. According to one account, "Immigration totals . . . dropped from 241,700 in 1930 to 97,139 in 1931 and to 35,576 in 1932."[14]

Roosevelt, who took the oath of office as the thirty-second president only a few weeks after Adolf Hitler became chancellor of Germany, did little to change immigration policy. Described most sympathetically, Roosevelt's approach was to comply with the restrictionist legislation while extending symbolic humanitarian gestures. As other historians have demonstrated, Roosevelt always listened to individual Jews and Jewish organizations, but did not make public statements or change policies to assist Jewish refugees. He was concerned that doing so would carry little if any political gain but would risk stirring up voters' emotions.[15]

Occasionally Roosevelt relaxed some of the administrative procedures that visa applicants faced, but overall, throughout the 1930s, American consular officers in Germany were liberal in their interpretation of restrictions imposed by the Hoover administration. "A stiff knee, a missing finger," or being underweight "after a two-year wait in refugee camps" were among the reasons used to deny applications. At the same time, the German government's economic policies, including different forms of private property confiscation, made it impossible for potential emigrants to show that they had sufficient assets not to become a public charge in the United States.[16]

Jewish organizations and individuals tried to work with government agencies to change the "public charge" policy. Judge Julian W. Mack of New York found a provision in the 1917 Immigration Act that "allowed the secretary of labor to accept a bond as a guarantee that a potential immigrant would not become a public charge." If a bond had been posted and accepted by the secretary, consuls abroad could not reject the application on public charge grounds. Mack was able to persuade Secretary of Labor Frances Perkins, who believed that more refugees should be admitted, to support the plan. But other officials in the Labor Department and, more important, the State Department were able to prevent the plan for public charge bonds from being administered.[17]

Moreover, widespread public and congressional support for the restrictionist immigration policy stood in the way of any administrative action to help European refugees. Despite very low immigration totals (23,068 in 1933, the lowest figure in American history since 1831), and despite the fact that between 1933 and 1937 more persons left the country than entered it ("a net loss of 47,172 individuals"), many Americans continued to call for more rigid restrictions on, or even the end of, all immigration.[18]

Mounting Fears

Nativism was on the rise in the 1930s. Years of economic insecurity, with as many as fifteen million individuals unemployed during the worst periods, led Americans, many of whom were no more than a generation removed from being immigrants, to endorse the nativist slogans "America for the Americans" or "100 percent Americanism." Gradually, the historical confidence in the nation's ability to absorb newcomers was destroyed. Fears that the Communist regime in the Soviet Union or Hitler might attempt to corrupt American institutions with the help of immigrants, as well as general anxiety about the preservation of American culture, added to the nativist and anti-alien sentiments. By 1940, 71 percent of the respondents to a Roper poll were convinced that Germany had already begun to form a "Fifth Column" in the United States.[19]

Anti-Semitism was also on the rise. Americans were not immune to the fear, popularized by Hitler, that "'Red Jews,' 'alien Jews,' 'Jewish-Bolshevists,' 'Jewish radicals,' and 'non-Aryans' were plotting to destroy the foundation of Anglo-Saxon civilization." Old-time patriotic organizations, panicked businessmen, and critics of Roosevelt's "Bolshevist" New Deal quickly embraced this anti-Semitic propaganda. The German American Bund, with 25,000 dedicated members, worked to frustrate any plan to harbor refugees from Germany. William Dudley Pelley's Silver Shirt Legion of America, with a claimed membership of 100,000, advocated a program of "Christian Democracy," including "an alien registration day for persons of 'Hebrew Blood,' imprisonment of Jews who attempted to use gentile names, prosecution of Jews who supported a Zionist state (on grounds of sedition), disenfranchisement of Jews, abrogation of all civil rights for Hebrews (including the right to hold property), and the establishment of an urban ghetto in one city in every state to pen up all Jews." More vocally, Father Charles E. Coughlin of Royal Oak, Michigan, helped spread Nazi propaganda through his tabloid newspaper *Social Justice*, "with a reported weekly circulation of one million," and his Sunday Radio broadcasting, "heard by a regular audience of 3,500,000."[20]

These groups and others, including the American Liberty League, organized in 1934 "to preserve the principles of the Declaration of Independence for succeeding generations of Americans," opposed not only Jews but also many, if not all, of the New Deal labor policies. Combining their political agendas, they "bombarded Congress" with objections to changes in immigration policy, claiming that new immigrants would make jobs scarce. This was a message that even more respectable organizations such as the American Federation of Labor (AFL) at times endorsed.[21]

Barriers and Facades

Meanwhile, the safety of Jews in Europe was deteriorating. Since the rise to power in early 1933 of the Nazi Party, German Jews, who constituted less than 2 percent of the Reich's population in 1933, were subject to political, economic, cultural, and physical persecution. Under the Nuremberg Laws, adopted in September 1935, Jews, who had already been banned from the professions, universities, and public service, lost their citizenship and were subject to business regulation that rapidly prevented them from pursuing, let alone making, a living.[22]

Then, on March 12, 1938, the German Army crossed the Austrian border. Within hours the *Anschluss* was complete, and the harsh Nuremberg Laws were imposed on Jews beyond the original boundaries of the Third Reich. The Nazis' goal was "to rid Austria of its Jews." Austrian Jewish leaders were arrested, anti-Jewish propaganda displayed on public buildings in Vienna, graveyards desecrated, and Jewish stores and offices looted. Jews were disenfranchised, thrown out of apartments, dismissed from schools and offices, and subjected to physical persecution. Austrian Jews were terrified. Within a couple of weeks "more than 30,000 persons queued up before the American consulate, and another 10,000 before the Australian consulate, in Vienna to seek visas. Officials estimated that 95 percent of these persons were Jewish." But the fear was not limited to countries under Nazi occupation. The march of Nazi soldiers across the Austrian border unleashed latent anti-Semitism throughout the continent. Terror was spreading among European Jews.[23]

As news of Nazi brutality began to arrive in the United States, editorials around the country harshly criticized the events. At a cabinet meeting on March 18, 1938, Roosevelt, too, expressed concerns about "the fate of European Jews." Yet while the American public was appalled by the events in Germany and Austria, it remained firmly opposed to the admission of refugees. With the recession of 1937, unemployment at nearly 20 percent, the popularity of Roosevelt and his New Deal policies at a new low, and strong isolationist sentiments throughout the country, the president was unwilling to shake up immigration policy.[24]

Without clear advice as to how the refugee problem might be solved, and given the explosiveness of any potential change in his immigration policies, Roosevelt determined to try an international solution. In March 1938, he invited representatives of foreign countries and private organizations to an international conference on the refugee crisis. Representatives of more than thirty nations and thirty-nine private organizations (of which twenty-one were Jewish) met in Evian-les-Bains, a small town in the French Alps, on July 6, 1938.[25] Roosevelt hoped to promote the settlement of refugees (not to be identified as any particular ethnic, political, or religious group) in "vacant spaces" on other continents (so that no nation would have to alter its immigration policies). He further insisted that funds for assisting the refugees would have to come from private groups, and that nothing should be done that might interfere with the work of existing relief organizations. Specifically, Roosevelt hoped that the Latin-American republics would offer settlement locations, but these countries' delegates dismissed this idea. Beyond that, the United States was only willing to accept refugees that fell within existing quotas, roughly 27,000 a year. Other countries followed suit. After a week, the meeting adjourned with the decision to create the Intergovernmental Committee on Refugees, a voluntary, privately funded organization to deal with the refugee problem, in which any member of the world community could participate and which ultimately was unable to act.[26] As one observer noted, Evian was "a façade behind which the civilized governments could hide their inability to act."[27] Within weeks of the Evian meeting, countries around the world enacted more rigid immigration laws. Doors were slammed in the faces of the refugees.

The Jewish Problem

In Europe, Jews were desperate. Beginning after midnight on November 10, 1938, the horrific *Kristallnacht,* the "Night of the Broken Glass," left synagogues, cemeteries, and Jewish businesses around Germany "in rubble." Supposedly provoked by the assassination of Ernst vom Rath of the German Embassy in Paris at the hands of a seventeen-year-old Jewish student, Herschel Grynszpan, *Kristallnacht* plunged Germany into a "bloodbath" that lasted several days. On November 12, 1938, the German government decreed that Jewish businesses, industries, and real estate had to be transferred to its control, with repairs to damaged properties made at the expense of the owners. The Jewish community was further required to pay one billion German marks "to compensate the [German] government for inconveniences sustained during *Kristallnacht."* The Nuremberg Laws of September 1935 had banned Jews from a wide range of professions, including the medical, legal, finance, sales, real estate, and tourist professions, and forced them to endure personal humiliation and degradation. After *Kristallnacht,* "Jews were [also] barred from all trades and ordered to divest themselves of all stocks, bonds, securities, gold, platinum, and silver."[28]

Again, the world was shocked. Holland, Belgium, Switzerland, and France responded by allowing Jews without funds or passports to enter their territories and, even "after closing the borders, continued to permit illegal immigrants to remain if they would stay in government camps." England, for a time, accepted immigrants at the American rate.[29]

Americans, too, responded with harsh condemnation. Republican and Democratic leaders alike chastised the Nazis. The Congress of Industrial Organizations (CIO), the AFL, churches, and other organizations issued statements deploring the actions of the German government. A poll conducted by the American Institute of Public Opinion in December 1938 revealed that "94 percent of those polled disapproved of the Nazis' treatment of the Jews. At the same time an increasing proportion of Americans (56 percent in October; 61 percent in December; 66 percent in April 1939) favored some form of boycott against German products. By April 1939, 78 percent of those polled approved a proposed 25 percent penalty tax on German imports."[30]

Still, immigration policies remained unchanged. Even the American Jewish community was unable to agree on the appropriate alternative. Until Hitler became chancellor of Germany, American Jews were similar to other American groups in their attitudes toward immigration.[31] Afterwards, Jewish-American organizations were divided, disordered, and, often, in disagreement. B'nai B'rith, the American Jewish Committee, the Zionist Organization of America, the Jewish Labor Committee, and the American Jewish Congress pressed Roosevelt for action to help their European brethren. But they failed to cooperate in a concerted effort. While some groups advocated opening American borders, others feared that increased Jewish immigration would result in rising anti-Semitism in America. Zionists wanted to settle Jewish refugees from Europe in Palestine, while religious organizations such as the Central Conference of American Rabbis, together with others who feared that Jewish nationalism only reinforced the idea that Jews were a distinctive race, opposed any such plan. Some historians maintain that, for the most part, these divisions reflected the general frustration of Jewish organizations at their inability to persuade Roosevelt and the State Department to act to save the refugees. Frustrated at their inability to achieve material results, "they blamed each other."[32] Others, however, suggest that these divisions prevented American Jews from doing much. As one historian pointedly put it, "Insecure themselves, constantly wary of raising the specter of double-loyalty which was the grist of anti-Semites," even Roosevelt's close Jewish advisers "ever exerted themselves to display their Americanism, their concern for this nation's welfare to the exclusion of all others, even when doing so meant the deaths of loved ones in Europe."[33]

The attitudes of Jewish organizations after *Kristallnacht* did not dramatically change. Many Jewish leaders continued to express fears that any attempt to modify immigration policy would lead to a devastating counterattack on the Jewish community. While a few newspapers immediately called for vigorous action, the General Jewish Council, which met on the day following the massive pogrom, did not discuss the issue, and when the leaders of the American

Jewish Congress, the American Jewish Committee, B'nai B'rith, and the Jewish Labor Council finally addressed it, they resolved that it was "the present sense of the General Jewish Council that there should be no parades, public demonstrations, or protests by Jews."[34]

The Alaska Development Plan

Refugee pressures from Germany caught "countries of potential refuge" around the world "unprepared, reluctant, and to some degree incredulous."[35] In the United States, where no specific immigration laws dealt with the question of refugees, several bills were introduced in Congress to try to help European Jews. Most celebrated among them—the Wagner-Rogers Bill, which Senator Robert Wagner of New York introduced in the Senate on February 9, 1939—called for the "admission of 20,000 German refugee children under age fourteen on a non-quota basis over the [following] two years." Edith Nourse Rogers introduced the bill in the House five days later. While the AFL, the CIO, many intellectuals, and thousands of others supported the bill, it failed to gain sufficient support in Congress. Anti-alien sentiments and the efforts of restrictionists, who were at the time promoting a bill to halt immigration indefinitely, diverted attention from the potential rescue of young children to fears that the children's parents would try to reunite with them, that the children would become a public burden, and that if they were adopted into American families, American children would be left in the streets. These concerns converged with anti-Jewish prejudices, which the bill's promoters were not able to overcome, even when they emphasized that many of the children were not Jewish. When the bill finally came out of committee, it simply gave priority to 10,000 children a year within the existing quota system. Disgusted, Wagner withdrew his support.[36]

A similar fate awaited a different attempt to bring refugees to the United States—specifically to the Alaska Territory. Conceived by Ickes and designed under Cohen's supervision, it became another pluralist experiment, one that could be described as the creation of refugee reservations in Alaska. When Congress and the American public rejected the plan, Cohen was forced to rethink his legal pluralist ideal. If his work on the IRA had taught him that important human needs transcended economic and political interests, his work on the Alaska Development Plan challenged Cohen to design legal rules to protect the human needs of diverse groups. Gradually he turned from a legal pluralist vision predicated on the protection of group autonomy to one based on the constitutional protection of group rights.

Alaska: The Final Frontier

Immediately after *Kristallnacht,* Ickes, who was disappointed both in the Jewish community and in Roosevelt, ordered Interior's lawyers to study the prospects of bringing Jewish refugees to Alaska. As Cohen wrote in retrospect, Ickes, "the custodian of the untapped resources that [made] up 95% of the Territory of Alaska," realized that "the resources of Alaska—its unsettled fertile lands, the timber and mineral resources, the vast water power, the fisheries and potential ports and industries—could comfortably support a population of at least ten million."[37]

Ickes's idea was not novel. Earlier that year, a group of European and American Jews established an "Association to Further Refugee Settlement in Alaska." They planned to establish manufacturing and industrial firms that would gradually become self-sustaining and contribute to Alaska's economic development. Similarly, a group of Protestants, Catholics, and Jews from Denver formed the "Alaska Colonization Society for Refugees" to settle Alaska with European refugees and unemployed Americans who would develop industry, business, and agriculture in Alaska on a cooperative basis.[38]

Eight days after *Kristallnacht,* Representative Charles A. Buckley, a Democrat from New York, sent "an open letter to Roosevelt" asking the president to allow European refugees in excess of immigration quotas to settle in Alaska. Buckley's motives were both humanitarian and political (he had a large Jewish constituency in the Bronx), but he stressed that the new settlement would benefit Alaska. "I'm sure that these immigrants will build Alaska as this country was built by immigrants who came to the United States from many lands during period[s] of persecution in the past," Buckley wrote. He believed that helping European refugees would demonstrate to the entire world that the United States, as it had always done, opened its borders to those oppressed in other countries.[39]

Roosevelt, who for the most part remained uninvolved in congressional debates about immigration, agreed that Alaska seemed suitable. But, warned by his advisors against involving the United States in the war, he was unwilling to change immigration policies. He suggested to Buckley that legislation exempting Alaska from immigration laws' restrictions would have to be supplemented by legislation restricting admission to the United States from Alaska.[40]

Interior's Plans

Buckley should have sent his proposal to Interior which, at Ickes's request, was already studying the possibilities of refugee settlements in Alaska as a way to develop the territory. Ernest Gruening, the son of German Jewish immigrants and the director of the Division of Territories and Island Possessions (who was soon to become governor of Alaska), was assigned the task of "developing a concrete colonization plan which was to include an analysis of the costs, required capital investments, and income possibilities in such diverse economic fields as the manufacture of paper and the processing of furs and hides." A news release based on the information collected was issued on April 13, 1939. But Interior made no recommendation because the colonization of Alaska involved questions outside its jurisdiction, including the interpretation of immigration laws and issues affecting national security.[41]

By August, however, in collaboration with the Departments of State, Commerce, Agriculture, and Labor, as well as outside organizations such as the National Lawyers Guild (NLG) and the Conference on Jewish Relations, Interior prepared "a draft of legislation" designed to solve two problems: "(1) The development of Alaskan resources and (2) the placement of refugees." A report "designed to awaken and enlighten popular interest in these objectives" was also prepared. Titled "The Problem of Alaska Development" and made public on August 16, 1939, it was signed by Undersecretary Harry Slattery after Assistant Secretary Chapman reportedly refused to sign it. It became known as the Slattery Report. Seven months later, after a series of delays, Senator Wagner, acting on behalf of Senator William H. King of Utah, and Representative Franck Havenner of California introduced the King-Havenner Bill (H.R. 8931, S. 3577) in the Senate and House, respectively.[42] Hearings were held before a Senate subcommittee of the Committee on Territories and Insular Affairs in May 1940. Cohen, who was working to find ways to help European refugees both as assistant solicitor and as a member of the NLG's International Law Committee, helped draft both the bill and the report.[43]

With Cohen at the helm, the Slattery Report provided brilliant packaging for Interior's attempt to help refugees. It began by describing Alaska's rich resources. It then went on to assess the problems of Alaska development—the territory's slow population growth, its unbalanced economy, "in which fishing and mining, mainly limited to summer work, accounted for 95 percent of employment," "a lack of investment capital," "random settlement," and the "high cost of living . . . caused by isolation, distance from markets and high freight rates." The solution was obvious. The report proposed the establishment of new settlements in Alaska, which would be based on year-round industries such as wood, minerals, fish, fur, and tourism. The report examined Baranof Island in southeast Alaska, the Kenai Peninsula, and the Matanuska-Susitna Valley as possible settlement sites.[44]

Cohen rejected the idea of individual settlement in Alaska. He believed that organized groups would guarantee group responsibility for the success of the project. Following the IRA model for tribal corporations, the Slattery Report recommended that "public purpose corporations" sponsor the new Alaska settlements.[45] These corporations would be privately financed but chartered by the federal government (specifically Interior) and include representatives chosen by governmental agencies on their boards of directors.[46] Titled "Alaska Development Corporations," these corporations' primary purpose would be to promote "permanent settlements in Alaska" and the development of "Alaskan industries so as to contribute to the needs of the national economy and the interest of the national defense."[47]

The corporations' powers were limited to the development of industries suitable for Alaska, and they could only employ a limited number of settlers. To assure compliance, Interior was to review each proposed development project, including the financial means of achieving it, the qualifications and number of settlers it would require, and the procedure for selecting settlers.[48]

The essence of Interior's plan was the method of selecting settlers. Interior emphasized that the majority of settlers would be unemployed Americans. But, as Ickes carefully put it, given the reluctance of American citizens to settle in Alaska, it was expected that settlers might include immigrants admitted under existing law and under a new category of quota-exempt immigrants.[49] (Quota-exempt or nonquota immigrants such as students, teachers, and ministers were allowed to enter the United States and its territories to engage in specific activities. They were not counted toward the quotas from their countries of origin.) Interior proposed that the new category of quota-exempt immigrants would include individuals in foreign countries between the ages of 16 and 45, as well as their spouses and children, who would agree to live in Alaska and engage in prescribed occupations. These immigrants would have the same legal status as other quota-exempt immigrants. They would be eligible to become quota immigrants only when possible under the quotas of their respective countries. To help in the selection of quota-exempt immigrants as settlers, the public-private corporations were empowered to certify settlers, furnish financial guarantees that they would not become public charges, train, transport, and support settlers, and enter agreements with settlers with respect to lands that they might acquire in Alaska.[50]

To preempt claims that the proposed settlement would introduce subversive influences into Alaska, Interior stressed that the quota-exempt immigrants would have to "meet prescribed conditions with respect to age, health and loyalty to the democratic institutions of the United States."[51] At the suggestion of the Departments of State, Labor, and Commerce, a provision was added to indicate that "at least 50 percent of the openings in each settlement [should] be given to citizens of the United States."[52]

"The needs of the national economy and the interest of the national defense"

Alaska was a perfect choice.[53] Not only was it under Interior's control, it was also sparsely settled, "with a population (half Eskimo and Indian) of one person per ten square miles" and with "industrial development at a minimum." Indeed, interest in Alaska development was budding in the 1930s as the published reports on the subject indicate. Given Alaska's proximity to Russia and Japan, many also believed that it was important to settle and develop Alaska to improve national defense. As the Slattery Report summarized the situation, Alaska represented "a weak spot in the national defense because it lack[ed] population and facilities for transportation, communication, housing, hospitalization, storage of supplies or repair of equipment, all of which [were] essential to defense and dependent upon population." Both the War and the Navy Departments were interested in promoting the settlement and economic development of Alaska to guard against potential conquest by hostile forces.[54]

Politically savvy, Interior emphasized both the importance of developing Alaska (turning to economists for detailed studies of the possibilities) and the significance of Alaska's economic development to national defense.[55]

Ickes set the tone during the hearings. Conceding that "the word 'humanitarian' is in bad odor these days," he went on to declare, somewhat wryly, that "if a proposition is good for business, and good for the national defense, and good for the American people, we ought not to turn it down merely because it has some humanitarian by-products."[56] Representatives of the Departments of Labor and of Commerce, the Division of Alaskan Fisheries, the U.S. Geological Survey, the Bureau of Mines, the Office of Indian Affairs, and the General Land Office followed his lead and "vouched for the practicality and the value to the nation" of the proposed plan. Other witnesses cited "excellent opportunities for the development of the cod, shrimp, and crab fisheries, the paper and pulpwood industries, mining, fur farming, and other enterprises" and stressed how the new settlements and businesses would create new jobs and promote consumption. Population growth in Alaska was presumed to follow.[57] Witnesses, including Vilhjalmur Stefansson, the Arctic explorer, added that "additional population and improvements such as roads and airports would mean easier defense of a vulnerable frontier."[58]

Interior described planned immigration, financed by philanthropic agencies and private investors, as the only way to settle Alaska. Cohen explained that the high cost of importing equipment and livestock and clearing the land, the inaccessibility of markets, and the lack of roads made individual settlement in Alaska too expensive. Group effort would not only reduce such costs, it would also allow for a decent existence by providing social services like hospitals and schools. Immigrants were essential to the plan because, as Interior put it, "Americans with the capital and training that would be needed to meet the problems of Alaskan living [did] not have the urge to leave the United States and start anew on the frontier." Acknowledging the need to help the many unemployed at home, Interior insisted that the initial settlement of Alaska required "foreign immigration of the proper sort under conditions which assure that immigration would make a positive contribution to the economic life of the Territory."[59] Dr. Frank Bohn, who came before the subcommittee as "the representative of a group of professionals, business and religious leaders, philanthropists, educators, artists and others," went so far as to suggest that establishing rural cooperatives in Alaska "consisting of the best physical strains in both America and Europe" would create a model of land settlement required to preserve America's "virility, physical strength and various other virtues." Americans ready to settle Alaska also appeared before the subcommittee.[60]

Planned group immigration was also described as the only way to attract to the territory American capital, which had traditionally "shown little interest in Alaskan development." As Interior cleverly put it, by allowing "persons and organizations interested in refugee settlement . . . to invest considerable amounts of capital in the development of Alaska," their program would attract to Alaska American capital that was otherwise being sent to Europe to help "victims of war and persecution."[61]

Departmental supervision of Alaska's economic development was a necessary element of the planned settlement. Interior was to supervise "the amount and type of capital investment per settler, the occupations to be pursued, the basis upon which settlers [were] to be selected, and other essential details of particular projects" (specifically limits on capital investment and distribution). Ickes and Cohen proclaimed that Interior's supervision would prevent corporations from bringing penniless refugees to Alaska and would assure continued reinvestment in the territory.[62]

While Interior would supervise the activities of the corporations, "the admission of nonquota immigrant settlers would be under the control of the Secretary of Labor."[63] Eager to allow deviations from the quota system, Interior's lawyers were keen on keeping the details of the program flexible, specifically the distribution of nationalities among settlers and any limit on the number of settlers. As Margold explained in a memorandum to Ickes, "rigid legislative restrictions upon administrative authority . . . is impractical and undesirable in legislation which for some years to come should be flexible enough to meet unforeseen conditions and developments, domestic and international."[64]

Neustadt

The Slattery Report generated new hopes in Europe. Throughout 1939 refugees sent inquiries to Interior. "Our emigration is *very urgent*. I beg you upon my knees to send the permission to entry into Alaska," wrote a manufacturer of clothing and linens in Breslau; and a group of Austrian Jews staying temporarily in France wrote, "No country wants us and [we] would rather die than go back to Austria." The most organized inquiry came from thirty members of the Jewish community in Neustadt, Germany. They wanted to emigrate to Alaska. They claimed to be "healthy, strong, and skilled" and stated that they "quite well" knew "the difficulties making the rough clime of Alaska" but that they had "no other choice, [being] German Jews."[65]

Neustadt was a typical village community—a small, centuries-old town northeast of Frankfurt. Its population in 1932 was 2,250 people, with "119 Jews, comprising 12 extended family groups." The Jews "made up a comfortable, prosperous and solidly middle-class community." "Their Judaism was liberal, restrained and unobtrusive; neither overly pious nor nationalistic," and they maintained good relations with their non-Jewish neighbors. "Gentile and Jewish children played together and attended the same school after the elementary level," and "Jews and non-Jews visited each other's homes, even attending religious celebrations of each on occasion." Bruno Rosenthal, who would become the leader in appealing to Interior, was descended from Neustadt merchants of the 1700s.[66]

Nonetheless, the Jewish community stood apart. The Jews attended synagogue regularly, observed Jewish holidays, adhered to Jewish law with respect to dietary restrictions and Sabbath observation, and rarely intermarried. They shared "a strong Jewish identification and a keen awareness that they were different from the rest of the community."[67]

These differences were magnified under the Third Reich, and the relationship between Jews and non-Jews in Neustadt rapidly deteriorated. Jewish businesses were boycotted, Gentiles and Jews avoided each other, and by the end of 1938 Jews were excluded from economic life throughout Germany. During *Kristallnacht* the Neustadt synagogue was destroyed, houses and apartments damaged by fire and stones, shop windows shattered, and shops looted and robbed. On November 10, all but two of the Jewish men over the age of eighteen were sent to Buchenwald for several months.[68]

By 1939, only forty-five Jews (comprising seven families) remained in Neustadt. The others had left, had been forcibly removed, or murdered. When, in honor of Hitler's birthday, men like Rosenthal were released from Buchenwald and returned to Neustadt, they clung to the possibility of settling Alaska. They read about it in the *Jüdisches Nachrichtenblatt,* the only Jewish publication permitted after 1938, which was intended to facilitate Nazi control. It "regularly carried accounts of mass resettlement plans, as Nazi policy until late 1941 encouraged Jews to leave Germany by every possible means."[69]

Rosenthal's first two letters were sent to the State Department and never received a response. Then, having read about Ickes's intentions to settle Alaska, Rosenthal directed his third letter, dated August 16, 1939, to Interior. In November 1939, Rosenthal received his first response from Washington. Signed by Undersecretary Slattery, it stated that Alaska was governed by quota laws and was therefore not under Interior's jurisdiction. Rosenthal was promised that his inquiry "would be sent to the 'appropriate governmental authorities to determine what disposition [could] be made' and that he would be 'advised of the results as soon as possible.'" A copy of the Slattery Report was enclosed.[70]

Rosenthal read the report and replied immediately, attempting to make a case "for the 'pioneering capital' of the community of Jews in Neustadt." His letter stated that they possessed all the "characteristics—industry, initiative, and one more that the Report [did] not mention, ideals—to successfully settle in Alaska. . . . Neither coldness nor other nature-forces [should] prevent [them] to do [their] duty. . . . Give us not charity, but assistance that will be the very thing for us Alaska new-pioneers," he asked. His letter listed "the names of 21 'German Jews . . . able-bodied and healthful' who want[ed] to go to Alaska as soon as possible."[71]

Interior did not respond. Rosenthal wrote again in November and December 1939, "expressing disappointment about the lack of reply" and reiterating the hopeless situation in Germany. "It is only the sorrow and the grief for all my coreligionists which are of the same mind as I and are willing, like myself, to bear with courage, energy, and patience our heavy destiny, us awaiting in Alaska," he pleaded, adding that "if 21 people were too much for the first 'pioneer wave', take numbers one to 13 on the list and the rest later."[72]

While Rosenthal waited for a reply, Interior struggled to defend its bill against its opponents' concerns about the possible detrimental effects of bringing Rosenthal, his neighbors, and other Jewish refugees to Alaska.

"A mass of misfits"

Reactions to Interior's Alaska Development Program were mixed. The idea of Alaska's economic development was received with wide support. In the first few months after the report became public, Interior received over four thousand letters approving of the idea (less than one percent were critical), and the editorials in no less than 388 newspapers were overwhelmingly favorable. The Cordova, Seward, Skagway, and Petersburg Chambers of Commerce also favored the idea and offered cooperation.[73]

Some potential sponsors expressed doubts, fearing that the problem of resettlement was too vast to be dealt with by private organizations. They wanted Interior to secure "the financial cooperation of governments."[74] But several organizations were already working with Interior on the details of the plan. In New York, the National Committee for Alaskan Development, formed as early as August 1939, merged with the Roland German American Democratic Society to create the Alaskan Development Committee, which became the main private group pressing for passage of the bill. Its main task was finding "financial backing for the proposed corporations, trying to show that people would put money into projects that would enable victims of persecution to become free and self-sufficient."[75] "The letters keep pouring in on Alaska," Cohen wrote to his father, "and I get a very deep satisfaction out of reading and answering them. Over a thousand now, and less than 10 adverse."[76]

The support for the bill was overwhelmed by strong opposition to the idea of bringing refugees to the territories. Members of the subcommittee suggested that Interior should focus its efforts on helping unemployed Americans. John Thomas Taylor of the American Legion and John Trevor of the American Coalition of Patriotic Societies testified that opening Alaska to settlement by aliens would increase the territory's vulnerability to attack. The State Department feared that creating this new category of quota-exempt immigrants could lead to the destruction of the entire system of protective immigration laws, while officials in Alaska stressed that it would separate Alaska from the rest of the United States. Anthony J. Dimond, Alaska's delegate to Congress, argued that the bill would make Alaska into a "sort of special land where people may reside who are not citizens and who are not permitted to be in the remainder of the United States"; it would create a "separate society or caste in [the] present casteless Territory." The Fairbanks Chamber of Commerce charged that the bill implied "virtual serfdom" for the refugees.[77] And the mayor of Fairbanks concluded that the proposal to make Alaska a haven for refugees "was almost as unpopular among Alaskans as the suggestion . . . that the territory be used for the location of penal colonies made up of convicts from prisons in the states."[78]

Alaskans were very conscious and resentful of proposals that tended "to the slightest extent to separate Alaska from the United States," Dimond similarly stressed.[79]

More pointedly, newspaper articles, radio stations, and residents of Alaska (with negligible exceptions) expressed concern about turning the territory into a home for Jewish refugees. Many of them never heard the voices of people like Rosenthal, many of them were horrified by the Nazis' actions and quick to denounce them, but they felt that the problem was European and should be left in Europe.[80]

Editorials in the *Fairbanks Daily News-Miner* asserted that Alaska could not "afford to carry on with a mass of misfits" and that "German-Jews are unsuited for Alaska settlers." "They are not the type of hardy Scandinavians who have had so much to do with the development of Alaska." The *Ketchikan Alaska Chronicle* pointed out that Alaskans had "a tendency to see a difference between 'colonization' and 'immigration,' and a further tendency to see a difference between immigration of Europeans and European Jews." Even the *Alaska Weekly,* which condemned "opposition to Jewish refugees based on racial antipathy," declared that "Jews would be the least desirable of immigrants because of being the least adaptable."[81]

Business organizations, including the Fairbanks, Juneau, Ketchikan, Wrangell, Valdez, Kodiak, and Anchorage Chambers of Commerce, made similar statements. They objected to populating Alaska with "foreign refugees of doubtful capacity for assimilation."[82] And the American Legion spokesman proclaimed that "instead of opening our doors wider to the Trojan horses of the enemies of our democracy . . . we should be taking steps to expel them and to close our doors to any more of their kind." Adding insult to injury, the representative of the American Coalition of Patriotic Societies asserted that Jews were persecuted "because of their beliefs in the Marxian philosophy."[83]

In a letter to Ickes, written shortly after the Slattery Report was made public, Gruening, by then governor of the territory, pointedly summarized these different critiques. Gruening, who viewed the governorship of Alaska as "his last chance for a political career," recognized that "it would be political suicide to push a plan that was stirring opposition in Alaska." He thus charged that the Slattery Report had concealed its true purpose of assisting refugees under the cloak of economic development. According to Gruening, by exempting Alaska from the quota system, the report violated Interior's policy of treating the territories and the states equally. Gruening further charged that by preventing immigrants from leaving the territory for five years, the measure included an unconstitutional prohibition on the freedom of movement, a rather ironic argument given the situation in Europe. Finally, Gruening, a confirmed atheist who complained when he was identified as "Jewish," proclaimed that the plan would turn Alaska into "a virtual 'concentration camp.'"[84]

Anti-Semitic sentiments converged with economic insecurity. Although many Alaskans had complained about the need to bring more settlers to Alaska, editorials in the *Fairbanks Daily News-Miner* were quick to assert that it would be impossible to assimilate masses of refugees into the territory's economic structure; moreover, an influx of immigrants would only add to the problems of poverty and unemployment in the territory. Similarly, Dimond emphasized that Alaskans were "free from racial and religious bigotry" but were concerned that even if the program was financed by private funds, the territory would have to spend large amounts of money for education, the construction of roads, and the provision of social services for the new settlers. Dimond further stressed that external bureaucratic control would only retard Alaska's economic development, which should (and would) occur naturally. In fact, according to Dimond, only the extension of roads was required to promote population growth in Alaska.[85]

It was, however, Robert Marshall, chief of recreation for the Forest Service and founder of the Wilderness Society, who expressed the most profound critique of the program. The son of Louis Marshall, "a prominent New York constitutional lawyer and the longtime president of the American Jewish Committee," Robert Marshall charged that the talk of the new frontier was an attempt to evade the nation's real economic problems. He did not oppose immigration per se, or even Jewish immigration. Rather, Marshall, who in 1934 worked with Cohen to draft the IRA and opposed some of Cohen's initial suggestions with respect to collective ownership of tribal lands, simply opposed collectivism. As he explained, Interior's plan would "take away from people the unique possibilities of individuality found in scantily populated countries where men are few and each one is distinctive."[86]

Dimond, Marshall, and Gruening criticized different aspects of the Alaska Development Plan. Dimond and Gruening were concerned, to varying degrees, about setting the territory apart from the United States and about settling Jews in Alaska. Marshall was more concerned about the collectivist ideas underlying Cohen's plan. But however different their views might have been, they were united in their opposition. In a journal note written after a dinner party at Marshall's house, at which all three were present, Gruening commented that "the refugee problem could be solved only by defeating the Fascist forces which originated it. But otherwise the problem was quantitatively overwhelming."[87]

Determination

Interior would not concede. The bill was intentionally drafted so that objection to the refugee issue could only be directed at two or three of its sections. As Cohen put it, it was meant to deprive opponents in Congress "of the usual weapons of delay and opposition" and limit them "to the weapons of amendment."[88] During the debates over the bill, Interior strongly asserted that the bill's major objective was Alaska's economic development. The refugee aspect was merely incidental. Interior emphasized that the bill included provisions to guarantee that the settlement of Alaska would not "deprive Americans of jobs," would not burden Alaska with "penniless refugees," and would not turn Alaska into "a stepping stone to illegal entry into the United States" or an inferior territory. Even against charges that unemployed Americans could settle Alaska and that, in fact, the corporations created by the bill had no special features but the ability to allow immigrants into the country, Interior was steadfast in its argument.[89]

Cohen pushed this point most adamantly. He proclaimed that the immigration features were simply "an essential means but not a fundamental purpose" of the bill and declared that he and Interior would support the bill "even though all of the immigration factors [were] stricken out," provided they were substituted by other means of bringing about Alaska's development like tax advantages or subsidies.[90] Even in a letter to his father, Cohen played down the refugee aspect of the program. "The proposed bill is not a humanitarian measure, except incidentally," he wrote. "Its primary justification is economic and military."[91] Still, Cohen believed that the arrangements in the King-Havenner Bill were "superior and preferable from the standpoint of general public policy to [the] other alternatives." Specifically, he pointed out that the bill would induce European companies, displaced by the war, to establish their businesses in Alaska and would thus foster the creation of employment opportunities for American citizens. He further emphasized that the plan could attract funds from individuals who were interested in helping friends and relatives in Europe as well as from refugee-owned industries.[92] When Morris, being cautious, encouraged his son to eliminate from the bill the reference to a new category of quota-exempt immigrants, Cohen refused.[93]

Cohen played down the fact that most immigrants would be Jewish. While he embraced pluralism with respect to other minority groups, he had trouble admitting it in his personal life. Like other Jewish intellectuals, Cohen endorsed the liberal division between the personal and the political and took the position that his religious or ethnic background was irrelevant to his position on the legal issues of restrictive immigration laws. The refugee problem was a universal, not a particular, one.[94]

Universalism was also practical. Cohen well knew that Interior's focus on Alaska's economic development and national defense was a means of diverting attention from the Jewish problem. He admitted that "concrete plans of development," which could "fit into the actual experience of Alaskans," would probably be discussed and received as such without reference to "racial or political considerations."[95] In this vein, the Slattery Report emphasized that race and religion would not be relevant in selecting immigrants to participate in the proposed program. Rather, immigrants would be selected based solely on their "physical, mental, and moral capacity to face the difficulties of Alaskan life, [their] experience and competence in the particular industries that are set up, and [their] ability to offer adequate guarantees that [they would] not become a public charge."[96] Cohen further stressed that their plan "should not be advocated as a sectarian affair." Rather, proponents of the plan should emphasize "the importance of joint action with groups of various faiths and with the increasing number of nationality groups that are vitally interested in the problem of refugee havens."[97]

Diverting attention from the Jewish refugee problem was intended to evade not only anti-Semitism but also opposition from Jewish organizations. Arthur Meyer, chairman of the Policy and Program Committee of the American Jewish Council (and a close friend of Morris Cohen), explained to Felix that the initial reaction of the American Jewish Committee and B'nai B'rith was "favorable," and he believed that the Jewish Labor Committee, while somewhat undecided, ultimately would support the program. Yet Meyer also reported that the American Jewish Congress was unsure as to whether Jewish organizations should act on this matter because of its potential damage to Zionist causes and, more important, because of their belief that endeavors to increase immigration to the United States would not only fail but would also result in more restrictive changes to the immigration law.[98]

This response was alarming. Senator Millard Tydings of Maryland, the chairman of the Committee on Territories who supported the program, was concerned about the potential opposition from Zionist organizations.[99] Cohen worked to convince leaders of the Jewish community to express their support. Tellingly, he wrote to Justice Louis Brandeis:

> The Bill is not intended as a solution to the Jewish refugee problem. Its greatest support thus far has come from Spanish groups, from non-Jewish German groups, and from representatives of Finnish groups. It would be a great tragedy, I feel, if those groups should come to believe that their interests are being sacrificed to the cause of another oppressed minority which can find a hope and salvation not shared by these groups in the land of Palestine. . . . I feel it my duty therefore to write and urge that if you consider that our proposed legislation would be of little help in solving the Jewish refugee problem, and that Palestine offers a greater source of hope to refugees of our faith—in which conclusions I should concur—you will nevertheless make it as clear as possible that you are not thereby disparaging a course of action on which many different groups of oppressed people have come to pin their hopes.[100]

Diverting attention from the Jewish refugee problem reflected Cohen's personal attitudes and his realism. But Cohen's arguments for settling Alaska with a diverse population ran deeper. Cohen believed that bringing various occupations and talents to Alaska would be a foundation for strengthening Alaska's economy and for promoting American values and culture. In a letter to Warner Brothers Pictures, discussing the possibility of a documentary on the Alaska Development Program, Cohen stressed the similarities between Alaska and the Western frontier in the late nineteenth century. "As the West was built through the pioneer spirit of persecuted and poor immigrants from Europe, so can Alaska be transformed into one more industrial and cultural star on the American shield," he explained.[101] According to Cohen, "The mixture of many different groups, representing various skills [had] been largely responsible for technological and industrial advance in the United States." He believed that a similar mixture would achieve the same ends in Alaska.[102]

Immigration and Pluralism

> All the causes with which I have identified my life seem to have been taking an awful licking in the last five years.
> —Felix S. Cohen to Morris Cohen, April 7, 1938 (MRCP)

Finding a place for the outsider in American society forced Cohen to re-assess his pluralist vision of the modern state. Stressing the role of collective institutions in American society or the importance of social integration was not a justification for opening the borders to strangers or for protecting those strangers' interests. Cohen had to resort to the normative argument in support of pluralism—to the role of diversity in individual and social life. He began to describe the diversity of groups (social, cultural, religious, economic, political) that characterized American society, not only as a means of reconciling the tensions created by relativism or a source of a comforting sense of belonging, but also as the ground for the strength of the American democratic tradition and institutions. In Cohen's writings in the early 1940s, tolerance bred freedom.

Take, for example, the debate over immigration. Arguments in support of a series of bills to prohibit or restrict immigration introduced in Congress in the late 1930s voiced common objections—"(a) that immigration threatens the American standard of living, (b) that immigration increases unemployment, and (c) that immigration lowers the cultural level, and menaces the American way of life."[103]

In an essay Cohen wrote for the NLG on "Exclusionary Immigration Laws," he used empirical data to refute each of these arguments. First, Cohen found a correlation between a high proportion of foreign-born in the population and high per capita annual income. He explained the correlation by emphasizing the importance of specialization and diversification of occupations to the development of industry and agriculture. In addition, he pointed to the contributions that immigrants had traditionally made as consumers of goods and as advocates of better employment conditions, especially in the union movement. Second, Cohen demonstrated a correlation between periods of heavy immigration and increasing numbers of available jobs. He explained this correlation by pointing to the role of immigrants as consumers and as creators of new industries. Finally, Cohen went on empirically to refute "popular fallacies"—that foreigners were more prone to criminal behavior than native-born Americans, that immigration raised illiteracy levels and harmed education levels, and that immigrants were likely to segregate themselves from American society.[104]

But Cohen's argument reached beyond the empirical refutation of common beliefs. As he saw it, attitudes toward immigration were not grounded in concerns about its economic and social consequences, but rather in "the psychology of hate." "If you hate a man, because of his color, manners, mode of dress, or speech," Cohen wrote, "you will think of the unpleasant things he may do, as a job-competitor, and pass lightly over his role as a consumer of the goods you produce." According to Cohen, hatred toward the foreign-born was not only against the American spirit of democracy, it was also counterproductive.[105]

Instead of hatred, Cohen wanted to cultivate tolerance. Instead of eliminating diversity, he turned to American constitutional values—"human equality, separation of church and state, and abrogation of ancestral titles"—as justifications for, and a means of, accommodating diverse races, traditions, cultures, and religions. Moreover, he wanted to convince the American public that commitment to these ideals and to "the spirit of tolerance" that infused them would strengthen American democracy. As he put it: American life was distinctive because it was "a product of the constant impact and interchange of diverse cultures, all contributing to a new civilization made possible by the spirit of tolerance." Accordingly, the utmost risk to American institutions came from those who wanted to restrict immigration and thus to "cut off the living stream" that made the American life.[106]

Cohen was an advocate. Seeking to refute common beliefs about the threats of immigration, he turned the threats upon themselves. If immigration was restricted or banned, he wrote,

> our standard of living would be lower, our illiteracy higher, our prejudice against minority races, minority creeds and foreigners generally would be more intense. Our governmental institutions based upon a many-party system would probably be superseded by other institutions based upon a one-party system, and the tenets of democracy based upon human freedom, race equality and religious tolerance would become slogans without substance.[107]

To Americans concerned about the loss of the frontier, the keystone of American democracy, Cohen proclaimed its existence. As he put it, "If anything had vanished it is the uprooted seeker of a new homeland, accustomed to hardship and willing to face the wilderness and tame it." The frontier was not lost, Cohen announced. "We just put a fence around it at the end of the first World War and declared that it could not be settled except by men and women who, being already comfortably settled within reach of roads, schools and movies, had no desire to subject their families to the hardships of wilderness life." He urged his audience to support opening American borders to refugees so as to bring back the "lost frontier" and its stimulating effects on American economics and politics.[108] According to Cohen, America's future was interdependent with the future of the world's dispossessed. "If America is destined in the decades or centuries ahead to create a culture and a civilization greater than any the earth has yet seen, it will be because each of the races of the earth is free here in America, as nowhere else, to make its highest contribution to the New World of the Future," he proclaimed.[109]

Here was Cohen's normative argument: his pluralism rested on the assumption that diversity was important to individual and social life. Allowing individuals to come together was not enough. The pluralist state would not fully protect the rights and interests of its own citizens unless it also protected those of the outsider. As Cohen put it, "The human rights of the citizen are safe only when the rights of the foreigner are protected." Furthermore, the pluralist state would not thrive unless it protected the needs of all human beings. "Hatred of the alien," he announced, was "the mark of a declining civilization, that has lost its capacity to grow and is no longer able to assimilate what is of value in other cultures."[110] In short, according to Cohen, liberty was born of tolerance. As we will see in the following chapter, this would become the premise of Cohen's new pluralist vision—a vision predicated not only on an ideal of constitutionally protected individual rights, as these quotes might suggest, but also, more essentially, on an ideal of constitutionally protected group rights. First, however, let us examine another of Cohen's attempts to help European refugees.

The Virgin Islands Option

A Different Alaska Bill

Cohen's argument in support of Alaska's settlement and immigration did not convince restrictionists, government officials, or Alaskans who were unwilling to admit refugees for the benefit of Alaska's development or American democracy. The subcommittee hearings on the King-Havenner bill ended on May 18, 1940. Numerous experts from the Bureau of Mines, the U.S. Geological Survey, and the Division of Alaska Fisheries testified in favor of the bill. Four witnesses opposed it (Don Carlos Brownell, the mayor of Seward; Dimond, Alaska's territorial delegate to Congress; Taylor, the representative of the American Legion; and Trevor, the representative of the American Coalition of Patriotic Societies), but "four was all it took."[111] At the close of the hearings, no further action was recommended or taken.

The bill died but the idea lived on. On January 29, 1941, Representative Samuel Dickstein, Democrat from New York and chairman of the House Immigration and Naturalization Committee, introduced a new bill (H.R. 2791) "to colonize Alaska with a highly trained and desirable class of citizens who are refugees from foreign persecution" for the purpose of strengthening national defense and creating a market for surplus production. To avoid criticisms for admitting nonquota immigrants, Dickstein proposed that the number of refugees who would be allowed to immigrate to Alaska would be limited to "the total of all unused quotas of all countries" for the preceding six years.[112]

Dickstein's bill was not a sufficient concession, and the debates over it repeated the arguments made earlier. Moreover, by the 1940s, the State Department and Alaskans were growing rapidly concerned about national security. Refugees were viewed as a potential fifth column, "spies and subversives," and hints were again made that "certain minorities in Germany were persecuted because of their subversive [Marxist] beliefs."[113] The bill's provisions requiring refugees to prove that they had never engaged in subversive activities and that they had renounced any allegiance to other countries or organizations did not calm such fears. Like the King-Havenner bill, the Dickstein bill "was laid to rest in a subcommittee."[114]

Refugees as Temporary Visitors

With the Alaska solution unable to pass the hearing stage in Congress, Interior searched for an alternative that would not require changing immigration laws. They concluded that existing laws allowed bringing a limited number of refugees into the Virgin Islands as temporary visitors, a category not subject to quotas. Normally, temporary visitors were required to return to their homelands, but Interior wanted to permit these refugees to stay in the Virgin Islands until they could receive an immigrant visa to the United States, move to South America, or return to postwar Europe.[115]

Interior specified that such temporary visas would be accompanied by a bond to ensure "that the visitor [would] not become a public charge"; that, while in the Virgin Islands, visitors "would rely on their own financial resources, on those of friends or relatives in the United States, or on help from American refugee agencies" (except for a limited number with special skills, visitors were forbidden gainful employment); that visitors would not "enter any other part of the United States, its Territories and possessions"; and that visitors would "depart from the Virgin Islands upon the expiration [of their temporary visa], unless prior to such date [they] should have received a quota visa."[116] While the Virgin Islands plan did not anticipate the creation of collective settlements, private organizations were expected to help sponsor individual immigrants and supervise their activities.[117]

The stated purpose of the Virgin Islands project was to allow several thousand refugees safely to wait in the Virgin Islands for their immigration visas to the United States.[118] Nonetheless, Interior justified the project in economic terms. They emphasized that the influx of support money would boost the islands' economy and that the expansion of housing and recreational facilities to meet refugee needs would help build the hotel and tourist industries. Cohen went as far as to suggest that a "liberalization of present regulations permitting the entry of refugee visitors into the Virgin Islands [might] help to solve one of the current problems of American shipping," that is, it might "provide passenger capacity for an important portion of the American merchant marine on westbound trips" from Europe.[119]

Most important, as Ickes explained to President Roosevelt, Interior wanted to make the Virgin Islands a laboratory for testing immigration policies, just as they had attempted to make Indian reservations laboratories for their democratic theories. Their "chief hope" was that "such economic contributions, in the form of new housing, construction, improvement of recreational and tourist facilities, etc. [would] constitute a laboratory demonstration of the economic value of a small group of carefully selected refugees."[120]

Legal Barriers

On November 18, 1938, the Legislative Assembly of the Virgin Islands passed a "Resolution offering the Virgin Islands of the United States as a place of safety for refugee peoples."[121] However, before the plan could be made operative, a major legal obstacle had to be removed. State Department regulations provided that "aliens who had already applied for permanent quota immigration would void their applications if they entered the United States or any of its possessions as temporary visitors." Because the main purpose of the plan was to allow refugees already on quota lists to wait in the Virgin Islands until their permanent applications were approved, these regulations undermined the entire project.[122]

Protecting holders of temporary visitor visas against withdrawal of their pending applications for entry into the United States as quota immigrants was a difficult obstacle to tackle.[123] On October 9, 1939, Margold issued a solicitor's opinion in which he declared that according to his interpretation of the Immigration Act of 1924, a grant of "a temporary visitor's visa for entry into a designated territory or possession of the United States" did not entail "a forfeiture of an application for an immigration visa to enter the United States." In any event, Margold suggested exempting the Virgin Islands from these administrative regulations.[124]

On November 25, 1939, Interior submitted to the Secretary of State and the Secretary of Labor "proposed amendments to existing regulations on the entry of alien visitors to the Virgin Islands." The amendments sought to allow such visitors to keep their applications for permanent visas. Secretary of Labor Frances Perkins believed that "the submitted regulations, subject to certain minor technical corrections, were consistent with existing law and unobjectionable from the standpoint of policy."[125] But the State Department was not convinced. In a memorandum to Ickes, Secretary of State Cordell Hull advised that in his opinion "the proposed regulations were incompatible with existing law." Hull conceded that if Congress enacted the necessary measures, his department would work with Interior to carry out the Virgin Islands project.[126]

By March 1940, Ickes was pressing Attorney General Robert Jackson for a ruling on the conflict of opinions between Interior and State. But the attorney general refused to express an opinion because, as he saw it, the question was within the jurisdiction of the State Department and could not be referred to him by the secretary of the interior.[127]

In August Ickes pressed again, at which time an attorney at Justice informally advised Margold that Interior's position on the compatibility of temporary visas and applications for permanent visas was sound but that "a serious legal question existed as to the power of the State Department to issue a limited visitor's visa requiring the holder to remain within a specified Territory until his departure from the United States." On Justice's suggestion, Margold provided an opinion concluding that "the Secretary of State had power to issue such a special visa."[128]

The different departments were at a stalemate, but Interior would not give in. In the fall of 1940 Margold proclaimed that the "power to achieve some of the objectives originally desired was vested in the Governor of the Virgin Islands" and not in the State Department. Specifically, while issuance of visas abroad required the cooperation of consuls working under the State Department, "a clause in an Executive Order of April 1938 authorized the governor of the Virgin Islands to allow alien visitors without visas to enter the islands in emergency cases."[129] Shortly thereafter, Cohen and his colleagues prepared "a draft of proclamation, specifying conditions under which discretionary power to waive passport and visa requirements vested in the Governor might be exercised." When the governor of the Virgin Islands, Lawrence W. Cramer, signed it, Interior began working on the regulations needed to implement the proclamation.[130] The cooperation of private organizations was suggested to assist the government of the Virgin Islands in verifying that the visitors without visas met the conditions upon which they could be admitted.[131]

The State Department was not convinced. Raising deep concerns about "a large-scale influx of foreigners to the Virgin Islands without adequate safeguards against undesirable elements," it continued to oppose the plan. Seeking a compromise, Interior stressed that "the process of selection and admission would be entirely in the hands of the consular offices" and that the visitors would not be allowed to travel to the United States. At the same time, at Ickes's request, Margold issued an opinion concluding that, given Interior's responsibility for the territories, the secretary of the interior could properly refer to the attorney general a question about the admission of alien visitors to the territories. But it was to no avail, and the attorney general remained reluctant to intervene unless the secretary of state referred the issue to him.[132] The final blow, however, came when the State Department referred the issue to the president.[133]

While Eleanor Roosevelt had expressed "a sympathetic interest in the possibility of establishing some kind of refugee haven in the Virgin Islands,"[134] the President sided with the State Department. In a memorandum to Ickes dated December 18, 1940, Roosevelt, "being perfectly frank in regard to the proposed proclamation by the Governor of the Virgin Islands in regard to the admission of this Island of certain refugees," told Ickes that matters of foreign relations and foreign policy were under the control of the State Department. "No matter what loyal counsel a legal adviser, etc. may give an opinion in regard to a case involving a portion of the United States," Roosevelt wrote, "the fact remains that the Secretary of State (and the President) must determine all matters relating to the foreign relations of each and every portion of the United States including its Insular possessions." "Tell Margold," Roosevelt ended on a scolding note, "that I have every sympathy but that if he has some better plan, to come and tell me about it and I will give it really sympathetic consideration. I cannot, however, do anything which would conceivably hurt the future of present American citizens. The inhabitants of the Virgin Islands are American citizens."[135]

Ickes, Margold, and Cohen would not admit defeat. Margold, after summarizing Interior's position in a memorandum that Ickes passed to Roosevelt, turned out a seventy-page paper defending the legality of Interior's proposal.[136] But by February 1941, Justice closed its file on the question and in April the State Department announced that its original decision would stand. Cohen, Margold, and Ickes were forced to concede.[137]

Aftermath

On February 25, 1941, Interior transferred Rosenthal's last letter, dated January 28, 1941, to the State Department. Rosenthal recognized that "there was no hope for him, his family or members of the Jewish community in Neustadt for resettlement in Alaska." Nonetheless, asserting that he and his wife were "ambitious people . . . anxious to go to Alaska as pioneers," he prayed: "Are there no exceptions?" Still waiting for his quota visa, Rosenthal added that his original American sponsor had died, and that due to "rotten luck" he had lost the address of his new sponsor. He wanted to know if the department could help him find the address.[138] Submitting the letter to the State Department, Interior wrote: "Matter comes within the jurisdiction of your department (State). Mr. Rosenthal's communication is referred to you for whatever action you feel it merits."[139]

Whatever action the State Department felt Rosenthal's case merited, it was too late. The war was well under way in Europe. Within a couple of months, emigration from Germany was prohibited. By December, the United States had entered the war. The ultimate fate of the Neustadt Jews "is clouded in discrepancies among the records," but it seems that on September 6, 1942, at the latest, the Jewish community of Neustadt (at that stage forcibly relocated to a different village) came to an end. Ten months earlier, Rosenthal and his wife were deported to a place unknown, where they perished.[140]

About 150,000 refugees, most of them Jewish, were able to reach the United States before Pearl Harbor, and perhaps 100,000 more came during and after the war. This was more than the number of refugees admitted by any other nation, but it was a very small number.[141] By 1945, six million Jews—two-thirds of the European Jewish population in 1939—had been murdered as part of Hitler's final solution. In 1952, eulogizing Harold Ickes, Cohen wrote the following:

> Perhaps, if fate had allowed a little more time for action the [Alaska Development Plan] might have cleared the Congressional obstacles laid in its path by isolationist North Carolina Senator Reynolds and other prophets of hatred against everything European. Perhaps, if some distinguished Zionist leaders had not regarded this program as a diversionary

scheme to block the settlement of Palestine; perhaps if some of Secretary Ickes' own lieutenants handling Alaskan affairs had not thrown their weight against the plan in numberless obscure ways,—perhaps a few hundred thousand victims of the Hitler Terror might have escaped to set- tle our northern wilderness. Perhaps there would today be a bastion of hardy souls and developing industries along our still vacant Northern frontier. But, whatever be the reason, America's golden opportunity faded in the northern twilight. . . . Somewhere in the heavens there still roll the echoes of [Ickes's] words of welcome to the world's dispossessed, some day perhaps to burst with fresh force upon ears that will yet hear.[142]

CHAPTER 7

The Intellectual Equipment
of a Generation

Democracy

The barbarities of totalitarianism affected American social scientists personally and professionally. Having devoted the early decades of the twentieth century to challenging absolutist theories in law, politics, and morals, American intellectuals in the late 1930s were forced to face the modern dilemma head on: was democracy as embodied in the American form of government ethically superior to other regimes? Could American democracy evade totalitarianism?[1]

Catholic thinkers recommitted to absolute moral values, describing a direct connection between ethical relativism, of which legal realists were often accused, and totalitarianism. To them, Thomistic rationalism, "by logically demonstrating the existence of God as the creator and supreme law-giver," offered "an absolute justification" for a democracy based on natural law and what they saw as its "consequent doctrine," natural rights.[2]

But most American intellectuals were not persuaded by the absolutist rhetoric. While many abandoned the social sciences' behaviorist position, which emphasized the ethical neutrality of scientific studies, they continued to think that "there was no intellectually legitimate way to demonstrate the truth of a moral judgment" and refused to endorse moral absolutism. In fact, they drew a connection between absolutism and authoritarianism, on the one hand, and between science and Western democracies, on the other. Choosing a middle ground between relativism and absolutism, they argued that the ethical goodness of American democracy was empirically demonstrable and called for studies of the working of democracy to demonstrate its virtue. Theirs was a "naturalistic and relativistic theory of democracy."[3]

Naturalist theories were not predicated on a "specific ethical theory or philosophical system." Viewing philosophical absolutism as "the real enemy of democracy," naturalists argued that "only social theories that recognized all truths, including ethical truths, as tentative, changing, and uncertain could support and justify democratic government." Furthermore, they proclaimed that ethical theories were important for the existence of democracy only as far as they were "reflected in a society's cultural forms." Democracy became "a social organization which celebrated diversity in all forms and on all levels." It was justified "not because anyone could prove or demonstrate certain ethical propositions, but because the idea of an absolute moral demonstration was itself a rational impossibility."[4]

So described, naturalism not only offered an ethical justification for democracy, it also described "the kind of cultural foundation that a democracy demanded"—democracy could embrace diversity because individuals in a democratic society shared a common culture. In turn, cultural consensus could only arise in a "philosophically relativistic and socially pluralistic society that allowed freedom and cherished diversity."[5]

Cohen's work at the turn of the 1940s followed similar lines. His writings on immigration stressed the important contributions of diverse cultures, races, and religions to the success of the American democratic experiment. According to Cohen, a reciprocal relationship existed between tolerance and freedom. Without diversity of interests, democracy could not thrive; in turn, diverse cultures, races, and religions could only flourish under a democratic regime. America could be a haven for European refugees, and the refugees would save American institutions.

Cohen was unwavering in his support for the American ideal of democracy, which he interpreted as promoting individual and social integration. Yet, unlike the naturalists, Cohen continued to search for an ethical foundation for democracy. He wanted to construct an ethical theory that would recognize the multiplicity of values in modern society but would not treat all of them as equally valid. This was the subject of his 1939 article, "The Relativity of Philosophical Systems and the Method of Systematic Relativism." It served as an anchor for Cohen's continuing work in the field of federal Indian law, specifically the *Handbook of Federal Indian Law* (*Handbook*). It also grounded his endeavors, particularly under the auspices of the Institute of Living Law that he helped create, to protect the workings of American democracy and to extend its benefits to the world. In this latter project, Cohen urged opening American borders to refugees and interpreting American law to protect the civil liberties of all individuals. He also engaged in elaborate studies of totalitarian propaganda and of plans for the governance of postwar Europe.

Systematic Relativism

In the early 1930s, Cohen tried to alleviate the tensions created by relativism in culture, politics, and philosophy by stressing the importance of groups as forums where individuals received meaning for their ideas and actions. By the late 1930s, such an emphasis was no longer sufficient. Cohen wanted to formulate an ethical theory that would recognize the multiplicity of value systems and attempt to encompass as many systems as possible.

In "The Relativity of Philosophical Systems," Cohen elaborated his new alternative. It rested on the assumption that while philosophical systems were different in form, that is, in "structure, or perspective, or emotional value, social symbolism or practical usefulness," they were compatible if not identical in content. If in "Transcendental Nonsense" Cohen had called for the redefinition of concepts based on a variety of interrelated particular and collective experiences, in 1939 he argued that the meaning of concepts depended on multiple external systems of reference. Legal change thus required not only the redefinition of legal reality but also the reconstitution of different legal systems as more inclusive. The legal philosopher's task was to correlate propositions in different systems and ultimately formulate an all-encompassing jurisprudential system.[6]

Cohen did not think the task was difficult. As he explained, legal philosophers merely needed to learn how to increase the scope of existing legal and philosophical systems, because when "divergent systems" grew more inclusive, they began to resemble each other. As Cohen further elaborated, the possibility of enlarging systems was not only philosophically plausible but also politically important. It pointed to a "principle of logical tolerance" based on an acceptance of diversity and change.[7]

Cohen's argument had political, social, and cultural significance. For one thing, John Collier described Cohen's approach as offering "the pluralistic way of looking at things," that is, the view that "we unify the disunited world . . . by accepting disunity as being properly of the nature of things."[8] Cohen, reflecting perhaps his father's critique of pluralism, did not like the label "pluralistic," but he appreciated Collier's understanding. In his response, Cohen wrote:

It is because I don't want to see either black or white suppressed or liquidated that I oppose any absolutism which would make either white or black "false," "unreal" or "secondary." It is perhaps because I . . . love . . . diversity and "irrepressible conflicts" that I reject absolutism.[9]

According to Cohen, conflicts had to be stabilized lest they end "in the annihilation of one side or both." "I think," Cohen concluded his letter to Collier, that "the relativist approach . . . justifies the stable kind of conflict that we find in music, art or mathematics, where neither side is ever annihilated."[10]

In short, Cohen's systematic relativism was an attempt to articulate a universal ideal, an integrated system that would include all particular systems of reference. It accepted cultural pluralism but rejected separatism, that is, the idea that different cultures were detached from each other. It opposed the forced assimilation of all cultural systems into one but envisioned all systems becoming one. It was motivated, at least in part, by Cohen's sense of identity as a Jewish American. Eager to be part of the polity, especially in the face of European totalitarianism and the many objections to his plans to bring refugees to America, Cohen wanted to define a middle position between assimilation and separatism. While "The Relativity of Philosophical Systems" had not worked out all the practical details of his philosophical argument, Cohen's work in the early 1940s, especially his work on the *Handbook*, attempted to do so.

The Handbook of Federal Indian Law

Federal Indian law was created with the new republic. In 1778, the United States initiated treaty-making with Indian tribes, the Constitution expressly mentions Indians, and in 1790 Congress passed the first Indian Trade and Intercourse Act. In the 1820s and 1830s, Chief Justice John Marshall defined the boundaries of Indian property rights, and in 1834 Congress formally defined Indian country as a zone within the boundaries of the United States where special laws applied. By 1846, the term Indian had a particular legal meaning, conveying particular status on individuals within the United States. And while Congress stopped making treaties with Indian tribes in 1871, not only had 348 treaties by then been ratified, but Congress also continued to approve negotiated agreements with Indian tribes.[11] By the 1930s there was thus a fully developed federal Indian law, including treaties, statutes, cases, and administrative decisions. Yet, given the multiplicity of sources and their complexity, it was not easily accessible.

Opportunity

The opportunity to make federal Indian law more accessible surfaced during the autumn of 1938. Carl McFarland, assistant attorney general, and Charles E. Collett, chief of the Trial Section of the Lands Division, asked Cohen to organize and head a survey of federal Indian law. The survey involved the compilation of statutes dealing with Indians that had never been compiled or codified hitherto, and their annotation with reference to cases, attorneys' general opinions, and solicitors' opinions. Based on these materials, a handbook was to be prepared for the legal and administrative officers of the Indian Service who, before 1938, had to search for legal authorities in hundreds of scattered sources. The work began, after some deliberation, as a cooperative project of the Justice Department's Lands Division and Interior under Cohen's supervision.[12] "I've finally become an Indian chief," Cohen wrote to his father, "—Chief of the Indian Law Survey, Dep't of Justice."[13]

Cohen recognized that "systematizing this law and preparing a comprehensive handbook on the subject" were "of peculiar difficulty." No treatise on the subject had ever been written, and, as Cohen had learned in the preceding five years, the law relating to Indian affairs was complex and difficult.[14] However, the survey's potential uses and the proposed handbook made the endeavor worthwhile.

Cohen envisioned a long-lasting, evolving book, similar to textbooks in other fields of law. It would explain the historical development of the laws as well as the legal interests of those affected by them. It would examine federal and state regulation of Indian affairs as well as changing Indian customs and laws. A statute for the American ideal of democracy, as Cohen viewed it, the handbook was meant to familiarize lawyers with the diverse aspects of Indian law. Cohen also hoped that together with the files of the broader survey, which included mimeographed collections of treaties, statutes, presidential letters, and departmental opinions, the handbook would help restore an age-old heritage to its warranted status. Federal and state laws, judicial and administrative decisions would then aim to fulfill the promise of this tradition.[15] Those engaged in the project, including his wife Lucy, soon realized that it was "monumental in its scope."[16]

Between Justice and Interior

Not everyone shared Cohen's aspirations. While Interior wanted to help Indian tribes understand their legal rights and how to exercise them, Justice wanted the work to help it respond to the many Indian land claims that were pending in the Court of Claims. (These claims amounted to "more than two billion dollars in face value.")[17] Cohen's eagerness (and Interior's willingness) to protect Indian tribes' rights aggravated many Justice officials. They believed that the handbook should be written to assist Justice attorneys litigating cases against Indians. They wanted to know what limited obligations the government had toward Indians, not what Indian rights were.[18]

Cohen's prophecy during the initial deliberations, that "this project would be resented by certain Justice Department employees," was quickly realized. From the start, Justice raised a variety of bureaucratic obstacles.[19] Then, as McFarland, who had a keen interest in the project, left the department and as World War II loomed on the horizon, "there wasn't much interest in this 'Indian thing.'"[20]

On August 3, 1939, Assistant Attorney General Norman M. Littell appointed an advisory committee to review the work on the handbook as it progressed. The committee was to confer with Cohen and to reach an agreement "as to the choice and arrangement of subject matter and the distribution of emphasis throughout this manual." The committee was also to develop "a satisfactory preliminary outline of the manual upon which the work [could] proceed with satisfaction to all parties interested in it."[21]

The committee's conclusions shocked Cohen and his team. Robert H. Fabian, chairman of the committee, wanted a trial manual for use by the Lands Division and discredited any thought of other manuals, specifically a prophylactic manual as Interior had in mind. According to Fabian, there was no value to Justice in an academic or administrative treatise or in long historical details. Justice wanted a book explaining how to win Indian cases, not an exegesis of the development and theoretical underpinnings of federal Indian law.[22]

Fabian and his committee, with Theodore Haas dissenting, also insisted that the federal government's concerns should determine each chapter's scope and content. They wanted the handbook to explain the extent to which the government was required to protect the Indians and the means it could use to do so and nothing more. While Cohen titled a chapter "Property Rights of Individual Indians," Fabian proposed changing it to "Rights of the United States with respect to Property Rights of Individual Indians."[23]

Those active on behalf of Indians were appalled. In his dissent from the committee report, Haas insisted that "as guardian of the Indians," the government had to be "acquainted with all of the rights and duties of its Indian wards" and with their historical origins, "even though there [might] not be any immediate need for it to take any legal action." Haas emphasized that such acquaintance would "prevent much litigation and . . . assist in law enforcement . . . [and] in the formulation of intelligent policies."[24]

Similarly, Cohen's response to the committee's report stressed that federal Indian law implicated not only the federal government's interests but also the interests of states, fiduciaries, attorneys, homesteaders, lessees, and contractors. How useful could a handbook be if cases involving Indian law, but in which the United States was not a party, were eliminated? Cohen asked. Then, using objectivity as a weapon, Cohen declared that, given the complexity of interests involved, the handbook had to offer an objective treatment of the law governing conflicts of interests rather than serve as a defense manual for one party only.[25]

Fighting a lost battle, Cohen was willing to concede that "most of the book . . . [should] stress current litigation." But he refused to allow the committee to determine that chapters or sections should be eliminated because the Trial Section did not find them valuable. The committee's view, Cohen pointed out, was "an extreme of bureaucratic provincialism."[26] Even in the face of defeat, Cohen remained confident and certain of his convictions. Concluding his memorandum to Fabian, he boldly wrote:

> I should like to take the opportunity to note that the majority of the Committee apparently contemplates a work very different from that which the undersigned was commissioned to prepare. . . . My own judgment, which is based upon a certain amount of experience in book writing generally and in Indian litigation and prevention of Indian litigation, is that a book based upon the principles laid down by the Committee majority . . . would be impossible to write and very nearly useless when written. I do not contemplate writing that sort of volume.[27]

Termination

Cohen's arguments fell on unreceptive ears. Without consulting with him, as it was required to do, the advisory committee recommended to Littell, ex parte,

that "all further work on the manual" be discontinued "forthwith." Their accusations were harsh: "All of the material submitted gives evidence of inadequate
research and lack of experience in the preparation of a law book designed to
serve as a complete and accurate handbook for lawyers engaged in actual litigation." Their main concern was Cohen's expansive view of Indians' rights in
land, water, and natural resources. "The preliminary drafts," the committee told
Littell, "give rise to the query of whether the manual may seriously embarrass
the sponsors of the project."[28]

On October 31, 1939, eight months into the project, with Cohen's rejoin-
der to the committee ignored, he was called before Littell, who advised him
that "he was dissatisfied with the work of the project and had determined to
put an end to it." On the following day, Cohen was "publicly relieved of [his]
command in the presence of [his] staff, which was then assigned to various
other units of the Lands Division."[29] Littell ordered the files inaugurated by the
survey completed under the direction of the chief of the Trial Section, who was
also assigned the responsibility of keeping them up to date and accessible to attorneys in the division.[30] Attacks on Cohen's scholarship and his character "before [his] superiors in the Interior Department and before various senators and
other officials" followed the termination of the project.[31]

For the most part, Littell, who lacked knowledge of Indian law or interest in
it, was troubled by the use that Indian tribes could make of the proposed handbook.[32] In April, while expressing some concerns about the necessity of including chapters on criminal procedure and Indian claims, Littell supported the
project. In light of the litigation pending in the Lands Division and other legal
problems incident to Indian affairs as well as the complexity of Indian law, Littell thought that a carefully prepared manual on Indian law "would be of inestimable value as an aid to government counsel, as well as to administrative officials and legal advisers in the Indian service."[33] Only weeks before he
discontinued the project, Littell stated that the work was "very interesting,
and . . . quite valuable."[34]

Having read his committee's report, however, Littell became concerned
about potential uses of the handbook. To the attorney general he explained that
the work on the handbook was terminated "because the drafts of chapters submitted were of such inferior quality that no practicable amount of revisions
would make them adequate to serve the needs of attorneys either in [Jus-
tice] . . . or . . . Interior."[35]

The handbook's staff was dismayed. Many wrote to Cohen stating how
much they enjoyed working with him.[36] Meanwhile Cohen sought to convince Littell to reverse his decision. In a hasty response to the charges against
him, which he wrote on October 31, Cohen concluded that "for reasons quite
other than those proposed in the memorandum of criticism, [he] should be
very glad to see the responsibility of the Department of Justice for [the] work
terminated, and the task of completion transferred to the Interior Department."[37] Yet, in a much calmer follow-up, written on November 1, he asked
Littell "in view of the erroneous statements and serious omissions in the mem-

orandum of criticism upon which [he had] relied, . . . to reconsider [his] announced determination in this matter, either upon the basis of a first-hand investigation . . . or on the basis of an independent inquiry by a person who [had] no possible interest in the termination of this project, such as the Chief of the Legislative Section, or the Chief of the Condemnation Section in this Division."[38]

"Dolce far niente"

Littell was not responsive, but Cohen's superiors at Interior were. Unimpressed by Littell's accusations, Acting Secretary E. K. Burlew advised Littell that in view of their knowledge of Cohen's prior work, Solicitor Margold and Acting Solicitor Frederic Kirgis found it difficult to accept the view that the material submitted was "hopelessly worthless." They "requested an opportunity fully to examine into the matter on the merits."[39] Following this examination, which repeated some of the criticisms but described them as reflecting the preliminary nature of the draft, Interior and its "pro-Indian" lawyers took over the project, putting Cohen again in a supervisory role, which included the authority to determine what material was important and what were disputed points of law.[40]

Cohen was happy to be back at Interior. Foregoing the additional salary was a "light cost to pay for the privilege of working once more for superiors who [knew] enough about [his] work to praise it intelligently instead of repeating, in parrot-like fashion, charges of disgruntled employees which show[ed] on their face that they emanate from prejudice, or ignorance, or both." Indeed, Cohen believed that the working conditions at Justice were so "inconsistent with ordinary standards of efficiency, economy and fair play in Government service" as to embarrass the administration if they became publicly known.[41]

Cohen and his team completed the *Statutory Compilation of the Indian Law Survey: A Compendium of Federal Laws and Treaties Relating to Indians* in 1940. Forty-seven staff members and contributors then completed the *Handbook*. It was officially released on August 25, 1941 under Interior's auspices.[42] In a congratulatory memorandum, Attorney General Jackson expressed regret over the differences of opinion between Justice and Interior and asked for a copy of the manual for the Lands Division's usage.[43]

As to Cohen, having just published "a year and a spring of [his] existence all wrapped up neatly in buckram and with thousands of footnotes,"[44] he was "trying to regain the mark of a civilized man," that is, "the capacity to doubt one's own first principles, which [had] entirely evaporated in the course of a year's strain of battle . . . over the [*Handbook*] . . . with colleagues, whose livelihood and prestige were threatened by the publication of trade secrets."[45] He did get "a certain mean personal satisfaction out of the fact that the Department of Justice, which tried to persuade the Secretary that no useful Handbook could be completed under [his] guidance," was anxious to secure hundreds of copies once the work was finished. "It was a tough and dirty fight while it lasted," Cohen concluded, "and the ensuing *dolce far niente* [sweet doing-nothing] is without blemish."[46]

Federal Indian Law and the Ideal of a Pluralist Democracy

Writing in retrospect, Felix Frankfurter observed that the *Handbook* was an attempt to bring "meaning and reason out of the vast hodge-podge of treaties, statutes, judicial and administrative rulings, and unrecorded practice in which the intricacies and perplexities, the confusions and injustices of the law governing Indians lay concealed."[47] While the *Handbook* did not presume to be encyclopedic, it was, as the editors of its 1982 edition noted, "a thorough and comprehensive treatise that attended to virtually every nook and cranny of the field."[48]

On its face, Cohen's analysis was informed by his realist (or functional) jurisprudence. It combined a historical approach, a systematic analysis of the different aspects of federal Indian law, and an examination of the actual functioning and consequences of legal rules and concepts. Reiterating the lessons of Cohen's scholarship, the introduction to the *Handbook* emphasized that it was not sufficient to study the law in books. Rather, it was necessary to study the law in action "which courts and administrators and the process of government have derived from the words of Congress."[49]

More deeply, Cohen's analysis was informed by his principle of systematic relativism. The *Handbook* examined not only how judges, administrators, and legislators viewed particular problems pertaining to Indian tribes but also how the Indians viewed these problems and their solutions. Cohen emphasized that such comparative studies and analysis were important to addressing the divergences of values that were common when groups with different traditions and experiences came in contact.[50]

Underlying Cohen's method of systematic relativism was his ethical ideal of socialized morality with its emphasis on the possibility and potential of social integration. The *Handbook* promoted the idea that the government's role was to bring about social integration by protecting individual and group rights. The foreword and introduction [drafted by Cohen and signed by Ickes and Margold, respectively] stressed that the *Handbook* was meant to assist the Indians in protecting collective rights they had due to their status as a political group as well as their position as a racial minority.[51] Cohen's acknowledgments suggested that this goal was grounded in "a set of beliefs that [formed] the intellectual equipment of a generation,"

> a belief that our treatment of the Indian in the past is not something of which a democracy can be proud, a belief that the protection of minority rights and the substitution of reason and agreement for force and dictation represent a contribution to civilization, a belief that confusion and ignorance in fields of law are allies of despotism, a belief that it is the duty

of the Government to aid oppressed groups in the understanding and appreciation of their legal rights, a belief that understanding of the law, in
Indian fields as elsewhere, requires more than textual exegesis, requires
appreciation of history and understanding of economic, political, social,
and moral problems.

These beliefs, Cohen concluded, represented the influence of "the American
mind" of his generation on "one tiny segment of the many problems" facing
modern democracy.[52]

A Set of Beliefs: A Group Right to Be Different

The set of beliefs that Cohen enumerated in his author's acknowledgments
formed his democratic ideal. In 1934, his vision for the IRA focused on the
government's obligation to protect Indian welfare. In the early 1940s, Cohen
argued that "the Federal Government undertook to protect . . . not only the
welfare of the Indians—a slippery phrase which might have been twisted to
justify a governmental oppression worse than that of private oppressors—but
the *rights* of the Indians."[53] More broadly, Cohen wanted to demonstrate that
the government had an affirmative duty to protect the rights of different
groups in society. Cohen was in a unique place to assess this obligation. As he
pointed out in the early 1940s, "probably the most vigorous defense of the
rights of a racial minority" within American jurisprudence could be found in
judicial decisions that challenged federal, state, and private actions involving Indian rights.[54]

What Cohen had in mind were not merely the rights that Indians could
claim as citizens, but also the rights arising out of their special legal status. These
rights included the right of self-government (subject only to absolute constitutional prohibitions such as the prohibition against slavery),[55] certain civil liberties enumerated in special statutes and administrative practices as well as the
civil liberties of every other minority group, and rights in Indian property.[56] As
the *Handbook* proclaimed, federal Indian law was based on four principles: the
political equality of races, tribal self-government, federal (rather than state) sovereignty in Indian affairs, and governmental protection of Indians.[57]

While drawing on federal Indian law, Cohen did not limit his normative
conclusions to the particular rights of Indian tribes. For one thing, the *Handbook* examined the civil liberties of Indians not only as a political but also as a
racial group. More important, the *Handbook* stressed the need to eliminate oppression against racial minorities in general. Because, as Cohen pointedly explained:

Oppression against a racial minority is more terrible than most other
forms of oppression, because there is no escape from one's race. The victim of economic oppression may be buoyed up in the struggle by the
hope that he can improve his economic status. The victim of religious

oppression may embrace the religion of his oppressors. The victim of political oppression may change his political affiliation. But the victim of
racial persecution cannot change his race. For these victims there is no
sanctuary and no escape.[58]

Given his experiences with the Alaska Development Plan, Cohen well knew
that the victims of racial oppression had no sanctuary and no escape, even in
the United States. He was thus determined to convince his audience that "the
asserted right to be immune from racial discrimination lies at the heart of
[American] democratic institutions." His reasoning was pragmatic: Americans
were as prone to bigotry and racism as other nations, but because American society was composed of multiple minority groups, each of which worried about
particular discriminatory laws, they all agreed upon the right not to suffer
racial discrimination.[59]

"The right to be immune from racial discrimination"

The 1940s were a transformative decade in the development of the modern
discourse of civil rights. In the early half of the twentieth century, legal scholars associated rights with economic and social needs, specifically the rights of
individuals to work, to livelihood, to social insurance, and to economic independence. The "cultural politics of the 1920s," including the rebirth of the Ku
Klux Klan and the passage of restrictive immigration laws, turned American intellectuals away from direct engagement with racial problems. Race and culture
were seen as divisive issues, especially after racial and cultural battles almost destroyed the Democratic Party in 1924. But in the second half of the twentieth
century, the concept of civil rights became associated with the rights of ethnic
and religious minorities, specifically the *right to be different*. The intellectual shift
from class to identity happened in the 1940s.[60]

Several factors helped turn the attention of lawyers, legal scholars, and government officials from the rights of labor to the rights of ethnic and racial minorities, including apprehension about the potential spread of European totalitarianism, fears of Japanese propaganda directed at African Americans, and
increased African American organization and protest. Despite the combined ascendance of both racial and labor related rights during the 1940s and the strong
correlation between racial discrimination and economic inequality, the concept of liberty in the postwar years became associated with the right not to suffer racial and ethnic discrimination. The concept of social and economic citizenship gradually lost its primacy.[61]

The shift from social and economic rights to racial and ethnic equality was
paralleled by a change in the perception of the role of the three branches of
government in protecting civil rights. In the early twentieth century and during the New Deal, legal scholars emphasized the role of the executive and legislative branches in promoting social and economic rights. With totalitarianism
in Europe, legal scholars grew concerned about the relationship between sta-

tism and tyranny.[62] Limiting the power of the legislative and executive branches became the underlying theme of scholarly writings about rights. (For instance, Robert Jackson indicated that the differences between Justice and Interior over the *Handbook* reflected the differences between the needs of the administrative and litigation branches of the government.)[63]

Moreover, if the state could become overpowering, so could groups and institutions. The early twentieth-century pluralist image of the state, with its collectivist undertones, rapidly came into disrepute, and legal scholars and political theorists turned their attention to the defense of the individual. Thus, the 1940s also witnessed a shift of intellectual and political focus from collective rights, specifically the workers' right to organize, to individual rights.

By the postwar years, these transformations—from class to ethnicity, from civil rights as an affirmative obligation of the state to civil rights as constraints on the government, from collectivism to individualism—were complete. The concept of civil rights was no longer associated with an affirmative obligation of the government to protect individuals and groups; rather, it was associated with the (liberal) judicial role of imposing constitutional constraints on the government to prevent it from violating individual liberties. This latter concept was articulated in a footnote in *United States v. Carolene Products Co.* (1938) and emphasized in the decisions of the Warren Court, the champion of a vision of democracy that focused on individual rights and liberties.[64]

"A principle of logical tolerance"

Cohen's approach was different. While recognizing the importance of preventing the government from discriminating against members of racial and ethnic minorities, he remained committed to the idea that the government had an affirmative obligation to protect social and economic rights. Furthermore, Cohen never abandoned the pluralist vision of the modern state, with its correlative emphasis on the executive branch's role. As the NAACP and others appealed to the courts to eliminate segregation and discrimination against African Americans, Cohen called on the judiciary as well as the legislative and executive branches to protect different groups in American society.

Fully embracing the ideas that groups were the bases for political and legal analysis and that the government had an affirmative obligation to protect diverse groups (and, through them, individuals), Cohen's work in the early 1940s sought to formulate a universal conception of group rights that would protect both political and economic groups and the needs of ethnic and religious minorities. He believed that by protecting group rights the government could promote social integration.

Cohen relied on his method of systematic relativism (the principle of logical tolerance) and its description of all concepts as relative to their context to argue that a conception of group rights was compatible with the American tradition of individual rights. As he explained in "The Relativity of Philosophical Systems":

Is it significant to ask whether I am *really* an individual or a great many individuals or only a part of some bigger individual? The thesis here advanced would require us to maintain that this question is invalid, that individuality is relative to system, that any group may be an individual from some viewpoint, that any individual may be a group from some viewpoint. . . . What we call a principle of individualism is, in effect, a formula for designating units of operation within a rational system. If alternative systems are valid, alternative principles of individuation are likewise valid.[65]

The comparable nature of individuals and groups, and thus the compatible nature of individual and group rights, justified of expanding the legal system through legislation and administrative action to include and protect the voices of various groups.

This was also the premise of Cohen's socialized morality. It, too, saw a correlation between the individual and the group. If traditional morality presupposed the metaphysical dogma that the individual was "an ultimate unity and society an ultimate plurality," Cohen's socialized morality rested on the metaphysical dogma that there was "something of the unity of the individual in society itself and something of the plurality of society in the individual life." By admitting that the social integration of diverse interests was similar to the adjustment and integration of conflicting interests in an individual life, Cohen's socialized morality made it easier for traditional understandings of society normatively to endorse pluralism.[66]

Cohen's systematic relativism and his socialized morality rejected theories centered on the individual because, as Cohen's argument implied, these theories resisted pluralism. Some positively denied pluralism, others normatively urged moral consensus as an attractive ideal. Still others created procedural mechanisms that could presumably constrain pluralism.[67] Instead, Cohen wanted to guarantee that the law favored solutions that encouraged the flourishing of diverse group ideas, beliefs, and values; he wanted law to promote solutions that would sustain the individual as a modern social being in a pluralist society. Accordingly, every law had to be examined in light of its effects on the enterprise of social integration. As Cohen explained in 1942, "Today, more than ever before, we need to study the legal relations that have served to bind together in common cause and common effort peoples of different races, different creeds, different social structures, and different ways of life." In so doing, he further emphasized, "we cannot afford to overlook the relations of the United States to the Indian tribes within our territory."[68]

Group Rights and Social Integration

Like many Jewish Americans, Cohen held a very positive image of the American democratic experience. Accordingly, he stressed that "the right to be immune from racial discrimination by governmental agencies" was "a moral right implicit in the character of democratic government" as well as affirmed by the Fifth, Fourteenth, and Fifteenth Amendments to the U.S. Constitution and, with respect to Indians, in a series of statutes and treaties.[69] Yet Cohen's argument reached deeper. At the dawn of the 1940s, Cohen had an emotional need to believe that an affirmative governmental duty to protect minority (individual and group) rights was both a fundamental legal principle and an already existing feature of the American experience. This duty formed the core of his belief in the possibility of social integration.

When he joined the New Deal, Cohen saw on Indian reservations a socialist structure that he wished the nation as a whole would imitate. In the 1940s, as he was seeking to promote his ideal of systematic relativism, especially his argument that the government had to protect group rights, he found supporting evidence, again, on Indian reservations. Cohen argued that a long line of conquerors, from the Spaniards to the federal government, had recognized tribal rights. American Indians were clearly widely oppressed under different colonial regimes, but Cohen asserted that "the oppression was in defiance of, rather than pursuant to, [colonial] . . . laws."[70]

Many have since accused Cohen of endorsing the fiction of conquest, that is, the idea that while tribes initially possessed all the powers of a sovereign nation, after conquest these powers were subject to qualification by the conqueror, like the federal government.[71] Cohen's writings during the early 1940s supported the argument that the conquerors were the arbiters of Indian rights. Yet he did not seek to encourage colonial or, more to the point, congressional intervention in Indian affairs. He truly wanted to defend tribal rights. Why, then, did he endorse the fiction of conquest?

One answer might be that Cohen adopted the fiction of conquest to deradicalize the *Handbook*'s argument in defense of tribal rights. Motivated by his faith in the feasibility of expanding legal and moral systems to create an inclusive system, Cohen hoped that by showing that the protection of tribal rights had been an important aspect of different legal traditions, including the American one, he would gain support for his advocacy of group rights, a claim that reached back to the IRA and "Powers of Indian Tribes." In this context, the historical analysis in the *Handbook* was a means to an end. Cohen hoped that the display of historical evidence would support the protection of tribal rights, including the right to self-government, without appearing to threaten congressional powers amid the growing expansion of federal powers during World War II.[72]

More likely, however, Cohen endorsed the fiction of conquest because it sat well with his jurisprudential approach and his vision of democracy. Cohen came to the New Deal to promote tribal self-government. Almost a decade at Interior and the rise of totalitarianism in Europe helped to shift his focus from sovereignty to racial discrimination. In the late 1930s, Cohen no longer believed that racial tensions would disappear once social or political conflicts were resolved. Rather, his systematic relativism and socialized morality envisioned social and cultural integration as an alternative to discrimination.[73]

In this vein, it seems that Cohen embraced the fiction of conquest not merely because it de-radicalized the message of the *Handbook,* but because endorsing it allowed him to celebrate tribal rights, on the one hand, and to argue, on the other, that tribes were not excluded from the mainstream of American life. It laid a foundation for a more general theory of group rights, a theory that admitted diversity, denied separatism, and made the sovereign the force of social integration. It was a theory that addressed culture and race but could avoid social divisions. For Cohen, the Jewish-American pluralist who at the time was struggling to keep American borders open to European refugees, both the possibility of inclusion and the role of the sovereign in battling racial discrimination were vital. His theory of group rights was meant to address the needs of Indian tribes as well as those of other minorities, including Jewish refugees.

Pluralism and Its Limits

Cohen's theory of group rights, as articulated in his writings in the early 1940s, drew on his ethical conception of the good society, his socialized morality, and on his method of systematic relativism. It grounded human equality in the celebration of human differences. The state was not a neutral night watchman. Rather, the government was charged with the affirmative protection of group rights. Such rights were need-based and historically construed through open social dialogues, defined and redefined through the interaction of particular groups and the relationship between groups and the polity. Furthermore, the obligation of the state to protect these rights did not sanction the trust doctrine, which viewed Indians and possibly other minority groups as wards of the state. Accordingly, the protection of group rights was subject to the limitation that it was for the welfare of those protected and in their interests.[74]

Embracing a conception of group rights, Cohen was faced with a dilemma, a variation on the modernist dilemma triggered by the acceptance of relativism: Should all groups be allowed to celebrate their values? Should groups whose expressed goals were against social integration or oppressive toward other groups be afforded the same protection as historically underprivileged groups? What were, in short, the limits of group autonomy?[75]

Given Cohen's rejection of moral relativism, his theory of group rights did not endorse all group values as equally valid. While struggling to protect the collective rights of Indian tribes and other minority groups in his role at Interior, Cohen tried in his writings and in his role at professional institutions outside the government to define the boundaries of his support for group rights. The task was difficult, not the least because the proponents of greater protection for individual civil rights and liberties in the 1940s were driven not only by fears that totalitarian ideas would reach American shores but also by concerns about repeating the repression of speech and political dissent that followed World War I.[76] Such concerns complicated any attempt to draw limits on group activities, especially group speech. But for Cohen, protecting the rights of certain groups while limiting those of others were intertwined ends. As he saw it, in order to protect the rights of minority groups, one needed to curtail the rights of other groups.

In Defense of American Democracy

In the late 1930s, together with a few friends and Lucy, Cohen formed the Institute of Living Law to defend the American ideal of democracy by promoting "a deeper knowledge and wider public participation in the life of the law." Membership and participation in its activities were open to lawyers and social scientists, including students, regardless of their opinions, as long as they accepted democracy "as an ideal"—specifically, the idea that "democracy, liberty, and tolerance are essential conditions for the achievement of human welfare."[77]

Initial membership was extended to friends and colleagues, many of whom were associated with the legal realist movement and Roosevelt's first New Deal. Cohen anticipated that Herbert Wechsler, Roger Baldwin, Harvey Laidler, Norman Thomas, Karl Llewellyn, Nathan Margold, Charles Beard, Louis Brandeis, Eugene Rostow, Walter Wheeler Cook, Hessel Yntema, and his own father would support the Institute's activities and potentially be active participants.[78]

Informed by legal realism, the institute's working assumption was that the law had to serve society and be evaluated according to "its success or failure in promoting the welfare of human beings of all races, creeds, and classes." Members of the institute wanted to use the legal theories of jurists such as Holmes, Brandeis, and Cardozo as "a powerful weapon in the defense of democracy." Specifically, the institute's members planned to engage in socio-legal research, similar to the Indian law survey that produced the *Handbook*, to explore the achievements and deficiencies of the American democratic experiment. The institute would then report to the American public "legal developments" justifying "public concern and critical analysis." Reporting tools included articles, radio discussions, and bills.[79]

Demonstrating their Progressive proclivities, Cohen and his colleagues were interested in studying a wide range of issues, including the New Deal legislation and its deficiencies, the development of federal bureaucracy, antitrust laws, consumer protection, cooperative laws, rent and housing legislation, transportation laws, and agricultural land tenures. Yet, already showing the impact of the intellectual transformation of the early 1940s, closest to their hearts were the issues of discrimination against historically marginalized groups and the role of law in protecting civil liberties. Their studies were thus intended to examine immigration laws, election laws, the subjection of quasi-public and private agencies exercising social controls to the constitutional guarantees of the Bill of

Rights, the role of international law with respect to minorities and refugees, as well as anti-democratic activities, totalitarian propaganda, and the potential development of a fifth column in the United States (the latter was to be examined in relationship to the refugee problem).[80]

Democracy's Boundaries: "Communists and fellow travelers"

The American left faced many challenges in the 1930s. The Spanish Civil War, the Moscow Trials, and the events preceding World War II, from the Hitler-Stalin Pact to the entry of the United States into the war, all raised serious questions about the American commitment to democratic institutions.[81]

In general, American intellectuals began to express growing fears of tyrannical and statist solutions. While opposition to and fears of dictatorship had always been a part of American ideology and culture, as late as the early 1930s one could still find statements of admiration for autocratic regimes like Mussolini's among American intellectuals. But Hitler's rise to power and the brutality and racism of the Nazi regime, as well as the Italian invasion of Ethiopia in 1935, the Spanish Civil War, and the growing visibility of Jewish refugees from Germany made American intellectuals fervently opposed to any form of dictatorship. By the early 1940s, American scholars were "denouncing autocracy as the greatest threat to democracy and peace" and defining American democracy as the antithesis to totalitarianism.[82]

Cohen's Institute of Living Law endorsed a particular vision of democracy, focusing not on the political process but on the protection of ethnic and religious groups. Cohen described the institute as "a legal aid society not for destitute individuals but for worthy causes." These causes included fighting for "racial and religious tolerance and civil liberties" and combating totalitarian forces. In this vein, the institute opposed "the efforts of vested interests in society" to preserve the status-quo and to repress critiques of the law as well as "all theories of race, religion or sex which attempt to bar any group from participation in law-making, law reform and effective legal criticism."[83]

If minority groups were at the core of the institute's democratic ideal, Cohen and his colleagues viewed advocates of any form of totalitarianism, specifically proponents of Nazi and Fascist ideas and Communists, as democracy's enemies. While Nazi and Fascist propaganda became the subject of many of the institute's studies, which the following sections examine, "Communists, 'fellow travelers,' and others" who did not recognize the methods of democracy as fundamental were excluded from participation in the institute's activities unless "invited to participate in discussions and otherwise to present their views."[84]

Cohen's adamant rejection of communism illustrates the normative limits of his commitment to pluralism. His pluralism was not a theory of ethical relativism; moreover, it was grounded in a strong endorsement of the American ideal of democracy. Not only in the Institute of Living Law, but also in the National Lawyers Guild (NLG), which he helped create and of which he was a member until October 1940, Cohen fought against Communist ideas.[85] As Cohen stated when he resigned from the NLG, in part due to its Communist bent, he believed that communism and fascism were united in their belief that the end justified the means, including lying and assassination, and only differed as to the ends they promoted. It seemed to him that the similarity in means was more important than the divergent ends. Accordingly, to "fight Fascism effectively," one had to "fight Communism."[86] As the following sections on Cohen's fight against Fascism illustrate, for Cohen pluralism was both a means and an end.

Democracy's Boundaries: Exposing Totalitarian Propaganda

For Cohen and his colleagues at the Institute of Living Law, fighting Fascism meant fighting totalitarian propaganda. This they defined as literature seeking to foster racial, ethnic, and religious divisions by attacking particular minority groups or pitting one minority group against another, literature attacking the American way of life or American democratic traditions and institutions, and literature seeking to incite individuals and groups to acts of espionage and sabotage.[87]

Totalitarian propaganda challenged the idea that the strength of American democracy was its diverse society. As Cohen and his colleagues saw it, by focusing on the divisions in American society propagandists hoped to create "a maze of mutually suspicious and antagonistic racial and religious groups" and undermine national unity.[88] Reiterating his *Handbook*'s call for fighting racial oppression, Cohen stressed that cleavages based on ancestry and race could potentially overpower "a nation founded upon the ideal of tolerance and having within it the blood of all races and all nations on earth."[89]

The issue was personal for Cohen. He believed that totalitarianism and anti-Semitism were joined at the root and that Jews had important contributions to make in the fight against totalitarianism. In a speech delivered a few days after the attack on Pearl Harbor, Cohen criticized American Jews who downplayed the anti-Semitic nature of totalitarian regimes and those who urged American Jews not to call attention to themselves in discussions about totalitarianism. He wanted Jews to act. As he pointedly put it,

> No nation crushes the Jews in its midst until it has come to despise reason and morality and the dignity of the human soul, and no nation has yet found a way to live in peace and secure prosperity without these moral qualities. . . . And so I think that we have a special responsibility to help safeguard our country against the forces that would destroy our Republic by undermining the moral principles of liberty and tolerance on which the Republic is based.[90]

Cohen and his colleagues refused to accept that pluralism was a double-edged sword. Recognizing that American society often exhibited racist atti-

tudes, they still wanted to believe that the diversity of cultural, religious, and social interests characterizing American society was the source of its strength.[91]
They thus looked for ways to prevent totalitarian propaganda from having an
impact. Their search forced them to face the limits of their commitment to
pluralism: if the strength of American democracy was its pluralism, how could
one fight certain kinds of propaganda, how could one fight speech, without
undermining the pluralist foundation of modern democracy?

Their solution was typical of the time. In a trilogy of articles, published
under the auspices of the institute, Cohen and his colleagues examined three
methods to combat totalitarian propaganda: suppression, exposure, and response "with a campaign of enlightenment." The method of suppression, which
the law of treason or the Espionage Act could implement, was dismissed not
only as unfit to address the subtlety of totalitarian propaganda but also as potentially over-inclusive. Cohen and his colleagues feared that "suppressive legislation" might be used during crises "to stifle all minority opinions."[92]

The method of disclosure gained the institute's support. It was easily justified as a necessary weapon, and it did not in their view threaten democracy.
After surveying different statutes requiring disclosure of the foreign connections of individuals and organizations disseminating totalitarian propaganda as
well as statutes requiring all aliens in the United States to furnish information
about their activities and statutes requiring subversive organizations to register,
Cohen concluded that they had "not been administered in a partisan or oppressive manner or in such a way as to interfere with the civil liberties of any
one."[93] Moreover, Cohen insisted that while Americans might have the right
"to calumniate [their] fellow citizens of other races or religions," their neighbors and government had, at the very least, the "reciprocal right . . . to investigate and expose the source and the substance of these calumnies." In the face of
Nazi propaganda, such a right had to be exercised to preserve the working of
the American democratic process and the unity of the nation.[94]

Cohen and his colleagues wanted mandatory disclosure to apply not only to
"the activities of foreign agents, subversive organizations, and aliens." They also
wanted to expose the names of authors and sponsors of "anonymous" totalitarian propaganda within the United States.[95] One of the first tasks the institute
undertook was drafting a bill, at the request of Senator Guy M. Gillette, to address "the problem of anonymous scurrilous literature attacking minority races
and religions." The bill required disclosure of the names and addresses of persons "writing, publishing, and circulating" such literature in connection with
political campaigns.[96] Tellingly, the bill did not propose to require general registration of all publications; Cohen and his colleagues feared that such a requirement might subject labor unions to "improper economic sanctions."[97]

The Gillette Bill also provided for certain penalties for lack of disclosure, including barring such anonymous propaganda "from the mails and from impor-
tation into the United States." Furthermore, informed by the assumption underlying many New Deal programs that prohibition alone could not achieve
social reform, the bill proposed to "set up special administrative machinery" to

investigate the organizations and individuals promoting scurrilous propaganda and make its inquiries public. After a series of different titles, this agency was labeled the Office of Minority Relations.[98]

The Office of Minority Relations bore the marks of Cohen's work at Interior. While the president would appoint the director from a list of three submitted by the chancellor and the board of regents of the Smithsonian, it was to be created within Interior and be subject to its secretary's supervision. The office's intended role was not to enforce the law. Rather, its primary purpose would be to study race relations. According to Cohen, this was a field for which Interior was "particularly fitted by its experience in dealing with misunderstandings, prejudices and fallacies affecting Indians and the populations of Puerto Rico, the Hawaiian Islands, and the Philippines, and other minority groups, and in coordinating the relations between these groups and their fellow Americans."[99] Interior was keen on controlling the office, just as it was keen on controlling other programs. Suggestions to place the office in the Department of Justice or State were viewed with suspicion by those in the institute who were familiar with the workings of these departments.[100]

Democracy's Promise: Combating Totalitarian Propaganda

Combating totalitarian propaganda through exposure was based on the belief that "more democracy" was "the cure for evils inherent in democracy."[101] In this vein, the institute's work emphasized that the government was responsible "only for supplying the public with relevant information concerning the connections and techniques of propagandists, relying upon the capacity of the American people to appraise propaganda fairly when the facts are known."[102]

The Gillette Bill received enthusiastic approval from Justice Louis Brandeis, Roger Baldwin of the ACLU, Stephen Raushenbush, Morris Cohen, and Norman Thomas, but it never gained congressional support.[103] Even Felix Cohen, despite his support for the bill, did not view it as the best method of combating totalitarian propaganda.

Unwavering in his embrace of American democratic traditions and institutions, Cohen wanted to pursue a third method of combating totalitarian propaganda, one he labeled "a campaign of enlightenment." Cohen described this method, which assigned a more active role to the government, as "an innovation in the framework of traditional liberalism." It rested on the assumption that it was the responsibility of the government, though not exclusively, to answer "totalitarian lies with democratic truths."[104] Felix and Lucy Cohen examined this method in the last of the three articles on combating totalitarian propaganda.

The Cohens emphasized that they did not have in mind a propaganda agency like the ones established by totalitarian regimes. Rather, they wanted the facts of American democratic institutions to speak for themselves. For one thing, they pointed to the New Deal programs as illustrating the great deeds of American democracy (including the Agricultural Adjustment Administration, which helped farmers maintain "the world's highest level of productive efficiency and the world's highest standard of rural living"; the National Labor Relations Board, which safeguarded "American workers in maintaining the highest wage levels in the world"; and the Tennessee Valley Authority, which helped efficiently to build and operate "the world's greatest dams and power systems"). More important, the Cohens wanted to showcase programs that they described as "helping Americans of diverse races and creeds to overcome ancient animosities in the building and safeguarding of a united nation."[105] Felix Cohen proclaimed the success of such programs because he wanted to believe in their success.

To allow these and other American successes to speak for themselves, Cohen wanted to repeal legislation that barred government agencies from reporting their activities to the public through restrictions and prohibitions on "the hiring of publicity experts, the issuance of magazines or journals, the use of photographs and other newfangled innovations in government printing, [and on] . . . the sale of government publications." He and Lucy concluded their analysis by calling on proponents of free speech to give the United States "the same measure of freedom which the United States allows to its enemies." At least during the war, they wanted Congress to suspend all laws preventing "the government from carrying out an effective counter-offensive against totalitarian propaganda."[106] As Cohen saw it, in the fight for pluralism, substance dominated form.

From a Pluralist Nation to a Pluralist World

While combating totalitarian propaganda was meant to protect the American ideal of democracy, two documents located in Felix Cohen's papers suggest that members of the Institute of Living Law were also interested in appropriating the American democratic ideal to create a new world order. These documents pertain to two proposals: the first involving the Pacific (including territories in the Western Pacific, Thailand, Burma, Malaya, Ceylon, India, Afghanistan, and the interior regions west of China but not including Siberia, Australia, and New Zealand), and the second addressing postwar Europe (excluding England and the Soviet Union). It was expected that these would become models for similar plans for Africa, the rest of Asia, and ultimately the entire international community.[107]

The idea expressed in these documents was simple. Following the New Deal example of using the corporation "as an instrument of social reform" as well as Cohen's mid-1930s *Socialist Constitution for the Commonwealth of the United States*, these proposals advocated the creation of a pluralist world—a world built as a pyramid with multiple incorporated groups at the bottom, followed by states, nations, and ultimately international organizations at the pyramid's top.[108] As demonstrated below, the working assumption of these proposals was the relationship between the strength of American democracy and the diversity that characterized American society and culture. They were meant to encourage the world community to follow the American pluralist model, to build on the multiplicity of groups in society to create strong democratic regimes.

"A Pacific Charter"

The document labeled "A Pacific Charter" declared the international community's responsibility for ending imperialism (conquest, aggression, and domination by governments or private corporations) and for promoting self-government by native groups in the Far East as independent entities or as units in regional federations and larger groupings. It called on the United States, Great Britain, France, Japan, and the Netherlands to relinquish their rights in territorial possessions and encourage native groups to self-govern.[109]

While Cohen believed that local self-government should be immediate and stressed that "there was no such thing as general superiority among cultures," the document reflected the belief that a supervised process of education in self-government was required.[110] To allow for supervision, each area included in the plan was to have a commission composed of members from the area and other regions as well as European and American members. All commissions were to be subject to the supervision of a "Pacific League," which would consist of "self-governing countries and regional federations."[111]

Each commission would have the effective powers of a democratic government, which it would use to teach the different peoples the administrative and technical knowledge required for self-government. Each area would be classified based on its state of development; as it moved from one class to another, its native population would become more active in its governance. Ultimately all regions would be democratically governed, following the model of the U.S. Constitution and the Bill of Rights.[112]

"The New World"

The document called "The New World" was published by the Council for Democracy.[113] The Institute of Living Law provided only comments on the subject. Written by Abraham C. Weinfeld and based on his essay "Towards a United States of Europe," they are worth examining as they embody a particular vision for postwar Europe, a vision that Cohen seemed to have endorsed.[114]

Weinfeld's comments rested on the assumption that Europe would adopt a federal structure and that most states would have a republican structure. Accordingly, while monarchies would be allowed, all states would incorporate a bill of rights to protect the rights of individuals and groups (including due process, the freedoms of speech, religion, and assembly, and the right to be free from discrimination on the account of nationality, race, religion, or sex).[115]

The plan was distinctively pluralist. While the rights of religious minorities were to be protected as they were protected under the U.S. Bill of Rights, it was anticipated that "every national minority" in a European state within the united states of Europe would be "organized as a public corporation," empowered to own property, make contracts, sue and be sued in courts, and levy taxes on its members. The membership of each corporation would "consist of all persons who, at the time of the census, [had] declared themselves to be members of the minority nation." Individuals' declaration would bind their children until they were twenty-one. Once members attained majority, they might cease their memberships by filing a declaration to that effect, waiting for a certain period (most likely six months), and paying all dues accrued up to the end of that period.[116]

The corporations of the different national groups and their members would be treated equally and given "a fair opportunity" to develop their social, cultural, and educational institutions. For example, national minorities would receive "a fair share" of federal and state appropriations for cultural and educational purposes. Furthermore, each such public corporation would "enjoy self-government within its sphere of cultural activities." Each minority would elect a legislative body authorized to legislate within the limited sphere of cultural activities and an executive body "to execute the laws and administer the affairs of the minority." The public corporation would also set up courts to deal with "disputes among members of the minority, touching minority matters only." The language of a minority group that composed five percent or more of the population of a state would be an official language (that is, it might be used "in courts and in all dealings with governmental authorities"). Even where the minority constituted "less than 5% of the population," government announcements were required to be published in its language "in those parts of the country where the minority form[ed] considerable settlements."[117]

It was assumed that the rights of all minorities would be guaranteed by the federal constitution and protected by federal and state courts. It was further recommended that an administrative body, a National Minorities Commission, would be established "to receive all minority complaints in the first instance, hold hearings, and render decisions, appealable to federal courts."[118]

Not surprisingly, special consideration was given to Jews, who were considered both a national minority and a religious group. It was decided that those Jews who chose to form a national minority corporation would be treated as such (including having the autonomy to determine their language), while religious Jews would enjoy "freedom of religious worship and organization, like any other religious group." It was anticipated that at least initially most Jews would choose to be treated as both a national minority and a religious group.[119]

Weinfeld's comments illustrated Cohen's and his contemporaries' pluralist dream. They were also among the last major statements in favor of an international or even a national community predicated upon a pyramid of self-governing groups. With the signing of the United Nations Charter in 1945, the international community brought to an end the experiment that began after World War I with the minorities' treaties of the League of Nations. The pluralist model, which seemed to resemble the League of Nations' approach, similarly ran into disrepute. Rather than protecting group rights, the international legal community became fixated on the need to protect individual human rights.[120]

Pluralism's Demise

At the 1919 Paris Peace Conference, a few delegates suggested requiring all the members of the League of Nations to guarantee the protection of religious and racial minorities within their boundaries. Unfortunately, no agreement was reached among the delegates.[121] Instead of a general obligation, a few treaties, imposed on certain nations, included explicit obligations for the protection of ethnic, national, and religious minorities so as to prevent "inter-state fictions and conflicts."[122]

In addition to protecting minority rights, these particular treaties guaranteed "full and complete protection of life and liberty to all inhabitants of the country or region concerned, without distinction of birth, nationality, language, race or religion." Furthermore, they guaranteed "that all nationals would be equal before the law and would enjoy the same civil and political rights, without distinction as to race, language or religion." Finally, they guaranteed that nationals belonging to minority groups could use their language and have the right "to establish social and religious institutions."[123]

The League of Nations treaties were "unprecedented limitations on national sovereignty under international law." But they were limited in scope. They were politically suspect as they were imposed by the victors on the defeated but not embraced by the victors themselves. They also applied only to a handful of countries, which constantly complained that they were being discriminated against when compared to countries without such obligations. Seeking to remedy these pitfalls, the Assembly of the League of Nations adopted a resolution in 1922 "expressing the *hope* that states not bound by such clauses would nevertheless observe in the treatment of their own minorities at least as high a standard of justice and toleration as required by these clauses." But recommendations for a more general convention determining the obligations of all League members toward minorities were rejected. More important, the treaties were not effective in preventing the rise of Nazism and Fascism. In October 1933, Germany simply withdrew from the League of Nations and the Disarmament Conference.[124]

Hence, by the time American and European intellectuals began to think about a postwar world order, the scheme adopted by the League of Nations was highly criticized. The proposed alternative was informed by the ideal of individual liberties that became dominant in the 1940s, especially in the United States. On January 6, 1941, President Roosevelt brought international and national law together. His State of the Union address, seeking to justify the entry of the United States into the war, announced that "freedom means the supremacy of human rights everywhere." The American support went "to those who struggle to gain these rights or keep them."[125]

Roosevelt's address included his famous assertion of the four freedoms. "In the future days, which we seek to make secure," Roosevelt announced, "we look forward to a world founded upon four essential freedoms": "the freedom of speech and expression, the freedom of worship, the freedom from want, and the freedom from fear." As Roosevelt elaborated, all individuals should have the economic benefits that the New Deal sought to promote (freedom from want), protection against oppression by their own countries and others (freedom from fear), and the classical list of civil liberties enumerated in the Bill of Rights for the U.S. Constitution (as represented by the freedom of expression and freedom of worship). Accordingly, the entry of the United States into World War II was meant not only to fight totalitarianism but also to bring the American democratic ideal to the world.[126]

Roosevelt's address set an ambitious goal for the international community—to protect all individuals, irrespective of race, religion, or national origin. As the Nazis' atrocities were revealed, the idea that the group was the basis for legal and political analysis was no longer viable. Collectivism of any sort seemed threatening. Scholars and world leaders brought individualism to bear upon the ideal of human rights. In 1945, the Charter of the United Nations incorporated the new emphasis, pushed, among others, by nongovernmental organizations in the United States, including several Jewish organizations.[127]

The creation of the United Nations, "envisioned as an international forum in which nations could peacefully resolve their differences,"[128] marked an end of an era. While the League of Nations was concerned about the claims of national minorities, the United Nations was focused on protecting individual human rights. National minorities, especially indigenous communities, received little support from international law for claims that did not involve individual civil and political rights. Article 1 of the United Nations Charter, which dealt with self-determination, was interpreted to apply only to those minorities "colonized from overseas" but not to "national minorities within a (territorially contiguous) state," even if they were subject to colonization and conquest. Article 27 of the International Covenant on Civil and Political Rights (1966), which promised "the right to enjoy one's culture," was interpreted "to include only negative rights of non-interference, rather than the positive rights of assistance, funding, autonomy or public recognition." In effect, it only reaffirmed that national minorities should be free "to exercise their standard rights of freedom of speech, freedom of association, freedom of assembly and freedom of conscience."[129]

Postwar discussions of civil rights and liberties in the United States similarly failed to address the special status of Native Americans. For one thing, in postwar American legal thought, especially after the rights revolution produced by the Warren Court, all individuals were considered equal and all were to be similarly treated. Treating groups (such as Indian tribes) differently was associated with discriminatory practices.[130] Furthermore, as the attention of legal scholars and political theorists turned to the protection of individual rights, "American tolerance for different cultural values, such as community responsibility and tribalism," rapidly diminished. A concept of collective rights was envisioned as being in direct opposition to the idea of individual liberty.[131]

Several decades would pass before the international community and the United States would begin to reassess indigenous communities' right to self-determination.[132] In this context, Cohen's work at Interior and his writings in the 1940s are extremely important. Perhaps because of his experience with Indian tribes or because of his personal struggle to belong to American society, Cohen never abandoned the pluralist vision. Throughout the 1940s, he looked for ways to accommodate the diverse needs of groups in a society committed to individual rights and liberties. His work during these years involved tribes' property claims to land, water, and natural resources. His conception of group rights and needs was thus tied to the issue of aboriginal title.

Applying his pluralist vision to property law, Cohen aimed to accommodate the meanings that particular groups attributed to ownership and occupancy. He wanted American law to embrace different legal ideals. As we have seen, such wishes underlay Cohen's conception of constitutionally protected group rights. Based on that conception, he wanted to remap the geographical terrain of the United States to accommodate the property claims of Native Americans and Alaska Natives. But, as he quickly learned, it was a lost battle. American legal institutions resisted any attempt to remap the terrain of legal definitions, especially the definition of property. Cohen was thus left to reassess his legal pluralist vision of the modern state. As we will see, his attention gradually shifted from the possibility of making legal systems more inclusive to the possibility of creating a dialogue between different legal cultures.

PART IV

Re-Mapping the Terrain,
1941–1947

CHAPTER 8

Property in (Group) Conflict

Dear Felix, Your letter of March 4 was explained to the Hualapais when they gathered to celebrate the first anniversary of the victory in the Hualapai case. Naturally they were all disappointed over the fact that you were unable to come and take part in their celebration. . . . I am sure your ears must have been ringing on that day. Your Indian friends and others really 'poured it on' as they expressed their appreciation of your friendship and your able handling of their interests in the Hualapai case.

Thomas H. Dodge, Superintendent, Hualapai Reservation, to Felix S. Cohen, March 14, 1948 (FSCP 51/773)

Aboriginal Title

Perhaps no other aspect of the relationship between American Indians and the United States had been a source of confusion and conflict more than the processes through which the United States (like other colonial powers) wrested lands from their original Indian owners. Beginning with Chief Justice John Marshall's decision in *Johnson v. M'Intosh* (1823), which divided property rights in Indian lands between the colonizing sovereign's ultimate title and the Indian tribes' occupancy rights, American courts helped legitimate conquest and unfulfilled treaties.[1]

According to Marshall, Indians' occupancy rights existed unless explicitly extinguished by the federal government; they encumbered any federal grant of the lands to others. As Marshall reiterated in *Worcester v. Georgia* (1832), a grant of the lands by itself did not extinguish aboriginal title. Indeed, Marshall went so far as to state that the Indians had to consent to an extinguishment of their title.[2]

Throughout the nineteenth century, the Supreme Court asserted these basic principles of the aboriginal title doctrine. But Indian tribes' visions of ownership and occupancy were sufficiently different from the American cultural understanding of ownership to allow courts to describe Indians as wandering on the land rather than occupying it and thus to justify taking that land, under the rule of law, without consent or compensation. Furthermore, because the federal government could extinguish Indian occupancy rights, many tribes were forced away from their lands. By the 1930s, Indians had lost most of their lands. The IRA attempted to correct historical injuries by reversing the devastating policy of allotment and allowing tribes to own their property collectively. But it did not resolve tribes' claims based on unfulfilled treaties for the sale of their lands. Nor did it protect Indians' title to their lands from being extinguished through future legal interpretations. Cohen's work in the 1940s sought to correct these wants.

As chapter 9 explores, in 1946 Cohen was able to secure the passage of the Indian Claims Commission Act, which dealt with tribal land claims. Though political compromises made it impossible to accomplish Cohen's goals for the act, it represented the culmination of his struggles in the 1940s to introduce aboriginal conceptions of property into American law. If in the mid-1930s Cohen wanted to protect tribal traditions by recognizing their autonomy, and if in the late 1930s he tried to articulate a theory of group rights to accommodate diverse interests, his work in the early 1940s focused on recognizing different cultural understandings of foundational concepts such as "occupancy" and "ownership"; he used culture and history to provide content to his idea of constitutionally protected group rights. His first opportunity to do so came in 1941, when the Supreme Court granted certiorari in the case of the Walapai (or, as they called themselves, Hualapai) against the Santa Fe Railroad Company. As Cohen described the case shortly after the decision was handed down, it was "one of the most important cases ever to reach the Supreme Court in the history of our Federal Indian law."[3]

Aboriginal Occupancy in Lands and Springs: The Hualapai Case

The Hualapai, literally "people of the tall pines," descended from the Hohokam culture. Together with the Yavapai and Havasupai Indians, they occupied north central Arizona for seven centuries, wandering over a large area north of the Mohave Desert to the Grand Canyon and extending their range after they had obtained horses from the Spaniards. The Hualapai (as well as the Havasupai and Yavapai) lived mostly on gathering and hunting, and while they had some knowledge of agriculture and farming, they were unsuccessful at them.[4]

Prior to 1864, whites "settled upon farming lands, commenced mining operations and grazed cattle on lands formerly exclusively used and occupied by the Hualapai Indians." The Hualapai and the white settlers maintained peaceful relations for a while, but with increased settlement, the United States tried to extinguish Indian occupancy rights.[5] On March 3, 1865, a month before the end of the Civil War and only seventeen years after the Mexican cession to the United States of southwest Texas, Arizona, New Mexico, Colorado, Wyoming, Utah, Nevada, and California, an act of Congress provided that "all that part of the public domain in the Territory of Arizona lying west of a direct line from Half-Way Bend to Corner Rock on the Colorado River, containing about seventy-five thousand acres of land, shall be set apart for an Indian reservation for the Indians of said river and its tributaries."[6] The Indians referred to in the act included the Hualapai, though due to want of funds they were forcibly removed onto the Colorado River Reservation only in 1874. "They were brought to the river but were unhappy and ran away almost immediately. In 1875 they were rounded up and brought back to the southern part of the reservation near La Paz, whence they again escaped and went back to Peach Springs." At that time, the Hualapai were allowed to stay near their springs. Eight years later, after "continuing border warfare with Anglo miners and cattlemen," a reservation was created for them there.[7]

Before the Hualapai returned home, an act of July 27, 1866 had granted title to some of their ancestral lands to the Atlantic and Pacific Railroad Company, a predecessor of the Santa Fe Pacific Railroad Company (hereafter Railroad). The 1866 act gave the Railroad title to "the odd-numbered sections of land within specified distances on each side of the line of railroad to be constructed, the specific sections to be identified later."[8] When in 1883 the new reservation was created for the Hualapai in Northwest Arizona, it included lands covered by the railroad grant, which vested on March 12, 1872. The railroad grant also included lands outside the 1883 reservation. Four decades later, in November 1925, the Hualapai asked the commissioner of Indian affairs for a map of their reservation so that they could protect the waters at Peach Springs against trespassers, specifically against the Railroad.[9]

The Hualapai expressed grave concerns about the Railroad's use of portions of their lands and waters both inside and outside their 1883 reservation. They offered ample evidence to show that they had used these areas, specifically Peach Springs, long before the Railroad had arrived. Thus, the Railroad was using the Hualapai's lands without their permission. The Railroad, in turn, claimed title to the odd-numbered sections inside and outside the reservation stemming from the 1866 grant.[10]

In part, the disagreement between the Railroad and the Hualapai had to do with the exact location of Peach Springs—were the waters on odd sections or even sections? More crucial, however, were the definition of aboriginal occupancy rights and how they might be extinguished. If the Hualapai had occupancy rights to the lands and waters of the 1883 reservation (and even outside the reservation) prior to the 1866 grant to the Railroad, then the Railroad received title subject to these rights. The 1866 grant was indeed limited to sections to which "the United States have full title, not reserved, sold, granted, or otherwise appropriated, and free from pre-emption or other claims or rights."[11]

Under American law, for the Hualapai to have recognized occupancy rights, they had to demonstrate that they had exclusively occupied the lands before the grant to the Railroad and that their occupancy rights had not been extinguished by the federal government. Alternatively, they had to demonstrate that the federal government, in treaty, executive order, or administrative act, had granted them such rights. As such an act of government did not exist, discussions of the Hualapai's rights focused on the nature of their occupancy prior to the grant to the Railroad.[12]

The Railroad and the lawyers assigned to the case at Justice and Interior maintained that the Hualapai had no occupancy rights. Even if one accepted, albeit reluctantly, the premise of Chief Justice Marshall's opinions, government attorneys and the Railroad insisted that different rules applied because the Hualapai's territory was part of the Mexican cession. Under the Treaty of Guadalupe Hidalgo, their rights were protected only if they were recognized prior to the cession. The Railroad and the government lawyers proclaimed that the Hualapai had no recognized rights prior to the Mexican cession because they had never possessed or occupied the lands. Instead, they wandered around without a definite home to which an occupancy right could be attached. Mexican and Spanish law did not recognize occupancy rights of wandering people. Neither did U.S. courts. Even if the Hualapai had long used the waters of Peach Springs, as oral testimony from the reservation suggested, so had the Railroad. In fact, the Railroad insisted that its use effectively pushed the Hualapai away. Furthermore, even if the Hualapai had rights in the land and even if the Railroad did not drive them away, the creation of the Colorado River Reservation extinguished their rights and rendered the lands vacant. Thus the grant to the Railroad was not subject to prior occupancy rights.[13]

These arguments prevailed during the 1920s, culminating in a 1925 act that authorized the division of the Walapai Reservation between the Indians and the Railroad.[14] But in 1932, after extensive hearings prompted by protests against the proposed division by Indians and their friends, the chairman of the Senate Indian Affairs Committee asked the secretary of the interior to inquire into the Hualapai's rights in reservation lands claimed by the Railroad.[15]

Interior's inquiry was a turning point. While government attorneys throughout the 1920s did their best to discourage the Hualapai from pursuing litigation, Margold, Cohen, and Collier did their best not only to get the case to the courts but also to win it. They went so far as to argue that the Hualapai had occupancy rights not only to the waters of Peach Springs but also to the entire reservation. In the fall of 1934, shortly after the passage of the IRA, Margold recommended bringing a suit on behalf of the Hualapai.[16]

Margold and his legal team viewed the nature and scope of occupancy rights as dependent on aboriginal conceptions of property and not on a conqueror's recognition. Because Indian customs and traditions determined the

scope of aboriginal title, it did not matter whether the lands so occupied originated in the colonies or in the Mexican cession. Furthermore, as Cohen and
Margold saw it, the laws of the United States, Mexico, and Spain recognized
the rights of wandering tribes. Margold and Cohen also rejected the idea that
the creation of the Colorado River Reservation or the forced removal of the
Hualapai onto it extinguished their title. If the Hualapai could prove that, based
on their tradition, they had occupied the lands prior to the grant, the Railroad's
title would be subject to these rights. Margold's office further concluded that
due to the absence of documentation, the Hualapai's oral evidence had to be
admitted in court.[17]

In late December 1935, at Ickes's recommendation, Justice hired Richard
Hanna, a Santa Fe lawyer with expertise in federal Indian law, as an independent attorney to oversee the Hualapai litigation. When he was hired, Hanna
was sharing a private practice in Albuquerque with the future commissioner of
Indian affairs, William Brophy. In late August 1937, after a few months in which
he studied the file and against the wishes of his superiors at Justice, Hanna filed
his complaint with the U.S. District Court for the District of Arizona. He
hoped to show not only that the entire 1883 reservation belonged to the
Hualapai but also that they did not give up rights to lands outside the reservation. Hanna estimated that the Hualapai ancestral home contained roughly
seven million acres, "extending as far west as the Colorado River on the present California border."[18]

The Railroad filed a motion to dismiss in April 1938, reiterating the claims
it had made throughout the 1920s: The Hualapai were "disunited bands of non-
agricultural nomadic savages who occupied exclusively no definable territory
and no place or places for any great length of time." They had no occupancy
rights under Mexican, Spanish, or American law prior to the creation of their
reservation. Even if they had such rights, the Railroad's evidence demonstrated
that various actions by Congress, including its dealings with the Hualapai and
with the Railroad, had extinguished those rights and opened the lands to white
settlement. Finally, the Railroad stressed that by the early 1920s, its own rights
had vested and been confirmed, beyond challenge, by political authorities.[19]

Judge David Ling agreed with the Railroad. On March 1, 1939, he dismissed
the government's suit, holding that the Hualapai had no rights to the lands
under the laws of Spain and Mexico and thus had no rights under the Treaty of
Guadalupe Hidalgo. As Congress had never granted them rights, they had
none. Furthermore, Ling accepted the Railroad's argument that even if the
Hualapai did have occupancy rights to the lands, such rights had undoubtedly
been extinguished. No evidence could change Ling's position. As he put it, "the
laws of Spain and Mexico, the Legislation of Congress, and the course of administration," all of which he considered "matters of judicial knowledge," determined his conclusion. It was thus "perfectly clear that no evidence adducible
would in any way affect the result of the case."[20]

Justice was happy to abandon the case. Its attorneys were increasingly skeptical about the possibility that a court would find any tribe living in the for-

merly Mexican territory to have occupancy rights like tribes elsewhere in the United States. Assistant Attorney General Norman Littell, who at the time was also fighting Cohen on the *Handbook* and who initially recommended an appeal, determined that the Hualapai had no property rights under Mexican law and that the Treaty of Guadalupe Hidalgo protected only titles valid under Mexican law. Justice was also becoming acutely aware that a holding for the Hualapai would support other tribes' aboriginal title claims against the government. Even if the Hualapai had occupancy rights, Justice concluded that the grant to the railroad extinguished them. Ironically, this possibility was denied by the words of the grant, which specified that Indian title could be extinguished only with the Indians' consent.[21]

Interior would not yield. In mid-July, after a long fight between the two departments, a decision was reached to appeal the case. By the beginning of October, Hanna and his partner Brophy had drafted a brief. But it was not filed. On December 11, 1939, Littell, ignoring the evidence that Hanna and the BIA had collected in support of the Hualapai's claim, filed a short brief with the U.S. Court of Appeals for the Ninth Circuit asking for recognition of the Hualapai's rights in lands inside their 1883 reservation and outside it. Immediately after filing the brief, Littell fired Hanna. Littell had determined to lose the case, and he did.[22]

The U.S. Court of Appeals for the Ninth Circuit rejected the Hualapai's claims with respect to the lands both within and outside the reservation. Curtly noting that the "word 'occupancy' is used interchangeably with 'possession' in appellant's brief," Judge Wilbur concluded that to be recognized by the federal government, the Hualapai's rights had to have been recognized under Spanish or Mexican law. As the Hualapai's rights were not so recognized because the Hualapai were wandering people, an explicit act of Congress was necessary to recognize their possessory rights. As no act of Congress recognized possessory rights of the Indians in Arizona "other than those existing under Mexican law or created by reservations after the Mexican cession to the United States," the Hualapai did not have possessory rights in their lands. Furthermore, according to Wilbur, even if the United States had recognized the Hualapai's possessory rights, subsequent acts of nonrecognition such as their forcible removal onto the Colorado River Reservation extinguished those rights. Like Judge Ling, Wilbur concluded that "evidence of which this court takes judicial notice which cannot be affected or overcome by testimony of possession" demonstrated that the Hualapai did not have occupancy rights to lands other than their 1883 reservation and that their rights in the latter were subject to the Railroad's vested rights to the odd-numbered sections.[23]

Hanna and Brophy wanted Interior and Justice to appeal to the Supreme Court, but attorneys at Justice expressed concern about their ability to help the Hualapai while simultaneously acting as defenders of the government. By the fall of 1940, as "many tribes were suing the government in the Court of Claims and several victories, totaling more than 10 million dollars, had been won in the Supreme Court," Justice "finally realized that they either had to fight or defend Indians." They solved their dilemma by letting Interior take over the Hualapai case. Hanna and Brophy were rehired, and within a few months Margold, Cohen, Hanna, and Brophy had won their first victory—on March 10, 1941, the Supreme Court issued a writ of certiorari.[24]

United States v. Santa Fe Pacific Railroad Company (1941)

"To protect . . . the rights of the Indians"

Interior was eager to protect Indian rights. Turning to Chief Justice Marshall's decisions, Interior's brief insisted that the term *Indian title,* which was used in the 1866 land grant to the Railroad, "had a well-understood meaning"—it meant "Indian possessory right based on aboriginal occupancy, whether or not that occupancy had been recognized by treaty, statute, or otherwise." Interior insisted that expert and Indian testimony demonstrated that the Hualapai were "peaceable, industrious people who engaged in irrigation farming long before white settlers came into the country," that, unless interrupted by troops or settlers, they "maintained permanent villages, settlements, and rancherias with well-recognized ownership rights applied to land and improvements," that their occupancy was continuous, and that they had always claimed the area as their own. Even if congressional recognition of occupancy rights was required, Interior insisted that Congress had granted it by allowing the Hualapai to stay on their lands. According to Interior, unless extinguished or limited by an explicit act of Congress or abandoned by the Hualapai, the Hualapai's possessory rights were "legally enforceable against everyone except the United States." Cohen and his colleagues concluded that Congress did not extinguish the Hualapai's rights and that they did not abandon them. Their appeal on behalf of the band rested upon two causes of action, "the first relating to lands inside, and the second, to lands outside" the 1883 reservation.[25]

Cohen went further. He wanted to refute once and for all the argument that different rules applied to lands originally under Mexican rule. First, Cohen argued that the doctrine of Indian title did not distinguish between the territories that came to the United States under the Mexican cession and those that came in other ways. Furthermore, he stated that "the Spanish and Mexican law accorded to Indian tribes rights of occupancy substantially similar to those accorded generally to Indian tribes by the United States."[26] In an article he published shortly after the decision was handed down, Cohen went so far as to argue that the recognition of tribal occupancy rights in American law developed out of the influences of Spanish law.[27]

The issue was the spirit of the law, not the law in action.[28] According to Cohen, the spirit of Spanish law anchored the four characteristics of federal Indian law (all elaborated in the *Handbook*): First, "the principle of legal equality of the races," which through a series of nineteenth-century legal cases was modified to protect the rights of Indians as "members of special political bodies." Second, "the principle of tribal self-government," which *Worcester v. Geor-*

gia and the doctrine of the law of nations recognized. It dictated that "a weaker power does not surrender its independence—its right to self-government—by associating with a stronger, and taking its protection." Accordingly, tribal decisions governed a wide range of fields of law, including property law, as long as their sovereign powers had not been "modified or repealed by act of Congress or by treaty." Third, "the principle of Federal sovereignty in Indian affairs," according to which federal law, not local or state law, governed the relationship between Indians and non-Indians, including the relationship between the Hualapai and the Railroad. Fourth, "the principle of governmental protection of Indians."[29]

The fourth principle, which included the federal government's responsibility for protecting Indian lands, was especially important for the Hualapai case. "By treaty and by statute," Cohen explained, "the United States undertook to protect the Indian tribes in their possession of vast areas of land." While the common law would not have recognized Indian possession as creating legal title to the lands, Cohen emphasized that such "subtleties of feudal legal theory . . . meant nothing to the Indians." More important was the fact that the Supreme Court had repeatedly upheld that "the Indian right of occupancy and use is as sacred as the fee title." As Cohen pointedly put it, it was "certainly more substantial than the naked legal title which legal theory locates in the Federal Government."[30]

While all of the principles were important for Cohen's vision of the relationship between the government and Indian nations, the fourth principle was vital to his developing theory of group rights. If in the nineteenth century the government was presumed to have protected Indian welfare and if in the 1930s the IRA aimed to protect tribal self-government, in the early 1940s Cohen proclaimed the duty of the federal government "to protect . . . the *rights* of the Indians," including "rights of personality, rights of self-government, and the rights of property." The most important of these protected Indian rights of property was "the right of the tribe to land occupied from time immemorial."[31]

In Court

Cohen was not a litigator. Like many of the New Deal lawyers, his work consisted of developing regulatory policies. The Hualapai case was the first major case on which he worked and, uncharacteristically, he felt uncertain about his ability to use ideas to achieve material results. Margold urged Cohen to argue the case, but Cohen refused. In a revealing letter to his father, written a day after Margold's argument before the Supreme Court, he explained that he "was scared, never having sat through a Supreme Court argument before, much less assisted in or made one."[32]

Cohen's letter suggested a second reason for rejecting Margold's offer—he believed that Margold would be more effective and that he deserved "the honor and prestige that goes with Supreme Court argument." But his concerns about his abilities as a litigator were real. Only after he had watched Margold preparing the case and arguing it did Cohen finally recognize his own aptitude. His letter to Morris elaborated both his desire to litigate cases and his personal need to fight for causes in which he believed. He was "rather glum," Cohen told his father, "about all the good points [they] had that Margold didn't make—he was interrupted every couple of minutes by the judges, and he hadn't slept at all the night before." Having felt the tension of preparation, Cohen wanted to have "the release of expression." As his letter to Morris concluded, "Every time Frankfurter or Stone or Black asked a question that I would have loved to answer the pressure within got worse. Well, if this experience has done nothing else, it may have helped shake a lawyer out of your son. Next time I get a chance to argue a case anywhere I'll grab it."[33]

For seven years Cohen was a New Dealer, a legislation drafter, a team worker, but in 1941, as power began to shift from the executive branch to the judiciary, he also wanted to litigate, to be "a lawyer," as he put it. He was no longer satisfied with working behind the scenes, being an anonymous lawyer; he wanted to argue cases. He wanted both the power to transform ideas and policies into actual judicial decisions, and he wanted, even if he was reluctant to admit it, the recognition and prestige that came with it. At least in part his first wish was fulfilled when the Supreme Court announced its decision in the Walapai case.

Victory

Interior's argument fell on receptive ears. Justice William O. Douglas, who wrote the Court's opinion, was a fellow realist and a known agitator against corporate power. In the battle between a large railroad and a small band of Indians, Douglas was sure to come out on the side of the latter. And so he did.

On December 8, 1941, the Supreme Court handed down its decision announcing that aboriginal occupancy, whether or not recognized by treaty, statute, or otherwise, was sufficient to establish Indian possession of lands irrespective of how these lands came to the United States. Douglas confirmed the principle, laid down by Chief Justice Marshall more than a century earlier, that tribes had a legal right to lands under aboriginal title unless extinguished by the United States "by treaty, by the sword, by purchase, by the exercise of complete dominion adverse to the right of occupancy, or otherwise." While, unlike Marshall, Douglas allowed the federal government to extinguish Indian title without the Indians' consent, he concluded that none of the federal government's actions, which the Railroad and the lower courts described as extinguishing the Hualapai's title, achieved this end, as there was no clear indication of congressional intent to that effect.[34]

Specifically, Douglas insisted that the forcible removal of the Hualapai to the Colorado River Reservation did not extinguish the Hualapai's title because Congress did not intend to achieve that result. Rather, the creation of a reservation was only an "offer" to the tribe, one that was not "accepted." Without the Hualapai's consent, their aboriginal title remained intact. When in 1883 a new reservation was created at the request of the Hualapai and many members moved there, their rights to lands outside the reservations were extinguished.[35]

Douglas's analysis made his conclusion seem obvious: the 1866 grant was subject to the Hualapai occupancy rights, but the establishment of the Hualapai Indian Reservation in Arizona in 1883, at the Hualapai's request and with their acceptance, amounted to the relinquishment of any tribal claims to lands outside the reservation. This relinquishment amounted to extinguishment. Hence, the Hualapai had occupancy rights to their reservation lands but not outside it. A petition filed by Interior for a rehearing with respect to lands outside the reservation was denied.[36]

The case went back to trial to determine "(a) . . . the area which the Walapai Indians aboriginally occupied, and (b) the amount of income which the railroad received from its use or disposition of these Walapai lands."[37] As he did in the past, Cohen turned to anthropologists in quest for ethnological studies proving the scope of the Hualapai's occupancy rights. By his own admission, their studies "demonstrated the relevance of anthropology to administrative problems" more effectively than his 1937 article on anthropology and Indian administration did.[38]

On March 13, 1947, the final consent decree was filed confirming the Hualapai's title to 502,870 acres within the reservation, together with about 6,480 acres of valuable springs outside the reservation and portions of the railroad station grounds at Peach Springs which were not used for railroad purposes. In a letter to Brophy, Cohen commented that the decree "makes the principles of law that were established in the Supreme Court decision more than high-sounding generalities, and makes me feel that my years at Interior have not been wholly wasted. Peace to the soul of old Judge Hanna, who must have seen the outcome before I knew of the existence of Walapai Indians."[39]

"The Spanish Origin of Indian Rights in the Law of the United States"

The Court's decision in the Hualapai case was a long-awaited victory. But Cohen's argument reached deeper than the Court's conclusions. His emphasis on the Spanish origin of federal Indian law was a means to an end broader than rebutting the Railroad's claims. The Hualapai case brought to the fore potential clashes between the interests of different groups and forced Cohen to distinguish between groups. After all, if one accepted Cohen's argument in support of group rights, as articulated in his writings in the early 1940s, how could one determine which group—the Hualapai or the Railroad—to protect?

Cohen used the similarities, as he described them, between the treatment of Indian tribes under Spanish and American law to justify using history as a means of distinguishing among groups. Moving away from his early 1930s emphasis on the need to protect the rights of different collective institutions, he turned to the need to protect the rights of certain groups, that is, groups that had historically occupied a unique place in the American and international polity. Aboriginal conceptions of property were to be recognized under American law because of the special historical relationship between Indian tribes and a line of conquerors. History obligated the federal government to protect Indian rights, including the right to be different (or to have different understandings of property).

Cohen wanted to make clear that Indian tribes' interests were different from those of corporations or other racial groups. He was not advocating special treatment based on racial characterization, a point that would have put him in direct conflict with his friends and colleagues at the NAACP and the ACLU. Rather, he was advocating special treatment based on historical distinction. As Cohen emphasized, what separated Indians from other groups was not their "racial character," but their particular relationship with the federal government that did not only protect their welfare and their rights but had traditionally recognized their right to self-government.[40]

Cohen must have realized that his argument went beyond supporting historical rights. Tribal rights were grounded in particular cultures. He used history to defend cultural rights, and he wanted to expand the argument to other, similarly situated groups around the world. Stressing the similarities between the treatment of Indian tribes under Spanish and American law permitted Cohen to make a statement about the treatment of minorities under international law. Appealing not only to the court but also to Americans concerned about their country's place in the world's fight against totalitarianism, Cohen emphasized that federal Indian law was not merely a "local adaptation of Anglo-American common law, or a pure product of independent national legislation." Rather, its spirit was universal and enduring. It could thus be "carried to other lands across wide waters and wider gulfs of polity, religion and culture."[41]

Amid a war against totalitarianism, Cohen pleaded with the Supreme Court to adopt a universal approach to the question of minorities. Spanish law, especially Vitoria's writings on international law and human rights, was Cohen's anchor. "Whether these ideas will play a still larger role in the development of inter-racial and inter-cultural adjustments in the future is one of the most important issues before our generation," he wrote.[42]

Protecting minority group rights was Cohen's foundation for a new world order. Upholding historically recognized aboriginal rights was one aspect of it. But Cohen saw the decision in the Hualapai case as reaching even further. As he worked to secure the rights of the Hualapai, Cohen was also working to protect the rights of Alaska Natives against canning companies eager to gain a monopoly over fishing in Alaska. The analogy between the occupancy rights of the Hualapai and of the Alaska Natives seemed obvious, but fishing rights were different from rights in lands and springs. Because under the common law, the waters of Alaska were in the public domain, there could be no exclusive fishing rights. Rather, the federal government granted fishing rights. To apply the holding in the Hualapai case in the case of Alaska Natives' fishing rights would mean applying a cultural concept far more foreign to the common law than aboriginal title. History was also not helpful. Only in the twentieth century did the question of aboriginal fishing rights come to the fore. There was no historical precedent (Spanish or other) to anchor Cohen's argument in favor of protecting diverse cultural interests. He had to address the question of cultural sovereignty directly. As he was working to guarantee the economic survival of indigenous peoples, the protection of cultural sovereignty for diverse groups became Cohen's key to promoting the world's political and economic success.

Setting: The Alaska Reorganization Act (1936)

The relationship between the federal government and the Alaska Natives was different from the relationship the government had with the aboriginal peoples of the lower forty-eight states. As the United States had only acquired Alaska in 1867 and as the land was distant, the federal government did not negotiate treaties with Alaska Natives for the acquisition of their lands, nor did it remove Alaska Natives from their territories or place them on large reservations. As if reflecting these differences, it was not until March 1931 that responsibility for the administration of Alaska Natives' affairs was given to the BIA.[43]

Given that neither Congress nor Interior considered Alaska Natives to be members of tribes and given that many of them did not reside on reservations, the IRA did not mention Alaska. During the hearings before the House Committee, Dimond, the territorial representative, insisted that Alaska Natives were eager to assimilate and that many of them had already enjoyed the status of their white neighbors (except that their lands were not taxed). Dimond introduced references to Alaska Natives in particular sections of the act, specifically those pertaining to education and benefits, including the right to organize business corporations. But these references were omitted from the final act.[44]

In 1935, at Dimond's urging, Cohen drafted a bill to amend the IRA to allow Alaska Natives to form business corporations. Cohen's hopes for Alaska Natives were similar to his dreams for American Indians. He wanted to provide for their economic development through the creation of corporations with exclusive rights to use the territory's resources. He thought that the bill should "permit groups of Indians already associated with each other in some enterprise [occupation, association, or residence] to adopt a constitution, regardless of past tribal or community affiliations." But in response to pressures from Alaska to allow the incorporation of groups regardless of their residence, Cohen stressed that, preferably, only groups that resembled a tribe or had exercised tribal powers in the past should be permitted to organize. He did not oppose the organization of "any group of partners or associates whose contacts [were] simply occupational," but he objected to opportunistic organization (of "groups of individuals who [had] not been associated together previously but [were] simply associated for the purpose of borrowing money" under the IRA). Furthermore, while Cohen argued that "where there [was] no community organization, groups [might] be organized purely as a business organization," he believed that "as a matter of policy, community organization and community responsibility" were preferable to "purely economic organization."[45]

Cohen's assessment of the needs of indigenous communities was changing. In the early 1930s he saw economic success as tied to political autonomy. By the 1940s, he saw a close connection between economic and cultural survival. Securing a geographical space for Alaska Natives was less urgent. The economic survival of Alaska Natives depended on the protection of Alaska Natives' economic interests as they culturally defined them.

Others at Interior were more insistent on the need to limit political sovereignty by setting geographical boundaries to it. According to Ickes, such boundaries, in fact reservations, would help identify different Native groups and draw the limits of their authority. Ickes saw the creation of reservations in Alaska as a means for the federal government "to fulfill its moral and legal obligations to protect the 'economic rights' of Alaska Natives."[46] Collier, the self-proclaimed cultural pluralist, similarly stressed that reservations would promote Alaska Natives' economic development. Collier believed that reservations were necessary to promote economic autonomy in Southeast Alaska, protect fur-bearing areas in interior Alaska against trespassing by non-Natives, and protect the interests of the Eskimos in the Arctic.[47]

The bill that Dimond introduced in January 1936 endorsed both positions. Section 1 of the bill authorized "Indian-chartered corporations in Alaska" to be organized "without regard to residence on any Indian reservations." It permitted "groups of Indians in Alaska not heretofore recognized as bands or tribes, but having a common bond of occupation, or association, or residence within a well-defined neighborhood, community or rural district" to adopt constitutions and organize corporations. Section 2 of the act authorized the secretary of the interior to designate as an Indian reservation "any area of land which has been reserved for the use and occupancy of Indians or Eskimos" by previous congressional or executive acts "together with additional public lands adjacent thereto, within the Territory of Alaska, or any other public lands which are actually occupied by Indians or Eskimos within said Territory."[48]

An act of May 31, 1938, strengthened the pro-reservation sentiment. It permitted the secretary "to withdraw and permanently reserve small tracts of not to exceed six hundred and forty acres each of the public domain in Alaska for schools, hospitals, and such other purposes as may be necessary in administering the affairs of the Indians, Eskimos, and Aleuts of Alaska." The 1938 act limited the creation of such reservations to situations where the applicants established that they used the land or areas in its vicinity or that the land had been reserved for them in the past.[49]

Ironically, Alaska Natives were uninterested in organization per se. Their concerns focused on economic survival, specifically the allocation of Alaska's natural resources. An Alaska native village typically consisted of a preexisting group sharing a common bond along axis of occupation or association or residence. They did not associate their tribal identity with a fixed geographical space or reservation. Rather, Alaska Natives viewed their survival as attached to their economic activities and to multiple sites. Despite pressures from Collier to create reservations, by 1938 only three villages had petitioned for reservations, and their requests were tied to economic survival—to the protection of fur, game, and fish.[50]

The struggle to protect Alaska Natives' rights thus brought together economic, cultural, and political (or geographical) concerns. It oscillated between the need to protect a geographical space where Alaska Natives could exercise their political, cultural, and economic sovereignty and the need to provide Alaska Natives with a sufficient land and resource base to enable them to be self-supporting. Initially, both the identification of a geographical space and the guarantee of a sufficient land and resource base were entangled with the question of aboriginal title. Interior wanted to guarantee that areas previously occupied by Alaska Natives would be part of their territory or, at the very least, their land and resource base. Yet, rapidly, the struggle for Alaska Natives' cultural and economic survival turned into a debate about the equal allocation of Alaska's resources between diverse collective entities, including non-Native canning companies.[51]

Many factors influenced this transformation, including the pressures of World War II, bureaucratic quarrels, territorial politics, and the distrust that permeated the interactions between Natives and non-Natives. But most detrimental to Alaska Natives' rights was American law as elaborated in adverse court decisions. Grounded in the post-Enlightenment individualist ideal, American law could not accommodate Cohen's vision with its fluidity and deep appreciation of culture, a vision that many attorneys for indigenous peoples in the late twentieth century have embraced. It could not even accommodate Collier's and Ickes's desires to create reservations in Alaska. Alaska Natives' forms of occupancy did not fit the pattern of occupancy or ownership recognized under American law; they did not even fit the exceptions created in law to accommodate the Native population in the United States. It was much easier for American lawyers to recognize the property rights of the different canning companies. The battle to promote Alaska Natives' political, economic, and cultural sovereignty was thus a losing battle, fought amid the demise of Roosevelt's New Deal. (Indeed, it remained unresolved when Ickes, Collier, and Cohen, within a couple of years of each other, tendered their resignations.) Alaska Natives gained neither a geographical space nor an equal share in Alaska resources. Their history and culture were ignored, but the stories they told about their title provided ammunition for future generations fighting for aboriginal rights. It was also the basis upon which Cohen drafted the Indian Claims Commission Act.

Economic Survival in Alaska: Aboriginal Title to Fish and Waters

Alaska's aquatic resources were the backbone of its economic life. Fishing and canning were the most common occupation and source of income for both Alaska Natives and whites.[52] The Fish and Wildlife Service (formerly the Bureau of Fisheries) promulgated annual rules for the conduct of Alaska's commercial salmon fishery during the fishing season. These regulations determined the allocation of trap sites and the limits of their usage. The 1939 transfer of the Fish and Wildlife Service from the Department of Commerce to Interior brought these seasonal regulations and, more important, "the protests of local Alaskans, Native and white, against absentee monopolization of fish traps" to Cohen's attention.[53]

Over the years, the Bureau of Fisheries' seasonal regulations granted de facto monopoly rights to a few cannery companies. Soon after the introduction of commercial fish traps, Alaska Natives began protesting. In 1918, the Supreme Court accepted the Metlakahtla Indians' argument that the Alaska Pacific Fisheries Company's fish trap was within their reservation. Expressing concern for the Indians' ability to sustain themselves, the Court held that the reservation embraced the surrounding waters and submerged lands and thus that permits for "erecting salmon traps at these islands" could only be issued to the Indians.[54] In 1924, the White Act required fishing regulations to adhere to an equal access rule and to avoid granting a fishing monopoly to any individual or group. Between 1924 and 1940 about half of the allowed fish traps were abolished.[55]

The equal access rule would be used in the late 1940s to undermine Alaska Natives' rights. But in the spring of 1941, a group of Alaska Natives used the concept of equal access to challenge certain fishing regulations. The group, which the BIA referred to the Solicitor's Office, wanted Interior to void the regulations because they excluded them from fishing within a certain distance of fishing traps of a commercial canning company. The argument was twofold: first, the group contended that "the fishing ground in question was theirs" and, second, that, at any rate, "it was unfair for the Department to grant a monopoly of the right to fish such waters to a commercial company and to exclude the Natives from the area."[56]

Intertwined, the two questions reflected two narratives that Alaska Natives wanted policymakers to hear. The first addressed the status and definition of aboriginal rights. The group wanted policymakers to realize that according to their laws and traditions certain fishing sites belonged to them. Second, even if policymakers could not recognize this claim of aboriginal ownership, the group insisted that it was unfair to grant a monopoly to white canning companies. This was not an issue of law and property rights, but of fairness—presumably a universal claim about the allocation of economic resources in the territory. Alaska Natives wanted to protect their rights to sufficient lands and resources. Informed by universal ideals of justice and by American concerns about monopoly, this argument bridged the gap between aboriginal conceptions of property and Western ones.

Concealed beneath these concerns was Alaska Natives' goal of asserting their ethnic and political identity. Fishing was more than a source of living for Alaska Natives. It was an activity imbued with cultural and spiritual meaning. Alaska Natives saw themselves as intertwined with nature. A successful hunting and fishing season depended on adherence to certain rules: nature's obligation was to surrender up certain life forms to satisfy Alaska Natives' needs, while Alaska Natives were required to refrain from abuse of the bounty. Alaska Natives believed that catastrophe would result if they failed to fulfill their commitment. In other words, fishing and hunting were parts of Alaska Natives' cultural identification.[57]

After reviewing the complaint, Margold concluded that the group made a *prima facie* case and that "about a dozen trap sites claimed by natives under aboriginal right should be eliminated from the pending regulations."[58] At Cohen's request, he also, albeit reluctantly, refrained from approving the yearly fishing regulations (the 1941 and 1942 regulations were approved by the undersecretary and the secretary).[59]

The Solicitor's Office then transformed the Alaska Natives' narratives about their economic culture, their identity, and fairness into legal questions about rights. The twofold claim thus became a twofold question: "Whether Indians of Alaska have any fishing rights which are violated by control of particular trap sites by non-Indians under departmental regulations, and whether such rights require or justify the closing down of certain trap sites or the allocation of trap sites to Indian groups or other remedial action by the Secretary of the Interior."[60]

In so transforming the Alaska Natives' claims, Cohen and Margold pushed a particular agenda. Recognizing the relationship between cultural sovereignty and economic survival, and thus the need to protect Alaska Natives' rights in fishing sites they had traditionally occupied, Cohen and Margold realized that the question had to be described as a matter of property law rather than one of administrative regulation. They described the question not as one involving the allocation of resources but as one requiring a determination regarding the scope of aboriginal title in Alaska. Consequently, any impact that their decision respecting aboriginal title would have on the cannery companies' ability to use certain trap sites would be accidental and not deliberate.

At least in part, Cohen and Margold's description of the issue was influenced by their recent victory in the Hualapai case.[61] But it was not obvious that the rule of that case could easily be applied to Alaska. The United States purchased the Alaska Territory from Russia, and an argument could be made that the rights of Alaska Natives were not recognized under Russian law. Furthermore, while the Hualapai claimed rights to lands and springs, Alaska Natives proclaimed possession of waters. Could Alaska Natives have an exclusive right to fish in waters which under the common law were in the public domain?

On February 13, 1942, Margold, in a solicitor's opinion drafted by Cohen and approved by Ickes, answered the question affirmatively. The argument about the need to determine whether Russia recognized aboriginal rights was easily dismissed. To Cohen, it seemed obvious. If the Hualapai's aboriginal title was valid irrespective of Mexican or congressional recognition, indeed despite ongoing encroachments upon it, then so was the Alaska Natives' aboriginal title. Only an explicit action by the conqueror could extinguish what Cohen viewed as the universal, international agreement about aboriginal claims. Margold's opinion pointed out that neither the Russian government nor the federal government had made any such attempt.[62]

Getting rid of the distinction between Russian and American law, Cohen and Margold turned to the argument about rights in waters. It was more difficult to tackle because the common law clearly did not recognize such rights. But Cohen and Margold did not think it mattered. As tribal traditions "recognized, *inter se,* private and exclusive rights to take fish in designated waters," the common law had to accommodate them (just as it accommodated Indian title to lands). If Alaska Natives could demonstrate that their aboriginal occupancy was "a continuous occupancy," analogous to the "use of uplands by an Indian tribe for agriculture, hunting, or seed-gathering, to the exclusion of other tribes," their occupancy of waters and submerged lands would be deemed occupancy under the Hualapai case. In other words, the fact that fishing rights in "ocean waters" or "land below the high water mark" were not recognized under the common law did not mean that "the extension of American sovereignty" over certain waters extinguished existing rights in such waters. Indian legal traditions were unaffected by the common law.[63]

Margold's opinion went further. Seeking to eliminate potential misunderstandings, it emphasized that neither the White Act nor the non–Native use of the waters harmed the aboriginal title of Alaska Natives. According to Margold, non–Native use was "a continuing wrong, rather than a wrong which, once committed, create supervening and inalienable rights in third parties." As to the White Act, while it prohibited "any grant of any exclusive right of fishery," it only referred "to grants under the statute and not to rights existing long prior to the statute." Even the White Act's requirement that "'in any area of the waters of Alaska where fishing is permitted by the Secretary of the Interior' no citizen of the United States shall 'be denied the right to take . . . fish'" was subject to aboriginal fishing rights. Margold stressed that any other construction of the act "would run counter to the well-established canon of construction" according to which federal statutes could extinguish or limit Indian rights only if they unmistakably expressed such intent.[64]

The accidental implications of Margold's opinion were obvious. Interior had no authority to allow public or private fishing in areas to which Alaska Natives could prove they had exclusive possessory rights.[65]

Even in the rare places where Alaska Natives did not have exclusive rights, Cohen was determined to protect their interests against potential encroachments by large cannery corporations. Margold's opinion explained that non-exclusive use created the equivalent of common-law easements, which were "property rights, and entitled to protection and respect." Cohen insisted that Interior did not have the legal power to open areas where Alaska Natives held easements for non–Indian use that would result in actual exclusion of interested Alaska Natives (for example, by allowing "the first comer" to set up a trap and ban others from fishing within a specified distance of that trap).[66]

Cohen feared that Alaska Natives, even when organized into corporations, would not be able to compete with the few large cannery corporations that, under the auspices of the Department of Commerce, were able to operate between 80 to 90 percent of the Alaskan salmon traps.[67] He thus announced that Alaska Natives' rights, exclusive or not, trumped the rights of canning companies eager to profit from the rich resources of Alaska. On March 20, another solicitor's opinion proclaimed that the companies did not acquire any vested rights in areas where Alaska Natives had rights.[68] According to Margold and Cohen, the violation of aboriginal occupancy rights by exclusive control of particular trap sites by non–Indians under departmental regulations was simply illegal, and the remedy simple. As Margold concluded his February opinion, "the Department might either forbid the establishment of fish traps except by persons having possessory rights in such areas, or forbid the establishment of any fish traps at all therein, or, as a final alternative, exclude such areas entirely from the domain of departmental control." Alaska Natives, Margold emphasized, did not need to be allocated fish trap sites. These sites were theirs, as long as they could prove that they had traditionally occupied them.[69]

Conflicting Claims: Aboriginal Occupancy, Property, and Sovereignty

Margold's February opinion tied Alaska Natives' economic survival to geographical space that was culturally appropriate for any given group of Alaska Natives. It allowed the creation of large reservations, including water, "based on aboriginal use and occupancy."[70]

Leaving open the "factual question of the extent of areas which have been continuously occupied by Indians or Indian groups," Margold's decision was meant to encourage Alaska Natives and those working on their behalf to claim their occupancy rights.[71] Many were quick to do so. Within a few weeks, Collier concluded that "the Alaska Natives were in continuous occupancy of their lands and adjoining water areas," analogous to the occupancy in the Hualapai case. Collier emphasized that Alaska Natives' villages "remained, almost without exception, at the identical spot or within the near neighborhood where they [were] first mentioned in early accounts." Their continuous occupancy was broken only when they were forcibly removed or where commercial interests took over their means of subsistence, events that, according to Justice Douglas's decision in the Hualapai case, could not extinguish aboriginal title. Collier recommended that Interior act without delay to clarify aboriginal title and restore to Alaska Natives their property.[72]

Cohen, too, pushed for a resolution. Together with Margold and Collier, he convinced Ickes to order the Fish and Wildlife Service to add a new regulation to their seasonal rules for the conduct of Alaska commercial salmon fisheries. The 1942 regulation prohibited the establishment of fish traps in "any site in which any Alaskan native or natives has or have any rights of fishery, by virtue of any grant or by virtue of aboriginal occupancy, by any person other than such native or natives." It further authorized "any native or natives" claiming a right of aboriginal occupancy to "petition the Secretary of the Interior for a hearing with respect to the validity of such claim." If others claimed rights to the same site, an administrative hearing would follow.[73]

Two Native claims to trap sites used by non-Natives were filed almost immediately, prompting the Solicitor's Office to recommend hearings without delay. In a memorandum drafted by Cohen, Margold explained that postponing the hearings would embarrass Interior when the Fish and Wildlife Service promulgated fishing regulations the following year. Margold emphasized that the industry, the Indians, and Interior would benefit from expeditious hearings and urged Ickes to send George W. Folta, who had represented Interior in Alaska, as a "field examiner to collect testimony" in the territory.[74]

But not everyone shared the sense of urgency displayed by Collier, Margold, and Cohen, or their commitment to protecting Alaska Natives' aboriginal title. Most vocal among their opponents were the canning companies. Shortly after the new regulation was adopted on March 13, 1942, the Association of Pacific Fisheries and the Northwest Salmon Canners Association "demanded its repeal."[75]

The canning companies had many supporters. Ira Gabrielson, the director of the Fish and Wildlife Service, strongly opposed Interior's plans to dismantle the traps of large cannery corporations "to afford Alaskan natives the exclusive right to catch millions of dollars worth of salmon." As he explained to Cohen, "The confusion and difficulties in the salmon fishery [had] become steadily worse. . . . It [was thus] doubtful that many areas [would] be fished at all." According to Gabrielson, it was not "good administration or for the national good to inject new elements into the situation at [that] time."[76]

More important, as lobbyists for the companies began accusing Ickes of disrupting food supply at a time of war, the old curmudgeon uncharacteristically gave in, indeterminably postponing the adjudication of aboriginal fishing rights that the new regulation required. "We need salmon too badly this year to run any chances, and we have the Japs to think of in addition," Ickes wrote in his diary on March 22.[77]

In the summer of 1942, the canning companies gained another supporter. On June 25, 1942, Margold was nominated, and on July 6 confirmed, to sit on the reconstituted District Municipal Court bench. Warner Gardner, who replaced him as solicitor, was not sympathetic to the cause of Alaska Natives' rights.[78] Now, in addition to Ickes, who continued to refuse to hold hearings during the war, Cohen had to fight the new solicitor who, within a few months of his appointment, teamed with Ira Gabrielson to undermine Cohen's agenda. The Tee-Hit-Ton Indians (a group belonging to the Tlingit Indians) gave them the opportunity to do so.

Back in April 1942, with the new fishing regulations as a weapon, William Paul, an Alaska Native who had fought for Alaska Natives' rights since the 1920s, petitioned Ickes to direct the Fish and Wildlife Service to order the Pacific American Fisheries Company to remove its trap from Point Colpoys; the trap "caught salmon that spawned at Salmon Bay on the north side of Prince of Wales Island in waters in which the Tee-Hit-Tons traditionally fished." The Fish and Wildlife Service's response was quick: "Because the Point Colpoys trap annually caught all of the fish that could be taken from the salmon run that spawned at Salmon Bay, the Fish and Wildlife Service had adopted a regulation that closed the bay to commercial fishing" (including Alaska Natives' fishing). In an act of civil disobedience, members of Paul's family and a few other Tee-Hit-Tons challenged the closure by setting their nets in Salmon Bay. They were promptly arrested for fishing in closed waters.[79]

The question was simple: did Alaska Natives' property rights trump the federal government's power to regulate fishing? The 1942 solicitor's opinion seemed to suggest that they did. While the opinion only held that government regulations should respect Alaska Natives' rights when allocating fishing sites, it seemed to prioritize aboriginal rights not only in relationship to canning companies but also in relationship to the government. Collier and Cohen insisted that while Alaska Natives' rights might be "subject to reasonable regulation," they were "sufficient to prevent a complete closing of the ancient fishing grounds." But Gabrielson saw the question differently. He strongly believed that the issue of aboriginal rights was irrelevant in this case; Indians were "subject to the fisheries regulations to the same extent as white persons." Gardner agreed with Gabrielson, although he noted that Interior had a moral obligation to modify its regulations to recognize aboriginal title.[80]

Cohen was outraged. As he wrote to Gardner, in his nine years of experience it was "the first case" in which Interior "upheld a deprivation of Indian property without compensation." He recognized that Alaska Natives' rights might have to yield to the needs of conservation, but he was pointedly accusatory of the lack of investigation or hearings prior to the decision.[81]

Gardner did not much care for Cohen's ire. In November 1942, he forwarded his advice to Ickes, who promptly authorized Gabrielson to amend the aboriginal fishing rights regulation to clarify that "this section shall not be construed as permitting any exercise of such rights contrary to any of the provisions of [the Fish and Wildlife Service's other fishing] regulations".[82] The federal government was put in the awkward position of protecting aboriginal occupancy rights and using its regulatory powers to limit them.

Adding insult to injury, in January 1943 Gabrielson proposed to eliminate the 1942 regulation. He decided that the postponement of the hearings had effectively revoked it.[83] Two months later, Senator Monrad Wallgren of Washington, an ally of the Alaska salmon canning industry, reintroduced a bill, previously introduced in January 1942, "to prohibit fish-traps from being closed except by future act of Congress." A clause that did not appear in the original bill mandated "that the Alaska commercial salmon fishery be open to all citizens 'free of all exclusive or several rights under any claim of occupancy, aboriginal or otherwise.'"[84]

Cohen viewed Gabrielson's and Gardner's support for nonresident corporations and, more crucially, Wallgren's proposed bill as undermining his plans for Alaska's economic development, plans that emphasized local self-government and protected aboriginal rights. He stressed that by dismissing "Indian occupancy rights," Wallgren's bill would grant existing operators "priorities with respect to the allocation of fishing privileges and locations which would . . . make it impossible effectively to curtail or prevent monopolistic tendencies, [and] place the Department in the position of being required by law to participate in the maintenance of monopolistic conditions."[85] According to Cohen, by requiring an act of Congress to close existing fishing traps, Wallgren's bill would "create vested rights of fishery in the maritime public domain for virtually the first time in the history of the Alaska fishery law, and . . . diminish both the scope and the flexibility of the legal powers of [Interior] to protect this extremely valuable public resource."[86]

Moreover, as Cohen saw it, by substituting "a system of individual permits and leases for major portions of the general regulatory powers" that were vested in Interior, the bill's equal access section threatened to perpetuate "a basically unjustifiable Colonial policy"—pitting cannery companies and their corporate lawyers against Alaska Natives whose rights had historically been less valued. "I am still of the opinion that this attempt of the 4 or 5 concerns that now hold about 80 percent of the fish traps in Alaskan waters to put this bill through Congress and secure for themselves a vested right in the high seas worth nearly 40 million dollar a year," Cohen wrote to a colleague, "represents the greatest raid on the public domain since the days of the Robber Barons."[87]

Cohen also stressed that by pitting the rights of Alaska Natives against the rights of other groups, the bill would turn the control over Alaska resources from Interior to the courts. Despite his recent success defending the Hualapai's cause, Cohen was well aware that American courts would not necessarily protect Alaska Natives' rights. Immersed in the common-law tradition, the courts, he feared, would be reluctant to recognize aboriginal fishing rights.[88]

While the bill was not enacted, dark clouds continued to hover above Alaska Natives' rights. But just when there seemed to be no hope, Ickes suddenly took action.

Breaking the Impasse

In 1943, with the hearings still pending, Interior took unexpected action. First, Assistant Secretary Oscar Chapman, who supervised the BIA's activities, "signed proclamations that established four reservations, one of which was a

1.8–million-acre reservation for the Gwich'in Indians." Two days later, "Ickes signed a land order that established a reservation at Karluk, a small village on the north shore of the Kodiak Island." In May 1944, the residents of Karluk voted to approve their reservation, as required by the Alaska amendments to the IRA.[89] In April 1944, Ickes "also closed fish traps operated by the salmon industry at eleven sites" where Alaska Natives claimed rights of aboriginal occupancy. Non-Natives who wanted to use these sites "were required to secure leases from their Native owners."[90]

Cohen was not satisfied. He wanted Ickes to schedule hearings to determine Alaska Natives' aboriginal rights. If Interior were to create reservations for Alaska Natives, they should be entitled to lands and waters that they had traditionally used. In April 1944, Cohen, again, "urged that the arguments for and against a prompt hearing of Indian claims [regarding their fishing rights] be presented to the Secretary." Ironically, given the public outrage that ensued following the creation of the reservations (motivated by fears that if Interior could establish reservations to give Alaska Natives exclusive rights to catch salmon in waters surrounding their villages, white fishermen would lose most of their access to Alaska resources), Ickes had no choice. When the matter was brought before him for a new decision in May 1944, Ickes approved scheduling hearings at the close of the fishing season then in progress.[91]

These were not the hearings for which Cohen prayed. Amid growing public uproar charging Interior with giving Alaska to its Native population without regard to the interests of others, Interior's press releases and memoranda took pains to emphasize that the hearings were only designed to determine "whether certain areas of land and water in Alaska" belonged to certain Indian villages "under existing statutes," and that Interior's power was limited to regulating fishing. Any decision as to whether lands should be returned to the Indians or whether Indians should be compensated for lands lost was to be left to congressional discretion once the facts were ascertained.[92]

Whatever the implications of such statements were, Alaska Natives did not dwell on them. Several petitions were immediately filed "for hearings to adjudicate aboriginal fishing rights" on behalf of the Natives of Klawock, Tongass, Hydaburg, Chilkat, Douglas, Juneau, Sitka, and Wrangell. They were also immediately rejected because the filing attorney, William Paul, was not approved by the secretary of the interior, as required by the IRA.[93]

Cohen decided to take matters into his own hands. In June 1944, together with Kenneth Simons, Cohen toured Alaska, specifically Metlakahtla, Hydaburg, Klawock, and Juneau.[94] He wanted to examine whether "any of the Indian groups concerned" could "present evidence in support of their claims," and whether they could "obtain, adequate private legal counsel in this matter or need legal aid from the Indian Office." Cohen concluded that there was sufficient evidence in support of these aboriginal claims, although most of it was oral. As he reported to the commissioner of Indian affairs, the evidence consisted "primarily of the testimony of older Indians, some over 80 years old, and other inhabitants of southeastern Alaska, as to the location of native winter homes, forts, summer camps, smoke-houses, fish traps and other areas of land and water use," but it was verifiable "by examination of available remains and by checking with historical and scientific reports and authorities."[95]

When he and Simmons visited Hydaburg, Kake, and Klawock, Cohen also secured the agreement of the members of their village councils to have Interior attorneys represent their communities. Upon their return, Cohen and Simons drafted new petitions for these three villages. They proposed that four hearings on Indian aboriginal claims be held in early September 1944.[96] Assistant Secretary Oscar Chapman scheduled the hearings as suggested and appointed Hanna, who had worked with Cohen on the Hualapai case, the administrative law judge to preside over them.[97]

Economic Survival in Alaska: The Limits of Aboriginal Title

The Haida and Tlingit residents of Hydaburg, Kake, and Klawock claimed exclusive use and occupancy of shore lands and waters for a distance of 3000 feet from the shore, lakes and streams emptying into said waters, and unpatented lands drained thereby. They emphasized that they had never "sold, ceded, relinquished or abandoned" these lands and waters, had "protested against all forms of trespass," and had asserted "present claim to exclusive use and occupancy."[98] They were represented by three Interior attorneys: Folta, counsel at large for Interior at Juneau, Alaska, who in 1943 reportedly "cast doubt upon the claim of the Tee-Hit-Ton tribe to any aboriginal fishing rights" by arguing in court that "the Indians of Southeast Alaska had no aboriginal fishing rights" (Folta was subsequently censured for unprofessionalism by Solicitor Gardner); Simons, a district counsel for the Indian Service at Billings, Montana, who accompanied Cohen to Alaska and "who purportedly privately believed that Felix Cohen's theory that the Indians of Southeast Alaska had aboriginal fishing rights was 'crazy' "; and Haas, "a forty-one-year-old attorney from the Solicitor's Office in Washington, DC." Haas had helped Cohen with the *Handbook* and more recently had been appointed as the BIA Chief Counsel. Cohen maintained direct contact with all three throughout the hearings.[99]

The cannery companies that collectively operated seventy-five traps in the waters surrounding Hydaburg, Kake, and Klawock had the support of the commercial establishment in Alaska and in the United States, as well as that of many individuals. The Juneau, Ketchikan, and Seattle Chambers of Commerce, the Alaska Miners Association, and the International Fishermen and Allied Workers of America sent letters to Interior expressing fears for the industry, the economy, and the nation if Alaska Natives were given priority in catching fish in streams. They described creating reservations for Alaska Natives as discriminatory and "un-American," as it deprived non-Natives, residents and nonresidents, of their livelihood. While agreeing that Alaska Natives might have to be compensated for lands and waters that were taken away from them, they insisted that everyone should be allowed to participate in Alaska's economic development and to use its natural resources.[100] Individual shareholders signed form letters to Hanna protesting the grant of exclusive rights to Indians "in patented lands, and even . . . whole incorporated cities" to the exclusion of "any other race of people who may have spent their lives and wealth" to develop those areas.[101]

The cannery companies sent five attorneys to the hearings; a sixth attorney represented the timber industry. The lead counsel was W. C. Arnold from Ketchikan, Alaska. Arnold was the chief counsel and managing director of Alaska Salmon Industry, the trade association of the cannery companies. On September 15, when Hanna called the Hydaburg hearing to order, Arnold announced that the Haidas' claims had "no basis in history or in law" and that "the entire proceeding is unfair to the white people of Alaska and the whole United States." Arnold went so far as to argue that the proceedings were "unsound as to the Indians themselves for the reason that it would make them mere wards of the government and deprive them of that personal independence which is essential to true equality." Arnold then asked that "these proceedings be dismissed on the ground that there is no legal authority for conducting the same." Invoking the White Act, Arnold declared that the secretary of the interior was not authorized to deny anyone the usage of trap sites and canneries or fishing privileges simply because such use or privilege interfered with "alleged aboriginal Indian rights." According to Arnold, only Congress or the judiciary had the power to recognize and enforce possessory rights in the public domain in some citizens to the exclusion of others.[102]

Without asking the petitioners to respond, Hanna rejected Arnold's request, reiterating Interior's position that the hearings were only a departmental inquiry into the facts. Hanna entered Arnold's objections as to the hearings' legal basis into the record, but the hearings were not dismissed. Rather, in the course of the next few months Hanna and his court moved from Hydaburg to Klawock to Kake, then to Ketchikan ("to allow representatives of such groups as the Ketchikan and Wrangell Chambers of Commerce and the Alaska Miners Association" to be heard), and finally to Seattle (where they "lasted a week and had to be moved three times to accommodate the hostile overflow crowd").[103]

In each location, Haas brought to the stand elderly Alaska Natives who testified, often through interpreters, about "the locations at which residents of their village traditionally fished," about the fact that, even prior to the turn of the twentieth century, "whites paid the Indians for the privilege of fishing in traditional areas," and about the harm to the village economy caused by the Fish and Wildlife Service regulations. Arnold consistently moved to strike the testimony, and Hanna consistently denied his motions.[104]

More to the substance of the claims, Arnold was determined to have the 1942 solicitor's opinion, which led to the hearings, overruled. His brief characterized the opinion not only as limiting public access to Alaska but also as making "the absurd statement that tribal law is superior to the law of the United States." Arnold also insisted that the claims should have been brought on behalf of individual petitioners, not bands of Indians. As he noted at the end of the hearings at Hydaburg, he was confused as to who the claimants were and what their claims were, as there was no "competent legal evidence establishing the boundaries or the claims or that the areas were ever aboriginally used and occupied."[105]

Arnold described the question of tribal occupancy as a question of law. Cohen, Haas, and their colleagues saw it as a question of fact—of culture and history. Accordingly, whether or not Congress recognized the band claiming aboriginal occupancy had no effect on the claim.[106] Haas repeatedly stressed that the villages' claims were collective in nature and reiterated the principle that American law protected Indian occupancy rights. Haas went so far as to accuse the canning companies of seeking to gain monopoly over fish traps. The petitioners' brief cleverly noted that "absentee private corporations who have monopolized and exploited for years the best fishing sites now proclaim the doctrine that no group should have special privileges. Furthermore, they assert the doctrine of a common right to fishery. In fact, it is the natives who are attacking the special privilege of a few. The general public will not suffer if salmon are caught in Indian-owned traps rather than traps owned by the absentee corporation."[107]

For the most part, Hanna, who was deeply concerned about Alaska Natives' rights, accepted the petitioners' interpretations of questions of law and policy. Against Arnold's strong objections, Hanna insisted that aboriginal occupancy could only be proven by making exceptions to the hearsay rules, that is, by testimony about the history and reputation of the community. Hanna pointedly told Arnold that he would not exclude the testimony of witnesses put forward by the petitioners. Rather, he hoped and expected that "the whole testimony would connect up in some way or other." When Arnold raised his objections again, Hanna ignored him.[108]

The testimony was vast, amounting to fifteen volumes and about 2,700 pages.[109] It included oral testimony by tribal members, non-Natives who used Alaska resources who testified on behalf of the respondents, and reports from anthropologists who testified on behalf of the petitioners and the respondents. But at the end, the testimony did not help the villages' cause. It revealed that the different villages allowed, first, Indians from other villages and, then, non-Indians to fish in their traditional areas. As Cohen realized when he toured Alaska, if a village had "sold traps or trap-sites to non-Indians or otherwise acted in a manner which may be held to constitute abandonment of particular areas formerly subject to Indian occupancy," the village residents' claim for aboriginal occupancy would be severely undermined.[110]

The question of Alaska Natives' occupancy reached beyond the ruling in the Hualapai case. Sufficient evidence supported the Hualapai's argument that they exclusively occupied the lands. The question before the court was simply whether American law recognized their aboriginal title. In contrast, in Alaska, as Arnold emphasized in every cross-examination, the evidence demonstrated that Alaska Natives did not exclusively occupy the waters; they allowed others to fish in them. If one were to apply the Hualapai ruling, the Alaska Natives' claim of aboriginal title would be rejected. If the residents of the villages did not try to prevent non-Natives and Natives from other villages from using their traps, how could they be injured by the cannery companies' use?[111]

Alaska Natives saw it differently. According to their legal traditions, they did not undermine their occupancy rights by allowing others to use the waters. They also thought that they did not abandon their traditional locations but rather were forced out of them.[112] But their understanding of occupancy was so far removed from the American vision of property rights that even those sympathetic to the Alaska Natives' claims could not endorse it.

For one thing, Hanna, who was expected to rule in the villages' favor, could not see the injury to the claimants from the development of commercial fisheries. In April 1945, while declaring that aboriginal occupancy was a question of fact independent of recognition by treaty, statute, or other government action, Hanna advised Ickes that there was "no substantial evidence in the record that [the Indians] engaged in [ocean-waters] fishing prior to the development of commercial fishing and the use of modern gear and power boats, or exercised any exclusive rights therein." Rather, their fishing was "for personal consumption and largely confined to small streams claimed by families or small groups, heads of houses or families." Furthermore, not only had Alaska Natives allowed non-Native fishermen to fish in their waters, they also abandoned their traditional practices in order to obtain employment with the commercial canneries. Hanna concluded that the residents of the three villages had aboriginal rights in certain lands and inland waters, albeit undefined based on the evidence produced at the hearings, but rejected the villages' claim for exclusive right in tidal waters except as to some small areas adjacent to the mouth of salmon streams flowing into tidal waters. As if seeking to soften the blow, Hanna suggested that Alaska Natives should be compensated for lands and waters that were forcefully taken from them and that Interior should respect the aboriginal rights of use and occupancy, which had not been extinguished or abandoned. He also left open the possibility of creating reservations that would include lands and waters for Alaska Natives.[113]

Ickes did not anticipate Hanna's conclusions but Cohen, at Ickes's request, confirmed their soundness. Even before he traveled to Alaska, Cohen expressed concerns about "the traditional ideas of property rights in land or fishing sites, whether such rights were considered exclusive, whether they were transferable, and how, if at all, they were inherited."[114] As we saw, his draft opinion for Margold back in 1942 sought to resolve situations where Alaska Natives could not prove exclusive ownership by suggesting that they at least had the rights associated with easements.[115]

Then, in November 1944, as Cohen evaluated the evidence at the hearings, he concluded that the three villages had allowed whites and Natives of all tribes freely to fish in the waters claimed by them "for a good many years." While he maintained that protecting Alaska Natives' property rights against infringement by non-Native corporations was immensely important both as a matter of fairness toward Alaska Natives and "from the standpoint of territorial development," he could not see any legal interpretation acceptable in American courts according to which the Alaska Natives' occupancy could be described as exclusive.[116] Cohen was forced to admit that, according to American law, Alaska Natives had abandoned their exclusive rights. In a memorandum to Folta, Simmons, and Haas, written amid the hearings, Cohen suggested that instead of pushing for a finding of exclusive occupancy, they might want to argue that the Indians had "abandoned any claim to exclusive fishing rights in deep water, retaining only a right or easement to fish, in common with others, at their accustomed fishing places."[117] As Cohen understood, American law's endorsement of cultural sovereignty was limited by its own culture.

Cohen wanted to protect Alaska Natives' rights, but could not find a legal doctrine in which to anchor them. He thus looked for a compromise that would protect Alaska Natives' rights even though their form of occupancy did not conform to American legal standards. His solution also took into account the interests of the cannery companies. Instead of enclosing large areas for the exclusive use of Alaska Natives, his solution proposed rights in common.

But the companies were unwilling to compromise. As the hearings progressed, their advocates began to use different rhetoric. Instead of focusing on the scope of aboriginal title, they began arguing that Alaska Natives would not use the territory's resources efficiently. Again, Cohen tried to compromise. He accepted that Alaska Natives did not need all the lands and waters they had claimed as theirs. But he wanted to ensure that they would be compensated when their possessions were taken. As he explained to Collier, Interior's policy in Alaska and in the states had always been and should remain "to respect and protect aboriginal possession against private trespass or pubic domain disposition until such time as Congress has compensated the Indians for the relinquishment of such possessions as they do not need."[118]

This became Cohen's argument. Seeking to convince the cannery companies to act in a manner consistent with Alaska Natives' rights, he declared that "if any part of the area in question is set aside or reserved for the Indians, neither the Department nor the Indians will exclude outsiders from using the resources of the area, upon payment of fair compensation." Moreover, Cohen added that no compensation would be required for usages that did not "seriously interfere with the enjoyment of an area by its owners."[119] A departmental press release in December 1944 expressed a similar attitude. "Should the result of these hearings be to vest in Indian groups areas more extensive than they can efficiently utilize," it stated, "the obvious remedy would be for Congress to secure the cession by the Indians of those land or fishing areas which they cannot officially utilize" by giving them fair compensation. "Areas so ceded would then become open to the usual forms of commercial development."[120]

Cohen hoped that by applying this policy to Alaska, while 99 percent of its area was still owned by the federal government, Interior could put Alaska's commercial development "on a sound legal and moral basis" and ensure that the economy of Alaska Natives was adjusted to the needs of the territory and the entire United States.[121] But even as Cohen was writing his suggestions, the question was already dissociated from morals (and compensation for lands taken) and instead was fixated "on the question of how much land Natives under given conditions would actually need or use." With no legal tools to protect cultural sovereignty, Cohen was forced to accept the fact that Alaska Natives could not regain title to lands and waters beyond what aboriginal groups of similar size and under comparable conditions needed for their subsistence. The anthropological and historical data, as well as studies of land use, seemed to indicate that four or five square miles per capita constituted typical usage.[122]

With this in mind, Cohen accepted Hanna's conclusions. Personally, he thought that "the Indian claimants were entitled to something better" than what Hanna's opinion gave them but, as Cohen explained to Solicitor Harper, in light of the evidence he doubted "that the Secretary could go beyond the conclusions reached . . . and make the result stick in the face of court or Congressional attack."[123] This was also Harper's recommendation to Ickes.[124]

Ickes followed his solicitor's instructions and signed a decision document accepting Hanna's conclusions of law and finding of fact. The decision recognized Alaska Natives' possessory rights in their beaches and streams and reiterated Interior's duty "to respect existing rights in disposing of the public domain," whether such rights were established in law, custom, or fact. Moreover, Ickes stressed that as a matter of law and policy, aboriginal rights in waters and tidelands could be recognized even though such recognition ran against the grain of the common law.[125]

Aboriginal possessory rights were protected in the United States and in Alaska, as long as "the possession [had] been continuous and exclusive." But it was almost impossible to prove such a pattern for most of the claims. Ickes acknowledged that the three villages had originally occupied 3.3 million acres of land and water but declared that since 1884 they had "ceased to maintain exclusive occupancy of approximately ninety-two percent" of these areas, "either by reason of voluntary abandonment of lands once claimed or by acquiescence in the superior power and authority of the Federal Government in patenting or otherwise disposing of or controlling certain lands which effectively interfered with Indian use." Furthermore, while Ickes recommended compensating Alaska Natives for lands where their exclusive possession was extinguished, he left the door open for future withdrawal of lands and waters from Indian ownership for public use, as long as "adequate compensation [was] secured." Ultimately, of the claimed area of 3,339,000 acres, even though Hanna's opinion indicated the impossibility of accurately defining areas continuously used by Alaska Natives, Ickes announced that the villages had exclusive rights only to 273,000 acres—101,000 acres for the Haidas of Hydaburg, 95,000 acres for the Tlingits at Klawock, and 77,000 acres for the Tlingits at Kake. Allocated per villager, Ickes's decision gave "approximately 190 acres for each petitioning Indian." Such allocation was much in accord with the traditional 160–acre homesteads given to each head of a family in the continental United States under the General Allotment Act.[126]

A balance was presumably struck among Alaska natives' aboriginal claims, the rights of cannery companies, and Alaska economic development.[127] But Haas and Arnold were not satisfied. Arnold was not willing to accept that Alaska Natives had rights even in a limited area, and Haas continued to insist that Alaska Natives exclusively occupied larger areas, especially the waters and submerged lands 3,000 feet from the shores. Both petitioned Ickes to reconsider his decision. Ickes granted their requests for reconsideration, but on January 11, 1946, he issued a second and final decision that, with slight modifications, reaffirmed the findings of fact and conclusions of law of his first decision.[128]

Compromises

Cohen's work in the 1940s sought to articulate a conception of group rights as the foundation for the modern discourse of civil rights and liberties. His work in Alaska attempted to translate his theoretical support for group rights into law and policy. He wanted to protect Alaska Natives' property rights as they had traditionally defined them. According to Cohen, aboriginal title trumped the rights of large, nonresident corporations. His argument thus focused on the nature, scope, and limits of aboriginal occupancy in lands and waters. He wanted to incorporate aboriginal conceptions of property into American law.

As the pressures of other groups and a legal system committed to a particular understanding of property, ownership, and occupancy mounted, Cohen compromised. First, he let go of his plan to protect aboriginal title to all lands and waters claimed by Alaska Natives and instead tried to protect Alaska Natives' rights to lands and waters where they could prove exclusive occupancy within the limits of American law. Then, as the canning companies turned to the rhetoric of efficiency, Cohen settled on compensation for lands and resources taken.

As we will see, this would become the premise of Cohen's work on Indian land claims in the continental United States. Maybe because his work in Alaska made him realize that lands would not be returned to their aboriginal owners, maybe because it was an unrealistic expectation, Cohen's resolution of the problem of Indian land claims focused on compensation for lands taken. Moreover, and maybe because his work in Alaska had also taught him the dangers of pitting aboriginal rights against large public corporations, Cohen's solution for Indian land claims set Indian rights against the federal government. Finally, as his experience in Alaska taught him the difficulties associated with a solution premised on property rights, Cohen's general solution for Indian land claims against the government was predicated upon the contractual relationship between the United States and Indian peoples.

CHAPTER 9

A Contract with America

The federal government signed 370 treaties with Indian nations in the nineteenth century, covering nearly two billion acres of land. It paid about ten cents per acre compared to $1.25 per acre, which was "the minimum purchase price for lands of the public domain." Because the United States as a sovereign could not be sued for a monetary judgment until it waived its privilege, Indian tribes could not rely on American courts to protect their lands from being taken without just compensation.[1]

In 1855, Congress created the Federal Court of Claims to "hear and determine all claims founded upon any law of Congress, or upon any contract, express or implied, with the government of the United States."[2] In 1863, however, Congress passed an amendment to the 1855 act, removing from its jurisdiction all claims arising out of treaties with the Indians.[3] While in 1881 Congress allowed individual tribes to request separate jurisdictional bills to adjudicate their claims before the Court of Claims, only a few claims were filed during the last decades of the nineteenth century. Federal Indian policy at the time, the allotment policy, sought to distribute tribal lands to individual Indians and, even if indirectly, open reservation lands to general usage. Compensating Indian tribes for historic land claims was inconsistent with this policy.[4]

After World War I and especially after the Indian Citizenship Act of 1924, Indian tribes filed increasing numbers of claims pursuant to jurisdictional bills. If before 1924, "only one year (1891) saw more than one award, and in only four years were as many as four cases filed," in 1924, five claims were filed, in 1925—seven, in 1926—ten, and in 1927—fifteen.[5] Still, a system based on special jurisdictional bills was unsatisfactory. For one thing, the tribe had to provide information about its claim and find legislators who would introduce the bill in Congress. Few tribes had access to the necessary documents, most of which were in Washington, and even fewer were trained to analyze them and draft a congressional bill. They could hire a lawyer, but tribes often needed the permission of the federal government (as guardian of their funds) before they could pay a lawyer, and "paying a lawyer to sue the government was something the government seldom deemed appropriate." Even if they were able to hire a lawyer and draft a bill, nothing guaranteed that it would pass Congress and obtain the president's signature.[6]

In 1928, the Meriam Report criticized the government's handling of Indian claims and recommended establishing a fairer and more efficient device to resolve them. The report stressed that individual Indians declined to work, cooperate with the government, or plan for the future as long as their claims had not been resolved. It recommended appointing nonpartisan experts to look into the claims and determine which should be sent to the Court of Claims.[7] In 1929, the Institute for Government Research retained Margold, then a New York attorney, "to study the Indian claims problem . . . and to draft a bill embodying a practical means for its solution." Margold proposed that Congress create and establish an Indian claims commission composed of six commissioners, to be appointed by the president. The commission would hear and decide "all claims of whatsoever nature," that is, claims based on the U.S. Constitution, U.S. laws, treaties, executive decisions, contracts, or equity. It would cease to exist on the complete fulfillment of its duties or fifteen years after its organization, whichever came first.[8]

Nothing came out of Margold's proposal, even after Margold's appointment as Interior's solicitor. But in the decade that followed, Congress passed several jurisdictional acts to allow different tribes to submit claims.[9] The 1930s also witnessed the introduction of numerous bills and extensive hearings on the question of Indian claims.

The first bills, introduced in the early 1930s, called for the creation of an Indian claims court. But beginning with H.R. 6655, which was introduced in March 1935 and which Cohen helped draft, bills called for the creation of a special Indian claims commission.[10] Those in favor of solving Indian claims came to believe that due to the questions of history and anthropology underlying many of the claims, an investigatory commission was preferable to the adversary process. It was also assumed that a commission "could better 'cut through' the red tape of bickering government agencies charged with the preparation of Indian cases." The commission was to be "a fact-finding body," empowered only to suggest remedies to Congress.[11] Then, on August 1, 1940, the most detailed bill, S. 4234, was introduced. Drafted by Justice with Interior's assistance, it made the commission an "independent agency of the executive branch of the government, to be known as the 'Indian Claims Commission.'"[12]

According to S. 4234, the commission would hear all claims, including "claims of whatsoever nature which would arise on a basis of fair and honorable dealings, even though not recognized by any existing rule of law or equity." In fact, the commission was to inform each band, Indian group, and tribe about the act and ask that they submit their claims. It was to investigate all ev-

idence pertinent to the claim, and would have "authority to make final determination of the claims on matters of fact *and* law." The commission's final decisions were to be subject to review by the Court of Claims only on "questions
of law." The commission would terminate after ten years because "efficiency
and expertness [could] be achieved through the handling of all the claims by
the same personnel familiar with the same records."[13]

Nothing came of these suggestions. Justice insisted on including offsets for
gratuitous government expenses, the Budget Bureau feared a flood of claims,
and President Roosevelt was not supportive. In a letter to Ickes, the president
noted that in light of the history of Indian claims, he did not think that "Indian
claims could be disposed of with finality through the establishment of an Indian Claims Commission." Roosevelt believed that once the commission declared its judgment, "dissatisfied Indians" and their lawyers would simply bring
the claim to Congress. At any rate, Roosevelt did not think that "failure to
enact this legislation should adversely affect the general welfare of our Indian
population."[14]

The Indian Claims Commission Act (1946)

Beginning in 1943, amid calls to end the special status of Indian tribes, which
were motivated in part by the positive role Indians played in World War II, the
House Committee on Indian Affairs pushed, again, for the resolution of tribal
claims. Having engaged in a detailed study of Indian reservations, which included listening to the testimony of tribal leaders, the committee members
concluded that "outmoded claims procedures kept Indians on reservations
waiting for future cash awards." A quick resolution of Indian claims would
eliminate the major obstacle on the path to Indian independence. In December 1944, the committee published H.R. 2091, calling on Congress to establish
an Indian claims commission. Immediately thereafter, the executive council of
the National Congress of American Indians drafted an Indian Claims Commission bill, which was introduced in Congress as H.R. 1198. It sought to create
an Indian claims commission with the authority "to determine tribal claims of
every nature against the United States." Pursuant to the bill, tribes would have
five years to file their claims and could select attorneys of their own choice to
represent them. The claims could not be barred by any rule of law or equity or
by the statute of limitations, and the Supreme Court would hear appeals on
questions of law. The commission was required to complete its work within ten
years, so as "to encourage the prompt resolution of all claims." H.R. 1198 also
required that at least one member of the commission should be "a duly en-
rolled member of some recognized tribe or band of Indians."[15]

Indian tribes viewed their lands in terms of utility and identity. Their cultures and lifestyles were seriously affected by conquest. They became "territorial minorities on their home ground." They wanted a resolution of their land
claims both because a remedy could put them on the road to economic self-

sufficiency and because it would represent a cultural victory.[16] Representatives of different tribes who testified at the hearings on H.R. 1198 before the House Indian Affairs Committee endorsed the bill, stressing how long they had waited for the resolution of their land claims.[17]

Congressional support for the creation of an Indian claims commission came about for several reasons. Many expected that the resolution of tribal claims would allow the federal government to "downsize [the BIA], remove Indians from federal guardianship, and let them independently manage their own affairs."[18] In June 1943, Senator Thomas of Oklahoma, who was overseeing the "Survey of the Conditions of Indians of the United States," initiated by the Senate in 1928, issued a partial report calling for the abolition of the BIA. In December 1944, the House Select Committee to Investigate Indian Affairs pointed to certain problems "retarding the progress of the Indian and perpetuating the need for maintaining the [BIA]." A few months later, Collier tendered his resignation. Brophy, whom Collier chose as his successor, was able to secure the passage of the Indian Claims Commission Act (ICCA), but, as we will see, he could not stop the attempt to put an end to the special status of Indian tribes, an attempt that would be remembered in the history of federal Indian law as "termination."[19]

Many in Congress were also concerned about recent decisions of the Court of Claims involving the Klamath and Shoshone tribes that granted substantial interest payments on claims awards.[20] With the economic boom of the postwar years, developers and business interests, especially in the Western states, home to most of the members of the committees on Indian affairs, also wanted to open up Indian lands to private development.[21]

Still, others felt that amid a war against totalitarianism it was important to uphold moral and legal obligations on the home front.[22] This was Interior's position. It wanted to do justice to the Indians, although its conception of justice was limited to compensating tribes for lands taken. At Ickes's instructions, Cohen worked with Ernest Wilkinson, a Washington lawyer who represented tribal claims in the 1930s, to introduce amendments into the original H.R. 1198. These amendments aimed to guarantee that the commission would have broad jurisdiction to hear different kinds of claims, including "claims of whatever nature which would arise on a basis of fair and honorable dealings, even though not recognizable by any existing rule of law or equity." This broad jurisdiction resembled the jurisdiction proposed in S. 4234. The amendments also turned the commission into an agent of Congress rather than an independent agency of the executive branch, and they made its judgment final, subject to review by the Court of Claims and the Supreme Court. Interior's amendments further limited allowable counterclaims and offsets to those permitted against non–Indian claimants.[23]

In addition to broadening the powers of the commission, Interior's amendments required the commission to notify tribes, bands, and Indian groups of the bill's provisions and formally to ask them to file their claims. Furthermore, they called for the establishment of an independent investigation division "to make a careful search of the voluminous records relating to each Indian tribe or group of tribes for the purpose of locating, assembling, digesting and collating the pertinent materials bearing upon the rights of the respective parties, including, of course, the United States." Finally, they gave jurisdiction to the Court of Claims to hear future land claims, without special jurisdictional acts.[24]

The committee accepted Interior's amendments and asked Cohen to redraft the bill. In addition to these changes, the redrafted bill did not require an Indian to serve on the commission. On December 20, 1945, the new bill, H.R. 4497, was reported to the Committee of the Whole House. The House passed the proposed legislation without dissent five months later.[25]

Things did not go as smoothly in the Senate. Since the bill's inception, Justice had opposed Interior's plans. For one thing, Attorney General Francis Biddle cautioned Congress that "the bill would cost 'huge sums' of money," a claim not supported by past experience; moreover, it would "create a court and bind Congress with its decisions." According to Biddle, the plan would effectively deprive Congress of its "prerogative to sift and control this unusual type of claim against the government."[26] In April 1946, Justice suggested numerous changes to the bill. These changes eliminated certain Indian groups from its scope, removed claims based on fraud, duress, mistake and taking without compensation from the commission's jurisdiction, denied the commission's judicial character and its power of final decision, eliminated the possibility of appeal to the Supreme Court from legal decisions of the Court of Claims, eliminated the proposed investigation division, increased the scope of offsets, and closed the Court of Claims to post-1946 claims.[27]

Cohen found Justice's attempt to deny the finality of the commission's decisions and increase the scope of offsets most objectionable. But he also opposed Justice's attempt to eliminate certain groups from the scope of the bill, to limit the nature of claims that the commission could hear, to eliminate the investigation division, and to eliminate appeals to the Supreme Court on legal questions.[28]

The Senate Committee, however, accepted Justice's suggestions. The bill, as passed by the Senate on July 17, 1946, reflected many of Justice's concerns. It limited the claims "to those in law or equity rather than those of a broader moral basis. It also made offsets less discretionary, disallowed transfer of suits from the Court of Claims, and, most importantly, struck the clause allowing final determination to the commission." But the House Committee objected and after conference was able to resurrect the larger part of its original bill. It was passed by the Senate and the House on August 2, 1946.[29]

On August 13, 1946, President Truman signed the bill with the following statement:

> This bill makes perfectly clear what many men and women, here and abroad, have failed to recognize, that in our transactions with the Indian tribes we have at least since the Northwest Ordinance of 1787 set for ourselves the standard of fair and honorable dealings, pledging respect for

all Indian property rights. Instead of confiscating Indian lands, we have purchased from the tribes that once owned this continent more than 90 per cent of our public domain, paying them approximately 800 million dollars in the process. It would be a miracle if in the course of these dealings—the largest real estate transaction in history—we had not made some mistakes and occasionally failed to live up to the precise terms of our treaties and agreements with some 200 tribes. But we stand ready to submit all such controversies to the judgment of impartial tribunals. We stand ready to correct any mistakes we have made.[30]

Cohen drafted Truman's statement.[31] As the following section explains, it endorsed one of his most controversial arguments in support of the ICCA.

"How We Bought the United States"

Aboriginal Title and Group Rights, Revisited

In January 1946, to encourage the passage of the ICCA, Cohen published an article that baffled his colleagues. Entitled "How We Bought the United States,"[32] the article stressed the "historic fact . . . that practically all of the real estate acquired by the United States since 1776 was purchased not from Napoleon or any other emperor or czar but from its original Indian owners."[33] At the hearings before the House Committee on Indian Affairs, Cohen used a map to demonstrate his argument. The transfer of land, he explained to the committee members, was complete. Tribal claims arose because the government had "failed to pay the considerations promised in these various treaties and at times had paid the wrong party."[34]

In a paragraph that was omitted in the original publication, Cohen emphasized that the history of dealings with Indians had its dark side: Americans had driven "hard Yankee bargains"; they often did not make the payments they promised; they did not always respect the boundaries of lands that the Indians reserved to themselves or other promises they made to the Indians in return for their land. Yet Cohen stressed that whenever Congress was apprised of such deviations, it had "generally been willing to submit to court decisions the claims of any injured Indian tribe. And . . . to make whatever restitution the facts supported for wrongs committed by blundering or unfaithful public servants." No nation, Cohen proclaimed, had "set for itself so high a standard of dealing with a native aboriginal people" or had been "more self-critical in seeking to rectify its deviations from those high standards."[35]

Many of Cohen's contemporaries and, more recently, legal historians criticized him for downplaying the darker side of America's dealings with Indian tribes.[36] In a letter to Cohen, Ickes, for example, commented that he "might be disposed to wonder" whether Cohen had not "placed too high a value upon the goods and services with which [the United States had] supplied the Indians in certain circumstances." Ickes wondered whether Cohen had been "too optimistic" in his positive assessment of the fairness of the United States actions. Having known Cohen to be "more disposed to discover wrongs and insist upon their being righted" than to take "a complaisant point of view," Ickes nonetheless concluded that "the article was a good one." "I only hope," he wrote, "that our record is as fair as you present it."[37]

Cohen was a lawyer, an advocate on behalf of Indian tribes. He wanted the Indian claims commission to address "all Indian claims, legal, equitable and moral." While he no longer called for the restoration of lands to Indian tribes, he wanted the commission to compensate tribes not only where the federal government had previously recognized their title to the land but also where it had not.[38]

To support his vision, Cohen turned to the federal government's contractual obligations toward Indian tribes. Disheartened by his failure to protect aboriginal conceptions of property in Alaska and by the American legal system's inability to reconceptualize property, he cast Indian claims in contractual terms. As Cohen saw it, the existence of treaties between the government and Indian tribes implied that the government, in its actions, had long recognized the aboriginal title of all Indian groups. Accordingly, explicit congressional recognition was not a necessary condition for a particular claim based on Indian title.

Cohen's argument went further. In an intellectual milieu increasingly committed to individual rights and formal equality, many saw the special treatment of Indians as sustaining the Indians' position of inferiority. They described the ICCA as a step toward ending this peculiar status. Once compensated, Indians would be on a par with the rest of American citizens.

Cohen's work stressed otherwise. He wanted Americans to see that the peculiar status of Indian tribes was not a diminution of full citizenship, a claim he suggested bureaucrats used to defend the erosion of the Indians' unique rights. Rather, it was an addition to full citizenship.[39] The ICCA was not a step toward terminating the particular relationship between the federal government and Indian tribes but an affirmation of it.

In the early 1940s, the terminology of conquest advanced Cohen's ideal of group rights. In the mid-1940s, his discussion of treaties served a similar cause. "How We Bought the United States" replaced the fiction of conquest, which the *Handbook* arguably promoted, with a contractual approach. If in the *Handbook* Cohen argued that a long line of conquerors had recognized Indian rights, his writings in the mid-1940s suggested that Indians were fortunate to have their needs recorded in abundant treaties. The different legal rules to which tribes were sometimes subjected, Cohen stressed, were the fruits of treaties, contracts, and statutes that Indians were able to secure from the federal government. "All the peculiar legal relationships that seem to encumber the Indian are in the final analysis really obligations of the Federal Government to the Indian which only the Indian himself can waive," he wrote in 1944. Hence, "the peculiar legal status of the Indian is not a matter of race or birth but is a matter of contract or consent."[40]

Reiterating the argument he had made in the *Handbook,* this time with respect to treaties, Cohen emphasized that without the earlier generations' recognition of Indian rights, there would have been no problem of Indian claims. Wrongs never created rights, he wrote. Using a comparison to illustrate his point Cohen asserted that there was "no problem of Negro Claims for the uncompensated labors of two and one-half centuries of slavery, because the Negroes had no legal rights during the period of slavery." The fact that Indian claims were considered a "problem" indicated not only that wrongs had been committed against Indians but also "that Indians [had] always occupied a high and protected position in the law of the land."[41]

Propaganda

To understand what seems to be a rather simplistic theory of race relations, we must recall that Cohen's work in the mid-1940s was informed by his concerns about the events in Europe and their potential ramifications in the United States. Cohen believed that the agents of totalitarianism had launched an attack on "the common beliefs that have held [Americans] together as a nation, the moral and intellectual foundations of [American] democracy."[42] Cohen's ongoing struggle to create a plural polity offered an internal critique of the American way of life. Yet, like many Jewish intellectuals, Cohen was determined to rebut comparisons between the history of race relations in the United States and totalitarianism in Europe. "The propaganda assaults of Nazism, Fascism and Communism have been skillfully organized and lavishly financed," Cohen wrote in the foreword to *Combating Totalitarian Propaganda* (1944), a compilation of the Institute of Living Law's articles on the subject. "With complete disregard for the canons of ordinary decency and honesty, the purveyors of totalitarian propaganda have insidiously and persistently sought to undermine loyalty to the American way of life."[43] Ironically, in an effort to combat totalitarian propaganda, Cohen's writings on the ICCA similarly ventured into propagandist aims.

In a letter to the editors of *Collier's* Cohen explained that he had "written up the story of 'How we Bought the United States' . . . in not too technical terms and illustrated the piece with a map of the United States showing the various Indian cessions." Amid growing concerns about the treatment of minority groups, Cohen wanted to call attention to "the story of our land dealings with the Indians," because he believed most Americans "[were] quite unfamiliar with the basic facts on this subject and accept[ed] without question the myth that Indian land rights [had been] ruthlessly disregarded in the growth of our country."[44]

Cohen believed that his article would help fight totalitarian propaganda. As he told Collier, who was then at the United Nations Assembly in England, "possibly, this piece will help you, as an American diplomat abroad, to live down the bad name of the United States in the field of native affairs."[45] Pointedly, Cohen noted his hope that, at the very least, the piece would refute the assertions of "Jap, Nazi and Fascist propagandists [who] lost no time in pointing out that what their countries were doing in Asia, Africa and Europe was no different from what the United States did years ago in taking a continent from the Indians in the name of a superior race."[46] Collier replied with approval. "This is the way *so much else* about Indians and about all dependent peoples could be put across," he wrote to Cohen.[47]

Cohen aimed his work at totalitarian propagandists outside the United States as well as at those Americans who voiced racial antagonism against Indians, blacks, Jews, and any other cultural group. He claimed that the ideals of the American Revolution guaranteed to Indians equal citizenship and, thus, that discrimination against Indians, or against any other group, deviated from American standards.

Cohen well knew that the ideals he attributed to American life were not always fulfilled. "I probably overstated the high standards embodied in our treaties and statutes," he confessed to Ickes, and the editors' deletion of darker paragraphs created an even more exaggerated picture. Perhaps, he added, "twelve years among the bureaucrats have made me less astute to criticize our Indian record than I should be." More to the point, as Cohen admitted, his goal was to counteract opposition to "righting Indian wrongs." He thought that objections were often founded "on the mistaken idea that we have consistently robbed the Indians of all they owned and that laying down any higher standard of public conduct now would be unprecedented, revolutionary, and terribly expensive." By recalling more positive aspects of the United States' dealings with the Indians, Cohen hoped to put the "program . . . for general Indian claims legislation in a more appealing setting." As he did with respect to Alaska, so he tried in this article to offer an olive branch to his opponents. Keenly, Cohen stressed

> in my own dealings with Congressmen and others in public life I have found much illumination in a saying of Epictetus: "Everything has two handles: one by which it may be borne, another by which it cannot. If your brother acts unjustly, do not lay hold on the affair by the handle of his injustice, for by that it cannot be borne; but rather by the opposite, that he is your brother, that he was brought up with you; and thus you will lay hold on it as it is to be borne."

Perhaps, Cohen concluded his letter to Ickes, "even an over-optimistic commentary on the high standards set by our Indian legislation may prove helpful in arousing critical attention to lapses from those standards."[48]

Obligations, Mitzvot, and Pluralism

Cohen wanted to develop new standards. Even as he knew that lands would not be returned to Indian tribes and that only compensation was available to them, his belief in the government's obligations toward Indian tribes ran deep. In the 1930s, Cohen (together with other New Dealers) envisioned a positive role for the government in promoting social welfare. In the 1940s, as scholars sought to limit the power of the state over individuals, Cohen made government obligations toward Indians contractual. But it was not a simple contract. Cohen made human and tribal rights part of the contractual obligation of the federal government toward its minority population. "Without attempting to enumerate such rights," he wrote, "I should like to suggest that by and large the rights that are important to Indians are not rights of citizenship, that is to say, rights accorded to all citizens and denied to non-citizens, but are either human rights or tribal rights."[49]

In the mid-1930s, Cohen's work anchored tribal rights in a conception of a political social contract. By the mid-1940s he had broadened that contract to embrace human rights and tribal rights. But it was only a rhetorical change. In the 1930s, Cohen's social contract embraced the New Deal vision of social and economic citizenship. In the 1940s, as intellectuals abandoned the New Deal ideal in favor of racial and ethnic equality, Cohen brought economic and social rights under the umbrella of human and tribal rights. Accordingly, "the right to be free from involuntary servitude, the right to be free from unreasonable restraints on person or property imposed without due process of law . . . and all the other rights which are set forth in the Bill of Rights" were universal rights, of citizens and non-citizens alike.[50]

Although he might not have recognized it, Cohen's understanding of the role of the government was informed by Jewish law. As Robert Cover explained, while the American liberal jurisprudence of rights emerged to counter the centralized force of the Western nation-state, the Jewish legal system, which having had "no centralized power and little in the way of coercive violence" for more than 1,900 years, used a discourse of obligations to reinforce the bonds of solidarity. Lacking "an hierarchically determined authoritative voice," it developed a jurisprudence grounded in the possibility of multiple meanings. Authority was diffuse, but such diffusion reinforced the significance of obligations. "The word 'mitzvah' which literally means commandment but has a general meaning closer to 'incumbent obligation'" occupied in Jewish law "a place equivalent in evocative force to the American legal system's 'rights.'"[51]

This concept of obligations was closely tied to Cohen's pluralist vision of the modern state. While emphasizing the federal government's obligations toward Indians as a group, not merely as individuals, Cohen also stressed that the government's failure to fulfill its obligations was not a problem of contract law. It was an act of oppression, banned by the U.S. Constitution. "Racial oppression," he cautioned, "has seldom destroyed the people that was oppressed, [but] it has always in the end destroyed the oppressor."[52]

This was indeed the gist of "How We Bought the United States." Cohen wrote it not only to proclaim the federal government's obligations toward Indian tribes but also to fight oppression. In a pluralist world, the most important *mitzvah* was to encourage coexistence. Cohen wrote "How We Bought the United States" because he wanted his audience to recognize that throughout American history Indians were not slaves or victims; they were active agents, sovereign peoples, with histories, traditions, and legal systems of their own, co-existing with the American people. They accepted the presence of non-Indians, they were capable of dealing with them, and they protected their own interests. In Cohen's mind, the fact that Indians were able to deal with American settlers suggested the possibility of dialogue between different value systems. When he wrote "How We Bought the United States," Cohen needed to believe that the ICCA was merely reviving an age-old tradition of ethnic and racial coexistence.

Cohen wanted to encourage dialogue. His vision of the federal government's obligations toward Indian tribes extended beyond the treaties they signed. Because the proof of aboriginal title or the existence of treaties would require the testimony of Indians and their experts, Cohen wanted the commission to provide a forum for Indian tribes and individual Indians to tell their stories of American history. Accordingly, he suggested that the commission operate not "on a purely legal level" but rather "as an administrative agency empowered to reach a just solution within broad limits established by law."[53] If the IRA set out to refute the antiquated policy of assimilation and the *Handbook* retold the history of the relationship between tribes and the federal government, Cohen wanted the commission to rewrite the future by telling a different narrative. He wanted it to offer Indian tribes a forum to voice their versions of American history.

In short, Cohen wanted the commission's proceedings to become exercises in hearing and learning from the testimony of the Indians. He wanted the commission to investigate "the entire field of Indian claims, even for those tribes which may be too poor to hire their own lawyers, and bring in within a reasonable period of time a report which will conclude once and for all this chapter of our national history."[54] The legal remedy was meant to bring closure. It was also intended to call attention to and memorialize a different historical narrative. For Cohen, the ICCA was a genuine attempt to use law as a tool of reconciliation and commemoration. He hoped that the commission would settle historical acts of political and cultural violence between particular groups while reconstructing new memories upon which they could build a pluralistic present.[55] The federal government's obligation, anchored in treaties with Indian tribes, became an obligation toward all minority groups and society at large.

Cohen embraced the possibility of dialogue as an alternative to totalitarianism in Europe and changing federal Indian policy in the United States. His work throughout the 1940s—defending indigenous peoples' property, drafting the ICCA, writing "How We Bought the United States"—aimed to establish new American standards through dialogue. In a world where victims were many, the preservation of diverse cultures seemed the only alternative to total annihilation. America's original owners, who reached agreements to preserve their traditions with immigrants to the new world, proved, in Cohen's view, the feasibility of such an alternative. By emphasizing the success of earlier cultural dialogues, Cohen hoped to provide an incentive for agreements in postwar

America: between Native Americans and non-Natives; between the old inhab-itants and European immigrants; between diverse groups of all kinds.

As the first decades of the commission's life proved, Cohen's hopes for it were both ambitious and extremely naïve. Few Americans were ready to hear the stories of Indian tribes; fewer still were willing to recognize the full scope of their aboriginal title. As we will see in the following part, in the postwar years, a different image of the state, the liberal night-watchman state, also re-placed Cohen's vision of governmental obligations and pluralism.

Law in Action

Cohen was a front-runner nominee for the position of Indian claims commis-sioner, "with letters of recommendation from the major Indian rights organiza-tions, the National Congress of American Indians, Secretary of the Interior Krug, Undersecretary of the Interior Oscar L. Chapman, and Indian Commis-sioner William Brophy." But President Truman turned down the opportunity to appoint an expert in Indian law to head the commission. Instead, he ap-pointed Texas Democrat Edgar Witt, "a lawyer who had recently chaired the Mexican Claims Commission, which had made settlements favorable to the United States." The two other commissioners were William McKinley Hold, an attorney from Lincoln, Nebraska, and Louis O'Marr, the attorney general of Wyoming.[56]

The three commissioners were sworn in on April 10, 1947, and in July the commission began its first full fiscal year of operation. By December, seventeen claims were filed. In almost all of them, the government filed requests to ex-tend the sixty days in which it was allowed to submit its answer.[57]

Most of the claims arose out of land cessions. Indian claimants asked for awards reflecting the difference between what the government paid them for their lands and the fair market value of the lands at the time of the purchase. Most of the remaining claims were for accounting; they focused on the gov-ernment's mismanagement of tribal funds, which it held in trust as the tribes' legal guardian.[58]

Proving a claim of either kind required sorting through old government documents and thousands of transactions. To establish an accounting award, the tribe had to prove the fiduciary culpability of the government. The proof of a land-claim award was more complex. First, the tribe had to establish title to the land, a task that required translating Indian conceptions of property into West-ern ones. The expert testimony of anthropologists and historians was indispen-sable in this stage. Once title was established, government documents were used to determine the compensation paid to the tribe, which was then compared to expert appraisals of the fair market value of the land at the time it was pur-chased or taken. The difference was the basis for the claim's award. Then, the commission would offset the award to account for gratuitous government ex-penditures on behalf of the tribe.[59] Given its different stages, the litigation process proved to be rather lengthy; the life of the commission was repeatedly extended, finally expiring in 1978.[60]

In the course of three decades, the commission accomplished a great deal. By September 1978, when the commission ceased to exist, "approximately 670 cases had been adjudicated and $774,222,906.64 awarded. About 80 cases remained uncompleted and were passed on, often subdivided into additional cases, to the Court of Claims for its determination. Since 1978, an additional $486,723,175.75 has been awarded, making a total of $1,260,946,082.39 as of March 1985."[61] Yet, despite such accomplishments, the fairness and success of the commission's processes and outcomes remain questionable.

First, the commission was set up to give money awards, but it could not restore lands to the Indians. The commission further limited the awards to the fair market value of the land at the time of the taking, without interest.[62] In addition, many Indian groups were excluded from the commission's jurisdiction. In 1948, Solicitor Mastin G. White, in response to the attorney general's request for an interpretation of the term "identifiable group of Indians" under the ICCA, ruled that "'identifiable' meant tribes or bands whose political existence was recognized by Congress or the executive branch." Approximately one hundred thousand people were excluded from the act based on White's interpretation. Finally, the commission, following Justice's lead, refused to hear individual claims "based on moral considerations and litigation concerning the negative impact of land allotment."[63]

The offsets for gratuitous expenditures were another source of contention. To be classified as offset, the expenditure had to have been made gratuitously for the benefit of the tribe as a whole, with no recognized government duty to make it and no obligation of the Indians to repay it. The commission was also bound by section 2 of the ICCA, which eliminated almost one-fourth of more than fifty categories of offsets. Thus, determining the nature of the offset required an understanding of the relationship between the federal government and the tribe, which often involved the commission in time-consuming investigations.[64]

Finally, the question of aboriginal title remained a difficult problem throughout the commission's life but particularly in its first decade. Following the ruling in the Hualapai case, the commission held that in order to establish aboriginal possession, a prerequisite for a claim of taking without compensation, the tribe had to prove "exclusive occupancy . . . in a definable territory . . . from 'time immemorial.'" This was a question of fact. For one thing, "if the government demonstrated that more than one tribe used a particular area, exclusivity was denied." In contrast, as Cohen realized when he wrote "How We Bought the United States," "if it was shown that the government had recognized the rights of a tribe to a specific tract, it was unnecessary for the tribe to prove its actual use and occupancy of that area." In such cases, determining tribal rights to the land became a question of law.[65]

In the decade following the creation of the commission, the Supreme Court handed down a few decisions crucial to the question of aboriginal title. On

November 25, 1946, almost four months after the passage of the ICCA, the Court approved Cohen's view of aboriginal title. Writing the opinion in *United States v. Alcea Band of Tillamooks,* a suit originating in the Court of Claims pursuant to a jurisdictional act, Chief Justice Fred Vinson declared that tribes could recover compensation for lands taken whether or not the federal government recognized their title to those lands. Tribes only had to identify themselves as entitled to sue, prove their original Indian title to designated lands, and demonstrate that their interest in such lands was taken without their consent and without compensation.[66] In a letter to a colleague who worked with him on the *Handbook,* Cohen expressed his joy:

> You will be happy to learn . . . that the Supreme Court this week handed down a most important decision on Indian claims . . . which relies very considerably on a portion of the Handbook that you wrote. It must be very gratifying to you, as it is to me, that the Supreme Court does not agree with some of our critics who made the historical portions of the Handbook an object of particular scorn. It is really a matter of poetic justice that the Department of Justice should have lost an important case on this issue.[67]

In an article he published shortly thereafter, Cohen reiterated his celebration of the decision in *Alcea.* The case, he wrote, gave "the final coup de grace to what has been called the 'menagerie' theory of Indian title, the theory that Indians are less than human and that their relation to their lands is not the human relation of ownership but rather something similar to the relation that animals bear to the areas in which they may be temporarily confined."[68]

But Cohen's excitement was short-lived. In a second *per curiam* decision in the same case, the Supreme Court declared that the early *Alcea* decision rested on a statutory provision mandating the payment and not on constitutional obligations. Compensation was thus a political question to be determined by Congress and not a legal matter to be decided by the courts.[69] Then, in *Tee-Hit-Ton Indians v. United States* (1955), a claim based on constitutional taking, the Supreme Court ruled that, unless the federal government recognized their title, Indians held title to their lands "by the grace of the sovereign," which could terminate whatever interest they had without compensation.[70]

The *Tee-Hit-Ton* case involved an alleged taking of timber in Alaska that occurred after the ICCA was passed. It did not come to the Supreme Court under the act and, according to the Court, was not associated with the act's legislative intent. The decision thus indicated that it might not affect cases before the commission. The same year, the Court of Claims, in *Otoe and Missouria Tribes of Indians v. United States,* upheld a commission's decision recognizing aboriginal title, albeit only under section 2 of the ICCA and in cases falling within the commission's jurisdiction, that is, those originating in takings that occurred before 1946.[71]

These conflicting decisions regarding aboriginal title reflected a deeper disagreement about the nature of the federal government's relationship to Indian tribes. As already noted, the history of the Indian claims commission, its successes and, even more so, its failures, was tied to major changes in federal Indian policy that took place during the first decade of its life, specifically to the policy of termination. Many believed that resolving tribal land claims against the government was a step toward termination; they wanted a quick resolution of what they viewed as historical claims, so that tribes could move forward in the present. They did not much appreciate tribal cultures and traditions. They simply hoped that the settlement of tribal claims would encourage Indians to assimilate and "fully share in the prosperity of America's postwar capitalist market economy."[72]

Given such assumptions, it is not surprising that the commission failed to fulfill Cohen's goals. But it is also important to remember that these goals were limited. The commission was created to compensate for past wrongs. It did not address, at least not directly, how respect for aboriginal title could affect the allocation of resources, such as land, in the present. This question was the focus of Cohen's work in Alaska. Before we turn to Cohen's struggles against termination, let us return to Alaska where, because the stakes were high, the ideal of economic progress had direct impact on the definition of aboriginal rights. As we will see, in the struggle between capitalism and cultural sovereignty, the latter had to yield.

Back to Alaska

What may be done to compensate [American] natives for losses they have suffered in past years is a wholly different problem—one that you and the Congress have wisely referred to an Indian Claims Commission. What is vital to our national honor, as you so well appreciate, is that the still remaining possessions and rights of our Alaskan natives should be scrupulously protected.
    —Felix S. Cohen to President Harry S. Truman, January 17, 1950 (FSCP 28/443)

By the late 1940s, it seemed that there was little that Alaska Natives could do to protect their natural resources. Both their occupancy patterns and their "inefficient" use of lands and waters, as the canning companies labeled it, stood in the way of their Native claims.

Dismayed, the villages of Kake and Klawock rejected the small reservations that Interior offered them as a consequence of the Kake, Klawock, and Hydaburg hearings. Hydaburg pondered the issue for a few more years and ultimately accepted a reservation in 1949. A couple of years later, though, the Alaska District Court declared the Hydaburg reservation void.[73]

Cohen, even as he approved Hanna's recommendations, was also disappointed. As he put it in a memorandum for Assistant Secretary Gardner:

What the natives of Alaska most want is to be treated fairly, on the same basis as white residents. We do not promulgate in the Federal Register our conceptions of how much land a white man or town or church or corporation should own in Alaska or whether the boundaries of his land should be such as to encourage infiltration by neighbors of another race. We refrain from this—notwithstanding many white corporations and churches may have staked out unjustified claims—because it would be paternalistic and unjudicial. Why should we do this to Indians? We do not denounce a white man's claims on the ground that he is not developing them as fast as he might. Why should we do this to Indian claims? Are we not in danger of assuming the very paternalism against which we would like to protest? I suggest that we refrain from laying down any rule applicable to Indians which we are not prepared to apply to non-Indians.[74]

Cohen was not one to give up. Shortly after the conclusion of the Kake, Klawock, and Hydaburg hearings, he urged Haas to collaborate with Walter R. Goldschmidt, an anthropologist at the University of California, to study Alaska Natives' rights in preparation for future hearings, especially the rights of the Haida and Tlingit Indians. Haas and Goldschmidt's report concluded that the Haida and Tlingit Indians had a "well-defined system of property ownership" and that they had "since time immemorial . . . continuously used and occupied" almost two million acres, "including land that anchored twenty-seven salmon traps." In response to accusations that creating reservations for Alaska Natives would prevent them from participating in Alaska's economic development, Haas and Goldschmidt made an even stronger point. "Without knowledge of writing, hard metals, or machinery," they wrote, the Haida and Tlingit Indians "developed one of the highest forms of civilization in aboriginal America north of Mexico. It was rich in ceremony and creative arts, and complex in its social, legal and political systems." According to Haas and Goldschmidt, Alaska Natives also demonstrated that they could preserve their native ways while contributing to the American economy.[75]

Haas and Goldschmidt's report was widely circulated and its findings of fact, for the most part, accepted. But the federal government was more concerned about the mass meetings held by non-Native settlers in Alaska to protest the outcome of the Kake, Klawock, and Hydaburg hearings. The cannery companies' charges that Interior was giving Alaska back to the Natives fell on receptive ears, as did their argument that Interior did not have the authority to decide these complex legal issues unilaterally. The cannery companies wanted Congress or a judicial tribunal to determine the merit of Alaska Natives' claims, and Gardner, who by 1945 was assistant secretary, saw their point.[76]

Cohen continued to compromise. He thought that forcing Alaska Natives to waive their rights in certain trap-sites required just compensation. ("Calling Indian property 'aboriginal' or 'reservation,'" he explained to the secretary, "does not detract from the measure of Indian rights.")[77] But he ultimately recommended that Alaska Natives accept an agreement, pursuant to which the P. E.

Harris Company would deliver the entire production of one of its fish traps to the Indian cannery at Hydaburg. In return Alaska Natives would avoid operating the eleven trap sites that, according to the decision in the Hydaburg, Kake, and Klawock hearings, were anchored to beaches held by them.[78] In a similar manner, in response to demands to allow financial interests to establish a pulp and newsprint mill in southeastern Alaska, Cohen drafted a bill to "authorize the Forest Service to cut timber in the Tongass National Forest," where the Haida and Tlingit peoples claimed aboriginal title. The bill allowed the Forest Service "to set aside small parcels of land for the pulp mills" but required it to "pay the Indians 10 percent of the gross proceeds from timber sales."[79]

These compromises did not satisfy the different industries. In the summer of 1947, at the urging of the pulp industry and the governor of Alaska, Truman signed into law an act that "gave the secretary of agriculture and secretary of the interior a free hand to appraise and sell timber on vacant unappropriated, and unprotected land in the Tongass National Forest." The act "did not recognize or deny the validity of native property rights based on aboriginal occupancy." Hence, instead of paying Alaska Natives a 10 percent royalty on sales of timber from these lands, the bill declared that proceeds of sales would be held in escrow, in a special U.S. Treasury account, until Congress determined Alaska Natives' claims.[80]

Cohen labeled the Tongass Timber Act Alaska's Nuremberg Laws.[81] Immediately after its passage, he began to work "to sell Indian timber to interested buyers and to block the government's trespass on Indian land." He wanted Alaska Natives to stake out their mineral claims, but he was also looking for another solution. Cohen began to urge Alaska Natives to organize "under the Alaska Reorganization Act to operate sawmills, and find customers to purchase their lumber." Describing the Tongass Timber Act as an imposition of "economic colonialism on Indians by allowing absentee corporations to steal their natural resources," he offered the creation of reservations in Alaska as a means of overcoming it.[82]

Fighting Economic Colonialism: Reservations

Back in 1934, Cohen warned that the "termination of governmental control" over Indian affairs "would not inaugurate Indian freedom. It would only exchange the slavery of bureaucracy for the slavery of poverty."[83] Beginning in the mid-1940s, he anxiously witnessed the fulfillment of his prophecy. As the federal government gradually reinterpreted or abrogated its duties to protect the rights of Alaska Natives, the latter were left to fend for themselves against large non-resident corporations. Writing in 1945, Cohen again stressed the differences and similarities between economic and political dominance. He wanted the government to "minimize the evils of political overlordship without increasing the evils of private economic exploitation."[84]

Against Cohen's wishes, throughout the late 1940s and 1950s government political overlordship joined forces with private economic powers to impose more barriers on the Alaska Natives' path for economic survival. Furthermore, Secretary Krug, at Gardner's advice, refused to hold additional administrative hearings "to determine the possessory rights of Indians other than those at the villages of Hydaburg, Kake, and Klawock."[85] Beginning in 1947, in a development that paralleled the shift toward termination in the continental United States, different bills were introduced in Congress to repeal the Alaska Reorganization Act, to rescind the executive orders that in 1943 established four reservations, and to transfer legal jurisdiction over Alaska Natives to the Alaska territorial government.[86]

Against these changing tides, Cohen and the few who shared his vision wanted to create reservations under the Alaska Reorganization Act to secure Alaska Natives access to land and resources. While Cohen strongly believed that Alaska Natives who would accept reservations should not be banned from claiming compensation for lands taken,[87] he wanted to define reservation boundaries so as to include waters or forests and provide Alaska Natives with resources for their economic survival.[88] Cohen repeatedly encouraged the different villages to accept their reservations.[89] But the opposition was too strong.

Letters written to Judge Hanna during the Hydaburg, Kake, and Klawock hearings already indicated the opposition of industries and individuals in Alaska to the idea of reserving land or water for the exclusive use of Alaska Natives. They described such plans as creating special classes and thus undemocratic. But unlike the missionary undertones of the attack on reservations in the continental United States, the attack on reservations in Alaska was motivated by fears that Interior was taking economic opportunity away from non-Natives. Letters suggested that creating reservations would "jeopardize investments and enterprises" and prevent "future expansion of business in Alaska."[90] "By herding [the Indians] together on Reservations," one letter noted, "they will lose their spark of freedom and Independence and we would destroy those great industries built up for the betterment of mankind in general."[91]

The industrial establishment emphasized its role in developing Alaska, or as one chamber of commerce put it, "It was not [Alaska Natives] who built up our commercial fishing industry, which was done through the investment of capital and the labor of fishermen and cannery workers over a period of many years."[92] But even groups who opposed the monopoly given to cannery companies joined the latter in opposing reservations for Alaska Natives. They wanted all workingmen and -women regardless of their race to have equal access to Alaska's resources.[93]

Many letters masked economic fears in the rhetoric of antidiscrimination that had come to dominate legal discourse in the 1940s. They emphasized the progress that Alaska Natives had made and described reservations as an obstacle on the Alaska Natives' road to full assimilation. But the fears about economic injustice were always apparent. One letter described reservations as "a monstrous injustice to the men and women who pioneered Alaska."[94] Another letter more pointedly suggested that giving "special privileges to Indians and those who marry the Indians" would "create racial or color hatreds, which fortunately, as yet are practically non-existent in Alaska." What was, then, the solution? According to this particular correspondent, "when you solve the problem for the poor white man you also solve the problem for the poor Indian"; in turn, a solution that would give Indians property and natural resources would simply give them the weapons, "which they now object to being wielded by white corporations."[95]

The bills introduced in Congress beginning in 1947 were similarly based on the view that reservations separated Alaska Natives from the white community, prevented prompt assimilation, protected tax-exempt property, and hindered the development of Alaska's industries for the benefit of the general public.

The debate ran deeper. The fight over the Alaska Natives' claims took place in a changing intellectual and political milieu. The pluralist ideal of the early 1930s and, more so, the notion that the government should protect the cultural and historical values of groups or groups' right to be different was no longer widely accepted. As scholars described different individuals and groups as equally situated, policymakers stressed the need to accommodate the interests of diverse groups in a neutral, preferably procedural, manner. As Gardner put it in a memorandum for Secretary Krug, in determining the policy with respect to Alaska Natives, Interior had two choices: it could emphasize its fiduciary duties toward Alaska Natives or it could emphasize its trusteeship toward all citizens. If the early New Dealers saw their role as trustees for American Indians, by the late 1940s Interior saw its role as protecting the interests of all groups. History and culture no longer mattered; all groups were equally found.[96]

Cohen continued to see the matter differently. Already in 1944, in a pointed memorandum to Assistant Secretary Chapman, he noted that the "assumption that a reservation is an area set aside for 'one race'" was erroneous. Drawing upon his theoretical argument in support of group rights, he elaborated:

> If a reservation that belongs to ten or two hundred Indians is a racial affair, then, it seems to me, a piece of property that belongs to ten or two hundred white persons is just as much a racial affair. But none of the opponents of the reservation policy have ever suggested, so far as I know, eliminating exclusive ownership of specific tracts of Alaskan land by white persons, even though it is on the land owned by white persons that racial discrimination most frequently occurs. The fact is, of course, that nobody has ever suggested the establishment of reservations for the "Indian race." All that has been suggested is that (a) Indian property rights should be respected, and (b) Indians should be permitted to acquire lands collectively rather than simply on an individual homesteader basis.[97]

But Cohen's keen critique could not change the general atmosphere. Even Alaska Natives viewed reservations negatively. First, like tribes in the continental United States who distrusted the BIA, many Alaska Natives viewed reservations as representing economic colonialism. But they rejected them for other reasons as well. By the late 1940s, many Alaska Natives accepted the white settlers' arguments that "reservations would restrict their freedom, promote racial discrimination, and jeopardize social security benefits and other rights enjoyed by American citizens."[98] Alaska Natives also feared—and, in light of the different bills in Congress to extinguish their title, had grounds to fear—that by accepting reservations they would relinquish any monetary claim against the federal government.[99] Moreover, after World War II, many lost faith in tribal self-government as a means of helping Native peoples in the United States and its territories. Not only was its success dubious, it also seemed antithetical to the emerging conceptions of individual rights and liberties that were the focus of legal attempts to protect minority groups.

The widely accepted individualist ideal was another form of colonialism. It went hand in hand with a growing acceptance of Keynesian economics, which viewed the state as responsible for compensating "for capitalism's inevitable flaws and omissions without interfering very much with its internal workings." It justified regulating the economy not through planning but by "accepting existing consumer preferences" and "manipulating aggregate demand." Postwar American liberals, who believed that the New Deal eliminated the dangerous features of corporate capitalism, detached liberalism from its earlier commitment to reform. They endorsed the view that "economic growth was the surest route to social progress" and that economic growth depended on consumption, not on production. In their hands, the individual consumer became the foundation of economic and political thought.[100]

As Alaska Natives soon realized, the rhetoric of consumption, individual preferences, and economic progress was detrimental to their needs. It helped characterize Alaska Natives not as a group claiming title to their lands and waters but as a group blocking universal progress. To paraphrase the Supreme Court decision in *Hynes v. Grimes Packing Company* (1949),[101] a case that encapsulated Cohen's work in Alaska and for which he wrote an amicus brief, Alaska Natives were an unprofitable race. In a world committed to economic progress, their cultural claims were bound to be ignored.

The Unprofitable Race: Aboriginal Title and Efficiency

Hynes v. Grimes Packing Company reached back to the establishment of the Karluk reservation. On May 22, 1943, Ickes created the reservation, pursuant to section 2 of the Alaska Reorganization Act, through departmental withdrawal of thirty-five thousand acres of land and water. It was meant to protect the interests of the two hundred Native Aleuts of Karluk who, every summer, just as "the red salmon that spawned up the Karluk River began migrating in from the ocean," were driven out of their fishing area by nonresident employees of the canning companies. The people of Karluk approved their reservation on May 23, 1944, and immediately thereafter, the village council marked "the outer boundary of an area at the mouth of the river within which it prohibited white fishermen to set nets."[102]

The cannery companies in Seattle and San Francisco were up in arms. As they saw it, if Interior established reservations to give Alaska Natives exclusive rights to catch salmon in waters surrounding their villages, white fishermen would lose most of their access to Alaska's resources. They promptly instructed their attorneys to block the creation of reservations.[103]

This was not a difficult task. A secretarial order and the vote of the particular group of Alaska Natives were sufficient to create a reservation, but they could not protect it against incursions. There was no specific criminal sanction for violating reservation boundaries. Moreover, the BIA did not have authority to enforce fishing regulations. It had authority to enforce actions for trespass on reservations, but Justice had to bring the action itself.[104] Given Justice's anti-Native biases, the process was likely to be ineffective.

Whether or not they were aware of these enforcement loopholes, the cannery companies took the law into their own hands. They continued to fish in the Karluk waters with complete disregard for the reservation's boundaries. In 1945, in an attempt to stop their activities, the Karluk village council required white fishermen to obtain a license to fish in reservation waters. The cannery companies ignored it, forcing Cohen and his colleagues to find an enforcement mechanism, which they did. In 1946, at Cohen's urging, the Fish and Wildlife Service promulgated a regulation pursuant to the 1924 White Act prohibiting white fishermen from fishing in the waters of the Karluk reservation unless authorized by the Karluk village council.[105]

The White Act was a tool the federal government used to regulate fishing in Alaska. It allowed the government to establish "fishing reserves for conservation purposes." The government could even exclude "all fishing within such reserves." But the White Act specifically banned granting exclusive fishing privileges to "any class of people." As the regulation Interior adopted guaranteed an exclusive fishing privilege to the Karluk Natives, it appeared to violate the White Act. Still, at the beginning of the 1946 fishing season, the Fish and Wildlife Service sent two Indian Service officers to protect the Karluk Natives' fishing rights.[106]

Sending these officers might not have been in the best interests of the Karluk Natives. It seems to have been a ploy by the Director of the Fish and Wildlife Service, who was "known to be extremely friendly to the plaintiff cannery companies," to push Alaska Natives out of their fishing grounds. His strategy was simple. While the inhabitants of Karluk were interested in protecting a relatively small fishing area for their use and requiring companies to apply for licenses to fish in other reservation areas, the Fish and Wildlife Service threatened an overall revamping of Alaska resources, vowing to arrest all white fishermen in reservation waters. These false threats "issued over the objection of the [BIA], helped the companies to paint a picture of ruin to their millions of dollars' worth of canning investment," a picture that the courts, when asked, were quick to adopt.[107]

The Profit Motive

Shortly after Interior promulgated its regulation, the Kodiak salmon packers filed suit in the District Court for the Alaska Territory, seeking to enjoin its enforcement.[108] In addition to arguing that the regulation violated the White Act, the cannery companies asked the court to invalidate the creation of the Karluk reservation because the Alaska Reorganization Act authorized the secretary of the interior "to withdraw 'public lands' as reservations," and "Congress did not intend the term 'public lands' to include water."[109]

Judge Harry Pratt of the District Court accepted the companies' argument and concluded that the secretary did not have the authority to issue the said regulation.[110] In 1947, the U.S. Court of Appeals for the Ninth Circuit affirmed Pratt's decision. The Court of Appeals held that the Alaska Reorganization Act authorized the secretary of the interior to reserve public lands for Alaska Natives, but it "did not empower him to reserve ocean lands below low water mark." Having invalidated the reservation, the Court of Appeals saw no reason to discuss the regulation because, as the Court put it, under the White Act, the regulation would be valid only if it protected reserved lands.[111]

The reasoning of the Court of Appeals was remarkable testimony to the postwar ideal of economic progress. The Court insisted that Congress could not have intended "to create in the Indians communal monopolies in such salmon fishing waters about the long established packing plants from which would be excluded the thousands of white fishermen employed in producing for the world, but principally the United States, its largest supply of canned fish food."[112]

In the competition between culture and capitalism, culture had to yield. The evidence showed that a large portion of the Alaska Native population lived at the mouths of streams into which salmon seeking to spawn ran. But the Indians were not packing companies. As the court explained, "prior to the coming of the canning and packing plants, the Indians smoked the salmon for winter use, that fish being their principal article of diet." In turn, the canning companies' use of salmon benefited the world community. Since the turn of the twentieth century, American canning enterprises had supplied "the world, particularly the United States," with canned salmon as well as thousands of jobs (including jobs for Alaska Natives). The Court went so far as to suggest that Alaska Natives benefited from the presence of the canning companies, which employed them and bought their merchandise.[113]

This was 1947. The court was sympathetic to minority groups (it was willing to accept the Alaska Reorganization Act as special legislation for Alaska Natives' benefit), but its compassion was limited to the protection of groups against discrimination. To allow groups, specifically Alaska Natives, to exercise their rights, on their terms, in ways that might impair the more efficient and profitable use of Alaska's resources as defined by the Court—that was unthinkable. "The American way of the profit motive," the Court elaborated, "often leaves unjustly behind minority groups of lesser education and initiative." Such realization required courts to construe statutes enacted to help minority groups liberally. But even given an empathetic interpretation of the Alaska Reorganization Act, the Court was determined that it did not give "monopoly-creating power" to the secretary of the interior. It could not have intended to exclude "great food producers . . . from their established fishing grounds."[114]

The Unprofitable Race

Cohen was outraged.[115] No longer in government service (having resigned in January 1948), he challenged the interpretation of the Court of Appeals in an amici curiae brief on behalf of the Native Village of Karluk, the Alaska Native Brotherhood, the National Congress of American Indians, the Association on American Indian Affairs, and the ACLU. Cohen insisted that the Alaska Reorganization Act authorized the secretary of the interior to include coastal waters as well as uplands in the Karluk Reservation.[116]

Cohen further argued that the White Act did not prohibit setting aside public property for federal use, specifically for the creation of Indian fisheries. It was only meant to prevent private monopolies. He sharply noted that as the White Act protected the rights of the first occupant of a fish trap site, "as long as he occupies it," the only question left was whether such protection should be "denied to groups which the court below has characterized as 'minority groups of lesser education and initiative.'" Cohen concluded that either the possessory and first occupancy rights of both Alaska Natives and the companies were recognized or they were not. In other words, if the Court were to deny the possessory rights of the Karluk Natives, it should open to the public all fishing sites in Alaska, even those to which cannery companies claimed a right.[117]

The Supreme Court accepted Cohen's argument with respect to the Alaska Reorganization Act but not with respect to the White Act. By a unanimous vote, the Court decided that Congress intended the term "public lands" in the Alaska Reorganization Act to include waters. The waters along the Karluk shore out as far as 3000 feet beyond low tide were thus a proper part of the Karluk reservation. But by a vote of 5 to 4, the Court also concluded that the White Act of 1924 prevented the Fish and Wildlife Service from adopting a regulation that prohibited white fishermen from fishing in the waters of the Karluk reservation. The Court declared that "whatever may be the powers of . . . Interior or the natives as to regulating the entrance of persons other than natives in possession of Karluk Reservation into or on the area of land and water in that reservation, they are not broad enough to allow the use of the White Act sanctions to protect the reservation against trespass."[118]

The Supreme Court's decision appeared to be based on a technical legal interpretation, but it incorporated many of the sentiments expressed by the Court of Appeals with respect to economic progress. Justice Stanley Reed, who delivered the opinion of the Court, noted that the canning companies had "canned fish from these waters for from seven to twenty-four years" and would suffer "irreparable injury . . . if they could not obtain the catch of the reservation." Reed added that the canners' investment was "substantial" and that they employed "over four hundred fishermen, chiefly residents of Alaska, and over six hundred cannery employees, chiefly nonresidents."[119]

Debates behind the scenes highlighted the Court's empathy for the canning companies. For one thing, the Court indicated that if it were required to determine whether the reservation was a permanent withdrawal, it would strictly interpret the secretary's powers under the Alaska Reorganization Act. Fearing just such an interpretation, Interior was compelled to argue that the act only granted the secretary power temporarily to withdraw lands and waters. While characterizing the reservation as temporary meant that as long as it existed the United States had authority to protect it against trespassers, it also implied that the reservation could be revoked without compensation to the Karluk residents.[120]

More important, in a private correspondence with Justice Reed, Justice William O. Douglas, who had written the decision in the Hualapai case and who was one of the four dissenting justices in *Hynes v. Grimes,* pointed out that the system of reservations was meant to create monopolies. Douglas contended that nothing in the White Act "was designed to effect a reversal in Indian policy." He stressed that "the problem in Alaska has been to protect the Indians and the public against the packing houses, not to protect the packing houses against the Indians." But Reed was not convinced. The decision, he told Douglas, was "best for the Indians." It was best because, according to Reed, "a monopoly of a three million dollar a year fishery" was "too much to give the Indians."[121]

A Lost Battle

By the late 1940s Cohen felt that he could no longer win fights for the rights of Native Americans and Alaska Natives from within Interior. In January 1948 Cohen left Interior to enter private practice, where he continued to work on behalf of indigenous peoples. In this capacity, he also wrote to the president of the Karluk Village Council to congratulate him on the *Grimes* "victory."[122]

Congratulations aside, Cohen took pains to explain the Supreme Court's decision and ways to enforce it. As Cohen pointed out, although the Court upheld Interior's authority to protect Alaska Natives' rights by establishing reservations for them, the Court rejected Interior's attempt to enforce exclusive rights in fisheries—a key reason for creating the Karluk reservation. The only remedy available to Alaska Natives was an action in trespass, which required not only adequate proof but also the Justice Department's agreement.[123]

Stressing the inability of the BIA to assist the Karluk people due to internal conflicts between the BIA and the Fish and Wildlife Service, Cohen's letter elaborated how the Karluk residents could protect themselves. He suggested that they "put up notices" to mark the reservation "fishing grounds," enforce their local "permit ordinance," identify trespassers, sue them, and hire private attorneys if government attorneys would not prosecute.[124] Writing to Alexander Lesser of the Association on American Indian Affairs six months after the decision was announced, Cohen noted that "it looks as if the canning industry has been willing to comply with the very modest Indian requirements." Perhaps, he concluded in the same spirit of compromise that characterized his work throughout the 1940s, "in the long run a policy of low license fees and cooperation with the industry will pay the best dividends."[125] Presumably liberated from political overlordship, Alaska Natives were free to fend for themselves against large corporations. In a world committed to "efficiency" defined by such corporations, Alaska Natives were free to compete and compromise. As Cohen well knew, they were also free to lose.

If anything could have been done in 1950 to protect the Karluk reservation, by 1952 the question became moot after the Alaska District Court delivered the last blow to the New Deal policy in Alaska. Assessing a legal suit by the United States against the Libby Packing Company for trespass on the Hydaburg reservation, one of the few created under the Alaska Reorganization Act, the court declared the reservation invalid.[126] Folta, one of the three attorneys who had represented the government at the Hydaburg, Kake, and Klawock hearings, was the district judge who decided the case.[127] After *Libby*, Alaska Natives were permitted to use fish traps under Interior regulations, but no serious attempt was made to enforce exclusive Native fishing rights or to create other reservations in Alaska. In 1971, the Alaska Native Claims Settlement Act brought to Alaska the same settlement methods enforced by the ICCA. It brought closure to Native claims to large areas of land by paying the claimants and recognizing their permanent rights to smaller areas.[128]

Part V

Doubts and Hopes, 1948–1953

CHAPTER 10

In the Shadows of the Law

"You will resign when your freedom . . . is denied"

When Mary Cohen died on June 8, 1942, Felix lost both a mother and a confidant. When Morris died less than five years later, on January 28, 1947, Felix lost a father, a friend, and a colleague. The letters of sympathy arriving at his residence were overwhelming. Writing to a friend, he noted, "the lines of Callimachus (in the Greek anthology) on Heraclitus keep running through the back of my throat":

> They told me, Heraclitus, they told me you were dead,
> They brought me bitter news to hear and bitter tears to shed.
> I wept, as I remembered, how often you and I
> Had tired the sun with talking and sent him down the sky.
> And Now that thou art lying, my dear old Carian guest,
> A handful of gray ashes, long, long ago at rest,
> Still are thy pleasant voices, thy nightingales, awake,
> For Death, he taketh all away, but them he cannot take.[1]

Less than a year after Morris's death, on December 15, 1947, Felix sent his letter of resignation to Secretary of the Interior Julius A. Krug. According to Lucy, the "unconscionable taking . . . without compensation or legal procedure" of timber in Alaska led to his resignation.[2] But Cohen revealed nothing. His letter reminded Krug that he had initially planned to stay at Interior for a year and "then return to private practice and teaching." It went on to say that "the many kindnesses" that colleagues extended to him, and his work's "fascinating variety and never-ending opportunities for defense of the public interest, [had] made leaving very difficult." He had thus "overstayed [his] appointed tour of duty by thirteen years and . . . largely outlived [his] usefulness." "You have a great team," Cohen's letter concluded, "and I wish you all the best of breaks in the contests ahead."[3]

"Usefulness" was the key word. The demise of the Indian New Deal left Cohen with less and less work. Constant debates with government officials left him frustrated. Shortly after Margold left the department, Morris Cohen, presumably without his son's knowledge, wrote to Ickes suggesting that Felix be appointed solicitor; Ickes refused.[4] In 1946, Krug, the secretary of the interior, and Brophy, commissioner of Indian affairs, recommended to the president that Felix Cohen be appointed chief commissioner of the first Indian Claims Commission; as we have seen, this appointment was never made.[5]

Back in 1933 Norman Thomas told Cohen: "You will resign when your freedom . . . is denied."[6] In 1947 Cohen concluded that he would be able to assist Indians (and other minorities) by representing them against the government.[7] The New Deal's zest had been suppressed, and Cohen felt that he "was no longer earning [his] salt." His "memoranda were being gratefully acknowledged and quietly pigeon-holed," and he felt a "sense of loneliness in the struggle for the defense of Indian rights." He failed "to get across to the right parties the significance of the current assaults on Indian lands which have reached a new high-water mark." He decided to continue the struggle from outside.[8] And so he did.

Shortly after leaving the government, Cohen accepted visiting teaching positions at CCNY and Yale Law School, where he taught on Fridays and Saturdays, respectively. While his teaching focused on jurisprudence and legal philosophy, his creative energies were seen in a course on legislative drafting that he designed. Building on his experience at Interior, Cohen viewed the course as teaching, through practical examples rather than lecture, the "unspeakable knowledge" of legislative drafting. Topics included "drafting of bills, committee reports, testimony before committees, and . . . the preparation of 'Reports to Clients.'" He wanted his students to get "the feel of legislative materials." Reflecting the lessons he learned, he also wanted them to gain "some realistic understanding of the give and take of the legislative process." It was a course that Cohen "enjoyed considerably."[9]

But the forty-year-old Cohen did not wish to enter academia as a full-time professor any more than the twenty-year-old Cohen did.[10] Academic life did not fit his temperament; he was an activist. He loved teaching and his students loved him, but he continued to believe that he was better suited to affect social and legal change as a lawyer, not as a scholar.

Cohen worked with the law firm of Curry, Bingham, and Cohen (the latter was his cousin Henry). The firm was involved in the struggle to protect Alaska Natives' rights, and in the postwar years it handled many Indian claims. It was agreed that because of Cohen's role in drafting the Indian Claims Commission Act he would not play a role in cases involving Indian claims so as not to violate ethics rules.[11]

In the summer of 1948, a bitter dispute between Cohen and Curry led Cohen to terminate his relationship with Curry, Bingham, and Cohen, which closed shortly thereafter.[12] Cohen became a consultant for the New York firm of Riegelman, Strasser, Schwarz, and Spiegelberg (it would later become Fried, Frank, Harris, Shriver, and Kampelman). It belonged to a group of twenty-one law firms—the Joint Efforts Group—which was formed in December 1948, with the permission of the Commissioner of Indian Affairs, "to set up a research office in Washington DC to expedite the formulation and prosecution of cases" before the Indian Claims Commission.[13] Cohen was to perform claims research from the Washington office. In this role, he compiled "tribal histories" as he had previously done in his work on the *Handbook*. He also studied and prepared summaries of the reports of the Committee on Indian Affairs prior to 1880 and trained a staff of four attorneys "in the methods and sources of research in Indian law and history." For this technical assistance, Cohen was paid an annual retainer of $15,000. As one of his partners, later complained, even when Cohen worked for a fee, he never charged what a professional lawyer would. Reportedly, the firm had to "reeducate" the clients they inherited from Cohen—they had to teach them the nature of "payment for professional service."[14]

In addition to his work on Indian claims, Cohen represented individual tribes in particular cases. The first case he argued in court as a private attorney secured the right to vote for Indians in New Mexico and Arizona.[15] Cohen also served as a general counsel to several tribes and to the Association on American Indian Affairs (AAIA). In this capacity, he argued cases that secured the right to participate in social security programs for Indians in Arizona and California.[16] As he described it, his work on behalf of Indian tribes embodied "the concept of a lawyer's obligation to the community that [he] learned from such devoted public servants and guides as Holmes, Brandeis, Cardozo, Roosevelt, Ickes, Margold, Fahy, and Chapman."[17]

Finally, Cohen continued to work with different organizations committed to protecting minorities' interests, including the New York Association for New Americans, the American Jewish Committee, the Conference on Jewish Relations,[18] and the Institute of Ethnic Affairs, organized by John Collier in 1945.[19]

As a member of these organizations and in his other endeavors, Cohen continued to defend and promote his pluralist vision, seeking to encourage group autonomy and, at the same time, limit group power toward other groups and individuals. In his work after he left Interior, promoting group self-government was not merely an end. It was also a means of achieving tolerance and understanding among diverse groups. Cohen's work thus encompassed a wide range of issues: assisting indigenous communities in the United States and the Territories to preserve their cultures and manage their economic and political affairs; helping migrant Mexican and Indian workers;[20] assisting immigrants; fighting exclusionary racism toward citizens, including African Americans[21] and Native Americans, as well as toward immigrants;[22] achieving fair employment practices;[23] fighting restrictive covenants;[24] fighting anti-Semitism and racist propaganda;[25] studying inter-minority relations, that is, what "the Indian problem" means to African Americans, Jewish Americans, and other minority groups; and attempting to foster international collaboration to achieve these goals.[26]

But the terrain in which Cohen operated had dramatically changed, both as a matter of personnel and as a matter of policy, especially in the field of federal Indian law. For one thing, the political focus shifted to the needs of African Americans and the needs of Native Americans were put on the back burner.[27] As we have also seen, in an intellectual milieu committed to individual rights, the special relationship of the federal government to Indian tribes seemed rather peculiar. Moreover, indigenous cultures seemed incompatible with a culture committed to the principles of consumption and economic progress. Postwar federal Indian policy thus sought to bring an end to the special status of Indian tribes.

Some supporters of termination were critical of the promotion of collectivism on Indian reservations. Others viewed the BIA's control over Indian reservations as denying freedom to individual Indians. For similar reasons some Indians, too, supported termination. Assimilated Indians wanted to own property individually, while others wanted to end the BIA's "paternalistic and pervasive control" over their affairs. Rapidly, "pressure increased to abolish the government's trust relationship with Indian nations" and, instead, to direct government efforts to helping individual Indians utilize their property responsibly.[28]

Cohen did not oppose eliminating the BIA's paternalistic control over Indian reservations. But while proponents of termination viewed the end of bureaucratic control as a step toward the Indians' assimilation as Americans, Cohen saw it as a step toward self-determination. Tellingly, Cohen, who rarely spoke publicly about Zionism, responded to the accusation that reservations were ghettos, which proponents of termination raised, by comparing reservations to the State of Israel. As he explained, while the term ghetto referred to "an area within which Jews were forcibly confined," reservations and the State of Israel were homelands to their peoples, who had such a passionate attachment to them that they were willing to risk their lives to defend them. "Those who use the shibboleth of 'emancipating the Indian from the ghetto' as a moral justification for their efforts to pry Indians loose from their lands, timber, minerals, and fisheries," Cohen noted with Jewish (and Indian) pride, "will be surprised, as were Arab armies, at the tenacity and effectiveness of Indian resistance."[29]

As we will see, even with such loaded comparisons, Cohen was not able to convince policymakers to endorse his pluralist vision. But he was able to win a few victories.

The Indian Quest for Justice: Changing Tides

One of the underlying difficulties of federal Indian law has been the tension between viewing Indian people as members of distinct, semi-sovereign nations and viewing them as citizens. Special laws govern Indian nations, while the laws applicable to all U.S. citizens apply to individual Indians. The General Allotment Act of 1887 attempted to break down tribal organization and assimilate individual Indians. In 1934, the IRA reversed the policy of allotment and focused on recreating tribal self-government and tribal communities. Beginning in the 1950s, federal Indian policy tried to do away with the unique field of federal Indian law and assimilate individual Indians into the polity.[30]

In 1948, the Eightieth Congress passed Public Law 62, establishing "a Commission on Organization of the Executive Branch of Government to make recommendations on how to promote economy, efficiency, and improved federal services." Former president Herbert Hoover chaired the commission. Among its tasks was a study of the administration of Indian affairs. The commission's report, issued in December 1948, reflected the particularities of postwar American thought. It suggested that tribal organization "had been dismantled for over a generation" and that most Indians wanted to assimilate into American society. It recommended that tribal governments established under the IRA be considered "a stage in the transition from federal tutelage to full Indian participation in state and local government." The Hoover Commission further recommended that the federal government "transfer responsibility for Indian law and order, education, public, health, and welfare to state governments" and that Indian corporations be redesigned to operate under state law without BIA supervision "as capitalist rather than socialist business enterprises."[31] Cohen sarcastically commented that these recommendations reflected yet another attempt to free Indians from evil, that is, from their possessions. Asserting that Indians, the original residents of America, had taught colonial forces many important lessons, he suggested that instead of trying so hard to "Americanize" the Indians, policymakers should work to "Americanize the white man."[32]

Despite opposition to the Hoover Commission's recommendations, President Truman pushed forward. In March 1950 he appointed Dillon S. Myer as commissioner of Indian affairs. Myer, who was head of the War Relocation Authority (WRA) from 1942 to 1946 and was directly responsible for the incarcerated Japanese Americans, had little knowledge of Indian affairs when he became commissioner; apparently, he had known even less about Japanese Americans when he took over the WRA. Nonetheless, he believed that "many Indians [were] still primitive," that they were "still like their hunting and fishing forefathers who had 'lived the life of the nomad, because they moved from place to place and many of the tribes lived in part by poaching on the richer tribes and stealing their produce.'" As his biographer concluded, under Myer's supervision "BIA officials did their level best to get back to the day . . . when reservations had in fact had many . . . earmarks of concentration camps."[33]

Myer treated Indian tribes as chance aggregates of individuals, indeed as collections of young children; in his view they were "wards of state, subject to his whims." He believed the Indian Reorganization Act was a mistake and wanted to discourage Indian self-government and eliminate federal support for Indian tribes.[34] Myer's goal was to promote tribal management of their own affairs under state jurisdiction, move unemployed Indians to cities, and provide Indians with better access to public education.[35]

Myer had the administration's support. He also gained the support of tribes and individual Indians who were disillusioned with the administration of their affairs under the IRA as well as the support of Indians who wanted individual freedom and economic opportunity. Myer's reforms enabled Indians "to spend their income from restricted property without supervision" and gave BIA directors "more authority to issue fee patents and remove restrictions on the sale of Indian real estate." But Myer also forced Indians to turn to commercial lenders and not to the federal government for credit. He closed BIA schools and transferred Indian children to state-sponsored schools. He funded a boarding-home placement program for Indian children in order to remove them from their homes and the influences of their parents and traditions, and he initiated a relocation program for adult Indians to allow, even force, Indians to leave reservations and resettle in urban communities.[36]

Myer spoke of ending the special status of Indian tribes, but at the same time he increased the BIA's power over Indian reservations. Not surprisingly, shortly after his appointment Myer found himself in an ongoing struggle with Cohen. Cohen wanted to end the BIA's paternalistic control over Indian reservations; he wanted the government to pull out because he wanted to encourage tribal self-government. The tension between his and Myer's visions was reflected in their interactions in the early 1950s. These exchanges, more accurately public fights, centered around the tribes' right to employ legal counsel of their choice, their right to their property, and their ability to impose law and order on their reservations. These were, after all, the powers that Cohen (and Margold) had attempted to secure for Indian tribes back in 1934.[37]

Cohen's interactions with Myer demonstrated that even though Cohen had left the government, he continued to rely on the methods he had used while at Interior to effect policy changes. He drafted memoranda and bills, he contacted members of Congress and the executive branch, and he used press releases to support his causes. Reading the accounts of these interactions, one might get the impression that Cohen was still at the Solicitor's Office.[38]

The Right to Counsel

The first battle between Cohen and Myer was over the ability of Indian tribes to hire their own attorneys. Since he had joined Interior, Cohen argued that tribes should select their own counsel. In 1938, he wrote regulations to govern the subject, which were approved by Assistant Secretary Oscar Chapman. These regulations addressed issues such as the selection of counsel, attorneys' qualifications, and the determination of fees and expenses. They encouraged tribes' involvement in the process of selecting their attorneys.

In the fall of 1950, Myer issued new regulations. They left the determination of attorneys' fees to the BIA, banned monthly retainer contracts, and required tribes to employ local attorneys. The BIA was also to determine in each case whether the tribe needed an attorney and whether it could afford one. Myer's goal was "to discourage Indian political activism and restrict awards by the Indian Claims Commission." As Cohen saw it, these regulations were intended to prevent attorneys from using his claims research, to monitor the activities of lawyers like himself and the Joint Efforts Group, and to make it more costly for them to litigate tribal claims.[39]

Cohen's response was bold and immediate. In collaboration with the ACLU and as a consultant to the AAIA, he wrote a brief entitled "Memorandum on the Right of Indian Tribes to Counsel." It was submitted to the secretary of the interior in December 1950 and circulated to members of Congress, civil rights groups, and Indian welfare organizations. As one scholar wrote, "It marked the beginning of a coordinated effort to derail Myer's plans to withdraw federal supervision over Indian affairs."[40]

The memorandum described Myer's regulations as authoritarian, as violating the constitutional principle of separation of powers as well as section 16 of the IRA, which guaranteed tribes the power to employ attorneys and fix their fees subject to the approval of the secretary of the interior. Its wide circulation led to a nationwide protest, which prompted Chapman, now the secretary of the interior, to ask Solicitor Mastin White for an opinion about the secretary's authority to revise the attorney contract regulations. White rejected Cohen's view, as expressed in "Powers of Indian Tribes," that tribes had inherent sovereign powers. Instead, he gave the secretary of the interior immense authority over Indian tribes, holding that under the plenary power the secretary of the interior could issue or deny approval of any tribal attorney contract for any reason.[41]

When Chapman followed White's advice and issued new regulations, he faced a wider public outcry. It included Indians and their friends (like Ickes, who described Myer as "a reckless, bullheaded fool" and "a Hitler and Mussolini rolled into one," and characterized White as a solicitor "who does not scruple to cheat [Chapman] when [the latter] ask for an opinion on Indian law").[42] It also included the American Bar Association (ABA). A special ABA committee studied the question of attorney contracts for seven months. Its report concluded that under section 16 of the IRA, the secretary's authority was limited to reviewing a tribe's choice of attorney and to fixing fees. In support of its conclusions, the ABA report cited a 1938 ruling by Acting Solicitor Frederic Kirgis, which directed superintendents to advise attorneys that "all other contract provisions were 'alterable at the pleasure of the tribe.'"[43]

Responding to the uproar, Chapman held departmental hearings on the subject in January 1952 following which he disapproved the new regulations and appointed a committee to study the adequacy of the 1938 regulations. Chapman also requested "a congressional review of his authority to regulate attorney contracts." In January 1953, the Senate subcommittee on Interior and Insular Affairs issued a report, noting that "it did not have authority to determine whether Secretary Chapman should relax or abandon federal supervision over Indians." According to the report, "until Congress decided otherwise, the Interior Department had a trust responsibility to regulate attorney contracts because of the questionable activities of [some] lawyers."[44]

The first battle between Cohen and Myer ended without an identifiable winner. The subcommittee's report was influenced by calls to terminate the trust relationship. It was very critical of the activities of lawyers, like Cohen, who advocated tribal self-government. Moreover, Myer continued to use his power to interfere with the ability of tribes to hire attorneys. But, at the same time, the ongoing public debate did much to discredit Myer's paternalistic approach, masked as it might have been in the rhetoric of self-determination. Furthermore, as the debates unfolded, Cohen was able to strengthen his position within the ABA. Having the support of other lawyers was helpful as he continued to fight Myer's policies.[45]

The Right to Property

Another interaction between Cohen and Myer revolved around the power of the Blackfeet tribe to exclude others, especially government employees, from their property. The question reached back to 1935, "when the Court of Claims deducted four million dollars in offsets for capital improvements on the reservation" against the Blackfeet claims award. These improvements included certain government buildings. In 1951, George Pambrun, chair of the Blackfeet Business Council, notified Superintendent Guy Robertson that the tribe owned these buildings because it had paid for them in 1935. Pambrun told Robertson that as long as the government was using the buildings, the business council would ask it to pay rent. On April 14, 1951, Pambrun, accompanied by Cohen, instructed the Indian police to serve federal employees who worked at the agency headquarters in Browning, Montana, with eviction notices. They also posted a "no trespassing" sign on the building.[46]

The act of the Blackfeet Indians was a bold act of self-government. For many years, their reservation had been a battleground between Indians seeking more autonomy over their affairs and "superintendents who treated them as young children or a primitive people." Repossessing their property was one of different actions the Blackfeet pursued, with Cohen as legal counsel, in their fight for self-determination. Shortly thereafter, Myer attempted to gain control over tribal funds by proposing an amendment to the Blackfeet constitution and manipulating voting processes on the reservation to have it approved. But a solicitor's opinion affirmed the right of the Blackfeet to self-government under the IRA. Solicitor White declared that voting rules on the reservation should be interpreted in light of the Blackfeet constitution, which was carefully prepared under the IRA and embodied the tribe's wishes. He declared that the amendment was not adopted.[47]

As to the Blackfeet title to their buildings—an 1951 FBI investigation into Cohen's role in the matter concluded by noting that "the appropriate U.S. at-

torney declined to press criminal charges and advised that the issue of ownership of the disputed buildings would be determined by civil action." Myer
and his BIA were forced to admit that the Blackfeet had "proper equity in such
buildings." But, as Cohen would later write, the BIA continued to collect the
rent, and "no tribal building of any substantial value [had] been turned over to
the Blackfeet." With Myer's approval, Superintendent Robertson simply retained the BIA's custody of the Blackfeet property.[48]

Law and Order

The final battle between Cohen and Myer took place in 1952. It focused on
S.R. 2543 and H.R. 6035 which authorized BIA's employees to "search, seize
and arrest Indians" for violations of BIA regulations.[49] As Cohen saw it, these
bills attempted to overturn the law and order regulations that he had drafted in
1935 to complement the IRA.

In a press release for the AAIA, Cohen, as legal counsel, warned that the bill
gave the BIA's law enforcement officers unprecedented power—"They could
arrest and imprison Indians without a search warrant for violating twenty-two
hundred federal regulations beyond the crimes identified in law codes used by
Courts of Indian Offenses." Cohen protested that Indian tribes were subject to
these regulations "just because they are Indians." He called it "an unprecedented invasion of American principles." The bill, Cohen warned his Indian
clients, was a direct repudiation of the Indian New Deal.[50]

Myer's response was short. In his testimony before the House Committee
on Interior and Insular Affairs, he asserted that Cohen's memorandum had used
"an argumentative technique that bears little resemblance to fair and honest
analysis—a technique seemingly designed to confuse and mislead." According
to Myer, Cohen engaged in "broad generalizations that do not even purport to
be based upon fact, in gross exaggerations, in the use of false analogies, and in
the use of slogans designed to arouse the emotions rather than contribute to a
considered judgment."[51]

The committee sided with Myer. But Cohen would not let go. Together
with Oliver La Farge, president of the AAIA, he continued to fight. In a letter
to the tribes for which he acted as general counsel (including the Blackfeet of
Montana, the Oglala Sioux of South Dakota, the San Carlos Apache of Arizona, and the Laguna Pueblo of New Mexico), Cohen stressed that the commissioner could not frighten the Indians because many tribes had retained
lawyers, "who acted as watchdogs and barked when trespassers threatened Indian rights." Then, Cohen and La Farge sent press releases to newspapers
around the country criticizing "Myer's approach toward law enforcement." A
"nationwide protest" ensued. Editorials around the country accused Myer of
"requesting gestapo power to oppress Indian wards." More important, Chapman refused to listen to Myer. After meeting with Cohen, Chapman asked the
Solicitor's Office to recall the bill.[52]

Termination

Cohen was an obstacle for Myer. As Myer harshly put it:

> Mr. Cohen's technique generally in serving as general counsel has been one that I would call a needling technique—needling the [BIA] on almost any issue he thinks he can bring up with the Indians that might make us unpopular and which might add to his prestige with certain Indians in key tribal positions. We disagree generally with Mr. Cohen both as to his general approach and in regard to his activities.[53]

Myer's attacks on Cohen were personal as well. He accused Cohen of having "a major financial interest in tribal claims presented under the Indian Claims Commission Act," which led to an FBI investigation to determine whether Cohen had violated the Hatch Act by "acting as an agent for tribes within two years of completing his government service."[54] Given Cohen's consultant role and the structure of his compensation (his partnership agreement with the firm of Riegelman, Strasser, Schwarz and Spiegelberg provided that he would have "*no share* in any fees which the firm may earn through the Joint Efforts Group"), the investigation concluded that he had no interest in the claims themselves and that no violation of the Hatch Act had occurred.[55]

Untiring, Myer was able to convince syndicated columnist Drew Pearson of the *Washington Post* that Cohen's attacks on Myer's policies were motivated by greed. As Pearson put it, Cohen was "a partner in a syndicate seeking more than 4 billion dollars in Indian claims against the government which [he] once represented." But like the FBI, Pearson had to withdraw his accusation. In September 1952, a month after the column was published, he reported that he learned that Cohen had "a partnership agreement specifically providing that he shall have no fees from these Indian claims."[56]

In March 1953, after Eisenhower's victory, Myer was required to resign. Some suggested that Cohen's article on "The Erosion of Indian Rights, 1950–1953: A Case Study in Bureaucracy," which detailed Myer's attack on Native Americans, had convinced powerful members of the incoming administration that Myer should be dismissed.[57]

But Myer had the upper hand. In August 1953, Congress passed P.L. 280, which transferred to five states—California, Minnesota, Nebraska, Oregon, and Wisconsin—civil and criminal jurisdiction over reservations within their territory. P.L. 280 had certain positive aspects. It exempted certain tribes from state jurisdiction after they asked to maintain their own legal systems. It did not allow states to exercise jurisdiction over tax-exempt Indian trust property. It recognized water and treaty rights. And it granted to tribal governments concurrent jurisdiction over civil cases. But it was the first bill to endorse state jurisdiction over Indian reservations since Margold's and Cohen's attempt to recognize Indian tribes' sovereignty. According to section 7 of P.L. 280, all states could assume jurisdiction over reservation lands "through legislation or by amending their statehood acts or constitutions." H.C.R. 108, which was also enacted in August 1953, sought to terminate the BIA's authority in several states and to end the special relationship between the federal government and certain tribes. It made termination the official federal Indian policy.[58]

Following the enactment of H.C.R. 108 and P.L. 280, the BIA tried to bring an end to federal supervision over reservations and to transfer federal responsibilities to Indians and to the states. Beginning in 1954, Congress passed individual termination acts, which ended federal recognition of approximately 110 tribes and bands in eight states.[59]

Many Indians preferred state health and education programs. Many others wanted to manage their own funds and lands. But, as one commentator described it, termination proved to be "assimilation with a vengeance."[60] Terminated tribal governments lost the status of separate sovereigns and, with it, the ability to regulate the activities of their members. Reservations were sold, in whole or in part, and many Indians were relocated. Terminated tribes lost revenues from tribal resources and benefits from federal Indian programs. Few Indians had sufficient education to engage in off-reservation employment, and even fewer Americans were willing to employ them. At the same time, Indians became responsible for payment of state income, property, and sales taxes. Very few Indians could support themselves, and many had to depend on welfare benefits. Most devastating, however, was the damage to their identity. With their trust relationship with the United States terminated, Indians were no longer different, legally, from other citizens; their source of autonomy and identification—the tribe—was destroyed.[61] In 1958, five years after Cohen's untimely death, a new edition of the *Handbook* eradicated the pluralistic characteristics of the original edition and suggested instead that Indians were wards of the state.

Proponents of termination wanted to bring an end to the Indian New Deal and Indian self-government. But as they pursued their agenda, Cohen continued to insist that the only solution to the Indian plight was a commitment to Indian self-government. He wanted policymakers and other Americans to recognize that the strength of American democracy was its endorsement of local self-government. "The great thing about American democracy," he wrote in 1951, was that most Americans had "an unprecedented power to shape [their] own lives, make [their] own mistakes, and attain new understanding and strength from mistakes [they] make." He wanted Indians to enjoy a similar freedom not least because he believed that group self-government and cultural tolerance were joined at the root.[62]

Indian Self-Government: The Philosophy of American Democracy

Two schools of thought emerged in the postwar years to explain why the United States did not and would not succumb to totalitarianism. For one group of scholars, the strength of American democracy was its basic societal consensus on fundamental values. For another group, the strength of American democracy was its political process, which allowed different groups to interact and trade ends. Both schools of thought converged in their acceptance of a morality of process independent of results. "If the advocates of consensus insisted that widespread agreement on procedure actually reflected a deeply substantive consensus—for otherwise nobody would acquiesce in an unfavorable outcome—the equilibrium theorists tended to emphasize value-free 'neutral principles' that could legitimate decisions independent of results."[63]

In this atmosphere, political scientists developed a new pluralist image of the state: a descriptive social theory, purportedly with no ethical conviction. It was inspired by a rejection of all absolutism, including any morally based pleas for social reform. Drawing on models of equilibrium derived from economics, their image of the state rested on the assumption that society was composed of multiple interest groups interacting, competing, and trading ends in neutral economic and political markets. Political compromises between diverse pressure groups were presumed to produce shared public goods. Robert Dahl's interest group pluralism was the ultimate example.[64]

The American ideal of democracy became a balancing theory. America was composed of interest groups, and group conflict reflected the dispersal of political power. Existing political institutions and cultural consensus, a "consensus rooted in the common life, habits, institutions, and experience of generations," were presumed to preserve the delicate balance between groups. The status quo became a normative theory.[65]

It was not a normative theory that Cohen endorsed. Remaining committed to the early twentieth-century pluralist image of the state, with its appreciation of group autonomy and diversity, Cohen drew on almost two decades of legal practice to promote his own pluralist vision of democracy both in the national and the international arena. In this vein, Cohen's work in the late 1940s and early 1950s brought together his support of group self-government and group rights, his understanding of the importance of a diversity of cultures and legal systems to the success of the American democratic experiment, and his hope of encouraging dialogue among diverse groups. Combined, these ideas grounded Cohen's call for greater cultural tolerance.

A Certain Blindness

Shortly after he left Interior, in an article for a conference sponsored by the AAIA to assess the Hoover Commission's recommendations, Cohen elaborated his ideal of Indian self-government. It was a harsh critique both of the Truman administration and of the BIA's historic approach to tribal autonomy, including the BIA under Collier's guidance and supervision.

Cohen's analysis began by stressing that self-government was a "form of government in which decisions are made not by the people who are wisest, or ablest, or closest to some throne in Washington or in Heaven, but, rather by the people who are most directly affected by the decisions."[66] He was speaking from experience. As he explained to a friend, as the tribes' lawyer and friend, he sometimes had "to appear ungracious, or to sound more doubtful" than he really was, or even "refuse to answer plain questions" to ensure that the Indians did not view him "as a tribal leader." He truly believed that the tribes should make their own independent decisions.[67]

Having established his definition of tribal self-government, Cohen went on to criticize the BIA's ongoing reluctance to allow tribes to exercise self-government. He went so far as to accuse Collier's BIA of trying to suppress a study that he had conducted in 1934. The study had uncovered that "the laws and court decisions clearly recognized that Indian tribes have all the governmental rights of any state or municipality except in so far as those rights have been curtailed or qualified by Act of Congress or by treaty, and such qualifications are relatively minor, in fact." At the time, he thought that such findings were extremely important to the New Deal policies. But, according to Cohen, the BIA found such conclusions "disturbing." As he remembered the events, "all copies of the opinion in the Indian Office had been carefully hidden away in a cabinet and . . . when an Indian was found reading this opinion, the copy was forthwith taken from his hands and placed under lock and key."[68]

The BIA's control over Indian affairs was even more paternalistic under Myer. Purporting to promote self-determination and the BIA's liquidation, Myer's policies immensely increased the scope of the BIA's supervision over reservations.[69] Cohen wryly wrote in another article that "the 'withdrawal' policies of Commissioner Myer have been stated, word for word, by several of his predecessor Commissioners during the past 160 years and in almost every case the alleged 'withdrawal' plans were followed by a vast increase in Indian Bureau appropriations."[70]

As Cohen saw it, the problem reached beyond the particular policies of any commissioner or administration, beyond the question of self-government, to the roots of the pluralist philosophy. Turning to the works of Ralph Barton Perry, his mentor at Harvard, Cohen described the problem as involving "the egocentric predicament," that is, "the fact that each of us is at the center of his world and cannot help seeing the world through his own eyes and from his own position." "It takes a certain amount of sophistication to realize that the vision of others who see the world from different perspectives is just as valid as our own," Cohen stressed.[71]

According to Cohen, "the administrative or bureaucratic mind" in particular lacked "such sophistication." Drawing on his experience in implementing Indian self-government, Cohen recalled how each division at Interior—Education, Forestry, Credit, and Law and Order—was in favor of self-government in general but was opposed to it in the field over which the division itself had jurisdiction. As Cohen put it, experts were reluctant to give up control over matters with which they were concerned, especially when they disagreed with tribal decisions. To guarantee that tribal decisions would not conflict with theirs, they limited the tribes' autonomy.[72]

While Cohen thought the bureaucratic mind was particularly prone to this egocentric predicament, he wanted to draw a stronger connection between his ideal of group self-government and cultural tolerance. For that purpose, he wanted his audience to realize that they, too, were blind to those different from them. He wanted them to understand the relationship between such blindness and the rejection of group autonomy; more to the point, he wanted them to see the connections between blindness and intolerance.

Half a century earlier, in a speech titled "On a Certain Blindness in Human Beings," William James declared that groups and individuals were all afflicted by blindness "in regard to the feelings of creatures and people different from [themselves]."[73] The speech, written as a critique of imperialism, especially the American policy toward the Philippines, involved two forms of blindness: blindness toward differences and blindness toward similarities.[74] James wanted his audience to realize how blind they were to ways of life different from their own, but he also wanted them to recognize that by focusing on external differences they were rendered blind to inner similarities. The individual will indicated for James the possibility of overcoming blindness and, more important, the possibility of unity within diversity.

The two forms of blindness corresponded to two themes in James's pluralist philosophy. On the one hand, James's pluralism celebrated diverse ways of life, each blind to the other. Recognizing the blindness of individuals and groups toward differently situated others, James suggested that distinct ways of life should be allowed to coexist, each within its separate sphere. On the other hand, James's pluralism also stressed the possibility of unity. Focusing on the ability of individuals to imagine or know themselves as the other, James urged not merely separate coexistence but the transcendence of boundaries. James was aware of the difficulty of adjudicating conflicting inner realities, but he believed that the possibility of a better relationship between individuals lay in their ability to sympathize with the inner realities of individuals different from them.[75] Similar themes grounded Cohen's pluralism. He believed that by protecting group autonomy one could promote tolerance.

Differences

Cohen's work in the 1940s aimed to learn and teach about diversity. In the mid-1940s, Cohen helped Collier establish the Institute of Ethnic Affairs "to deal with the profoundly disturbing problems of group tension and conflict, problems commonly referred to as 'racial' in origin, which imperil human affairs at home and abroad."[76] Following the agenda of the Institute of Living Law, although not explicitly, Collier, Cohen, and other members of the Institute of Ethnic Affairs planned to employ the social sciences to study group conflict and tensions. Their attention focused on indigenous communities and minorities both inside and outside the United States. They wanted "to organize, plan, and render social services on behalf of groups in need thereof, to furnish information and issue reports and documents based upon such research and investigation and such social service projects and to contribute to the education of interested persons and agencies." In the spirit of pluralism, although already reflecting the prioritization of science over values, they stressed that the institute would "seek to operate not with the one-sided seal of the reformer but with the scientist's passion for discovering the many-sided causes of things."[77]

Cohen and Collier wanted to help unlettered populations achieve literacy without abandoning their languages. They wanted to assist community organizations in bringing professional health services to disease-ridden areas. They hoped to create economic development plans appropriate for indigenous organization and custom. By studying these questions, they hoped to understand and call attention to "the economic, political, social, and psychological factors which contribute . . . to the creation of ethnic tension and conflict."[78]

Cohen and Collier wanted to understand how to connect groups—within which personality is formed and the human relationship lived out—into nations and nations into an international community. They strongly believed that self-government was the key to helping indigenous communities. But their pluralism, unlike Cohen's 1930s pluralism, which encompassed all groups, was limited to ethnic and cultural groups. Exclusionary practices by voluntary associations (clubs, professional associations, labor unions, churches, and others) were to be studied as throwing "an unpleasant light upon the working of [American] democracy." They wanted to uncover the "causes of this widespread social malady" and develop "programs for its cure."[79]

With this in mind, Cohen's analysis of self-government resembled James's argument about blindness. Cohen believed that groups could make important cultural and social contributions; in fact, he stressed that Indians had made distinctive contributions to American culture and law, especially in the field of property rights.[80] He also believed that by allowing groups to cultivate their own ideas without expert intervention, one could promote tolerance. In this respect, his ideal of group self-government was a means to an end. In the mid-1940s, Cohen articulated a conception of constitutionally protected group rights predicated upon the obligation of the sovereign state to bring about social integration. Among the beliefs expressed in the *Handbook,* Cohen counted "a belief that it is the duty of the Government to aid oppressed groups in the understanding and appreciation of their legal rights."[81] In the late 1940s, while still endorsing the ideal of group rights, Cohen suggested that it was "not the business of the Indian Bureau or of any other federal agency to integrate Indians or Jews or Catholics or Negroes or Holy Rollers or Jehovah's Witnesses into the rest of the population as a solution of the Indian, Jewish, Negro, or Catholic problem, or any other problem." It was nonetheless "the duty of the federal government to respect the right of any group to be different so long as it does not violate the criminal law."[82]

Because Cohen believed that the protection of religious, ethnic, and linguistic minorities against oppression was likely to be curtailed by domestic democratic processes, and because such protection invoked sympathies across borders, Cohen's work in the late 1940s emphasized the role that organs of the United Nations could play in protecting minorities. Cohen, who began his career a socialist and political pluralist, who came to Interior in 1934 seeking to impose certain economic universals on Indian reservations, had come to believe that the assault on minorities rights was a threat to world peace that was "far more menacing than any threat arising out of the oppression of single individuals or of voluntary economic or political organizations of individuals."[83]

"The miner's canary"

Disappointed at the failure of the New Deal administration to create a pluralist polity, Cohen, no longer in government service, wanted the government to step out, to let local self-government flourish. More important, he wanted the international community to protect the right of groups to be different. Like his interactions with Myer, Cohen's argument about the egocentric predicament was bold. As Cohen saw it, the bureaucratic mind, in fact the modern mind, was afflicted with racial attitudes. Opposition to Indian self-government was rooted in particular cultural and ethnic biases.

Cohen's analysis of Indian self-government (and of colonialism) ended with an appeal which he hoped would help Americans grasp the dangers of intolerance. His plea was personal. He wanted Americans to understand the potentially horrible consequences of racial attitudes, to recognize that what happened in Europe could happen here. In the early 1940s, in his writings about immigration, Cohen argued that diversity was important to the country's social and economic progress. In these writings, tolerance was, at least to an extent, instrumental. In the late 1940s and early 1950s, self-government became the means, with tolerance the end, and Indians the key group helping Americans recognize and realize both the end and its means.[84] "The Indian plays much the same role in our American society that the Jews played in Germany," Cohen wrote:

> Like the miner's canary, the Indian marks the shifts from fresh air to poison gas in our political atmosphere; and our treatment of Indians, even more than our treatment of other minorities, reflects the rise and fall in our democratic faith. Here, as in other parts of the world, the undermining of that faith begins with the glorification of "expert administrators" whose power-drives are always accompanied by soft music about "the withering away of the state" or the ultimate "liquidation" of this or that bureau. . . . [W]hat we need another John Maynard Keynes to remind us of, is that in the long run we are all dead, and that while the means we use may be moulded by the ends we seek, it is the means we use that mould the ends we achieve.[85]

After fourteen years in government service, Cohen no longer trusted policymakers to create a plural polity. He also no longer believed that cultural and ethnic tensions would disappear once groups gained economic and political autonomy. Indians had taught Cohen the need to cherish cultural pluralism both because they were most discriminated against and because Indian philosophy was predicated upon respect for diverse opinions. The Holocaust had crystallized the need. "The Indian tribe is the miner's canary," Cohen concluded his piece on Indian self-government, "and when it flutters and droops we know that the poison gasses of intolerance threaten all other minorities in our land. And who of us is not a member of some minority?"[86]

Like James's analysis of the second form of blindness, blindness toward similarities, Cohen's question "who of us is not a member of some minority?" was meant to invoke empathy. Cohen wanted to believe that once individuals overcame their blindness toward differences and became aware of the experiences and cultures of those different from themselves, they would be able to see the similarities between themselves and others. Indeed, Cohen's jurisprudential theory in the 1950s aimed to help judges and lawyers overcome blindness. It was intended to uncover hidden assumptions and visions of judges and policymakers so that they could see through their biases and prejudices.

Logic, Law, and Ethics: Field Theory and Judicial Logic

In 1935, in "Transcendental Nonsense and the Functional Approach," Cohen examined law as a system of group violence. Four years later, in "The Relativity of Philosophical Systems," he proclaimed that if legal systems could be enlarged to incorporate other systems, the violence inherent in each system might be eliminated. Slightly more than a decade later, Cohen returned to the question of group violence. It seemed to him that before any given legal system could incorporate the values of another system, law-making agencies would have to recognize the hidden value fields in which they operated. Cohen's "Field Theory and Judicial Logic" (1951) attempted to uncover the concealed cultural and value assumptions in judicial decisions. According to Cohen, it offered further reflections on his earlier work. As he put it, everything was derived from his dissertation.[87]

"Field Theory and Judicial Logic" was divided into three parts, each corresponding to a distinct part in "Transcendental Nonsense." The first part, "The Paradoxes of Judicial Logic," built on Cohen's earlier examination of the heaven of abstract concepts. The second part, "Public Policy: A Field Theory of Values," drew on Cohen's functional approach as a basis for policymaking. Finally, the third part, "Through the Blind Alleys of Jurisprudence," replaced Cohen's functional theory of adjudication. Together, the three parts explored Cohen's new jurisprudential approach. Informed by over fourteen years of advocacy on behalf of minority groups, it used Einstein's field theory to help individuals realize their blindness toward others and to overcome it. It was meant to promote tolerance.

The Paradoxes of Judicial Logic

Cohen's early critique of the use of abstract concepts attempted to shift legal scholars' attention from concepts to questions of social fact and social policy.[88] In 1951, Cohen's analysis turned from the critique of jurists' reliance on abstract concepts to the critique of their' reliance on precedent. Many Progressive legal scholars and realists argued that law lagged behind society because judges paid too much attention to precedent.[89] But Cohen saw the issue differently.

In 1935, Cohen described abstract concepts as capable of receiving multiple meanings. In turn, in 1951 he stressed that every judicial decision could be traced to multiple precedents. The question was "not *whether* judges should follow precedent . . . [but] rather, *how* they should draw the lines of similarity that connect past cases and present cases."[90]

Cohen's reformulation of the question emphasized the value judgment involved in selecting precedents, "a judgment that similarities between the precedent and the following decision are important and that dissimilarities are relatively unimportant." But Cohen's analysis went further. If in 1935 he wanted his readers to see how the use of abstract concepts sustained law's violence toward particular groups, in 1951 he stressed that the use of precedent was a form of group violence. Judges employed different "patterns of selectivity" in examining precedents. These patterns increased "the force and scope" of decisions the judges agreed with and limited "the scope and force" of decisions they thought were wrong. Cohen stressed that these patterns were influenced by judges' own biases and prejudices.[91]

Cohen knew that judges resented the accusation that they let their biases influence their decisions. He dismissed such reactions as indicating that "judges are like other human beings. . . . We are none of us aware of our own prejudices."[92]

Demonstrating that judges' biases affected their decisions was not a novel idea. Already in "Transcendental Nonsense" Cohen explained that diverse social forces, including the political, economic, and professional background and activities of a judge, and the judge's biases shaped judicial decisions.[93] The originality of "Field Theory" was its solution. In "Transcendental Nonsense" Cohen proposed social scientific studies of the ways social forces influenced law so that lawyers and legal scholars could predict how a case would be decided. In comparison, in "Field Theory" he wanted to uncover hidden value assumptions not only because he thought this analysis would allow one to predict the outcome of any given case but also, more crucially, because he thought it would help eliminate prejudice and bias.[94] If in "Transcendental Nonsense" Cohen wanted to redefine abstract concepts to reflect the multiplicity of interests that characterized American society, in "Field Theory" he used language as a tool, as a means of overcoming blindness.

Public Policy: A Field Theory of Values

Uncovering judges' hidden value patterns required differentiating between what Cohen labeled "large-scale" and "small-scale" patterns. As Cohen clarified, national phenomena such as racism created group-reinforced, large-scale value patterns. These patterns explained, for example, why "precedents that point to the protection of civil liberties suddenly dwindle in times of public hysteria, but after the hysteria subsides they may resume their original force and direction."[95]

Cohen was more interested in the small-scale value patterns, those that reflected a judge's own biases and prejudices. These patterns, according to Cohen, were seen in a judge's "reaction to day-to-day problems of statutory construction, . . . in the choices [a judge] makes between competing interpretations of fact, in the selection of value-charged words to describe given facts, and in the implicit and inarticulate premises of his arguments."[96]

Of particular concern to Cohen were hidden race- and class-value judgments, judgments that indicated how blind judges were to those different from them. Drawing upon examples from federal Indian law, he demonstrated how the words used to describe a particular activity or right differed based on whether the participant in the activity or the bearer of the right was an Indian or non-Indian. "In many cases," Cohen wrote, "the courts apply to Indians terms that are ordinarily applied to animals, thus conveying the impression that the relation of an Indian to his land is similar to that of an animal to its habitat and therefore not a subject of enforceable rights." In such cases, he wrote, "while a white person 'travels' or 'commutes' an Indian (like a buffalo) 'roams.'" In a similar manner, courts assigned positive labels such as "'corporate' or 'partnership' or 'family' property'" to "land held by a group of white men in accordance with an intricate apportionment of individual rights." But, as the decision of the Court of Appeals for the Ninth Circuit in *Hynes v. Grimes* demonstrated, when describing "land held by a group of Indians under arrangements of equal or greater intricacy," courts used terms evoking negative connotations such as "communally occupied." A system of double-talk was also seen in the calls for termination. As Cohen pointedly put it, "If a government repudiates its obligations to a white man we speak of 'government bankruptcy'; if a government repudiates its obligations to an Indian, this is commonly referred to as 'emancipating the Indian.'"[97]

In other cases, judges used terminology that associated Indians and members of other historically underprivileged groups with "something mean or revolting or contemptible" in the experience of the majority. They used religious or racial adjectives that were irrelevant to the question under discussion.[98] Moreover, they used "we" words to describe the actions of those with whom they felt an affinity, and "they" words to describe those from whom they wanted to dissociate themselves. They described a white person "as a citizen, a taxpayer, a father, a husband or a veteran," thus grouping themselves with that person. In turn, white judges used an "out-grouping line of demarcation," describing defendants as "Negro, Indian or savage," to separate themselves from these defendants.[99] Every group, Cohen wrote, had "a special term, generally carrying a downgrading connotation, by which it refers to outsiders."[100]

Thus described, language became an indicator of one's social position, a distinguishing mark between the oppressor and the oppressed, between the privileged and the underprivileged. Cohen wished his readers to see that when judges used particular terms, they sanctioned cultural, social, and political assumptions about the allocation of power in society.

More important, Cohen hoped that a "greater tolerance of cultural diversity" would develop once the inarticulate value premises were revealed. As he explained, "the technique of semantic analysis" could help individuals recognize their and others' egocentric limitations and thus help them identify and eliminate prejudice.[101]

Cohen's analysis reached further. Once the different hidden value judgments or indicators were revealed, they formed a value field. Once a value field was defined, its content could be exported into a different field. This was the gist of Cohen's application of Einstein's field theory to law. It rejected the "absolute space of unchanging rules and unmoving precedents that characterized traditional jurisprudence" and assumed "a 'life space' with many 'value regions.'" "Whatever passes from one region to another,—a rule a precedent, or a statement of facts—changes its weight, its shape, and its direction in accordance with 'the lay of the geodesics of that region.'" According to Cohen, the significance of Einstein's theory was the "development of formulae by which many different accounts of the same physical event may be correlated with each other."[102]

By uncovering judges' hidden value judgments and the value fields in which they operated, Cohen's application of Einstein's field theory to law opened up the possibility of translation between different value systems. It was a foundation for dialogue. "If we understand a proposition in the context of its own field," he wrote, "we can translate the proposition into language that will convey the same informational content in any other value field we understand."[103] Indeed, we can show how those individuals who seem different from us are also very similar to us.

Through the Blind Alleys of Jurisprudence: Tolerance and Pluralism

The early 1950s were not hopeful years. In a letter to a friend Cohen commented that "it is so easy in these days to fall prey to attitudes of helplessness and hopelessness in the face of spreading forces of evil that seem so deeply entrenched."[104] Writing to another friend he described "the Government atmosphere" at the time as full of false charges, adding "almost any sort of thinking is suspect."[105]

But Cohen held on to his faith in democracy and in the American people. "For the self-styled 'realist' observers of the international scene, Europe and America are finished, freedom and democracy are finished," Cohen told the Yale Philosophy Club. But, he continued, "perhaps it is time for the cynics to step aside and yield the helms of state to hands of greater faith in humanity and human reason."[106] "I feel sure," he similarly wrote about the struggle to improve the conditions on Indian reservations, that "if we make the American people aware of such things as have been going on at Blackfeet and elsewhere, I have no doubt of the ultimate result."[107]

Cohen's last paragraphs of "Field Theory and Judicial Logic" reflected both his despair and his optimism. They dealt not with a theory of adjudication, as might have been expected in light of the title of the subsection, but with the general history of jurisprudence. Cohen wanted his audience to recognize the similarities between different schools of thought. "The house of jurisprudence have many mansions," he wrote. And "each line of exploration is likely to disclose landmarks which will prove of value to other explorers moving in different directions and starting from different approaches." He wanted to bring the semantic analysis to bear upon struggles among jurists, to make legal scholars realize how similar their theories were.

Why was Cohen so interested in resolving conflicts in academia? In part, he wanted to assure himself of the similarities between his and his father's approaches to law. More important, he fully recognized how wasteful academic struggles were. In a world where hope was limited, there was no time to spare. As he put it, "Even the forbidding formalism of Kant," which Morris endorsed and Felix criticized, made "practical sense" if one appreciated Kant's concern with "the problem of how men pursuing radically different social goals and capable of destroying each other with the weapon of modern science can possibly evolve a pattern of living together in mutual respect, a pattern more fundamental than any of the things that mark off nation from nation, class from class, and man from man."[108]

Cohen wanted jurists and legal scholars to abandon their mundane debates about the novelty of their theories and instead focus on the important question of promoting tolerance. As he told the audience at a symposium on "Ethical Values and the Law in Action":

> All of us who face the obligations that our democracy attaches to the study and the practice of law have a responsibility towards our fellow citizens that is a greater responsibility than those in other fields and professions. Ours is the responsibility for deepening public consciousness of the hopes, the ideals, and the values that are written into our constitutions and our laws. We have a responsibility for broadening the consciousness of the ways in which we fail to meet those hopes and those ideals. Our society, by and large, has marked out its aspirations in the books of the law, for those who can read them; and we who are charged with the reading of those books have a special responsibility for keeping alive the vision of our country's highest hopes and deepest aspirations.[109]

In the 1930s, Cohen's hopes and aspirations focused on promoting certain political and economic goals. His legal pluralism was predicated upon the idea that self-governing collectivities would become the foundation of the modern state. In the early 1940s, Cohen emphasized the need to protect diverse groups. His pluralism rested on the assumption that group rights, be it the rights of Native Americans or Jewish refugees, were constitutionally protected. In the 1950s, Cohen seemed to have lost faith in the ability of law to bring about change. He used law as a tool to analyze prejudice so that individuals and groups might learn to be more tolerant of others. His pluralism was predicated upon the possibility of translation and dialogue between different value systems. Group autonomy and group rights became means to an end; they were tools that could be used to encourage and promote tolerance. In a world where racial attitudes often dominated law and policymaking, Cohen made tolerance of different ethnic, racial, and religious values the end of law, politics, and society.

In an address given at CCNY on March 12, 1953, Cohen described what he labeled the American faith—"a faith different from the Catholic faith, the Protestant faith, the Jewish faith, different from all these, and yet somehow inclusive of them, inclusive too of the faith of good Americans who have been Mormons, Buddhists, Theosophists, Pagans, Atheists and Agnostics." According to Cohen, the core of the American faith was tolerance. Emphasizing the importance of cherishing different cultural identities, including his own, Cohen, who in the early 1930s rejected ethnic particularities, endorsed in 1953 Horace Kallen's ideal of cultural pluralism. His address concluded with the following:

> When the Fathers of our country sought to put what I am trying to say into a few words, they selected the motto, E Pluribus Unum, one out of many. I venture to think that they were not trying to describe an historical incident, the vanishing of the many and the appearance of the one, but rather were trying to describe an ideal of symbiosis. They were describing not the lifelessness of the melting pot in which every metal with its distinctive use sinks into a vast, monotonous, useless amalgam. That we can leave to Nazis and communists and other totalitarians. I venture to think that in this motto, far-seeing statesmen sought to describe the entity of the symphony. The symphony orchestra plays and every man in it remains an individual human being, more than individual and more human because he is a part of the great orchestra. Here in this great orchestra that is America, every creed, every culture, every people, every skill can make its great contribution. And that, I submit, is the meaning of the American flag, 13 stripes and 48 stars, soon I hope, 49, and perhaps 50 and more. Where else in the world will one find this glorification of diversity, set as the seal upon the life of a people?[110]

Tolerance was the essence of Cohen's life.

Epilogue

> I particularly appreciate your observations that in causes of this charac-
> ter one has to be content to have done the best he can do, even
> though the achievement in actuality seems at best to move between
> giant failure and microscopic success.
>
> Felix S. Cohen to Felix Frankfurter, August 28, 1953 (FSCP 64/1025)

Felix Cohen has left many legacies. His article "Transcendental Nonsense and the Functional Approach" has remained a classic example of the legal realists' critique of conceptualism. His *Handbook of Federal Indian Law,* despite a hostile revision in 1958, has remained the most comprehensive treatise on federal Indian law. The Indian Reorganization Act and the Indian Claims Commission continue to provide models for addressing the problems of indigenous communities.

Each of these legacies was born out of Cohen's ongoing efforts to find ways out of the dilemma of modernism—to define the normative limits of cultural and moral pluralism. At least since Oliver Wendell Holmes, Jr. challenged the description of law as a body of natural and neutral rules,[1] legal scholars had struggled with this dilemma. On the one hand, to allow the state to exercise power over diverse groups risked imposing one's own concededly partial interests and beliefs in the name of a general public good. On the other hand, the alternative of deferring to groups risked moral relativism, maybe even nihilism.[2]

Faced with diverse social and cultural interests and hence with a variety of visions of what law ought, as a social and political matter, to be, many adopted one system of beliefs and treated it as the primary guiding light in their analysis of law. In the 1930s, many legal realists, for example, assumed the existence of correct answers to policy and legal questions and the inability of conservative judges to reach them.[3] The IRA was similarly predicated upon the plausibility of a universal solution to the Indian problem. In the postwar years, interest group pluralists, and the legal process school they influenced, adopted a different approach. Instead of endorsing any particular vision of the good, these process theorists found refuge in creating conceptions of neutral processes in which different groups supposedly interact, compete, and trade ends.[4] In federal Indian law, such assumptions substantiated the policy of termination.

The turn to process attracted criticism, however, from those who saw law as necessarily embracing substantive norms.[5] In the 1960s, the Warren Court and the civil rights movement helped focus legal thought on the concept of individual rights and liberties. The 1960s also brought renewed hope to the field of federal Indian law. In 1961, Indian leaders from seventy tribes met at the University of Chicago; they called for an end to termination and demanded self-government for Indian groups as the IRA promised. In 1970, President Nixon publicly repudiated the termination policy, and in 1975 Congress passed the Indian Self-Determination and Education Assistance Act, guaranteeing Indian participation in their government and education.[6]

By the 1980s, growing interest in natural resources on Indian reservations brought some economic gain to certain tribes although it also raised the risk of harm to tribal land base and tribal identity. Also in the 1980s, critical legal studies, the new institutional economics, and feminist legal theory, to name a few jurisprudential movements, sought to focus legal debates on questions of power and identity.[7] In the late 1990s, we have seen the resurgence of formalism, especially in judicial decisions;[8] while on Indian reservations, the struggle for the appropriate balance between self-determination and individualism continues.

In this context, Cohen's legal pluralist image of the state, which offered the conceptual anchor for his attempts to accommodate the interests of diverse groups without either promoting certain moral absolutes or succumbing to moral relativism, is of enduring importance. While in the early 1930s, informed by political pluralism, he believed that economic and political equality could be achieved through universal schemes, by the mid-1930s, Cohen recognized the multiplicity of cultural and value systems in society and thus the implausibility of universal solutions. His ongoing efforts to protect the rights of groups—Native Americans, Alaska Natives, Jewish refugees, African Americans, and other underprivileged minorities—offer an important insight into the history of civil rights and liberties in the first half of the twentieth century. While Cohen's failure to achieve many of his goals is testimony to the limits of the American legal and political traditions, Cohen's attempts to promote cultural dialogue, as seen in his work in the 1950s, offer a plausible archetype for addressing issues involving indigenous peoples and religious or cultural groups today. Cohen's changing interpretations of legal pluralism and their relationship to his sense of identity as a Jewish American also demonstrate the interconnections among ideology, identity, and the law.

Early in 1953, Felix Cohen eulogized his mentor and friend Jerry Michael of Columbia Law School. Cohen compared Michael to Morris Cohen, Laski, Brandeis, and Cardozo, a generation of thinkers who were students and heirs both of "a Hellenic tradition that cradles the eternal pursuit of a truth that is never fully caught" and of "a Hebraic tradition that cradles the eternal pursuit of a social justice that is never duly achieved." "For in the Hebraic tradition," Cohen asserted, "the profession of the law teacher is the highest of all human professions." According to Cohen, the most important command in the Hebraic tradition was found in Deuteronomy:

It is not in heaven, that thou shouldst say, Who will go up for us to heaven, and fetch it down unto us, and cause us to hear it, that we may do it? Neither is it beyond the sea, that thou shouldst say, Who will go over the sea for us, and fetch it unto us, and cause us to hear it, that we may do it? But the word is very nigh unto thee, in thy mouth, and in thy heart, that thou mayest do it.[9]

Cohen's eulogy of Michael reflected "a beauty of diction, a perceptiveness of analysis and a depth of feeling."[10] It concluded with the prayer that, according to Cohen, encompassed Michael's whole life:

A prayer that begins for us in an ancient Aramic tongue, *Yisgadal, v'yiskadash, sh'meh rabo,* a prayer that expresses the eternal hope that no tyranny can quite destroy, the hope that a righteousness which as yet exists only in the world of our ideals may yet prevail on our earth as in God's heaven. And so in that tradition we who were Jerry Michael's students, and will continue to be his students all our lives, say amen to the prayer that was Jerry Michael's life. . . . He who maketh peace to rule in His high heavens may bring peace and comfort in the days to come.[11]

In the spring of 1953, Cohen was diagnosed with cancer of the lining of the pleura. As the tumor grew, his chest filled with fluid, making breathing difficult. He was often sick, but no one was to know how sick he really was, except for Lucy. Even his daughters were not told, and his brother learned the diagnosis from Harry Rosenfield, their brother-in-law, with whom Cohen happened to have had a close working relationship.[12]

Cohen was determined not to make his struggle with cancer an excruciating experience for his family. Those were six wonderful months, Lucy later said. He was also a good patient. He urged his doctors to experiment with certain medications and kept detailed records of their effectiveness and side effects so that others could benefit from his experience. He only feared that he would stop being productive. He avoided medicine to reduce pain, so his mind could remain clear.[13]

Gradually, Cohen transferred responsibility to others in his law firm, but he did not explain why. When he checked into a hospital in Washington, D.C., he told them he was in the Adirondacks, and when they called his house in the Adirondacks, they were told that he was hiking in the mountains. When a relative drove to the Adirondacks, Lucy told him that Cohen was busy writing and could not see him. As friends later noted, Cohen had a tremendous drive to win—to understand, to win a case, to win a tennis match; the thought of losing to a disease, to nature, must have been hard to accept.[14] "The Roof it has a lazy time, a lying in the sun; The Walls, they have to hold it up, they do not have much fun," Cohen wrote to his secretary, Pearl Ann. "I have been quite roof like and want to thank you and all the rest of the staff for holding me up in these past two weeks."[15]

Not wanting to disappoint his students, Cohen tried to arrange for another professor to share responsibility with him for courses he was to teach at Yale and CCNY in 1953.[16]

As much as he could, he kept working. When he needed to stay in bed, he worked at home. If someone joined him, it was on condition that no cognizance of his illness would be taken. Cohen spent his last months reviewing the galley proofs of the second edition of Morris's *Reason and Nature* and the first edition of Morris's *American Thought*.[17] He testified against a termination bill about a month before his death.[18]

Walter Fried, a partner at Cohen's law firm, described Cohen as "a fighter." "His battles were almost exclusively on behalf of the oppressed and inarticulate," Fried noted. "He carried into every fight his great ability as a lawyer and his tireless energy, but he won because of his overwhelming convictions and his shining enthusiasm."[19]

On Sunday October 19, 1953, the *Review of Jewish Interests* published Cohen's review of Morroe Berger's book *Equality by Statute: Legal Controls over Group Discrimination*. "The legal framework of American democracy," Cohen began his comments, "had been fashioned, in large part, as a response to four great challenges": first, Americans faced and fought against the political tyranny of King George III; then, they encountered the contradiction between chattel slavery and the American ideal of equality. "When the abolition of slavery had been achieved, the perspective of American idealism shifted to the challenge of economic autocracy," which the New Deal sought to end. The fourth challenge, emerging just as the other causes could no longer "kindle in the hearts of young or old idealists the strong moral drives that are prerequisite to basic legal change," was the challenge of racism.[20]

Cohen was adamant about the need to fight racial discrimination. In an intellectual world that had become committed to neutrality, Cohen called for federal and local legislation to eliminate segregation and racism. "The notion of law as neutral in race relations," he explained, "is as unrealistic as the notion of a neutral battlefield. Law is the battlefield in which all great social struggles take place, and the contours, natural or artificial, of the battlefield are as important as the magnitude of the opposing forces in determining the outcome of the struggle." While admitting the importance of cases eliminating white primaries, segregation in interstate buses, racially restrictive covenants, and segregation in public higher education, Cohen stressed the importance of legislative and administrative efforts such as the Fair Employment Practices Committee's drive to eliminate racial discrimination in employment.[21]

Cohen did not live to continue the fight against racism. He died on the day on which his review was published. "He spent the day out in the sun, stripped to the waist, and working feverishly on a book review" of Milton Konvitz's *Civil Rights in Immigration*.[22] To support Konvitz's critique of the McCarran-Walter Act of 1952, which attempted to restrict immigration. Cohen's review reiterated his argument that oppression of "small and friendless" groups like the Indians, African Americans, Mormons, the Chinese laborer, or aliens would ultimately be extended to society at large.[23]

"He moved his chair and writing paraphernalia and thermos jug and pills, as the sun moved." At 5 p.m. "he finished with a flourish." After dinner "he read from Thomas Jefferson's collected works on the Indians, wrote out his time sheet of hours spent on work that day (6 hours writing the review and an hour and 20 minutes reading Jefferson's papers, altogether 7 hours and 20 minutes), prepared his pills and nightly chart of when he expected to awaken and what pills to take, transferred his pen, papers, etc. to his office suit for the next day, and retired to bed at around 10:30." He died shortly after midnight of a ruptured blood vessel.[24]

Rabbi Norman Gerstenfeld of the Washington Hebrew Congregation officiated at the ceremony at the Danzansky Funeral Home. The honorary pallbearers were Justice Felix Frankfurter; Minnesota Democratic Senator Hubert H. Humphrey; North Dakota Republican Senator William Langer; Judges David L. Bazelon, Henry W. Edgerton, Charles Fahy, and William H. Hastie; and Deans Wesley Sturges of Yale Law School and George Johnson of Howard University Law School. Eulogies were delivered by Oscar L. Chapman, former secretary of the interior; Walter J. Fried, Cohen's legal associate; and Professors Ernest Nagel of the Philosophy Department at Columbia University, Eugene V. Rostow of Yale Law School, and Benjamin Kaplan of Harvard Law School. Also participating were Brendon Brown, dean of Catholic University Law School, Professor Milton Konvitz of Cornell University, Arthur L. Strasser, Cohen's senior partner, Norman Thomas, Joel Wolfsohn, former assistant secretary of the interior, William Zimmerman, John Collier, Roger Baldwin of the ACLU, and Oliver La Farge, president of the AAIA.[25]

Shortly after the publication of *The Legal Conscience,* the collected works of Felix Cohen, Justice William Douglas wrote the following:

The first book—Logic, Law and Ethics—reveals the author as a worthy companion of his eminent father. . . . He sees in lawyers' and judges' talk not logic but feelings, not immutable principles but the visceral reactions of differing individuals. He is devastating in his analysis of court decisions when he uses what he calls "word magic." The stimulating first book in this volume might be summed up in one of the closing sentences, "We are all blind men reporting on an elephant." . . . [The second book] reflects the philosophy behind Cohen's monumental work "Handbook of Federal Indian Law." . . . No mind that ever delved into Indian affairs was keener, more discerning, more enlightened. There is wisdom, companion and depth of understanding. The job of "Americanizing the white man" seemed to him to come ahead of "Americanizing the Indian." . . . No minority ever had a more faithful advocate. . . . [In the] final book— the Philosophy of American Democracy . . . [t]he problems of the pluralistic society at home and across the world are put in new perspective.[26]

On Cohen's desk, a handwritten page indicated the agenda for 1953: "Immigration and Indian articles . . . Indian policy . . . Indian legislative program . . . Indian litigation . . . joint efforts . . . complete administration of Morris Cohen's estate . . . Finish *American Thought* volume . . . Reissue *Reason and Nature* . . . and develop immigration and international practice."[27]

Felix Solomon Cohen's life was a prayer for pluralism. The Blackfeet Indians called him "A Double Runner" because he moved between two peoples and because he did so at an extremely fast pace.[28] As a friend beautifully captured the essence of Cohen's life, "He had a personal and mental equipment to enable him to climb into the seats of the mighty but he chose instead to do justice and to walk with the humble."[29] "He was a great and noble teacher," Professor Ralph S. Brown Jr. of Yale Law School wrote, "a teacher whose whole life was part of the lesson he had to give us."[30] In the words of Micah, "What does the Lord require of thee, but to do justice and to love mercy and to walk humbly with thy God."[31]

Abbreviations

FSCP   Felix S. Cohen Papers, Yale Collection of Western Americana, Beinecke Rare Book and Manuscript Library, Yale University, New Haven, Connecticut (material is cited by box/folder).

HP   Handbook of Federal Indian Law Papers, Yale Collection of Western Americana, Beinecke Rare Book and Manuscript Library, Yale University, New Haven, Connecticut (material is cited by folder).

JCP   John Collier Papers, Sterling Memorial Library, Yale University, New Haven, Connecticut (microfilm; material is cited by reel number).

JPLP   Joseph P. Lash Papers, Franklin D. Roosevelt Presidential Library, Hyde Park, New York (the material cited is from boxes 50, 51. These boxes include transcripts of interviews that Joseph Lash conducted with members of the Cohen family, relatives, and friends. Names of individual interviewees were omitted).

Legal Conscience   *The Legal Conscience: Selected Papers of Felix S. Cohen*, ed. Lucy Kramer Cohen (New Haven, 1960).

MRCP   Morris R. Cohen Papers, Special Collections Research Center, Joseph Regenstein Library, University of Chicago, Chicago, Illinois (the material cited is from boxes 6,7,8,9).

RG   The National Archives Record Groups 46 (U.S. Senate) 48 (Interior), 75 (BIA), and 233 (U.S. House of Representatives) (material is cited by entry, part, box, or folder).

PHN   ProQuest Research Library Plus, Historical Newspapers.

RB   Records and Briefs of the U.S. Supreme Court.

NOTES

Chapter 1. A Second Generation

1. Felix S. Cohen (FSC) to Joseph Lash, October 11, JPLP.

2. Arthur A. Goren, *The Politics and Public Culture of American Jews* (Bloomington: 1999), 32; David A. Hollinger, *Morris R. Cohen and the Scientific Ideal* (Cambridge, MA: 1975), 19–27; Delia Caparoso Konzett, "Administered Identities and Linguistic Assimilation: The Politics of Immigrant English in Anzia Yezierska's *Hungry Hearts*," *American Literature* 69 (1997): 597.

3. Lawrence A. Cremin, *American Education: The Metropolitan Experience, 1876–1980* (New York: 1988), 622–23.

4. Ibid., 623; Morris R. Cohen, *A Dreamer's Journey: The Autobiography of Morris Raphael Cohen* (Boston: 1949), 96–97; Hollinger, *Morris Cohen*, 25; records of burials in Mt. Zion Cemetery, New York, www.shtetlinks.jewishgen.org/nesvizh/mtzion.html; obituary, Mrs. Morris R. Cohen, *New York Times*, June 13, 1942, PHN; Interviews, JPLP. On the Triangle fire, see Richard A. Greenwald, *The Triangle Fire, The Protocols of Peace, and Industrial Democracy in Progressive Era New York* (Philadelphia: 2005); Irving Howe and Kenneth Libo, *How We Lived: A Documentary History of Immigrant Jews in America 1880–1930* (New York: 1979), 185; Meredith Tax, *The Rising of the Women: Feminist Solidarity and Class Conflict, 1880–1917* (New York: 1980), 234–36; Dave Von Drehle, *Triangle: The Fire that Changed America* (New York: 2003); www.ilr.cornell.edu/trianglefire/. On the Women's Trade Union League, see Nancy Schrom Dye, "Creating a Feminist Alliance: Sisterhood and Class Conflict in the New York Women's Trade Union League, 1903–1914," *Feminist Studies* 2 (1975): 24; Jone Johnson Lewis, womenshistory.about.com/od/worklaborunions/a/wtul_2.htm. On the Women's International League for Peace and Freedom, see Florence Brewer Boeckel, "Women in International Affairs," *Annals of the American Academy of Political and Social Science* 143 (1929): 243, 246.

5. Cremin, *American Education*, 623–24. On the Ethical Culture Society, see www.aeu.org/adler1.html; "Miscellaneous City News: A School for Ethical Culture," *New York Times*, April 10, 1883, PHN.

6. Declaration of Appointee, FSCP 92/1473.

7. Howe and Libo, *How We Lived*, 17–26; Hollinger, *Morris Cohen*, 31–32. On the immigrants' vision of New York City as the Promised City, see Selma C. Berrol, "Education and Economic Mobility: the Jewish Experience in New York City, 1880–1920," in *East European Jews in America, 1880–1920: Immigration and Adaptation*, ed. Jeffrey S. Gurock (New York: 1998), 983.

8. Hadassa Kosak, *Cultures of Opposition: Jewish Immigrant Workers, New York City, 1881–1905* (Albany, NY: 2000), 37.

9. FSC, Testimonial Dinner, January 17, 1948, FSCP 92/1470.

10. Howe and Libo, *How We Lived,* 55; James R. Barrett, "Americanization from the Bottom Up: Immigration and the Remaking of the Working Class in the United States, 1880–1930," *Journal of American History* 78 (1992): 997.

11. Kosak, *Cultures of Opposition,* 134. See also Howe and Libo, *How We Lived,* 20; Gerald Sorin, *The Jewish People in America: A Time for Building: The Third Migration, 1880–1920* (Baltimore: 1992), 117.

12. Howe and Libo, *How We Lived,* 161, 174.

13. Sherry Gorelick, *City College and the Jewish Poor: Education in New York, 1880–1924* (New Brunswick: 1981), 31.

14. Kosak, *Cultures of Opposition,* 11, 92–93, 98.

15. Hollinger, *Morris Cohen,* 19.

16. Ibid., 27. See also Cremin, *American Education,* 619; Interviews, JPLP; James A. Good, "The Value of Thomas Davidson," *Transactions of the Charles S. Peirce Society,* 40(2004): 289; discussion paper: "Philosophy as Teaching: James's 'Knight Errant,' Thomas Davidson," www.american-philosophy.org/archives/past_conference_programs/pc2004/submissions/dp-10.htm.

17. Gorelick, *CCNY and the Jewish Poor,* 34, 37. On the Marx Circle, see Cremin, *American Education,* 619.

18. William S. Berlin, "The Roots of Jewish Political Thought in America," Ph.D. diss., Rutgers University, 1975, 215.

19. Gorelick, *CCNY and the Jewish Poor,* 32–38; Good, "The Value of Thomas Davidson."

20. Hollinger, *Morris Cohen,* 29, 35, 48–49. Morris pursued undergraduate studies at CCNY.

21. Interviews, JPLP.

22. Hollinger, *Morris Cohen,* xii, 18–19. See also Simon Agranat, "Reflections on the Man and His Work," *Israel Law Review* 16 (1981): 283. On anti-Semitism in academia in the early-twentieth century, see Susanne Klingenstein, *Jews in the American Academy, 1900–1940: The Dynamics of Intellectual Assimilation* (New Haven: 1991).

23. Morris Cohen, *A Dreamer's Journey,* 233–34. See also Klingenstein, *Jews in the American Academy,* 53.

24. Hollinger, *Morris Cohen,* 56–57.

25. Werner Sollors, *Beyond Ethnicity: Consent and Descent in American Culture* (New York: 1986), 66, 97; David A. Hollinger, "Ethnic Diversity, Cosmopolitanism and the Emergence of the American Liberal Intelligentsia," *American Quarterly* 27 (1975): 142; Elmer N. Lear, "On the Unity of the Kallen Perspective," in *The Legacy of Horace M. Kallen,* ed. Milton R. Konvitz (London: 1987), 116; Sidney Ratner, "Horace M. Kallen and Cultural Pluralism," in *The Legacy of Horace M. Kallen,* 50.

26. Horace M. Kallen, "Democracy versus The Melting-Pot," in *Culture and Democracy in the United States* (New York: 1924), 67, 125. Originally published in *The Nation* (February 18 and 25, 1915). Kallen, whose family immigrated to the United States from Germany when he was five and whose father was a Boston rabbi, wanted to be identified as an American, not as a Jew. But at the influence of his professors at Harvard, especially Barrett Wendell and William James, Kallen accepted that being a Jew was not inconsistent with being an American. Interestingly, Kallen's concept of cultural pluralism was traceable to the scientific, even racist, assumptions of anti-immigrationists and their racial determinism. "Men," Kallen wrote, "may change their clothes, their politics, their wives, their religions, their philosophies, to greater or lesser extents, but they cannot change their grandfathers." Yet Kallen made race and ethnicity positive elements of American society. Louis Menand, *The Metaphysical Club: The Story of Ideas in America* (New York: 2001), 388–93.

27. Morris R. Cohen, "Zionism: Tribalism or Liberalism?" in *The Faith of a Liberal: Selected Essays by Morris Cohen* (New York: 1946), 327–29. The article was first published in the *New Republic* in 1919 as a critique of Zionism, which Morris Cohen associated with Kallen's pluralism. See also Klingenstein, *Jews in the American Academy,* 50–51; Hollinger, "Ethnic Diversity."

28. Hollinger, "Ethnic Diversity," 133–40. As Hollinger further indicates, "The concept of the 'cosmopolitan Jew' has long been a stereotype of adulation and of anti-Semitism." Ibid., 138n21.

29. Hollinger, *Morris Cohen,* 6–7. See also Klingenstein, *Jews in the American Academy,* 64; Morton J. Horwitz, "Jews and Legal Realists," 16 (unpublished manuscript).

30. Hollinger, "Ethnic Diversity," 139.

31. On the dialogue between the Jewish immigrant culture and the American middle-class culture, see Deborah Dash Moore, *At Home in America: Second Generation New York Jews* (New York: 1981).

32. Morris Cohen, *A Dreamer's Journey,* 25, 121, 132; Leonora Cohen Rosenfield, *Portrait of a Philosopher: Morris R. Cohen in Life and Letters* (New York: 1962), 239. See also interviews, JPLP.

33. Cohen Rosenfield, *Portrait of a Philosopher,* 362.

34. Hollinger, *Morris Cohen,* 9–11.

35. Interviews, JPLP.

36. Cremin, *American Education,* 621–26. On gender roles, see Paula E. Hyman, "Culture and Gender: Women in the Immigrant Jewish Community," in *East European Jews in America,* 931.

37. Cremin, *American Education,* 625.

38. Interviews, JPLP.

39. Theodore H. Haas, ed., *Felix S. Cohen: A Fighter for Justice* (Washington, D.C.: 1956), 19; Interviews, JPLP.

40. Interviews, JPLP.

41. Hollinger, *Morris Cohen,* 12.

42. Moore, *At Home in America,* 89–121.

43. Ibid., 82; FSC's Resume, FSCP 92/1472.

44. Eileen F. Lebow, *The Bright Boys: A History of Townsend Harris High School* (Westport, CT: 2000), 22–24, 61, 198.

45. Ibid., 30–31, 36.

46. Haas, ed., *Felix S. Cohen,* 17; FSC's Resume, FSCP 92/1472.

47. Interviews, JPLP; FSC, Report of the Secretary of Housing to Morris and Mary Cohen, n.d., MRCP.

48. FSC to Mary Cohen, Sunday, ca. 1940s, MRCP.

49. Interviews, JPLP.

50. Interviews, JPLP. See also David Silve, "Morris Raphael Cohen as Educator," Ph.D. diss., SUNY Buffalo, 1985.

51. FSC to Joseph Lash, October 11, JPLP.

52. Charles S. Peirce, "The Fixation of Belief," in *Chance, Love, and Logic: Philosophical Essays,* ed. Morris R. Cohen (Lincoln: 1998) (1923), 20.

53. As his friends remembered, Felix Cohen read this poem on his commencement night in 1926. Cited in Haas, ed., *Felix S. Cohen,* 32.

54. Gorelick, *CCNY and the Jewish Poor,* 62; James Traub, *City on a Hill: Testing the American Dream at City College* (Reading, MA: 1994), 9, 21, 24.

55. Gorelick, *CCNY and the Jewish Poor,* 62–70; Traub, *City on a Hill,* 23–24.

56. Gorelick, *CCNY and the Jewish Poor,* 61–83; Traub, *City on a Hill,* 26.

57. Traub, *City on a Hill,* 27–28; Gorelick, *CCNY and the Jewish Poor,* 83, 137. Gorelick adds that "by the turn of the century three-quarters of the students at CCNY were Eastern European Jews, although German Jewish names predominated among the graduates at least until the 1930s, the dropout rate being extremely high." Ibid., 123. On quotas, see John Higham, *Strangers in the Land: Patterns of American Nativism, 1860–1925* (New Brunswick: 1992), 278; Beth S. Wenger, *New York Jews and the Great Depression: Uncertain Promise* (Syracuse, NY: 1999), 23.

58. Gorelick, *CCNY and the Jewish Poor,* 83; Traub, *City on a Hill,* 31–33. Gorelick challenges the relationship between education and upward mobility.

59. Gorelick, *CCNY and the Jewish Poor,* 85, 138.

60. Traub, *City on a Hill,* 9, 32.

61. Berrol, "Education and Economic Mobility," 984.

62. Interviews, JPLP.

63. Traub, *City on a Hill,* 40.

64. Haas, ed., *Felix S. Cohen,* 18.

65. Later in life, Felix learned Hebrew and Spanish. Haas, ed., *Felix S. Cohen,* 18–19. He also taught himself Yiddish so that he could follow the serialization of Morris Cohen's *A Dreamer's Journey* in *Der Tog* (*The Day*) and studied Spanish so that he could make a speech in Spanish to a lawyers' convention in Mexico. Interviews, JPLP. In a 1942 application for an attorney position, Felix listed French, Spanish, German and reading knowledge of Greek and Latin as languages he was able to read, write, or speak with reasonable fluency. See also FSC's Resume, FSCP 92/1472.

66. Interviews, JPLP.

67. Correspondence between FSC and his parents, 1924–1926, MRCP. On participatory sports as middle-class fads in the 1920s, see Lynn Dumenil, *The Modern Temper: American Culture and Society in the 1920s* (New York: 1995), 77. Felix's love for the outdoors ran deep, "with an emotional and scientific interest akin to Thoreau's." He "knew the names of many trees, plants (including mushrooms—of special interest to him), and animals." He loved the Adirondacks and its mountains and climbed some forty of the forty-six Adirondacks peaks over 4,000 feet in height. At home in Washington, he cultivated "a large, strange garden, complete with grape arbor and a fig tree. Succulent vegetables and fruits were frequently harvested by the Cohen household just before mealtime." Haas, ed., *Felix S. Cohen,* 26–27.

68. Moore, *At Home in America,* 10. The generation paradigm could be misleading, given the long period of mass migration into the United States. As other historians have concluded, it is more accurate to label each of the generations a different cultural generation. The second generation is thus a generation "born out of the process of 'scurrying between [the] two worlds' of a confined immigrant environment and an increasingly familiar American society. . . . 'At home both in American urban culture and immigrant Jewish culture, second generation Jews could synthesize the two.'" Wenger, *New York Jews and the Great Depression,* 7.

69. FSC to Morris Cohen, August 7, 1925, MRCP.

70. Hollinger, *Morris Cohen,* 43–57. On the revolt against formalism, see Morton G. White, *Social Thought in America, the Revolt against Formalism* (New York: 1949). On the similarities between Morris Cohen's evaluation of this revolt and White's assessments, see Hollinger, *Morris Cohen,* 246–48.

71. Hollinger, *Morris Cohen,* 123; Peter Novick, *That Noble Dream: The "Objectivity Question" and the American Historical Profession* (New York: 1988), 143; Dorothy Ross, *The Origins of American Social Science* (New York: 1991).

72. JPLP.

73. Interviews, JPLP.

74. "In Memoriam Felix S. Cohen '26," *The City College Alumnus,* December 1953, FSCP 91/1467. See also *Columbia Law School News,* November 11, 1953. On Morris's style, see Hollinger, *Morris Cohen,* 69–75.

75. Robert Cohen, *When the Old Left was Young: Student Radicals and America's First Mass Student Movement, 1929–1941* (New York: 1993), 24; Howe and Libo, *How We Lived,* 188; Moore, *At Home in America,* 201–30.

76. Robert Hyfler, *Prophets of the Left: American Socialist Thought in the Twentieth Century* 121–26 (Westport, CT: 1984). On the idea of the best men, see John G. Sproat, *The Best Men: Liberal Reformers in the Gilded Age* (New York: 1968). On Progressive ideology, see Gorelick, *CCNY and the Jewish Poor,* 83–84.

77. Joseph P. Lash, interview, "The Student Movement of the 1930s," newdeal.feri.org/students/lash.htm#26.

78. On the League for Industrial Democracy, see Robert Cohen, *When the Old Left was Young,* 31; Lash, "The Student Movement."

79. FSC to Morris Cohen, 1924, MRCP.

80. FSC to Morris and Mary Cohen, 1926, MRCP.

81. Eileen Eagan, *Class, Culture, and the Classroom: The Student Peace Movement in the 1930s* (Philadelphia: 1981), 110–11; S. Willis Rudy, *The College of the City of New York: A History 1847–1947* (New York: 1949), 405–7. On Felix's election as editor of *Campus,* see "City Brevities," *New York Times,* May 26, 1925, PHN.

82. Hyfler, *Prophets of the Left,* 123.

83. Dumenil, *The Modern Temper,* 152.

84. Charles Chatfield, *For Peace and Justice: Pacifism in America, 1914–1941* (Knoxville: 1971), 146.

85. See www.princetonreview.com/cte/articles/military/rotchist.asp.

86. Chatfield, *For Peace and Justice,* 152–53.

87. Rudy, *The College of the City of New York,* 366.

88. This history of military science at CCNY is described in *The Lavender* 3 (December 1925): 3–5 (Military Science Issue), John Hay Library, Brown University, Providence, Rhode Island. See also Rudy, *The College of the City of New York,* 405.

89. The selected excerpts were: "The object of all military training is to win battles"; "The principles of sportsmanship and consideration for your opponent have no place in the practical application of this work"; "To finish an opponent who hangs on, or attempts to pull you to the ground, always try to break his hold by driving the knee or foot to his crotch and gouging his eyes with your thumbs"; "This inherent desire to fight and kill must be carefully watched for and encouraged by the instructor"; and "America needs invincible infantry." *Lavender,* 5.

90. Rudy, *The College of the City of New York,* 404–6.

91. Ibid.; *Lavender,* 4–5.

92. FSC, "The Last Word," *Lavender,* 6–7.

93. Ibid.

94. FSC to Joseph Lash, May 1, [1935], JPLP.

95. Chatfield, *For Peace and Justice,* 154.

96. FSC, "The Last Word," 6.

97. Ibid.

98. Morris R. Cohen, "The Case against Compulsory Military Science," letter to the President and Faculty, December 8, 1925, *Lavender,* 9.

99. FSC, "The Last Word," 7.

100. Rudy, *The College of the City of New York,* 406.

101. The quotes are from letters reprinted in *Lavender,* 13–26.

102. Ibid., 14, 17, 19, 25.

103. Rudy, *The College of the City of New York,* 406–7.

104. "Mezes Lifts Ban on Student Paper," *New York Times,* December 21, 1925, PHN. Shortly thereafter, Felix was elected by CCNY's students to attend the Princeton Intercollegiate World Court Conference of the National Student Federation. After President Mezes attempted to prevent him from attending, Felix went and raised the question whether delegates were to be selected by the student body or by the faculty. An attempt by Mr. Fulle of Princeton (a friend of Mezes) to prevent Felix from addressing the delegates was futile. The other members supported the opponent of compulsory military training and a resolution was adopted "that all the representatives of colleges in the Federation be appointed by the students, and not by the faculties." For detailed stories, see MRCP; "College Reforms, Aim of Students," *New York Times,* December 14, 1925, PHN.

105. JPLP.

106. FSC to Morris Cohen, 1926, MRCP.

107. *Microcosm,* Class of 1926, at the Morris R. Cohen Library, CCNY. See also JPLP.

108. "Military Training in Colleges Scored," *New York Times,* December 31, 1926, PHN.

109. Opponents of military training believed that the course continued to receive a favored position in the curriculum. Each student was required to take two years of Hygiene, "but those who took the two-year military course were exempted from a third prescribed year of hygiene." Throughout the early thirties *The Campus* continued to call for a curriculum reform to eliminate the favored position of the elective in Military Science. In September, 1935, the General Faculty finally voted to make the change; "the third year of hygiene was voted elective for all undergraduates by a unanimous resolution, and Military Science was at last placed on a purely elective basis." Rudy, *The College of the City of New York,* 408–9. See also Robert Cohen, *When the Old Left was Young,* 28.

110. As a friend relayed the story, they all agreed in advance that they would refuse to accept their keys as long as Felix was kept out. At the induction meeting, one of the candidates stepped forward and, speaking on behalf of the new candidates, refused to accept the keys "because a fellow student, as deserving as the rest of [them], has been denied a key for reasons having nothing to do with scholarship." From that moment on, everyone was blackballed. Interviews, JPLP.

111. FSC to Mary Cohen, 1926, MRCP.

112. Rudy, *The College of the City of New York*, 405–11.

113. FSC to Morton Gottschall, May 8, 1947, FSCP 87/1368.

114. Morris Cohen, *A Dreamer's Journey*, 154–55; "City College Phi Beta Kappa Picks 18," *New York Times*, November 27, 1928, PHN.

Chapter 2. Multiple Destinies

1. Gorelick, *CCNY and the Jewish Poor*, 68.

2. Interviews, JPLP.

3. At least since his days at Harvard, as a roommate to Felix Frankfurter, Morris hoped to bring philosophy and law together. In a paper he delivered at the meeting of the American Philosophical Association in December 1912, "Jurisprudence as a Philosophical Discipline," Morris argued that acquaintance with general jurisprudence would enrich the discussion and teaching of logic, epistemology, and metaphysics. When, as he remembered, his plea "left the waters of academic philosophy unrippled," Morris worked to bring together representatives of legal and philosophical thought. The product of his efforts, the Conference on Legal and Social Philosophy, met only a few times during the 1910s, fading quietly after that. But during its short life it brought together some of the leading figures in academia, including John Dewey (who acted as chairman of the Conference), W. E. Hocking, Roscoe Pound, Felix Adler, John Wigmore, and Albion Small. Morris Cohen, *A Dreamer's Journey*, 175–80; Leonora Cohen Rosenfield, "Aristotelianism in Morris R. Cohen's Legal Philosophy," *Israel Law Review* 16 (1981): 294. See also Morris R. Cohen, "Jurisprudence as a Philosophical Discipline," The *Journal of Philosophy* 10 (1913): 225.

4. Correspondence between Felix and Morris, summer 1926, MRCP. See particularly FSC to Morris Cohen, July 12, 1926.

5. Hollinger, *Morris Cohen*, 55.

6. FSC, "Government and the Social Contract: Ethical Evaluations in the Law," address before the Eastern Law Students Conference, New York University School of Law, New York City, March 7, 1936, in *Legal Conscience*, 362–63. On Morris's generation's attraction to ideas, see David Joseph Singal, "Towards a Definition of American Modernism," *American Quarterly* 39 (1987): 12, cited in *1915: The Cultural Moment: The New Politics, the New Woman, the New Psychology, the New Art, and the New Theater in America*, ed. Adele Heller and Lois Rudnick (New Brunswick: 1991), 6.

7. See also interviews, JPLP.

8. On this intellectual generation, see James T. Kloppenberg, *Uncertain Victory: Social Democracy and Progressivism in European and American Thought, 1870–1920* (New York: 1986).

9. Interviews, JPLP. But see FSC to Morris Cohen, MRCP, on the subject:

Dear Dad,
Just got a note from Woods asking if I'd accept his nomination for the Henry Bromfield Rogers Fellowship, for the study of Ethics in its relation to Jurisprudence or to Sociology. 700 bucks. Sounds like a lot of money and I'll have to consider it at my leisure. But I have no leisure right now. My gov. essay is overdue and I haven't started writing it yet. . . .

10. FSC to Dr. John Haynes Holmes, chairman, board of directors, ACLU, December 30, 1949, FSCP 86/1341. On scientism in American thought, see Ross, *Origins of American Social Science*.

11. On the intellectuals' reconfiguration of modernity as radically interdependent, see Thomas L. Haskell, *The Emergence of Professional Social Science: The American Social Science Association and the Nineteenth Century Crisis of Authority* (Urbana: 1977), 13–15.

12. Ann Douglas, *Terrible Honesty: Mongrel Manhattan in the 1920s* (New York: 1995), 3–28. See also Gorelick, *CCNY and the Jewish Poor,* 72.

13. FSC, "What City College will Contribute to the Development of the Law," *The Barrister* (1938): 5–7 (1938), FSCP 69/1095.

14. Ibid., 4–5.

15. Correspondence between Felix and his parents, 1926–27, MRCP.

16. Ibid.

17. Ibid.

18. He studied logic of relatives with H. M. Sheffer, metaphysics with A. N. Whitehead, ethics with Raphael Demos, symbolic logic with Langford, theory of value with Ralph Perry, metaphysics with E. A. Burtt, and philosophy of the state with W. E. Hocking. FSC's Resume, FSCP 92/1472.

19. Bruce Kuklick, *The Rise of American Philosophy, Cambridge, Massachusetts, 1860–1930* (New Haven: 1977), 524–32, 569–70, 255, 441–42, 505–10.

20. Ibid., 505–15.

21. Ibid., 225; Bruce Kuklick, *A History of Philosophy in America* (Oxford: 2001), 189–91.

22. FSC, *Ethical Systems and Legal Ideals: An Essay on the Foundations of Legal Criticism* (Camden, N.J.: 1933), 1.

23. FSC to Morris Cohen, 1926–27, MRCP.

24. Ibid.

25. Douglas, *Terrible Honesty,* 143, 444–45.

26. FSC to Morris Cohen, 1926–27, MRCP.

27. Ibid.

28. Novick, *That Noble Dream,* 144.

29. *A History of the School of Law, Columbia University* by the staff of the foundation for research in legal history under the direction of Julius Goebel Jr. (New York: 1955), 337.

30. Interviews, JPLP; FSCP 92/1472.

31. The term *classical legal thought* was originally coined by Duncan Kennedy in *The Rise and Fall of Classical Legal Thought* (unpublished manuscript). A portion of this manuscript was published as Duncan Kennedy, "Toward an Historical Understanding of Legal Consciousness: The Case of Classical Legal Thought in America, 1850–1940," *Research in Law and Society* 3 (1980). See also Morton J. Horwitz, *The Transformation of American Law, 1870–1960: The Crisis of Legal Orthodoxy* (New York: 1992), 9–31, 273; Arnold M. Paul, *Conservative Crisis and the Rule of Law: Attitudes of Bar and Bench, 1887–1895* (Gloucester: 1976); Robert Gordon, "Legal Thought and Legal Practice in the Age of American Enterprise, 1870–1920," in *Professions and Professional Ideologies in America,* ed. Gerald L. Geison (Chapel Hill, NC: 1983), 70.

32. Laura Kalman, *Legal Realism at Yale, 1927–1960* (Chapel Hill, NC: 1986), 11–12.

33. Horwitz, *Transformation of American Law, 1870–1960,* 193–212. On the relationship between realism and pragmatism, see White, *Social Thought in America;* Jerome Frank, "A Conflict with Oblivion: Some Observations on the Founders of Legal Pragmatism," *Rutgers Law Review* 9 (1954): 425; James R. Hackney Jr., "The Intellectual Origins of American Strict Products Liability: A Case Study in American Pragmatic Instrumentalism," *American Journal of Legal History* 39 (1995): 443.

34. Oliver Wendell Holmes Jr., "The Path of the Law," *Harvard Law Review* 10 (1897): 457. See also White, *Social Thought in America,* 69–70.

35. Jerome Frank, *Law and the Modern Mind* (New York: 1931), *cited* in Kalman, *Legal Realism at Yale,* 8.

36. Roscoe Pound, "Law in Books, Law in Action," *American Law Review* 44 (1910): 15.

37. Roscoe Pound, "Mechanical Jurisprudence," *Columbia Law Review* 8 (1908): 609–10. See also Roscoe Pound, "A Practical Program of Procedural Reform," *Green Bag* 22 (1910): 438; Horwitz, *Transformation of American Law, 1870–1960,* 188; David Wigdor, *Roscoe Pound: Philosopher of Law* (Westport, CT: 1974), 187.

38. Robert L. Hale, "Coercion and Distribution in a Supposedly Non-Coercive State," *Political Science Quarterly* 38 (1923): 470.

39. Horwitz, *Transformation of American Law, 1870–1960,* 49–50.

40. Arthur L. Corbin, "Offer and Acceptance, and Some of the Resulting Legal Relations," *Yale Law Journal* 26 (1917): 206.

41. John P. Dawson, "Economic Duress: An Essay in Perspective," *Michigan Law Review* 45 (1947): 253.

42. Holmes, "The Path of the Law," 469.

43. Wigdor, *Roscoe Pound,* 146–82.

44. *Muller v. Oregon,* 208 U.S. 412 (1908); Philippa Strum, ed., *Brandeis on Democracy* (Lawrence, KS: 1995), 7–13.

45. *Lochner v. New York,* 198 U.S. 45, 75 (1905).

46. *A History of the School of Law,* 297–98.

47. Similar attempts were undertaken at Yale. William Douglas "combined half a dozen separate so-called fields of law into a single course called 'Business Units,' [and] Wesley Sturges did the same in a course called 'Credit Transactions.'" Thurman Arnold, "Book Review of American Legal Realism: Skepticism, Reform and the Judicial Process by Wilfrid E. Rumble, Jr.," *Political Science Quarterly* 84 (1969): 668.

48. *A History of the School of Law,* 297–303.

49. Ibid., 303–4.

50. Ibid., 305.

51. Interviews, JPLP.

52. *A History of the School of Law,* 312–13.

53. Ibid., 311–20.

54. Horwitz, *Transformation of American Law, 1870–1960,* 49–50.

55. Dalia Tsuk, "Corporations without Labor: The Politics of Progressive Corporate Law," *University of Pennsylvania Law Review* 151 (2003): 1888.

56. *A History of the School of Law,* 317.

57. Ibid., 311–12.

58. The address was delivered on Station WPCH, August 20, 1927. William L. Twining, *Karl Llewellyn and the Realist Movement* (London: 1973), 341–49. On the trial, see Dumenil, *The Modern Temper,* 225.

59. *A History of the School of Law,* 281.

60. "Riotous Marchers Routed by Police," *New York Times,* August 10, 1927, PHN.

61. Interviews, JPLP.

62. FSC to Harry N. Rosenfield (brother-in-law), JPLP.

63. Horwitz, *Transformation of American Law, 1870–1960,* 49.

64. Jerold S. Auerbach, *Unequal Justice: Lawyers and Social Change in Modern America* (New York: 1976), 21–22.

65. See, for example, Morris Cohen, "Justice Holmes and the Nature of Law," *Columbia Law Review* 31 (1931): 352; Roscoe Pound, "The Call for a Realist Jurisprudence," *Harvard Law Review* 44 (1931): 697; John Dickinson, "Legal Rules: Their Function in the Process of Decision," *University of Pennsylvania Law Review* 79 (1931): 833; Lon L. Fuller, "American Legal Realism," *University of Pennsylvania Law Review* 82 (1934): 429; Hermann Kantorowicz, "Some Rationalism about Realism," *Yale Law Journal* 43 (1933–34): 1240.

66. Fuller, "American Legal Realism," 430.

67. Horwitz, *Transformation of American Law, 1870–1960* 211.

68. Pound, "A Realist Jurisprudence," 697.

69. Ibid., 697–700.

70. Morris Cohen, "Justice Holmes," 360.

71. Horwitz, *Transformation of American Law, 1870–1960,* 211. Compare Fuller, "American Legal Realism," 461, which noted that "the cleft between Is and Ought causes acute distress to the realist. . . . The Is may be compelled to conform to the Ought, or the Ought may be permitted to acquiesce in the Is." But as it is often impossible to say what the Ought is, "the easier course . . . [is] to let the Ought acquiesce in the Is, to let law surrender to life." See also N. E. H. Hull, "Some Realism about the Llewellyn-Pound Exchange over Realism: The Newly Uncovered Private

Correspondence, 1927–1931," *Wisconsin Law Review* (1987): 933–40; Hollinger, *Morris Cohen*, 181–91.

72. Ajay K. Mehrotra, "Law and the 'Other': Karl N. Llewellyn, Cultural Anthropology, and the Legacy of The Cheyenne Way," *Law and Social Inquiry* 26 (2001): 750–51.

73. Dumenil, *The Modern Temper*, 145.

74. Novick, *That Noble Dream*. See also Horwitz, *Transformation of American Law, 1870–1960*, 180–82; Richard H. Pells, *Radical Visions and American Dreams: Culture and Social Thought in the Depression Years* (Urbana: 1998), 4.

75. Horwitz, *Transformation of American Law, 1870–1960*, 210–12.

76. Horwitz, "Jews and Legal Realists," 9–10. Cf. Morton J. Horwitz, "Why is Anglo-American Jurisprudence Unhistorical?" *Oxford Journal of Legal Studies* 17 (1997): 581.

77. Horwitz, *Transformation of American Law, 1870– 1960*.

78. Interviews, JPLP.

79. Walter Shepard, "Book Review," *Philosophy Review* 43 (1933): 624.

80. Duncan Kennedy, *A Critique of Adjudication (fin de siècle)* (Cambridge, MA: 1997), 88.

81. Joel R. Cornwell, "From Hedonism to Human Rights: Felix Cohen's Alternative to Nihilism," *Temple Law Review* 68 (1995): 201.

82. FSC, *Ethical Systems*, 11, 15, 17.

83. Ibid., 69, 49, 111.

84. Ibid., 101.

85. Ibid., 107.

86. Ibid., 111–12.

87. Cornwell, "From Hedonism to Human Rights," 206.

88. FSC, *Ethical Systems*, 227.

89. Ibid. See also Shepard, "Book Review," 624.

90. Cornwell, "From Hedonism to Human Rights," 206.

91. Kuklick, *Rise of American Philosophy*, 510. See also Ralph B. Perry, *General Theory of Value: Its Meaning and Basic Principles Construed in Terms of Interest* (New York: 1926).

92. George H. Sabine, "Book Review," *Cornell Law Quarterly* 19 (1933): 165.

93. FSC, *Ethical Systems*, 229.

94. Max Radin, "Book Review," *Harvard Law Review* 47 (1933): 147.

95. Sabine, "Book Review," 164.

96. FSC, *Ethical Systems*, 231, 234, 285.

97. Ibid., 233.

98. Ibid., 289.

99. Ibid., 292.

100. Jean Wahl, *The Pluralist Philosophies of England and America*, trans. Fred Rothwell (London: 1925), 101.

101. Ibid., 317–18, 155; Hilary Putnam, *Pragmatism: An Open Question* (Cambridge: 1995), 30–31. See also Nelson Goodman and Catherine Z. Elgin, *Reconceptions in Philosophy and Other Arts and Sciences* (Indianapolis: 1988), 24–25.

102. William James, *A Pluralistic Universe: Hibbert Lectures at Manchester College on the Present Situation in Philosophy* (Lincoln, NE: 1996) (1909), 321–22.

103. Compare Roderick A. Macdonald, "Metaphors of Multiplicity: Civil Society, Regimes and Legal Pluralism," *Arizona Journal of International and Comparative Law* 15 (1998): 71.

104. Horace M. Kallen, "A Pluralistic Universe: Professor James on the Present Situation in Philosophy," *Boston Evening Transcript*, June 16, 1909. See also William James, *Pragmatism, A New Name for Some Old Ways of Thinking* (New York: 1907); James, *Pluralistic Universe*.

105. Hilary Putnam, "James's Theory of Truth," in *The Cambridge Companion to William James*, ed. Ruth Anna Putnam (New York: 1997), 166.

106. Radin, "Book Review," 146.

107. C. E. Ayres, "Book Review," *Yale Law Journal* 43 (1933): 158.

108. Hessel Yntema, "Book Review," *American Political Science Review* 27 (1933): 654.

109. Walter Nelles, "Book Review," *Columbia Law Review* 33 (1933): 763.

110. Radin, "Book Review," 145.

111. Malcolm Sharp, "Book Review," *International Journal of Ethics* 44 (1934): 263–64.

112. George P. Adams, "Book Review," *California Law Review* 21 (1934): 632.

113. Kingsley Davis, "Book Review," *American Sociological Review* 5 (1940): 800.

114. Radin, "Book Review," 145.

115. FSC, *Ethical Systems,* 287–88.

116. FSC, "The Bauer-Bonbright Proposal for the Revision of the New York Public Service Commission Law and its Constitutionality," *Columbia Law Review* 30 (1930): 548 (unsigned). See also Horwitz, *Transformation of American Law, 1870–1960,* 160–64.

117. FSC, "The Vestal Bill for the Copyright Registration of Designs," *Columbia Law Review* 31 (1931): 477 (unsigned).

118. On group rights, see, for example, FSC, "The Privilege to Disparage A Non-Competing Business," which suggested that courts should accord groups and associations the same freedom of speech granted to individuals (at least with respect to commercial and industrial information). *Columbia Law Review* 30 (1930): 511, 521 (unsigned).

119. FSC, "The Judicial Resolution of Factional Disputes in Labor Unions," *Columbia Law Review* 30 (1930): 1025–27 (unsigned).

120. Ibid., 1039.

121. James, *Pluralistic Universe,* 321–22.

122. See, for example, W. Y. Elliott, *The Pragmatic Revolt in Politics: Syndicalism, Fascism, and the Constitutional State* (New York: 1928); Paul Q. Hirst, ed., *The Pluralist Theory of the State: Selected Writings of G. D. H. Cole, J. N. Figgis, and H. J. Laski* (New York: 1989). See also Elisabeth S. Clemens: *The People's Lobby: Organizational Innovation and the Rise of Interest Group Politics in the United States, 1890–1925* (Chicago: 1997); R. Jeffrey Lustig, *Corporate Liberalism: The Origins of Modern American Political Theory, 1890–1920* (Berkeley, CA: 1982), 109–49; John Buenker, "The New Politics," in *1915: The Cultural Moment,* 15; Daniel R. Ernst, "Common Laborers? Industrial Pluralists, Legal Realists, and the Law of Industrial Disputes, 1915–1943," *Law and History Review* 11 (1993): 59; Ellis W. Hawley, "The Discovery and Study of a 'Corporate Liberalism,'" *Business History Review* 52 (1978): 309; Ellis W. Hawley, "Herbert Hoover, the Commerce Secretariat, and the Vision of an 'Associative State,' 1921–1928," *Journal of American History* 61 (1974): 116–22. On functionalism as an alternative to class analysis, see Pells, *Radical Visions,* 21.

123. Arthur Bentley, *The Process of Government* (Bloomington, IN: 1908), 465–80. See also Earl Latham, *The Group Basis of Politics* (Ithaca, NY: 1952), 12–13.

124. Harold J. Laski, "The Sovereignty of the State," in *Studies in the Problem of Sovereignty* (New Haven: 1917), 1, 5. See also John Dewey, *The Public and Its Problems* (New York: 1927); Mary P. Follett, *The New State: Group Organization the Solution of Popular Government* (New York: 1918); Laski, *Problem of Sovereignty.* For a recent analysis of theories of political pluralism, see Avigail I. Eisenberg, *Reconstructing Political Pluralism* (Albany, NY: 1995).

125. Elliott, *Pragmatic Revolt,* 142.

126. FSC, "Judicial Resolution," 1026.

127. FSC, "What City College will Contribute to the Development of the Law," 8.

128. Eisenberg, *Reconstructing Political Pluralism,* 63.

129. Mark M. Hager, "Bodies Politic: The Progressive History of Organizational 'Real Entity' Theory," *University of Pittsburgh Law Review* 50 (1989): 579–80.

130. The classic critique of the distinction between public and private power remains Hale's "Coercion and Distribution."

131. FSC, "Politics and Economics," in *Socialist Planning and a Socialist Program: A Symposium* ed. Harry W. Laidler (New York: 1932), 69, 70–71, 75.

132. Gregor McLennan, *Pluralism* (Buckingham, UK: 1995), 33. Compare Louis L. Jaffe, "Law Making by Private Groups," *Harvard Law Review* 51 (1937): 201.

133. FSC, "Address before the Columbia Law School Liberal Club" (1939), JPLP. See also FSC, "Government and the Social Contract," 362.

134. In the mid-1930s, together with a few friends, FSC composed a *Proposed Constitution for the Socialist Commonwealth of America* (JPLP). It promoted decentralized control of the means of

production by democratically governed groups coordinated through governmental planning. It also protected individual rights.

135. See, for example, Kallen, "Democracy versus the Melting Pot."

136. Nathan Irvin Huggins, *Harlem Renaissance* (New York: 1971), 50. See also Buenker, "New Politics," 23, which notes that Socialists "shared the anti-black biases of white America generally, even though their animus took the form of neglect and ignorance more often than it did overt hostility."

137. Morris R. Cohen, *Reason and Nature: An Essay on the Meaning of Scientific Method* (New York: 1931).

138. Morris Cohen to Justice Holmes, February 28, 1931, in Cohen Rosenfield, *Portrait of a Philosopher,* 357.

139. FSC to Gerald Katcher, February 11, 1948, FSCP 87/1381.

140. Haas, ed. *Felix S. Cohen,* 22.

141. Felix Frankfurter to Mary Cohen, December 21, 1930, in Cohen Rosenfield, *Portrait of a Philosopher,* 256; Interviews, JPLP.

142. Interviews, JPLP.

143. FSCP 49/736.

144. Interviews, JPLP.

145. Interviews, JPLP.

146. FSC to Morris Cohen, July 25, 1937, MRCP.

147. FSCP 49/736.

148. Interviews, JPLP.

Chapter 3. A Time Ripe for Change

1. FSC to Morris Cohen, n.d., MRCP.

2. Interviews, JPLP. On anti-Semitism in the corporate bar, see Lawrence E. Mitchell, "Gentleman's Agreement: The Antisemitic Origins of Restrictions on Stockholder Litigation," Social Science Research Network.

3. Margold and Cohen worked together in preparation of a brief in the CCNY student rights fight. FSC to Norman Thomas, November 8, 1933, JPLP.

4. Interviews, JPLP.

5. Wenger, *New York Jews and the Great Depression,* 24; Jerold S. Auerbach and Eugene Bardach, "Born to an Era of Insecurity: Career Patterns of Law Review Editors, 1918–1941," *American Journal of Legal History* 17 (1973): 6–7.

6. Cohen continued to handle miscellaneous legal issues through 1938 and had an office at Seligsberg and Lewis in New York. FSCP 92/1473; FSC to William E. Friedman, FSCP 84/1314.

7. John Collier, FSC testimonial dinner, January 17, 1948, FSCP 92/1470.

8. Theodore Haas, FSC memorial service, December 4, 1953, FSCP 93/1466.

9. FSC to Joseph Lash, October 26, 1933, JPLP. See also Elmer R. Rusco, *A Fateful Time: The Background and Legislative History of the Indian Reorganization Act* (Reno, NV: 2000), 183.

10. JCP 6 (correspondence between Margold, Collier, Ickes and Frankfurter); JCP 15 (Margold's resume); *New York Times,* March 24, 1933, PHN; T. H. Watkins, *Righteous Pilgrim: The Life and Times of Harold L. Ickes, 1874–1952* (New York: 1990), 328–39. On Margold's role in framing the NAACP's legal drive for equality that led to *Brown v. Board of Education* (1954), see Richard Kluger, *Simple Justice: The History of Brown v. Board of Education and Black America's Struggle for Equality* (New York: 1975), 133–39; Mark Tushnet, *The NAACP's Legal Strategy against Segregated Education, 1925–1950* (Chapel Hill, NC: 1987), 15–29.

11. Collier's view was shaped by the "deep physical and spiritual depression" which he experienced at the age of sixteen, after his mother died from addiction to a relaxant drug and his father committed suicide. Donald Craig Mitchell, *Sold American: The Story of Alaska Natives and their Land, 1867–1959* (Hanover, NH: 1997), 255; Kenneth R. Philp, *John Collier's Crusade for Indian Reform, 1920–1954* (Tucson: 1977), 4–5. See also Lawrence C. Kelly, *The Assault on Assimilation: John Collier and the Origins of Indian Policy Reform* (Albuquerque: 1983), 3–17.

12. Donald L. Parman, *The Navajos and the New Deal* (New Haven: 1976), 15; Philp, *Collier's Crusade*, 2, 12–25, 117; Watkins, *Righteous Pilgrim*, 544; Everett Helmut Akam, "Pluralism and the Search for Community: The Social Thought of American Cultural Pluralism," Ph.D. diss., University of Rochester, 1990; Kenneth R. Philp, "John Collier and the American Indian, 1920–1945," in *Essays on Radicalism in Contemporary America*, ed. Leon Borden Blair (Austin, TX: 1972), 65–67.

13. Mitchell, *Sold American*, 254.

14. Ibid., 254–55; Kelly, *Assault on Assimilation*, 268; Philp, *Collier's Crusade*, 115.

15. Wilcomb E. Washburn, *Red Man's Land/White Man's Law: A Study of the Past and Present Status of the American Indian* (New York: 1971), 78.

16. FSC to Joseph Lash, October 26, 1933, JPLP.

17. 31 U.S. 515, 559 (1832).

18. Rusco, *Fateful Time*, 1; Graham D. Taylor, *The New Deal and American Indian Tribalism: The Administration of the Indian Reorganization Act, 1934–45* (Lincoln, NE: 1980), 1–3; Washburn, *Red Man's Land*, 65–69; Robert N. Clinton, "Redressing the Legacy of Conquest: A Vision Quest for a Decolonized Federal Indian Law," *Arkansas Law Review* 46 (1993): 77; L. Scott Gould, "The Consent Paradigm: Tribal Sovereignty at the Millennium," *Columbia Law Review* 96 (1996): 809; Tadd M. Johnson and James Hamilton, "Self-Governance for Indian Tribes: From Paternalism to Empowerment," *Connecticut Law Review* 27 (1995): 1251; Robert A. Williams, " 'The People of the States Where They Are Found Are Often Their Deadliest Enemies': The Indian Side of the Story of Indian Rights and Federalism," *Arizona Law Review* 38 (1996): 981.

19. 21 U.S. 543 (1823).

20. 30 U.S. 1 (1831).

21. Ramona Ellen Skinner, *Alaska Native Policy in the Twentieth Century* (New York: 1997), 4–5.

22. Ibid. On the trail of tears, see Joan Gilbert, *The Trail of Tears across Missouri* (Columbia, MO: 1996); Gloria Jahoda, *The Trail of Tears* (New York: 1995); Elliott West, *Trail of Tears: National Historic Trail* (Tucson: 2000); Jeanne Williams, *Trail of Tears: American Indians Driven from Their Lands* (Dallas: 1992).

23. Kelly, *Assault on Assimilation*, 145–47. See also Skinner, *Alaska Native Policy*, 5.

24. Ch. 119, 24 Stat. 388 (1887); Skinner, *Alaska Native Policy*, 5; Taylor, *American Indian Tribalism*, 1–5; Watkins, *Righteous Pilgrim*, 531–32; Kenneth H. Bobroff, "Retelling Allotment: Indian Property Rights and the Myth of Common Ownership," *Vanderbilt Law Review* 54 (2001): 1565; Johnson and Hamilton, "Self-Governance for Indian Tribes," 1257; E. Richard Hart, foreword, *Indian Self-Rule: First-Hand Accounts of Indian-White Relations from Roosevelt to Reagan*, ed. Kenneth R. Philp (Logan, UT: 1995), 6–8; Yuanchung Lee, "Rediscovering the Constitutional Lineage of Federal Indian Law," *New Mexico Law Review* 27 (1997): 277–85.

25. On the classical vision of private property, see Horwitz, *Transformation of American Law, 1870–1960*, 145–67. See also Joseph William Singer, "Sovereignty and Property," *Northwestern University Law Review* 86 (1991): 1, which demonstrates how, despite the rhetoric of private property, Indian property was not protected.

26. Bobroff, "Retelling Allotment," 1572. As examples of tribes with individual systems of property ownership, Bobroff counts the Yakima, who were primarily hunters and fishers, the Salish and Kootenai Indians on the Flathead reservation, the Oneida Indians of Wisconsin, the Santee Dakota Indians, "on the Santee Sioux Reservation in Nebraska, the Lake Traverse Reservation, on the border between North and South Dakota, and the Devil's Lake Reservation in North Dakota," and the Indians of the Yankton Sioux reservation. Ibid., 1594–96.

27. Ibid., 1612–16.

28. Ibid., 1610; Curtis Berkey and Lynn Kickingbird, *The Indian Reorganization Act of 1934* (Washington, D.C.: 1977), 2–3; Vine Deloria Jr. and Clifford M. Lytle, *The Nations Within: The Past and Future of American Indian Sovereignty* (Austin, TX: 1998), 188.

29. FSC, Margold's Address (draft), ca. 1934, FSCP 10/137.

30. Watkins, *Righteous Pilgrim*, 532.

31. Many Indians were forced to sell their lands once the trust period expired due to their inability to pay taxes, or because the land was parceled out to many units, which prevented effective use or lease by individuals. Between 1915 and 1920 about twenty thousand patents were issued to

Indians "of less than one-half Indian blood" in the Great Lakes and the Dakotas against the recipients' protests due to their inability to pay property taxes. These actions set the scene for later conflicts between landless mixed-blood Indians who lost their lands and full-blood Indians who kept their allotments. Taylor, *American Indian Tribalism,* 5; Washburn, *Red Man's Land,* 75. See also Berkey and Kickingbird, *The Indian Reorganization Act of 1934,* 3–4; Watkins, *Righteous Pilgrim,* 533; Bobroff, "Retelling Allotment," 1610–11.

32. Berkey and Kickingbird, *The Indian Reorganization Act of 1934,* 4–5; Rusco, *Fateful Time,* 56–57; Washburn, *Red Man's Land,* 75–76. No clearly stated policy toward Indian governments existed. Furthermore, because tribal governments did not disappear, the BIA was at times "forced" to acknowledge their existence and deal with them, rather than with individual Indians. Rusco, *Fateful Time,* 1–34.

33. Skinner, *Alaska Native Policy,* 13–14; Alan Trachtenberg, *The Incorporation of America: Culture and Society in the Gilded Age* (New York: 1982), 29.

34. Brian W. Dippie, *The Vanishing American: White Attitudes and U.S. Indian Policy* (Lawrence, KS: 1982), 209; Kelly, *Assault on Assimilation,* 148.

35. Kelly, *Assault on Assimilation,* 148.

36. Taylor, *American Indian Tribalism,* 4.

37. Ch. 2523, 34 Stat. 1221 (1907).

38. Indian Commissioner Sells, A Declaration of Policy, Extract from the Annual Report of the Commissioner of Indian Affairs, October 15, 1917, in *Documents of U.S. Indian Policy,* ed. Francis Paul Prucha, 3d ed. (Lincoln, NE: 2000), 213–15. See also Kelly, *Assault on Assimilation,* 150.

39. Ch. 95, 41 Stat. 350 (1919).

40. Ch. 115, 42 Stat. 208 (1921); Johnson and Hamilton, "Self-Governance for Indian Tribes," 1258.

41. Ch. 233, 43 Stat. 253 (1924).

42. See generally *Walter Benn Michaels, Our America: Nativism, Modernism, and Pluralism* (Durham, NC: 1995), 30–31. On federal Indian policy during the first decades of the twentieth century, particularly the 1920s, see Larry A. DiMatteo and Michael J. Meagher, "Broken Promises: The Failure of the 1920's Native American Irrigation and Assimilation Policies," *University of Hawaii Law Review* 19 (1997): 1.

43. Dippie, *The Vanishing American,* 228–34.

44. Gorelick, *CCNY and the Jewish Poor,* 139.

45. Trachtenberg, *Incorporation of America,* 34–35.

46. Pells, *Radical Visions,* 23–33.

47. Gorelick, *CCNY and the Jewish Poor,* 142.

48. Dumenil, *The Modern Temper,* 167–68. See also George W. Stocking Jr., *The Ethnographer's Magic and Other Essays in the History of Anthropology* (Madison, WI: 1992), 98–102.

49. On Alain Locke, see Johnny Washington, *Alain Locke and Philosophy: A Quest for Cultural Pluralism* (New York: 1986). On the Harlem Renaissance, see Houston A. Baker Jr., *Modernism and the Harlem Renaissance* (Chicago: 1987); Mark Irving Helbling, *The Harlem Renaissance: The One and the Many* (Westport, CT: 1999); Cary D. Wintz, ed., *Remembering the Harlem Renaissance* (New York: 1996).

50. Donald Young, *American Minority Peoples: A Study in Racial and Cultural Conflicts in the United States* (New York: 1932), 460, cited in Dippie, *The Vanishing American,* 305.

51. Trachtenberg, *Incorporation of America,* 37. On nativism, see Higham, *Strangers in the Land,* 264–99.

52. See generally Winifred L. Frazer, *Mabel Dodge Luhan* (Boston: 1984); Lois Palken Rudnick, *Mabel Dodge Luhan: New Woman, New Worlds* (Albuquerque: 1984); Lois Palken Rudnick, ed., *Intimate Memories: The Autobiography of Mabel Dodge Luhan* (Albuquerque: 1999).

53. Kelly, *Assault on Assimilation,* 118–20.

54. Philp, *Collier's Crusade,* 2–3.

55. Randolph C. Downes, "A Crusade for Indian Reform, 1922–1934," *Mississippi Valley Historical Review* 32 (1945): 331, 334. The Pueblo Lands Bill, which was introduced by Senator Holm O. Bursum of New Mexico on July 20, 1922, allowed Anglo and Spanish settlers to gain title to

Pueblo land, if they could prove continuous possession, "with color of title, before or after 1848," and "since June 29, 1900, without color of title." Philp, *Collier's Crusade,* 26–45.

56. Philp, *Collier's Crusade,* 53.

57. Berkey and Kickingbird, *The Indian Reorganization Act of 1934,* 8; Rusco, *Fateful Time,* 62–93; Downes, "Crusade for Indian Reform," 340.

58. Lewis Meriam et al., ed., *The Problem of Indian Administration* (Baltimore: 1928); Prucha, ed., *Documents of U.S. Indian Policy,* 219–22; Johnson and Hamilton, "Self-Governance for Indian Tribes," 1258.

59. Philp, *Collier's Crusade,* 90; Washburn, *Red Man's Land,* 77; Frederick J. Stefon, "Significance of the Meriam Report of 1928," *The Indian Historian* 11 (1978): 2–7. Three years later, the National Advisory Committee on Education similarly noted that the government's educational policy had "in large degree pauperized the Indian and left him almost helpless in the face of a strange economic civilization as he was before." Downes, "Crusade for Indian Reform," 333.

60. Philp, *Collier's Crusade,* 97.

61. Ibid., 71–91; Watkins, *Righteous Pilgrim,* 534–35; Kenneth R. Philp, "Introduction: The IRA Fifty Years Later," in *Indian Self-Rule,* 15, 16–17.

62. Rusco, *Fateful Time,* 105–6. See also Deloria and Lytle, *The Nations Within,* 56–58.

63. See generally Rusco, *Fateful Time,* 137–76.

64. Ibid., 114–76.

65. Watkins, *Righteous Pilgrim,* 535.

66. Rusco, *Fateful Time,* 183.

67. The Department of Indian Emergency Conservation Work was mostly active in Arizona, Oklahoma, Montana, New Mexico, South Dakota, and Washington. It built roads in reservation forests, and constructed storage dams, fences, and wells. Indians working for the department (approximately 85,000 between 1933 and 1942) received thirty dollars a month and were taught land management and how to operate mechanized equipment. Philp, *Collier's Crusade,* 121–22.

68. Allocations from the Agricultural Adjustment Administration founded herds on a number of reservations and prevented overgrazing by purchasing surplus animals on others. On the Navajo reservation the purchase of surplus animals led to a bitter controversy, which was among the reasons for the Navajos refusal to come under the IRA. Ibid., 122–23.

69. Funds from the Federal Emergency Relief Administration paid Indians to examine and assess economic and social conditions on their reservations. Ibid., 123.

70. The Civil Works Administration employed Indians to repair government and tribal buildings, construct roads and wells, do clerical work, and make clothes. The administration also "hired fifteen Indian artists to paint murals on government buildings and twenty-five craftsmen to manufacture rugs, pottery, and jewelry, which Collier placed in Indian Service facilities." Ibid., 123–24.

71. The Public Works Administration, which was established under the National Industrial Recovery Act (NIRA), built day schools, hospitals, roads, irrigation projects, and sewer systems on reservations. It also constructed several museums for demonstrating and marketing Indian products. With NIRA funds Interior also established a Subsistence Homestead Division, which supported "five subsistence Indian homesteads [for landless Indians] at Burns, Oregon; Great Falls, Montana; Chilocco, Oklahoma; Rosebud, South Dakota; and at the Sacramento Agency in northern California." Ibid., 124–25.

72. The Works Progress Administration employed over 10,700 Indians annually, usually to index and file BIA documents. Ibid., 125.

73. Young Indians who participated in the National Youth Administration received six dollars a month for "clothing, supplies, and lunches at day schools." In New York, Onondaga Indians were trained "to act as counselors for city children during summer vacation." Ibid.

74. Watkins, *Righteous Pilgrim,* 535–37.

75. Philp, *Collier's Crusade,* 122, 133. See also Deloria and Lytle, *The Nations Within,* 63.

76. This advisory group included: "Robert Marshall, director of Indian forestry; Ward Shepard, principal planning specialist; H.L. Shapiro, assistant curator at the Museum of Natural History; J. G. Townsend, chief of the development of industrial hygiene at the Public Health Service; Ralph Linton, professor of anthropology at Columbia University; Edward Kinnard, specialist on Indian

languages; and Jay Nash, emergency unemployment." Philp, *Collier's Crusade*, 119–20. See also Oliver La Farge, ed., *The Changing Indian* (Norman, OK: 1942), vii–x.

77. Notes for the Preparation of Material in the Rough for Mr. Margold, September 24, 1937, attached to John Collier, Memorandum for Nathan Margold, October 1, 1937, FSCP 10/138. See also Philp, *Collier's Crusade*, 118.

78. John Collier to Superintendents, August 12, 1933, approved by Harold Ickes, August 14, 1933, 74792, FSCP 5/58, cited in Rusco, *Fateful Time*, 183.

79. Assistant Chief, Division of Appointments, to FSC, October 19, 1933, FSCP 49/741; Assistant Chief, Division of Appointments, to FSC, November 16, 1933, FSCP 49/740. Little information exists about Melvin Siegel's background and later activities. Apparently, Cohen and Siegel were hired for a year, but Siegel stayed only a few months. He then moved to the Justice Department. Rusco, *Fateful Time*, 177–93. See also Oral History Interview with Isaac N. P. Stokes, July 3, 1973, Truman Presidential Library, www.trumanlibrary.org/oralhist/stokes.htm.

80. [FSC], Memorandum: The Problem of Law and Order on Indian Reservations in Relation to the Wheeler-Howard Bill, ca. 1934, FSCP 1/11. My attribution of this memorandum to Cohen is based on its content and style and on a note from Fred Daiker to Harry Edelstein, August 13, 1937, FSCP 1/11, which identifies Cohen as the author. See also Rusco, *Fateful Time*, 200.

81. FSC to Norman Thomas, November 8, 1933, JPLP. Cohen was aware that real estate interests saw in "unrestricted Indian ownership of individual lands an opportunity to grab good land at low prices or simply to shift local taxes." Yet, he believed that "the officials in the service" shared "an honest idealism" not found "in private business or private law practice to nearly the same extent." Ibid. Thomas's reply was positive, emphasizing (a) the importance of "real service"; (b) the opportunity to train for administrative work, a training that could, in the future, help the Socialist Party; and (c) Cohen's freedom in the Department of the Interior to implement his policies. "You will resign when your freedom in this respect is denied," Thomas concluded. Norman Thomas to FSC, November 14, 1933, JPLP.

82. Lucy Kramer Cohen et al., "Felix Cohen and the Adoption of the IRA," in *Indian Self-Rule*, 70. See also Mitchell, *Sold American*, 257.

83. On the middle-class attraction to nature and the natural, see T. Jackson Lears, *No Place of Grace: Antimodernism and the Transformation of American Culture, 1880–1920* (Chicago: 1984), 144–49.

84. FSC to Norman Thomas, November 8, 1933, JPLP.

85. Interviews, JPLP.

86. L. S. Zacharias, "Repaving the Brandeis Way: The Decline of Developmental Property," *Northwestern University Law Review* 82 (1988): 619–20.

87. Michael J. Sandel, *Democracy's Discontent: America in Search of a Public Philosophy* (Cambridge: 1996), 211–17.

88. Pells, *Radical Visions*, 3.

89. Kallen, "Democracy versus the Melting Pot," 125.

90. Herbert Hovenkamp, "Labor Conspiracies in American Law, 1880–1930," *Texas Law Review* 66 (1988): 960.

91. Ibid., 959–60; James Gray Pope, "The Thirteenth Amendment versus the Commerce Clause: Labor and the Shaping of American Constitutional Law, 1921–1957," *Columbia Law Review* 102 (2002): 1.

92. Pells, *Radical Visions*, 49, 98.

93. Compare Jordan A. Schwarz, *The New Dealers: Power Politics in the Age of Roosevelt* (New York: 1993), xi.

94. Sandel, *Democracy's Discontent*, 252–55. On collectivism in the New Deal, see also Gary Dean Best, *The Retreat from Liberalism: Collectivists versus Progressives in the New Deal Years* (Westport, CT: 2002).

95. FSC, Margold's Address (draft), ca. 1934, FSCP 10/137; FSC, Law and Order (Memorandum), ca. 1934, FSCP 1/11.

96. FSC, Memorandum for the Solicitor, March 4, 1936, FSCP 7/104.

97. Assistant Solicitor, Memorandum for FSC, July 20, 1937, FSCP 8/119.

98. On legal realism and ethnicity, see "Note: Legal Realism and the Race Question: Some Realism about Realism on Race Relations," *Harvard Law Review* 108 (1995): 1607.

Chapter 4. Ideals and Compromises

1. FSC, Memorandum of work, July 16, 1934, FSCP 49/740. On the tribal incorporation movement, see Rusco, *Fateful Time,* 114–36.
2. FSC to Joseph Lash, October 26, 1933, JPLP. See also FSC to Mary Ryshpan Cohen, November, 1933, MRCP.
3. FSC, Memorandum of work, July 16, 1934, FSCP 49/740.
4. FSC to Morris Cohen, 1934, MRCP.
5. Superintendent L. W. Shotwell, Fort Belknap Agency, Montana, December 20, 1933, RG48//Entry 809/Box 3.
6. Circular of November 20, 1933, RG75//4984–1934–066/Part 10–A/Folder 1/1.
7. Ibid. Boas and his students were the main advocates of cultural anthropology. They believed that cultural phenomena were influenced by a wide range of historical influences and, therefore, did not follow any necessary historical sequence in their development. The alternative—evolutionary anthropology—viewed cultural development as subsumed within a deterministic scientific framework. Stocking, *The Ethnographer's Magic,* 119–20.
8. Kenneth M. Chapman, Curator, Laboratory of Anthropology, Santa Fe, New Mexico, January 5, 1934, RG75//4984–1934–066/Part10–A/Folder 1/3.
9. Elsie Clews Parsons, Harrison New York, ca. April 30, 1934, RG75//4984–1934–066/Part 10–A/Folder 2/3; A. L. Kroeber, Department of Anthropology, University of California at Berkeley, December 13, 1933, RG75//4984–1934–066/Part 10–A/Folder 3/3.
10. Cora Du Bois, Department of Anthropology, University of California at Berkeley, December 13, 1933, RG75//4984–1934–066/Part 10–A/Folder 1/3.
11. Fred Eggan, Department of Anthropology, University of Chicago, January 11, 1934, RG75//4984–1934–066/Part 10–A/Folder 3/3.
12. Ralph L. Beals, University of California at Berkeley, to John Collier, December 12, 1933 (reporting on the Southern Maidu), RG75//4984–1934–066/Part 10–A/Folder 1/3.
13. Philp, *Collier's Crusade,* 137.
14. W. C. McKern, Department of Anthropology, Public Museum, Milwaukee, Wisconsin, ca. December 27, 1933 (reporting on the Patwin at Colusa Sacramento Valley, Winnebago, Wisconsin Rapids, and Menomini, Wisconsin), RG75//4984–1934–066/Part 10–A/Folder 2/3.
15. H. Scudder Mekeel, Social Science Research Fellow (Anthropology), Harvard University, December 12, 1933 (commenting on the Teton-Dakota), RG75//4984–1934–066/Part 10–A/Folder 2/3.
16. Ralph Linton, University of Wisconsin, Madison, Wisconsin, ca. December 9, 1933, RG75//4984–1934–066/Part 10–A/Folder 3/3.
17. Among the letters that Cohen found helpful were A. L. Krober's report on the tribes of northwestern California, which recommended a system of a large number of small reservations as a basis for organization; Alfred W. Bowers's review of the Mandans, Hidatsas, and Arikaras; Cora Du Bois's letter, which emphasized that "a small inalienable tracts of land which offer adequate resources" should be the foundation for organizing small local groups as in California; and Martha Beckwith's report, which indicated that if the Indian were to "be made to gain value as an individual [he could] do this only by a sense of pride in his group." "If lands were shared and crops and herds tended as a communal responsibility," Beckwith concluded, "the local legislation might well, with care in the selection of a legislative body, be left in the hands of the Indian themselves, who would be directly responsible to the cabinet official in Washington in charge of Indian affairs." RG75//4984–1934–066/Part 10–A/Folder 1/3.
18. FSC, Memoranda for Mr. Shepard (1) January 2, 1934 and (2) undated, RG75//4984–1934–066/Part 10–A/Folders 1&2 of 3. See also Rusco, *Fateful Time,* 190 (quoting FSC). According to Rusco, because many anthropologists did not submit their responses to the ques-

tionnaire until after the bill was sent to Congress, the impact of these anthropological studies on the bill is unclear. Ibid., 188–90.

19. Fred Eggan, Department of Anthropology, University of Chicago, January 11, 1934, RG75//4984–1934–066/Part 10–A/Folder 3/3.

20. FSC, Memorandum of work, July 16, 1934, FSCP 49/740; RG75//4984–1934–066/Part 10–C.

21. Deloria and Lytle, *The Nations Within,* 63–64; Philp, *Collier's Crusade,* 135; Rusco, *Fateful Time,* 179–88; Taylor, *American Indian Tribalism,* 19–20.

22. Robert Marshall devoted his life's work to the causes of conservation and environmentalism. He served as the Assistant Agriculturist at the Northern Rocky Mountain Experiment Station from 1925 to 1928. From 1929 to 1931 Marshall engaged in exploration, ecological studies, and anthropological research in northern Alaska. Between 1933 and 1937 Marshall served as Director of Forestry in the Office of Indian Affairs. In 1937 Marshall was appointed Chief of Division of Recreation and Lands at the U.S. Forest Service in the Department of Agriculture. He held this position until his death in 1939. See Robert Marshall Papers, The Jacob Rader Marcus Center of the American Jewish Archives, Cincinnati, OH.

23. Ward Shepard was a member of the Forest Service and then the Office of Indian Affairs.

24. Rusco, *Fateful Time,* 194. Cohen was Chairman of the Provisional Committee on Tribal Organization, FSCP 7/100.

25. John Collier, "America's Handling of its Indigenous Indian Minority," speech broadcast over the Blue Network of N.B.C., at 10:30 p.m. EST December 4, 1939, FSCP 11/152.

26. Parman, *Navajos and the New Deal,* 30–31.

27. FSC, Margold's Address (draft), ca. 1934, FSCP 10/137.

28. Ibid.

29. See Recent Developments in Indian Tribal Organization, n.d., FSCP 9/124.

30. Senate Journal, 73rd Congress, 2nd Session, February 6, 1934, 114; U.S. Congress, House, Committee on Indian Affairs, Hearings on H.R. 7902, Readjustment of Indian Affairs, 73rd Congress, 2nd Session, 1934, RG233, 1. The following sections provide a short summary of the drafting processes and the ultimate bill. For a more detailed examination, see Deloria and Lytle, *The Nations Within*; Philp, *Collier's Crusade*; Rusco, *Fateful Time*; Taylor, *American Indian Tribalism.*

31. Philp, *Collier's Crusade,* 140–43; Taylor, *American Indian Tribalism,* 19–21.

32. Commissioner Collier, memorandum for Zimmerman, February 6, 1934, RG75//4894–1934–066/Part 11–C/Folder 1/4.

33. Hearings on H.R. 7902, 1–2; Deloria and Lytle, *The Nations Within,* 67–71.

34. FSC and Melvin Siegel (draft), RG75//4894–1934–066/Part 11–C/Folder 2/4.

35. FSC, Law and Order (Memorandum), ca. 1934, FSCP 1/11.

36. Hearings on H.R. 7902, 2–3.

37. Ibid., 3–5.

38. Deloria and Lytle, *The Nations Within,* 68–69.

39. FSC, Memorandum for Commissioner of Indian Affairs, January 17, 1934, RG75//4984–1934–066/Part 11–C/Folder 1/4; Deloria and Lytle, *The Nations Within,* 70.

40. Hearings on H.R. 7902, 2.

41. FSC and Siegel, Draft, RG75//4894–1934–066/Part 11–C/Folder 2/4.

42. Deloria and Lytle, *The Nations Within,* 71–72.

43. Ibid., 72.

44. Lawrence's comment touched on a dilemma that had plagued not only Collier's efforts on behalf of Indian tribes, but also his 1910s work on behalf of immigrants. Philp, *Collier's Crusade,* 24–25.

45. FSC and Siegel, Draft, RG75//4894–1934–066/Part 11–C/Folder 2/4.

46. FSC, Margold's Address (draft), ca. 1934, FSCP 10/137.

47. Ibid.; FSC, Memorandum for John Collier, December 5, 1938, FSCP 10/138.

48. FSC, Margold's Address (draft), ca. 1934, FSCP 10/137; Rusco, *Fateful Time,* 197–98.

49. FSC and Siegel (draft), RG75//4894–1934–066/Part 11–C/Folder 2/4. See also Rusco, *Fateful Time,* 198.

50. FSC, Margold's Address (draft), ca. 1934, FSCP 10/137. See also FSC, Law and Order (Memorandum), ca. 1934, FSCP 1/11.

51. FSC to Joseph Lash, May 27, 1934, JPLP.

52. Marshall explained that "if the Indians held their tribal land in fee simple, a little poor business on their part, and we have got to expect that at first with many tribes, would often make them lose their land to some person to whom they were in debt. With the government holding the land this danger . . . would be obviated." Robert Marshall, Memorandum on Bills submitted by Messers. Stewart, Shepard, Siegel, and Cohen RG75//4984–1934–066/Part 11-C/Folder 2/4.

53. Shepard's Draft, RG75//4984–1934–066/Part 11-C/Folder 2/4.

54. Hearings on H.R. 7902, 8.

55. Deloria and Lytle, *The Nations Within,* 73–74.

56. Ibid., 74–75.

57. FSC, Law and Order (Memorandum), ca. 1934, FSCP 1/11.

58. Ibid.

59. The community courts' jurisdiction was limited to cases involving fines that did not exceed $500 or terms of imprisonment that did not exceed six months. As Cohen explained, this mimicked the jurisdiction vested at the time in the tribes, the secretary of the interior, or Indian judges responsible to him. Ibid.

60. The court's original jurisdiction, "either exclusive or concurrent with the jurisdiction of State or local Indian courts," would cover:

> (1) Prosecutions for crimes against the United States committed within the territory of a reservation or chartered Indian community; (2) cases to which an Indian tribe or chartered community is a party; (3) cases arising out of commerce between tribal Indians and other persons; (4) cases arising under the laws or ordinances of a chartered community and involving a non-member as a party; (5) cases involving the interpretation of Federal laws, departmental regulations and charter provisions defining the powers and regulating the affairs of an Indian tribe or chartered community (. . . [including] the assigned jurisdiction to render declaratory judgments covering the interpretation of charter powers and other like matters); (6) cases involving any right to allotment of land (this branch of jurisdiction [was to be] greatly diminished by the provisions of [the pending IRA bill] . . . which halt the operation of the allotment system); (7) cases involving heirship, probate and partition of Indian lands or the guardianship and competency of Indians (. . . matters in which the discretionary powers of the Secretary of the Interior [were] severely limited by the provisions of . . . the pending bill).

Ibid.

61. FSC and Siegel (draft), RG75//4894–1934–066/Part 11-C/Folder 2/4.

62. FSC, Law and Order (Memorandum), ca. 1934, FSCP 1/11; Rusco, *Fateful Time,* 197–201.

63. Section 4 of the title terminated "all jurisdiction heretofore exercised by the United States district courts" in cases that would fall under the jurisdiction of the Court of Indian Affairs. Hearings on H.R. 7902, 12; Deloria and Lytle, *The Nations Within,* 76.

64. FSC and Siegel, Draft, RG75//4894–1934–066/Part 11-C/Folder 2/4.

65. Robert Marshall, Memorandum on Bills submitted by Messers. Stewart, Shepard, Siegel, and Cohen, RG75//4984–1934–066/Part 11-C/Folder 2/4.

66. For example Marshall recommended that "some provision should be made to the effect that the liberties guaranteed in the bill of rights of the U.S. Constitution should be operative within the tribal jurisdiction." Ibid.

67. FSC, "Civil Rights of Indians," FSCP 1/13.

68. See constitutions drafted by Cohen and discussion in chapter 5.

69. FSC, Law and Order (Memorandum), ca. 1934, FSCP 1/11.

70. Hearings on H.R. 7902, 12–13. See also Deloria and Lytle, *The Nations Within,* 76–78.

71. See Outline of Bill on Indian Self-Government, ca. 1934, FSCP 9/120.

72. Rusco, *Fateful Time,* 198.

73. FSC, Margold's Address (draft), ca. 1934, FSCP 10/137.

74. Hearings on H.R. 7902, 18.

75. John Collier, February 19, 1934, RG46//Box 33/Folder 8 (submitted to Congress).

76. FSC, The Decline of Dictatorship in the Indian Country, FSCP 66/1056.

77. House Committee on the Judiciary (Hatton W. Summers, Texas, Chair) to Edgar Howard, March 15, 1934, U.S. Congress, House, 73rd Congress, Papers Accompanying Specific Bills and Resolutions, RG233//HR73A–D12/Folder 1/3.

78. Hearings on H.R. 7902, 315.

79. Ibid., 63–65; Philp, *Collier's Crusade,* 143.

80. Deloria and Lytle, *The Nations Within,* 87–89.

81. Hearings on H.R. 7902, 311.

82. Ibid., 89. Collier invited those who worked on the bill to the hearings. They introduced certain elements of the bill and responded to questions. Cohen explained the nature of the Federal Court of Indian Affairs, and answered questions about the tribal corporations' legal liability. Ibid.

83. Ibid.

84. Ibid., 95. Cohen's comment was made in response to questions about the incorporated tribes' liability. Committee members wanted tribal corporations to be liable whenever they breached a commercial contract, even if such liability exceeded the debt limits written into each tribal charter. Unwilling to accept Cohen's analogy between tribes and federal corporations, the liability of which was similarly limited by their assets, the committee members instructed Collier to submit a revised version of this section of the bill. Ibid., 102.

85. John Collier, February 19, 1934, RG46//Box 33/Folder 8 (submitted to Congress).

86. Ibid.

87. Deloria and Lytle, *The Nations Within,* 85–87.

88. Hearings on H.R. 7902, 64.

89. Hearings on S. 2755, RG233, 152.

90. Collier asked Howard for 3000 copies of the printed hearings for "distribution to those Indians [and others] who request them." John Collier to Edgar Howard, February 26, 1934, U.S. Congress, House, 73rd Congress, Papers Accompanying Specific Bills and Resolutions, RG233//HR73A–D12/Folder 1/3.

91. Collier sent another circular to anthropologists on April 3, 1934, asking for their comments. RG75//4984–1934–066/Part 10–B.

92. Central Avenue Christian Reform Church, Michigan, April 30, 1934, U.S. Congress, House, 73rd Congress, Papers accompanying Specific Bills and Resolutions, HR 73A–D12, committee on Indian Affairs, RG233//HR6275–HR7902/Folder 2/3. Compare Parman, *Navajos and the New Deal,* 68–69.

93. Statement of Sam Lapointe, Chairman of the Rosebud Sioux council and Chairman of the Sioux Nation Council after the Congress at Rapid City, Hearings on H.R. 7902, 330–31.

94. Deloria and Lytle, *The Nations Within,* 92.

95. Flora Warren Seymour, Chicago, Illinois, An Open Letter to the President of the United States, April 23, 1934, RG233//Box 75/Folder 2/3. See also Taylor, *American Indian Tribalism,* 24; Michael T. Smith, "The Wheeler-Howard Act of 1934: The Indian New Deal," *Journal of the West* 10 (1971): 527.

96. Hearings on H.R. 7902.

97. Zimmerman to Supt. C. R. Whitlock, Yakima Indian Agency, Toppenish, Washington. March 28, 1934, RG75//4894–1934–066/Part 1–A/Folder 3/8 (the letter was drafted by Cohen).

98. Ibid.

99. Collier's circular called attention to specific issues of tribal organization: law and order, lands administration and creating a firm economic basis, and the possibility of organizing tribes as municipal corporations. Collier suggested that these matters be the subject of discussion and consideration on reservations. The circular also encouraged tribes to discuss specific questions like the appropriate number of elected officials and their titles, the manner of elections, membership rules,

methods of legislation (representative or popular), the possibility of recalling or impeaching officers, the function of government (ordinances, cooperative marketing and purchasing, contribution to community projects, charity), land matters, control of funds, control of employees, and the appropriate jurisdiction of Indian communities. RG75//4894–1934–066/Part 8/Folder 1/2.

100. FSC, Memorandum for Commissioner of Indian Affairs, January 17, 1934, RG75//4984–1934–066/Part 11–C/Folder 1/4.

101. Ibid.

102. Ibid.

103. Collier's circular, January 20, 1934, RG75//4894–1934–066/Part 8/Folder 1/2, emphasis in original.

104. Jasper Long and 36 others, Crow Agency, Montana, March 9, 1934, RG75//4894–1934–066/Part 11–A/Folder 1/1.

105. Philp, *Collier's Crusade,* 139–40.

106. Ibid.

107. The Southern Ute tribal council, Consolidated Ute Agency, Colorado, to John Collier, February 12, 1934, RG75//4894–1934–066/Part 1–A/Folder 8/8.

108. Franz Boas, Department of Anthropology, Columbia University, to John Collier, December 7, 1933, RG75//4984–1934–066/Part 10–A/Folder 1/3; F. H. Roberts, Bureau of American Ethnology, ca. December 17, 1933 (reporting on the Zuni), RG75//4984–1934–066/Part 10–A/Folder 2/3.

109. Generally, anthropologists' letters emphasized tribe members' positive emotions toward their traditional authorities, even when tribal organization had been severely disrupted. Ralph L. Beale, Department of Anthropology, University of California at Berkeley, December 12, 1933 (reporting on the Southern Maidu), RG75//4984–1934–066/Part 10–A/Folder 1/3. Yet anthropologists also reported that younger members tended to seek a different form of government. Harold S. Colton, Museum of Northern Arizona, Northern Arizona Society of Science and Art, December 15, 1933 (reporting on the Hopi), RG75//4984–1934–066/Part 10–A/Folder 1/3. In some places, while the older generation kept to its traditions, the middle-aged and young persons were almost completely acculturated, owning property individually and earning their living as individual farmers. H. E. Driver, Anthropology Department, University of California at Berkeley, April 9, 1934 (reporting on the Geyserville reservation in Sonoma Co. California), RG75//4984–1934–066/Part 10–A/Folder 1/3.

110. W. O. Roberts, Superintendent, Report to Collier from Rosebud Indian Agency, January 31, 1934, RG75//4984–1934–066/Part 1–A/Folder 1/8.

111. Taylor, *American Indian Tribalism,* 25.

112. Deloria and Lytle, *The Nations Within,* 102, citing Theodore Haas.

113. Indian Congresses were held at Rapid City, South Dakota, March 2–5, 1934 (for the Plains Indians); Salem, Oregon, March 8–9, 1934 (for the Indians of the Northwest, including Indians from Idaho, Washington, Oregon and Northern California); Santo-Domingo, New Mexico, March 11, 1934 (the All Pueblo Council); Fort Defiance, Arizona, March 12–13, 1934 (Navajo Council); Phoenix, Arizona, March 15–16, 1934 (for Indians from Southern Arizona); Riverside, California, March 17–18, 1934 (for Mission and Yuma Indians); Anadarko, Oklahoma, March 20, 1934; Muskogee, Oklahoma, March 22–23, 1934; Miami, Oklahoma, March 24, 1934; and Hayward, Wisconsin, April 23–24, 1934 (for the Great Lakes Indians). See Hearings on H.R. 7902.

114. RG75//4894–1934–066/Part 1–B/Folder 2/8.

115. Albert Folsom (Oklahoma City, Oklahoma) to Edgar Howard, March 17, 1934, U.S. Congress, House, 73rd Congress, Papers Accompanying Specific Bills and Resolutions, RG233//HR73A–D12/Folder 3/3.

116. Deloria and Lytle, *The Nations Within,* 106.

117. Cited ibid.

118. See generally RG75//Entry 1011; Deloria and Lytle, *The Nations Within,* 101–21.

119. Deloria and Lytle, *The Nations Within,* 117, 111.

120. FSC to Morris and Mary Cohen, March 10, 1934, MRCP.

121. Deloria and Lytle, *The Nations Within,* 111.

122. Hearings on H.R. 7902, 194–95. See also Rusco, *Fateful Time,* 220–49.

123. Hearings on H.R. 7902, 310–11.

124. Franklin D. Roosevelt to Burton Wheeler, April 28, 1934, in Report No. 1080 to accompany S. 3645.

125. See Senate Journal, 73rd Congress, 2nd Session, May 10, 1934, 428, 435; June 6, 1934, 554, 577, 594, 598, 607, 612, 636; June 15, 1934, 812, 833, 861, See also House Journal, 73rd Congress, 2nd Session, June 13, 1934, 748; June 15, 1934, 783, 787.

126. Representative Edgar Howard, Speech, June 15, 1934, in U.S. Congress, Committee on Interior and Insular Affairs: Indian Affairs Investigating Committee, Sen. 83A–F9 (1928–1953), RG46//Box 33/Folder 13.

127. Notes for the Preparation of Material in the Rough for Mr. Margold, September 24, 1937, FSCP 10/138.

128. Taylor, *American Indian Tribalism,* 27–28.

129. Ibid.; Philp, *Collier's Crusade,* 158–59; Prucha, ed., *Documents of U.S. Indian Policy,* 229–30; John Collier, "The Genesis and Philosophy of the Indian Reorganization Act," in *The Western American Indian: Case Studies in Tribal History,* ed. Richard N. Ellis (Lincoln, NE: 1972), 151.

130. John Collier, Facts about the New IRA (90027): An Explanation and Interpretation of the Wheeler-Howard Bill as Modified, Amended and Passed by Congress, RG75// 4894–1934–066/Part 11–C/Section 2/Folder 2/2. While the initial departmental draft subjected these powers to the secretary's discretion, New Dealers like Cohen believed that these powers would ultimately be transferred to the Indians. Members of Congress rejected wholeheartedly the idea of decentralizing power, even gradually, and creating self-governing Indian communities. Deloria and Lytle, *The Nations Within,* 143.

131. Taylor, *American Indian Tribalism,* 29.

132. FSC, Memorandum for Acting Solicitor, August 5, 1936, FSCP 3/36.

133. Notes for the Preparation of Material in the Rough for Mr. Margold, September 24, 1937, FSCP 10/138.

134. Taylor, *American Indian Tribalism,* 28, citing John Collier, *The Indians of the Americas* (1947), 265. See also Notes for the Preparation of Material in the Rough for Mr. Margold, September 24, 1937, FSCP 10/138.

135. Taylor, *American Indian Tribalism,* 28.

136. Ibid., 27–31, citing John Collier, *From Every Zenith: A Memoir* (1962), 224; Philp, *Collier's Crusade,* 158–60. For a critical evaluation of Collier's role in forcing Indian tribes to come under the IRA, see Rebecca L. Robbins, "Self-Determination and Subordination: The Past, Present, and Future of American Indian Governance," in *The State of Native America: Genocide, Colonization, and Resistance,* ed. M. Annette Jaimes (Boston: 1992), 95–98.

Chapter 5. In Flux

1. Deloria and Lytle, *The Nations Within,* 172.

2. Ibid.; Lawrence E. Kelly, "The Indian Reorganization Act: The Dream and Reality," *Pacific Political Review* 44 (1975): 301; Taylor, *American Indian Tribalism,* 32–33, 94. But see Russel Lawrence Barsh, "Another Look at Reorganization: When Will Tribes Have a Choice?" *Indian Truth,* October 1982, 4.

3. John Collier, Facts about the New IRA (90027): An Explanation and Interpretation of the Wheeler-Howard Bill as Modified, Amended and Passed by Congress, RG75//4894– 1934–066/Part 11–C/Section 2/Folder 2/2. See also Thomas Biolsi, *Organizing the Lakota: The Political Economy of the New Deal on the Pine Ridge and Rosebud Reservations* (Tucson: 1992), 79, which reports that "some Lakota people believed that liberal credit funds would be given as a reward for voting favorably for the IRA"; Paul C. Rosier, *Rebirth of the Blackfeet Nation, 1912–1954* (Lincoln: 2001), 96, which notes that the Blackfeet and Flathead nations "embraced the IRA because it gave them access to credit and the statutory power to stage elections to reduce or eliminate federal control of the tribe's financial and natural resources."

4. Solicitor's Opinion, Papago-Wheeler-Howard Act, October 12, 1934, *Opinions of the Solicitor of the Department of the Interior Relating to Indian Affairs, 1917–1974,* vol. 1 (U.S. GPO), 441.

5. See www.airpi.org/research/tdlead.html.

6. M. 27810, Solicitor's Opinion Wheeler-Howard Act—Interpretation, December 13, 1934, *Opinions of the Solicitor,* 485; M. 27810, Synopsis of Solicitor's Opinion, December 13, 1934, FSCP 8/117; Assistant Commissioner Zimmerman, Memorandum for Secretary of the Interior, October 15, 1934, FSCP 6/78; Memorandum of Work of Assistant Solicitor Felix S. Cohen, July 29, 1935, FSCP 49/741. See also "Indian Affairs Abruptly Halted by Two Mysterious Commas: A Grammarian's Funeral Knell Sounds as House Committee Asks Plaintively, Who Put Those Distressing Punctuations in Act?" *Washington Post,* February 15, 1935, PHN.

7. Deloria and Lytle, *The Nations Within,* 171–72. See also M. 27903, Synopsis of Solicitor's Opinion, February 5, 1935, FSCP 8/117; Kelly, "The Indian Reorganization Act," 303, which notes that "of approximately 97,000 Indians who were declared eligible to vote, only 38,000 actually voted in favor of the act. Those who voted against it totaled 24,000, while those who did not vote at all, approximately 35,000, were nearly equal in number to those who voted in favor."

8. American Indian Policy Center, The Formation of Contemporary American Indian Tribal Governments, www.airpi.org/research/tdcontemp.html; Deloria and Lytle, *The Nations Within,* 151.

9. M. 27903, Solicitor's Opinion, February 5, 1935. See also Draft of M. 27810, Solicitor's Opinion, October 20, 1934, FSCP 6/78.

10. Deloria and Lytle, *The Nations Within,* 172.

11. Ibid., 173–74. In the first year, only one quarter of the $12.5 million authorized by the act was provided, and in the following years, the revolving credit fund was cut "to $2.5 million, the annual land purchase fund to $1 million, the funds allocated for tribal organization to $150,000, and educational loans to $175,000." Ibid.

12. Immediate Program for Organization of Indian Tribes, July 31, 1934, FSCP 8/117.

13. Memorandum of Work of Assistant Solicitor Felix S. Cohen, July 29, 1935, FSCP 49/741; John Painter et al., "Implementing the Indian Reorganization Act," in *Indian Self-Rule,* 80–82.

14. Initially, the organization unit recommended the organization of 30 tribes, believing that some will be eliminated in the process of deliberation because of unseen obstacles. Immediate Program for Organization of Indian Tribes, July 31, 1934, FSCP 8/117.

15. Theodore H. Haas, *Ten Years of Tribal Government under the Indian Reorganization Act* (1947), online at thorpe.ou.edu/IRA/IRAbook/index.html. The organization unit was so impressed with the Fort Belknap reservation's cattle industry and local livestock cooperative associations, which they set up on their initiative, that it recommended that the Fort Belknap Indians be allowed to exercise business powers without departmental review within a few years (as compared to the usual ten years set for other groups). Indian Organization Unit, Memorandum for Mr. Zimmerman, April 2, 1936, FSCP 7/102.

16. Immediate Program for Organization of Indian Tribes, July 31, 1934, FSCP 8/117; FSC, Memorandum for Mr. Venning, October 18, 1934, FSCP 7/100; FSC, Memorandum for Mr. Gord and Mrs. Welpley, November 1, 1934, FSCP 8/117; FSC, Memorandum for Mr. Shepard, August 1, 1934 re changes in land policy and the need to study tribal traditions, FSCP 7/95; FSC, Memorandum for Mr. Collier, July 17, 1934, FSCP 6/75, requesting statistical data on each tribe re assimilation and economic and social conditions; Sources (n.d.) FSCP 7/100; Memorandum of Work of Assistant Solicitor Felix S. Cohen, July 29, 1935, FSCP 49/741; Memorandum of Work of Assistant Solicitor F.S. Cohen, July 1, 1935 to June 1, 1936, July 11, 1936, FSCP 49/742; FSC to Ambrose Doskow, October 25, 1935, FSCP 7/104, asking about limited dividend corporations and housing corporations in connection with his work on charters for Indian corporations; FSC to Richard B. Morris, November 5, 1936, FSCP 43/647, sending sample Indian constitutions and a general memo on constitution drafting for Morris's reaction as a political scientist. For model constitution and bylaws, see FSCP 7/100. See also Taylor, *American Indian Tribalism,* 36–38.

17. FSCP 7/101. See also FSC, Memorandum for Mr. Jennings, August 19, 1935, FSCP 8/106; Criticisms of Stockbridge and Munsee Constitution, December 27, 1935, FSCP 7/90; FSC, Memorandum for Mr. Daiker, October 7, 1938, FSCP 5/64, commenting that the election provi-

sions in the Yuma constitution were not "ridiculous," "anachronistic," "unwise" or "unworkable" but rather innovative and commendable, accommodating the specific social structure of the reservation.

18. Basic Memorandum on Drafting of Tribal Constitutions, FSCP 7/101. See also Cohen's criticism of the Wisconsin Oneida Constitution, December 14, 1935, FSCP 7/90, noting that a section was copied without choosing between the two alternatives and adding that "it is a fair inference that the tribal representatives have not embodied any constructive thought on self-government in this constitution and it would be my suggestion that they be encouraged to talk over the constitution at popular meetings for a few weeks and suggest any needed modifications. Even if no modifications are suggested the process of discussion would, I think, be a useful part of adult education in self-government."

19. FSC to Arthur Schiller, Columbia Law School, March 2, 1935, FSCP 43/645.

20. Basic Memorandum on Drafting of Tribal Constitutions, FSCP 7/101.

21. FSC to Maurice K. Townsend, July 7, 1950, FSCP 89/1427.

22. In his analysis of the IRA, Rusco notes that "nothing in the IRA was designed to impose any particular structure of government on an Indian society." Rusco, *Fateful Time*, 296. While the IRA on its face did not adopt one structure, imitation created it. Of course, as Cohen noted in 1950, imitation of legal systems and constitutions was common throughout the world. FSC to Maurice K. Townsend, July 7, 1950, FSCP 89/1427. See also Haas, *Ten Years of Tribal Government*, which noted that the provisions "designed to enable . . . tribes to take advantage of the specific powers and benefits provided for in the Act" were often the same in many constitutions, but that there were "wide variations in the provisions regarding tribal membership, the governmental organization, the safeguards available to individual members, the methods of handling tribal business and the extent of the supervision of the Secretary of the Interior." For a discussion of constitution drafting, see, for example, Biolsi, *Organizing the Lakota*, 86–98. On the need to revise tribal constitutions, see Kenneth R. Philp, *Termination Revisited: American Indians on the Trail to Self-Determination, 1933–1953* (Lincoln, NE: 1999), 7.

23. Memorandum of a Proposed Tribal Organization in conformity with the Provisions of Section 16 of the Wheeler-Howard Act, FSCP 6/76.

24. Painter et al., "Implementing the Indian Reorganization Act," 85.

25. On May 15, 1934, the acting solicitor gave an opinion on the pending IRA, "a move that was virtually without precedent in legislative history." Titled *Indian Corporations—Federal Charters,* the opinion described the draft bill as "in effect, a general incorporation law for a defined class of Federal corporations, to wit, incorporated Indian tribes or communities." Deloria and Lytle, *The Nations Within,* 156. While Congress never endorsed Interior's plans, the idea of federal incorporation of Indian tribes remained alive. On federally chartered corporations, see A. Michael Froomkin, "Reinventing the Government Corporation," *University of Illinois Law Review* (1995): 543; Carrie Stradley Lavargna, "Government-Sponsored Enterprises Are 'Too Big to Fail': Balancing Public and Private Interests." *Hastings Law Journal* 44 (1993): 1004–10.

26. Rules and Regulations adopted pursuant to IRA, FSCP 3/37.

27. Taylor, *American Indian Tribalism,* 30–36. While numbers vary slightly in different reports, the pattern is accurate. See also Philp, *Collier's Crusade,* 163; Indian Organization, Memorandum for Mr. Cohen, October 7, 1936, FSCP 43/647. By September 15, 1938, eighty-eight tribes had constitutions and bylaws (including Oklahoma), and sixty had charters. Memorandum 37037, September 15, 1938, FSCP 8/107.

28. John Collier, Memorandum 120508 for Superintendents, re: Organization of Indian Tribes not under the IRA (Circular 3160), May 5, 1938, FSCP 9/132; Solicitor Margold, Memorandum for John Collier, November 23, 1936, FSCP 9/132; Deloria and Lytle, *The Nations Within,* 174; Taylor, *American Indian Tribalism,* 38.

29. The Alaska Reorganization Act (1936) made all the IRA's provisions applicable to Alaska Indians except those pertaining to tribal lands and reservations. The Oklahoma Indian Welfare Act (1936) made Oklahoma Indians, who could establish business corporations and obtain federal credit under the original IRA, eligible to participate in a program of self-government. The Oklahoma act permitted "groups of ten or more Indians to organize into cooperatives," which could

draw "an appropriation of two million dollars, administered by the Oklahoma Indian Credit Cor-poration. This fund was also to be made available to individual Indians who lived in the state. . . . [T]wenty tribal constitutions and fifteen corporate charters were adopted under the Oklahoma act." But only a small number of Indians came under the act. "None of the Five Civilized Tribes, with the exception of three Creek towns and the Cherokee Keetoowah band, adopted either a constitution or a charter under the law." Deloria and Lytle, *The Nations Within*, 176–77.

30. Taylor, *American Indian Tribalism*, 37–38.

31. Kelly, "The Indian Reorganization Act," 304–5.

32. Taylor, *American Indian Tribalism*, 41–45.

33. Ibid., 51. See also Biolsi, *Organizing the Lakota*, 78; Scudder Mekeel, "An Appraisal of the Indian Reorganization Act," *American Anthropologist* 46 (1944): 210–11.

34. See, for example, Cohen's remarks during the congress for the Indians of the Northwest, FSCP 2/17.

35. Taylor, *American Indian Tribalism*, 51.

36. During the congress for the Indians of the Northwest, Cohen, for example, explained that self-government meant that the Indians would create the laws that would govern their affairs and property, choose their officials, and control their funds, rather than having the BIA determine these matters. FSCP 2/17.

37. Philp, *Collier's Crusade*, 164.

38. Painter et al., "Implementing the Indian Reorganization Act," 84.

39. Taylor, *American Indian Tribalism*, 49–52. See also Biolsi, *Organizing the Lakota*, 80–84.

40. Taylor, *American Indian Tribalism*, 51–53.

41. M. 27810, Solicitor's Opinion Wheeler-Howard Act—Interpretation, December 13, 1934, *Opinions of the Solicitor*, 487; Deloria and Lytle, *The Nations Within*, 164. See also Carole Goldberg, "Members Only? Designing Citizenship Requirements for Indian Nations," *Kansas Law Review* 50 (2002): 446–47.

42. Deloria and Lytle, *The Nations Within*, 164–65. Margold's opinion contained one impor-tant interpretation of the act, of which many Indians were unaware. Margold ruled that section 16 of the act allowed small groups, separate tribes, or bands to organize "without the consent of a majority of the adult Indians living on a reservation if they occupied a definite geographical area and desired to have an organization to deal specifically with their own property." According to Margold, if a small group so organized, it was entitled to receive a charter. Such interpretation could have provided a way for full-blood Indians to separate and protect their interests from "a reservation-wide tribal government." But this aspect of Margold's ruling was not highly publi-cized, and most Indians believed that the tribal government had to represent the entire reserva-tion. Ibid., 165.

43. Prior to the reservation policy, dissident Indian groups often resolved their disputes by breaking from the tribe and setting off on their own course. After reservations were created, they could rarely do that. Taylor, *American Indian Tribalism*, 45–49. According to Taylor, only thirty-one of the ninety-three tribal governments formed under the act in its first decade rep-resented sufficiently cohesive groups to be deemed communities. For the most part, this was true of bands in California, Nevada, Michigan, and Minnesota "where there was virtually no re-maining reservation land base, even in the form of allotments." In places "where a potential land base still existed on a reservation in the form of either tribal lands or allotted land held in trust," the BIA worked to create a "reservation-wide tribal organization." Once tribal organization was in place, the BIA might be more flexible in allowing smaller community groups to orga-nize. Ibid., 63–69.

44. Deloria and Lytle, *The Nations Within*, 161–64.

45. Kelly, "The Indian Reorganization Act," 305–9.

46. Mekeel, "An Appraisal," 211–14; Taylor, *American Indian Tribalism*, 113.

47. These powers included:

The establishment of civil and criminal codes by the tribe; levying of taxes on tribal members and non-members residing on the reservation; licensing of traders; issuance of permits and setting of fees for hunting, grazing, and fishing; appropriation of tribal funds not under the control of Congress; assignment of tribal lands and resources; regulation of inheritance of property by individual tribal members or descendants of tribal members; chartering of subordinate economic or political organization such as cooperatives; and excluding non-tribesmen from the reservation.

In addition, tribal membership was to be based on the official census rolls, and changes to the regulations with respect to induction of new members into the tribe were to be subject to review. "Boundaries for electoral districts could likewise be altered only with approval by the secretary of the interior. . . . Furthermore, the ratification of the constitution itself and any amendments was subject to review." Taylor, *American Indian Tribalism,* 93–103. See also Lucy Kramer Cohen et al., "Felix Cohen and the Adoption of the IRA," 83; FSCP Box 3, discussing credit regulations that restricted the governing powers of tribes who asked to use the credit funds.

48. Deloria and Lytle, *The Nations Within,* 189. See also H. Scudder Mekeel, Field Representative in charge of Applied Anthropology, December 30, 1935, FSCP 7/104.

49. FSC, Memorandum for the Commissioner of Indian Affairs, March 5, 1935, FSCP 49/741; FSC, Memorandum for the Commissioner of Indian Affairs, April 10, 1935, FSCP 49/741. For the argument that the tribal constitutions under the IRA in fact reduced tribal sovereignty, see Richmond L. Clow, "The Indian Reorganization Act and the Loss of Tribal Sovereignty: Constitutions on the Rosebud and Pine Ridge Reservations," *Great Plains Quarterly* 7 (1987): 125–34.

50. Taylor, *American Indian Tribalism,* 94.

51. Ibid. See also Rosier, *Rebirth of the Blackfeet Nation,* 96–97.

52. Deloria and Lytle, *The Nations Within,* 184–85.

53. FSC, Memorandum for Acting Solicitor, August 5, 1936, FSCP 3/36.

54. Rough Draft, Notes for the Preparation of Material in the Rough for Mr. Margold, September 24, 1937 attached to John Collier, Memorandum for Nathan Margold, October 1, 1937, FSCP 10/138. In addition to solicitor's opinions, Interior also endeavored to introduce new bills to convince Congress to consider further the matters of tribal courts, selection of BIA officials, Indian inheritance, tribal powers, and tribal claims. FSC, Margold's Address (draft), ca. 1934, FSCP 10/137.

55. Ch. 576, § 16, 48 Stat. 984, 987 (1934). Of particular concern to Congress was the title on *Indian Self-Government* in Interior's draft. Section 2 of that title authorized the secretary of the interior to issue charters that would grant to any Indian community any or all of the powers of government fitting its experience, capacities, and desires. Section 4 of the title authorized the secretary to grant to any community chartered under the act any or all of ten enumerated governmental powers. The final act reflected, however, congressional intent to limit tribal jurisdiction to consenting members. Furthermore, Interior's draft contemplated that where an extensive consolidation of Indian land and population existed, tribes would have civil and criminal jurisdiction over members and nonmembers. The final act eliminated all the compulsory provisions, especially Indian communities' ability to make laws on their reservations. Gould, "The Consent Paradigm," 832–33, referring to Bradley B. Furber, "Two Promises, Two Propositions: The Wheeler-Howard Act as a Reconciliation of the Indian Law Civil War," *University of Puget Sound Law Review* 14 (1991): 241–50; Donald Craig Mitchell, "Alaska v. Native Village of Venetie: Statutory Construction or Judicial Usurpation? Why History Counts," *Alaska Law Review* 14 (1997): 394–95n176.

56. Solicitor's Opinion, Powers of Indian Tribes, October 25, 1934, *Opinions of the Solicitor,* 445.

57. Ibid. See also Deloria and Lytle, *The Nations Within,* 175–76.

58. Solicitor's Opinion, Powers of Indian Tribes, October 25, 1934, *Opinions of the Solicitor,* 445–46. See also Deloria and Lytle, *The Nations Within,* 159. Many late twentieth-century scholars have criticized Cohen's endorsement of the fiction of conquest as dispelling "any lingering hopes that congressional intervention in tribes' domestic affairs could be limited by treaties." Russel Lawrence Barsh and James Youngblood Henderson, *The Road: Indian Tribes and Political Liberty* (Berkeley, CA: 1980), 112. See also chapter 7, infra.

59. Solicitor's Opinion, Powers of Indian Tribes, October 25, 1934, *Opinions of the Solicitor,* 445–46.

60. Ibid.

61. FSC, Legal Doctrine, FSCP 1/12; Deloria and Lytle, *The Nations Within,* 158. See also Mitchell, "Alaska v. Native Village of Venetie," 394–95n176.

62. Solicitor's Opinion, Powers of Indian Tribes, October 25, 1934, *Opinions of the Solicitor,* 447; FSC, Legal Doctrine, FSCP 1/12. See also Deloria and Lytle, *The Nations Within,* 160; Rusco, *Fateful Time,* 5; Mitchell, "Alaska v. Native Village of Venetie," 394–95n176.

63. FSC, Memorandum for the Commissioner of Indian Affairs, March 5, 1935, FSCP 49/741; Deloria and Lytle, *The Nations Within,* 160.

64. American Indian Policy Center, Traditional American Indian Leadership, www.airpi.org/research/tdintro.html.

65. See, for example, Outline of Tribal Constitutions and Bylaws 96589, FSCP 8/106; Membership Agreement, FSCP 8/116.

66. FSC, "Transcendental Nonsense and the Functional Approach," in *Legal Conscience,* 33. Originally published in *Columbia Law Review* 35 (1935): 809.

67. Solicitor's Opinion, Powers of Indian Tribes, October 25, 1934, *Opinions of the Solicitor,* 446. See also Deloria and Lytle, *The Nations Within,* 159.

68. *Opinions of the Solicitor,* 531, 536; FSCP 1/2. See also Philp, *Termination Revisited,* 8.

69. Department of the Interior, Memorandum for the Press, January 8, 1935, in FSC, *Law and Order Regulations—Draft and Report,* 1934–1935, FSCP 3/31; FSC to Morris Cohen, July 21, 1935, MRCP. See also Philp, *Termination Revisited,* 8.

70. Philp, *Termination Revisited,* 8.

71. Ibid. See also FSC, *Law and Order Regulations—Draft and Report,* 1934–1935, FSCP 3/31.

72. *Opinions of the Solicitor,* 891, 892, 899. As Cohen summarized in 1941, the penal codes adopted by tribes organized under the act (after deliberation among members of the tribe) typically included 40–50 offenses (as compared with 800–2000 in a typical state code) and did not contain catch-all provisions "found in state penal codes (vagrancy, conspiracy, criminal syndicalism, etc.), under which almost any unpopular individual [could] be convicted of crime." The maximum punishment allowed under these penal codes seldom exceeded imprisonment for six months, even when state codes imposed imprisonment for twenty years or more (or death) for similar offenses. Indian courts were given large discretion to adjust the penalty "to the circumstances of the offense and the offender." And the form of punishment was, "typically, forced labor for the benefit of the tribe or of the victim of the offense." FSC, "Indian Rights and the Federal Courts," *Minnesota Law Review* 24 (1940): 155–56.

73. Deloria and Lytle, *The Nations Within,* 166–68; Philp, *Termination Revisited,* 8–9.

74. "Transcendental Nonsense" is one of the most cited articles in recent decades, ranking 72nd in Fred Shapiro's list of most-cited law review articles. This is rather an achievement, given that only four other articles on the list preceded 1940 (Holmes's "The Path of the Law" (1897) [no. 5], Samuel D. Warren and Louis D. Brandeis, "The Right to Privacy" (1890) [no. 9], Lon L. Fuller and William R. Perdue Jr., "The Reliance Interest in Contract Damages" (1936–37) [no. 43], and James B. Thayer, "The Origin and Scope of the American Doctrine of Constitutional Law" (1893) [no. 83]). Other articles by legal realists (Llewellyn, Pound Hohfeld) did not qualify for the all-time listing but would have qualified had the data included pre-1956 citations. Fred R. Shapiro, "The Most-Cited Law Review Articles Revisited," *Chicago-Kent Law Review* 71 (1996): 751. See also Fred R. Shapiro, "The Most-Cited Law Review Articles," *California Law Review* 73 (1985): 1540.

75. Allen R. Kamp, "Between-the-Wars Social Thought: Karl Llewellyn, Legal Realism, and The Uniform Commercial Code in Context," *Albany Law Review* 59 (1995): 327–28.

76. Ibid., 345–47.

77. Cited ibid., 350.

78. FSC, "Transcendental Nonsense," 33.

79. Ibid., 34–37. See also "Introduction" to the *Handbook of Federal Indian Law* with reference table and index (Washington, D.C.: 1942), xi, which noted that there were "more than 200 differ-

ent Indian languages, some of them as distinct from each other as English and Chinese. . . . Linguistic diversity was paralleled by diversities in the conditions and legal problems of more than 200 different Indian reservations."

80. Robert W. Gordon, "American Law Through English Eyes: A Century of Nightmares and Noble Dreams" (book review), *Georgetown Law Journal* 84 (1996): 2224–25.

81. FSC, "Socialism and the Myth of Legality," *American Socialist Quarterly* 4 (1935): 8.

82. FSC, "Transcendental Nonsense," 37, 40–42, 46. Apparently, Cohen urged piracy in trade names to "make it easier for servant and mistress to wear clothes that looked the same." Cohen labeled his approach "a democracy of the cloth." Interviews, JPLP.

83. See discussion in chapter 2, *supra*.

84. Gordon, "American Law Through English Eyes," 2224. Compare FSC, "The Problems of a Functional Jurisprudence," in *Legal Conscience*, 78, originally published in *Modern Law Review* 1 (1937): 5; Thomas O. Sargentich, "The Contemporary Debate about Legislative-Executive Separation of Powers," *Cornell Law Review* 72 (1987): 439.

85. FSC, "Transcendental Nonsense," 46–47. On functionalism, see Kalman, *Legal Realism at Yale*, 17–18; Edward A. Purcell Jr., *The Crisis of Democratic Theory: Scientific Naturalism and the Problem of Value* (Lexington, KY: 1973), 23; Thomas Carlson, "James and the Kantian Tradition," in *Cambridge Companion to William James*, 368–69; Thomas C. Grey, "Holmes and Legal Pragmatism," *Stanford Law Review* 41 (1989): 793–98; Joseph W. Singer, "Legal Realism Now," *California Law Review* 76 (1988): 468–69. On Cohen's interest in the implications of logical positivism and functionalism, see also FSC to Morris Cohen, ca. 1934, MRCP; Martin P. Golding, "Realism and Functionalism in the Legal Thought of Felix S. Cohen," *Cornell Law Review* 66 (1980–81): 1032.

86. FSC, "Transcendental Nonsense," 52, 55.

87. Ibid., 55–59.

88. FSC, "A Factual Study of Rule 113," *Columbia Law Review* 32 (1932): 830–33. According to Shientag, he planned the study several years earlier but his appointment to the Supreme Court of New York made it impossible to carry on the investigation personally. When Cohen came to his chambers, he engaged the study under Shientag's "supervision and direction." Bernard Shientag, "Foreword to Summary Judgments in the Supreme Court of New York," *Columbia Law Review* 32 (1932): 829.

89. Purcell, *The Crisis of Democratic Theory*, 24–46. See also Robert C. Bannister, *Sociology and Scientism: The American Quest for Objectivity 1880–1940* (Chapel Hill, NC: 1987); Ross, *Origins of American Social Science*, 428–29.

90. Compare Robert W. Gordon, "Critical Legal Histories," *Stanford Law Review* 36 (1984): 61–71.

91. FSC, "Problems of Functional Jurisprudence," 79–80.

92. See, for example, FSC, "Lecture: Realistic Jurisprudence and the Nature of Law," FSCP 58/915, criticizing the American Law Institute and the Restatement project for attempting to harmonize a mass of conflicting decisions in numerous sovereign states.

93. FSC, "Anthropology and the Problems of Indian Administration," in *Legal Conscience*, 213–21. Originally published in *Southwestern Social Science Quarterly* 18 (1937): 1.

94. FSC to Franz Boas, May 15, 1936, FSCP 1/7.

95. Correspondence between Leslie Spier, editor of *The American Anthropologist*, and FSC, FSCP 1/7. Spier indicated that applied anthropology was appropriate for "journals of sociology, political science, or the like, where there was concern with the practical manipulations of social groups in . . . modern community." But he had "never been convinced that the so-called applications have any contribution to make to anthropological science." According to Spier, only new principles of the nature of culture or its growth were of concern to anthropological science. See also FSC, Memorandum for John Collier, April 14, 1936, FSCP 1/7, noting that Scudder Mekeel thought that the article should be published in the *American Journal of Political Science*; FSC to Alexander Goldenweiser, April 15, 1936, FSCP 1/7, explaining that the article was "on the border line of anthropology and politics."

96. Robert Lowie to FSC, May 27, 1936, FSCP 1/7. Collier, too, thought that Cohen's article was "a particularly lucid, concrete and stimulating discussion." He sent out copies to superintend-

ents. John Collier to superintendents, November 3, 1937, FSCP 1/9. See also correspondence in FSCP 1/9. M.E. Opler thought it was an "admirable paper." M.E. Opler to FSC, March 27, 1937, FSCP 1/7. Alexander Goldenweiser was supportive, too. Alexander Goldenweiser to FSC, March 2, 1936, FSCP 1/7.

97. Robert Lowie to FSC, May 27, 1936, FSCP 1/7.

98. FSC, "Socialism and the Myth of Legality," 24–28.

99. FSC, "Transcendental Nonsense," 60–61; FSC, "Socialism and the Myth of Legality," 16. The social and economic changes that helped to make the foundations of classical legal thought obsolete also supported a growing trend towards deference to the legislator. Faced with conflicting social interests and a court unsympathetic to social-welfare legislation, many Progressives put their faith in the legislator; the post-bellum constitutional ideals of equality were gradually transformed into the procedural recognition "that the only way to preserve pluralism [and democracy] is by accepting the primacy of institutions—primarily the legislature—that can incorporate multiple ideological perspectives." G. Edward White, "Chief Justice Marshall, Justice Holmes, and the Discourse of Constitutional Adjudication," *William and Mary Law Review* 30 (1988): 147.

100. FSC, "Letter to the Editor of the Fordham Law Review," *Fordham Law Review* 5 (1936): 551.

101. FSC, "Transcendental Nonsense," 61, 66.

102. Ibid., 61–69.

103. Joseph C. Hutcheson Jr., "The Judgment Intuitive: The Function of the 'Hunch' in Judicial Decision," *Cornell Law Quarterly* 14 (1929): 274.

104. Frank, *Law and the Modern Mind*.

105. FSC, "Socialism and the Myth of Legality," 14n9.

106. FSC, "Transcendental Nonsense," 70–72.

107. For a critique of "Transcendental Nonsense," see the debate between Cohen and Walter B. Kennedy: Walter B. Kennedy, "Functional Nonsense and the Transcendental Approach," *Fordham Law Review* 5 (1936): 272; FSC, "Letter to the Editor of the Fordham Law Review"; Walter B. Kennedy, "More Functional Nonsense—A Reply to Felix S. Cohen," *Fordham Law Review* 6 (1937): 75.

108. FSC, "Problems of a Functional Jurisprudence," 84.

109. Ibid., 89–90. Cohen saw his functional approach as following in the tradition of Progressive legal thought, specifically sociological jurisprudence. Unlike other realists of his generation, he did not see realistic and sociological jurisprudence as antithetical but rather as stemming from "a common, skeptical, scientific, anti-supernatural, functional outlook" and thus complementary in part and overlapping in part. He cited with approval Cardozo, who wrote that "the spirit of the age, as it is revealed to each of us, is too often only the spirit of the group in which the accidents of birth or education or occupation or fellowship have given us a place," as well as Laski, who, more pointedly (and radically), wrote that "once we realize that the legal relations of society are, broadly speaking, the expressions of class relations, . . . the processes of law begin to clarify themselves in a fundamental way." Ibid., 80–85.

110. FSC, "Review of *The Folklore of Capitalism* by Thurman W. Arnold," in *Legal Conscience*, 446–47. Originally published in *National Lawyers Guild Quarterly* 1 (1938): 161.

111. FSC, "Review of *Bentham's Theory of Fictions* by C. K. Ogden and *The Theory of Legislation* by J. Bentham, ed. by C. K. Ogden," in *Legal Conscience*, 181. Originally published in *Yale Law Journal* 42 (1933): 1149; FSC, "A Factual Study of Rule 113," 834–45.

112. FSC, "Transcendental Nonsense," 74–76.

113. FSC, "The Socialization of Morality," in *Legal Conscience,* 337. Originally published in *American Philosophy Today and Tomorrow*, ed. Horace M. Kallen and Sidney Hook (New York: 1935).

114. Ibid., 339–43.

115. Ibid., 344.

116. Ibid., 340–45.

117. Ibid.

118. Ibid. 346–48.

119. Ibid., 348–49.

120. James, *Pragmatism,* 64.

121. Kennedy, "More Functional Nonsense," 78.
122. Kennedy, "Functional Nonsense," 274.
123. Kennedy, "More Functional Nonsense," 79.
124. Kennedy, "Functional Nonsense," 284.
125. FSC, *Ethical Systems*, 8.
126. Morris Cohen to Roscoe Pound, July 9, 1938, in Cohen Rosenfield, *Portrait of a Philosopher*, 307.
127. Morris R. Cohen, "On Absolutism in Legal Thought," *The University of Pennsylvania Law Review* 84 (1936): 681.
128. Dumenil, *The Modern Temper*, 147.
129. Interviews, JPLP.
130. FSC to Morris Cohen, April 22, 1935, MRCP. See also FSC, "Modern Ethics and the Law," in *Legal Conscience*, 22–23, originally published in *Brooklyn Law Review*. 4 (1934): 33, which criticized Kantians, and Morris among them, for positioning the moral world in the domain of human will which was supposed to be without cause and effect. Informed by the utilitarian tradition, Cohen opposed the assumption that if one willed what was right, one was moral; he saw rightness as dependent upon the effects of a particular conduct on the lives of other people. Cohen complained that by turning logic into a supreme moral guide, Kantians freed ethics from doubt or change. But with such freedom ethics had no recourse to basic questions of social value.
131. FSC to Morris Cohen, July 11, 1937, MRCP.
132. FSC to Morris Cohen, July 25, 1937, MRCP.
133. FSCP 43/652; FSC to Franz Boas, August 1, 1939, FSCP 67/1074.

Chapter 6. First Americans, Misfits, and Refugees

1. FSC, "Government and the Social Contract: Ethical Valuation in the Law" (address before the Eastern Law Students Conference, New York University School of Law, March 7, 1936) in *Legal Conscience*, 352–61.
2. Ibid., 362.
3. Ibid., 363.
4. Ibid.
5. Wheeler, who introduced the IRA but opposed Collier throughout the hearings, introduced one of the bills to repeal it. He proclaimed his concern that the act was designed to "preclude Indians from becoming self-sufficient and operating within the mainstream of white society." The collectivist ideology underlying the IRA went against Wheeler's commitment to the idea of "rugged individualism." He was also concerned about the power reserved for the BIA under the act. Deloria and Lytle, *The Nations Within*, 177–78.
6. FSC, "How Long Will Indian Constitutions Last?" in *Legal Conscience*, 226. Originally published in *Indians at Work* 6 (1939): 40.
7. FSC, Memorandum for Commissioner of Indian Affairs, March 5, 1935, FSCP 49/741.
8. Assistant Solicitor, Memorandum for Organization Division, July 15, 1937, FSCP 8/119.
9. FSC, "How Long Will Indian Constitutions Last?" 227–29. In the original draft, a paragraph stated the following:

Where the demand for local autonomy is found, there is ground to hope that a tribal constitution is a relatively permanent institution. Where this demand is not found, there is reason to believe that the tribal government will not be taken very seriously by the governed, that Indian Service control of municipal functions will be superseded by state control, and that the tribe will disappear as a political organization.

FSCP 1/3. Compare FSC, "Invisible Indian Resources," FSCP 1/5, a short article that Cohen was not able to publish. It criticized the moral overtones of the BIA's attempts to address the tribes' economic life and called on the BIA to recognize the multiple Indian cultural resources that could be used to provide an economic basis for Indian life (that is, the Indian tradition of design, the Indian heritage of wildcraft, and the tradition of adventure). It concluded with the following:

> The Indian is likely to draw from work within the Indian historical tradition something that few Indians have drawn from the occupation of farming, something without which no Indian and few white men will do worthwhile work—that is, a sense of pride and joy in workmanship, nourished by the appreciation of those who enjoy the products of the work. . . . It is up to the Indian . . . to establish himself as a living and valued part of American life, and in the course of this to establish the basis of his future economic security in the invisible resources that remain to him.

10. FSC to Morris Cohen, April 30, MRCP, explaining Ickes's reasons for not appointing him First Acting Solicitor and noting that "according to Margold's account there was no criticism of [Cohen] involved,—all the criticism was directed to the fact that Margold was vulnerable to attack, had made good use of a western non-Jew, Fred Kirgis, to appear at committee hearings, etc., and needed that kind of aid." For Ickes's account of this incident (or at least a similar one), see Harold L. Ickes Papers, MSS Div., LC, Diaries, Reel 4 (with thanks to Dan Ernst for finding it).

11. Richard Breitman and Alan M. Kraut, *American Refugee Policy and European Jewry, 1933–1945* (Bloomington, IN: 1987), 7.

12. Ibid.

13. David S. Wyman, *Paper Walls: America and the Refugee Crisis, 1938–1941* (New York: 1985), 4. See also Roger Daniels and Otis L. Graham, *Debating American Immigration, 1882–Present* (New York: 2001), 24–25.

14. Cited in Saul S. Friedman, *No Haven for the Oppressed: United States Policy toward Jewish Refugees, 1938–1945* (Detroit: 1973), 22.

15. Breitman and Kraut, *American Refugee Policy,* 222–28.

16. Friedman, *No Haven for the Oppressed,* 23–24.

17. Breitman and Kraut, *American Refugee Policy,* 11–27.

18. Ibid., 27; Roger Daniels, *Guarding the Golden Door: American Immigration Policy and Immigrants Since 1882* (New York: 2004), 59–60; Friedman, *No Haven for the Oppressed,* 24–25.

19. Breitman and Kraut, *American Refugee Policy,* 117. See also Friedman, *No Haven for the Oppressed,* 22–25; Claus-M. Naske, "Jewish Immigration and Alaskan Economic Development: A Study in Futility," *Western States Jewish Historical Quarterly* 8 (1976): 139. Friedman explains that "the refugee policy of the Roosevelt administration between 1938 and 1945 . . . was a policy based at first on fear—fear of complicating the domestic employment situation, fear of arousing nativists and neo-Nazis, fear of allowing foreign agents intent on wrecking the industrial capacity of America to filter into the country." Friedman, *No Haven for the Oppressed,* 225.

20. Friedman, *No Haven for the Oppressed,* 25–28.

21. Ibid., 28–31.

22. Wyman, *Paper Walls,* 27–29.

23. Friedman, *No Haven for the Oppressed,* 37–41.

24. Ibid., 42–44.

25. Including Canada, Great Britain, the Dominions, Denmark, France, Belgium, Norway, Luxembourg, Sweden, Switzerland, the Netherlands, Panama, Mexico, Costa Rica, Honduras, Nicaragua, Cuba, Haiti, the Dominican Republic, Columbia, Venezuela, Peru, Ecuador, Chile, Brazil, Paraguay, Argentina, Bolivia, and Ireland. Ibid., 55–56.

26. Ibid., 56–64; Wyman, *Paper Walls,* 43–63.

27. Ira Hirschmann, cited in Naske, "Jewish Immigration," 141. Immigration quotas in the United States remained set at about 20,000 German immigrants a year, and even they were not filled. According to historical reports, "between 1933 and 1941, 137,000 Jews reached America under the quota for Germany. That was more than were taken in by any other single country, but it was less than of the allowable quota." Tom Kizzia, "Beacon of Hope (Sanctuary: Alaska, The

Nazis, and the Jews)," *Anchorage Daily News*, May 16, 1999. See also Friedman, *No Haven for the Oppressed*, 52–55.

28. Friedman, *No Haven for the Oppressed*, 31, 72–73.

29. Wyman, *Paper Walls*, 72.

30. Friedman, *No Haven for the Oppressed*, 84–86.

31. Naske, "Jewish Immigration," 140.

32. Breitman and Kraut, *American Refugee Policy*, 80–111.

33. Friedman, *No Haven for the Oppressed*, 45–50.

34. David Morrison, *Heroes, Antiheroes, and the Holocaust: American Jewry and Historical Choice* (Jerusalem, Israel: 1995), 129–30. See also David Brody, "American Jewry, the Refugees and Immigration Restriction (1932–1942)," in *American Jewish History, vol. 7: America, American Jews, and the Holocaust*, ed. Jeffrey S. Gurock (New York: 1998), 181–209.

35. Daniels and Graham, *Debating American Immigration*, 136.

36. Friedman, *No Haven for the Oppressed*, 90–104; Wyman, *Paper Walls*, 79–92.

37. FSC, "Harold L. Ickes: The Champion of the Dispossessed," *Freeland* (1952), FSCP 65/1036. On Ickes's disgust with the Jewish organizations' lack of action, see Morrison, *Heroes, Antiheroes*, 131.

38. Naske, "Jewish Immigration," 142.

39. Ibid., 143; Kizzia, "Beacon of Hope."

40. Naske, "Jewish Immigration," 143; Wyman, *Paper Walls*, 99.

41. Naske, "Jewish Immigration," 146. On Gruening's objection to the plan, see Claus-M. Naske, *Ernest Gruening: Alaska's Greatest Governor* (Fairbanks, AK: 2004), 33–39.

42. Report to the Executive Committee on the Proposal for the Development of Alaska, FSCP 29/461; Nathan Margold to Senator William H. King, March 11, 1940, FSCP 24/396; Nathan Margold, Memorandum for Undersecretary, August 4, 1939, FSCP 18/309. As Margold conveyed the story, he believed that "the report would carry greater weight" if Chapman signed it and the secretary agreed. In turn, Chapman thought that because he had not visited Alaska and the undersecretary had, it would be better if the undersecretary issued the report. Margold indicated that he agreed with Chapman's reasoning, although he was also happy "to recur to the original plan of signing the report" if the undersecretary so preferred. See also Report to Secretary of the Interior on the Problem of Alaskan Development, signed by Harry Slattery, August 9, 1939, FSCP 18/310; Wyman, *Paper Walls*, 103.

43. FSC to Melvin M. Fagen, January 11, 1939, FSCP 22/365; FSC to Arthur S. Meyer, Chairman of Policy and Program Committee, General Jewish Council, January 3, 1939, FSCP 22/365; Minutes of the Committee on Alaska Meeting, July 10, 1939, FSCP 25/408, indicating that "it was agreed that the report, 'New Horizons for Alaska,' should be printed as a government document, sponsored by Assistant Secretary of the Interior Oscar Chapman, with FSC, Mrs. Schalet, Mr. Stefansson, and Mr. Pickett listed among the collaborators." Cohen also consulted with his father, who was at the time the president of the Conference on Jewish Relations. See FSC to Bee Schalet, August 4, 1939, FSCP 18/307. It should be noted that Representative May and Senator Gibson introduced a different bill prior to the one described here. Cohen described that bill as "very poorly thought out and poorly drafted . . . purporting to throw open Alaska to refugee settlement." FSC to Arthur S. Meyer, Chairman of Policy and Program Committee, General Jewish Council, July 31, 1939, FSCP 25/408.

44. Naske, "Jewish Immigration," 147; Tom Kizzia, "Give Us This Chance (Sanctuary: Alaska, The Nazis, and the Jews)," *Anchorage Daily News*, May 17, 1999.

45. FSC, Memorandum for Wolfsohn, February 26, 1940, FSCP 24/397; Memorandum on Proposed Alaskan Development Corporation Bill, FSCP 19/331. Most accounts of the Alaska Development Corporations also note the similarity between the proposed public purpose corporations and the London, Plymouth and Dutch West India Companies. Naske, "Jewish Immigration," 147.

46. FSC, "Harold L. Ickes"; FSC to Arthur S. Meyer, Chairman of Policy and Program Committee, General Jewish Council, April 21, 1939, FSCP 25/406; Harold Ickes to Secretary of War, June 2, 1939, FSCP 24/405.

47. Summary of Proposed Alaska Development Corporation Act of 1941, FSCP 17/304; Settlement and Development of Alaska: Hearings on S. 3577 before a Subcommittee of the Committee on Territories and Insular Affairs, U.S. Senate, 76th Congress, 3rd Session, 1.

48. Summary of Proposed Alaska Development Corporation Act of 1941, FSCP 17/304; Summary of proposed Alaska Development Corporation Act, March 15, 1940, FSCP 19/330; Hearings on S. 3577, 3.

49. Harold Ickes to Secretary of War, June 2, 1939, FSCP 24/405.

50. Summary of Proposed Alaska Development Corporation Act of 1941, FSCP 17/304. See also a 1941 version of the bill, M. 134880–1, FSCP 17/304 (this bill limited the number of "non-quota settlers that [might] be admitted during any fiscal year, under the act, to 10,000."); Hearings on S. 3577, 3–4; Wyman, *Paper Walls*, 104.

51. A Brief Summary of Undersecretary Slattery's Report on the Problem of Alaska Development, FSCP 18/307. See also FSC, Memorandum, January 5, 1939, FSCP 25/407; Harold Ickes to Secretary of War, June 2, 1939, FSCP 24/405.

52. Nathan Margold, Memorandum for Undersecretary, August 4, 1939, FSCP 18/309.

53. Other places were suggested, too. See Assistant Solicitor to Ralph Jonas, July 14, 1939, FSCP 25/408, noting that Phillips Ranch (adjoining the Fort Belknap Indian Reservation) "and similar areas in the Mountain States could be developed in such a way as to demonstrate the value of refugee settlers to the country and in this way to dissipate some of the existing prejudice against immigrants and aliens."

54. FSC, Memorandum, January 5, 1939, FSCP 25/407. See also Summary: New Horizons for Alaska, 62320, FSCP 18/316; A Brief Summary of Undersecretary Slattery's Report on the Problem of Alaska Development, FSCP 18/307; Civil Preparedness in the Territories: A National Defense project (Department of the Interior), FSCP 18/309. On earlier reports on Alaska Development, see Orlando W. Miller, *The Frontier in Alaska and the Matanuska Colony* (New Haven: 1975), 161–66.

55. See Maurice Parmelee (consultant economist), Memorandum for Joel D. Wolfsohn and FSC, June 6, 1940, FSCP 23/391; Assistant Secretary to Charles B. Henderson, Director, Reconstruction Finance Corporation, August 10, 1940, and enclosures (*Industrial Factors for National Defense in Alaska and Strategic and Critical Minerals in Alaska*), FSCP 18/309.

56. Statement by Harold L. Ickes in support of S. 3577 before the special subcommittee of the Senate Committee on Territories and Insular Affairs, May 13, 1940, FSCP 23/390; Hearings on S. 3577, 7. See also Tom Kizzia, "Are There No Exceptions? (Sanctuary: Alaska, The Nazis, and the Jews)," *Anchorage Daily News,* May 19, 1999.

57. Wyman, *Paper Walls,* 107; Hearings on S. 3577; A Brief Summary of Undersecretary Slattery's Report on the Problem of Alaska Development, FSCP 18/307. See also FSC to Warner Brothers Pictures, October 28, 1939, FSCP 29/459.

58. Naske, "Jewish Immigration," 153. See also Statement by Harold L. Ickes in support of S. 3577 before the special subcommittee of the Senate Committee on Territories and Insular Affairs, May 13, 1940, FSCP 23/390; Harold Ickes to Millard E. Tydings, Chairman, Committee on Territories and Insular Affairs, U.S. Senate, April 25, 1940, FSCP 19/330. The following individuals also testified in favor of the bill—Clarence Pickett, executive secretary of the Friends Service Committee; Alvin Johnson, director of the New School for Social Research and head of the immigration resettlement project in North Carolina; Frank Bohn, authority on land settlement; and Edmund I. Kaufmann, manufacturer and investor. Hearings on S. 3577; David J. Speck and FSC, Memorandum for Secretary of the Interior, May 21, 1940, FSCP 23/390.

59. Memorandum on Proposed Alaskan Development Corporation Bill, FSCP 19/331; Hearingss on S. 3577, 85; FSC to Warner Brothers Pictures, October 28, 1939, FSCP 29/459.

60. Naske, "Jewish Immigration," 153–54; Hearings on S. 3577, 179–94.

61. Memorandum on Proposed Alaskan Development Corporation Bill, FSCP 19/331.

62. Ibid.

63. Statement by Harold L. Ickes in support of S. 3577 before the special subcommittee of the Senate Committee on Territories and Insular Affairs, May 13, 1940, FSCP 23/390.

64. Nathan Margold, Memorandum for Secretary Ickes, January 20, 1940, FSCP 25/417.

65. Naske, "Jewish Immigration," 149; Gerald S. Berman, "From Neustadt to Alaska, 1939: A

Failed Attempt at Community Resettlement," *Immigrants and Minorities* 6 (March 1987): 68. See also Kizzia, "Beacon of Hope" and "Alaska Wants No Misfits (Sanctuary: Alaska, The Nazis, and the Jews)," *Anchorage Daily News,* May 18, 1999.

66. Berman, "From Neustadt to Alaska," 69–70; Kizzia, "Beacon of Hope."

67. Berman, "From Neustadt to Alaska," 70–71.

68. Ibid., 71–73.

69. Ibid., 73–74.

70. Ibid., 74–75.

71. Ibid., 75.

72. Ibid., 75; Kizzia, "Give Us This Chance."

73. Gerald S. Berman, "Reactions to the Resettlement of World War II Refugees in Alaska," *Jewish Social Studies* 44 (1982): 273; Naske, "Jewish Immigration," 148–51. See also Hearings on S. 3577, 221–22; Unsigned Letter to Dr. Robert Morse Lovett, Government Secretary of the Virgin Islands, December 7, 1939, FSCP 93/1482. For a detailed analysis of the responses of the different Chambers of Commerce, see *Responses to Department Report on Alaska by Alaskan Chambers of Commerce,* FSCP 24/392.

74. Confidential Minutes of Meeting held at Dr. Isador Lubin's office in the Department of Labor, FSCP 25/408.

75. Berman, "Resettlement of World War II Refugees in Alaska," 273; Wyman, *Paper Walls,* 104–5.

76. FSC to Morris Cohen, September 14, 1939, MRCP.

77. Hearings on S. 3577, 85, 119, 163, 230, 232, 245. See also Berman, "Resettlement of World War II Refugees in Alaska," 274–75.

78. Naske, "Jewish Immigration," 144.

79. Anthony J. Dimond to Senator James W. Head, October 9, 1939, FSCP 24/398; Hearings on S. 3577, 228.

80. Criticism of *Preliminary Report on Refugee Colonization in Alaska,* FSCP 24/405; Berman, "Resettlement of World War II Refugees in Alaska," 273; Kizzia, "Alaska Wants No Misfits."

81. Wyman, *Paper Walls,* 106; Naske, "Jewish Immigration," 144; and Berman, "Resettlement of World War II Refugees in Alaska," 274–75.

82. Unsigned Letter to Dr. Robert Morse Lovett, Government Secretary of the Virgin Islands, December 7, 1939, FSCP 93/1482; Hearings on S. 3577.

83. Hearings on S. 3577, 119, 170; Wyman, *Paper Walls,* 106–7.

84. Kizzia, "Give Us This Chance"; Berman, "Resettlement of World War II Refugees in Alaska," 276–77. Ickes, who had little patience for opposition, responded by pointing out the explicit discussion of the refugee problem in the Slattery Report. Wyman, *Paper Walls,* 101.

85. Anthony J. Dimond to Senator James W. Head, October 9, 1939, FSCP 24/398; Hearings on S. 3577, 231–33. See also Berman, "Resettlement of World War II Refugees in Alaska," 275.

86. Robert Marshall, "Should We Settle Alaska?" *New Republic,* February 8, 1940; Kizzia, "Give Us This Chance."

87. Kizzia, "Give Us This Chance."

88. FSC to Morris Cohen, July 23, 1939, FSCP 18/307.

89. Memorandum on Proposed Alaskan Development Corporation Bill, FSCP 19/331; Wyman, *Paper Walls,* 108–10.

90. Hearings on S. 3577, 150–53; Wyman, *Paper Walls,* 109; Berman, "Resettlement of World War II Refugees in Alaska," 276.

91. FSC to Morris Cohen, July 23, 1939, FSCP 18/307.

92. Hearings on S. 3577, 151–53; Wyman, *Paper Walls,* 109; Berman, "Resettlement of World War II Refugees in Alaska," 276.

93. Morris Cohen (as President of the Conference on Jewish Relations) to FSC, July 20, 1939, FSCP 18/307. See also FSC to Morris Cohen, July 23, 1939, FSCP 18/307.

94. On the Holocaust and Jewish-American identity, see Pnina Lahav, "The Eichman Trial, The Jewish Question, and the American-Jewish Intelligentsia," *Boston University Law Review* 72 (1992): 561–62.

95. FSC to Mr. Wolfsohn, August 3, 1940, FSCP 29/463. See also FSC to Arthur Meyer, Chairman of Policy and Program Committee, General Jewish Council, April 21, 1939, FSCP 25/406.

96. A Brief Summary of Undersecretary Slattery's Report on the Problem of Alaska Development, FSCP 18/307.

97. FSC to M. D. Mosessohn, August 7, 1940, FSCP 29/463.

98. Arthur S. Meyer, Chairman of Policy and Program Committee, General Jewish Council, August 11, 1939, FSCP 25/414. See similarly Minister Merrill Fowler Clarke, Congressional Church of New Canaan, to FSC, May 24, 1939, FSCP 25/407, noting that the plan might cause others to think that refugees should only be admitted to Alaska. For an examination of Jewish attitudes toward the refugee problem, see Brody, "American Jewry"; Rafael Medoff, "Alaska Could Have Saved Jews," *Jerusalem Post,* January 10, 1991. See also FSC to Morris Cohen, May 21, MRCP, asking Morris to ask Judge Mack for help in convincing Jewish organizations to support the plan.

99. Senator Tydings was important not only because he was the chair of the committee but also because many of his constituents in Baltimore were interested in the refugee problem; several of them were particularly interested in the bill. FSC to Arthur S. Meyer, Chairman of Policy and Program Committee, General Jewish Council, July 31, 1939, FSCP 25/408.

100. FSC to Louis D. Brandeis, February 7, 1940, FSCP 43/652. Brandeis's response suggested that he opposed the plan on broad grounds. Justice Louis D. Brandeis to FSC, February 7, 1940, FSCP 25/414. See also FSC to Arthur S. Meyer, Chairman of Policy and Program Committee, General Jewish Council, July 31, 1939, FSCP 25/408, asking Meyer to indicate to Senator Tydings a sympathetic interest in any legislation that could help with refugee settlement; FSC to Arthur M. Lamport, June 14, 1940, FSCP 29/462, asking for a note indicating that Zionist organizations did not oppose the bill.

101. Draft, "Object of this short motion picture," FSCP 25/408. Cohen's suggestions included the following:

> By montage effects we see shots of Pilgrims leaving Layden bound for New England; the Mayflower; Plymouth Rock. Rapid shots of stoning of Quakers in London; William Penn; the settlement of Pennsylvania by Penn and his followers; the St. Bartholomew massacre; the persecution of the Huguenots; their subsequent settlement of Delaware. A reportorial comment throughout by a narrator whenever necessary to point up the theme of settlement of these American Colonies by persecuted refugees. A covered wagon; a camp fire at night; settlers opening the West—an Irishman, an Englishman, a Scotchman, a German, a Frenchman—the Mormons being stoned out of Nauvoo; trek to Utah. The steerage of an ocean liner; the Irish from the potato famine areas; the Jews from Poland and Russia.

See also FSC to Warner Brothers Pictures, October 28, 1939, FSCP 29/459.

102. FSC to Beatrice Schalet, Alaskan Development Committee, Washington, D.C., February 26, 1940, FSCP 29/460. See similarly Nathan Margold, Memorandum for Secretary Ickes, January 20, 1940, FSCP 25/417.

103. FSC, "The Social and Economic Consequences of Exclusionary Immigration Laws," *National Lawyers Guild Quarterly* 2 (1939): 171.

104. Ibid., 172–89.

105. Ibid., 184–85.

106. Ibid., 189–91.

107. Ibid., 191.

108. FSC, "Mythology of Immigration," in *Legal Conscience,* 388–89. Originally published in *Freeland* 2 (1946): 12–13, 16.

109. FSC, "Exclusionary Immigration Laws," 191–92.

110. Ibid.

111. Watkins, *Righteous Pilgrim,* 674–75.

112. H.R. 2791, FSCP 18/305; Congressional Record—Appendix, February 5, 1941, FSCP

18/305; Congressional Record—Appendix, July 2, 1942, FSCP 18/306. See also Wyman, *Paper Walls*, 111; Berman, "Resettlement of World War II Refugees in Alaska," 272.

113. Berman, "Resettlement of World War II Refugees in Alaska," 278.

114. Wyman, *Paper Walls*, 111.

115. FSC's comments, in Minutes of Meeting Held November 15, 1940 in the Secretary's Conference Room, Interior, on the Use of the Virgin Islands of the United States as a Temporary Haven for Refugees, FSCP 35/547; Wyman, *Paper Walls*, 112. See also FSC to Clarence E. Pickett, Cosmos Club Washington, D.C., October 25, 1940, FSCP 35/545. Cuba served a similar purpose for a while. In 1940, when the Cuban government made it almost impossible for Jewish refugees to enter Cuba, Mexico opened its gates. But American consuls abroad refused to issue transit certificates to refugees heading to Mexico. This prevented the refugees from leaving Europe because there was "only one little freight line running every six weeks or so from Genoa to Verz Cruz and accommodating at most eight to ten passengers." Albert F. Coyle to FSC, February 6, 1940, FSCP 93/1482. Cohen and his colleagues discussed other places as well, including the Dominican Republic (a manuscript on Refugee Settlement in the Dominican Republic for a meeting at the Town Hall Club, NYC, February 15, 1940, FSCP 35/545), and the Philippines (confidential memorandum on refugee immigration in the Philippines attached to a letter from Emery H. Komlos, Assistant Secretary, Refugee Economic Corporation, to FSC, November 26, 1940, FSCP 35/547; FSC to Camilo Osias, Technical Assistant to the President of the Philippines, June 20, 1939, FSCP 31/485).

116. Secretary of the Interior to Secretary of Labor / Secretary of State, November 25, 1939, FSCP 36/553; Nathan Margold, Supplementary Memorandum on Power to Issue Limited Visitor's Visa, October 30, 1940, FSCP 37/570. See also Wyman, *Paper Walls*, 113.

117. Proposed Agenda for Conference on Virgin Islands Refuge Plan, FSCP 35/547; Minutes of Meeting Held November 15, 1940 in the Secretary's Conference Room, Interior, on the Use of the Virgin Islands of the United States as a Temporary Haven for Refugees, FSCP 35/547; Tentative Draft of Regulations on Admission of Alien Visitors to Virgin Islands, FSCP 36/559.

118. Harold Ickes to Attorney General (draft), August 10, 1940, FSCP 36/554; Wyman, *Paper Walls*, 113.

119. Solicitor, Memorandum for Secretary of the Interior, November 17, 1939, FSCP 36/554.

120. Secretary of the Interior to President Roosevelt, n.d., FSCP 36/554.

121. Secretary of the Interior, Draft Memorandum for Secretary of State / Secretary of Labor, November 25, 1939, FSCP 36/553. According to Interior, "this resolution was prompted both by the Assembly's desire to relieve the suffering of refugees and by its realization that such a program would be of great economic value to the Islands." Frederic L. Kirgis, Acting Solicitor, Memorandum for Secretary of the Interior, August 9, 1940, FSCP 36/554. See also Wyman, *Paper Walls*, 113–15.

122. Wyman, *Paper Walls*, 112–13.

123. Solicitor, Memorandum for Secretary of the Interior, November 17, 1939, FSCP 36/554.

124. See Frederic L. Kirgis, Acting Solicitor, Memorandum for Secretary of the Interior, August 9, 1940, FSCP 36/554. See also Solicitor, Draft Memorandum for Mr. Burlew, May 24, 1941, FSCP 36/559.

125. Frances Perkins, Secretary of Labor, to Secretary of the Interior, February 3, 1940, FSCP 36/554; Frederic L. Kirgis, Acting Solicitor, Memorandum for Secretary of the Interior, August 9, 1940, FSCP 36/554.

126. Department of State to Secretary Ickes, December 15, 1939, FSCP 36/554. See also Appendix C: Chronological Account of Inter-Departmental Negotiations on Admission of Alien Visitors into Virgin Islands, FSCP 35/540; Solicitor, Memorandum for Secretary of the Interior, FSCP 36/562; Frederic L. Kirgis, Acting Solicitor, Memorandum for Secretary of the Interior, August 9, 1940, FSCP 36/554; Wyman, *Paper Walls*, 113.

127. Appendix C: Chronological Account of Inter-Departmental Negotiations on Admission of Alien Visitors into Virgin Islands, FSCP 35/540; Solicitor, Memorandum for Secretary of the Interior, FSCP 36/562; Frederic L. Kirgis, Acting Solicitor, Memorandum for Secretary of the In-

terior, August 9, 1940, FSCP 36/554. Ickes went as far as to write the opinion for the Attorney General. See Secretary Harold Ickes to Attorney General, August 10, 1940, FSCP 36/554.

128. Appendix C: Chronological Account of Inter-Departmental Negotiations on Admission of Alien Visitors into Virgin Islands, FSCP 35/540. See also Solicitor, Memorandum for Secretary of the Interior, November 17, 1939, FSCP 36/554.

129. Nathan Margold, Memorandum on the Correct Interpretation of the Term "Emergency" as used in Executive Order No. 8430, November 22, 1940, FSCP 35/543; Wyman, *Paper Walls,* 113.

130. Proclamation by the Governor of the Virgin Islands, FSCP 36/559. See also Richard Flournoy (Secretary of State office) to FSC, November 30, 1940, FSCP 35/543.

131. Suggestions on the Effecting of the Proclamation of the Governor of the Virgin Islands Concerning the Admission of Non-Immigrant Aliens to the Islands, ca. November 1940, FSCP 35/546; FSC to Arthur Lamport, November 8, 1940, FSCP 37/565; Synopsis of Solicitor's Opinion (M. 31295), FSCP 37/567.

132. Solicitor, Supplementary Memorandum on the Propriety of a Request from the Secretary of the Interior for an Opinion of the Attorney General on Matters Affecting Alien Visitors to the Territories, November 14, 1940, FSCP 35/551; Nathan Margold, Memorandum for the Secretary, November 18, 1940, FSCP 34/538; Nathan Margold, Memorandum for Harold Ickes, December 26, 1940, FSCP 34/538. See also Harold B. Hoskins, The Problem of Foreign-Born Citizens, April 16, 1941, FSCP 37/571.

133. Solicitor, Memorandum for Secretary of the Interior, n.d., FSCP 36/558.

134. Frederic L. Kirgis, Acting Solicitor, Memorandum for Secretary of the Interior, August 9, 1940, FSCP 36/554.

135. Franklin D. Roosevelt, Memorandum for Harold Ickes, Secretary of the Interior, December 18, 1940, FSCP 34/538; Wyman, *Paper Walls,* 114.

136. Solicitor, Draft Memorandum for Mr. Burlew, May 24, 1941, FSCP 36/559.

137. Nathan Margold, Memorandum for Secretary of the Interior, February 13, 1941, FSCP 35/540, noting that he heard that Attorney General Jackson, after conference with the president, had decided not to respond to Interior's questions on admission of refugees to the Virgin Islands and other territories, and mark the file closed. Margold suggested that Ickes might want to talk with the attorney general. Ickes did, but to no avail. Harold Ickes, Memorandum for the Attorney General, February 21, 1941, FSCP 35/540. See also Wyman, *Paper Walls,* 114.

138. Berman, "From Neustadt to Alaska," 76; Kizzia, "Are There No Exceptions?"

139. Berman, "From Neustadt to Alaska," 76.

140. Ibid., 76–79.

141. Daniels and Graham, *Debating American Immigration,* 29.

142. FSC, "Harold L. Ickes." Cohen did not name any of the opponents of the Alaska Development Plan. When pressed on the issue by *Freeland's* editor, he explained that he was "reluctant to use the occasion of a man's death for criticism of the people who blocked the Alaskan Development Program—especially since the 2 or 3 more vigorous blockers [were by then] dead." FSC to Ada Siegel, *Freeland,* May 24, 1952, FSCP 65/1036. See also Ada Siegel to FSC, May 1, 1952, FSCP 65/1036.

Chapter 7. The Intellectual Equipment of a Generation

1. Purcell, *The Crisis of Democratic Theory,* 138.
2. Ibid., 168–69.
3. Ibid., 189–202.
4. Ibid., 202–5.
5. Ibid., 209–11, 231.
6. FSC, "The Relativity of Philosophical Systems and the Method of Systematic Relativism," in *Legal Conscience,* 97–99. Originally published in *The Journal of Philosophy* 36 (1939): 57.
7. Ibid., 98–103.
8. John Collier to Allan Harper, March 10, 1939, JCP 14/108; John Collier, Memorandum for FSC, March 10, 1939, JCP 12/300. While Collier's letter and memorandum did not mention

the title of Cohen's essay, their content and respective dates suggest that they refer to FSC, "The Relativity of Philosophical Systems."

9. FSC to John Collier, March 13, 1939, JCP 12/301. Cohen was responding to a comment made in a letter from Allan Harper to Collier. Harper suggested that Cohen's "thesis proved unpalatable" because "he seems to say that there is no substantial difference between colors like black and white; there is only our emotional attitude and approach to the question." Allan Harper, Director, TC-BIA (Denver, Colorado), to John Collier, March 7, 1939, JCP 14/107.

10. FSC to John Collier, March 13, 1939, JCP 12/301.

11. Thomas Biolsi, *"Deadliest Enemies": Law and the Making of Race Relations on and off Rosebud Reservation* (Berkeley, CA: 2001), 6–7.

12. FSC, Memorandum for Mr. Stull, December 5, 1938, HP F6; FSC, Report of Work as Chief of Indian Law Survey: 1939–1940, attached to FSC, Memorandum for Solicitor of the Interior, February 10, 1940, HP F7; Memorandum, FSCP 12/173; Agreement for Inter-Departmental Services, entered March 18, 1939, FSCP 11/156; Jill E. Martin, "'A Year and A Spring of My Existence': Felix S. Cohen and the Handbook of Federal Indian Law," *Western Legal History* 8 (1995): 36; Rennard Strickland and Gloria Valencia-Weber, "Observations on the Evolution of Indian Law in the Law Schools," *New Mexico Law Review* 26 (1996): 155–57. On April 19, 1939, Theodore Haas was appointed Special Attorney in the Department of Justice and designated to assist Cohen. Attachment, FSCP 12/173.

13. FSC to Morris Cohen, May 8, 1939, MRCP.

14. FSC, Memorandum for Mr. Stull, December 5, 1938, HP F6. See also excerpt from classification sheet submitted by Solicitor Margold, December 12, 1938, and approved by Civil Service Commission March 11, 1938, FSCP 12/171.

15. FSC, Report of Work as Chief of Indian Law Survey, HP F7; Theodore Haas, Memorandum for Norman Littell, August 4, 1939, FSCP 13/184; Martin, "A Year and A Spring," 37.

16. Theodore Haas, Memorandum for Norman Littell, August 4, 1939, FSCP 13/184.

17. Office of Indian Affairs, Press Release, August 5, 1940, FSCP 15/264.

18. Vine Deloria Jr., "Reserving to Themselves: Treaties and the Powers of Indian Tribes," *Arizona Law Review* 38 (1996): 964; Martin, "A Year and A Spring," 42.

19. In particular, they engaged in petty administrative warfare—for example, barring Cohen's assistants from entering the Justice Department building after hours or failing to provide mimeographing when required. Cohen, Report of Work as Chief of Indian Law Survey, HP F7.

20. Strickland and Valencia-Weber, "Evolution of Indian Law," 156. See also FSC to Carl A. McFarland, September 4, 1941, FSCP 15/266.

21. Norman Littell, August 3, 1939, FSCP 13/179; FSC, Memorandum for Norman Littell, FSCP 12/168. The committee was composed of Robert H. Fabian (chair), Theodore Haas, W. H. Churchwell and Mr. Pedro Capo-Rodriguez from the Trial Section, and Mr. Joseph T. King Jr. from the Legislation Section.

22. Robert H. Fabian, Memorandum for the Advisory Committee on the Indian Book, September 9, 1939, FSCP 12/168. See also Christian McMillen, "Rewriting History and Proving Property Rights: Hualapai Indian Activism and the Law of Land Claims in the Twentieth Century," Ph.D. diss., Yale University, 2004; Martin, "A Year and A Spring," 42–48.

23. Robert H. Fabian, Memorandum for FSC, September 19, 1939, FSCP 12/168; Martin, "A Year and A Spring," 43–44.

24. Theodore Haas, Memorandum for FSC re Committee Report, September 20, 1939, FSCP 12/168.

25. FSC, Memorandum for Robert H. Fabian, September 25, 1939, FSCP 12/168.

26. Ibid.

27. Ibid.

28. Memorandum for Norman Littell re Indian Law Survey, n.d., FSCP 12/168.

29. FSC, Memorandum for Solicitor of the Interior, February 10, 1940, HP F7.

30. Norman Littell, Memorandum for all persons affected, November 1, 1939, FSCP 12/168.

31. FSC, Memorandum for Solicitor of the Interior, February 10, 1940, HP F7.

32. Cohen, Report of Work as Chief of Indian Law Survey, HP F7.

33. Norman Littell, Memorandum for Attorney General, April 14, 1939, FSCP 11/154. See also FSC, Memorandum for Norman Littell, April 20, 1939, FSCP 12/172.

34. Cited in FSC, Memorandum for Solicitor of the Interior. February 10, 1940, HP F7.

35. Attorney General [Frank Murphy] to Harold Ickes, December 13, 1939, HP F1. For Cohen's response, see HP F6.

36. See, for example, Letter, November 1, 1939, FSCP 15/263.

37. FSC, Memorandum for Norman Littell, October 31, 1939, FSCP 13/181.

38. FSC, Memorandum for Norman Littell, November 1, 1939, FSCP 13/181.

39. FSC, Memorandum for Solicitor of the Interior, February 10, 1940, HP F7; E.K. Burlew, Memorandum for Attorney General, January 16, 1940, HP F2.

40. Assistant Solicitor W. H. Flannery, Memorandum for Solicitor, n.d., FSCP 14/247; Frederic L. Kirgis, Memorandum for Secretary, July 13, 1940, FSCP 12/170; FSCP 11/154. Apparently, Cohen went to his father's friend, Felix Frankfurter, who then went to see the president. Roosevelt said that he could not "overrule the Attorney General," but Frankfurter convinced him that no "overruling" was required, just "re-establishing." Roosevelt agreed to do that, and the task force moved from the Justice Department to Interior. Strickland and Valencia-Weber, "Evolution of Indian Law," 156. See also Nathan Margold to Felix Frankfurter, January 3, 1941, FSCP 16/279. Ickes noted that the examination revealed that Littell's evaluation was based on a memorandum submitted to him "which was not based on adequate research or inquiry." Ickes further pointed that when the project was undertaken, it was understood that it should serve "the needs of [Interior] in presenting litigation as well as the needs of [Justice] in conducting litigation." In Ickes's opinion, "the assumption of a basic divergence between the interests of . . . Justice and the interests of [Interior] in the field of Indian law [was] . . . unfortunate." Different government agencies and departments, Ickes explained, had to work together, especially as the Justice Department's work often involved litigation under statutes drafted by Interior. Secretary Ickes, Memorandum for Attorney General, July 24, 1940, HP F2.

41. FSC, Memorandum for Solicitor of the Interior, February 10, 1940, HP F7.

42. "Introduction" to *Felix Cohen's Handbook of Federal Indian Law,* ed. Rennard Strickland et al. (Charlottesville, VA: 1982), viii. For a detailed examination of the writing process, see Martin, "A Year and A Spring."

43. Robert H. Jackson to Secretary Ickes, August 2, 1940, FSCP 12/170, commenting on Ickes's and Kirgis's memoranda dated July 24, 1940.

44. FSC to Bernard L. Shientag, New York Supreme Court, August 23, 1941, FSCP 15/265.

45. FSC to Sam Thorne (ca. 1941), JPLP.

46. FSC to Arthur S. Meyer, Chairman of Policy and Program Committee, General Jewish Council, September 15, 1941, FSCP 15/266. See also FSC to Carl A. McFarland, September 4, 1941, FSCP 15/266; FSC to Charles E. Collett, September 4, 1941, FSCP 15/266; FSC to Adolf A. Berle Jr., September 4, 1941, FSCP 15/266.

47. Felix Frankfurter, Foreword, "Symposium: Felix S. Cohen," *Rutgers Law Review* 9 (1954): 356.

48. "Introduction" to *Handbook* (1982), viii.

49. Ibid., xxviii.

50. *Handbook of Federal Indian Law* (Washington, D.C.: 1942), 173.

51. "Foreword" to *Handbook* (1942), xix.

52. "Author's Acknowledgments" in *Handbook* (1942), xviii.

53. FSC, "The Spanish Origin of Indian Rights in the Law of the United States," in *Legal Conscience,* 237. Originally published in *Georgetown Law Journal* 31 (1942): 1.

54. FSC, "Indian Rights and the Federal Courts," *Minnesota Law Review* 24 (1940): 146. See also *Handbook* (1942), 173, which explained that the legal issues involved in protecting the civil liberties of Indians were different from those arising in dealing with other groups. While with respect to all groups, infringement upon civil liberties involved government action, with respect to Indian tribes, government action constituted "a special, and in many ways peculiar, body of law and administration." "In the mass of special legislation and special administration," Cohen wrote, "we find a number of civil liberties problems that have not arisen elsewhere in American law."

55. The right of self-government included "the power of an Indian tribe to adopt and operate under a form of government of the Indians' choosing, to define conditions of tribal membership, to regulate domestic relations of members, to prescribe rules of inheritance, to levy taxes, to regulate property within the jurisdiction of the tribe, to control the conduct of members by municipal legislation and to administer justice." According to Cohen, tribal autonomy included the tribe's procedural, civil, and criminal jurisdiction on the reservation. FSC, "Indian Rights," 147, 149–53, 158–59.

56. Ibid., 146–47.

57. "Introduction" to *Handbook* (1942), xxiii.

58. FSC, "Indian Rights," 185.

59. Ibid.

60. Alan Brinkley, *The End of Reform: New Deal Liberalism in Recession and War* (New York: 1995), 165; Risa Goluboff, "The Work of Civil Rights in the 1940s: The Department of Justice, the NAACP, and African Americans Agricultural Workers," Ph.D. diss., Princeton University, 2003.

61. John T. Elliff, *The United States Department of Justice and Individual Rights, 1937–1962* (New York: 1987); William E. Forbath, "Civil Rights and Economic Citizenship: Notes on the Past and Future of the Civil Rights and Labor Movements," *University of Pennsylvania Journal of Labor and Employment Law* 2 (2000): 697; Risa L. Goluboff, "The Thirteenth Amendment and the Lost Origins of Civil Rights," *Duke Law Journal* 50 (2001): 1609; Goluboff, "The Work of Civil Rights"; Herbert Hovenkamp, "The Political Economy of Substantive Due Process," *Stanford Law Review* 40 (1988): 379. Forbath traces the turn from class to race to the collapse of the political alliance between Northern and Southern Democrats. According to Forbath, initial support for New Deal programs came from Northern and Southern Democrats. This alliance guaranteed that the New Deal programs would remain focused on workers' rights to the exclusion of any reference to the "melding of class and caste" in the Southern labor market. As Roosevelt's social and economic rights talk "grew more and more robust and universal," the alliance fell apart. By the late 1930s, Southern democrats were attacking the New Deal as a coalition of blacks and Marxists, and by the 1940s they openly joined ranks with Republicans to defeat the 1940s reforms that would have supported a more active national labor market (including Roosevelt's "second Bill of Rights"). At the same time, the mass migration of blacks from the rural South to Northern cities forced Northern Democrats to address the issue of equal rights. See Forbath, "Civil Rights," 697–708. Goluboff traces the transformation to the work of the Civil Rights Section of the Justice Department, which was established in 1939. Goluboff, "The Thirteenth Amendment," 1614. See also Mary L. Dudziak, *Cold War Civil Rights: Race and the Image of American Democracy* (Princeton, NJ: 2000).

62. See, for example, Brinkley, *End of Reform*, 154–65.

63. Robert H. Jackson to Secretary Ickes, August 2, 1940, FSCP 12/170.

64. *Carolene Products* (304 U.S. 144) involved a due-process challenge to economic regulation. Justice Stone agreed with the New Dealers that the Supreme Court should exercise judicial restraint and defer to the judgment of elected legislatures on economic and social issues. But he enumerated three exceptions to the presumption of judicial restraint, situations where it might be necessary to exercise a "more exacting judicial scrutiny": (1) when the legislation appears to violate one of the provisions of the Bill of Rights, (2) when the legislation "restricts those political processes which can ordinarily be expected to bring about repeal of undesirable legislation," and (3) when the legislation was "directed at particular religions or national or racial minorities." Justice Stone reasoned that "prejudice against discrete and insular minorities may be a special condition, which tends seriously to curtail the operation of those political processes ordinarily to be relied upon to protect minorities, and which may call for a correspondingly more searching judicial inquiry." Morton J. Horwitz, *The Warren Court and the Pursuit of Justice* (New York: 1998), 76–78.

65. FSC, "The Relativity of Philosophical Systems," 109.

66. FSC, "The Socialization of Morality," 347–48.

67. More recently, Joshua Cohen has offered a similar critique. Joshua Cohen, "Pluralism and Proceduralism," *Chicago-Kent Law Review* 69 (1994): 589.

68. FSC, "Spanish Origin," 231.

69. "Introduction" to *Handbook* (1942), xxiv.

70. FSC, "Spanish Origin," 239–52.

71. See, for example, Russel Lawrence Barsh and James Youngblood Henderson, *The Road: Indian Tribes and Political Liberty* (Berkeley, CA: 1980), 112, 278.

72. Among these rights were also ownership rights (including the rights of alienation). In this respect, Cohen's *Handbook* set the foundation for his later work on the Indian Claims Commission by documenting how the different conquerors negotiated with Indian tribes for the purchase of their lands. See Office of Indian Affairs, Press Release, June 15, 1942, FSCP 16/284; *infra* Chapter 9.

73. On the typical early twentieth-century turn to economics as a solution to cultural and racial problems, see Brinkley, *End of Reform,* 165–66.

74. See, for example, FSC, "Spanish Origin," 244–47.

75. The question of group autonomy also encompasses the relationship between the group and its own members. This is a subject discussed in great detail in late twentieth-century scholarship. In part because his goal was to empower Indian tribes, in part because the realities of group power were not fully explored at the time, Cohen paid less attention to the question of group power toward its individual members. However, in all his writings on group rights, he stressed the importance of individual rights. See, for example, FSC, review of Osmond K. Frankel, *Our Civil Liberties,* FSCP 62/974, which noted that "if our liberties are valuable they need to be protected not only against governments but against employers, labor unions, landlords, news associations, churches, espionage agents of foreign powers, and various other nongovernmental associations and agencies." See also Chapter 2, *supra.*

76. Goluboff, "The Work of Civil Rights."

77. Notes on a "Projected Institute of Living Law," FSCP 77/1209; Articles of Association, FSCP 77/1209. Apparently, the title "living law" was derived from Eugen Ehrlich's 1912 book *Fundamental Principles of the Sociology of Law,* trans. Professor Moss, 1937. FSC, book review, in *Legal Conscience,* 189–90.

78. Notes on a "Projected Institute of Living Law," FSCP 77/1209; Articles of Association, FSCP 77/1209.

79. Institute of Living Law: Statement of Purpose, FSCP 77/1209; Notes on a "Projected Institute of Living Law," FSCP 77/1209; Institute of Living Law: List of Proposed Projects, February 1941, FSCP 77/1209. See also FSC to Professor Eugene Rostow, Yale Law School, July 22, 1941, FSCP 77/1211; FSC to Karl N. Llewellyn, Columbia Law School, July 28, 1941, FSCP 77/1211.

80. The institute's studies were intended to focus on the actions of the federal government but with respect to several issues research was also extended to the states. Notes on a "Projected Institute of Living Law," FSCP 77/1209; Institute of Living Law: List of Proposed Projects, February 1941, FSCP 77/1209; Jim [Curry] to FSC, March 30, 1941, FSCP 77/1211; Institute of Living Law (Notice), July 30, 1941, FSCP 79/1246; Secretary of Institute of Living Law to the Attorney General, July 1941, FSCP 77/1211.

81. See generally, Milos Calda, *The American Left and the Challenges of the 1930s* (Prague, Czech Republic: 1998).

82. Brinkley, *End of Reform,* 154–55.

83. Program of Activities, FSCP 77/1209; Institute of Living Law: Statement of Purpose, FSCP 77/1209.

84. Notes on a "Projected Institute of Living Law," FSCP 77/1209; Articles of Association, FSCP 77/1209. According to Cohen, a Communist was a member of the Communist Party, while a fellow traveler was a person who did not join the Party but who voted "on the side of the Communists on all important issues." In turn, "innocents" were those who voted "on the side of the Communists in all important issues without knowing that it is the Communist side, either because [they think] that it is the side of true liberalism or because [they have] been conditioned to the sound of epithets like 'red baiter,' 'friend of the Dies Committee' and 'disrupter' to a point where [they] will respond satisfactorily to the verbal pressure of Communist or fellow traveler as-

sociates." FSC to Lester P. Schoene, Secretary, District of Columbia Chapter, NLG, October 1, 1940, FSCP 77/1216.

85. Cohen was a member of the NLG's National Executive Board, the Executive Committee of the District of Columbia Chapter, the Professional Employment Committee of the Chapter, and the staff of the *National Lawyers Guild Quarterly*. FSC to Lester P. Schoene, Secretary, District of Columbia Chapter, NLG, October 1, 1940, FSCP 77/1216.

86. Ibid. In his three years at the NLG, Cohen was involved in different debates over foreign policy, including the debates about the United States isolationist position and the Spanish embargo. He maintained that his position on these issues reflected his assessment of the particular facts of each scenario, rather than an endorsement of one rule as applicable to all situations, a behavior of which he accused many of the Communists in the NLG. Ibid. See also Affidavit of FSC, November 12, 1948, FSCP 89/1417, in which he notes his participation in a campaign to eliminate Communists and Communist sympathizers from positions as chapter delegates to the NLG Convention in the spring of 1940 and from other offices in the NLG. On the NLG, see Percival Roberts Bailey, "Progressive Lawyers: A History of the National Lawyers Guild, 1936–1958," Ph.D. diss., Rutgers University, 1979.

87. Remarks of Senator Guy M. Gillette in the Senate, prepared by the Institute of Living Law, Thursday March 6, 1941, FSCP 79/1243; Summary of Memorandum on Nazi Activities in the United States, May 14, 1940, FSCP 42/627; FSC and Edith Lowenstein (for the Institute of Living Law), "Combating Totalitarian Propaganda: The Method of Suppression," *Illinois Law Review* 37 (1942–43): 194.

88. Transcript for Radio Program (WEVD), March 20, 1942, FSCP 79/1244.

89. FSC and Lowenstein, "Totalitarian Propaganda: Suppression," 196.

90. FSCP 90/1451.

91. On cultural attitudes portraying racism as un-American and on the perverse racism in America during World War II, see Mary L. Dudziak, "Desegregation as a Cold War Imperative," *Stanford Law Review* 41 (1988): 68–73.

92. FSC and Lowenstein, "Totalitarian Propaganda: Suppression," 193, 209.

93. James E. Curry, FSC, and Bernard M. Newburg (for the Institute of Living Law), "Combating Totalitarian Propaganda: The Method of Exposure," *University of Chicago Law Review* 10 (1942–43): 138. See also the Foreign Agents Registration Act, 52 Stat. 631 (1938), the Alien Registration Act, 54 Stat. 670 (1940), and the Voohris Act, 54 Stat. 1201 (1940); Affidavit of FSC, FSCP 94/1519. On the institute's work on the Foreign Agents Registration Act and the institute's critique of its administration, see Transcript for Radio Program (WEVD), New York, May 15, 1941, FSCP 78/1231; Institute of Living Law, Report No. 3, The Administration of the Foreign Agents Registration Act, ca. 1941, FSCP 78/1232; News Release by the Institute, FSCP 77/1213.

94. FSC to Dr. Carl J. Friedrich, Chairman, Executive Committee, Counsel for Democracy, New York, February 1, 1941, and enclosed draft legislation, FSCP 79/1242.

95. Curry et al., "Totalitarian Propaganda: Exposure," 139.

96. Ibid., 140. See also "Urges New Campaign Ban," NYT, February 28, 1941, PHN; Remarks of Senator Guy M. Gillette in the Senate, prepared by the Institute of Living Law, Thursday March 6, 1941, FSCP 79/1243; Transcript for Radio Program (WEVD), March 20, 1942, FSCP 79/1244; FSC to Dr. Carl J. Friedrich, Chairman, Executive Committee, Counsel for Democracy, New York, NY, February 1, 1941, and enclosed draft legislation, FSCP 79/1242. Iowa Democrat Guy Gillette (1879–1973) was elected to the House of Representatives in 1932, and then to the Senate in 1936. During World War II, Gillette expressed concerns about the plight of European Jews and called on Roosevelt to set up an independent rescue agency. Gillette also worked with the State Department to draft the United Nations Charter.

97. FSC to Frank N. Trager, March 3, 1941, FSCP 77/1211.

98. The original title was the Office of Race Relations, but many supporters of the bill objected to it. The Office of Cultural Unity was another suggestion, but most institute members thought that it "was too 'fine-arty.'" The titles Office of Political Unity or Office of National Unity seemed "too totalitarian." And they finally settled on Office of Minority Relations. FSC to Stephen Raushenbush, March 3, 1941, FSCP 77/1211. Another office recommended by the Insti-

tute of Living Law was the Office of Propaganda Exposure or Investigation. See Order establishing the Office of Propaganda Exposure, FSCP 47/714; Nathan Margold, Memorandum for Secretary, March 14, 1941, FSCP 47/714; Chart of Proposed Office of Propaganda Exposure, FSCP
47/714.

99. FSC to Dr. Carl J. Friedrich, Chairman, Executive Committee, Counsel for Democracy,
New York, February 1, 1941, and enclosed draft legislation, FSCP 79/1242; Remarks of Senator
Guy M. Gillette in the Senate, prepared by the Institute of Living Law, Thursday March 6, 1941,
FSCP 79/1243; Transcript of radio program (WEVD), March 20, 1942, FSCP 79/1244; FSC to
Stephen Raushenbush, March 3, 1941, FSCP 77/1211; Curry et al., "Totalitarian Propaganda: Ex-
posure," 141.

100. FSC to Frank N. Trager, March 3, 1941, FSCP 77/1211.

101. Remarks of Senator Guy M. Gillette in the Senate, prepared by the Institute of Living
Law, Thursday March 6, 1941, FSCP 79/1243; Transcript for Radio Program (WEVD), March 20,
1942, FSCP 79/1244; Curry et al., "Totalitarian Propaganda: Exposure," 141.

102. Cohen and Lowenstein, "Totalitarian Propaganda: Suppression," 213.

103. FSC to Frank N. Trager, March 3, 1941, FSCP 77/1211.

104. Cohen and Lowenstein, "Totalitarian Propaganda: Suppression," 193, 213–14. Already in
the late 1930s Cohen helped draft regulations requiring that any suggested controversial speech
on national parks property would not be banned but rather advertised in advance to allow for responses. FSC to Morris Cohen, August 23, MRCP.

105. Lucy M. Kramer and FSC (for the Institute of Living Law), "Combating Totalitarian Propaganda: The Method of Enlightenment," *Minnesota Law Review* 27 (1942–43): 548.

106. Ibid., 562–73.

107. "A Pacific Charter," n.d., FSCP 78/1238.

108. FSC to James T. Ramsey, January 14, 1941, FSCP 85/1333.

109. "A Pacific Charter," n.d., FSCP 78/1238. See also Ezra Glaser to Jim, February 17, 1943,
FSCP 78/1237. Different references to a pacific charter are found in the 1940s and early 1950s.
On September 8, 1954, the delegates of Australia, France, New Zealand, Pakistan, the Philippines,
Thailand, the United Kingdom, and the United States signed a "Pacific Charter" designed to
maintain peace and security in Southeast Asia and the Southwest Pacific. The charter upheld the
principles of equal rights and self-determination of peoples. Similarities between the 1954 charter
and the one examined in this section reflect public concerns about self-determination and the
rights of indigenous peoples at the end of World War II that are beyond the scope of the discussion here. It should be noted that interest in a pacific charter seems to have originated after the
signing of the "Atlantic Charter" between the United Kingdom and the United States on August
8, 1941. The "Atlantic Charter" sought to establish a foundation for a postwar world. The text of
the "Atlantic Charter" (1941) and the "Pacific Charter" (1954) can be found online at the Avalon
Project at Yale Law School, www.yale.edu/lawweb/avalon.

110. Proposed Plans for A Pacific Charter, n.d., FSCP 78/1238.

111. "A Pacific Charter," n.d., FSCP 78/1238.

112. Ibid. Cohen also participated in similar plans, suggested by Collier and Ickes to President
Roosevelt, to apply Indian reorganization-like programs to Pacific islands occupied by the United
States. See Haas, ed., *Felix S. Cohen*, 11; Kenneth William Townsend, *World War II and the American
Indian* (Albuquerque, NM: 2000), 209–14.

113. Council for Democracy, *The New World* (New York: 1942).

114. See also Abraham C. Weinfeld, *Towards a United States of Europe, Proposals for a Basic Structure* (Washington, DC: 1942).

115. FSC to Professor C. J. Friedrich, Chairman, Executive Committee, Council for Democracy, November 28, 1941, and enclosed Memorandum for the Council for Democracy (furnished
to the Institute by Abraham C. Weinfeld), FSCP 77/1211.

116. Ibid.

117. Ibid.

118. Ibid.

119. Ibid.

120. See, for example, Second Draft: What is the Pragmatic Justification for the existence of the Sub-Commission on Prevention of Discrimination and Protection of Minorities? Prepared for the Consultative Council of Jewish Organizations, December 1, 1948, FSCP 50/764.

121. President Wilson proposed to include "an obligation of all League members to respect religious freedom and to refrain from discrimination on the basis of religion." The British delegate wanted an even stronger statement, which Wilson thought went too far because it gave the Council of the League "a right of intervention against states that would disturb world peace by a policy of religious intolerance." Finally, the Japanese delegate "proposed to add . . . an obligation of all member states to refrain from discrimination on the basis of race or nationality against foreigners who would be nationals of the League members." While the commission supported the Japanese proposal, it was rejected by the United Kingdom and the United States. Moreover, given this development, the American delegation withdrew its own proposal. Jan Herman Burgers, "The Road to San Francisco: The Revival of the Human Rights Idea in the Twentieth Century," *Human Rights Quarterly* 14 (1992): 449.

122. Carol Weisbrod, "Minorities and Diversities: The 'Remarkable Experiment' of the League of Nations," *Connecticut Journal of International Law* 8 (1993): 367–68. As Weisbrod points out, between 1919 and 1920, treaties were signed by the Allies with Poland, Czechoslovakia, Romania, Yugoslavia, and Greece. Peace treaties with four defeated states—Turkey, Austria, Bulgaria, and Hungary—also included minority clauses. Ibid. They were also included in declarations that Albania, Estonia, Finland, Latvia, and Lithuania had to make "as a condition for their admission to the League of Nations." Finally, "similar clauses were included in two bilateral treaties, namely between Germany and Poland regarding Upper Silesia and between Germany and Lithuania regarding the Memel Territory. . . . All these instruments assigned certain supervisory powers to the Council of the League of Nations." Burgers, "The Road to San Francisco," 449–50; Joseph S. Roucek, "The Problem of Minorities and the League of Nations," *Journal of Comparative Legislation and International Law* 15 (1933): 67.

123. Burgers, "The Road to San Francisco," 450.

124. Weisbrod, "Minorities and Diversities," 370–71; Burgers, "The Road to San Francisco," 450–59.

125. Burgers, "The Road to San Francisco," 448, 459.

126. Ibid., 468–70.

127. Ibid., 474–77.

128. Dudziak, "Desegregation," 93.

129. Will Kymlicka, "Theorizing Indigenous Rights," *University of Toronto Law Journal* 49 (1999): 283–84 (review of S. James Anaya, *Indigenous Peoples in International Law*). As Kymlicka explains, unil the 1990s debates about national minorities have centered on the "middle area" between these two articles: "about the right to use a minority language in courts or local administration; the funding of minority schools; the extent of local or regional autonomy; the guaranteeing of political representation for minorities; the protection of minority homelands from economic development or settlement and so on."

130. See similarly Moses Moskowitz to FSC, December 6, 1948, FSCP 50/764.

131. Rebecca Tsosie, "Separate Sovereigns, Civil Rights, and the Sacred Text: The Legacy of Thurgood Marshall's Indian Law Jurisprudence," *Arizona State University Law Journal* 26 (1994): 530.

132. See, for example, Draft Declaration on the Rights of Indigenous Peoples (1994); Proposed American Declaration on the Rights of Indigenous Peoples (Approved by the Inter-American Commission on Human Rights, February 26, 1997).

Chapter 8. Property in (Group) Conflict

1. Joseph W. Singer, "Well Settled? The Increasing Weight of History in American Indian Land Claims," *Georgia Law Review* 28 (1994): 492.

2. *Johnson v. M'Intosh*, 21 U.S. 543 (1823); *Worcester v. Georgia*, 31 U.S. 515, 559 (1832).

322   NOTES TO PAGES 192-199

3. FSC to Dr. A.L. Kroeber, University of California at Berkeley, February 25, 1942, RG48//Entry 824/Box 1/Folder 4.

4. See www.swirc.org/res_hualapai.cfm?ep=7&ec=1.

5. *The Hualapai Tribe of the Hualapai Reservation, Arizona v. United States,* before the ICC, Docket No. 90, decided November 19, 1962, in Robert A. Manners, *Hualapai Indians II: An Ethnological Report on the Hualapai (Walapai) Indians of Arizona* (New York: 1974), 453.

6. 13 Stat. 541, 559.

7. Edward H. Spicer, *Cycles of Conquest: The Impact of Spain, Mexico, and the United States on Indians of the Southwest, 1533–1960* (Tucson: 1962), 271. For a detailed narrative of these events, see Dennis G. Casebier, *Camp Beale's Springs and the Hualapai Indians* (Norco, CA: 1980). See also RG48//Entry 824/Box 1/Folder 1.

8. Act of July 27, 1866, 14 Stat. 292.

9. McMillen, "Rewriting History." McMillen's is the most comprehensive study of the Hualapai case. Unless otherwise necessary I relied on his excellent archival research for factual background. As McMillen notes, only with the creation of the reservation did the different Hualapai bands became a unified political entity—a tribe.

10. Ibid.

11. Act of July 27, 1866, 14 Stat. 292.

12. On tribal property rights under American law, see Singer, "Well Settled?"

13. McMillen, "Rewriting History."

14. 43 Stat. 954.

15. Solicitor Gardner, Memorandum (drafted by FSC), November 30, 1942, RG48//Entry 824/Box 1/Folder 1.

16. RG48//Entry 824; McMillen, "Rewriting History."

17. For these different arguments, see RB (Walapai).

18. McMillen, "Rewriting History."

19. Memorandum of Points and Authorities in Support of Defendant's Motion to Dismiss Plaintiff's Complaint, RB (Walapai), 26–132; RG48//Entry 824/Box 2.

20. *United States v. Santa Fe Pacific Railroad Company,* U.S. District Court for the District of Arizona, October 1938 Term, RB (Walapai), 190–95.

21. McMillen, "Rewriting History."

22. Ibid.

23. *United States v. Santa Fe Pacific Railroad Company,* 114 F. 2d 420, 426 (1940).

24. McMillen, "Rewriting History."

25. *United States as Guardian of the Hualapai Indians of Arizona v. Santa Fe Pacific Railroad Co.* 314 U.S. 339 (1941); Brief for the U.S., RB (Walapai), 92–98. See also Petition for Writ of Certiorari to the U.S. Circuit Court of Appeals for the Ninth Circuit, Reply Brief in Support of Petition for Certiorari, and Brief for the U.S., RB (Walapai).

26. Petition for Writ of Certiorari to the U.S. Circuit Court of Appeals for the Ninth Circuit, RB (Walapai), 16.

27. FSC, "Spanish Origin," 250.

28. Max Radin, a fellow legal realist and a friend, who represented the Railroad, accused Cohen of abandoning the legal realist position by prioritizing general propositions over concrete facts. Respondent's Brief Part 2: An analysis of the Laws of Spain and Mexico, RB (Walapai). But Radin seemed to have missed the point. A legal realist might recognize that the law in action was apart from the law in books, and still admire the ideals to which the law in books aspired.

29. FSC, "Spanish Origin," 232–39.

30. Ibid., 237–39.

31. Ibid., 237. See also FSC, Memorandum on Walapai Tribal Occupancy in Reservation Area, n.d., RG48//Entry 824/Box 1/Folder 1.

32. FSC to Morris Cohen, 1941, MRCP.

33. Ibid.

34. *United States v. Santa Fe Pacific Railroad Company* (1941). See also Caroline L. Orlando,

"Aboriginal Title Claims in the Indian Claims Commission: *United States v. Dann* and its Due Process Implications," *Boston College Environmental Affairs Law Review* 13 (1986): 246.

35. *United States v. Santa Fe Pacific Railroad Company* (1941). See also John P. Lowndes, "When History Outweighs Law: Extinguishment of Abenaki Aboriginal Title," *Buffalo Law Review* 42 (1994): 92–94; Singer, "Well Settled?" 487–88, 516–17, which argues that the court's statement regarding ways in which Indian title could be extinguished misinterpreted Marshall's opinions.

36. Petition for Rehearing, RB (Walapai). See also *United States as Guardian of the Indians of the Tribe of Hualapai v. Santa Fe Pacific Railroad Company*, 314 U.S. 716 (1942).

37. Solicitor Gardner, Memorandum (drafted by FSC), November 30, 1942, RG48//Entry 824/Box 1/Folder 1.

38. See, for example, FSC to Robert McKennan, Dartmouth College, February 20, 1942, RG48//Entry 824/Box 1/Folder 4.

39. FSC to Commissioner Brophy, March 14, 1947, FSCP 86/1350. See also FSC, Memorandum for Solicitor of the Interior, March 27, 1947, FSCP 43/642.

40. FSC, "Spanish Origin," 251–52.

41. Ibid., 230–31.

42. Ibid., 230–31. As Spain was the first European nation extensively to colonize peoples in the New World, Vitoria's writings had immensely influenced other theorists on the subject of international law and he is considered the founder of the Spanish School of International Law. See Robert A. Williams Jr., "The Algebra of Federal Indian Law: The Hard Trail of Decolonizing and Americanizing the White Man's Indian Jurisprudence," *Wisconsin Law Review* (1986): 240n65.

43. Mitchell, *Sold American*, 253.

44. Ibid., 259.

45. See FSC, Memorandum for Mr. Harper, October 14, 1936, FSCP 24/403; Assistant Solicitor, Memorandum for Mr. Harper, December 18, 1936, FSCP 24/403; Assistant Solicitor, Memorandum for Mr. Harper, December 21, 1936, FSCP 24/403.

46. David S. Case and David A. Voluck, *Alaska Natives and American Laws* (Fairbanks, AK: 2002), 84.

47. Mitchell, *Sold American*, 275.

48. Act of May 1, 1946, 49 Stat. 1250; Mitchell, *Sold American*, 271; Skinner, *Alaska Native Policy*, 37–38.

49. 52 Stat. 593; Statement of Policy on the Development of Alaska Resources, July 13, 1946, FSCP 21/361.

50. Collier instructed his field agents to require "each village to obtain an [IRA] constitution that, when approved by the secretary of the interior, authorized the Native residents of the village to elect a village council that then could petition for a reservation." Between 1938 and 1941, Ickes approved forty-four village constitutions which authorized the village residents to elect a village council. But Collier's guidelines to his field agents insisted that village councils would have "no governmental authority until a reservation had been established for [their] villages." Mitchell, *Sold American*, 275–76. See also Skinner, *Alaska Native Policy*, 40.

51. Case and Voluck, *Alaska Natives*, 85. The struggle involved the BIA acting on behalf of the Indians, on the one hand, and other governmental agencies, for example the General Lands Office, seeking to maintain Alaska open for whites, on the other. As late as 1944, there were "half a dozen [public land] orders establishing Alaska reservations . . . hung up in one or another of the Interior Department bureaus—principally the Lands Office." Mitchell, *Sold American*, 276.

52. Francis Joseph Weiss, Chemical Utilization of Fish Products in Alaska, April 1941, National Economic and Social Planning Association, FSCP 19/329.

53. FSC, Letter to the Editor, *Ketchikan Alaska Chronicle*, April 19, 1948, cited in Mitchell, *Sold American*, 280.

54. *Alaska Pacific Fisheries v. United States*, 248 U.S. 78 (1918).

55. Act of June 6, 1924, 43 Stat. 464; FSC, Memorandum for Assistant Secretary Gardner, December 3, 1946, FSCP 21/361.

56. FSC, Memorandum for Solicitor of the Interior, January 28, 1943, FSCP 22/370.

57. Karen Ferguson, "Indian Fishing Rights: Aftermath of the Fox Decision and the Year 2000," *American Indian Law Review* 23 (1998–99): 104–5.

58. FSC, Memorandum for Solicitor of the Interior, January 28, 1943, FSCP 22/370.

59. FSC, Memorandum for Solicitor of the Interior, February 26, 1944, FSCP 22/370.

60. M. 31634, Solicitor's Opinion, Fishing Rights of Alaskan Indians, February 13, 1942, *Opinions of the Solicitor,* 1096.

61. Ibid.; Margold, Memorandum for Secretary of the Interior, November 29, 1941, FSCP 20/345.

62. M. 31634, Solicitor's Opinion, Fishing Rights of Alaskan Indians, February 13, 1942, *Opinions of the Solicitor;* FSC, Memorandum for Solicitor of the Interior, January 28, 1943, FSCP 22/370; Draft note, FSCP 19/333.

63. M. 31634, Solicitor's Opinion, Fishing Rights of Alaskan Indians, February 13, 1942, *Opinions of the Solicitor,* 1096–98.

64. Ibid., 1100–5.

65. Ibid., 1106.

66. Ibid. See also FSC, Memorandum for Solicitor of the Interior, January 28, 1943, FSCP 22/370; FSC, Memorandum for Solicitor of the Interior, February 26, 1944, FSCP 22/370.

67. Notes on Alaska Fishery Regulations, FSCP 21/350, mentioning that "in 1937, out of 453 traps, some 214 were controlled by 9 operators of whom the five principal operators controlled 171."

68. The opinion was approved by the attorney general on April 8. Harold Ickes to Senator W. Warren Barbour, June 17, 1942, FSCP 19/333.

69. M. 31634, Solicitor's Opinion, Fishing Rights of Alaskan Indians, February 13, 1942, *Opinions of the Solicitor,* 1106. See also Solicitor Margold, Memorandum for Secretary of the Interior, March 5, 1942, FSCP 20/346.

70. Case and Voluck, *Alaska Natives,* 85.

71. Solicitor Margold (written by FSC) to George S. Folta, Counsel at Large, Juneau, Alaska, April [2?] 1942, FSCP 19/333.

72. John Collier, Memorandum for Secretary of the Interior, March 4, 1942, FSCP 19/334.

73. Solicitor Margold, Memorandum for Harold Ickes, March 5, 1942, FSCP 20/346.

74. Solicitor Margold, Memorandum for Harold Ickes, April 11, 1942, FSCP 19/333.

75. Solicitor Harper, Memorandum (drafted by FSC) for Assistant Secretary Chapman, April 27, 1944, FSCP 19/334; Mitchell, *Sold American,* 283–84.

76. Ira N. Gabrielson, Memorandum for FSC, February 16, 1942, FSCP 20/346. See also correspondence in FSCP 20/346, specifically FSC, Memorandum for Solicitor of the Interior, January 21, 1942 (approved by Margold on February 3, 1942).

77. Cited in Mitchell, *Sold American,* 281–82. The term curmudgeon is in reference to Harold L. Ickes, *The Autobiography of a Curmudgeon* (New York: 1943).

78. "Biographical Sketches of 8 New Judges," *Washington Post,* June 26, 1942, PHN; "8 Municipal Court Judges Confirmed," *Washington Post,* July 7, 1942, PHN; "Ickes Appoints Gardner Solicitor for Interior Dept.," *Washington Post,* August 27, 1942, PHN. "A native of Indiana, Gardner was educated at Swarthmore College, Rutgers University and the Columbia University Law School. He served Chief Justice Harlan F. Stone of the Supreme Court as a law clerk from 1934 to 1935 and later was employed in the office of the Solicitor General before [becoming the solicitor of] the Department of Labor." Ibid.

79. Mitchell, *Sold American,* 282–83.

80. Solicitor, Memorandum for Secretary of the Interior, November 11, 1942, FSCP 28/450; Mitchell, *Sold American,* 283.

81. FSC to Warner Gardner, October 15, 1942, cited in Mitchell, *Sold American,* 283.

82. Mitchell, *Sold American,* 283 (brackets in original).

83. Angrily, Cohen pointed out the "difference between postponing a hearing on a question and abrogating a complainant's rights." FSC, Memorandum for Solicitor of the Interior, January 28, 1943, FSCP 22/370.

84. S. 2227, 77th Cong., 2d. Session, January 26, 1942; Mitchell, *Sold American,* 283–84.

85. Discussed in S. 1446, H.R. 3859 (1947–1948): A bill to give America's most valuable fishing grounds to half a dozen large packing companies is the White-Tollefsen Bill, hearing on January 30, FSCP 22/370. See also Solicitor Margold, Memorandum for Harold Ickes, March 5, 1942, FSCP 22/370, approved and referred to the Fish and Wildlife Service on March 11, 1942.

86. FSC to Walter V. Woehlke, Esq., April 17, 1943, FSCP 22/370.

87. Ibid.

88. FSC, Memorandum for Mr. Wright, February 23, 1943, FSCP 21/356. See also The Problem of Alaskan Development, 5–16, 41, 42, FSCP 18/310.

89. Mitchell, *Sold American,* 277–78.

90. Philp, *Termination Revisited,* 35–36.

91. Mitchell, *Sold American,* 285–86.

92. Department of Interior, Press Release, December 14, 1944, FSCP 20/340; Department of Interior, Press Release, September 3, 1944, FSCP 20/338. See also Solicitor Harper, Memorandum for Secretary of the Interior, December 15, 1944, RG48//Entry 825/Box 1/Folder 4; Naske, *Ernest Gruening,* 233–35.

93. Mitchell, *Sold American,* 286–87.

94. FSC to Louise Devlin, Office of Solicitor, June 10, 1944, FSCP 19/335. See also correspondence between FSC and Kenneth R.L. Simmons, District Counsel, Office of Indian Affairs, Billings, Montana in FSCP 19/335, specifically letters dated May 19 and May 22, 1944.

95. FSC, Report to Commissioner of Indian Affairs re Work in Alaska June 15 to July 1, FSCP 19/335.

96. Solicitor Harper, Memorandum for Secretary of the Interior, July 13, 1944, FSCP 20/336.

97. Mitchell, *Sold American,* 286–88. See also Solicitor Harper to Richard H. Hanna (Night Letter, drafted by FSC), August 25, 1944, RG48//Entry 825/Box 1/Folder 4; Solicitor Harper to Norman Littell, Department of Justice, August 29, 1944, FSCP 20/337; Richard Hanna, Telegram to the Department of the Interior, August 26, 1944. Cohen initially supported appointing Hanna's partner, Brophy, as the administrative judge. Solicitor of Interior to Acting Secretary, August 25, 1944, FSCP 20/337. But he was happy with Hanna's appointment as Hanna had "acquired a very considerable knowledge of public land and Indian law." FSC to Theodore Haas, August 29, 1944, FSCP 20/337.

98. Notices re Hearings, FSCP 20/336. See also different petitions, RG48//Entry 825/Box 1/Folder 1.

99. Transcript of Proceedings, 3, RG48//Entry 825; Mitchell, *Sold American,* 287–88; Correspondence in FSCP, Box 20.

100. RG48//Entry 825/Box 1/Folder 3. See also Report of Presiding Chairman, Judge Richard Hanna, RG48//Entry 825/Box 1/Folder 1.

101. See letters from individual shareholders of J. R. Heckman and Company to Hanna, RG48//Entry 825/Box 10/Folder 24.

102. Transcript of Proceedings, 35–39, RG48//Entry 825; Mitchell, *Sold American,* 288.

103. Transcript of Proceedings, 40–41, RG48//Entry 825; Mitchell, *Sold American,* 288.

104. Mitchell, *Sold American,* 288; Transcript of Proceedings, RG48//Entry 825/Boxes 6–10.

105. Transcript of Proceedings, RG48//Entry 825.

106. See, for example, Transcript of Proceedings, 56–69, RG48//Entry 825.

107. Reply brief and proposed amended finding of fact and recommendation of petitioners, RG48//Entry 825/Box 5/Folder 8.

108. Transcript of Proceedings, 92–96, RG48//Entry 825.

109. Report of Presiding Chairman, Judge Richard Hanna, RG48//Entry 825/Box 1/Folder 1. See also transcripts, RG48//Entry 825/Boxes 6–10.

110. FSC, Report to Commissioner of Indian Affairs, re Work in Alaska June 15 to July 1, FSCP 19/335; Mitchell, *Sold American,* 288–89.

111. Mitchell, *Sold American,* 289.

112. Brief, Proposed Finding of Fact, Conclusions of Law, and Recommendations of Petitioners, RG48//Entry 825/Box 1/Folder 1; Transcript of Hearings, 462, RG48//Entry 825.

113. Report of Presiding Chairman, Judge Richard Hanna, RG48//Entry 825/Box 1/Folder

1; Mitchell, *Sold American,* 289–90; Claims of the Natives of Hydaburg, Klawock, and Kake, Alaska, "Statement of Facts," July 27, 1945, Summary File 9–1–52, Reservation of Lands for Natives, RG126, cited in Naske, *Ernest Gruening,* 237; Robert E. Price, *The Great Father in Alaska: The Case of the Tlingit and Haida Salmon Fishery* (Douglas, AK: 1990).

114. FSC to Theodore Haas, Chief Counsel, Office of Indian Affairs, May 27, 1944, FSCP 19/335.

115. M. 31634, Solicitor's Opinion, Fishing Rights of Alaskan Indians, February 13, 1942, *Opinions of the Solicitor,* 1096.

116. In Cohen's words: "Fisheries owned by a native town, as at Metlakahtla, contribute substantially to the wealth and development of the Territory, while the 'take' of corporate pirates tend to keep the Territory in the strait-jacket of a colonial economics." FSC, Report to Commissioner of Indian Affairs re Work in Alaska June 15 to July 1, FSCP 19/335.

117. FSC to George [Folta], Kenneth [Simmons], and Ted [Haas], November 13, 1944, FSCP 20/339. See also George Folta to Theodore H. Haas, December 7, 1944, RG48//Entry 825/Box 1/Folder 4.

118. Case and Voluck, *Alaska Natives,* 86.

119. FSC to George [Folta], Kenneth [Simmons], and Ted [Haas], November 13, 1944, FSCP 20/339.

120. Department of Interior, Press Release, FSCP 20/336.

121. Draft of Press Release, December 14, 1944, FSCP 20/340.

122. FSC to Gene Weltfish, Department of Anthropology, Columbia University, October 14, 1944, FSCP 20/338; Gene Weltfish to FSC, October 18, 1944, FSCP 20/338; Kenneth Simmons to Theodore Haas, October 25, 1944, FSCP 20/338; Studies of land use, FSCP 20/339; FSC to Theodore Haas, November 9, 1944, FSCP 20/339.

123. FSC, Memorandum for Solicitor of the Interior, June 22, 1945, FSCP 20/341.

124. Solicitor Harper, Memorandum for Secretary of the Interior, July 13, 1945, FSCP 20/341.

125. Harold Ickes, Claims of the Natives of Hydaburg, Klawock and Kake, Alaska, July 27, 1945, RG48//Entry 82/Box 1/Folder 1; Mitchell, *Sold American,* 290.

126. Harold Ickes, Claims of the Natives of Hydaburg, Klawock and Kake, Alaska, July 27, 1945, RG48//Entry 825/Box 1/Folder 1; Acting Commissioner Zimmerman, Memorandum for Secretary Warne, re: Alaska Reservation and Possessory Rights, FSCP 21/361; Department of Interior, Press Release, July 29, 1945, FSCP 20/341; FSC, Memorandum for the Under Secretary, October 22, 1947, FSCP 24/399; Mitchell, *Sold American,* 290; Naske, *Ernest Gruening,* 237.

127. See, for example, Warner W. Gardner, Memorandum for Secretary Krug December 26, 1946, RG48//Entry 825/Box 4/Folder 6.

128. Petitions for rehearing, RG48//Entry 825/Boxes 2–3; Order and Opinion No. 123903, January 11, 1946, RG48//Entry 825/Box 1/Folder 4. See also Case and Voluck, *Alaska Natives,* 86; Mitchell, *Sold American,* 290–91.

Chapter 9. A Contract with America

1. H. D. Rosenthal, *Their Day in Court: A History of the Indian Claims Commission* (New York: 1990), 3–5.

2. Ch. 122, 10 Stat. 612.

3. Ch. 92, § 9, 12 Stat. 765, 767. See also Charles F. Wilkinson et al., "The Indian Claims Commission," in *Indian Self-Rule,* 151; Michael Lieder and Jake Page, *Wild Justice: The People of Geronimo vs. The United States* (New York: 1997), 53.

4. Philp, *Termination Revisited,* 17; Rosenthal, *Their Day in Court,* 5–18.

5. Rosenthal, *Their Day in Court,* 18–19.

6. Lieder and Page, *Wild Justice,* 53–55.

7. Philp, *Termination Revisited,* 18. Wilkinson et al., "The Indian Claims Commission," 151–52.

8. Statement of Nathan R. Margold, Attorney at Law, "Survey of Conditions of Indians in the United States," Hearings before Subcommittee of Senate Committee on Indian Affairs,

70th and 71st Congress, part 25, pp. 13670–77, in *Legislative History of the Indian Claims Commission Act of 1946,* ed. Robert W. Barker and Alice Ehrenfeld (1976). See also "A Bill to create an Indian claims commission to provide for the powers, duties, and functions thereof, and for other purposes," in *Indian Claims Against the Government, Survey of Conditions of the Indians in the United States,* 72nd Congress, 1st session (Washington, D.C., 1932); Rosenthal, *Their Day in Court,* 20–27, 47–53.

9. For example, "In 1929, Congress permitted twenty-five thousand California Indians to submit a claim of $12.8 million for land lost after the Senate refused to ratify eighteen treaties in 1852" (in 1944, the Court of Claims awarded them $5 million). And "The Blackfeet, Klamath, Paiute, Shoshone, and Ute tribes hired Ernest Wilkinson, a Washington DC attorney, to present their cases before the Court of Claims." Other tribes followed suit. Philp, *Termination Revisited,* 18–19.

10. FSC, Memorandum of Work of Assistant Solicitor Felix S. Cohen, June 29, 1935, FSCP 49/741.

11. Rosenthal, *Their Day in Court,* 53–71. These bills are included in *Legislative History,* ed. Barker and Ehrenfeld.

12. S. 4234, 70th Congress, 2nd Session, August 1, 1940, Secretary of Interior to Elmer Thomas, U.S. Senate, n.d., Solicitor, Memorandum for the Secretary, ca. March 1941, all in *Legislative History,* ed. Barker and Ehrenfeld.

13. Ibid. See also Rosenthal, *Their Day in Court,* 71.

14. President Roosevelt to Secretary of the Interior, August 18, 1941, in *Legislative History,* ed. Barker and Ehrenfeld. The Solicitor's Office responded by suggesting the inclusion of a section in the proposed legislation that would require lawyers representing tribal claims to have their contracts approved by the secretary of the interior. According to Margold, this, together with a section prohibiting the secretary from approving such contracts if the commission had already disposed of the claims, would guarantee the finality of the commission's decisions. Nathan Margold, Memorandum for the Secretary, October 29, 1941, ibid.

15. H.R. 1198 was introduced together with H.R. 1341, an almost identical bill, although it did not require that one member of the commission would be an Indian. Hearings before the Committee on Indian Affairs House of Representatives, 79th Congress, 1st Session, on H.R. 1198 and H.R. 1341, March 2, 3, and 28; June 11 and 14, 1945, ibid. See also Philp, *Termination Revisited,* 19–21.

16. "Prolegomena," in *Irredeemable America: The Indians' Estate and Land Claims,* ed. Imre Sutton (Albuquerque: 1985), 4–5.

17. Philp, *Termination Revisited,* 21–22.

18. Ibid., 21.

19. Fredrick J. Stefon, "The Irony of Termination, 1943–1958," *The Indian Historian* 11 (1978): 4–5.

20. Testimony of Ernest Wilkinson, Hearings on H.R. 1198 and H.R. 1341, 109. See also Rosenthal, *Their Day in Court,* 27.

21. Mark A. Michaels, "Indigenous Ethics and Alien Laws: Native Traditions and the United States Legal System," *Fordham Law Review* 66 (1998): 1578–79; Michael C. Walch, "Terminating the Indian Termination Policy," *Stanford Law Review* 35 (1983): 1185–86.

22. Philp, *Termination Revisited,* 21–22.

23. Hearings on H.R. 1198 and H.R. 1341, 112–33, 140.

24. Ibid., 112–33; Philp, *Termination Revisited,* 23–25.

25. Hearings on H.R. 1198 and H.R. 1341, 133, 160; *Legislative History,* ed. Barker and Ehrenfeld; Lieder and Page, *Wild Justice,* 63; Rosenthal, *Their Day in Court,* 85–89.

26. Rosenthal, *Their Day in Court,* 87.

27. FSC, Memorandum for Commissioner of Indian Affairs, April 22, 1946, in *Legislative History,* ed. Barker and Ehrenfeld. See also Rosenthal, *Their Day in Court,* 85–90.

28. FSC, Memorandum for Commissioner of Indian Affairs, April 22, 1946, in *Legislative History,* ed. Barker and Ehrenfeld.

29. Rosenthal, *Their Day in Court,* 90–91.

30. Statement of the President, August 13, 1946, in *Legislative History,* ed. Barker and Ehrenfeld.

See also FSC, "Original Indian Title," in *Legal Conscience,* 304. Originally published in *Minnesota Law Review* 32 (1947): 28.

31. Lieder and Page, *Wild Justice,* 64.

32. FSC, "How We Bought the United States," *Collier's* 117 (January 19, 1946): 22, reprinted with adaptation in FSC, "Original Indian Title," 279–88. The material was also presented in a speech to the Indian Rights Association. FSC to John Collier, United Nations Assembly, England, January 11, 1946, FSCP 65/1041.

33. FSC, "Original Indian Title," 280.

34. Hearings on H.R. 1198 and H.R. 1341, 69–70. Cohen offered the Hualapai case as an exception to the general rule of transfer of land by treaty because the Supreme Court held that the Hualapai's acceptance of their reservation completed the transfer of land.

35. FSC, "Original Indian Title," 288.

36. See correspondence in FSCP 65/1041. See also Aviam Soifer, "Descent," *Florida State University Law Review* 29 (2002): 269.

37. Harold Ickes to FSC, January 17, 1946, FSCP 65/1041.

38. FSC, "Indian Claims," in *Legal Conscience,* 266. Originally published in *The American Indian* 2 (1945): 3.

39. FSC, "Indians are Citizens!" in *Legal Conscience*, 253. Originally published in *The American Indian* 1 (1944): 12.

40. FSC, "Indians are Citizens!" 254–55. For a contemporary contractual approach, see the discussion of "treaty federalism." Barsh and Henderson, *The Road,* 279–87.

41. FSC, "Indian Claims," 268.

42. FSC, "Foreword" to *Combating Totalitarian Propaganda: A Legal Appraisal,* (Washington, DC: 1944), i.

43. Ibid.

44. FSC to Editors of *Collier's,* January 26, 1945, FSCP 65/1040.

45. FSC to John Collier, United Nations Assembly, England, January 11, 1946, FSCP 65/1041.

46. FSC, "How We Bought the United States," 22.

47. John Collier to FSC, January 18, 1946, FSCP 65/1041.

48. FSC to Harold Ickes, January 22, 1946, FSCP 65/1041.

49. FSC, "Indians are Citizens!" 257.

50. Ibid.

51. Robert Cover, "Obligation: A Jewish Jurisprudence of the Social Order," in *Narrative, Violence, and the Law: The Essays of Robert Cover,* ed. Martha Minow, Michael Ryan, and Austin Sarat (Ann Arbor, MI: 1995), 239. Originally published in *Journal of Law and Religion* 5 (1987): 65.

52. FSC, "Indians are Citizens!" 257.

53. FSC, "Indian Claims," 266–72.

54. Ibid., 272.

55. Ironically, in practice, government attorneys transferred the Court of Claims' procedures to the commission, transforming it into a court and eliminating the flexibility that Cohen hoped to achieve by creating an investigatory commission. Vine Deloria Jr., *Behind the Trail of Broken Treaties: An Indian Declaration of Independence* (Austin, TX: 1985), 222–26.

56. Philp, *Termination Revisited,* 29. See also Ernest Wilkinson to the President, December 3, 1946, FSCP 53/819, recommending Cohen for the position.

57. Rosenthal, *Their Day in Court,* 112–15. The claims arrived very slowly. Many tribes found it hard to secure representation, and many lawyers preferred to delay filing to see decisions in the early cases. Only 263 claims were filed by early 1951. Then, in the last weeks of the five-year filing period, tribes and their attorneys rushed to file their claims. By the end of the filing period, 852 claims were filed, which were "consolidated into 370 dockets representing about 600 claims." The government's responses also came in slowly. By 1956, more than 5,000 requests for the extension of time to respond were filed and 200 of the 852 claims remained unanswered. Ibid.

58. Ibid., 135–37. Accounting claims were slightly different and most of them were filed only late in the second decade of the commission's life. Ibid., 139.

59. Ibid., 119–27, 137–39. On expert testimony, see Ralph L. Beals, "The Anthropologist as

Expert Witness: Illustrations from the California Indian Land Claims Case," in *Irredeemable America,* 139. On appraisals and offsets, see Leonard A. Carlson, "What Was It Worth? Economic and Historical Aspects of Determining Awards in Indian Land Claims Cases," in *Irredeemable America,* 87.

60. Wilcomb E. Washburn, "Land Claims in the Mainstream of Indian/White Land History," in *Irredeemable America,* 24; Ward Churchill, "The Earth is Our Mother: Struggles for American Indian Land and Liberation in the Contemporary United States," in *The State of Native America,* 139, 147.

61. Washburn, "Land Claims," 24.

62. James E. Officer, "Termination as Federal Policy: An Overview," in *Indian Self-Rule,* 114, 118; Wilkinson et al., "The Indian Claims Commission," 152; Michaels, "Indigenous Ethics," 1578. It is important to note that the ICCA brought about conflicts between tribal members who wished to settle the claims and those who wished a "full accounting by the United States of its illegal acts against the tribe." Deloria, *Behind the Trail of Broken Treaties,* 226–28.

63. Philp, *Termination Revisited,* 30–31.

64. Harvey D. Rosenthal, "Indian Claims and the American Conscience: A Brief History of the Indian Claims Commission," in *Irredeemable America,* 48.

65. Ibid., 48–52.

66. *United States v. Alcea Band of Tillamooks,* 329 U.S. 40 (1946).

67. FSC to Mary-K Morris Bell, November 29, 1946, FSCP 71/1132.

68. FSC, "Original Indian Title," 301–4.

69. *United States v. Alcea Band of Tillamooks,* 341 U.S. 48 (1951); Rosenthal, *Their Day in Court,* 148.

70. *Tee-Hit-Ton Indians v. United States,* 348 U.S. 272 (1955); Rosenthal, *Their Day in Court,* 149.

71. *Otoe and Missouria Tribes of Indians v. United States,* 131 Ct. Cl. 593 (1955); Rosenthal, *Their Day in Court,* 149. On Cohen's role in protecting timber rights in Alaska, see *infra.*

72. Philp, *Termination Revisited,* 29.

73. Case and Voluck, *Alaska Natives,* 86.

74. FSC, Memorandum for Assistant Secretary Gardner, December 3, 1946, FSCP 21/361.

75. Dr. Walter R. Goldschmidt and Theodore H. Haas, A Report to the Commissioner of Indian Affairs, Possessory Rights of the Natives of Southeastern Alaska: A Detailed Analysis of the Early and Present Territory Used and Occupied by the Natives of Southeastern Alaska, except the Natives of Kake (partially treated), Hydaburg, and Klawock, December 3, 1946, RG48//Entry 825/Box 4/Folder 6. See also Philp, *Termination Revisited,* 37.

76. Warner W. Gardner, Memorandum for Secretary Krug, January 30, 1947, RG48//Entry 825/Box 4/Folder 6; Warner W. Gardner, Memorandum for Secretary Krug, December 26, 1946, RG48//Entry 825/Box 4/Folder 6. See also Philp, *Termination Revisited,* 36.

77. FSC, Memorandum for the Secretary, June 19, 1946, FSCP 25/410.

78. Associate Solicitor, Memorandum for Assistant Secretary Warne re: S.1446, H.R. 3859, FSCP 25/412; Warner W. Gardner, Memorandum for Secretary Krug, December 26, 1946, RG48//Entry 825/Box 4/Folder 6; FSC, Memorandum for the Secretary, June 19, 1946, RG48//Entry 825/Box 1/Folder 4. For the agreement, see W.C. Arnold, Managing Director of the Alaska Salmon Industry, Inc. to Warner Gardner, June 11, 1946, RG48//Entry 825/Box 1/Folder 4. According to the agreement the Hydaburg Cooperative Association would pay the Harris company half of the cost of operating the fish trap and transferring the fish. See also Philp, *Termination Revisited,* 36.

79. Philp, *Termination Revisited,* 39–40. See also Secretary of Interior, Memorandum for Speaker of the House of Representatives, Joseph W. Martin Jr., M. 19471, RG48//Entry 825/Box 4/Folder 6.

80. Philp, *Termination Revisited,* 40–41, 241–43; Naske, *Ernest Gruening,* 239–40. For a copy of the bill see Secretary of Interior, Memorandum for the Speaker of the House of Representative, Joseph W. Martin Jr., 19471, RG48//Entry 825/Box 4/Folder 6.

81. FSC, "Alaska Nuremberg's Laws: Congress Sanctions Racial Discrimination," *Commentary*

6 (1948): 136–43. See also FSC, "Breaking Faith with Our First Americans," *Indian Truth* 25 (1948): 1–8; Letter, July 28, 1948, FSCP 63/995.

82. Philp, *Termination Revisited,* 43. See also "Cohen Raps Alaska Colonialism," *Alaska Federationist,* Juneau Alaska, May 1948, FSCP 27/438; Memorandum on Native Economic Enterprises in Alaska, FSCP 21/351. On Interior's plans with respect to the Tongass Act, see also Under Secretary, Memorandum for Secretary of Agriculture, October 8, 1947, FSCP 24/399.

83. FSC, Margold's Address (draft), FSCP 10/137; FSC, Law and Order (Memorandum), FSCP 1/11.

84. FSC, "Colonialism: A Realistic Approach," in *Legal Conscience,* 380. Originally published in *Ethics* 55 (1945): 167.

85. Philp, *Termination Revisited,* 37.

86. See, for instance, Memorandum on Butler-Watkins-D'ewart Bill to Abolish Alaska Native Reserves, FSCP 24/401; Memorandum of Information re S. 2037 (to transfer to the Territorial Government of Alaska the administration within such territory of laws relating to Indians), FSCP 24/401. See also Naske, *Ernest Gruening,* 242.

87. FSC to Don Foster, January 5, 1950, FSCP 28/443.

88. See, for example, Solicitor Mastin G. White, Memorandum for Secretary of the Interior, October 15, 1947, FSCP 27/442, indicating that the order designating the Hydaburg reservation could include water within the reservation; FSC, Memorandum for the Files, December 10, 1947, FSCP 42/639.

89. See, for example, FSC to Mr. Clarence Peele, Hydaburg, Alaska, February 18, 1950, FSCP 28/443.

90. See, for example, E. G. Griggs (President) and T. A. Stevenson (Manager), Tacoma Chamber of Commerce, Resolution, November 13, 1944, attached to letter to Hanna, November 13, 1944, RG48//Entry 825/Box 10/Folder 24.

91. Marvin H. Coleman, Sunset Incorporated, to Judge Richard Hanna, November 3, 1944, RG48//Entry 825/Box 10/Folder 24.

92. Cordova Chamber of Commerce, Protest, sent to Secretary Ickes and Judge Hanna, November 13, 1944, RG48//Entry 825/Box 10/Folder 24.

93. Alaska Board of Examiners in Optometry to Richard Hanna, November 5, 1944, RG48//Entry 825/Box 10/Folder 24.

94. W. O. Carlson, president, and Chas W. Carter, secretary, Igloo No. 6 Pioneers of Alaska, to Hanna, October 3, 1944, RG48//Entry 825/Box 10/Folder 24.

95. Alaska Board of Examiners in Optometry to Richard Hanna, November 5, 1944, RG48//Entry 825/Box 10/Folder 24.

96. Warner Gardner, Memorandum for Secretary Krug, March 12, 1947, RG48//Entry 825/Box 4/Folder 6.

97. FSC, Memorandum for Assistant Secretary Chapman, August 28, 1944, FSCP 20/337, attacking Governor Gruening's pronounced objection to the reservation policy.

98. Philp, *Termination Revisited,* 48–49; Naske, *Ernest Gruening,* 243–44; Don Foster to FSC, March 21, 1950, FSCP 28/443; FSC to Cyrus Peck, Grand President, Grand Camp, Alaska Native Brotherhood, Sitka, Alaska, January 17, 1950, FSCP 28/443.

99. FSC to Cyrus Peck, Grand President, Grand Camp, Alaska Native Brotherhood, Sitka, Alaska, January 17, 1950, FSCP 28/443.

100. Sandel, *Democracy's Discontent,* 251–62; Brinkley, *End of Reform,* 269. See also Alan Brinkley, "The New Deal and the Idea of the State," in *The Rise and Fall of the New Deal Order, 1930–1980,* ed. Steve Fraser and Gary Gerstle (Princeton, NJ: 1989), 112.

101. 337 U.S. 86 (1949).

102. Mitchell, *Sold American,* 278.

103. Ibid.

104. Case and Voluck, *Alaska Natives,* 87.

105. Mitchell, *Sold American,* 278–79; Case and Voluck, *Alaska Natives,* 87–88; Association on American Indian Affairs, Press Release, October 16, 1948, FSCP 26/426.

106. Case and Voluck, *Alaska Natives,* 88.

107. "A Fishy Decision?" FSCP 27/431.

108. Case and Voluck, *Alaska Natives,* 88.

109. Mitchell, *Sold American,* 279.

110. *Grimes Packing Company v. Hynes,* 67 F. Supp. 43 (1946).

111. *Hynes v. Grimes Packing Company,* 165 F. 2d 323, 324–25 (1947).

112. Ibid., 325.

113. Ibid., 325–26.

114. Ibid., 330.

115. In fact, he believed that the whole suit was an attempt by the canning companies and the Director of the Fish and Wildlife Service to deprive Alaska Natives of their rights. FSC to Roger Baldwin, ACLU, September 28, 1948, FSCP 26/426.

116. This was not an obvious conclusion. In 1936, Cohen noted that the term "public lands" did not necessarily include waters and that such interpretation might "arouse a good deal of protest by white interests in Alaska." FSC, Memorandum for Harper, December 21, 1936, FSCP 24/403.

117. RB (Hynes v. Grimes).

118. *Hynes v. Grimes Packing Company,* 337 U.S. 86, 122–23 (1949).

119. Ibid., 95–96.

120. Case and Voluck, *Alaska Natives,* 88.

121. Cited in Mitchell, *Sold American,* 279–80.

122. FSC to Larry M. Ellanak, President, Council of Karluk Native Village, June 11, 1949, FSCP 26/427.

123. Ibid.; Case and Voluck, *Alaska Natives,* 89.

124. FSC to Larry M. Ellanak, President, Council of Karluk Native Village, June 11, 1949, FSCP 26/427; Case and Voluck, *Alaska Natives,* 90. See similarly Memorandum on Native Economic Enterprises in Alaska, FSCP 21/351.

125. FSC to Alexander Lesser, January 5, 1950, FSCP 26/428.

126. *United States v. Libby, McNeil and Libby* 107 F. Supp 697 (1952). See also Naske, *Ernest Gruening,* 244. The Hydaburg reservation was created by Secretary Krug on his last night in office (November 30, 1949). Unexpectedly Krug signed orders that established reservations for the villages of Hydaburg, Barrow, Shungnak, and Kobuk (making the reservations contingent upon Alaska Natives waiving any claims for fisheries and minerals). All villages except Hydaburg rejected the proposed reservations. The condition, which Cohen and Ickes criticized, was removed by Secretary Chapman a month later. Price, *The Great Father in Alaska,* 128.

127. Price, *The Great Father in Alaska,* 132–33.

128. Case and Voluck, *Alaska Natives,* 62–63, 92–93.

Chapter 10. In the Shadows of the Law

1. FSC to Samuel E. Thorne, Yale Law Library, February 5, 1947, JPLP. For the words of Callimachus, see FSC to Florence Shientag (upon the death of her husband, Judge Bernard Shientag), May 26, 1952, FSCP 89/1421. Cohen seems to have used William Johnson Cory's 1891 translation of the epigram of Callimachus. See also FSC to Robert L. Hale, Columbia Law School, February 28, 1947, FSCP 87/1371; FSC to Harold J. Laski, May 16, 1947, FSCP 87/1387.

2. Lucy Kramer Cohen to Benjamin Kaplan, Harvard Law School, February 18, 1955, FSCP 93/1490. See also Stephen Haycox, "Felix S. Cohen and the Legacy of the Indian New Deal," *Yale University Library Gazette* 68 (1994): 147.

3. FSC to Secretary Krug, December 15, 1947, FSCP 92/1473. See also FSC, testimonial dinner, January 17, 1948, FSCP 92/1470; FSC to S. I. Hayakawa, University of Chicago, February 9, 1949, FSCP 87/1371; *Ketchikan Daily News,* FSCP 90/1446. As expected, Krug's response indicated Cohen's tremendous contributions to the public interest. "Your brilliant mind, your untiring energy, your zeal for the defense and promotion of the public interest, and your broad comprehension of the place of law in modern society," Krug wrote, "have made you one of the

Government's most valuable employees." Secretary of Interior (signed Cap) to FSC, December 16, 1947, FSCP 92/1473.

4. Interviews, JPLP.

5. Haas, ed., *Felix S. Cohen*, 23.

6. Norman Thomas to FSC, November 14, 1933, JPLP.

7. D'arcy McNickle, testimonial dinner, January 17, 1948, FSCP 92/1470.

8. FSC to William A. Brophy, February 11, 1948, FSCP 90/1445. See also FSC, testimonial dinner, January 17, 1948, FSCP 92/1470:

> All who came to Washington in 1933 will remember that many of us thought then that we were not far from the Divine Throne. The fate of the world seemed to rest on the wisdom and the power that the President brought to bear on the great problems that faced him during those critical days. It seemed to me that when the problems really became peculiarly difficult or novel, the President usually turned to the Secretary of the Interior. . . . And the Secretary of the Interior, when he found novel problems which could not be solved by time-honored procedures, problems which called for the drafting of new laws or the breaking of new legal paths, would generally turn them over to Solicitor Margold, who turned them over to me. . . . I would be blind if I didn't see that the President and the Secretary and the Solicitor are not quite as close to the Throne as I thought they were in 1933. Perhaps I have grown older and I have changed. The fact remains that year by year, I got fewer and fewer central problems. Perhaps the problems of the Department are less important now; perhaps these problems are of a different kind. They are not problems of trail blazing. I believe that we have made solid gains which are still on the statute books. But I have learned that it is not enough to achieve the reality of words. The words of statutes are important to the solution of a problem, but they must be implemented, defended, maintained. That calls for efforts and abilities which I don't feel that I can contribute. The tasks that I could not finish will be carried on better by others.

9. Cohen to Thomas I. Emerson, Yale Law School, April 25, 1947, FSCP 86/1364; Notes for Legislative Seminar Meeting, FSCP 59/930.

10. Cohen to Dean Sturges, Yale Law School, January 4, 1946, FSCP 58/519.

11. Philp, *Termination Revisited*, 109–10.

12. Ibid.

13. Rosenthal, *Their Day in Court*, 118.

14. Interviews, JPLP.

15. *Trujillo v. Garley* (D.N.M., August 3, 1948, unreported) and *Harrison and Austin v. Laveen*, 196 P.2d 456 (1948).

16. See *Acosta v. County of San Diego*, 272 P.2d 92 (1954); *Arizona v. Hobby*, 221 F.2d 498 (1954). See also FSC to Mr. Royal D. Marks, Phoenix, Arizona, October 9, 1948, FSCP 52/791; FSC to Mr. Royal D. Marks, Phoenix, Arizona, November 17, 1948, FSCP 52/791. See generally "Symposium: Felix S. Cohen," 348–49.

17. FSC to Drew Pearson, August 21, 1952, FSCP 94/1503.

18. The conference studied issues such as the sociological and ideological significance of concentration camps as instruments of the totalitarian state; transferring property of German origin to the custody of the Jewish Cultural Reconstruction Inc.; economic adjustment and resettlement, including the psychological and sociological characteristics of survivors of extermination camps, and factors affecting immigration to Latin American countries; the status and trends of American Jews in the professions; Jewish demography; and anti-Semitism. FSCP 84/1319.

19. Philp, *Collier's Crusade*, 214–15.

20. FSC, Circular to Indian Communities, February 29, 1952, FSCP 52/795.

21. See, for example, FSC to Mr. Jacob Billikopf, Philadelphia, October 10, 1950, FSCP 50/755. In 1939, Cohen helped guarantee that African-American singer Marian Anderson could sing from the Lincoln Memorial after the Daughters of the American Revolution had denied her access to Constitution Hall. The free event drew a crowd of 75,000 and was broadcast to millions.

In July 1939 Eleanor Roosevelt presented Anderson with the NAACP's Spingarn Medal. See www.library.upenn.edu/exhibits/rbm/anderson/

22. FSC, Communist Double Talk: Trap for Good Americans, FSCP 63/1010, criticizing different immigration bills; FSC, "Enacting Entry Bans," *New York Times*, July 6, 1952, FSCP 64/1043; FSC to Harry Rosenfield, July 13, 1950, FSCP 88/1414, enclosing a bill to pool unused immigration quotas; FSC to Javits, September 12, 1951, FSCP 63/999; FSC to Harry Rosenfield, October 1, 1951, FSCP 88/1414; FSC to Read Lewis, Executive Director, Common Council for American Unity, FSCP 88/1414; Sidney Liskofsky to Jules Cohen, February 12, 1952 (cc FSC), FSCP 50/757.

23. FSC to John Slawson, executive vice president, American Jewish Committee, January 18, 1950, FSCP 50/755.

24. Institute of Living Law, Minutes, July 7, 1947, FSCP 78/1226.

25. FSC to John Slawson, American Jewish Committee, February 25, 1948, FSCP 50/751.

26. See American Institute of Ethnic Affairs, FSCP 51/776; FSC to John Collier, March 3, 1945, FSCP 51/780; FSC to Moses Moskowitz, Consultative Council of Jewish Organizations, March 3, 1950, FSCP 51/770; FSC, Testimony on migrant Indian workers before the Senate Committee on Labor and Labor Management, delivered March 28, 1952, FSCP 52/795. See also FSCP 51, containing information about Cohen's work with the Consultative Council of Jewish Organizations to draft a memorandum to the Commission on Human Rights and its Sub-Commission on the Prevention of Discrimination and Protection of Minorities, January 1950.

27. FSC, "Our Country's Shame," *The Progressive* 13 (1949): 9–10.

28. Michaels, "Indigenous Ethics," 1578–79; Walch, "Terminating the Indian Termination Policy," 1185–86.

29. FSC, letter to *The Progressive*, March 7, 1951, FSCP 63/1008.

30. Thomas Biolsi, *"Deadliest Enemies,"* 13–14.

31. Philp, *Termination Revisited,* 77–79.

32. FSC, Draft, FSCP 10/145. See also FSC, "Americanizing the White Man," in *Legal Conscience,* 315. Originally published in *The American Scholar* 21 (1952): 177.

33. Richard Drinnon, *Keeper of Concentration Camps: Dillon S. Myer and American Racism* (Berkeley, CA: 1987), 21–25, 217.

34. Ibid., 215–17, 170.

35. Philp, *Termination Revisited,* 87–88. For the different programs Myer initiated, see ibid., 89–107.

36. Ibid., 93–99.

37. See Solicitor's Opinion, Powers of Indian Tribes, October 25, 1934, *Opinions of the Solicitor.* The following sections rely on Kenneth Philp's and Richard Drinnon's excellent research for factual background. Philp and Drinnon offer very comprehensive accounts of Myer's actions as commissioner of Indian affairs. The following sections offer only a few examples focusing on Myer's interactions with Cohen. See Philp, *Termination Revisited* and Drinnon, *Keeper of Concentration Camps.*

38. Cohen's first encounter with Myer took place in 1943, when Myer's WRA "negotiated a memorandum of understanding" with Interior "covering the relocation of ten thousand Japanese on the Gila River Indian Reservation in Arizona." Cohen objected to the term "Japanese" used in reference to native-born Americans of Japanese descent, as distinguished from Japanese evacuees, and Collier agreed. Drinnon, *Keeper of Concentration Camps,* 30–31.

39. Philp, *Termination Revisited,* 111–14. See also Robert Yellowtail, chairman, Crow Tribal Council, Lodge Grass, Montana, Selection of Indian Counsel—Pro and Con (weekly newsletter to all Indians), FSCP 94/1503.

40. Philp, *Termination Revisited,* 113.

41. Ibid., 115–16.

42. Drinnon, *Keeper of Concentration Camps,* 194–95.

43. Philp, *Termination Revisited,* 116–18.

44. Ibid., 118–23. See also FSC to John W. Smith, mayor, Council Annette Islands Reserve, Metlakatla, Alaska, March 9, 1953, FSCP 27/437.

45. FSC, "The Erosion of Indian Rights, 1950–1953: A Case Study in Bureaucracy," *Yale Law*

Journal 62 (1953): 355–56; Drinnon, *Keeper of Concentration Camps,* 208–13; Philp, *Termination Revisited,* 123–24.

46. Philp, *Termination Revisited,* 125–31.

47. Ibid., 125–39. See also M. 36141, Solicitor's Opinion, Eligibility to Vote on Amendment to Blackfeet Constitution, July 18, 1952, *Opinions of the Solicitor,* 1582–85; FSC, "The Erosion of Indian Rights," 353–55.

48. Drinnon, *Keeper of Concentration Camps,* 221; FSC, "The Erosion of Indian Rights," 368.

49. Philp, *Termination Revisited,* 148.

50. Newspapers, JCP 34/307; FSCP 67/1069; FSC, "The Erosion of Indian Rights," 358; Philp, *Termination Revisited,* 148–49.

51. Statement of Commissioner of Indian Affairs Dillon S. Myer regarding the Testimony of FSC on H.R. 6036, April 21, 1952, FSCP 67/1069. See also Philp, *Termination Revisited,* 149.

52. Philp, *Termination Revisited,* 150. As Philp notes, Chapman also did not support Myer's six bills seeking to subject reservations to state jurisdiction. See also Drinnon, *Keeper of Concentration Camps,* 224–28.

53. Dillon S. Myer, Testimony before the Committee on Appropriations, House of Representatives, March 9, 1951, FSCP 94/1503. For Cohen's response, see FSC to Dillon S. Myer, May 16, 1951, FSCP 94/1503.

54. Drinnon, *Keeper of Concentration Camps,* 223–24.

55. Richard Shifter to Fred Blumenthal, August 15, 1952, FSCP 94/1503 (emphasis in original). Cohen had no financial interest in the outcome of the cases as he acted as a consultant whose fees were paid "out of the pockets of attorneys in the Group." These fees were "under no circumstances chargeable to the Indians or the Government, [and were] the same whether the cases [were] won or lost." Ibid. See also Interviews, JPLP; Drinnon, *Keeper of Concentration Camps,* 223–24.

56. Drinnon, *Keeper of Concentration Camps,* 231–32. See also FSC to Drew Pearson, August 21, 1952, FSCP 94/150.

57. Drinnon, *Keeper of Concentration Camps,* 245–46. See also FSC to Arthur Meyer, March 27, 1953, FSCP 64/1024, noting, that he was "much gratified by the acceptance of Commissioner Myer's resignation, but [he] should doubt that there was any direct connection between the article and the resignation. On the other hand, [he felt] reasonably sure that there was a close connection between the incidents reported in the article and the resignation—which is as it should be."

58. Philp, *Termination Revisited,* 151–69; Stefon, "The Irony of Termination," 7.

59. Walch, "Terminating the Indian Termination Policy," 1185–86.

60. Judith V. Royster, "The Legacy of Allotment," *Arizona State University Law Journal* 27 (1995): 18; Sharon O'Brien, *American Indian Tribal Governments* (Norman, OK: 1989), 85–86.

61. Walch, "Terminating the Indian Termination Policy," 1188–90.

62. FSC, "Colonialism: U.S. Style," *The Progressive* 15 (1951): 16–18.

63. Horwitz, *The Transformation of American Law, 1870–1960,* 250–58.

64. Ibid. See, for example, Robert A. Dahl, *A Preface to Democratic Theory* (Chicago: 1956); Robert A. Dahl, *Pluralist Democracy in The United States: Conflict and Consent* (Chicago: 1967).

65. Purcell, *The Crisis of Democratic Theory,* 253–66.

66. FSC, "Indian Self-Government," in *Legal Conscience,* 305. Originally published in *The American Indian* 5 (1949): 3–12.

67. FSC to Sister Providencia, College of Great Falls, Montana, June 10, 1950, FSCP 88/1410.

68. FSC, "Indian Self-Government," 307. See also *supra* Chapter 5.

69. FSC, "Colonialism: U.S. Style."

70. FSC, "The Erosion of Indian Rights," 387.

71. FSC, "Indian Self-Government," 308–9.

72. Ibid.

73. William James, "On a Certain Blindness in Human Beings" (1899), in *The Writings of William James,* ed. John J. McDermott (Chicago: 1977), 629.

74. George Cotkin, *William James, Public Philosopher* (Baltimore: 1990).

75. Anthony Skillen, "William James, 'A Certain Blindness' and an Uncertain Pluralism," in *Philosophy and Pluralism,* ed. David Archard (Cambridge, UK: 1996), 33–45.

76. John Collier, president, to FSC, director, June 14, 1946, FSCP 51/781.

77. The American Institute of Ethnic Affairs, Inc., FSCP 57/776; Certificate of Incorporation, FSCP 57/777.

78. The American Institute of Ethnic Affairs, Inc., FSCP 57/776; Certificate of Incorporation, FSCP 57/777.

79. The American Institute of Ethnic Affairs, Inc., FSCP 57/776; Certificate of Incorporation, FSCP 57/777.

80. FSC, "Americanizing the White Man," 315, 324; FSC to Richard R. Powell, Columbia University, August 10, 1948, FSCP 88/1409.

81. "Author's Acknowledgments" in *Handbook* (1942), xxi.

82. FSC, "Indian Self-Government," 308.

83. Second Draft of Final Chapter (Chapter VII: Summary, Conclusions and Recommendations), attached to FSC to Moses Moskowitz, Secretary, Consultative Council of Jewish Organizations, February 21, 1949, FSCP 50/765. Cohen explained to Moskowitz that "human beings have a legitimate interest in what happens on the other side of a boundary line and . . . any international arrangement which ignores this fact is, from the standpoint of minority protection, self-defeating." FSC to Moses Moskowitz, March 28, 1949, FSCP 51/770.

84. FSC to Felix Frankfurter, August 28, 1953, FSCP 64/1025, noting that the Indian was "a key figure in the whole world problem of interracial and international relations that is, in some ways, the number one challenge of the twentieth century to western man."

85. FSC, "Erosion of Indian Rights," 390. See also FSC (unsigned), "Experiment in Immortality," *The Nation,* July 26, 1952, FSCP 64/1027. FSC's draft title was "Indian Bureau Double Talk."

86. FSC, "Indian Self-Government," 313–14. See also FSC, Testimony before the Senate Sub-Committee on Labor and Labor Management (March 1952), FSCP 52/795; Drinnon, *Keeper of Concentration Camps,* 268–69.

87. FSC to Lt. Col. F.V. Cahill, September 10, 1951, FSCP 62/966.

88. FSC, "Transcendental Nonsense," 45.

89. FSC, "Field Theory and Judicial Logic," in *Legal Conscience,* 128. Originally published in *Yale Law Journal* 59 (1951): 238.

90. Ibid., 129 (emphasis in original).

91. Ibid., 130–32.

92. Ibid., 131. See also FSC, "The Reconstruction of Hidden Value Judgments: Word Choices as Value Indicators," in *Symbols and Values,* ed. Lyman Bryson (New York: 1954), 545.

93. FSC, "Transcendental Nonsense," 70.

94. FSC, "Field Theory," 131.

95. Ibid., 133–35.

96. Ibid., 148.

97. Ibid., 149–50.

98. As Cohen put it, "The adjective, *Negro,* may be entirely relevant to a discussion of the medical effects of sunburn, and the adjective, *Jewish,* may be entirely relevant to a discussion of religious ritual. The relevance of these adjectives to a report of a crime wave, however, may depend upon the inarticulate premise that Negroes or Jews are especially disposed to criminal activity. Such inarticulate premises make the difference between sympathetic and unsympathetic accounts of the same event." FSC, "Hidden Value Judgments," 545–48.

99. FSC, "The Vocabulary of Prejudice," in *Legal Conscience,* 430–35. Originally published in *Fellowship Magazine* 19 (1953): 5–10. See also FSC, "Hidden Value Judgments."

100. FSC, "Hidden Value Judgments," 549, 551.

101. Ibid., 561; FSC, "Vocabulary of Prejudice," 435.

102. FSC, "Field Theory," 134, 126.

103. Ibid., 150–51.

104. FSC to Sister Providencia, who helped Cohen in his work on the Blackfeet reservation, College of Great Falls, Montana, January 4, 1951, FSCP 88/1410.

105. FSC to Charlotte Anschuetz Bleistein, August 3, 1951, FSCP 86/1341.

106. FSC, "The Democratic Faith," Address before the Yale Philosophy Club, New Haven, January 1951, in *Legal Conscience,* 428.

107. FSC to Sister Providencia, Sacred Heart Hospital, Washington, July 13, 1950, FSCP 88/1410.

108. FSC, "Field Theory," 156–57.

109. FSC, "Judicial Ethics," Address at symposium on "Ethical Values and the Law in Action" at the College of Law, Ohio State University, February 25, 1950, in *Legal Conscience,* 170. Originally published in *Ohio State Law Journal* 12 (1951): 3.

110. FSC, "The Making of Americanism," FSCP 71/1140.

Epilogue

1. Holmes, "The Path of the Law."

2. Compare Ernst, "Common Laborers?" 60.

3. Kennedy, *Critique of Adjudication,* 88.

4. Dahl, *A Preface to Democratic Theory* and *Pluralist Democracy.*

5. See, for example, Laurence H. Tribe, "The Puzzling Persistence of Process-Based Constitutional Theories," *Yale Law Journal* 89 (1980): 1063.

6. Declaration of Indian Purpose (June 1961), President Nixon, Special Message on Indian Affairs (July 8, 1970), and Indian Self Determination and Education Assistance Act (January 4, 1975), all in Prucha, ed., *Documents of U.S. Indian Policy,* 245–47, 256–58, 275–77.

7. See, for example, *The Politics of Law: A Progressive Critique,* ed. David Kairys (New York: 1998).

8. See, for example, "Symposium: Formalism Revisited," The *University of Chicago Law Review* 66 (1999): 527.

9. Deut, 30:12–14.

10. Max Goldman to Louis Lowenstein Jr., January 29, 1953, FSCP 87/1368.

11. FSC, "A Student Homage: Jerome Michael," *Columbia Law Review* 53 (1953): 312–14.

12. Interviews, JPLP.

13. Lucy Kramer Cohen to Dr. James J. Feffer, January 14, 1954, FSCP 93/1488; Interviews, JPLP.

14. Interviews, JPLP.

15. FSC to Pearl Ann, August 11, 1953, FSCP 88/1390.

16. FSC to Dean Sturges, Yale Law School, September 4, 1953, FSCP 60/947; FSC to Daniel Bronstein, CCNY, September 4, 1953, FSCP 60/954.

17. Interviews, JPLP.

18. Lucy Kramer Cohen et al., "Felix Cohen and the Adoption of the IRA," 71.

19. Cited in Haas, ed., *Felix S. Cohen,* 20.

20. FSC, "The Challenge of Racism," *A Review of Jewish Interests,* October 19, 1953, 12–13, FSCP 62/969.

21. Ibid.

22. Lucy Kramer Cohen to Dr. James J. Feffer, January 14, 1954, FSCP 93/1488.

23. FSC, "Law for the Immigrant," *The New Leader,* November 9, 1953, FSCP 62/975.

24. Lucy Kramer Cohen to Dr. James J. Feffer, January 14. 1954, FSCP 93/1488. See also FSCP 62/975.

25. Newspapers, JCP 34/306.

26. William O. Douglas, "Some Pertinent Reflections on Democratic Institutions," *New York Times Book Review,* entered in the Congressional Record at the suggestion of Senator Humphrey on March 28, 1961, pp. 4683–84, FSCP 72/1145.

27. FSCP 92/1475.

28. FSCP 93.

29. Joseph Rosenfarb, cited in Haas, ed., *Felix S. Cohen,* 29.

30. Cited in Haas, ed., *Felix S. Cohen,* 16.

31. Micah, 6:8 cited in FSC, "The Menace of Government by Experts," FSCP 70/1128.

Selected Bibliography

Archival Collections

Bureau of Indian Affairs, Records, RG 75, The National Archives, Washington, D.C.

Felix S. Cohen Papers, Yale Collection of Western Americana, Beinecke Rare Book and Manuscript Library, Yale University, New Haven, Connecticut.

Handbook of Federal Indian Law Papers, Yale Collection of Western Americana, Beinecke Rare Book and Manuscript Library, Yale University, New Haven, Connecticut.

Office of the Secretary of the Interior, Records, RG 48, The National Archives, College Park, Maryland.

John Collier Papers (microfilm), Sterling Memorial Library, Yale University, New Haven, Connecticut.

Joseph P. Lash Papers, Franklin D. Roosevelt Presidential Library, Hyde Park, New York.

The Lavender, John Hay Library, Brown University, Providence, Rhode Island.

Morris R. Cohen Papers, Special Collections Research Center, Joseph Regenstein Library, University of Chicago, Chicago, Illinois.

U.S. House of Representatives, Records, RG 233, The National Archives, Washington, D.C.

U.S. Senate, Records, RG 46, The National Archives, Washington, D.C.

U.S. Supreme Court, Records and Briefs (microform).

Printed Works

Adams, George P. "Review of *Ethical Systems and Legal Ideals* by Felix S. Cohen." *California Law Review* 21 (1934): 631–32.

Agranat, Simon. "Reflections on the Man and His Work." *Israel Law Review* 16 (1981): 282–90.

Akam, Everett Helmut. "Pluralism and the Search for Community: The Social Thought of American Cultural Pluralism." Ph.D. diss., University of Rochester, 1990.

Alexander, Gregory S. *Commodity and Propriety: Competing Visions of Property in American Legal Thought, 1776–1970*. Chicago: University of Chicago Press, 1999.

Anaya, S. James. *Indigenous Peoples in International Law*. 2nd ed. New York: Oxford University Press, 2004.

Arnold, Thurman. "Book Review of *American Legal Realism: Skepticism, Reform and the Judicial Process* by Wilfrid E. Rumble Jr." *Political Science Quarterly* 84 (1969): 668–69.

Auerbach, Jerold S. *Unequal Justice: Lawyers and Social Change in Modern America*. New York: Oxford University Press, 1976.

Auerbach, Jerold S., and Eugene Bardach. "Born to an Era of Insecurity: Career Patterns of Law Review Editors, 1918–1941." *American Journal of Legal History* 17 (1973): 3–26.

Ayres, C. E. "Review of *Ethical Systems and Legal Ideals* by Felix S. Cohen." *Yale Law Journal* 43 (1933): 158–60.

Bailey, Percival Roberts. "Progressive Lawyers: A History of the National Lawyers Guild, 1936–1958." Ph.D. diss., Rutgers University, 1979.

Baker, Houston A. *Modernism and the Harlem Renaissance*. Chicago: University of Chicago Press, 1987.

Ball, Milner S. "John Marshall and Indian Nations in the Beginning and Now." *The John Marshal Law Review* 33 (2000): 1183–95.

Bannister, Robert C. *Sociology and Scientism: The American Quest for Objectivity, 1880–1940*. Chapel Hill: University of North Carolina Press, 1987.

Barker, Robert W., and Alice Ehrenfeld. *Legislative History of the Indian Claims Commission Act of 1946*. New York: Clearwater Publishing, 1976.

Barret, James R. "Americanization from the Bottom Up: Immigration and the Remaking of the Working Class in the United States, 1880–1930." *Journal of American History* 78 (1992): 996–1020.

Barsh, Russel Lawrence. "Another Look at Reorganization: When Will Tribes Have a Choice?" *Indian Truth* (October 1982): 4.

Barsh, Russell Lawrence, and James Youngblood Henderson. *The Road: Indian Tribes and Political Liberty*. Berkeley: University of California Press, 1980.

Beals, Ralph L. "The Anthropologist as Expert Witness: Illustrations from the California Land Claims Case." In *Irredeemable America: The Indians' Estate and Land Claims,* ed. Imre Sutton. Albuquerque: University of New Mexico Press, 1985.

Bentley, Arthur. *The Process of Government*. Bloomington, IN: Principia Press, 1908.

Berkey, Curtis, and Lynn Kickingbird. *The Indian Reorganization Act of 1934*. Washington, D.C.: Institute for the Development of Indian Law, 1977.

Berlin, William S. "The Roots of Jewish Political Thought in America." Ph.D. diss., Rutgers University, 1975.

Berman, Gerald S. "From Neustadt to Alaska, 1939: A Failed Attempt at Community." *Immigrants and Minorities* 6 (1987): 66–83.

———. "Reactions to the Resettlement of World War II Refugees in Alaska." *Jewish Social Studies* 44 (1982): 271–82.

Berrol, Selma C. "Education and Economic Mobility: The Jewish Experience in New York City, 1880–1920." In *East European Jews in America, 1880–1920: Immigration and Adaptation,* ed. Jeffrey S. Gurock. New York: Routledge, 1998.

Best, Gary Dean. *The Retreat from Liberalism: Collectivists Versus Progressives in the New Deal Years*. Westport, CT: Praeger, 2002.

Biolsi, Thomas. *"Deadliest Enemies": Law and the Making of Race Relations on and off Rosebud Reservation*. Berkeley: University of California Press, 2001.

———. *Organizing the Lakota: The Political Economy of the New Deal on the Pine Ridge and Rose-bud Reservations.* Tucson: University of Arizona Press, 1992.

Blair, Leon Borden, ed. *Essays on Radicalism in Contemporary America.* Austin: University of Texas Press, 1972.

Bobroff, Kenneth H. "Retelling Allotment: Indian Property Rights and the Myth of Common Ownership." *Vanderbilt Law Review* 54 (2001): 1559–1623.

Boeckel, Florence Brewer. "Women in International Affairs." *Annals of the American Academy of Political and Social Science* 143 (1929): 230–48.

Breitman, Richard, and Alan M. Kraut. *American Refugee Policy and European Jewry, 1933–1945.* Bloomington: Indiana University Press, 1987.

Brinkley, Alan. *The End of Reform: New Deal Liberalism in Recession and War.* New York: Alfred A. Knopf, 1995.

———. "The New Deal and the Idea of the State." In *The Rise and Fall of the New Deal Order, 1930–1980,* ed. Steve Fraser and Gary Gerstle. Princeton: Princeton University Press, 1989.

Brody, David. "American Jewry, the Refugees and Immigration Restriction (1932–1942)." In *American Jewish History, vol. 7: America, American Jews, and the Holocaust,* ed. Jeffrey S. Gurock. New York: Routledge, 1998.

Buenker, John. "The New Politics." In *1915: The Cultural Moment: The New Politics, The New Woman, The New Psychology, The New Art, and the New Theater in America,* ed. Adele Heller and Lois Rudnick. New Brunswick: Rutgers University Press, 1991.

Burgers, Jan Herman. "The Road to San Francisco: The Revival of the Human Rights Idea in the Twentieth Century." *Human Rights Quarterly* 14 (1992): 447–77.

Calda, Milos. *The American Left and the Challenges of the 1930s.* Prague, Czech Republic: University of Karlovy, 1998.

Carlson, Leonard A. "What Was It Worth? Economic and Historical Aspects of Determining Awards in Indian Land Claims Cases." In *Irredeemable America: The Indians' Estate and Land Claims,* ed. Imre Sutton. Albuquerque: University of New Mexico Press, 1985.

Carlson, Thomas. "James and the Kantian Tradition." In *The Cambridge Companion to William James,* ed. Ruth Anna Putnam. New York: Cambridge University Press, 1997.

Case, David S., and David A. Voluck. *Alaska Natives and American Laws.* 2d ed. Fairbanks: University of Alaska Press, 2002.

Casebier, Dennis G. *Camp Beale's Springs and the Hualapai Indians.* Norco, CA: Tales of the Mojave Road, 1980.

Chatfield, Charles. *For Peace and Justice: Pacifism in America, 1914–1941.* Knoxville: University of Tennessee Press, 1971.

Churchill, Ward. "The Earth Is Our Mother: Struggles for American Indian Land and Liberation in the Contemporary United States." In *The State of Native America: Genocide, Colonization, and Resistance,* ed. M. Annette Jaimes. Boston: South End Press, 1992.

Clemens, Elisabeth S. *The People's Lobby: Organizational Innovation and the Rise of Interest Group Politics in the United States, 1890–1925.* Chicago: University of Chicago Press, 1997.

Clinton, Robert N. "Redressing the Legacy of Conquest: A Vision Quest for a Decolonized Federal Indian Law." *Arkansas Law Review* 46 (1993): 77–160.

Clow, Richmond L. "The Indian Reorganization Act and the Loss of Tribal Sovereignty: Constitutions on the Rosebud and Pine Ridge Reservations." *Great Plains Quarterly* 7 (1987): 125–34.

Cohen, Felix S. "Alaska Nuremburg's Laws: Congress Sanctions Racial Discrimination." *Commentary* 6 (1948): 136–43.

———. "Americanizing the White Man." In *The Legal Conscience: Selected Papers of Felix S. Cohen*, ed. Lucy Kramer Cohen. New Haven: Yale University Press, 1960. Originally published in *The American Scholar* 21 (1952): 177–91.

———. "Anthropology and the Problems of Indian Administration." In *The Legal Conscience: Selected Papers of Felix S. Cohen*, ed. Lucy Kramer Cohen. New Haven: Yale University Press, 1960. Originally published in *Southwestern Social Science Quarterly* 18 (1937): 1–10.

———. "The Bauer-Bonbright Proposal for the Revision of the New York Public Service Commission Law and its Constitutionality." *Columbia Law Review* 30 (1930): 548–62 (unsigned).

———. "Breaking Faith with Our First Americans." *Indian Truth* 25 (1948): 1–8.

———. "The Challenge of Racism." *A Review of Jewish Interests* 20 (October 19, 1953): 12–13.

———. "Colonialism: A Realistic Approach." In *The Legal Conscience: Selected Papers of Felix S. Cohen*, ed. Lucy Kramer Cohen. New Haven: Yale University Press, 1960. Originally published in *Ethics* 55 (1945): 167–81.

———. "Colonialism: U.S. Style." *The Progressive* 15 (1951): 16–18.

———. "The Democratic Faith." In *The Legal Conscience: Selected Papers of Felix S. Cohen*, ed. Lucy Kramer Cohen. New Haven: Yale University Press, 1960.

———. "The Elements of Fair Trial in Disciplinary Proceedings by Labor Unions." *Columbia Law Review* 30 (1930): 847–62 (unsigned).

———. "The Erosion of Indian Rights, 1950–1953: A Case Study in Bureaucracy." *Yale Law Journal* 62 (1953): 348–90.

———. *Ethical Systems and Legal Ideals: An Essay on the Foundations of Legal Criticism*. New York: Falcon Press, 1933.

———. "A Factual Study of Rule 113." *Columbia Law Review* 32 (1932): 830–58.

———. "Field Theory and Judicial Logic." In *The Legal Conscience: Selected Papers of Felix S. Cohen*, ed. Lucy Kramer Cohen. New Haven: Yale University Press, 1960. Originally published in *Yale Law Journal* 59 (1950): 238–72.

———. "Foreword." In *Combating Totalitarian Propaganda: A Legal Appraisal*, ed. Felix S. Cohen. Washington, D.C.: Institute of Living Law, 1944.

———. "Government and the Social Contract: Ethical Evaluations in the Law." In *The Legal Conscience: Selected Papers of Felix S. Cohen*, ed. Lucy Kramer Cohen. New Haven: Yale University Press, 1960.

———. "Harold L. Ickes—Champion of the Dispossessed." *Freeland* (1952): 7–8.

———. "How Long Will Indian Constitutions Last?" In *The Legal Conscience: Selected Papers of Felix S. Cohen*, ed. Lucy Kramer Cohen. New Haven: Yale University Press, 1960. Originally published in *Indians At Work* 6 (1939): 40–43.

———. "Indians Are Citizens!" In *The Legal Conscience: Selected Papers of Felix S. Cohen*, ed. Lucy Kramer Cohen. New Haven: Yale University Press, 1960. Originally published in *The American Indian* 1 (1944): 12–22.

———. "Indian Claims." In *The Legal Conscience: Selected Papers of Felix S. Cohen*, ed. Lucy Kramer Cohen. New Haven: Yale University Press, 1960. Originally published in *The American Indian* 2 (1945): 3–11.

———. "Indian Rights and the Federal Courts." *Minnesota Law Review* 24 (1940): 145–200.

———. "Indian Self-Government." In *The Legal Conscience: Selected Papers of Felix S. Cohen*, ed. Lucy Kramer Cohen. New Haven: Yale University Press, 1960. Originally published in *The American Indian* 5 (1949): 3–12.

———. "Judicial Ethics." In *The Legal Conscience: Selected Papers of Felix S. Cohen*, ed. Lucy Kramer Cohen. New Haven: Yale University Press, 1960. Originally published in *Ohio State Law Journal* 12 (1951): 3–13.

——. "The Judicial Resolution of Factional Disputes in Labor Unions." *Columbia Law Review* 30 (1930):1025–39 (unsigned).

——. "Law for the Immigrant." *The New Leader,* November 9, 1953.

——. "Letter to the Editor of the Fordham Law Review." *Fordham Law Review* 5 (1936): 548–51.

——. "Modern Ethics and the Law." In *The Legal Conscience: Selected Papers of Felix S. Cohen,* ed. Lucy Kramer Cohen. New Haven:Yale University Press, 1960. Originally published in *Brooklyn Law Review.* 4 (1934): 33–50.

——. "Mythology of Immigration." In *The Legal Conscience: Selected Papers of Felix S. Cohen,* ed. Lucy Kramer Cohen. New Haven:Yale University Press, 1960. Originally published in *Freeland* 2 (1946): 12–13, 16.

——. "Original Indian Title." In *The Legal Conscience: Selected Papers of Felix S. Cohen,* ed. Lucy Kramer Cohen. New Haven:Yale University Press, 1960. Originally published in *Minnesota Law Review* 32 (1947): 28–59.

——. "Our Country's Shame." *The Progressive* 13 (1949): 9–10.

——. "Politics and Economics." In *Socialist Planning and a Socialist Program:A Symposium,* ed. Harry W. Laidler. New York: Falcon Press, 1932.

——. "The Privilege to Disparage a Non-Competing Business." *Columbia Law Review* 30 (1930): 510–21 (unsigned).

——. "The Problems of a Functional Jurisprudence." In *The Legal Conscience: Selected Papers of Felix S. Cohen,* ed. Lucy Kramer Cohen. New Haven:Yale University Press, 1960. Originally published in *Modern Law Review* 1 (1937): 5–26.

——. "The Reconstruction of Hidden Value Judgments: Word Choices as Value Indicators." In *Symbols and Values,* ed. Lyman Bryson. New York: Harper, 1954.

——. "The Relativity of Philosophical Systems and the Method of Systematic Relativism." In *The Legal Conscience: Selected Papers of Felix S. Cohen,* ed. Lucy Kramer Cohen. New Haven:Yale University Press, 1960. Originally published in *The Journal of Philosophy* 36 (1939): 57–72.

——. "Review of *Bentham's Theory of Fictions* by C. K. Ogden and *The Theory of Legislation* by J. Bentham, ed. by C. K. Ogden." In *The Legal Conscience: Selected Papers of Felix S. Cohen,* ed. Lucy Kramer Cohen. New Haven:Yale University Press, 1960. Originally published in *Yale Law Journal* 42 (1938): 1149–52.

——. "Review of *The Folklore of Capitalism* by Thurman W. Arnold." In *The Legal Conscience: Selected Papers of Felix S. Cohen,* ed. Lucy Kramer Cohen. New Haven: Yale University Press, 1960. Originally published in *National Lawyers Guild Quarterly* 1 (1938): 161–64.

——. "Review of *Fundamental Principles of the Sociology of Law* by Eugen Ehrlich." In *The Legal Conscience: Selected Papers of Felix S. Cohen,* ed. Lucy Kramer Cohen. New Haven:Yale University Press, 1960. Originally published in *Illinois Law Review* 31 (1937): 1128–34.

——. "The Social and Economic Consequences of Exclusionary Immigration Laws." *National Lawyers Guild Quarterly* 2 (1939): 171–92.

——. "Socialism and the Myth of Legality." *American Socialist Quarterly* 4 (1935): 3–33.

——. "The Socialization of Morality." In *The Legal Conscience: Selected Papers of Felix S. Cohen,* ed. Lucy Kramer Cohen. New Haven:Yale University Press, 1960. Originally published in *American Philosophy Today and Tomorrow,* ed. Horace M. Kallen and Sidney Hook. New York: Lee Furman, 1935.

——. "The Spanish Origin of Indian Rights in the Law of the United States." In *The Legal Conscience: Selected Papers of Felix S. Cohen,* ed. Lucy Kramer Cohen. New Haven: Yale University Press, 1960. Originally published in *Georgetown Law Journal* 31 (1942): 1–21.

——. "A Student Homage:Jerome Michael." *Columbia Law Review* 53 (1953): 312–14.

——. "Transcendental Nonsense and the Functional Approach." In *The Legal Conscience: Selected Papers of Felix S. Cohen,* ed. Lucy Kramer Cohen. New Haven:Yale University Press, 1960. Originally published in *Columbia Law Review* 35 (1935): 809–49.

——. "The Vestal Bill for the Copyright Registration of Designs." *Columbia Law Review* 31 (1931): 477–94 (unsigned).

——. "The Vocabulary of Prejudice." In *The Legal Conscience: Selected Papers of Felix S. Cohen,* ed. Lucy Kramer Cohen. New Haven:Yale University Press, 1960. Originally published in *Fellowship Magazine* 19 (1953): 5–10.

——. "What City College will Contribute to the Development of the Law." *The Barrister* [City College of New York] 2 (1938): 4–16.

Cohen, Felix S., ed. *Handbook of Federal Indian Law.* Washington, D.C.: U.S. Government Printing Office, 1942.

——. *Combating Totalitarian Propaganda: A Legal Appraisal.* Washington, D.C.: Institute of Living Law, 1944.

Cohen, Felix S., and Lucy Kramer Cohen. "Combating Totalitarian Propaganda: The Method of Enlightenment." *Minnesota Law Review* 27 (1942–43): 545–74.

Cohen, Felix S., and Edith Lowenstein. "Combating Totalitarian Propaganda: The Method of Suppression." *Illinois Law Review* 37 (1942–43): 193–214.

Cohen, Joshua. "Pluralism and Proceduralism." *Chicago-Kent Law Review* 69 (1994): 589–618.

Cohen, Lucy Kramer et al. "Felix Cohen and the Adoption of the IRA." In *Indian Self-Rule: First-Hand Accounts of Indian-White Relations from Roosevelt to Reagan,* ed. Kenneth R. Philp. Logan: Utah State University Press, 1995.

Cohen, Lucy Kramer, ed. *The Legal Conscience: Selected Papers of Felix S. Cohen.* New Haven: Yale University Press, 1960.

Cohen, Morris R. "On Absolutism in Legal Thought." In Morris R. Cohen, *Reason and Law: Studies in Juristic Philosophy,* Glencoe: The Free Press, 1950. Originally published in *The University of Pennsylvania Law Review* 84 (1936): 681–715.

——. *A Dreamer's Journey: The Autobiography of Morris Raphael Cohen.* Boston: Beacon Press, 1949.

——. *The Faith of a Liberal: Selected Essays by Morris R. Cohen.* New York: Henry Holt, 1946.

——. "Jurisprudence as a Philosophical Discipline." In Morris R. Cohen, *Reason and Law: Studies in Juristic Philosophy* Glencoe: The Free Press, 1950. Originally published in *Journal of Philosophy, Psychology, and Scientific Methods* 10 (1913): 225–32.

——. "Justice Holmes and the Nature of Law." *Columbia Law Review* 31 (1931): 352–67.

——. *Reason and Law: Studies in Juristic Philosophy.* Glencoe: The Free Press, 1950.

——. *Reason and Nature: An Essay on the Meaning of Scientific Method.* New York: Harcourt, Brace and Company, 1931.

——. "Zionism: Tribalism or Liberalism?" In *The Faith of a Liberal: Selected Essays by Morris R. Cohen.* New York: Henry Holt, 1946. Originally published in *New Republic.* March 19, 1919.

Cohen, Morris R., ed. *Chance, Love, and Logic: Philosophical Essays.* Lincoln: University of Nebraska Press, 1998 (1923)

Cohen, Robert. *When the Old Left was Young: Student Radicals and America's First Mass Student Movement 1929–1941.* New York: Oxford University Press, 1993.

Cohen Rosenfield, Leonora. "Aristotelianism in Morris R. Cohen's Legal Philosophy." *Israel Law Review* 16 (1981): 291–300.

——. *Portrait of a Philosopher: Morris R. Cohen in Life and Letters.* New York: Harcourt, Brace and World, 1962.

Collier, John. *From Every Zenith: A Memoir.* Denver: Sage Books, 1963.

——. "The Genesis and Philosophy of the Indian Reorganization Act." In *The Western American Indian: Case Studies in Tribal History,* ed. Richard N. Ellis. Lincoln: University of Nebraska Press, 1972.

Corbin, Arthur L. "Offer and Acceptance, and Some of the Resulting Legal Relations." *Yale Law Journal* 26 (1917): 169–206.

Cornwell, Joel R. "From Hedonism to Human Rights: Felix Cohen's Alternative to Nihilism." *Temple Law Review* 68 (1995): 197–222.

Cotkin, George. *William James, Public Philosopher.* Baltimore: Johns Hopkins University Press, 1990.

Council for Democracy. *The New World.* New York: Edward Finston Company, 1942.

Cover, Robert. "Obligation: A Jewish Jurisprudence of the Social Order." In *Narrative, Violence, and the Law: The Essays of Robert Cover,* ed. Martha Minow, Michael Ryan, and Austin Sarat. Ann Arbor: University of Michigan Press, 1995. Originally published in *Journal of Law and Religion* 5 (1987): 65–74.

Cremin, Lawrence A. *American Education: The Metropolitan Experience, 1876–1980.* New York: Harper and Row, 1988.

Curry, James E., Felix S. Cohen, and Bernard M. Newburg. "Combating Totalitarian Propaganda: The Method of Exposure." *University of Chicago Law Review* 10 (1942–43): 107–41.

Dahl, Robert A. *Pluralist Democracy in the United States: Conflict and Consent.* Chicago: University of Chicago Press, 1967.

——. *A Preface to Democratic Theory.* Chicago: University of Chicago Press, 1956.

Daniels, Roger. *Guarding the Golden Door: American Immigration Policy and Immigrants since 1882.* New York: Hill and Wang, 2004.

Daniels, Roger, and Otis L. Graham. *Debating American Immigration, 1882–Present.* Lanham, MD: Rowman and Littlefield, 2001.

Davis, Kingsley. "Review of *Ethical Systems and Legal Ideals* by Felix S. Cohen." *American Sociological Review* 5 (1940): 799–801.

Dawson, John P. "Economic Duress: An Essay in Perspective." *Michigan Law Review* 45 (1947): 253–90.

Deloria, Vine Jr. *Behind the Trail of Broken Treaties: An Indian Declaration of Independence.* Austin: University of Texas Press, 1985.

——. "Reserving to Themselves: Treaties and the Powers of Indian Tribes." *Arizona Law Review* 38 (1996): 963–80.

Deloria, Vine Jr., and Clifford M. Lytle. *The Nations Within: The Past and Future of American Sovereignty.* Austin: University of Texas Press, 1998.

Dewey, John. *The Public and its Problems.* New York: H. Holt and Co., 1927.

Dickinson, John. "Legal Rules: Their Function in the Process of Decision." *University of Pennsylvania Law Review* 79 (1931): 833–68.

DiMatteo, Larry A., and Michael J. Meagher. "Broken Promises: The Failure of the 1920's Native American Irrigation and Assimilation Policies." *University of Hawaii Law Review* 19 (1997): 1–36.

Dippie, Brian W. *The Vanishing American: White Attitudes and U.S. Indian Policy.* Lawrence: University Press of Kansas, 1982.

Douglas, Ann. *Terrible Honesty: Mongrel Manhattan in the 1920s.* New York: Farrar Straus and Giroux, 1995.

Downes, Randolph C. "A Crusade for Indian Reform, 1922–1934." *Mississippi Valley Historical Review* 32 (1945): 331–54.

Drinnon, Richard. *Keeper of Concentration Camps: Dillon S. Myer and American Racism.* Berkeley: University of California Press, 1987.

Dudziak, Mary L. *Cold War Civil Rights: Race and the Image of American Democracy.* Princeton: Princeton University Press, 2000.

——. "Desegregation as a Cold War Imperative." *Stanford Law Review* 41 (1988): 61–120.

Dumenil, Lynn. *The Modern Temper: American Culture and Society in the 1920s.* New York: Hill and Wang, 1995.

Dye, Nancy Schrom. "Creating a Feminist Alliance: Sisterhood and Class Conflict in the New York Women's Trade Union League, 1903–1914." *Feminist Studies* 2 (1975): 24–38.

Eagan, Eileen. *Class, Culture, and the Classroom: The Student Peace Movement in the 1930s.* Philadelphia: Temple University Press, 1981.

Eisenberg, Avigail I. *Reconstructing Political Pluralism.* Albany: State University of New York Press, 1995.

Elliff, John T. *The United States Department of Justice and Individual Rights, 1937–1962.* New York: Garland, 1987.

Elliot, W. Y. *The Pragmatic Revolt in Politics; Syndicalism, Fascism, and the Constitutional State.* New York: The Macmillan Co., 1928.

Ellis, Richard N., ed. *The Western American Indian: Case Studies in Tribal History.* Lincoln: University of Nebraska Press, 1972.

Ernst, Daniel R. "Common Laborers? Industrial Pluralists, Legal Realists, and the Law of Industrial Disputes, 1915–1943." *Law and History Review* 11 (1993): 59–100.

"Felix S. Cohen," Symposium. *Rutgers Law Review* 9 (1954): 348–475.

Ferguson, Karen. "Indian Fishing Rights: Aftermath of the Fox Decision and the Year 2000." *American Indian Law Review* 23 (1998–99): 97–154.

Follett, Mary P. *The New State, Group Organization the Solution of Popular Government.* New York: Longmans, Green, 1918.

Forbath, William E. "Civil Rights and Economic Citizenship: Notes on the Past and Future of the Civil Rights and Labor Movements." *University of Pennsylvania Labor and Employment Journal* 2 (2000): 697–718.

"Formalism Revisited." Symposium. *The University of Chicago Law Review* 66 (1999): 527–942.

Frank, Jerome. "A Conflict with Oblivion: Some Observations on the Founders of Legal Pragmatism." *Rutgers Law Review* 9 (1954): 425–63.

——. *Law and the Modern Mind.* New York: Brentano's, 1931.

Frankfurter, Felix. Foreword. In "Symposium: Felix S. Cohen." *Rutgers Law Review* 9 (1954): 355–56.

Fraser, Steve, and Gary Gerstle, eds. *The Rise and Fall of the New Deal Order, 1930–1980.* Princeton: Princeton University Press, 1989.

Frazer, Winifred L. *Mabel Dodge Luhan.* Boston: Twayne, 1984.

Friedman, Saul S. *No Haven for the Oppressed: United States Policy toward Jewish Refugees, 1938–1945.* Detroit: Wayne State University Press, 1973.

Froomkin, A. Michael. "Reinventing the Government Corporation." *University of Illinois Law Review* (1995): 543–634.

Fuller, Lon L. "American Legal Realism." *University of Pennsylvania Law Review* 82 (1934): 429–62.

Furber, Bradley B. "Two Promises, Two Propositions: The Wheeler-Howard Act as a Reconciliation of the Indian Civil Law War." *University of Puget Sound Law Review* 13 (1991): 211–82.

Geison, Gerald L., ed. *Professions and Professional Ideologies in America.* Chapel Hill: University of North Carolina Press, 1983.

Gilbert, Joan. *The Trail of Tears across Missouri.* Columbia: University of Missouri Press, 1996.

Goldberg, Carole. "Members Only? Designing Citizenship Requirements for Indian Nations." *Kansas Law Review* 50 (2002): 437–71.

Golding, Martin P. "Realism and Functionalism in the Legal Thought of Felix S. Cohen." *Cornell Law Review* 66 (1980–81): 1032–57.

Goluboff, Risa L. "The Thirteenth Amendment and the Lost Origins of Civil Rights." *Duke Law Journal* 50 (2001): 1609–85.

———. "The Work of Civil Rights in the 1940s: The Department of Justice, the NAACP, and African American Agricultural Workers." Ph.D. diss., Princeton University, 2003.

Good, James A. "The Value of Thomas Davidson." *Transactions of the Charles S. Peirce Society* 40 (2004): 289–318.

Goodman, Nelson, and Catherine Z. Elgin. *Reconceptions in Philosophy and Other Arts and Sciences.* Indianapolis: Hackett, 1988.

Gordon, Robert W. "American Law through English Eyes: A Century of Nightmares and Noble Dreams." *Georgetown Law Journal* 84 (1996): 2215–43.

———. "Critical Legal Histories." *Stanford Law Review* 36 (1984): 57–125.

———. "Legal Thought and Legal Practice in the Age of American Enterprise, 1870–1920." In *Professions and Professional Ideologies in America,* ed. Gerald L Geison. Chapel Hill: University of North Carolina Press, 1983.

Gorelick, Sherry. *City College and the Jewish Poor: Education in New York, 1880–1924.* New Brunswick: Rutgers University Press, 1981.

Goren, Arthur A. *The Politics and Public Culture of American Jews.* Bloomington: Indiana University Press, 1999.

Gould, L. Scott. "The Consent Paradigm: Tribal Sovereignty at the Millennium." *Columbia Law Review* 96 (1996): 809–902.

Greenwald, Richard A. *The Triangle Fire, the Protocols of Peace, and Industrial Democracy in Progressive Era New York.* Philadelphia: Temple University Press, 2005.

Grey, Thomas. "Holmes and Legal Pragmatism." *Stanford Law Review* 41 (1989): 787–870.

Gurock, Jeffrey S., ed. *American Jewish History, vol. 7: America, American Jews, and the Holocaust.* New York: Routledge, 1998.

———. *East European Jews in America, 1880–1920: Immigration and Adaptation.* New York: Routledge, 1998.

Haas, Theodore H. *Ten Years of Tribal Government under the Indian Reorganization Act.* Tribal Relations Pamphlets, Haskell Institute Printing Department, 1947.

Haas, Theodore H., ed. *Felix S. Cohen: A Fighter for Justice.* Washington, D.C.: Chapter of the Alumni of the City College of New York, 1956.

Hackney, James R. Jr. "The Intellectual Origins of American Strict Liability: A Case Study in American Pragmatic Instrumentalism." *American Journal of Legal History* 39 (1995): 443–509.

Hager, Mark M. "Bodies Politic: The Progressive History of Organizational 'Real Entity' Theory." *University of Pittsburgh Law Review* 50 (1989): 575–654.

Hale, Robert. "Coercion and Distribution in a Supposedly Non-Coercive State." *Political Science Quarterly* 38 (1923): 470–94.

Hart, E. Richard. Foreword. In *Indian Self-Rule: First-Hand Accounts of Indian-White Relations from Roosevelt to Reagan,* ed. Kenneth R. Philp. Logan: Utah State University Press, 1995.

Haskell, Thomas L. *The Emergence of Professional Social Science: The American Social Science Association and the Nineteenth Century Crisis of Authority.* Urbana: University of Illinois Press, 1977.

Hawley, Ellis W. "The Discovery and Study of a 'Corporate Liberalism.'" *Business History Review* 52 (1978): 309–20.

——. "Herbert Hoover, the Commerce Secretariat, and the Vision of an 'Associative State,' 1921–1928." *Journal of American History* 61 (1974): 116–40.

Haycox, Stephen. "Felix S. Cohen and the Legacy of the Indian New Deal." *Yale University Library Gazette* 68 (1994): 135–56.

Helbling, Mark Irving. *The Harlem Renaissance: The One and the Many.* Westport, CT: Greenwood Press, 1999.

Heller, Adele, and Lois Rudnick, eds. *1915: The Cultural Moment: The New Politics, The New Woman, The New Psychology, The New Art, and the New Theater in America.* New Brunswick: Rutgers University Press, 1991.

Higham, John. *Strangers in the Land: Patterns of American Nativism, 1860–1925.* New Brunswick: Rutgers University Press, 1992.

Hirst, Paul Q., ed. *The Pluralist Theory of the State: Selected Writings of the G. D. H. Cole, J. N. Figgis, and H. J. Laski.* New York: Routledge, 1989.

A History of the School of Law, Columbia University. New York: Columbia University Press, 1955.

Hollinger, David A. "Ethnic Diversity, Cosmopolitanism and the Emergence of the American Liberal Intelligentsia." *American Quarterly* 27 (1975): 133–51.

——. *In the American Province: Studies in the History and Historiography of Ideas.* Baltimore: Johns Hopkins University Press, 1985.

——. *Morris R. Cohen and the Scientific Ideal.* Cambridge: MIT Press, 1975.

Holmes, Oliver Wendell Jr. "The Path of the Law." *Harvard Law Review* 10 (1897): 457–78.

Horwitz, Morton J. "Jews and Legal Realists." Unpublished manuscript.

——. *The Transformation of American Law, 1870–1960: The Crisis of Legal Orthodoxy.* New York: Oxford University Press, 1992.

——. *The Warren Court and the Pursuit of Justice.* New York: Hill and Wang, 1998.

——. "Why Is Anglo-American Jurisprudence Unhistorical?" *Oxford Journal of Legal Studies* 17 (1997): 551–86.

Hovenkamp, Herbert. "Labor Conspiracies in American Law, 1880–1930." *Texas Law Review* 66 (1988): 919–66.

——. "The Political Economy of Substantive Due Process." *Stanford Law Review* 40 (1988): 379–447.

Howe, Irving and Kenneth Libo. *How We Lived: A Documentary History of Immigrant Jews in America 1880–1930.* New York: Richard Marek Publishers, 1979.

Huggins, Nathan Irving. *Harlem Renaissance.* New York: Oxford University Press, 1971.

Hull, N. E. H. "Some Realism about the Llewellyn-Pound Exchange over Realism: The Newly Uncovered Private Correspondence, 1927–1931." *Wisconsin Law Review* (1987): 921–70.

Hutcheson, Joseph. "The Judgment Intuitive: The Function of the 'Hunch' in Judicial Decision." *Cornell Law Quarterly* 14 (1929): 274–88.

Hyfler, Robert. *Prophets of the Left: American Socialist Thought in the Twentieth Century.* Westport, CT: Greenwood Press, 1984.

Hyman, Paula E. "Culture and Gender: Women in the Immigrant Jewish Community." In *East European Jews in America, 1880–1920: Immigration and Adaptation,* ed. Jeffrey S. Gurock. New York: Routledge, 1998.

Ickes, Harold L. *The Autobiography of a Curmudgeon.* New York: Reynal and Hitchcock, 1943.

Jaffe, Louis L. "Law Making by Private Groups." *Harvard Law Review* 51 (1937): 201–53.

Jahoda, Gloria. *The Trail of Tears.* New York: Wings Books, 1995.

Jaimes, M. Annette, ed. *The State of Native America: Genocide, Colonization, and Resistance.* Boston: South End Press, 1992.

James, William. "On a Certain Blindness in Human Beings." 1899. In *The Writings of William James,* ed. John J. McDermott. Chicago: University of Chicago Press, 1977.

———. *A Pluralistic Universe: Hibbert Lectures at Manchester College on the Present Situation in Philosophy.* Lincoln: University of Nebraska Press, 1996.

———. *Pragmatism, A New Name for Some Old Ways of Thinking.* New York: Longmans, Green and Co., 1907.

Johnson, Tadd M., and James Hamilton. "Self-Governance for Indian Tribes: From Paternalism to Empowerment." *Connecticut Law Review* 27 (1995): 1251–80.

Kairys, David, ed. *The Politics of Law: A Progressive Critique.* 3d ed. New York: Basic Books, 1998.

Kallen, Horace M. *Culture and Democracy in the United States.* New York: Boni and Liveright, 1924.

———. "Democracy versus the Melting Pot." In Horace M. Kallen, *Culture and Democracy in the United States.* New York: Boni and Liveright, 1924. Originally published in *The Nation.* February 18 and 25, 1915.

———. "A Pluralistic Universe: Professor James on the Present Situation in Philosophy." *Boston Evening Transcript.* June 16, 1909.

Kallen, Horace M., and Sidney Hook, eds. *American Philosophy Today and Tomorrow.* New York: Lee Furman, 1935.

Kalman, Laura. *Legal Realism at Yale, 1927–1960.* Chapel Hill: University of North Carolina Press, 1986.

Kamp, Allen R. "Between-the-Wars Social Thought: Karl Llewellyn, Legal Realism, and the Uniform Commercial Code in Context." *Albany Law Review* 59 (1995): 325–97.

Kantorowicz, Hermann. "Some Rationalism About Realism." *Yale Law Journal* 43 (1934): 1240–53.

Kelly, Lawrence C. *The Assault on Assimilation: John Collier and the Origins of Indian Policy Reform.* Albuquerque: University of New Mexico Press, 1983.

———. "The Indian Reorganization Act: The Dream and Reality." *Pacific Political Review* 44 (1975): 219–312.

Kennedy, Duncan. *A Critique of Adjudication (fin de siècle).* Cambridge: Harvard University Press, 1997.

———. *The Rise and Fall of Classical Legal Thought.* Unpublished manuscript.

———. "Toward an Historical Understanding of Legal Consciousness: The Case of Classical Legal Thought in America, 1850–1940." *Research in Law and Sociology* 3 (1980): 3–24.

Kennedy, Walter B. "Functional Nonsense and the Transcendental Approach." *Fordham Law Review* 5 (1936): 272–300.

———. "More Functional Nonsense—A Reply to Felix S. Cohen." *Fordham Law Review* 6 (1937): 75–89.

Kizzia, Tom. "Sanctuary: Alaska, the Nazis, and the Jews." 4 parts. *Anchorage Daily News.* May 16–19, 1999.

Klingenstein, Susanne. *Jews in the American Academy, 1900–1940: The Dynamics of Intellectual Assimilation.* New Haven: Yale University Press, 1991.

Kloppenberg, James T. *Uncertain Victory: Social Democracy and Progressivism in European and American Thought, 1870–1920.* New York: Oxford University Press, 1986.

Kluger, Richard. *Simple Justice: The History of Brown v. Board of Education and Black America's Struggle for Equality.* New York: Knopf, 1975.

Konzett, Delia Caparoso. "Administered Identities and Linguistic Assimilation: The Politics of Immigrant English in Anzia Yezierska's *Hungry Hearts.*" *American Literature* 69 (1997): 595–619.

Konvitz, Milton R., ed. *The Legacy of Horace M. Kallen*. London: Associated University Presses, 1987.

Kosak, Hadassa. *Cultures of Opposition: Jewish Immigrant Workers, New York City, 1881–1905*. Albany: State University of New York Press, 2000.

Kuklick, Bruce. *A History of Philosophy in America, 1720–2000*. Oxford: Clarendon Press, 2001.

———. ed. *The Rise of American Philosophy, Cambridge. Massachusetts, 1860–1930*. New Haven: Yale University Press, 1977.

Kymlicka, Will. "Theorizing Indigenous Rights," *University of Toronto Law Journal* 49 (1999): 281–93.

———. *The Rights of Minority Cultures*. New York: Oxford University Press, 1995.

La Farge, Oliver, ed. *The Changing Indian*. Norman: University of Oklahoma Press, 1942.

Lahav, Pnina. "The Eichman Trial, the Jewish Question, and the American Jewish Intelligentsia." *Boston University Law Review* 72 (1992): 555–75.

Laski, Harold J. *Studies in the Problem of Sovereignty*. New Haven: Yale University Press, 1917.

Latham, Earl. *The Group Basis of Politics*. Ithaca: Cornell University Press, 1952.

Lavargna, Carrie Stradley. "Government-Sponsored Enterprises Are Too Big to Fail: Balancing Public and Private Interests." *Hastings Law Journal* 44 (1993): 991–1038.

Lear, Elmer N. "On the Unity of the Kallen Perspective." In *The Legacy of Horace M. Kallen*, ed. Milton R. Konvitz. London: Associated University Presses, 1987.

Lears, T. Jackson. *No Place of Grace: Antimodernism and the Transformation of American Culture, 1880–1920*. Chicago: University of Chicago Press, 1994.

Lebow, Eileen F. *The Bright Boys: A History of Townsend Harris High School*. Westport, CT: Greenwood Press, 2000.

Lee, Yuanchung. "Rediscovering the Constitutional Lineage of Federal Indian Law." *New Mexico Law Review* 27 (1997): 273–357.

"Legal Realism and the Race Question: Some Realism about Realism on Race Relations." *Harvard Law Review* 108 (1995): 1607–24.

Lieder, Michael and Jake Page. *Wild Justice: The People of Geronimo vs. The United States*. New York: Random House, 1997.

Lissak, Rivka Shpak. *Pluralism and Progressives: Hull House and the New Immigrants, 1890–1919*. Chicago: University of Chicago Press, 1989.

Lowndes, John P. "When History Outweighs Law: Extinguishment of Abenaki Aboriginal Title." *Buffalo Law Review* 42 (1994): 77–118.

Lustig, R. Jeffrey. *Corporate Liberalism: The Origins of Modern American Political Theory, 1890–1920*. Berkeley: University of California Press, 1982.

Macdonald, Roderick A. "Metaphors of Multiplicity: Civil Society, Regimes, and Legal Pluralism." *Arizona Journal of International and Comparative Law* 15 (1998): 69–91.

Manners, Robert A. *Hualapai Indians II: An Ethnological Report on the Hualapai (Walapai) Indians of Arizona*. New York: Garland, 1974.

Marshall, Robert. "Should We Settle Alaska?" *New Republic*. February 8, 1940.

Martin, Jill E. "'A Year and Spring of My Existence': Felix S. Cohen and the Handbook of Federal Indian Law." *Western Legal History* 8 (1995): 34–60.

McDermott, John J., ed. *The Writings of William James*. Chicago: University of Chicago Press, 1977.

McLennan, Gregor. *Pluralism*. Buckingham, United Kingdom: Open University Press, 1995.

McMillen, Christian. "Rewriting History and Proving Property Rights: Hualapai Indian Activism and the Law of Land Claims in the Twentieth Century." Ph.D. diss., Yale University, 2004.

Medoff, Raphael. "Alaska Could Have Saved Jews." *The Jerusalem Post.* January 10, 1991.

Mehrotra, Ajay K. "Law and the 'Other': Karl N. Llewellyn, Cultural Anthropology, and the Legacy of the Cheyenne Way." *Law and Social Inquiry* 26 (2001): 741–75.

Mekeel, Scudder. "An Appraisal of the Indian Reorganization Act." *American Anthropologist* 46 (1944): 209–17.

Menand, Louis. *The Metaphysical Club: The Story of Ideas in America.* New York: Farrar Straus and Giroux, 2001.

Meriam, Lewis et al. *The Problem of Indian Administration.* Baltimore: Johns Hopkins Press, 1928.

Michaels, Mark A. "Indigenous Ethics and Alien Laws: Native Traditions and the United States Legal System." *Fordham Law Review* 66 (1998): 1565–84.

Michaels, Walter Benn. *Our America: Nativism, Modernism, and Pluralism.* Durham: Duke University Press, 1995.

Michelman, Frank I. "The Supreme Court, 1985 Term: Foreword: Traces of Self-Government." *Harvard Law Review* 100 (1986): 4–77.

Miller, Orlando W. *The Frontier in Alaska and the Matanuska Colony.* New Haven: Yale University Press, 1975.

Minow, Martha. *Between Vengeance and Forgiveness: Facing History after Genocide and Mass Violence.* Boston: Beacon Press, 1998.

Minow, Martha, Michael Ryan, and Austin Sarat, eds. *Narrative, Violence, and the Law: The Essays of Robert Cover.* Ann Arbor: University of Michigan Press, 1995.

Mitchell, Donald Craig. "*Alaska v. Native Village of Venetie*: Statutory Construction or Judicial Usurpation? Why History Counts." *Alaska Law Review* 14 (1997): 353–442.

———. *Sold American: The Story of Alaska Natives and their Land, 1867–1959: The Army to Statehood.* Hanover, NH: University Press of New England, 1997.

Mitchell, Lawrence E. "Gentleman's Agreement: The Antisemitic Origins of Restrictions on Stockholder Litigation." Social Science Research Network.

Moore, Deborah Dash. *At Home in America: Second Generation New York Jews.* New York: Columbia University Press, 1981.

Morrison, David. *Heroes, Antiheroes, and the Holocaust: American Jewry and Historical Choice.* Jerusalem, Israel: Gefen Publishing House, 1995.

Naske, Claus-M. *Ernest Gruening: Alaska's Greatest Governor.* Fairbanks: University of Alaska Press, 2004.

———. "Jewish Immigration and Alaskan Economic Development: A Study in Futility." *Western States Jewish Historical Quarterly* 8 (1976): 139–57.

Nelles, Walter. "Review of *Ethical Systems and Legal Ideals* by Felix S. Cohen." *Columbia Law Review* 33 (1933): 763–68.

Novick, Peter. *That Noble Dream: The "Objectivity Question" and the American Historical Profession.* New York: Cambridge University Press, 1988.

O'Brien, Sharon. *American Indian Tribal Governments.* Norman: University of Oklahoma Press, 1989.

Officer, James E. "Termination as Federal Policy: An Overview." In *Indian Self-Rule: First-Hand Accounts of Indian-White Relations From Roosevelt to Reagan,* ed. Kenneth R. Philp. Logan: Utah State University Press, 1995.

Opinions of the Solicitor of the Department of the Interior Relating to Indian Affairs 1917–1974. 2 vols. Washington, D.C.: Government Printing Office, 1979.

Orlando, Caroline L. "Aboriginal Title Claims in the Indian Claims Commission: *United States v. Dann* and its Due Process Implications." *Boston College Environmental Affairs Law Review* 13 (1986): 241–80.

Painter, John et al. "Implementing the Indian Reorganization Act." In *Indian Self-Rule: First-Hand Accounts of Indian-White Relations from Roosevelt to Reagan,* ed. Kenneth R. Philp. Logan: Utah State University Press, 1995.

Parman, Donald L. *The Navajos and the New Deal.* New Haven: Yale University Press, 1976.

Paul, Arnold M. *Conservative Crisis and the Rule of Law: Attitudes of the Bar and Bench, 1887–1895.* Gloucester, MA: P. Smith, 1976.

Peirce, Charles S. "The Fixation of Belief." In *Chance, Love, and Logic: Philosophical Essays,* ed. Morris R. Cohen. Lincoln: University of Nebraska Press, 1998 (1923).

Pells, Richard H. *Radical Visions and American Dreams: Culture and Social Thought in the Depression Years.* Urbana: University of Illinois Press, 1998.

Perry, Ralph B. *General Theory of Value: Its Meaning and Basic Principles Construed in Terms of Interest.* New York: Longmans, Green and Company, 1926.

"Philosophy as Teaching: James's 'Knight Errant,' Thomas Davidson." Discussion paper. www.american-philosophy.org/archives/past_conference_programs/pc2004/submissions/dp-10.htm. Accessed July 19, 2006.

Philp, Kenneth R. "Introduction: The Indian Reorganization Act Fifty Years Later." In *Indian Self-Rule: First-Hand Accounts of Indian-White Relations from Roosevelt to Reagan,* ed. Kenneth R. Philp. Logan: Utah State University Press, 1995.

———. "John Collier and the American Indian, 1920–1945." In *Essays on Radicalism in Contemporary America,* ed. Leon Borden Blair. Austin: University of Texas Press, 1972.

———. *John Collier's Crusade for Indian Reform, 1920–1954.* Tucson: University of Arizona Press, 1977.

———. *Termination Revisited: American Indians on the Trail to Self-Determination, 1933–1953.* Lincoln: University of Nebraska Press, 1999.

Philp, Kenneth R., ed. *Indian Self-Rule: First-Hand Accounts of Indian-White Relations from Roosevelt to Reagan.* Logan: Utah State University Press, 1995.

Pommersheim, Frank. *Braid of Feathers: American Indian Law and Contemporary Tribal Life.* Berkeley: University of California Press, 1995.

Pope, James Gray. "The Thirteenth Amendment Versus the Commerce Clause: Labor and the Shaping of American Constitutional Law, 1921–1957." *Columbia Law Review* 102 (2002): 1–122.

Pound, Roscoe. "The Call for a Realist Jurisprudence." *Harvard Law Review* 44 (1931): 697–711.

———. "Law in Books, Law in Action." *American Law Review* 44 (1910): 12–36.

———. "Mechanical Jurisprudence." *Columbia Law Review* 8 (1908): 605–23.

———. "A Practical Program of Procedural Reform." *Green Bag* 22 (1910).

Price, Robert E. *The Great Father in Alaska: The Case of the Tlingit and Haida Salmon Fishery.* Douglas, AK: First Street Press, 1990.

"Prolegomena." In *Irredeemable America: The Indians' Estate and Land Claims,* ed. Imre Sutton. Albuquerque: University of New Mexico Press, 1985.

Prucha, Francis Paul, ed. *Documents of United States Indian Policy.* 3d ed. Lincoln: University of Nebraska Press, 2000.

Purcell, Edward A. Jr. *The Crisis of Democratic Theory: Scientific Naturalism and the Problem of Value.* Lexington: University Press of Kentucky, 1973.

Putnam, Hilary. "James's Theory of Truth." In *The Cambridge Companion to William James,* ed. Ruth Anna Putnam. New York: Cambridge University Press, 1997.

———. *Pragmatism: An Open Question.* Cambridge: Blackwell, 1995.

Putnam, Ruth Anna, ed. *The Cambridge Companion to William James.* New York: Cambridge University Press, 1997.

Radin, Max. "Review of *Ethical Systems and Legal Ideals* by Felix S. Cohen." *Harvard Law Review* 47 (1933): 145–48.

Ratner, Sidney. "Horace M. Kallen and Cultural Pluralism." In *The Legacy of Horace M. Kallen,* ed. Milton R. Konvitz. London: Associated University Presses, 1987.

Robbins, Rebecca L. "Self-Determination and Subordination: The Past, Present, and Future of American Indian Governance." In *The State of Native America: Genocide, Colonization, and Resistance,* ed. M. Annette Jaimes. Boston: South End Press, 1992.

Rosenblum, Nancy L. *Membership and Morals: The Personal Uses of Pluralism in America.* Princeton: Princeton University Press, 1998.

Rosenthal, Harvey D. "Indian Claims and the American Conscience: A Brief History of the Indian Claims Commission." In *Irredeemable America: The Indians' Estate and Land Claims,* ed. Imre Sutton. Albuquerque: University of New Mexico Press, 1985.

———. *Their Day in Court: A History of the Indian Claims Commission.* New York: Garland, 1990.

Rosier, Paul C. *Rebirth of the Blackfeet Nation, 1912–1954.* Lincoln: University of Nebraska Press, 2001.

Ross, Dorothy. *The Origins of American Social Science.* New York: Cambridge University Press, 1991.

Roucek, Joseph S. "The Problem of Minorities and the League of Nations." *Journal of Comparative Legislation and International Law* 15 (1933): 67–76.

Royster, Judith V. "The Legacy of Allotment." *Arizona State Law Journal* 27 (1995): 1–78.

Rudnick, Lois Palken. *Mabel Dodge Luhan: New Woman, New Worlds.* Albuquerque: University of New Mexico Press, 1984.

Rudnick, Lois Palken, ed. *Intimate Memories: The Autobiography of Mabel Dodge Luhan.* Albuquerque: University of New Mexico, 1999.

Rudy, S. Willis. *The College of the City of New York: A History 1847–1947.* New York: Arno Press, 1949.

Rusco, Elmer R. *A Fateful Time: The Background and Legislative History of the Indian Reorganization Act.* Reno: University of Nevada Press, 2000.

Sabine, George H. "Review of *Ethical Systems and Legal Ideals* by Felix S. Cohen." *Cornell Law Quarterly* 19 (1933): 164–65.

Sandel, Michael J. *Democracy's Discontent: America in Search of a Public Philosophy.* Cambridge: Belknap Press, 1996.

Sargentich, Thomas O. "The Contemporary Debate about Legislative-Executive Separation of Powers." *Cornell Law Review* 72 (1987): 430–87.

Schlegel, John Henry. *American Legal Realism and Empirical Social Science.* Chapel Hill: University of North Carolina Press, 1995.

Schwarz, Jordan A. *The New Dealers: Power Politics in the Age of Roosevelt.* New York: Knopf, 1993.

Shapiro, Fred R. "The Most-Cited Law Review Articles." *California Law Review* 73 (1985): 1540–54.

———. "The Most-Cited Law Review Articles Revisited." *Chicago-Kent Law Review* 71 (1996): 751–79.

Sharp, Malcolm. "Review of *Ethical Systems and Legal Ideals* by Felix S. Cohen." *International Journal of Ethics* 44 (1934): 262–64.

Shepard, Walter. "Review of *Ethical Systems and Legal Ideals* by Felix S. Cohen." *The Philosophical Review* 43 (1934): 623–25.

Shientag, Bernard. Foreword to "Summary Judgments in the Supreme Court of New York." *Columbia Law Review* 32 (1932): 825–29.

Silve, David. "Morris Raphael Cohen as Educator." Ph.D. diss., State University of New York at Buffalo, 1985.

Singal, David Joseph. "Toward a Definition of American Modernism." *American Quarterly* 39 (1987): 7–26.

Singer, Joseph William. "Legal Realism Now." *California Law Review* 76 (1988): 465–544.

——. "Sovereignty and Property." *Northwestern University Law Review* 86 (1991): 1–56.

——. "Well Settled? The Increasing Weight of History in American Indian Land Claims." *Georgia Law Review* 28 (1994): 481–532.

Skillen, Anthony. "William James, 'A Certain Blindness' and an Uncertain Pluralism." In *Philosophy and Pluralism,* ed. David Archard. Cambridge: Cambridge University Press, 1996.

Skinner, Romana Ellen. *Alaska Native Policy in the Twentieth Century.* New York: Garland, 1997.

Smith, Michael T. "The Wheeler-Howard Act of 1934: The Indian New Deal." *Journal of the West.* 10 (1971): 521–34.

Soifer, Aviam. "Descent." *Florida State University Law Review* 29 (2001): 269–76.

——. *Law and the Company We Keep.* Cambridge: Harvard University Press, 1995.

Sollors, Werner. *Beyond Ethnicity: Consent and Descent in American Culture.* New York: Oxford University Press, 1986.

Sorin, Gerald. *A Time for Building: The Third Migration, 1880–1920, The Jewish People in America.* Vol. 3. Baltimore: Johns Hopkins University Press, 1992.

Spicer, Edward H. *Cycles of Conquest: The Impact of Spain, Mexico, and the United States on Indians of the Southwest, 1533–1960.* Tucson: University of Arizona Press, 1962.

Sproat, John G. *The Best Man; Liberal Reformers in the Gilded Age.* New York: Oxford University Press, 1968.

Stefon, Frederick J. "The Irony of Termination: 1943–1958." *The Indian Historian* 11 (1978): 3–14.

——. "Significance of the Meriam Report of 1928." *The Indian Historian* 8 (1974): 2–7.

Stocking, George W. Jr. *The Ethnographer's Magic and Other Essays in the History of Anthropology.* Madison: University of Wisconsin Press, 1992.

Strickland, Rennard et al., eds. *Felix S. Cohen's Handbook of Federal Indian Law.* Charlottesville, VA: Bobbs-Merrill, 1982.

Strickland, Rennard, and Gloria Valencia-Weber. "Observations on the Evolution of Indian Law in the Law Schools." *New Mexico Law Review* 26 (1996): 153–68.

Strum, Philippa, ed. *Brandeis on Democracy.* Lawrence: University Press of Kansas, 1995.

Sutton, Imre, ed. *Irredeemable America: The Indians' Estate and Land Claims.* Albuquerque: University of New Mexico Press, 1985.

Tax, Meredith. *The Rising of the Women: Feminist Solidarity and Class Conflict, 1880–1917.* New York: Monthly Review Press, 1980.

Taylor, Graham D. *The New Deal and American Indian Tribalism: The Administration of the Indian Reorganization Act, 1934–45.* Lincoln: University of Nebraska Press, 1980.

Townsend, Kenneth William. *World War II and the American Indian.* Albuquerque: University of New Mexico Press, 2000.

Trachtenberg, Alan. *The Incorporation of America: Culture and Society in the Gilded Age.* New York: Hill and Wang, 1982.

Traub, James. *City on a Hill: Testing the American Dream at City College.* Reading, MA: Addison-Wesley, 1994.

Tribe, Laurence H. "The Puzzling Persistence of Process-Based Constitutional Theories." *Yale Law Journal* 89 (1980): 1063–80.

Tsosie, Rebecca. "Separate Sovereigns, Civil Rights, and the Sacred Text: The Legacy of

Thurgood Marshall's Indian Law Jurisprudence." *Arizona State Law Journal* 26 (1994): 495–533.

Tsuk, Dalia. "Corporations Without Labor: The Politics of Progressive Corporate Law." *University of Pennsylvania Law Review* 151 (2003): 1861–1912.

Tushnet, Mark. *The NAACP's Legal Strategy Against Segregated Education, 1925–1950.* Chapel Hill: University of North Carolina Press, 1987.

Twining, William L. *Karl Llewellyn and the Realist Movement.* London: Weidenfeld and Nicholson, 1973.

Von Drehle, Dave. *Triangle: The Fire that Changed America.* New York: Atlantic Monthly, 2003.

Wahl, Jean. *The Pluralist Philosophies of England and America.* Trans. Fred Rothwell. London: Open Court Co., 1925.

Walch, Michael C. "Terminating the Indian Termination Policy." *Stanford Law Review* 35 (1983): 1181–1215.

Washburn, Wilcomb E. "Land Claims in the Mainstream of Indian/White Land History." In *Irredeemable America: The Indians' Estate and Land Claims,* ed. Imre Sutton. Albuquerque: University of New Mexico Press, 1985.

———. *Red Man's Land/White Man's Law: A Study of the Past and Present Status of the American Indian.* New York: Charles Scribner's Sons, 1971.

Washington, Johnny. *Alain Locke and Philosophy: A Quest for Cultural Pluralism.* New York: Greenwood Press, 1986.

Watkins, T. H. *Righteous Pilgrim: The Life and Times of Harold L. Ickes, 1874–1952.* New York: H. Holt, 1990.

Weinfeld, Abraham C. *Towards a United States of Europe, Proposals for a Basic Structure.* Washington, DC: American Council for Public Affairs, 1942.

Weisbrod, Carol. *Emblems of Pluralism: Cultural Differences and the State.* Princeton: Princeton University Press, 2002.

———. "Minorities and Diversities: The 'Remarkable Experiment' of the League of Nations." *Connecticut Journal of International Law* 8 (1993): 359–406.

Wenger, Beth S. *New York Jews and the Great Depression: Uncertain Promise.* Syracuse, NY: Syracuse University Press, 1999.

West, Elliott. *Trail of Tears: National Historic Trail.* Tucson: Southwest Parks and Monuments Association, 2000.

White, Edward G. "Chief Justice Marshall, Justice Holmes, and the Discourse of Constitutional Adjudication." *William and Mary Law Review* 30 (1988): 131–48.

White, Morton G. *Social Thought in America, The Revolt Against Formalism.* New York: Viking Press, 1949.

Wigdor, David. *Roscoe Pound: Philosopher of Law.* Westport, CT: Greenwood Press, 1974.

Wilkinson, Charles F. *American Indian, Time, and the Law: Native Societies in a Modern Constitutional Democracy.* New Haven: Yale University Press, 1987.

Wilkinson, Charles F. et al. "The Indian Claims Commission." In *Indian Self-Rule: First-Hand Accounts of Indian-White Relations From Roosevelt to Reagan,* ed. Kenneth R. Philp. Logan: Utah State University Press, 1995.

Williams, Jeanne. *The Trail of Tears: American Indians Driven from their Lands.* Dallas: Hendrick-Long, 1992.

Williams, Robert A. Jr. "The Algebra of Federal Indian Law: The Hard Trail of Decolonizing and Americanizing the White Man's Indian Jurisprudence." *Wisconsin Law Review* (1986): 219–99.

———. *The American Indian in Western Legal Thought: The Discourses of Conquest.* New York: Oxford University Press, 1990.

———. "'The People of the States Where They Are Found Are Often Their Deadliest Enemies': The Indian Side of Indian Rights and Federalism." *Arizona Law Review* 38 (1996):
981–98.

Williston, Samuel. *Life and Law: An Autobiography.* Boston: Little, Brown and Company, 1940.

Wintz, Cary D., ed. *Remembering the Harlem Renaissance.* New York: Garland, 1996.

Wyman, David S. *Paper Walls: America and the Refugee Crisis, 1938–1941.* New York: Pantheon
Books, 1985.

Yntema, Hessel E. "Review of *Ethical Systems and Legal Ideals* by Felix S. Cohen." *American
Political Science Review* 27 (1933): 654–56.

Young, Donald. *American Minority Peoples: A Study in Racial and Cultural Conflicts in the United
States.* New York: Harper and Brothers, 1932.

Zacharias, L. S. "Repaving the Brandeis Way: The Decline of Developmental Property."
Northwestern University Law Review 82 (1988): 596–645.

Cases

Acosta v. County of San Diego, 272 P.2d 92 (1954).

Alaska Pacific Fisheries v. United States, 248 U.S. 78 (1918).

Arizona v. Hobby, 221 F.2d 498 (1954).

Brown v. Board of Education, 347 U.S. 483 (1954).

Cherokee Nation v. Georgia, 30 U.S. 1 (1831).

Grimes Packing Company v. Hynes, 67 F. Supp. 43 (1946).

Harrison and Austin v. Laveen, 196 P.2d 456 (1948).

Hynes v. Grimes Packing Company, 165 F.2d 323 (1947).

Hynes v. Grimes Packing Company, 337 U.S. 86 (1949).

Johnson v. M'Intosh, 21 U.S. 543 (1823).

Lochner v. New York, 198 U.S. 45 (1905).

Muller v. Oregon, 208 U.S. 412 (1908).

Otoe and Missouria Tribes of Indians v. United States, 131 Ct. Cl. 593 (1955).

Tee-Hit-Ton Indians v. United States, 348 U.S. 272 (1955).

Trujillo v. Garley, D.N.M. 3 August 1948. Unreported.

United States v. Alcea Band of Tillamooks, 329 U.S. 40 (1946).

United States v. Alcea Band of Tillamooks, 341 U.S. 48 (1951).

United States v. Carolene Products Co., 304 U.S. 144 (1937).

United States v. Libby, McNeil & Libby, 107 F.Supp. 697 (1952).

United States v. Santa Fe Pacific Railroad Co., 114 F.2d 420 (1940).

United States v. Santa Fe Pacific Railroad Co., 314 U.S. 339 (1941).

United States v. Santa Fe Pacific Railroad Co., 314 U.S. 716 (1942).

Worcester v. Georgia, 31 U.S. 515 (1832).

INDEX